A HISTORY OF THE UNITED STATES
SINCE THE CIVIL WAR

A HISTORY

OF

THE UNITED STATES

SINCE THE CIVIL WAR

BY

ELLIS PAXSON OBERHOLTZER

IN FIVE VOLUMES
(Volume V: 1888–1901)

NEGRO UNIVERSITIES PRESS
NEW YORK

Originally published in 1917-37
by The Macmillan Company, New York

Reprinted 1969 by
Negro Universities Press
A DIVISION OF GREENWOOD PUBLISHING CORP.
NEW YORK

SBN 8371-2646-0

PRINTED IN UNITED STATES OF AMERICA

AUTHOR'S NOTE

The completion of this volume fulfils the plan with which the author set out when he projected "A History of the United States Since the Civil War." He has been much longer in coming to the end than he had anticipated because of the variety and amount of detail entering into the narrative. The work was begun more than twenty years ago not without misgivings as to the time which might be required before it could be finished, but with no full understanding of the labor involved in the development of the theme.

It may be thought, as it doubtless will be thought on some sides, that a History having such a title in 1936 should invade a later period and treat of more recent occurrences. However papers bearing on a more recent time are not yet available. The correspondence of Presidents and other prominent figures even in the nineteenth century are still in some instances impounded and, if in the Library of Congress and other depositories, they are subject to restricted use. The author's indebtedness to such sources as have been opened to him is acknowledged and it is his object here merely to express regret that the work must be completed without his gaining access to the papers, for instance, of Benjamin Harrison, Thomas F. Bayard and others which he should have liked to explore.

Anyhow treatment of recent events is an unhistorical exercise. Such a narrative, in the best case, must be, in a degree, polemical on the side of the author, or, if it be not so, it must seem to have this quality in the view of the reader who, having lived through the period, knows it from his own standpoint and is ready to dispute opinion, if it be uttered, the appraisal of personalities and even plain facts. The appearance of the United States in the galaxy of nations as a "world power" at the conclusion of the war with Spain must be regarded as an appropriate point at which to bring the investigation to a close, and here it ends.

CONTENTS

CHAPTER XXXIII

THE CAMPAIGN OF 1888

CHAPTER XXXIV

HARRISON'S ADMINISTRATION

vii

CHAPTER XXXV

CLEVELAND OR HARRISON AGAIN

CHAPTER XXXVI

CLEVELAND'S SECOND TERM

CHAPTER XXXVII

BRYAN

CHAPTER XXXVIII

THE WAR WITH SPAIN

CONTENTS

CHAPTER XXXIX

AFTER THE WAR

CHAPTER XL

MATERIAL PROGRESS AND SOCIAL REFORM

A HISTORY OF THE UNITED STATES
SINCE THE CIVIL WAR

A HISTORY OF THE UNITED STATES SINCE THE CIVIL WAR

CHAPTER XXXIII

THE CAMPAIGN OF 1888

FROM the moment that President Cleveland sent his message to Congress, on the subject of the tariff, in December, 1887, the issue in the campaign of 1888 was made. The Republicans accepted it through the New York Tribune's interview with Mr. Blaine in Paris. Their hope of wresting the control of the government from the Democrats and of resuming their accustomed sway was high. Nor was there certainty that they could be prevented from gaining the object in view in the minds of the politicians who surrounded the President and who, whether they liked his course or not, must advocate his cause. Some of his friends had used their endeavors to deter him from making the tariff the preeminent issue, but he was intent upon it and he was to be seen for a brave crusader, who had taken up the gage of battle for the people as against the rich man and the "trust." It was to be an alignment of the masses against wealth and privilege, if it could be made into such a contest, with wealth and privilege denying that they were now acting, or had ever acted, in contravention of the popular interest, and with the frank declaration, indeed, as the campaign progressed, that the people could enjoy prosperity only while the rich were rich and directed the country's destinies.

The Republicans, hitherto in Presidential years, since 1860, had been the first to hold their convention and present their platform, and the candidates who would stand upon it. They issued the challenge and the other party followed with its answer. Now in 1888 the situation was reversed. The Democrats were in power, their President invited battle on the subject which he had chosen for his appeal to the country, and it remained for them merely to name him formally for reelection and to publish a statement of principles, which they would do at the earliest suitable day. The Republicans would await the action of the Democratic convention and would govern their movements by what might be revealed to them of the intended movements of the enemy. Mr. Cleveland was still one whom they pretended to view with a kind of contempt; they still held, concerning him, a superior attitude which indicated that they felt it demeaning to deal with him. But it was plain that he had the advantage of entrenchment in place which had been theirs for so many years, and that the most powerful exertions must, and would be, made on their side to recapture control of the government.

Sapping and mining went forward in reference to the administration, nowhere so actively as in New York, where Tammany in the city, and Hill as a leader of sinister interests in the state, would have gladly assisted in bringing about the President's overthrow.[1] Politicians, to whom government was merely an agency to enable those who could seize it to advance their private interests, and newspapers like the New York Sun, gravely advocated the nomination of Hill. He should be the party's candidate for the Presidency. But the logic of events was too great and overwhelming for obstruction of any kind to stand in the way of a renomination of the only man who, in twenty-five years, had led the party to success, of an endorsement of his administration and a ratification of the platform with which he had provided it.

Randall and his following were defeated in the organization of the Democratic state convention in Pennsylvania. Cleveland's friend, W. L. Scott, a rich man in Erie, supplanted the "Republican agent" in Philadelphia, who had had dominance in the councils of the party in his own state and, in a degree, in the nation at large. The President's tariff message was commended.[2] Randall's defeat disposed of his pretensions as one in whom the

---

[1] McElroy, Grover Cleveland, vol. i, pp. 279–80.
[2] A. Nevins, Grover Cleveland, pp. 371, 386; N. Y. Nation, Jan. 26, 1888.

opposition might find a standard bearer in the approaching contest. In Massachusetts, where the Democrats in the preceding year had set the President at defiance, new things were seen. The state committee declared that they were "a unit in their support of Cleveland in the policy recommended by him in his last annual message to Congress." [1] The wire pulling which was in progress in the interest of Hill in New York promised to come to naught. He would be fortunate, men said, if he should be renominated for governor. [2] It was plain, already in February, that Cleveland would have a majority of the delegates; his enemies had the hope only of preventing his getting two-thirds of the number needed for victory. [3] Reminders that Cleveland had intimated in his letter accepting the nomination in 1884 that one term was enough for our Presidents met no response. [4] Hill and his friends saw that there was nothing left of his "boom." Tammany and the other factions came, if apathetically and with little loyalty, [5] under the Cleveland banner, and the New York state committee in April declared itself in hearty sympathy with his policies and the plan to renominate him. This event presaged the choice of a "solid Cleveland delegation" in the national Democratic convention from the President's own state. [6] Everywhere the Democrats fell into line behind Cleveland unitedly, and, to outward appearance, enthusiastically, thus making his nomination sure. [7] Not one of the state conventions, when they met, withheld approval of the candidate; not one expressed dissent from his tariff message and nearly all, in varying terms, gave it emphatic endorsement. [8]

The national convention when it assembled in the Exposition Hall in St. Louis on June 5th, therefore, held no surprises, and

[1] N. Y. Nation, Feb. 2, 1888.
[2] Ibid.
[3] Ibid., Feb. 9, 1888.
[4] Ibid., April 12 and June 7, 1888; McElroy, Grover Cleveland, vol. i, p. 274.
[5] McElroy, op. cit., vol. i, p. 289.
[6] N. Y. Nation, April 12, 1888.
[7] Ibid., May 10, 1888.
[8] Ibid., May 24, 1888; N. Y. Times, June 2 and 7, 1888.

was wanting in dramatic interest. Richard Croker, an Irishman who had followed John Kelly as the "Boss" of Tammany Hall, said that the nominating speech should be made by Daniel Dougherty, the "silver tongued" orator who had presented Hancock's name in the convention of 1880, then from Philadelphia but now a member of the New York delegation. Cleveland's friends gave no very warm welcome to the suggestion. One said that Dougherty was not "well balanced." [1] But he had written his speech and he assumed that he was to deliver it.[2] His persistent entreaties had won a place in the civil service for his son,[3] and he had the necessary enthusiasm, as well as the forensic talent, for the work in hand. He "ascended the rostrum," he said in his Irish accents, "to name the next President of the United States." Mr. Cleveland had been unknown eight years ago, but he had "met and mastered every question as if from youth trained to statesmanship." He was not "a hope," he was a "realization." With disregard of self he had "courageously" declared to Congress that "the supreme issue" was "reform, revision, reduction of national taxation." A "privileged class" who had been "shaping legislation for their personal gain" was levying by law "contributions for the necessaries of life from every man, woman and child in the land." To lower the tariff was not free trade; he who asserted that it was so insulted intelligence. There had been no "pilfering" in this administration, no "jobs." Public office was a public trust. Above all, "sectional strife as never before" had been brought to an end. "I give you," the orator said, as he brought his eloquent discourse to a conclusion, "a name entwined with victory." The usual scene at such times in national nominating conventions—a roaring hubbub which lasted for near half an hour—ensued, coming to an end with strains from the band of the "Star Spangled Banner" and "Yankee Doodle." The nomination was seconded in a humorous speech by a

---

[1] Magone to Lamont, May 28, Dougherty to Lamar, May 26, Bissell to Lamont, May 3, Hoadly to Lamont, June 1 and Croker to Lamont, June 2, 1888, in Cleveland Papers.

[2] Croker to Lamont, June 4, 1888, in ibid.

[3] Cleveland Papers.

delegate from Kentucky and by other men from other states. With a shout, without a ballot, Cleveland was nominated unanimously by acclamation. No more than one hour and fifteen minutes had been consumed in making the President his party's candidate for a second term.[1]

To find a "running mate" was not quite so easy a feat. But in the hall, as in the galleries, the aisles and the streets, bandana handkerchiefs were displayed. This red cotton rag was a symbol. It caught the mist of tobacco which was expelled by a sneeze of Allen G. Thurman. It hung from the coat tail pocket in the pictorial papers wherever the figure of the "old Roman" of Ohio was seen. He adhered to the polite but now obsolete habit of putting snuff to his nose.[2] He had been, it was said, too carelessly dismissed by Cleveland when the new government had been organized in 1885. Such a Nestor of Democracy should have been called to some high place in the councils of the President.[3] The hour was at hand when the party should pay him the homage to which his eminent services abundantly entitled him. Men spoke, too, of the commissioner of pensions, General Black, and, with still more favor, of Governor Isaac P. Gray of Indiana who, however, was described by William H. English and other Democrats in that state as a "renegade Republican."[4] Thurman's age—he was now or soon would be 75 years old—and his physical infirmities were emphasized. As well, said William H. Barnum, chairman of the Democratic National Committee, nominate "a corpse."[5] At any rate his character and history unfitted him for a place on the ticket with Cleveland. The newspapers recalled a speech of his in 1861 when he had said that it would be impossible to subjugate the South. Coercion, if it should be attempted, would be a violation of the Constitution. In 1867 he had opposed the giving of the franchise to the negro. He was notoriously unsound on the money question. His

[1] N. Y. Times, July 7, 1888.
[2] Cf. ibid., June 8, 1888.
[3] Cleveland Papers; N. Y. World, June 5, 1888.
[4] English to Cleveland, Jan. 15, 1888, in Cleveland Papers.
[5] N. Y. Times, June 8, 1888.

nomination would put the party "on the defensive from the start." It would be a "return," a Democrat wrote to Lamont, "to the whirlpools and quicksands" in which they so long had floundered.[1] In no case could it be expected that Thurman would develop the power to take his state of Ohio from the Republicans on election day, while it was plain that Indiana remained "doubtful." It was to some "vote getter" there that the convention should turn its face; a Hoosier should be given the second place on the ticket, if victory were to be achieved in November.

Mr. Cleveland was asked for his preferences. He declined to express a choice. It was not his task, he said, but the convention's to select the candidates. No argument seemed likely to avail. Thurman, his friends averred, would awaken the enthusiasm of the "old Democracy." In Indiana, as everywhere, there would be an outpouring of affectionate sentiment at mention of his name. He was "irresistibly popular." His nomination, it was believed, several days before the convention met, would be an "inevitable result." [2] And it was, for, on June 7th, the third and last day of the meeting, when the call of states was at an end, it was seen that there were 684 votes for Thurman, 105 for Gray and 31 for Black. Thurman, by the withdrawal of the names of his two opponents, was declared to be the unanimous choice of the convention for Vice President.[3]

The platform was another matter. There were delegates, and they were men of high position in the party, for whom Mr. Cleveland's message was too strong a meat. They would use their influences in favor of resolutions calculated to cool the ardor of the leaders in Congress who were endeavoring to give expression to the President's principles as they were stated in the "Mills bill," and would go to the country with a modified plan for tariff revision. One of these was Chairman Barnum of the National Committee; another Edward Cooper, one time

[1] June 2, 1888, in Cleveland Papers; cf. George Hoadly to Lamont, June 1, 1888, in ibid., where he says that the nomination would be "disastrous."
[2] N. Y. Times, June 4, 1888.
[3] Ibid., June 8, 1888.

mayor of New York, and a generous contributor of funds raised to prosecute Democratic campaigns, both, it was pointed out, "beneficiaries" of high tariffs, since they were actively engaged in the iron trade. Ex-Senator Davis of West Virginia, with large industrial interests, was also on the ground; he made himself active in the same sense. Senator Gorman of Maryland, powerful in party management, let it be supposed that he had espoused the anti-Cleveland cause. His loyalty was frankly doubted on several counts.[1] A "Randall Club" from Philadelphia reminded the delegates of the "assistant Republicans" in Pennsylvania, who were led by him whose name their organization bore.

These men and others, either for personal, or for tactical political reasons, would have the convention adopt a platform which should make no mention of the President's tariff message, but should simply reiterate the statement on this subject found in the platform of 1884. Much would depend upon the committee on resolutions of which it was proposed that that facile journalist, Henry Watterson, "the star eyed goddess of reform," who had written another national platform for the party, should be the chairman. It was difficult to set aside so aggressive a leader and Watterson, the radical, won over Gorman, the conservative, but by a majority of only two votes,[2] and the work of preparing a statement of principles was begun. The victory of the tariff reform wing of the party was complete, though Watterson himself was kept under restraint by the energetic action of those who knew the President's wishes in the case, and he had but little to do with the wording of the paper.[3] In making his report to the convention Watterson said that the resolutions had been agreed upon in the committee unanimously.

In the platform of 1888 the declarations in the platform of 1884 were reaffirmed; "the views expressed by President Cleveland in his last earnest message to Congress" which were

[1] Cf. Writings of Carl Schurz, vol. iv, p. 492.
[2] N. Y. Times, June 6, 1888.
[3] Cf. N. Y. World, June 7 and 8, 1888; A. Nevins, Grover Cleveland, pp. 401-2.

proclaimed to be "the correct interpretation of that platform upon the question of tariff reduction" were endorsed. The Republican party was resisting "a reformation of unjust and unequal tax laws" which had "outlasted the necessities of war." The Democratic party would continue, "with all the power confided to it, the struggle to reform these laws. Prices were raised; the cost of the necessaries of life" was "unjustifiably" increased by a system which was "unduly enriching the few that combine and rob the body of our citizens by depriving them of the benefits of natural competition." The surplus in the Treasury, while it represented unnecessary and onerous taxation, was, at the same time, "demoralizing." The Republican party was "debauched by this immense temptation" and was an advocate of "extravagant appropriation," while the Democratic policy was "to enforce frugality in public expense."

Established domestic industries would not be "endangered" by the "reduction and correction of the burdens of taxation." Manufacturers would gain extended markets. Labor would have a cheapened cost of living, with steady and remunerative employment.[1] A separate resolution specifically endorsed and recommended the early passage of the "Mills bill."

Whatever else was said was of little import. The platform was an endorsement of the President, a restatement, and the adoption by the party, of the issue which he had made. It was, by the convention, with Cleveland and Thurman as its candidates for President and Vice President, sent to the people who were, after five months of unexampled agitation, to give their judgment upon it. In Wall Street bets at the rate of two to one were made that Cleveland and Thurman would be elected.

Cleveland's "prestige, no less than his courage," said the Atlanta Constitution, "his courage, no less than his almost omnipotent common sense, make him the sturdiest and safest and best leader either party has had since Abraham Lincoln." [2] He was the "natural" choice, the logical candidate, said the

[1] N. Y. Times, June 8, 1888. For a description of the part that President Cleveland himself is thought to have had in shaping the platform see McElroy, Grover Cleveland, vol. i, pp. 290–1.

[2] Quoted in N. Y. Times, June 7, 1888.

New York World, as it endeavored to overcome some of the disfavor in which the President was held by many of its readers. He should be elected because he had "espoused a great principle involving the highest welfare of the people and the just conduct of the government." [1] He had "put a new song into the mouth of the Democratic party," said the New York Herald. Thurman commended himself to "the everlasting common sense of the people." [2] It was "an ideal ticket," and "as good a platform as was ever adopted by a convention." [3]

Ratification meetings were held; fireworks were exploded. Turkey red bandana handkerchiefs appeared in all parts of the country. The Democratic party, made strong by three years' enjoyment of Federal power, presented a solid front to the determined and angry foe.

The Mugwumps would be rather guarded in their praise of the platform until after the Republican nominations were announced. But they were, for the most part, revenue reformers, and James Russell Lowell, as the presiding officer at a dinner of the Massachusetts Reform League in Boston on December 29, 1887, expressed the views which they generally entertained, as judged by the applause with which the statement was received on the one side and the ridicule which it excited on the other, when he said that Mr. Cleveland was "the best representative of the higher type of Americanism" who had been seen since Lincoln's day. [4]

The Mugwumps were also advocates of civil service reform which they had done so much to put forward and make into a leading issue in the campaign of 1884. They were not loath to express their disapprobation of the President's course on this topic in a number of specified particulars. George William Curtis had voiced their sentiments in his presidential address to the National Civil Service Reform League at its meeting held in New York upon the eve of the assembling of the St.

[1] Issue of June 7, 1888.
[2] N. Y. Herald, June 9, 1888.
[3] Ibid., June 8, 1888.
[4] N. Y. Times, Dec. 30, 1887; cf. Silas Burt to Lamont, Jan. 5, 1888, in Cleveland Papers.

Louis convention.[1] Schurz expressed his disappointment in the plainest terms. He would go as far as the President's severest critics. By concessions to the "spoils element" within the Democratic party Mr. Cleveland had lost a great opportunity for leadership of a people eager "for homage to the intrepidity of his rectitude." [2] For Cleveland's "deviations from the path" which he had marked out for himself, the New York Times declared, there were "no words of excuse or palliation." [3]

But, said the New York Nation, if the President had "fallen short of his promises" concerning civil service reform, he had, "as a matter of fact, done far more for it than any of his predecessors." The consciousness of minor inconsistencies in the giving out of offices, to which all men could point, was lost in the sight of his "struggles to ward off attempts" to wring from him concessions of a far worse character than anything the reformers have had to reproach him with." [4] The New York Evening Post and the Nation would support Cleveland on the tariff question, and also, in spite of his shortcomings, on the subject of civil service reform. An inspection of the Republican leaders and the record of the uses which they, when in power, had made of public office would cause all intelligent men to "rise up cured of any nausea" created by a study of Mr. Cleveland's administration.[5]

Cleveland, said the New York Times, represented and led "the popular demand for a just conduct of the public business." He was known and trusted by the people. His "great ability" had come to be "candidly recognized." His "perfect honesty and sincerity" were no longer questioned, "save by reckless and malignant partisans." [6] The best thing which had been done by the convention at St. Louis, said the Springfield Republican, was its nomination of Mr. Cleveland. There was "no possible

[1] N. Y. Times, May 30 and 31, 1888.
[2] Writings of Schurz, vol. iv, p. 511.
[3] Issue of July 7, 1888.
[4] Issue of June 14, 1888.
[5] Ibid.
[6] N. Y. Times, June 7, 1888.

doubt of his superiority as a candidate over any and all other Democrats." [1]

What the Republican organs would say on the occasion was clearly anticipated. By extravagance in denunciation and the emphasis which they could put upon their malice the editors hoped to procure greater notice for what they wrote. As a matter of fact the platform which had been adopted at St. Louis was brief, sincere, forthright and a creditable statement of purpose. It was drafted and bore the seal of approval of the President and his friends. No demagogic or clap trap utterance marred the paper. Nothing was said in it about "free trade." Plainly taxation was excessive, as a surplus of moneys in the Treasury proved. Plainly expenditure could be increased; the President preferred prudence and frugality to the distribution of redundant revenues in support of ill advised enterprises. Plainly there might be, for popular advantage, a reduction of taxes so that the necessaries of life might be lowered in price to consumers. Plainly whiskey and tobacco were not necessaries— the reduction must be in import duties. Plainly the tariff could and should be revised—the Republicans themselves had distinctly said this but a few years since in party platforms, through their leaders in Congress, through their press and in a report of a commission in which no avowed revenue reformer had had a place. They were reminded of the facts. Thomas Nast drew a series of cartoons of Grant, Garfield and Arthur, quoting their statements in regard to tariff reform. "Was Grant, was Garfield, was Arthur," he asked, "bought by British gold?" Was any one of these "a Democratic Hessian" as Cleveland was declared to be? [2] One Republican platform after another, one Republican President after another, one Republican Secretary of the Treasury after another, said Carl Schurz, had advocated a revision and reduction of tariff rates. [3]

The platform of 1888 distinctly disclaimed, on the part of the Democrats, any wish to disturb industry—to unsettle either

[1] Quoted in N. Y. Tribune, June 8, 1888.
[2] The President's Message of 1887, a pamphlet published by Putnams in 1888.
[3] Writings of Schurz, vol. iv, p. 515.

investment in manufacturing enterprise or the employment of labor. Discretion and moderation marked the paper throughout. Yet the answer to it was what had filled every Republican partisan mouth in Congress and on the stump in 1884, and ever since, what had flowed from every Republican editorial pen— that Mr. Cleveland was a "free trader," that his party was a "free trade" party, that they were British and in league with England to break down and destroy work and wages in America. They were banded together to sell out the country and overset its institutions. By raising again and swelling this hue and cry the Republicans would, so they hoped, put the Democracy out and recapture the government. Barring some manufacturers and industrialists, who were certainly benefited by the tariff, as they were free to declare, saying at the same time that in their own prosperity lay the prosperity of the republic, the contest was to be, at ground, a knock down and drag out fight for office and power.

The President, the New York Tribune said, had "nailed the free trade flag to the mast." The "selfish ambition and the ignorance of one man" would be overruled by the American people. The way was prepared "for the final triumph of protection to home industry." [1] He was weak "morally," the Tribune said, weak "intellectually," weak "in his hypocritical professions of reform," on which account he was a "weak candidate," though a dangerous one, now that he was the avowed "champion" of free trade.[2] The Philadelphia Press told its readers that Cleveland was "more of a dictator than Jackson and less of an intellect than Frank Pierce." The "only success of his administration" was in "what it did not do," and so on.[3] "Since the time of the grosser successors of Augustus Caesar," said the New York Mail and Express, there had been "no such display of the power of one man." Money to elect him would be spent like water by the "agents of the English manufacturers." Four years ago, the Boston Journal remarked, it

---

[1] N. Y. Tribune, June 7, 1888.
[2] Ibid.
[3] Quoted in ibid., June 8, 1888.

had been a common thing to hear Cleveland spoken of as "better than his party." It was so no longer—he was now at home in his party; he was "a Democrat of Democrats." [1]

Thurman was "a Bourbon of the Bourbons," said the Chicago Inter-Ocean; his name, in the opinion of the Indianapolis Journal, would not "help to carry any state." [2] His nomination, it was plain to see, had been made against the better judgment of the President's sincerest friends. His name on the ticket, George Hoadly said, would "alienate many and attract none." The convention should have chosen a Liberal Republican who had come into the party in the Greeley movement, or a War Democrat.[3] It was a political mistake, another Democrat wrote. Thurman's long record overshadowed the President's. The party was put in the position of trying to "drive upon two diverse lines," and, since the days of Janus, it had been "hard to look both ways." [4]

Scandal mongering was revived. Now that Mr. Cleveland was married to one whose graces had captivated the nation some new turn must be given to malice. It would be within the bounds of belief, so enemies supposed, if they were to start and spread the tale that he got drunk and abused his wife. The state of affairs was so dreadful, it was said, that Mrs. Cleveland was on the point of leaving him. Her mother, Mrs. Folsom, had departed the White House and had made a resolution never to return; she could not endure the sight of the cruelties which her daughter suffered. A preacher sponsored the story, as one or more of the cloth had served in the same interest during the campaign of 1884. It was told in large denominational conferences. Clergymen went home with the news to their congregations. One talebearer, female as well as male, passed it to another until, in a twinkling, it had spread over the land. A pamphlet appeared in the St. Louis convention detailing the allegation so discreditable to the President. A man who had earlier been in the employ of the New York Tribune, though

[1] N. Y. Tribune, June 8, 1888.
[2] Quoted in ibid., June 9, 1888.
[3] Hoadly to Cleveland, July 3, 1888, in Cleveland Papers.
[4] W. P. Thompson to Lamont, June 25, 1888, in ibid.

that newspaper rather vigorously disclaimed responsibility for what was being done, was identified as the colporteur of the book.[1]

Such offensive activity came to the attention of the President, but to make denial of, or even to notice, calumny of this kind dignifies it and widens the circle in which it receives comment.[2] Anyhow, as it was an aspersion upon his manhood, denial could be made more effectively by others, and action was deemed advisable as the date of the convention drew near and the nature of the plot which would, it was hoped, damage the party, as well as him who would again be its candidate for the Presidency, came to be clearly understood. Mrs. Folsom, and Mrs. Cleveland herself, pluckily made statements to silence, if possible, defaming tongues. Mrs. Folsom who, it was alleged, would not again be seen at the White House was found in Paris by a reporter of the New York Herald. She made it clear that she would in a few days return home and would go directly to Washington. The charge was "a foolish campaign story without a shadow of foundation."[3] Mrs. Cleveland's statement was definitely to the point. The opportunity was found in a reply to a woman in Boston who had asked for information. Mrs. Cleveland "pitied" the man who had been "made the tool to give circulation to such wicked and heartless lies." Continuing she said that she could "wish the women of our country no greater blessing than that their homes and their lives may be as happy, and that their husbands may be as kind, as attentive, considerate and affectionate as mine."[4] Friends gave their testimony. Richard Watson Gilder would do his part to "kill the damnable lie." He and Mrs. Gilder declared that the allegations were "grotesquely, outrageously, totally false in every respect."[5] However, as might have been expected, in spite of all denials, stories of a similar nature

[1] N. Y. Times, June 7, and N. Y. Tribune, June 8, 1888.
[2] N. Y. Herald, June 7, 1888.
[3] Ibid., June 6, 1888.
[4] Boston Globe, June 7, 1888; cf. N. Y. World, June 8, 1888; N. Y. Evening Post, June 6, 1888; McElroy, Grover Cleveland, vol, i, pp. 285–9.
[5] Gilder to Lamar, June 9, 1888, in Cleveland Papers; cf. Cleveland to Bissell, June 17, 1888, in ibid.

continued to be circulated in all parts of the country throughout the campaign.[1]

The course to be taken by the Republicans, if they were to accomplish their design which was the overthrow of an enemy for whom they professed so much aversion, was not entirely clear. The party had fallen into the hands of Blaine and his friends who still pretended to think him a leader of such eminence as to preclude the nomination of any one else. The New York Tribune in a particular way among newspapers, B. F. Jones of Pittsburgh, the chairman of the Republican National Committee, and other men in control of the machinery of the party, whose chagrin at the result of the election in 1884 had been so keen that they had not yet recovered their aplomb, were certain that no other would serve their uses so well. He must be renominated—he could denounce free trade more vigorously than any one else, and he should be put forward in another campaign when he would, they professed to think, meet a better fate. Whitelaw Reid said that Henry Cabot Lodge and Theodore Roosevelt, who had been hostile to Blaine in 1884, now advocated his nomination as the one most likely to bring party success.[2] How honest more than a few men were in this belief may not be known—they at any rate would hold their organization together under Blaine's name and prevent the advantage from slipping away from them until the causes of other candidates could be improved. The Mugwumps continued their warfare. No opportunity to state their unchanging opposition to Blaine on the grounds upon which they had based their declarations of his unsuitability as a candidate in 1884 was allowed to escape, to meet, of course, the undiminished fury of his friends, made the

---

[1] N. Y. Nation, Nov. 29 and Dec. 13, 1888; N. Y. Tribune, Dec. 8, 1888, where denial and correction are made by Mrs. Wm. C. Whitney with a particular view to stilling the tongue of Chauncey M. Depew. To what lengths traduction could proceed, even in high quarters, is illustrated in an article by the presiding officer of the United States Senate, J. J. Ingalls, in a leading American magazine, the North American Review. See issue of June, 1888.

[2] Cortissoz, Life of Reid, vol. ii, p. 115. But see Corr. of Roosevelt and Lodge, vol. i, pp. 61–2.

angrier by a consciousness that defeat in that year could be
laid at the door of the Independents.

Sage Republicans concerned for victory in 1888 well understood that it would not do to present the name of their beaten
candidate. Blaine had virtually wrung the nomination from
the party after it had been refused him in 1876 and 1880. He
was an "old man of the sea" who must be thrown off the
shoulders of the political organization upon which he had fastened his person and his name. If the party had "no higher
aim" than to nominate Blaine, Conkling told Senator Farwell,
"it had better die and be decently buried." If, as Blaine's
friends believed, he could be nominated by acclamation he
would be defeated, Conkling said, in the same way.[1] The
beloved leader was abroad for prolonged rest and travel and
he had been heard from in February in Florence. He addressed
Chairman Jones. "My name," he said in his statement, "will
not be presented to the national convention called to assemble
in Chicago in June next." The reasons for his "decision"
were "entirely personal" to himself. He went on to express
his "deep sense of gratitude" to the many thousands of his
countrymen who had "sustained" him "so long and so cordially." He would remember such "loyalty of friendship"
until the end of his life. The rest of the letter was an argument
to show by how little the party had failed of success in 1884,
and in justification of his leadership. The position of the
Republicans had improved, as had been demonstrated by the
elections of 1886 and 1887; they would display "irresistible
strength" in 1888 because of what President Cleveland had
"fortunately" done to clear the air. The issue was plain.
Should the "industrial system" which had so greatly increased
the wealth of the country be "recklessly abandoned," or
should "a new trial be made of an old experiment which has
uniformly led to national embarrassment and widespread individual distress?"[2]

Whether the statement was meant to be frank, or merely an

[1] Farwell to Gresham, Feb. 9, 1888, in Gresham Papers.
[2] N. Y. Tribune, Feb. 13, 1888.

essay to discover, if possible, the feeling of the party as to his candidacy in another campaign neither friend nor enemy knew. After all was said and done nothing appeared in the lengthy epistle touching upon a renomination except the rather oracular assertion—"My name will not be presented," etc. The New York Tribune, upon a first reading of the statement, took it to be a withdrawal. Blaine had been "dragooned" by his friends into running in 1880 and 1884; nothing, until this letter came, could have prevented his renomination in 1888, and more in a like sense.[1] But the Tribune's view underwent change as the weeks passed;[2] the possibility became a probability that Blaine would again be the party's candidate. Politicians and newspapers held to the opinion that, if it were the unanimous wish of the convention, he could be prevailed upon to accept the place of leadership another time. He should be nominated by acclamation—then he could not refuse. The question as to whether his name would be presented was beyond his control. He was "the greatest living Republican" and "the man of all others who could defeat Mr. Cleveland." He had no right to decline any position which the party might assign to him.[3]

There were Republicans who held different views. There were other candidates.[4] In the sight of many the prospect of party victory would be made immeasurably more certain by Blaine's elimination from the canvass.

The Democrats saw plainly enough, and said, that, while the "magnetic man from Maine" was in retreat, he had not burned his bridges behind him. The sincerity of the writer of the letter, when he had used such studied and ambiguous language to announce his retirement was, they declared, wholly questionable. It was in no way a final pronouncement. The Mugwumps expressed the same view, though they were called

[1] N. Y. Tribune, Feb. 13, 1888.
[2] N. Y. Nation, May 3 and June 7, 1888; Cortissoz, Whitelaw Reid, vol. ii, pp. 115–7.
[3] Cf. extracts from newspapers and interviews with politicians in N. Y. Tribune after Feb. 15, 1888; N. Y. Nation, Feb. 16 and 23, 1888.
[4] N. Y. Nation, March 22, 1888.

weeks prior to the meeting of the convention passed, but it was very clear that something of the enthusiasm necessary to secure the nomination was wanting in the Ohio delegation. It would vote for Sherman, as it was told to do, but faithless men in the group were spreading suspicion and distrust. They spoke of supporting him "as long as there was any chance" of nominating him—that kind of support meant defeat.[1]

Sherman had a new and valuable friend, a rich business man in Cleveland, Marcus Alonzo Hanna, known to his familiars as Mark Hanna. As a delegate in the national convention in 1884 he had supported the Ohio candidate rather than Blaine —he would now be actively useful. He was a mixture of various racial strains. Through his father he was of Irish Quaker lineage, the family having come into Ohio by way of Pennsylvania and Virginia; through his mother he had New England ancestry. While he was still a lad his parents left a farm to live in Cleveland, a place at the time of about 60,000 inhabitants. His education had been interrupted at an early age that he might engage in the wholesale grocery trade, in which he prospered. He abandoned this activity at the importunity of his father-in-law for a lucrative iron and coal business out of which in 25 years he took millions of dollars in profits, largely because of his own tenacious and capable management of its affairs. Investments widened his interests. Mining, manufacturing, banking, shipping, street railways, the publication of a newspaper and the control of a theatre were fields into which his energies carried him, while politics, as his life advanced, claimed his attention to satisfy a love of adventure as well as an ambition for power.

Hanna had been "snowed up" for four days in Atlantic City during the memorable blizzard of March, 1888. He employed his time in conferring with politicians, similarly marooned, in the interest of Sherman. When the railways were reopened he continued his conversations—with Wharton Barker, Charles Emory Smith and other men in Philadelphia, with John D.

---

[1] W. M. Bateman to Sherman, March 31 and April 5, 1888, in Sherman Papers.

Rockefeller, Whitelaw Reid and Thomas C. Platt in New York, but without receiving too much encouragement.[1]

Walter Q. Gresham, who had been in the Arthur cabinet and now was a Federal judge, made definite advances. His was an honorable figure. He had a good mind, moral force and clean hands. But he would not serve the uses of the party in the opinion of the protectionist interests in the East. He was held to be unsound on the tariff question.[2] John Wanamaker questioned him upon this point.[3] He had not voted for Blaine in 1884, said that man's advocates, a statement which was denied,[4] though no one rose to say, or could say, that he had done so of choice and with good will. He, nevertheless, would have support in Illinois where he had won the admiration of Joseph Medill and the Chicago Tribune.[5] Senator Farwell was his friend. The delegation from Illinois was instructed to vote for him in the convention. He was that state's candidate for President and he was offered, with a side look at Blaine, as one who could make "an aggressive and not a defensive campaign."[6]

Senator Allison of Iowa was a figure of whom some spoke, though his views concerning the tariff, like Gresham's, made the suggestion of his nomination unpalatable to those who would keep the party, for this campaign at least, in the most erect position on this subject.

Russell A. Alger of Michigan was mentioned; he was a rich man who was not averse to being thought eligible for the nomination, though no one believed that he could possibly be a serious contender for so great a place.

It was clear enough that, while there were other doubtful states to be won, New York and Indiana, since they controlled the greater number of electoral votes, would be of prime importance in 1888. They had been gained by Cleveland in 1884; they must not be his now. The field was scanned for leaders

---

[1] Hanna to Sherman, March 16, 17 and 19, 1888, in Sherman Papers.
[2] N. Y. Nation, March 22, 1888.
[3] May 30, 1888, in Gresham Papers.
[4] Foster to Gresham, May 8, 1888, in ibid.
[5] Mrs. Gresham, Life of Gresham, vol. ii, p. 568.
[6] N. Y. Nation, May 10, 1888; cf. ibid., May 24, 1888.

who promised to give the ticket strength on debatable ground, and public attention was being directed to one who bore a distinguished name and carried himself with personal dignity in Indiana. In New York the party was offering no more imposing a figure than Chauncey M. Depew. Such a candidacy, while it indicated a veering away from Blaine, could, on no side, be taken seriously. It was a blind—behind it lurked no one knew what realities. Mr. Depew had been, for a brief time, a "reformer"—he had been a candidate for a state office on the "Greeley ticket" in 1872. He had since celebrated his full attachment to the Republican organization in New York. The Vanderbilts had seen his value and had appointed him president of the New York Central Railroad, a connection which Republicans in the West said would so affect him that, if he were nominated, he could not carry one state west of Ohio.[1] But it was as an "after dinner speaker" that he had made his way into public notice and affection. He had post prandial gifts which were accounted to be rare, and by jest making and story telling he had laughed his way into politics. If New York were to present his name, as it would, Indiana was on strong ground. It would ask, with hope of being heard, for the nomination of its "favorite son," General Benjamin Harrison.

It is true that Harrison's pretensions were being contested by Judge Gresham. Indiana was Gresham's native state and his friends believed that it would be "plain sailing" for his "boom," if they could control the delegation,[2] a result of which they soon discovered there was little hope. The Harrison forces were well organized. Gresham said that he was not a candidate. He was putting forth no efforts to secure, and did not expect to receive, the nomination—he was simply pursuing a course which he thought the proprieties of his position as a judge on the bench required. The advocacy of his claims by the Chicago Tribune, which was accused of an interest in free trade, was embarrassing to him. "I have never said anything that 'squints' at free trade," he declared, "and no one who knows me thinks I am a

[1] N. Y. Tribune, June 15, 1888.
[2] J. W. Foster to Gresham, Feb. 24 and March 16, 1888, in Gresham Papers; M. A. Tyner, Indiana Mag. of History, vol. 29, p. 317.

free trader." [1] William Walter Phelps was seeking a ticket on which he could run as Vice President. George W. Childs of Philadelphia, a not very potential patron, said that the convention should nominate Gresham and Phelps. Other men expressed similar views.[2]

It was observed that Harrison's record as a liberal in reference to the restriction of Chinese immigration might alienate voters on the Pacific coast. He had been elected a senator of the United States from Indiana in 1881. Finding a Democratic majority in the legislature in 1887, he, at the expiration of his term, had returned to law practice in Indianapolis. In the discussion of the Chinese question during the administration of President Arthur he had voted with the minority, in which respect it was remarked, however, that he was in no worse case than Allison and John Sherman, who on this occasion, in this matter, had acted in a like way.[3] If the West and Northwest were of a mind to bolt the ticket, in the absence of any promise of tariff reform, as some pretended to think, they might not very greatly object to Harrison. Whatever his opinions on this topic the fact that he was a resident of the West might be expected, in the long run, to insure him the support of all the elements in the party in that section. That he was not known, as Allison and Gresham were, for sympathy with the movement for a lower tariff would improve his chances in the East. The more the situation was pondered the clearer did it become that Harrison was "available," probably the most "available" of those under consideration, for leadership in the campaign. He was fairly obscure, an advantage in Presidential candidates—he had not made enemies on account of opinions which he held, and the Republican party, through him, might be able to reinstate itself in the places which had been vacated so reluctantly and with so much bitterness when Cleveland came in. Harrison

[1] Gresham to Erastus Brainerd, March 17, 1888, and Andrew Hall to Gresham, Feb., 1888, in Gresham Papers.
[2] Gresham Papers
[3] N. Y. Nation, March 1, 1888; McPherson's Handbook for 1882, pp. 92–107; cf. letter of July 1, 1888, in Cleveland Papers; Foster to Gresham, Feb. 24, 1888, in Gresham Papers.

was known to be a "cold" man. But the "workers" were not acquainted with the degree of his frigidity—they would assume that he held sentiments which were kindlier with reference to Republicans than Democrats, and that it might be worth their while to "take off their coats" to effect his nomination.

But the prize was not yet in his hands. The other aspirants were still in the field and no one certainly knew what the convention, which would meet on June 19th, would bring forth. As the day drew near the men who were still for Blaine and who held that, in spite of his statements, he was "in the hands of his friends" and was "subject to draft"—including the delegates from his own state of Maine who with delegates "instructed" for him from other parts of the country numbered, in all, the Philadelphia Press said, 377 persons[1]—were in a quandary as to the course which they should take. Manifestly he could not and should not be nominated unless the call for his leadership was practically unopposed. It was not so, and Blaine himself, seeing this, made another declaration, on May 17th, which was published in the New York Tribune on May 30th. It was written in Paris and was addressed to Whitelaw Reid. In the letter Blaine expressed regret that his position should have been misunderstood. He would "mislead" no one "among the millions" who had given him "their suffrages and their confidence." Even assuming that the Presidential nomination should, "by any possible chance," be offered to him he could not, he said, "accept it without leaving in the minds" of the people the impression that he had "not been free from indirection"; therefore he "could not accept it at all." He concluded his message with observations about the "pauper labor" of Europe, which had touched his sympathies deeply during his foreign residence. He wished that every voter of the republic could see, as he had seen, the condition of workingmen abroad—in this case "the party of free trade in the United States would not receive the support of one wage worker between the two oceans." Europe concerned us as the "philanthropists" that we ought to be. "The rewards

[1] N. Y. Nation, June 7, 1888.

of labor everywhere," he said, would be "advanced" if we should "steadily refuse to lower the standard at home." [1]

The pins at long last seemed to be quite knocked from under the Blaine men. How insincere they had believed their leader's words to be when he had spoken to them from Florence in February now appeared. They scurried about, talked, telegraphed and wrote to one another and were in a great pother. The New York Tribune untruthfully said that "of late," until this letter came to its editor, there was "little doubt among either friends or foes" that Blaine would be nominated. His retirement was "an act of magnanimous self abnegation rare in political history, and sure to command the appreciation of his regretful but admiring countrymen." Now it would be necessary to make "another choice." [2] Nevertheless, politicians, whose myopia was such that they could see no one else in the political skies, still said that he would be nominated "by acclamation," [3] a statement which, in some degree, was meant to conceal a desire to hold the faction in leash until plans could be formulated for new alignments.

When the convention met Blaine's two sons and his friend, Stephen B. Elkins, were on the ground. Even yet there was apparently no reason to suppose that the "Plumed Possum of the Kennebeck" would decline to run if the delegates could be stampeded into giving him the nomination.[4]

Sherman stood in the way and made no concealment of the object which he had in view. If he could not be nominated Blaine should not be. It was General Raum's aim to secure for Sherman the support on the first ballot of almost the entire body of delegates from the South, largely blacks and mulattoes, and about 100 from the North. He had been asking for money to transport the negroes to the state conventions and then to bring them to Chicago, and some had been provided for the use.[5] But Sherman and his friends did not have the funds to

[1] N. Y. Tribune, May 30, 1888.
[2] Ibid.
[3] Ibid., May 31, 1888.
[4] Cf. J. M. Scovel to Sherman, March 22, 1888, in Sherman Papers.
[5] Raum to Sherman, March 21, 1888, in ibid.

compete in this activity with Alger who had knocked the head out of his "barrel." [1] Hanna had not yet interested himself in politics to the degree necessary to gain results by such methods. Nevertheless he was "terribly in earnest," [2] and he told Sherman that from the time he got to Chicago "things would be hot." [3] "My one sole aim, ambition and desire is to make you President of the United States." [4]

Conferences, demands upon Sherman and Gresham for cabinet posts and other offices in case of election, in return for the votes of blocks of delegates in the convention, suggestions of trades and deals to seduce unstable followings filled the air by day and by night. Foraker would have made the speech nominating Sherman—support outside of Ohio was sought and, to invite it, Senator Hoar of Massachusetts was addressed. He declined [5] and a sponsor was found in General Daniel H. Hastings of Pennsylvania. Quay, under the influence of Cameron, who had lately taken for a second wife a niece of Sherman, was showing a sympathy more or less sincere for the senator from Ohio, and a number of votes, it was believed, could be secured in the Pennsylvania delegation. Foraker would second the name when it should be presented to the convention, although Sherman's friends repeated their expressions of suspicion directed at his loyalty. There was an "unseen hand" in the Ohio delegation, they said. [6] Foraker had opened his own headquarters where he displayed a sign, "No rebel flags will be returned while I am Governor," a reference to the most famous of his political performances. [7] He would not work with McKinley, Hanna, Grosvenor, Butterworth, Charles Foster and Sherman's other lieutenants. [8] The man was "wild

[1] Raum to Sherman, June 19, 1888, in Sherman Papers.

[2] F. B. Baird to Sherman, June 14, 1888, in ibid.

[3] Hanna to Sherman, June 11, 1888, in ibid.

[4] Hanna to Sherman, May 30, 1888, in ibid.

[5] Foster to Gresham, May 20, 1888, in Gresham Papers.

[6] Hedges to Sherman, June 20, 1888, in Sherman Papers.

[7] Doan to Sherman, June 30, 1888, in ibid. Foraker was "one of the most conspicuous of the Grand Army beggars and blatherskites," said the New York Nation. He waged his campaigns by "waving the bloody shirt." —Issue of Nov. 7, 1889.

[8] Grosvenor to Sherman, June 21, 1888, in Sherman Papers.

with ambition." [1] Apparently his object was to gain the nomination for the Vice Presidency on a ticket headed by Blaine.[2]

Nothing of moment occurred in the convention until the 22nd when the platform was brought in and adopted, and the roll of states was called for the presentation of the names of Presidential candidates. Judge Gresham's sponsor was Leonard Swett of Illinois, a friend and associate of Lincoln in the early years of the Republican party. After a number of orators had extolled Gresham ex-Governor Albert G. Porter of Indiana brought forward Benjamin Harrison, with many a reference to his great-grandfather of the same name who, as a delegate in the Continental Congress from Virginia, had signed the Declaration of Independence, and to his grandfather William Henry Harrison, the first governor of Ohio, who had performed service of value in the Northwest Territory, the hero of the battle of Tippecanoe, where he had met Tecumseh and had won a victory over that bellicose Indian chieftain, and then, for a reward, in 1840, had been elected to the Presidency of the United States. Indiana offered, amid loud cheering, the name of the grandson of "Old Tippecanoe."

Iowa presented the claims of Senator Allison, Michigan General Alger, New York, through Senator Hiscock, Chauncey M. Depew. General Hastings of Pennsylvania then nominated and Governor Foraker of Ohio seconded the nomination of John Sherman. Senator Spooner delivered a eulogy on the character and services of Governor Rusk of Wisconsin, an old stage driver, rail splitter and tavern keeper.[3]

The balloting began at once. There were 831 delegates and 416 were necessary for a choice. Sherman on the first ballot received 229 votes, not so many as his adherents had claimed for him. His strength, in spite of Alger's inroads, lay in the South,

---

[1] Hedges to Sherman, June 20, 1888, in Sherman Papers. Sherman spoke of Foraker's "egotism."—Sherman to Hedges, June 29, 1888, in ibid.

[2] Hanna to Sherman, June 24, 1888, in ibid.

[3] "A rough diamond," who, it was believed, might be "made to sparkle under the polishing influence of Senator Spooner's eloquence."—Indianapolis Journal, quoted in N. Y. Tribune, June 15, 1888.

where it had been in 1880 and 1884. His position appeared to be more advantageous than in any previous convention from the standpoint of numerical strength, though it was clear enough that the Blaine leaders, knowing that he had resisted the movement in behalf of their favorite in 1884, and that he was active now with the same ends in view, were not of a mind to increase his following. Gresham received 111 votes on the first ballot,[1] Depew 99, Alger 84 and Harrison 79. Blaine's name had not been formally presented to the convention, though it was loudly cheered when it was mentioned by his admirers in the course of speech making—35 delegates voted for him. Lieutenants were despatching cablegrams to him deluding him with their flatteries and pledges of support.[2]

As candidates for whom delegations cast their votes in mere maneuvering for recognition were withdrawn, Sherman, Gresham and Alger made gains, but they were inconsiderable. Three ballots were taken on the 22nd. An evening session was held. It was adjourned so that the delegates might hear a speech by Colonel Robert G. Ingersoll, who was in the hall working for Gresham, perhaps to little advantage because of his reputation as an "atheist,"[3] and who had been called for by a unanimous and vigorous shout. He, trespassing upon hospitality, as many believed, took the occasion to espouse the cause of his candidate amid disorder which, when his purpose became clear, soon drowned his voice.

Men began to talk of William McKinley. If Sherman could not be nominated the young advocate of protectionism from Ohio who held himself well in the House of Representatives on the tariff question might be made the nominee.[4] Depew's candidacy was seen to be an absurdity and his name was withdrawn. Two more ballots on Saturday brought Harrison's vote, with the aid of a large body of the released delegates from

[1] Outside of Illinois he had strength in the delegation from Minnesota and Missouri.—Proceedings of Republican Convention of 1888, pp. 159–60.
[2] Medill to Gresham, May 8, 1888, in Gresham Papers.
[3] J. H. Wilson to Bluford Wilson, June 2, 1888, in Gresham Papers.
[4] N. Y. Tribune, June 25, 1888.

New York,[1] from 94, where he had ended on Friday, to 213 with a slight, though no significant, gain for Alger. The Blaine men studied the situation and the most devoted of his friends still pretended to think, when adjournment was taken until Monday morning, the 25th, without the choice of a candidate, that the convention, in its helplessness, might turn to their idol. And but for Sherman they might have started the stampede upon which they rested their hopes.

New York continued to repel the advances of Sherman's managers, although Warner Miller and Depew were looked upon as his friends. They were overborne by Platt whose hostility to the Ohio candidate was active and open.[2] The Illinois delegates, with the abettance of Medill and the Chicago Tribune, still gave Sherman no favor.[3] Foraker had further confirmed suspicions regarding his loyalty by voting against the seating of a contesting delegation from Virginia, led by ex-Confederate General Mahone, who was counted in Sherman's following. Clearly he was dickering with the Blaine men and would go off with them when and if he could. Quay was "panicky."[4]

McKinley discouraged the use of his name in definitive terms,[5] though Senator Hoar of Massachusetts, Phelps, Farwell and others brought forward the candidacy and advocated such a diversion in the balloting. Hanna, in prophecy of his later attachments, favored the movement until the suggestion was rejected by Sherman, who bore himself proudly and honorably until the end. A resolution had appeared in the Senate on June 13th requesting the President to apply the principle of arbitration on "fit occasions" in the settlement of international disputes. Sherman had introduced it as chairman of the Committee on Foreign Relations.[6] The Irish, at the instigation

[1] Proceedings of Convention of 1888, p. 178.
[2] Sherman to a friend, June 26, 1888, and A. E. Bateman to Sherman, June 6, 1888 in Sherman Papers; C. M. Depew, Memories of 80 Years, p. 132.
[3] Cf. Sherman to Butterworth, June 16, 1888, in Sherman Papers.
[4] Charles Foster to Sherman, June 27, 1888, in ibid.
[5] Proceedings of Convention of 1888, pp. 173–4.
[6] Cong. Record, 50th Cong. 1st sess., pp. 5195–6, 5239.

of the Blaine men, set upon him at once.[1] "What has the Chicago convention to do with a question of this kind?" Sherman asked. Why was he singled out for abuse? Anyhow, he wrote Butterworth, "the Quakers [2] are worth more to us than dynamiters or bellicose anarchists. It is about time we should understand," he said, "that peace and friendly intercourse with foreign nations ought not to turn upon the injustice done by such nations to their own citizens." [3]

Sherman would not be shaken—he would not release Ohio from its pledge of support. "My withdrawal is the nomination of Blaine," he said, when his friends asked him by telegraph wire to Washington for instructions. More than half of the Ohio delegates would follow Foraker in that direction. To name Blaine would be to "commence the campaign with distrust and accusation." [4] Putting such a candidate before the country would be "resented," as he believed, "by an overwhelming defeat at the polls." [5] Blaine's course had been "deceptive" and, Sherman thought, "dishonorable." [6] It was necessary to make the contest "if for no other reason than to unmask the hypocrisy of Blaine." [7] "He is a candidate as much as I. If he beats me under the circumstances all right." The "only safe thing to do is to stick." Sherman would not "run from battle." He preferred "defeat to retreat." To withdraw would be a breach of faith; it would be unjust to others. "The better way," he declared, "is for all of us to stand together and suffer defeat, if that is in store for us," [8] a fate which was not far away.

The sixth ballot, the first on Monday, disclosed a gain for Harrison, and on the eighth ballot, with the withdrawal of Allison's name and a disintegration of the Sherman, Alger and Gresham followings, which could not be prevented now that

[1] Butterworth to Sherman, June 18, 1888, in Sherman Papers.
[2] Who always interested themselves in arbitration.
[3] Sherman to Butterworth, June 18, 1888, in Sherman Papers.
[4] Sherman to Hanna, June 22, 1888, in ibid.
[5] Sherman to Hedges, June 12, 1888, in ibid.
[6] Sherman to Raum, June 23, 1888, in ibid.
[7] Sherman to a friend, June 26, 1888, in ibid.
[8] To McKinley, Hanna, Raum and others, June 23 and 24, 1888, in ibid.

Blaine was seen to be out of the way, Harrison received the votes of 544 delegates. The nomination was made unanimous and he was declared to be the party's candidate for President. No time was lost in naming, in accordance with expectation, Levi P. Morton of New York for the Vice Presidency. He was chosen on the first ballot over William Walter Phelps, brought forward as a "polished scholar," [1] and one or two other candidates. The convention adjourned. News came in from all parts of the country of booming cannon, flags flung to the breeze, "rousing" ratification meetings, parades of campaign clubs. The Republicans were in battle line for the great contest with Cleveland and "free trade."

Five men at the end had still voted for Blaine. That paragon of Republicanism was at the moment on a coach, with his wife, two daughters and his Boswell, Miss Dodge, (Gail Hamilton),[2] the guest of Andrew Carnegie for a trip behind horses through England and up into Scotland to Cluny Castle on Speyside, which the rich American ironmaster was occupying for the summer. [3] Carnegie was a stout advocate of the renomination of Blaine [4] whose movements were chronicled from day to day for the Tribune by its London correspondent, George W. Smalley. There would be "no travelling on Sundays, of course." The journey would cover 700 miles and occupy about thirty days.[5] Blaine was, at the moment, taking no interest in American politics, though he, now and again, sent a message to the United States through Mr. Smalley to say that nothing which purported to come from him would be genuine unless it bore his name,[6] and, finally, as the convention neared the end of its labors, cablegrams from Edinburgh, in which city he had arrived, to his representatives at Chicago, requesting them to "respect" his wishes and to "refrain" from voting for him, while he stood at the end of the Atlantic cable, not without

[1] Proceedings, p. 218.
[2] Blaine's Egeria, with "White House aspirations."—N. Y. World, June 23, 1888.
[3] B. J. Hendrick, Life of Carnegie, vol. i, pp. 326–8.
[4] Cortissoz, Life of Whitelaw Reid, vol. ii, p. 117.
[5] N. Y. Tribune, June 6, 1888.
[6] See e.g. ibid., June 21, 1888.

hope that he would again be called to party leadership.[1] The
Blaine men were lowering themselves as gracefully as they
could—

> "We'll vote this year for Tippecanoe,
> And for James G. Blaine in '92." [2]

Blaine had done "the most magnanimous thing in the history
of American politics," said the New York Tribune. He could
and would have been nominated on Saturday but for the action
of his friends, and even on Monday, but for his "peremptory
cables" from Scotland.[3] Harrison had been chosen by the
Blaine men—no one could have been nominated without their
favor and assent.[4]

Sherman thanked his friends generously. They had "preserved their honor." Hanna, who had made a fine impression
upon those with whom he was brought into association, described by Butterworth as a "prince," [5] was particularly singled
out for praise for his "manly, disinterested and persistent
support." [6] Hanna, on his side, in return, renewed his devotion
to his leader, "the greatest living American statesman," and
spoke of mistakes—if he had made them it was due to a "want of
experience in dealing with unknown quantities," and, he added
with point, to his "not knowing that in politics promises go for
nothing." [7] McKinley's conduct was "heroic." [8] Unless he
should "become insane," Sherman assured his friends that "no
temptation of office" would induce him to "seek further political
honors," a resolution in which Mrs. Sherman joined him.[9] From

---

[1] Proceedings of Convention of 1888, p. 187; N. Y. Nation, June 28,
1888; cf. daily cablegrams of N. Y. World correspondent who followed the
coaching party in Scotland; N. Y. Tribune, June 26, 1888.

[2] N. Y. Tribune, June 26, 1888.

[3] Ibid; also issue of July 5, 1888. His friend "Joe" Manley of Maine
said, while still in Chicago, that Blaine could have been nominated on
Saturday, if those who spoke for him had permitted it.—Chicago despatch
to ibid., June 25, 1888.

[4] Ibid., June 27, 1888.

[5] Butterworth to Sherman, June 21, 1888, in Sherman Papers.

[6] Sherman to Hanna, June 26, 1888, in ibid.

[7] Hanna to Sherman, June 25, 1888, in ibid.

[8] Hanna to Sherman, June 25, and Sherman to Hanna, June 26, 1888,
in ibid.

[9] Sherman to Hedges and other friends, June 26, 1888, in ibid.

the beginning he had been the leading candidate in the convention; it was Sherman "against the field"; he had been defeated by "a combination, unnatural and illogical," growing out of his "prominence" and the disappointment of the Blaine men.[1] The Ohio delegation gave him but cool support. Foraker had wavered under the weight of his own importance. He was "too weak to be true to his friend or honest with himself."[2] A corrupt clique had dominated the New York delegation.[3] Alger had bought the negroes "like sheep." They needed his money and he confined a parcel of them in a room in a hotel after the purchase price had been paid, so that they could not escape. Alger's canvass, Sherman said, would "always be stained with dishonor and bribery." The country had reached the last stages in the history of the Roman Empire, when offices were sold at public auction to the highest bidders.[4] Sherman wrote to the successful Harrison—he could not agree to Blaine's proposition "that all of us should decline, or be killed off in detail, to leave the field clear for him." That was an assumption of "superiority and distinction" which Sherman resented.[5] He and his friends had "lifted the Blaine cloud from the Republican horizon."[6] The most useful men, ex-President Hayes observed in condoling with Sherman, must leave the Presidency to "the less conspicuous and less deserving."[7] Long public service, said John Hay, aroused so much envy and hatred as to make conventions "cowardly." He feared that, under our system, the "best man" would never again be President of the United States.[8] Sherman must share the fate of Webster, Clay and Seward. He announced

---

[1] Sherman to Hanna and Halstead, June 26, 1888, in Sherman Papers.
[2] Hedges to Sherman, June 27, 1888, in ibid.
[3] Sherman to a friend, June 28, 1888 in ibid. Recollections of John Sherman, pp. 1029–30.
[4] Sherman to Hanna, June 15, to Charles Foster, June 27, and to other friends June 28, 1888, in Sherman Papers; Recollections of Sherman, pp. 1029, 1032.
[5] Sherman to Harrison, June 30, 1888, in Sherman Papers.
[6] A. M. Jones to Sherman, June 25, 1888, in Sherman Papers; cf. Hedges to Sherman, June 27, 1888, in ibid.
[7] Hayes to Sherman, June 27, 1888, in ibid.
[8] Hay to Sherman, June 25, 1888, in ibid.

that he would give the nominee of the convention his "hearty support."

Morton was taken for what he was—a rich man who would aid the managers in financing the campaign. He would link New York with Indiana and make two doubtful states safe for the Republicans.

The platform was a wonderful compilation. It went the whole distance on the subject of protection and declared that, in dealing with the surplus, rather than make any concession in the rates of duties on imports, which, if upheld, meant prosperity to employer and workingman, manufacturer and farmer, all alike and all together, the internal taxes on liquor and tobacco should be swept away. Those elements in the party which in recent years had suggested reform of the tariff and revision of the schedules in the interest of cheaper living were held now in complete disregard. As the Republican leaders in Congress advocated a reduction of the surplus by greater appropriations, so now the convention, in the platform upon which the electoral contest of 1888 would be waged, declared itself, directly or by inference, in favor of enlarged expenditures for soldiers' pensions, rivers and harbors, coastal fortification, the navy, Blair's scheme to do away with illiteracy in the South and like enterprises. The platform was a statement of a design, the New York Nation said, "to squander the public revenue in order to make opportunity for high and unnecessary taxes." [1]

To catch votes that might be straying and were not safely within the Republican compound there was a "plank" condemning the Democratic administration "in its efforts to demonetize silver," by which it was hoped, by implication, to characterize Mr. Cleveland as a gold monometallist and gain the support of the friends of "free coinage"; another, looking to the Irish and the Gloucester fishermen, which declared the pending treaty with Great Britain to be "a pusillanimous surrender" to England. To bring in the Prohibitionists, whose numbers were sufficient to make them far from negligible factors in doubtful states, the convention, as an afterthought, lest the party be

[1] N. Y. Nation, June 28, 1888.

accused of advocating "free whiskey," by reason of the plan to repeal the internal taxes rather than touch the tariff, adopted a resolution expressing its sympathy "with all wise and well directed efforts for the promotion of temperance and morality."

Harrison's nomination was an escape from Blaine and for so much citizens of high ideals were grateful. Democrats of discrimination respected the chosen candidate. George Hoadly had come to know him and his father in the practise of the law. They were his clients. Mr. Hoadly told President Cleveland of the Republican who would oppose him during the canvass. He is "an honest gentleman of high private character, without any sense of humor at all, rather disposed to be narrow and bigoted than wide and open to new thought, but very sincere and true in all his relations, public and private." He had "a strong constitution and firm temper"—any one who "counted him" an "inferior" man would discover that he had made a mistake.[1]

It was plain, however, that few Mugwumps could, or would, be brought back within the party fold as a result of Mr. Harrison's nomination and the bids for their return in the platform adopted by the Chicago convention. The charges of the New York Tribune and such newspapers that the Independents of 1884 had merely made Blaine's record an excuse for bolting the ticket, that they were in reality, and at ground, Democrats, free traders and enemies of their country were now, it was held, susceptible of proof. They would not support the Republican candidates no matter whom the nominees might be. The evil in their being was at last completely revealed. They had been in 1884, and were now again in 1888, for Cleveland because they were for free trade.

The Prohibitionists were to share with the Mugwumps the reprobation of the Republican managers. That they should dare to leave the "Grand Old Party," which had freed the slave, saved the Union and stood for all that was of good report, met with disapproval which could not be couched in moderate language. The Prohibitionists had done their part in three or

[1] Hoadly to Cleveland, July 3, 1888, in Cleveland Papers; cf. J. W. Foster, Diplomatic Memoirs, vol. ii, p. 253.

four states in 1884 to turn these states from Blaine to Cleveland. They had a militant organ, called the Voice, which was published in New York. The Tribune and other Republican journals put this paper under fire,[1] and, if, by the vituperative arts, they could stop its presses and shame its readers into abandoning the separate political movement for the outlawing of the liquor traffic, they could, it was conceived, prevent other men from stultifying themselves and committing the folly of deserting the party of Lincoln, Grant and the heroes of the struggle for the preservation of the republic. The Prohibitionists were in favor of temperance; they could gain no such end through a pitifully small defection from the great party of moral reform. The Democrats were notoriously unfriendly to the ideals of the Prohibitionists, whose only hope lay within the Republican party. To keep them in their old places so-called Anti-Saloon Republican associations continued to meet and make statements; plainly a ruse with no sincerity in the leadership of the movement, though individuals were now and again deceived by it, especially if they were in quest of excuses to satisfy a conscience which was quick as to temperance, but well settled on the subject of Democratic delinquency.[2]

A considerable body of men who were attached to the Prohibition movement in 1884 and had voted for Governor St. John were not to be intimidated or beguiled, and they called a national nominating convention which met in Indianapolis on May 30, 1888. It was, in effect, a mass meeting—no less than 1800 delegates from every state in the Union attended— a large sum of money was subscribed for the purpose in view, namely the destruction of the "saloon power in politics." Honest enthusiasm marked the speeches and the proceedings generally. It but increased the zeal of their enemies, the Republicans—the Democrats were not affected by the movement—that the platform contained declarations in favor of a reduction of the surplus by a removal of the "burdens of taxation" from the "necessaries of life." They, too, therefore,

---

[1] Cf. N. Y. Tribune, June 9, 1888.
[2] Cf. N. Y. Nation, May 10, 1888; vol. iv of this work, p. 431.

like the Mugwumps, could be dismissed with that contempt which was felt for "free traders." General Clinton B. Fisk, a respectable philanthropist, whose interest in the negroes and the Indians was of national notoriety, living in New Jersey, was nominated for President, and the name of a preacher, a Rev. Dr. Brooks of Kentucky, more recently of Kansas City, a former Democrat, "a chaplain in the rebel army," [1] was added to the ticket as the candidate for Vice-President. The party had polled upwards of 150,000 votes in 1884—adding together the totals in various state elections in 1886 it was computed that it had, in that year, come to number about 295,000 men. [2]

The canvass was under way and its rancors reached expression at once. On June 26th, the day after the nomination of Harrison at Chicago, President Cleveland received the delegation from the St. Louis convention whose duty it was to notify him of his nomination. He was surrounded in the East Room of the White House by members of his cabinet and leaders in Congress. Mrs. Cleveland and a number of ladies, the wives of cabinet officers, had places in the background. The President's reply to the committee rang with that good frankness and honesty which had won him the admiration of intelligent men of independent mind in 1884 and which would now determine them to support him for reelection. [3] He knew at the beginning of his administration, he said, "that abuses and extravagances had crept into the management of public affairs," but he did not know "their numerous forms nor the tenacity of their grasp." He knew "something of the bitterness of partisan obstruction"; he did not know "how bitter, how reckless and how shameless it could be." The record of his administration was "open to every citizen of the land." He had "yielded obedience only to the Constitution" and the "solemn obligation" of his oath of office. Continuing, the President said in his own behalf—"I have done

---

[1] N. Y. Tribune, June 1, 1888.
[2] N. Y. Nation, June 7, 1888.
[3] N. Y. World, June 21, 1888.

those things which, in the light of the understanding God has given me, seemed most conducive to the welfare of my country-men and the promotion of good government.   I would not, if I could, for myself or for you, avoid a single consequence of a fair interpretation of my course."

The committee went home and the canvass progressed.   "I mean to be as good a candidate as I can," the President wrote his old law partner, Bissell.[1]   But he was surrounded by trou-bles brought to him by his friends, as well as by those who wished to destroy him.   To Bissell a month later he said: "I am beginning to feel very much indeed the need of rest and freedom from the terrible nagging I have to submit to here." He was not permitted to work, he complained, "until after other people were abed and asleep." [2]

The appointment of Lamar as a justice of the Supreme Court had been buffeted about in the Senate in the most dis-respectful way before it was confirmed, and the naming of Melville W. Fuller, a few months later, to the Chief Justiceship in succession to Mr. Waite, though the President had given the choice the most conscientious consideration,[3] led to like unpleasantness.   Lamar had been called a "rebel"; Fuller was a "copperhead." [4]   Mr. Fuller was appointed in April, but was not confirmed by the Senate until late in July, 1888.   The vote was 41 to 20.[5]   The vote for Lamar in the preceding January had been 32 to 28.[6]

The President resisted suggestions that he make appoint-ments to office to forward the canvass.   Powderly, the head of the Knights of Labor, who was using that organization for his own advancement, wished to be Commissioner of Labor. The President, in the midst of the campaign, again now, as in 1885, declined suggestions that he put the labor leader in

[1] June 17, 1888, in Cleveland Papers.
[2] July 22, 1888, in ibid.
[3] The field which he went over included the names of James C. Carter, F. R. Coudert, A. H. Garland, George Gray, E. J. Phelps and Richard Olney.
[4] Cramer to Sherman, May 29, 1888, in Sherman Papers.
[5] Senate Ex. Journal, vol. 26, pp. 252, 254, 287, 313.
[6] Ibid., p. 140; cf. Cleveland Papers.

the place.[1] The Mugwumps, through Seth Low, could still say of Mr. Cleveland—

> "This rock shall fly
> From its firm base as soon as I."[2]

Harrison was notified of his nomination at his home in Indianapolis on the 4th of July amid the implications of patriotism associated with the anniversary of the country's independence from Great Britain. The weather was insufferably hot but a crowd assembled for the ceremony which drew a prepared speech from the candidate. He said little except with reference to the anniversary. The Republican party had "walked in the light of the Declaration of Independence." It had "lifted the shaft of patriotism upon the foundation laid at Bunker Hill." It had "made the more perfect union secure by making all men free." Mr. Harrison had "examined the platform with some care" and he would stand upon it. He was "deeply sensible" of the honor and "very grateful"; he would accept the nomination.[3]

The Republican plan of campaign was simple. It was plain to every one now, it had been clear for a long time, that it would be what was known as "working the free trade racket." Those at Cleveland's right hand who had urged him to step more softly, and not to invite a direct contest, that his reelection might be the more easily accomplished, had foreseen the event. The country would be put in an uproar until November about "free trade," the breaking down of industry and the end of good wages, decent profits and prosperity generally. The people's pockets were to be touched by Cleveland; they were to be impoverished and beggared by the lowering of customs barriers and a deluge of foreign made goods, especially out of England, about which country there was a singular want of understanding because of the great number of recently arrived Irish in the electorate, the traditional enmity resting upon the Revolution, the War of 1812 and the sympathy felt and uttered by press and govern-

[1] P. A. Collins to Cleveland, July 8 and 9, 1888, in Cleveland Papers.
[2] Speech in Cooper Union before the Reform Club, Oct. 17, 1888.
[3] N. Y. Tribune, July 5, 1888.

ment in Great Britain for the South in the late Civil War, supported by the teaching in the public schools, 4th of July oratory and the formulæ of patriotic associations.   The average American boy of the period knew little of history except what came to him from the text books used in the common schools and these were entirely anti-British in their tendency.   Every utterance in an English newspaper, every remark, however casual, by an Englishman at home or in this country, which indicated a want of sympathy with Blaine, who so long had baited England for his own advancement, was gleaned, quoted and brought forward by the New York Tribune and the elements in the Republican party which followed such leadership, as proof that it was American to be for the Republican ticket and un-American to be for Mr. Cleveland.

It was not to be wondered at that British opinion would be anti-Blaine and pro-Cleveland, but the fact was ascribed to the existence of a conspiracy of the Cobden Club, and indeed of the whole British nation, all alike "free traders," who would, if they could, destroy our industry and the government itself. To give such a direction to the canvass was, it was said by such journals as the New York Evening Post, to "insult the intelligence" of the people.   It pre-supposed that they were not much less than "a pack of fools," which, alas, might be the case in a Presidential campaign.   The people were, or had been, by a large majority, Republican in their leanings in the North and West, which sections were still the battle ground of the parties.   They were little enamored of the name Democrat or of the South, and, if they could be given excuses, even not very worthy ones, for remaining true to their political allegiances they might in national, if not in local, elections be kept in their olden ways.

Upon these considerations the Republican procedure was based and nothing remained for the managers of the Harrison campaign but to shout and re-shout their shibboleths in newspaper, on stump, in pamphlet, through cannon, brass band and parade up and down the country, without ceasing, until election day.   Other things would be said—about rebels, about broken pledges, about the cold and narrow obstinacy of the President, about his treatment of Mrs. Cleveland, a scandal which could not be quieted in the bitterness of a great electoral contest, harking back as it did to the other scandal which had been worked so industriously in 1884, about the "Solid South," about the Democracy prior to Cleveland's advent as its leader, which clearly was not, and did not deserve to be, very well entrenched in the public confidence and love.

To effect as much as the managers had in mind called for a large outlay of money. In each quadrennial party wrangle for power there was increased demand for funds. The manner in which the campaigns were waged made small sums of little use. The experts in the manipulation and marshalling of votes needed not thousands but hundreds of thousands of dollars for their operations. The Republican organizations in the South were small bodies of mercenaries who were kept in order, for the most part, by Federal offices. Anyhow, by this time, the hope of carrying states in that part of the Union for the Republican ticket had been nearly abandoned, and to send money in that direction was to throw it away. Funds were needed in the doubtful Northern states, in Congressional districts where seats were in danger. The growth of cities with prizes in the shape of taxes on the riches concentrated there, in franchises, in contracts, in administrative jobbery had produced a new kind of politician, one whose business it was to herd bodies of men and mass their votes. Behind the "machine" thus created the whole business of collecting and expending revenues proceeded. These corrupt rings produced leaders who must be reckoned with in national elections. Tammany in New York was known about. Other cities had similar organizations. They spoke in terms of advantage to themselves, not of the public welfare. They must be dealt with, if states were to be carried by Republican or Democrat. Their ideas concerning their own magnitude grew as their cities grew in tax paying capacity and in budgetary importance. When Mr. Cleveland's friends had expressed doubt of the wisdom of his staking his reelection upon the outcome of a controversy over the tariff question they had rested their reasoning on the knowledge that the Republican party contained more rich men than the Democratic party. On such an issue the Republican managers could turn to the presidents of "trusts," the manufacturers and other magnates in the business world and obtain from them voluntarily, or under pressure, great amounts for the prosecution of the canvass. A full treasury at the disposal of expert politicians who could deal with the "bosses" of cities and corruptible groups of whatever kind anywhere, in addition to the building up of a great organization for making the contest a "campaign of education" on the subject of "protection" and "free trade," would in all probability, as well informed and candid men knew, lead to Cleveland's defeat.

The recent party canvasses, on the Republican side, had had the skilful direction of Chandler, Dorsey, Elkins, and men of similar outlook whom they had gathered about them for the "practical" work. Now another would come into prominence, Matthew Stanley Quay. His rise had been gradual but sure. He was the son of a Presbyterian clergyman in the western part of Pennsylvania, and his opportunity to make for himself a political career was at hand when he had been chosen to be private secretary of Andrew G. Curtin, the "War Governor" of that state. His appointment as the colonel of a regiment of volunteers gave him a military title, though he had seen but brief service in the field. At the end of the war he entered the legislature of Pennsylvania where, by a strange natural political acumen, he at once won for himself a place as the leader of the Curtin forces, passing from this side to Simon Cameron's retinue when that sage Scot took the direction of affairs in the state.[1] In the service of such a leader Quay gained facility in the management of campaigns and elections. It was an entirely impudent proposal, a mere piece of trickery, with the open object of making a lucrative position for Quay, when the legislature of Pennsylvania, at dictation, in 1877, created the office of "recorder" in Philadelphia. It would yield about $30,000 a year and Quay was appointed to the place. He removed to Philadelphia, of which he was not a citizen, and where

[1] Cf. A. K. McClure, Old Time Notes of Pa., vol. i, pp. 456–65.

his reception was far from warm. To have a non-resident quartered upon them at so much cost to the taxpayers met with expressions of resentment. He soon found it necessary to abandon his sinecure, and he returned to the West where his successful activities were continued. Unhappy speculation with public moneys threatened him with complete ruin. But friends saved him and he remained "the absolute arbiter of Republican movements and policy in Pennsylvania."[1]

Cameron and his son, James Donald, who had been sent to the United States Senate in his father's place in 1877, and Quay had had no friendship for Blaine in 1876; they were numbered with the "306" who stood solidly for Grant in 1880.[2] The sentiment in Blaine's behalf was so powerful in 1884 that no attempt was put forth to stem the tide,[3] but in the convention of 1888 it had been a different matter. So omnipotent had Quay become that in 1885 he had announced his candidacy for, and had had himself elected to, the state treasurership, and in 1887 he advanced, with almost no opposition, upon the United States Senate where, with Donald Cameron, he represented Pennsylvania. The two men were, for the campaign of 1888, as we have seen, in Sherman's following. A block of delegates from the eastern end of the state, for strategic reasons, had voted on the first ballot for Edwin H. Fitler, a manufacturer of cordage who had just been elected mayor of Philadelphia. Thus such friends in the delegation as Blaine had would be held together for later use. Charles Emory Smith who was put forward to guide this coterie of delegates was outwitted—they scattered soon. Many came to Sherman and, when it was seen that he could not be nominated, the group, under Quay's iron hand, which was raised at times in a menacing way, to keep the Blaine "boomers" from making outburst, had been turned to Harrison.[4] What now could be more natural or deserved than the appoint-

---

[1] A. K. McClure, Old Time Notes of Pa., vol. ii, p. 505. See vol. iv of this work, pp. 473-4.

[2] A. K. McClure, op. cit., vol. ii, pp. 505-6, and chap. xcvii.

[3] Ibid., p. 549.

[4] Hanna to Sherman, June 22, 1888, in Sherman Papers; N. Y. Nation, July 5, 1888; Philadelphia Press, June 30, 1888.

ment of Quay to be chairman of the Republican National Committee, entrusted with the direction of the campaign. The personality of the management of the canvass, the possibilities of a tariff contest for levies upon the rich beneficiaries of the protective system, the nice balance between the parties in two or three crucial states were an assurance that money would be used to shape the result as never before.

The idea came to forceful expression in a statement sent out by James P. Foster, president of the "Republican League of the United States," which had been formed in New York in December, 1887, and which, it was said, in April, 1888, had 300,000 members enrolled in 3625 separate clubs.[1] This rather more frank than tactful man issued a "confidential" circular in which he quoted a United States senator to the effect that he would "put the manufacturers of Pennsylvania under the fire and fry all the fat out of them." So unfortunate a statement was at once turned against the party by the opposition press and the opposition stump until "fat" became synonymous with contributions to the Republican party and "fat frying" was descriptive of the work which so fully engrossed the attention of the managers of the campaign.[2]

The organization of a committee on the Democratic side to cope with such men and their methods was not easy. Democrats with money bags were few. Such as there were had been welcomed, and, because of the sums which they might contribute, as well as because of their proven administrative capacity, were put in positions where they could be useful, but they had undergone some dampening of ardor by reason of Cleveland's tariff message. They could not lend very much enthusiasm to a tariff reform campaign. Chairman William H. Barnum, who had been chairman of the National Committee in 1884, was a rich business man in Connecticut. He wanted to retire. Gorman who had taken an active part in the campaign of that year, and who joined to his connections with wealth a high reputation for political finesse, refused "point blank" to take the chairman-

---

[1] Sherman Papers, particularly a circular dated April 2, 1888.
[2] N. Y. Nation, July 26, Aug. 2, 9 and 16, 1888.

ship.[1] William L. Scott, a capitalist, made rich by coal, iron and railways, had come to Erie, Pa., from Virginia. He had recently wrested a Congressional district from the Republicans and now, on the tariff question, had overcome the protectionist, Randall, as the leader of the party in Pennsylvania. "I confess I cannot see," he wrote to Cleveland in vigorous English, "what in the hell we are to do for the head of the committee." He spoke of ex-Senator William A. Wallace of Pennsylvania. But if they won he would "want all the earth," Scott observed. However they might "give him a small island." [2] After all the possibilities had been discussed Barnum agreed to remain in the chairmanship of the general committee, while Calvin S. Brice would direct the campaign committee. It was but a makeshift. Brice had but little heart for tariff reform. He had made money, and a great deal of it, out of the tariff, and he, as well as others in charge of the canvass, knew that rich men would not contribute of their means to effect the overthrow of a system by which they had come to affluence. Brice advanced money from his own stores,[3] but there was never enough. The committee received advice from all sides—they should stop "chasing rainbows" and abandon hope of carrying certainly Republican states. They knew their duty and it was their wish to concentrate their "means and thoughts" on New York, New Jersey, Connecticut and Indiana where there was an "even chance" of success.[4] But those who visited the party headquarters in New York complained of the indifference which seemed to reign there. Bissell observed an "amateurish air" in the office,[5] a criticism which, until Quay took hold of the subject earnestly, might have been directed with equal force at the Republican campaign organization.

It was difficult to develop enthusiasm for the Republican ticket until Blaine came home. His friends had been overruled at Chicago. They were sulking. For the most part they were

[1] F. W. Dawson, to Cleveland, July 12, 1888, in Cleveland Papers.
[2] Scott to Cleveland, July 9, 1888, in ibid.
[3] Scott to Lamont, Sep. 14, 1888, in ibid.
[4] Brice to Lamont, Aug. 4, 1888, in ibid.
[5] Bissell to Lamont in September in ibid.

"commercial politicians" who sought wide opportunities for
investment or speculation. In Blaine's retinue they could have
advanced upon Washington. In him they had visions of a
reckless administration of public affairs. In Harrison they saw
a man through whom, probably, nothing would come to them.
Respect even for a policy so necessary to prosperity as they
held the protective system to be was subordinate to getting
hold of office so that the government could be administered for
their benefit. Harrison's name was seldom mentioned in the
Republican organs—it was coldly received. Blaine must be
given a chief place in the cabinet; he must be assured of a
leading part in the direction of affairs under the headship of
one so little known as, and manifestly so inferior in intellect
to, the great man from Maine.[1]

That his *amour propre*, and that of his ambitious family,
had suffered much from the turn taken at Chicago was increasingly clear as the facts in regard to his equivocal declinings
came to public knowledge. That the convention had found
another of sufficient magnitude to lead the party was an unconcealed disappointment. Blaine's arrival in New York
would be celebrated by his great following,—a parade of campaign clubs from several states was being organized with a
grand marshal, a hundred aides and a multitude of brass bands.
He would leave Liverpool on August 1st on a ship flying the
American flag.[2] Many enthusiasts went down the bay to meet
the *City of New York*; it was her maiden voyage and she was
late. They cruised about until sunset and then returned to
resume their watch on the ensuing morning. Again they were
disappointed. Mass meetings on deck, speeches, music from a
band kept the waiting company in good spirits. The parade
could not be delayed. The expense of maintaining in New York
marching Republicans from distant states until the arrival of
a ship of which there was still no report was immense. On the
night of August 9th some thousands of persons, come to honor
"the idol of so many American hearts," whose name had been

[1] Cf. N. Y. Nation, Aug. 2, 1888.
[2] N. Y. Tribune, July 31, 1888.

abroad "the synonym of national interests and at home the chief word in the councils of a mighty party," [1] tramped in a great torchlight procession down Fifth Avenue. The many clubs, numbering, the New York Tribune said, 40,000 men, were mobilized in no less than 35 "divisions." Flags, transparencies, mottoes, such as the following, were carried aloft—

"Protection to American Labor, No Free Trade for us."
"American Wages for American Workingmen."
"Cleveland Runs Well in England."
"We are not Going to Vote Away Our Wages."
"New Jersey is All Right."
"Welcome Home, James G. Blaine."
"Turn the Rascals out."
"America for the Americans—No Free Trade." [2]

Finally, the next day, the 10th, the *City of New York* appeared in the bay. It was said that 2,000 people were included in the number who went down to the entrance of the harbor to hail the return of the "First Republican." The whole atmosphere was "light and buoyant with that strange inspiration, the Blaine magnetism." [3] The old cry, "Blaine, Blaine, James G. Blaine," rang out over the water long before the ship which bore him back to his native shores came to rest. He left the vessel on a tender. Every kind of craft in the bay opened its steam whistle and joined in the uproar. The president of a Republican club, as soon as Blaine was safely on board the boat prepared for his reception, made a speech. History was repeating itself. When "the armed hosts of treason sought to destroy the government the Republican party saved the nation." Now, when the Democratic party, "intrenched in power," had adopted a policy that would "prostrate our industries and compel our wage earners to compete with the pauper labor of the Old World," the Republican party stood forth "once more as the saviour of the country." Under a Democratic administration the "Solid South" had been "encouraged by English

[1] N. Y. Tribune, Aug: 10, 1888.
[2] Ibid.
[3] Ibid., Aug. 11, 1888.

sympathy, as was the Confederacy in the dark years of our civil struggle." Where he, Blaine, led the Republican hosts would follow.

Blaine, in reply, expressed the wish that every voter in the United States might have seen what he had seen in the past year. His stay abroad had apparently been full of horrors— it was a proud moment, now that he was again in the land of the free, out of sight of the low wages and the misery which had so deeply touched his sensitive nature as he travelled, particularly in the British Islands. It was "the opportunity of England" to overwhelm us with her "cheaper fabrics" and "lower the standard of American wages to the European level." Like the man who had made the speech of welcome Blaine said that the pending contest to overthrow the Democratic administration was one directed against "those elements in the Union which lately sought its entire destruction." The crowd sang a song to the tune of "America"—

> "Welcome with one acclaim,
> Plumed Knight of loyal fame,
> Great son of Maine.
> Welcome to thee we bring,
> Welcome our forests ring,
> Welcome the prairies sing,
> Welcome to Blaine."

At his hotel individuals met the returning traveller; delegations extended their greetings. Another parade was organized, a so-called "Labor Parade." Blaine was serenaded by a band and, brought out to the reviewing stand, he was soon in the midst of a ringing speech telling American workingmen how grateful they should be that they did not live in Europe and were not in the squalid poverty which prevailed among those who toiled with their hands in lands across the sea, where Cleveland was loved and admired, but were settled by Providence in the great American republic, clothed with the suffrage for their own defense in such a contest to degrade them as now impended.[1]

[1] N. Y. Tribune, Aug. 11, 1888.

His words, the Tribune said, would "echo through the land." He "could not keep them back." They pressed for utterance after what he had witnessed in England where there was "an army of unemployed in every town," and "another great horde" which must "either emigrate or starve." Capital could take care of itself—labor needed the protection of tariff laws.[1]

Blaine passed on to Boston for another reception, and then to Maine where a campaign was in progress to culminate in an election in September, which would serve, as usual, as an index of what might be expected in the nation at large in November.

The letters of the candidates accepting the nomination came in September to invigorate the canvass during its final weeks, Mr. Cleveland's on the 8th. This paper was devoted entirely to revenue reform. It was a restatement in restrained and temperate language of the President's position with reference to the surplus and the reduction of public income that the people might be relieved of the burden of redundant taxation. They were offered "free tobacco and free whiskey" by the Republican party. They asked for bread and they were given a stone. The President hoped that he might have the support of his countrymen for the vindication of his attempt "to inaugurate a righteous and beneficial reform." [2]

Harrison's letter of acceptance followed Cleveland's on September 11th. The Democrats, he said, were making "an assault upon our protective system." They were endeavoring to place the tariff laws "upon a purely revenue basis." This was "practical free trade—free trade in the English sense." Mr. Harrison denied that the tariff was a tax, that it enhanced, by the amount of the duty, the price of the article on which the duty was laid. Those who said this were "students of maxims and not of the markets." The Democratic party declared protection to be unconstitutional; the Republicans held it to be "constitutional, wholesome and necessary." It was essential that the American market be preserved for American producers, and, at the same time, that the "American scale of wages" should be maintained.

[1] N. Y. Tribune, Aug. 11, 1888.
[2] N. Y. Times, Sep. 10, 1888.

Wage earners in this country received higher rewards for their labor and lived more comfortably than those in any other part of the world. It was for them to decide whether they were to enjoy these "substantial advantages" or dally with "the deceptive promises and forecasts of theorizing reformers." They were to determine whether the protective system should be "continued or destroyed." Those who were "hostile to protective customs duties" had "magnified and nursed the surplus." Excessive revenues could be employed in the purchase and retirement of government bonds. Mr. Harrison spoke of other issues before the people as they had been catalogued in the party platform. He gave these questions attention with a view to making the best possible impression upon the electorate whose favor he and his party required, if the victory in this angry contest was to be theirs.[1]

The canvass was now in full swing. Such Republicans as seemed to be for Blaine first and the party afterward were, upon his return, ready to attack the business in hand with augmented zeal over all the country, but with particular industry in the "doubtful states." The Republican journals, led by the Tribune in New York and the Press in Philadelphia, whose editors held the intelligence of their readers in so little esteem, daily scattered their stories about the "rebels" of the South and about England—about the high wages which were inseparable from a protective tariff, about the poverty and starvation which would afflict the country at the mere mention of "free trade." Men who had passed through colleges and were numbered among the higher intellectual classes of the people shouted in print and on the stump sentiments which they must have thought of with wonder after the ardor of this year had cooled. Frankly all the wild bedlam into which otherwise reasonable persons were plunged was for no other object than to put out of office a party, or men in that party, whom they disliked: some on their selfish personal accounts, since their commercial adventures or other private plans would not prosper, as they thought, while Mr. Cleveland was President; some, the mass, perhaps,

[1] N. Y. Times, Sep. 12, 1888.

in a mere frenzy of prejudice and passion which the Republican politicians went to all lengths to arouse.

Harrison, in truth, was of a reserved nature, the reverse of Blaine who undoubtedly had qualities which drew men to him. One had a stiff dignity while the other exuded a certain friendly enthusiasm. One spoke with care and precision, while the other shot out words and phrases with the greatest facility. Harrison was born in 1833 in Ohio—therefore 55 years ago. He was a stocky, bearded man. A large head on a very short neck and a height not greater than five feet and seven inches lent him an appearance which was unimposing. He was not an orator, though he had cultivated the art of effective speaking. His methods were described as painstaking, but little ability to remember names and faces and an indisposition, which was ill concealed, to mingle with men socially on familiar terms, gave him a reputation for aloofness which was not undeserved. Those who knew him described him as wanting in sentiment. He was just, they said, without being grateful.[1] He was making speeches to delegations which visited him in Indianapolis, but he could not electrify the atmosphere around him. His soundness as a Republican was under review. With reference to his attitude toward the Chinese question, while he had been in the Senate, since it affected vote getting on the Pacific coast, there were explanations and apologies for the uses of the campaign. He had voted for the "Blair bill" and seemed to be an advocate of "centralization" rather than state rights. He had been sturdy and unashamed in his attitude toward larger appropriations for soldiers' pensions. He had supported the Hennepin canal scheme.[2] He was assuredly no fanatic on the subject of civil service reform. While he had been a United States senator from Indiana, and Blaine had been Secretary of State, during the Garfield administration, Blaine had complained that Harrison had asked for 13 more first class missions than there were on the diplomatic list.[3]

[1] Cf. N. Y. World, June 26, 1888.
[2] N. Y. Nation, July 19, 1888.
[3] Ibid., June 28, 1888; cf. Writings of Schurz, vol. iv, p. 513.

It was clear that he was "sound" on the tariff question. He had said one day in a speech in Chicago that some things might be "too cheap." He was not in full sympathy with the demand for "cheaper coats" which involved, so he thought, a "cheaper man" under the coat. The Democrats rang the changes on this development of the phrase "cheap and nasty" and found pleasure in suggestions that proof was at hand, as had been suspected from the first, that all of the Republican talk about protection and high wages was in the interest of high prices.[1] The Republicans were, of course, no friends of the poor man at all; they were the friends of the rich man, the manufacturer, the trust, the beneficiary of the tariff, whose virtues they so loudly proclaimed. Imported British clothing at low prices would convert the blessed American workingman into something contemptible, an absurdity laid at Harrison's door, which, whether it made or lost him votes, was, invited to do its part in the turmoil of the campaign.

To warm the people it was guessed that some connection could be established between this canvass and that historic one in 1840 when the candidate's grandfather, William Henry Harrison, had been swept into office on the reputation of his victory over Tecumseh. The cry of "Tippecanoe and Tyler too," was raised. Log cabins, hard cider and raccoons were brought into the torchlight processions. Why these things should be revived after 48 years, and what they meant was in no sense clear, though the object was to connect Harrison with the soil, give him points of contact with the "plain people" and make everyone understand that he was the bearer of a name which had an honored place in American history.[2] The retort of the enemy was obvious. The candidate and his sponsors, finding that he was awakening no popular enthusiasm for his own person, were calling upon his ancestor. The political caricaturists gave him a great beaver hat—a bewhiskered pygmy under grandfather's hat which was too large for him and covered his entire frame made the rounds of the Demo-

[1] N. Y. Nation, July 5, 12 and Aug. 9, 1888.
[2] Cf. ibid., July 26, 1888.

cratic press. "Fat frying" went on at a merry rate. The
"Mills bill" was passed by the House on July 21st and made
its appearance in the Senate, which would stifle it and compile
a bill of its own after consulting this and that manufacturer
and the interests concerned. This bringing to Washington
of men whose business was affected by tariff rates was ostensibly for the instruction of the makers of laws. Practically,
at any rate at a time like this, it was to impress the heads of
"trusts," "combines," corporations, manufacturers and others
with the fact that the Democrats were free traders and would
harm, if not ruin, their industries, while the Republicans (who
controlled the Senate) would give them more considerate
treatment. The Senate hearings and the preparation of
schedules dragged on through the summer into October until
the day of adjournment, within a fortnight, therefore, of the
election.

While the Republicans promised the manufacturers tender
attentions in their bill, or at any rate the defeat of the "Mills
bill," Quay and his like who were directing the canvass on its
material side were plying them with requests for money to save
the country from Cleveland and free trade. The politicians
came, carried away and came again as the weeks passed. Always the demand was for more that the result might be safe.
The danger was constantly kept before the manufacturers; it
was exaggerated; fright, even panic, overtook many to whom the
bugbear of free trade seemed the more awful the more closely
they viewed it. Foster's Republican League, the Home Market
Club in Boston,[1] the Manufacturers' Club in Philadelphia
directed by a rich man, Thomas Dolan; Swank's Iron and Steel
Association,[2] Joseph Wharton's Industrial League and other
organizations were collecting agencies. They girded Quay's
loins so that he could attack the practical work which confronted him in New York and so that his associate, Dudley,

[1] Cf. N. Y. Nation, Sep. 27, 1888.
[2] See Swank's letters to Sherman in Sherman Papers. He was distribut-
ing tracts where "dense ignorance" prevailed.—Swank to Morrill, April 18,
1888, in Morrill Papers.

the late Commissioner of Pensions, could take needful measures in Indiana.[1]

The Democrats spoke of the "trusts." They declared in their speeches and in their newspapers, and President Cleveland said, that manufacturers were forming combinations in order to monopolize the supply of one or another commodity with a view to fixing prices. Such operations were made the easier behind tariff walls with security against foreign competition.[2] The House had been carrying on a detailed investigation of these combines and a report of a thousand pages condemning their methods was numbered among the events of these turbulent months.[3] The Republicans in their platform had been impelled to declare their opposition to organizations of capital formed with a view to controlling trade and oppressing the people by increasing the charges on the necessaries of life. But in the main their leaders and their press made but little of the trusts, and noticed them only as much as the exigencies of the canvass required. It was not long after Blaine's return home when he gave the party the keynote on this subject. The trusts are "largely private affairs," said he, "with which neither President Cleveland nor any private citizen has any particular right to interfere." Anyhow they had nothing to do with a protective tariff, for, under a system of free trade, England, which he had come to know about during his recent view of the country from the top of Mr. Carnegie's coach, was "literally plastered all over with trusts." [4]

Blaine was soon done with the campaign in Maine and was free to take the stump in other parts of the country. He had a characteristic view of the election in his own state in September. The result, he said, was "not simply a great victory,"

[1] Many in the group quite lost their equilibrium. Joseph Wharton of the Industrial League wrote to John Sherman, after he had made his speech on the tariff before the Home Market Club in Boston, complimenting him on his "good natured murder" of James Russell Lowell, who had been "so conspicuously absurd" [in joining Cleveland's name with Lincoln's], and "the whole lesser brood of dudes and eunuchs." Wharton to Sherman, Feb. 11, 1888, in Sherman Papers.

[2] Cf. Writings of Schurz, vol. iv, pp. 524–7.

[3] House Reports, 50th Cong. 1st sess., no. 3112.

[4] N. Y. Nation, Aug. 23 and Sep. 6, 1888.

it was "almost a political revolution." The fact was that party lines in Maine remained substantially as they had been in 1884.[1] The vote, if it meant anything, indicated a close contest throughout the country and there could be assurance on neither side of the final issue. The canvass proceeded with increasing vigor and bitterness. The Republican hymn was—

"Protection, oh, Protection, the joyful sound proclaim
Till each remotest nation has heard the Tariff's name." [2]

The Cobden Club, every quotable phrase or sentence in the London Times or any other British newspaper whatever, if it indicated sympathy with Mr. Cleveland or the objects of the Democratic party, every statement from the mouth of an Englishman of current or earlier dates which could be put to similar use were made to bear upon the canvass. Utterances emanating from Great Britain were invented and distorted, and were given circulation by Quay's committee or some affiliated body of political managers in handbill or in newspaper.[3] Cleveland's name, under the British flag, was printed beside Harrison's, under the American flag.[4] Circulars containing pictures of women in England hammering on anvils for "36 cents a day," of girls in trousers with picks and shovels working in collieries, of man and wife making chairs, earning both together $4 a week, while the children played on the earth floor, with descriptions of those who, it was alleged, had seen such sights on journeys in England, were distributed in mills and factories.[5] A cartoonist depicted John Bull discovering Cleveland in a small basket among the bulrushes. "Ah," said he, "this is the Moses that will open the American Land of Milk and Honey to the products of my Pauper Labor." [6]

Such a tilting at windmills by the New York Tribune and the journals which followed its lead, and by the pamphleteers

[1] N. Y. Nation, Sep. 13, 20 and 27, 1888.
[2] Cf. ibid., Sep. 13, 1888.
[3] Cf. ibid., Sep. 20 and 27, Oct. 4 and 11, 1888.
[4] Cf. a handbill in German circulated during the campaign.
[5] See "Free Trade Toilers," a circular issued during the campaign of 1888.
[6] In a pamphlet issued by Judge Publishing Company in 1888.

presupposing and alleging a dark plot in England to impose
free trade upon the United States in the interest of British
industrial supremacy, and our consequent vassalage, had never
been seen before.　The tariff reformers within the Republican
party in the West, who had made a brave show a few months
since, were reduced to silence.　They could not withstand
such an impeachment of their intelligence as protest would
have invited and fell into place as defenders of the ticket.[1]

The Republican Senate bill as a substitute for the Democratic "Mills bill," which had been passed by the House, was
the platform on which the party rested its hopes.　One was
synonymous with protection, the other with free trade.　Thurman's son, Allen E. Thurman, found that men, women and
children, boys and girls, had "all gone crazy on the subject
of politics" in Indiana.[2]　Bandana clubs, bandanas on hats,
around girls' waists, at their necks, were the symbols of Democracy.　Raccoons, log cabins, cider barrels and grandfathers'
hats distinguished the excited Republicans.　Men and boys
tramped the streets with transparencies and torches shouting
the Democratic and Republican slogans.　Red fire, roaring
cannon, banners, streamers and flags, poles of hickory and
ash, surmounted by brooms which would give one party or
the other a "clean sweep," crowing cocks, mass meetings out
of doors and in halls and theatres, leather lunged oratory,
argument and debate, papers that put news aside for "politics"
testified to the absorption of all classes of the people in a
contest which they had been brought to believe meant so
much to them and the republic.

The defeat of the treaty with Great Britain by the Republican
Senate converted the Canadian fisheries imbroglio into a mere
device still further to involve England in the canvass.　That
Cleveland felt himself compelled, for the sake of his own and
his party's success, to use the ruffianly tactics of the opposition
cast an unpleasant sidelight on the American character, while

[1] Cf. N. Y. Nation, Sep. 13, 1888.
[2] Thurman to Lamont, Oct. 22, 1888, in Cleveland Papers.

it was disturbed by a political campaign.[1] His counsellors urged him to action. Any even casual study of the subject confirms the impression that his very anti-English message of August 23rd [2] was issued to wean the Irish voters from the Republican party. It was an old game and it was always played with a reference to New York City in order to capture the electoral vote of New York state. Irishmen demanded it. Irishmen rejoiced after Cleveland had spoken. His words, one said, were "worthy of a Washington or an Emmet." They had "thrilled the Irish heart." Resolutions praising him were adopted by meetings of "Irish-American citizens." Salutes were fired by the Irish. Fishermen in New England who might have voted against Cleveland, it was said, would now give him their support.[3]

Likewise the Chinese were to be assailed; California would turn its electoral votes to Harrison in spite of his record on this subject, if action aimed at this hated race were not immediate. Hysterical appeals reached the President and his friends. W. L. Scott's principal contribution to the campaign, in addition to his gifts of money, was the bill bearing his name which he drove through the House and the Senate and which Cleveland, on October 1st, signed. California shouted. Grown men when the news reached San Francisco embraced and danced in the streets like school boys. They lighted bonfires, formed torchlight processions and behaved as if they were bereft of reason or the common impulses of human beings, while celebrating the enactment of a barbarous law.[4]

Mr. Cleveland was marring his fine record as a public man, as he joined in the rivalry for fleeting favor in this turbulent political campaign. The ill mannered usage of England and the shameful treatment of the Chinese gave added proof of the entirely self centered and parochial state of feeling in the

[1] See vol. iv of this work, pp. 491–9.
[2] Richardson, Messages and Papers, vol. viii, pp. 620–7.
[3] Cleveland Papers.
[4] Cf. a letter, Oct. 3, 1888, in Cleveland Papers; also vol. iv of this work, pp. 501–2.

United States. Men said again "What do we care for abroad?"
Foreign relations were no matter when balanced against
personal and party success in a Presidential canvass. The
honor of the people as a people, and of the commonwealth
as a member of the family of nations was put in the background. The statesman became a small politician. The party
became a body of contriving men hating the other party more
than they loved the reputation of their country, while they
engaged in a mad scramble for votes. The New York Nation
remarked, not without reason, that it could not recall a Presidential campaign since slavery had been abolished which was
"marked by such abnegations of manhood in the higher counsels of the nation" as that one which would end in November.[1]

Even yet all was not done; the lion's tail must have further
twisting lest some Irishman should escape. At the very end
of the canvass a plot to entrap the British minister at Washington and make him serve the uses of the Republican managers
was unfolded. No one had come to feel, in such degree as
this minister had felt, the unfriendly hand of the American
politician with reference to a fine international measure.

Labors to which he had given his time and attention in
connection with a settlement of disputes between two great
peoples of common origins speaking the same tongue, had
just been brought to naught by a number of Republican leaders
in the United States Senate. President Cleveland, Secretary
Bayard and the administration had tried to treat the fisheries
question fairly until they saw that they must run a race in
demagogy with the other party. The British minister's sympathies were, in the nature of the case, with them. He could
not but resent such utterances concerning the treaty as fell
from the lips of Republican leaders in the United States Senate.
Such anti-English tirades as marked the debates of both houses
of Congress and the scurrility aimed at Great Britain on the
Republican stump, and in the New York Tribune and other
Republican newspapers, such systematic and deliberate lying

[1] N. Y. Nation, Sep. 13, 1888.

about his country and his countrymen with a view to pro-
pitiating the Irish had never before been seen.

The British minister belonged to a distinguished old family
in the county of Kent. He had come here as Mr. West, was
knighted to be known as Sir Lionel Sackville Sackville-West
and, very recently, during the bitter progress of the campaign,
he, at the death of his elder brother, Mortimer, fell heir to
a barony, so that he was to be known hereafter as Lord Sackville.
In September a man in California, who called himself Mur-
chison, but whose real name seems to have been Osgoodby,
a small fruit farmer in Pomona in that state, baiting his hook
with the statement that he was a naturalized Briton, wrote to
Lord Sackville to ask for whom he and others of British nativity
should cast their ballots in the coming election.[1] The minister
of Great Britain in the United States, not without interest in
the result, replied guardedly, marking his latter "private." He
intimated that there was a greater sympathy on the side of
the "party in power" with the "mother country," at any rate
when not in the heat of a political campaign, than in the
other party, which had rejected the fisheries treaty. Any party,
"at the present moment" which "openly favored" England
would "lose popularity." That was a fact of which the Democrats were "fully aware"; they were "still desirous," Lord
Sackville said, of "settling all questions with Canada." [2] There
was in the letter not a word which was not true, not a word
which any one of intelligence did not know to be true.[3] To have
made the inquiry and to have sought to involve the minister
in our party politics was a petty and an unworthy trick. But
its success was complete from the standpoint of the Republican
managers who may, probably, have instigated it, to whom
anyhow the product was taken by the recipient of the letter
and by his friends.[4]

---

[1] House Ex. Doc., 50th Cong. 2nd sess., no. 150, pp. 2-3.
[2] Ibid., p. 3.
[3] London Times, Oct. 29, 1888.
[4] Cf. R. B. Mowat, Diplomatic Relations of Great Britain and the U. S.
p. 242; Los Angeles Times, Oct. 21, 1888, and Jan. 8, 1889; H. G. Otis to
Sherman, Feb. 19, 1889, in Sherman Papers.

At first all the possibilities of the letter seem not to have been discerned, but the New York Tribune, which, on October 22nd, printed it in an obscure position, soon transferred the subject to its first page. The New York Sun, which was forwarding the Republican campaign, as it could, following the course which it had taken in 1884 with reference to Mr. Cleveland, led in demanding that Lord Sackville should be handed his passports.[1] "Bounce him!", said the New York World speaking to its ignorant audience.[2] The letter was printed in black-face or double-leaded type in the most prominent positions in Republican newspapers day by day for all to see. Van loads of reprints of it were sent through the streets, and were put into the hands of the people.[3] The cat was now out of the bag. Here was proof that Cleveland was "the English candidate."[4] He was ready to yield to British influence and favor "British interests at the sacrifice of American rights" in the matter of the fisheries question, as in reference to the tariff.[5] "The English government, through its official representative at Washington," said the Brooklyn Times, had, "openly taken the stump for Grover Cleveland." "The ox knoweth his master and John Bull his profits," said the Philadelphia Press. The letter ought to defeat Cleveland. It would defeat him. Those who were willing to be marched to the polls "with the British flag flying," said the Pittsburgh Times, could now do so boldly. By Lord Sackville's letter, Chauncey M. Depew observed, Grover Cleveland's advocacy by the English was "officially established."[6] "The interference of the British government with an election in this country," said the New York Tribune, was "deeply resented by all Americans."[7]

The letter was published on the eve of a "monster mass meeting" of Irishmen in Madison Square Garden in New York.

[1] See issues of Oct. 23, 25, 26, 27 and 29, 1888.
[2] Issue of Oct. 27, 1888.
[3] N. Y. Nation, Nov. 1 and 8, 1888; N. Y. Tribune, Oct. 26, 1888.
[4] N. Y. Tribune, Oct. 23, 1888; cf. ibid., Oct. 24, 1888.
[5] Ibid., Oct. 26, 1888.
[6] Ibid., Oct. 27, 1888.
[7] Issue of Oct. 29, 1888.

This assemblage, on October 25th, was to be adressed by Blaine who entered the great hall with "Steve" Elkins, Patrick Egan, one time president of an Irish American League, and Patrick Ford who had been cooperating during the campaign with Quay and the officers of the Republican National Committee. Amid the old cries of "Blaine, Blaine, James G. Blaine," and "No, No, No, Free Trade" it was clear that the "Plumed Knight" was among his friends. When he came in speakers were denouncing the Cobden Club to which, so it was said, the heads of the Cleveland administration belonged, and in which they stood side by side with Balfour and the "murderers" of Irishmen in England. When Blaine reached the Sackville incident he declared that three ministers to the United States, two certainly, had received their "walking papers" for less reason. Were we to have a British minister at Washington, he inquired, to tell us "what we should do in our political and domestic contests"? It was an insult to the Republican party, an insult to the Democratic party and he, Blaine, would protest in the name of the Democratic party against Lord Sackville's saying "that the rejection by the Republican Senate of an outrageous and miserable and dastardly fisheries treaty was a mere political ruse for the campaign," when it was known that what was done was for "the honor of the American flag," and the protection of the "race of hardy fishermen of America," and so on.[1]

Secretary Bayard at first was disposed to "pooh pooh the affair."[2] But he could not do so long. The embarrassment of the administration, fighting for its life with an unscrupulous enemy which every day, throughout the campaign, in Congress, on the stump and in the press, had been charging it with being more British than American, was such that the President and the Secretary of State must take note of the incident. Challenge and taunt filled the air—they would not dare to move upon their British allies. Democratic party managers

[1] N. Y. Tribune, Oct. 26, 1888.
[2] London Times, Oct. 29 and Nov. 1, 1888; cf. Bayard to Cleveland, Oct. 25, 1888, in Cleveland Papers.

said that the "Irish vote" was "slipping away from them." [1]
They fell upon the President. John Boyle O'Reilly who edited
an Irish paper in Boston, was asked for advice. Others offered
their counsel. "Now knock out Lord Sackville with your
biggest boot and best kick, and you've got 'em," said A. K.
McClure.[2] Only prompt and decisive action would dispose
of "Quay, Blaine & Co." Hesitation would be death. Some
would have had Cleveland go farther. He should "fire" Bayard
and "get himself an American Secretary of State." [3]

Sackville attempted no defence. He simply said to Secretary
Bayard that the letter was "private" and, plainly, "the whole
affair," as it appeared, had been a "trick" to make use of
him. He repeated, in writing, the "disclaimer," which he
had made in conversation at the Department of State, "of
any thought or intention of meddling in domestic politics," [4]
but unwisely talked to newspaper reporters who, as might
have been expected, turned his words and made the matter
worse.[5] There could be no delay. Only a few days of the
campaign remained and Cleveland must be reelected. The
British government was informed of the facts, opening the way
for the minister's recall.

Everywhere in England as in the United States it was agreed
that the writing of the letter was a stupid lapse on the part
of a representative of a first rate power. But the London
Times spoke of the "undignified vulgarity" of the outcry. It
was, perhaps, nothing to the discredit of the minister that he
was not "up to all the dirty tricks of American politicians."
The people of the United States in the heat of one of their
quadrennial electoral contests seemed to be "without regard
for the dictates of good manners." [6] No action being in immediate contemplation by Lord Salisbury,[7] the President,

[1] N. Y. Tribune, Nov. 1, 1888.
[2] To Cleveland, Oct. 27, 1888, in Cleveland Papers.
[3] Nordhoff to Lamont, Oct. 25, 1888, in ibid.
[4] Sackville to Bayard, Oct. 25, 1888, in ibid.
[5] See e.g. N. Y. Tribune, Oct. 24, 1888; House Ex. Doc., 50th Cong.
2nd sess., no. 150, pp. 13, 62, 63.
[6] London Times, Oct. 29, 1888.
[7] House Ex. Doc., 50th Cong. 2nd sess., no. 150, pp. 4–5.

through the Department of State, on October 30th, notified
Lord Sackville that he was no longer *persona grata* and his
passports were delivered to him.[1] Government, people and
press in London were amazed. The tone of the demand for
the minister's surrender of his exequatur seemed to be need-
lessly importunate and abrupt. While "an angry king whis-
pers," the London Spectator said, "a vexed democracy bellows."
American diplomats were, the Spectator continued, "the
spoiled children of diplomacy" for which reason, though offense
had been done in this instance, "a little latitude" should be
allowed the representatives of other countries.[2] "A more
ridiculous spectacle," said the London Times, "has rarely been
witnessed in any civilized country." Secretary Bayard has
proven to the world that he could be "as contemptuously
disregardful of the decencies of international intercourse as
Mr. Blaine."[3] The justice of such an indictment Mr. Bayard
would not have denied, but the rules of comity now, as in
reference to the fisheries treaty, Cleveland's retaliatory measures
regarding Canada and the Chinese treaty, must be subordinated
to the requirements of a rampant struggle for party power.

Those in America who knew the minister, though they may
have deplored such precipitate action in his case, wasted
little sympathy upon him. He had thought so ill of the state
of society in this country that, in coming to Washington, he
had brought with him, to preside over his household, three
daughters by a Spanish dancer whose acquaintance he had
made at Madrid, and to whom he had not been married.
He had not felt free to have them accompany him to other
capitals. It was a matter of surprise that England, under
Queen Victoria, should keep and advance an officer in her
foreign service for whom those of correct standards of conduct
could feel so little respect.[4]

What the effect of such a really petty incident had upon the

---

[1] House Ex. Doc., 50th Cong. 2nd sess., no. 150, p. 7.
[2] Issue of Nov. 3, 1888.
[3] Issue of Nov. 1, 1888.
[4] R. B. Mowat, Dip. Relations of Great Britain and the U. S., p. 241;
J. W. Foster, Dip. Memoirs, vol. ii, p. 319.

course of the mind of any considerable body of "red hot" Americans who were to be influenced to vote for Harrison and against Cleveland is indeterminable. It is likely that fewer citizens who may have made up their minds to support Cleveland deserted him for this reason than on other accounts. The factionalism within the Democratic party in New York state was a more powerful influence in deciding the result. Ostensibly friendly relations subsisted between Hill, who had followed Cleveland as governor of New York, and the President. Efforts were made on both sides, by correspondence and by invitations to Albany and to Washington for personal meetings, to create an appearance of a common purpose. But it was plain that there was no congenial ground for the two men; they personally, and their respective followings, had entirely opposite ideals. Cleveland's objects were honest public service and good government, while Hill was a cunning spoilsman, as all could see. His administration of the governorship was founded on bargains and trades. Offices and "jobs" for himself and his adherents were his highest end and Cleveland, in the nature of the case, was unloved by the rank and file of the party in New York who made a living from politics. In the Presidency he had frustrated many of their dearest projects. To lead them away from the head of their ticket was not a difficult feat.

The conflict of aims and interests had been obvious in the Presidential campaign of 1884. Hill's claims upon the nomination for governor in 1885 were unsuccessfully contested by Abram S. Hewitt, which caused the Independents to support the Republican candidate, Davenport. Hill's plurality in the election was more than 11,000. His term had expired—would he be renominated? Cleveland was importuned to take a part in the impending contest. Committees were formed. Cards were distributed asking voters to enroll their names for Cleveland, while declaring their intention of voting against Hill, should he be the party nominee, as it seemed certain that he would be.[1] The New York Evening Post, the New York Times

[1] Specimens of these cards are in the Cleveland Papers.

and other Independent newspapers, which were ably engaged in the effort to reelect the President, opposed the pretensions of Hill.[1] If Cleveland should express a wish for Hill's success would he not forfeit the respect of his Independent following? Hill had written to the President commending his letter of acceptance [2] and, in the usual course of events, Cleveland might have taken the opportunity to voice his approval of Hill's design to seek another term.

But, if he had wished to do so, his friends would have stayed his hand. They wrote to warn him of the trading which would proceed on election day at his expense and for the governor's advantage. Hill's renomination would weaken, if it should not defeat, the ticket.[3] He was "so unscrupulous and wicked, so craftily dishonest," a friend of the President said, that his reelection would be "the shame of the state." [4] What shreds of character had still been his were being destroyed by revelations concerning frauds in connection with the construction of the Croton aqueduct, in which it was shown that he had corrupt complicity.[5] Ex-Mayor Grace told Cleveland that expressions of favor for Hill would be "absolutely suicidal." He would so greatly damage his record, that it would be "more than the Presidency was worth." [6]

Soon it would be too late to obstruct the governor's progress. Failure on Cleveland's side "to indicate a different desire," Roswell P. Flower observed, meant Hill's renomination.[7] It was a difficult situation and there was no desire on the Republican side, or among Hill's motley band, to make it the easier for the President to extricate himself from the corner into which he had been pressed. He chose to say that it would be improper for him, as President, to interfere in a state contest, and to have taken another course would, probably, have

---

[1] Cf. N. Y. Nation, Sep. 27, 1886.
[2] Sep. 10, 1888, in Cleveland Papers.
[3] Cf. Stetson to Cleveland in ibid.
[4] W. M. Ivins to Lamont, July 18, 1888, in ibid.
[5] Simon Sterne to Cleveland, July 18, 1888, in ibid; A. Nevins, Abram S. Hewitt, pp. 516–20.
[6] W. R. Grace to Cleveland, Sep. 20, 1888, in Cleveland Papers.
[7] Flower to Lamont, July 24, 1888, in ibid.

been a very great mistake. At any rate, as he wrote Bissell, he was "determined to let the gubernatorial question alone." [1]

Hill had the support of Tammany, the New York Sun and all the forces arrayed against honest and efficient public service dissociated from self interest. While Cleveland's sympathies were not to be mistaken by well informed men, he said, when asked for public statements, that expressions of preference on his part would have the character of dictation, and recommended his friends to abide, as he would abide, by the "judgment" of the organization to which they all adhered. [2] Hill would be the candidate to oppose ex-Senator Warner Miller whom the Republicans had nominated for the governorship.

Abram S. Hewitt's term as mayor of New York City was coming to an end. Croker refused him the support of Tammany Hall and presented one of its catspaws, Hugh J. Grant, as the candidate for the office, while Hewitt was left with the support of the "County Democracy" which feebly contested Tammany's pretensions. [3] In the interest of harmony he was asked to retire from the contest. [4] He refused. For two years he had given the city an honest administration; he would not stand aside for a gang whose corruptions were notorious throughout the country and, indeed, the civilized world. [5] A poetaster who betrayed more enthusiasm for Hill than for Grant stated "The Duty of the Hour"—

"Ye friends of Grover Cleveland, all the gallant men who train
In Democratic legions for the cause and not for gain,
You surely know your duty now, so step right up and do it,
For Cleveland, Thurman, Hill and Jones, and also Abram Hewitt.
Ye friends of Allen Thurman, that old Roman, grand and good,
The man who sucked Democracy with his very earliest food.
Your duty is to firmly stand, as rightly now you view it,
For Cleveland, Thurman, Hill and Jones and also Abram Hewitt,
&c. &c. [6]

[1] Cleveland to Bissell, July 17, and Cleveland to W. R. Grace, July 14, 1888, in Cleveland Papers.
[2] McElroy, Grover Cleveland, vol. i, pp. 292–3.
[3] A. Nevins, Abram S. Hewitt, p. 522.
[4] Ibid., p. 524; also Cleveland Papers.
[5] Cf. N. Y. Nation, Sep. 20, Oct. 4 and 11, 1888.
[6] N. Y. Sun, Oct. 24, 1888.

The ranks of the Mugwumps were little broken in spite of the fact that Cleveland's policies had not been such as to fulfil all of his promises or all of their hopes. The most eminent of the defections, perhaps, was Henry C. Lea of Philadelphia, and his action was influenced by his views concerning the tariff.[1] Many professors in the colleges, and other men of high ideals of Republican leanings were added, indeed, to the list of those who had voted with the Independents in 1884.[2] As in that year the press in New York was preponderantly for Cleveland. No changes were to be noted except the establishment of a new Republican daily morning paper called the Press, edited by Robert P. Porter, an Englishman, who had been brought to see the delights of "protection," and a strengthening by new ownership of a Republican pictorial weekly, Judge, to counteract the influence of Puck which was employed so effectively in the Democratic interest.[3]

The issue four years ago, however, in so far as the Mugwumps were concerned, had been Blaine and, while the effort was made to have it appear that his record as a public character was still the issue, since the Republican party in 1888 found more inspiration in the sound of his voice than in that of Harrison,[4] the fact is that at least as many Independent voters were leaving Cleveland on the question of the tariff as were coming to him on this question. The Mugwumps in New York could not, and would not, support Hill or Grant. They made it plain day by day that they, while voting for Cleveland for President would cast their ballots for Warner Miller, the Republican candidate for governor, and for Hewitt for mayor.

Breaches were to be closed by a final "business men's" parade in New York on Saturday, October 27th, when Tam-

[1] N. Y. Nation, Oct. 25, 1888, and Oct. 27, 1892; E. S. Bradley, Henry Charles Lea, p. 235.
[2] N. Y. Nation, Sep. 27 and Oct. 25, 1888.
[3] Gillam who had served Puck so well, tempted by the new publisher of Judge, now turned his talents against Cleveland. Puck was founded in 1877, Judge in 1881. W. J. Arkell purchased Judge in 1886. The first number issued under his management was dated Jan. 16 of that year.—Files in N. Y. Public Library.
[4] Cf. Writings of Schurz, vol. iv, p. 513.

many and Mr. Hewitt's friends, Hill men and Cleveland men, would have a happy reunion. Cleveland would be present; Hill, it was believed, would be also. Factional lines would be obliterated and there would be harmony, where discord had been, under the banners of Jefferson, Andrew Jackson and other leaders gone to join the saints.

Hill was employed in campaigning in another part of the state,[1] but Grant and Hewitt publicly shook hands in the presence of Cleveland who, with the mother of Charles Stewart Parnell, "Ireland's uncrowned king," in a green velvet dress, at his side, to stir the hearts of Erin's sons endued with the voting franchise in America, stood to watch 30,000 or 35,000 men, many of them of prominence and wealth, known the country over, pass by in a pelting rain. But for the storm there would have been 100,000, said the New York Herald.[2] "Four, four, four years more" was the song that resounded up Broadway. "Grover, Grover has a walkover," "Grover, Grover, he'll hold over," "No, no, no Jim Blaine," "Don't, don't, don't be afraid, Tariff Reform is not Free Trade" and other cries rose from the clubs as they passed along waving their bedraggled red bandanas, the symbols of the stirring canvass.[3]

On the following Saturday afternoon, again in the rain, the Republicans filled the streets of New York with their battalions of marching men, shouting "Sack, Sack, Sackville West," "Grover, Grover, your time's over," as they filed before a stand on which Levi P. Morton, the candidate for Vice-President, Warner Miller, Chauncey Depew and others stood, while Blaine, who saw the propriety of keeping himself in the background, was ensconced at the window of a hotel. This demonstration was followed at night by a great Democratic torchlight parade reviewed by Hill, when it was said that 50,000 men were in line.[4]

---

[1] N. Y. Sun, Oct. 27, 1888.
[2] The Tribune said there were only 14,420 "by actual count."—Issue of Oct. 29, 1888.
[3] N. Y. Herald, Oct. 28, 1888.
[4] Ibid., Nov. 4, 1888.

The New York Herald succinctly stated the meaning of the campaign from the standpoint of the Democrats—

"Republican success on Tuesday means—More trusts; more monopolies; more subsidized millionaires—Carnegies, Dwights, Algers and Dolans; the rich richer and the poor poorer; increased taxation on all the necessaries of life; continued white slavery in iron and textile industries; highly 'protected' wages, 85 cents to 95 cents a day; total destruction of American shipping interests; the return to power of Dorseys, Bradys, Dudleys and Credit Mobilier swindlers who formerly disgraced the nation, and the closing of all American woolen mills." [1]

The pluralities were sufficiently large to make it possible to know the result the day after the ballots were cast. Hope on the Democratic side of another determination upon the receipt of later returns was not extinguished, but it was clear to unbiassed observers that Harrison and Morton had been elected and that the important factors had been New York and Indiana. The number of voters who went to the polls was 11,388,038 and, while 100,476 more cast their ballots for the Democratic than for the Republican ticket,[2] Mr. Cleveland was not elected. Mr. Harrison carried New York by a plurality of 13,002, as compared with Cleveland's plurality of 1,047 in 1884. Harrison carried Indiana by 2,348 in 1888 as against Cleveland's plurality of 6,512 in 1884. New Jersey remained faithful to Cleveland by a plurality of 7,149, nearly 3,000 in excess of that of four years ago. Connecticut's Democratic plurality was reduced in four years from 1,284 to 336. The Republican pluralities were smaller in Pennsylvania, Ohio, Illinois, Rhode Island, New Hampshire and Minnesota; they were somewhat larger in Iowa, Kansas, Maine, Massachusetts, Nebraska, Vermont and Wisconsin.[3] The frantic call for the Scott bill to hound the Chinese, and its enactment, had not brought the President California. Harrison's plurality in that state was 7,000.

[1] N. Y. Herald, Nov. 4, 1888.
[2] The Democratic plurality in the popular vote in 1884 had been 62,683.
[3] App. Ann. Cyclop. for 1888, pp. 782, 826-8.

Harrison was assured of 233 electoral votes, while Cleveland would have 168. All again had hinged upon the 36 votes of New York. Had these been for Cleveland instead of for Harrison the President would have had 204 electoral votes and Harrison 197. It could be said that Cleveland had thrown away the Presidency when he had sent to Congress his message in December, 1887, and had committed the party to tariff reform.[1] But examination of the returns gives but little confirmation to any theory that the cause which Mr. Cleveland espoused had been rejected, or that he personally had been repudiated. The great mass of contemptuous abuse of the President and his party and its principles which had descended upon the country during the canvass must have seemed pitifully unavailing to the Republican managers when they were able afterward coolly to contemplate the scene. Blaine, Whitelaw Reid and other men who were directing the great manipulation of the minds of the voting citizenry had made a spectre of "British free trade."[2] More men, as measured by the popular vote, were repelled by, than were pleased to approve and endorse, these methods.

As for Mr. Cleveland he contemplated retirement from the troubled scene with but little personal regret. "You know how I feel in the matter and how great will be the personal compensations of defeat," he wrote Dr. S. B. Ward, on November 6th, election day. "I am sure," he continued, "that any choice I may have for success rests upon the conviction that the triumph of my party at this time means the good and the prosperity of the country."[3] Letters and telegrams offered sympathy and consolation and voiced the sense of loss felt by his friends. He had fallen in a battle for a principle. It was better to be right than to be President. Truth crushed to earth would rise again. John Bigelow sent Mr. Cleveland

[1] McElroy, Grover Cleveland, vol. i, chap. xi; N. Y. Nation, Nov. 8, 1888.

[2] "They gave you no fair fight," Professor Alexander Johnston of Princeton wrote to Cleveland after the election; "nothing but English flags, forged quotations and appeals to ignorance, terror and the basest prejudices and passions of men."—Cleveland Papers in November.

[3] To S. B. Ward, Nov. 6, 1888, in ibid.

congratulations "upon the prospect of once more belonging to himself." That, in itself, Mr. Bigelow said, is "the recovery of a great estate. Like Phaeton you have the satisfaction of knowing that you fell in attempting great things." [1]

One prediction was confirmed by the election. The Republicans, by the President's tariff message, had been put in a position where they could demand money of manufacturers, and other men of large means whose private interests made them high tariff advocates. They had been able to collect a campaign fund which exceeded by many times any sum which the Democrats could hope to assemble. It fell into the hands of Quay, Dudley and other "practical" campaigners who had a prominent part in giving the election to Mr. Harrison. [2] The situation in New York was carefully studied. In the first place Warner Miller, the Republican candidate for governor, had declared himself in favor of "high license," and had taken a stand against the "saloon" by reform of the excise system, [3] which reduced the vote of the separate Prohibition party from 36,000 in 1886 and 42,000 in 1887 to 30,000 in 1888. [4] While he thus gained from the "temperance" elements he lost the favor of German-Americans who were proverbially hostile to restrictions upon conviviality, [5] and the liquor interests generally with which his opponent, Hill, had made profitable alliances. This situation affected the vote for President. [6]

Many said, and the well informed knew, that there had been treachery, in spite of Croker's and other disclaimers. [7] Cleveland had been "stabbed" just as Hancock had been "assassinated" in 1880. [8] Hill's corrupt connections, and Croker's rise to responsible leadership of the Tammany machine in New York

[1] Bigelow to Cleveland, Nov. 8, 1888, in Cleveland Papers.
[2] Cf. N. Y. Nation, Nov. 22, 1888.
[3] Ibid., Nov. 22, 1888.
[4] Cf. ibid.
[5] McElroy, Grover Cleveland, vol. i, pp. 298-9.
[6] E. P. Wheeler to Lamont, Aug. 14, 1888, in Cleveland Papers. Hill had recently vetoed a high license law which had been passed by the legislature. See Warner Miller's speech at Cooper Union, Sep. 18, 1888; cf. N. Y. Nation, Nov. 22, 1888.
[7] Croker to Cleveland, Nov. 16, 1888, in Cleveland Papers.
[8] Blanton Duncan to Cleveland, Nov. 11, 1888, in ibid.

City, which pushed the claims of Grant for mayor against Hewitt, with a Republican in the canvass to take the place which Roosevelt had occupied in the Hewitt-George campaign in 1885,[1] invited bargains and deals to Cleveland's disadvantage. The low and corruptible men in Hill's following who were pleased at the prospect of his continued occupancy of the place would go to any length in his behalf. Croker was without scruple in his contest to elect Grant and to win control of the taxing and spending power in New York City. Quay who knew the game which these elements played was at hand. He would exchange Democratic votes for Harrison for Republican votes for Hill and Grant. This trade was engaged in with profit to both sides and with loss, incidentally, to Cleveland. It was buying a victory "by giving a vote for Hill and a vote for Grant in exchange for a vote for Harrison," [2] a process by which Miller fell "outside the breastworks."

While Harrison's plurality in New York state was more than 14,000, that of Hill's was in excess of 19,000, in spite of the well known fact that the Mugwumps, whatever their number, as well as many respectable Democrats, had voted for Cleveland, but had "scratched" Hill.[3] In New York City Hill had received some 4,000 votes more than Cleveland, in Erie county 3,500.[4] If this disparity were not entirely due to wicked contrivance a part of it was ascribable, as all well informed and candid men knew, to simple barter and sale.[5] Hundreds of thousands of dollars were taken in one city alone, Philadelphia, from merchants and manufacturers, excited to it by apparent belief that ruin would overtake them and their businesses and industries, if Cleveland were continued in power.[6] It is likely that $3,000,000 in all were collected and expended by the Republican managers, up to this time an unheard of sum to be raised by any party for an electoral campaign—$400,000 had

[1] N. Y. Nation, Oct. 25, 1888.
[2] N. Y. Times, Oct. 30, 1888; cf. A. Nevins, Abram S. Hewitt, p. 526.
[3] N. Y. Nation, Nov. 15, 1888.
[4] N. Y. Tribune, Nov. 19, 1888.
[5] Cf. N. Y. Times, Nov. 8 and 9, 1888; A. K. McClure, Old Times Notes of Pa., vol. ii, pp. 568–9.
[6] A. K. McClure, Old Time Notes of Pa., vol. ii, pp. 570–1.

been sought and secured in the last week of the canvass [1]— and, with a view to defeating future Congressional inquiries, the officers of the Republican National Committee had made a bonfire of their records.[2] Quay was wont to say afterward that he and those in his retinue were near "the gates of the penitentiary" for what they had done to make Harrison President.[3]

It was generally and quite truly stated that Dudley in the West had pursued methods not more correct as judged by any proper rule of morals with reference to the conduct of elections. He had issued a circular on October 24th directing the "workers" to "divide the floaters into blocks of five and put a trusted man with necessary funds in charge of these five, and make him responsible that none get away, and that all vote our ticket." He was ready for the fray. "The Rebel crew," he said, "can't steal this election from us as they did in 1884 without some one getting hurt."[4] Purchased, and herded to the polling places, with money taken from the rich, Dudley's "floaters" turned the tables upon Cleveland in Indiana.[5] "Fat frying" and "blocks of five" were the eloquent phrases which the campaign of 1888 contributed to the American political vocabulary.

No Republican of correct ethical standards for our public life could look back with pride upon such a canvass. But in the result great satisfaction was taken by highly respectable classes of men in the North and West who knew little of the methods which had brought the victory and, in innocence or indifference, gave no credence to accounts in the opposition press of the wickedness of the processes by which the end had been gained. It was the triumph again of the loyal population over the Secessionist South; of the old party of "moral ideas" over a party whose often repeated stupidities none could excuse or forget; of prosperity over impending disaster to industry; of

[1] N. Y. Nation, Nov. 22, 1888.
[2] Ibid., Dec. 13, 1888.
[3] A. K. McClure, Old Time Notes of Pa., vol. ii, p. 573.
[4] A copy of this circular is in Cleveland Papers. Cf. N. Y. Nation, Nov. 8 and 22, 1888.
[5] W. H. English to Cleveland, Nov. 13, 1888, in Cleveland Papers. Mr. English observed that a change of one vote in each precinct in Indiana would have given Cleveland a plurality of 1,000.

work and wages for native labor over imports of products of disliked foreign rivals; of protection over free trade. Quay had been astute and capable in a necessary business. It was not an hour to inquire too narrowly into the manner in which he had comported himself in New York.

CHAPTER XXXIV

HARRISON'S ADMINISTRATION

THE election of Harrison set in motion the ambitious energies of Quay and the politicians who were glad to take the credit for the victory, which would reestablish the Republican party in power in Washington. The construction of a cabinet for the new President immediately occupied the attention of the press. Guesses and prognostications filled the columns of the newspapers while Harrison gave his mind to the problem of organizing a government and framing the policies which should distinguish his administration.

The one thing which seemed certain was that Blaine would be appointed Secretary of State, although the friends of John Sherman pretended to think that he had more valid claim to the place.[1] The Blaine following took umbrage at suggestions that any one but their leader who, in the nominating convention, had stepped aside, as they said, in favor of the President-elect, should have the "premiership." He had held the office before and was in the midst of a brilliant administration of the nation's foreign affairs when Garfield had been shot. He might be disposed, as Harrison knew, to dominate the situation and make himself in fact, if not in name, the head of the government.[2] But he was now an older man than when he had overborne Garfield, and plainly his health was impaired so that the same militancy might not be expected of him.[3] It was suggested that he could be disposed of by his appointment as minister to England, a highly humorous idea. The New York Evening Post said that he would not be received by the British government were he to present his credentials, a rejection for which there

[1] N. Y. Nation, Dec. 6, 1888.
[2] Cf. Gail Hamilton, Biography of Blaine, p. 651.
[3] Thomas F. Bayard, seeing Blaine in 1889 for the first time in seven years, thought him "a very enfeebled man."—Writings of Schurz, vol. v, p. 18; cf. A. F. Tyler, Foreign Policy of J. G. Blaine, p. 183.

would be full warrant, were that government willing to give itself the trouble to study his utterances and plumb a mind which seemed, for political purposes at least, to be so passionately anglophobic.[1] It was said, too, that he would prefer to return to the United States Senate—he did not wish a cabinet post.[2] But it was soon taken for granted that Blaine would be Secretary of State.

It was confidently expected that Senator Allison would be Secretary of the Treasury. His knowledge of finance was accounted to be intimate, though he was a man, as appeared, who was not certain of himself and, under pressure, would not stand unshaken in his place.[3] He declined, and William Windom was called to Indianapolis. He had been Secretary of the Treasury in the brief Garfield administration, when he was accredited to Minnesota. Since his retirement from office he had been residing in New York.[4]

Another appointment which was regarded as certain was that of John Wanamaker of Philadelphia to be Postmaster General. On its face no choice seemed more unfit to be made. It was notorious that Mr. Wanamaker had collected a large sum of money which was put in the hands of "Matt" Quay for use in the campaign to elect Mr. Harrison. Whatever the amount, which was variously stated, it was unquestionably applied in dubious manipulations which had given Harrison ascendency over Cleveland in New York state. The success of the Republican ticket by any device was held to be a sufficient justification for the means of gaining it and no explanations, under criticism, came from Mr. Wanamaker, or his friends, beyond a denial of the charge that he had burned his records. The collection and expenditure of the money was not looked upon by him as a public·matter, and the papers, if they remained in his custody, were not for the information of those who were questioning him in uncivil ways. His action was held to be the more unseemly since it was known to all men that he was prominent

---

[1] N. Y. Nation, Dec. 27, 1888.
[2] Halstead to Sherman, Nov. 19, 1888, in Sherman Papers.
[3] N. Y. Nation, Feb. 7, 1889.
[4] Ibid., Feb. 21 and March 7, 1889.

in the church. Moreover he was a man, it appeared, without the slightest prior contact with public life. His direction of a department of the government gave no promise of service valuable to the people. He had not yet opened a shop in New York, to influence with advertising patronage the opinion of the newspaper press in that city, as the same press stood under his influence in Philadelphia, and criticism of his movements was free. He had come forward during the campaign with his "money bags." He had been distinguished only in the "clothing trade," lately extending his interest to the sale, by "seductive advertisements," of "almost everything that is used by civilized man or woman." Of speeches he had made none; his writing was confined to "puffs" of "Yankee notions." He had no wisdom, so ran the comment in New York, except "in the keeping of a large variety store." Wanamaker, "the most religious Republican in the world," with probable exception for Colonel Elliott F. Shepard, of the New York Mail and Express, which kept a Bible text at the head of its editorial columns, would take his place in the President's cabinet because he had bought and paid for it.[1]

The unfavorable public impression created by the collection of money in Pennsylvania to influence the election was intensified by revelations in New York as to the expenditure of the money. Small party henchmen in that city were charged with receiving funds without giving the expected return. They were paid for what, it was complained, they did not do. Results which were promised, when money was put into their hands, were not achieved and they were held to account, not for the corruption of the franchise, but for their bad faith.[2] Reform in election systems was demanded. Various plans to insure uninfluenced and secret voting for candidates in order to confound those who made it their business to send men to the polls in "blocks," and to deliver majorities in answer to payment in cash or remunerative office, were under discussion. Some states, following

---

[1] Writings of Schurz, vol. v, pp. 13–5, 18–21; N. Y. Nation, Nov. 29, Dec. 13 and 27, 1888, and Jan. 3 and March 14, 1889.

[2] N. Y. Nation, Nov. 29 and Dec. 6 and 13, 1888.

Massachusetts, were experimenting with the Australian ballot, or some modified form of that system, which would render the vote unsalable, in that the buyer would have no assurance that what he had bought had been received.[1]

Corrupt practices acts which would require parties and candidates of parties to publish the names of contributors and the amount of money given in canvasses, and to punish bribery were advocated. Bills calling for the publication of expenditures in political campaigns appeared in Congress and in some of the state legislatures, to receive discussion in the press.[2] The Mugwumps and their reforms could not be laughed to scorn in the face of such incidents as those which had scandalized the Presidential canvass of 1888. The movement was stimulated by the publication, late in this year, of James Bryce's "The American Commonwealth."[3] Intelligent Americans knew how their political system had fallen from the standards set for it at its foundation. A competent and respected foreign observer now told us, in clear and simple terms, how astounding and how very many were the evils which had crept into our public life, especially in the cities and states. Young men in the colleges, the heads of which, in nearly all instances, were open and courageous reformers and inspiring examples to the youth committed to their care,[4] were stimulated in a wish and a purpose, as they went out into politics and journalism, to lead the people to a higher plane of thought and action with regard to civic affairs. There were men to resent the words of Senator Ingalls of Kansas when he said that the "purification of politics" was an "iridiscent dream," that "the Decalogue and the Golden Rule had no place in a political campaign," and that a

[1] N. Y. Nation, March 14 and 21, Apr. 18, May 16 and 30, and June 6, 1889, Jan. 16 and Apr. 3, 1890. See John H. Wigmore, The Australian Ballot System. Before September 1, 1889, no less than 11 states had enacted laws requiring the ballots used at elections to have an official character, and providing for secrecy in the casting of these ballots. (N. Y. Nation, Aug. 29, 1889.) By March, 1891, there were 25.—Ibid., March 12, Apr. 30 and May 21, 1891.

[2] N. Y. Nation, Dec. 27, 1888, and May 9, 1889, Apr. 17, 1890, Feb. 12, 1891.

[3] Cf. ibid., March 6, 1890.

[4] Ibid., Oct. 10 and Dec. 26, 1889.

politician who should be defeated because of his principles was like a commander who should lose a battle "through the activity of his moral nature—the derision and jest of history." [1]

While Harrison, at his home in Indiana, was under siege by the men, many of them corrupt, who had been influential factors in electing him, and he was formulating his plans for the cabinet with which he would begin his administration, Cleveland was bringing his term of office to an end. Congress would meet in December, 1888, and he gave it his fourth and last message. Unlike the third it was a general statement of the condition of the country and touched a great variety of subjects, many of which demanded the attention of the legislative branch of the government. The retiring President did not fail, however, to re-direct public notice to the tariff and the surplus. He spoke of "combinations, monopolies and aggregations of capital" which were rewarded not "solely" as a result of "sturdy industry and enlightened foresight," but through "the discriminating favor of the .government." They were "largely built upon undue exactions from the masses of the people," he said. Two classes were being formed, "one comprising the very rich and powerful," the other "the toiling poor." Aggregated capital fared on triumphantly, while the citizen was "struggling far in the rear," or was "trampled to death beneath an iron heel." Corporations which should be "the carefully restrained creatures of the law and the servants of the people" were "fast becoming the people's masters."

The government persisted in exacting in taxes millions which lay dormant in the Treasury, "unapplied and useless." To the extent to which the citizens were thus burdened "beyond any useful purpose, and for the benefit of a favored few," the government was entering "gratuitously into partnership with these favorites, to their advantage and to the injury of a vast majority of our people," which was, Mr. Cleveland said, "not equality before the law." The existing situation was "injurious to the health of our entire body politic." Communism was "a hateful thing," but the "communism of combined wealth and capital,"

[1] Writings of Schurz, vol. v, pp. 77, 101; N. Y. Nation, Nov. 3, 1890.

working insidiously, was "not less dangerous than the communism of oppressed poverty and toil," which, when exasperated by injustice, attacked, "with wild disorder, the citadel of rule." "He mocks the people," said the President, harking back to the noise of the recently ended campaign, "who proposes that the government shall protect the rich and that they, in turn, will care for the poor." For the relief of the people "a just and sensible revision of our tariff laws" should be made at once. "As public servants," the President concluded, "we shall do our duty well, if we constantly guard the rectitude of our intentions, maintain unsullied our love of country and, with unselfish purpose, strive for the public good." [1]

Cleveland had learned nothing by his defeat, the Republican newspapers declared. The message, said the New York Tribune, was "the snarl of a beaten candidate." He was scolding 60 millions of people "for failing to appreciate his transcendent wisdom and devoted patriotism," and more in a similar strain. [2]

The New York Evening Post commended the "boldness of the message." The President was right when he spoke of the protective tariff as a species of socialism. From the theory propounded by the Republicans, which Cleveland denounced, it was not a "long step" to declare that it was the duty of the government "to furnish remunerative employment to everybody." If the "capitalistic class" be given a "shock" by the message it is "precisely what they need," said the Evening Post. [3]

The message, in so far as it contained allusions to the tariff, added nothing to the prospect of action on the bills relating to this topic, the discussion of which had been interrupted by the adjournment of Congress in October. The Mills bill would not be passed by the Senate, nor would the substitute bill which had been put forward by that chamber make progress toward enactment into law in the present complexion of the national

[1] Richardson, Messages and Papers, vol. viii, pp. 773–6.
[2] N. Y. Tribune, Dec. 4, 1888.
[3] N. Y. Nation, Dec. 6, 1888.

legislature in the few weeks remaining to a waning administration. All pertaining to the tariff was gall and rancor.

Now and again private pension bills were vetoed in the courageous spirit in which the President had attacked this question, with new thrusts at the transparently improper claims of persons whom Congress had chosen for the grant of benefits. A final order on the civil service, extending the provisions of the law to cover employees of the Post Office Department at work on the railways, a group which the reformers had greatly desired to be included in classes removed from the reach of party politics, met with widespread commendation.[1] Dorman B. Eaton had not commanded the confidence of the civil service reformers, nor did Mr. Edgerton whom Cleveland had put in the place as the president of the commission. There had been no reason to think, indeed, that this valetudinarian, who so long had lived apart from public life, and who was, it appeared, without sincere interest in the success of the law, nor in sympathy with the principle underlying it, would be an efficient public servant.

In 1889 he was dismissed for utterances unfriendly to the cause which he had been appointed to advance,[2] and Hugh S. Thompson of South Carolina, one time governor of his state and lately Assistant Secretary of the Treasury, was nominated for the place. The Senate refused its approval of his name and the work of reorganizing the commission was passed on to Mr. Harrison.

A scheme to pay back to the states and territories and the District of Columbia "all moneys collected under the direct tax," levied for war purposes by act of August 5, 1861, aggregating about $17,000,000, had occupied much attention in the last session, while the campaign raged, at which time the bill passed the Senate. It was plain, of course, that the fund would be distributed in the North and the West, since a very small part of the collections had been made in the states which had seceded

---

[1] Cf. Richardson, vol. viii, pp. 844 et seq; N. Y. Nation, March 19, 1889.
[2] Cf. N. Y. Nation, Dec. 13, 1888, Feb. 14 and 21, 1889. Edgerton called civil service reform "a hollow and extravagant fraud."

from the Union. Though it had been collected by mediation
of the states on a quota plan, the tax had been laid by the
Federal government, and it in no way belonged to them.
It was plain, too, that the money when, and if, it should be
received by the states would be expended in many, if not in all,
instances fruitlessly and foolishly. Nevertheless the measure
was approved by Congress as one aimed at the reduction of
the surplus and it was sent to the President, who promptly
vetoed it. The states, Mr. Cleveland said, should be supported
by the states; their funds should be furnished by their own
citizens, an element of "purity and strength" not "safely
exchanged for the threatened demoralization and carelessness
attending the custody and management of large gifts from the
Federal Treasury." Nearly a generation had passed away
since this tax had been collected and expended. It was collected
for a purpose not standing in any relation to present necessities.
It was still the "people's money," and better use could be found
for it than the distribution of it, "upon the plea of a reimburse-
ment of ancient taxation." Such a payment to the states would
be "a sheer, bald gratuity," and it would be "unconstitutional." [1]

The Senate, actuated by unabated enmity to the President,
at once passed the bill over the veto, by a vote of 45 to 9, but no
action ensued in the House.[2]

The Congress before it came to its end, with the installation of
Harrison, considered the cases of the Western territories and
voted to admit four of them to statehood, subject to appropriate
preliminary action in those territories. This "Omnibus bill"
was approved by President Cleveland on Washington's Birthday, 1889. Dakota was divided into North and South Dakota,
thus ending a long standing dispute as to the proper course to be
pursued with reference to that large territory. Both states
would carry the name to which the people were attached, while
the convenience, and necessities, indeed, of the growing popula-

[1] Richardson, vol. viii, pp. 837–43; McPherson's Handbook for 1890,
pp. 18–20; ibid., for 1888, pp. 173–4; N. Y. Nation, Dec. 13, 1888, and
March 7, 1889.
[2] McPherson's Handbook for 1890, p. 21.

tion would be served. Washington, in the Northwest, with its great harbor on the Pacific Ocean, its natural wealth and its increasing settlements would be favored, while Montana, though its immediate claims were less pressing, despite its manifestly rich resources and the assurance of its growth, was also invited to come into the Union. Democrats who desired to bring in New Mexico, since it was expected to return popular majorities for their party, yielded, when the bill emerged from the conference committee, and the execution of that design was accordingly deferred.[1]

The Congress before adjournment also passed a bill authorizing the incorporation of the Maritime Canal Company of Nicaragua to forward the construction of the much and long discussed interoceanic waterway which should cross that Central American state, now that the adventure at Panama had failed under circumstances so notorious. This measure was approved by the President.[2]

The day for Cleveland's retirement and for Harrison's taking over of the Presidential office, March 4, 1889, came and the usual ceremonies attended the inauguration. Harrison had left Indianapolis on February 25th with Mrs. Harrison, his son, Russell Harrison, and his daughter, Mrs. McKee, and their families, and several secretaries and friends, a party which filled a "Pullman palace car." He had said farewell to a crowd of well wishers at the railway station in Indianapolis, and was welcomed at the national capital by many friends as well as by office seekers. He awaited the appointed hour in a house operated as an annex of the Arlington Hotel.

Rain and piercing winds made the day of the inauguration as unpleasant as it had been enjoyable four years before. Thousands paraded the streets, nevertheless, and at night there was a ball in the Pension Building at which Mrs. Harrison and the

---

[1] Cong. Record, 51st Cong. 2nd sess., pp. 2095–2104, 2113–6; McPherson's Handbook for 1890, pp. 7–13; App. Ann. Cyclop. for 1889, pp. 193–203; N. Y. Nation, Feb. 28, 1889.

[2] Cong. Record, 51st Cong. 2nd sess., pp. 1402–4, 1488–91, 1520–31, 1565–74, 1590; McPherson's Handbook for 1890, pp. 15–8; App. Ann. Cyclop. for 1889, pp. 206–10; N. Y. Nation, Feb. 14, 1889.

Republican ladies, for the satisfaction of the New York Tribune and those who shared its patriotic spirit, appeared in dresses made from American fabrics. The new President took possession of the White House and his administration was begun amid jubilation in Republican circles. Mr. Cleveland who had felt himself estranged from Buffalo, in view of the unfriendliness of many of its citizens, as exhibited, particularly, in their spread of the scandals affecting his private life,[1] would make his residence in New York City where he would resume the practise of the law as a partner in the firm of Bangs, Stetson, Tracy and MacVeagh. He and Mrs. Cleveland occupied apartments at the Victoria Hotel until they could find a house.

The Republican newspapers, and the leaders of the party which was returning to power, continued to allude to the Cleveland administration as one of the greatest degradations in the history of the country. They may have believed that it had been what they would have it to be. Mr. Cleveland himself doubted whether what he had tried to accomplish would ever be understood or appreciated.[2] Many, even of those who had been his friends, turned away from him, now that his power appeared to be at an end. The New York Evening Post was not uncritical; but it averred that he had "materially advanced the cause of civil service reform," whatever his "aberrations from the path of duty" in this direction. Moreover he had rendered a great service in resisting the tendency toward "paternalism in government." He had been "one of the best Presidents," the Evening Post continued, that we had ever had—"a model of industry, an exemplar of honesty, a representative of common sense, an embodiment of courage; in short, an excellent type of those homely virtues upon which the future of the republic depends."[3] "No jobbery or fraud" had been traced to the White House, or in its direction, while Cleveland had occupied it. He was the first President since Lincoln to quit it "without leaving behind a single scandalous memory."[4]

[1] See N. Y. Tribune, Feb. 27, 1889, and Cleveland Papers.
[2] R. W. Gilder, Grover Cleveland, p. 22.
[3] N. Y. Nation, March 7, 1889.
[4] Ibid., March 14, 1889.

His bravery was attested to by the number of his vetoes. During his administration he had returned, either to the Senate or the House, 304 bills, with messages, stating the reasons for his disapproval of them. He had "pocketed" 109 more, a total, therefore, of 413, of which 297 were private pension bills. All the Presidents preceding Mr. Cleveland, their administrations covering a period of 96 years in our national history, had vetoed by message, it was said, only 109 bills sent to them by Congress.[1]

Mr. Harrison's cabinet was completed and the names of its members were announced. Although Blaine was more frequently spoken of as one likely to receive the appointment as Secretary of State it had been intimated on several occasions that Sherman would be called to the office.[2] But no proffer of the place came to him from the President-elect, or other communication, barring a thankyou for a letter of congratulation and a promise of a conference at a later time.[3] In a similar way Blaine had been ignored by Harrison, who was told by many, and who was ready to believe, that such an appointment would make mischief in his cabinet. Moreover it would be confirmatory of the charge, iterated and reiterated during the canvass, that Harrison was a "mere proxy of Blaine."[4] It was said that Blaine's brother who held a small public office in Washington, had confronted "Jim" with an inquiry as to whether he would enter the cabinet. He, at first, evaded the question but, when pressed, answered—"I am going into that cabinet, or I'll know the reason why."[5] At last the summons came, Blaine would be Secretary of State.[6]

John Wanamaker was appointed Postmaster General, as it was predicted that he would be. For some time it had been

[1] McPherson's Handbook for 1890, p. 26.
[2] Richard Smith and Murat Halstead to Sherman in Sherman Papers.
[3] Sherman Papers, supported by A. T. Volwiler who has had access to the Harrison Papers.
[4] H. C. Johnson to Sherman, Nov. 9, 1888, in Sherman Papers.
[5] Walter Wellman to Gresham, Jan. 12, 1889, in Gresham Papers.
[6] The position was tendered him on Jan. 17, and accepted on Jan. 21, 1880; cf. Gail Hamilton, Biography of Blaine, pp. 651-3; Letters of Mrs. Blaine, vol. ii, p. 231; T. H. Sherman, Twenty Years with Blaine, pp. 107-10.

clear that William Windom would be Secretary of the Treasury. Redfield Proctor, once the governor of Vermont, became Secretary of War. It was again difficult to satisfy the antagonistic factions in New York. "Tom" Platt had a determination to be Secretary of the Treasury.[1] Only eight years since this man, henchman of Conkling, had left the United States Senate because too few Federal offices were put at his master's disposal. He had been discredited when he, with his master, sought reelection on this issue, and he had been relegated to private life. But he had risen from his obscurity. He was the state "boss." He had had a hand in bringing about the defeat of Warner Miller for reelection as a United States senator in 1887.[2] He had promised Miller the Republican nomination for the governorship of New York to sidetrack a movement in the New York delegation in the Chicago convention toward Sherman,[3] but was held to have given Miller reluctant support at the polls. Miller would have been glad to have had the appointment as Secretary of the Treasury where, however, he would have been antagonized again by Platt. For a member of the cabinet from New York Platt commended to the President a schoolmate and a family friend, not unacceptable to the opposing faction, General Benjamin F. Tracy,[4] though if he were to be in the cabinet at all he might better, it was said, have been Attorney General, a place reserved for Mr. Harrison's confidential friend and law partner in Indianapolis, William Henry Harrison Miller. John W. Noble, a lawyer in St. Louis, was chosen to be Secretary of the Interior, while the new Department of Agriculture, created in the closing days of the Cleveland administra-

[1] Platt said that the office had been promised to him. When he heard of Windom's selection he felt, he said pompously, "that there was little use of pinning my faith upon anybody or training myself for high office." (Autobiog. of Platt, p. 207.) He attributed his failure to receive the appointment to Cornelius N. Bliss—the "source of one half our woes in the party"—and the Union League club in New York, "an aristocratic and semi-disloyal body."—Platt to Tracy, Feb. 2, 1891, in Tracy Papers.

[2] N. Y. Nation, Jan. 27, 1887.

[3] Sherman to a friend, June 26, 1888, in Sherman Papers.

[4] Tracy, while Secretary of the Navy, was freely called upon by Platt for appointments and other favors. Tracy continued to give attention to his law business, while holding a cabinet post, and received $600 a month from the firm for the use of his name and for his services.—Tracy Papers.

tion to dignify farming and give it a place at the President's council table,[1] was entrusted to ex-Governor Jeremiah M. Rusk of Wisconsin who had been that state's choice as a Presidential candidate in the convention which had nominated Harrison.

Though Blaine was a member of the cabinet it seemed quite certain that his active personality would not dominate the President. If he had offered counsel it was plain that it had fallen upon ungrateful ground. It was made very clear to him by the President that in coming to the Department of State he might not bring with him any of his lieutenants.[2] When he had asked that his son, Walker, should be appointed Assistant Secretary the request was declined by Mr. Harrison though the young man was soon attached to the office in another capacity. Blaine chafed under what was considered the President's "narrowness,"[3] though he was trying to control a nature which could be fairly called inflammable.[4] It was certain, too, that Quay was receiving but few rewards for his activity in the direction of the late successful campaign. If he had brought forward Wanamaker it was a Pyrrhic victory, for that man was not obedient to masters, and signed or recognized no treaties of lasting alliance with such a politician. The cabinet was respectable. While it would be definitely Republican it gave promise of some chastening of character which would set it apart from the administrations of that party's Presidents prior to the advent of Cleveland, with the wholesome lessons which he had given the country in the four years just past.

Harrison's inaugural address was a rather platitudinous restatement of the principles of his party, as they had been expounded in its platform and by the Republican newspapers and stump speakers during the campaign. However, it spoke of no excited or urgent striving after any object. The new

[1] Act of Feb. 9, 1889; Cong. Record, 50th Cong. 2nd sess., pp. 1399, 1764; Richardson, Messages and Papers, vol. ix, p. 51.

[2] Letters of Mrs. Blaine, vol. ii, p. 344.

[3] Walter Wellman to Gresham, March 20, 1889, in Gresham Papers.

[4] In an apology to John W. Foster, for an outburst in the State Department Blaine wrote—"I have a very quick and very unfortunate temper." —Dec. 24, 1891, in Foster Papers.

Congress, which would have large working Republican majorities in both branches, would not meet until December and the
President and the heads of the departments of government in
the intervening period might install themselves in their places
and gain acquaintance with their duties. Mr. E. J. Phelps, our
minister to England, had found his situation, after Lord
Sackville's dismissal, not too comfortable. Any nation could
not but have considered our action in that connection to be
brusque, as indefensible as was the British minister's writing of a
letter to an unknown correspondent on the subject of a pending
election. The British government took no steps to appoint
another representative in this country. At his earnest request
Mr. Phelps was granted a leave of absence from his post in
January, 1889, and he sailed for home. Now, with the incoming
of a new administration, it was announced that Sir Julian
Pauncefote, an affable man of large experience, would be sent to
Washington, where he arrived in April, 1889.[1]

A suggestion for an appointment in Mr. Phelps's room was as
grotesque as that which linked the name of Blaine with the
mission. Whitelaw Reid must be rewarded for his fervent
activities in behalf of the party in general, and Blaine in particular. Those who knew him were convinced that his tastes drew
him to diplomacy and as the post at the Court of St. James was
the most honorable on the list it was assumed, in some quarters,
that he would be asked to represent us at London. How the
editor of a newspaper which had now for some years, and never
so acridly as in the campaign of 1888, assailed England and the
entire British people could be regarded as suitable for such a
place was not obvious. His thrusts had been malicious—no day
passed without some expression of suspicion or charge of evil
purpose directed at the nation to which it was quite clear that he
would like to be accredited as a diplomatic representative.
England, in the sight of the newspaper which he edited, was an
active enemy engaged in enterprises that would somehow
overset our republic. It was believed that Reid had his tongue
in his cheek when he said much of what was said on this topic,

[1] N. Y. Tribune, April 22, 1889.

and it was somehow taken for granted that a journalist would be forgiven for speech that manifestly was intended for ignorant men with a view to taking votes from one political party and giving them to another. But his virulence was a matter of record. The files of the paper were emblazoned with words that were as a million to one in any scale which should be set for Reid in a comparison with Sackville-West. The British minister's mild utterances in a letter were a peccadillo beside the columns of falsehood and insinuation that Reid had launched against the country to which it was gravely said that he might be sent as our representative.

John Hay thought that Reid might receive the appointment. William Walter Phelps spoke to Blaine who was "hot for it." Finally the President called the editor to the White House where he was told that there had never been a time since the election when it had not been intended to offer him a worthy and an honorable official post. But the President wondered whether Reid would be happy in London, since his newspaper had been so outspoken in its advocacy of "Home Rule" for Ireland and in its friendliness for Gladstone, rather than Lord Salisbury who was now in power—a very polite avenue of approach—and urged the claims of France, which, Mr. Harrison alleged, was in many respects, a more desirable mission. Seeing the entire impropriety of a plan to send Reid to England, even if his name were *persona grata* to the British government, the President asked the editor as a personal favor to take the mission to France, and to that place he was appointed and to Paris he promptly repaired to remain until it was urgent for him to return to participate in the campaign of 1892.[1]

Robert T. Lincoln received the English mission. His appointment as the son of the President for whom esteem was increasing—not only in America but throughout the world—was a healing measure. Frederick D. Grant, son of another President, whose name all Europe knew, was sent to Austria. Both were named quite distinctly because they were their father's sons. Reid having been assigned to France, two more

[1] Cortissoz, Life of Reid, vol. ii, pp. 121-5.

editors who had served the party, Allen Thorndike Rice, the wealthy owner and enthusiastic editor of the North American Review, and Murat Halstead of the Cincinnati Commercial Gazette were nominated for the Russian and German missions respectively. Halstead was rejected by the Senate for having lately cast imputations upon a member of that body,[1] and the place was given to William Walter Phelps who had vied with Reid in his interest in clearing the name and spreading the fame of Blaine. Rice died in May, before he had proceeded to his post, which opened a way to the reward of Charles Emory Smith, editor of the Philadelphia Press, whose journalistic services in behalf of the Republican party were not much inferior, in want of reservation, to Whitelaw Reid's.[2] Other editors were put in lucrative and influential places to recompense and to increase the diligence of their pens, none more prominent than J. S. Clarkson who had been vice-chairman of the Republican National Committee, associate of Quay in the management of the campaign, and who controlled a newspaper in Iowa. For him a place was found in the Post-Office Department. Robert P. Porter, a newspaper editor in New York, an Englishman who had gained the confidence of the protectionists, was appointed to take the eleventh decennial census.[3] The finding of posts for the relations of the President, of his wife, and of his son Russell, revived charges of nepotism, which had not been heard since the Grant era.[4]

The rush for the offices was mighty; it was, said the New York Evening Post, "almost like the march of the Barbarians on Rome." [5] The earlier protestations of the President were, it would appear, forgotten in the stress of the vexatious situation in which he had been plunged. He had declared, in his letter accepting the nomination, that "only the interest of the public service should suggest removals from office." In the Re-

---

[1] Senate Ex. Journal, vol. 27, pp. 44, 47, 49, 51, 55; N. Y. Nation, April 4, 1889.
[2] Cf. N. Y. Nation, Feb. 13, 1890.
[3] Ibid., April 25, 1889.
[4] Ibid., May 23 and 30 and July 18, 1889.
[5] Ibid., March 14, 1889; cf. ibid., March 28, 1889.

publican national platform, upon which he had stood as a
candidate, it was said that "the spirit and purpose" of civil
service reform "should be observed in all executive appointments." [1] For four years the Republican press had outdone the
party's stump speakers in condemning Cleveland and the
Democratic party for their insincerity in regard to the reform,
and the Republicans gave pledges of better conduct, if they
should be returned to power. Civil service reformers themselves, preeminently those in Indiana who had been so
grievously disappointed with Cleveland and in 1888 had voted
instead for Harrison, confessed that they had been deceived.

The result was seen—corrupt or causeless removals, bad or
unfit appointments,[2] a "clean sweep" in so far as the offices had
not been brought into protected classes, and, even then, violation and disregard of the plain purposes of the restricting rules.
Officials who had performed useful service were relieved of duty
before the expiration of their terms merely because they were
adherents of the opposite party, a course which Cleveland had
honestly tried to avoid. It was openly said by heads of departments making the dismissals that the reasons were "political." Newspapers which had been outspoken advocates of the
reform, when, in the last administration, Republicans were to be
displaced, now found no value in it. Republican party platforms in the states which had rung with praise of the principle,
while Cleveland had been President, now had nothing to say
about the civil service.[3] It was plain, as sober men had anticipated, that the professions of virtue on the Republican side had
been but party devices to beguile the Mugwumps and other
high-minded citizens and to take away votes from Mr. Cleveland. Clarkson was the headsman of the Post Office Department. In one week in June, 1889, it was said that he had
removed over 1,000 Democratic postmasters to make way for
Republicans which, it was computed, was one for every three
minutes of each working day.[4] He served under Wanamaker

[1] N. Y. Nation, May 2, 1889.
[2] Cf. ibid., May 2, 1889.
[3] Ibid., Aug. 15 and 22, 1889.
[4] Ibid., June 20, 1889; cf. ibid., May 16, 1889.

whose religious professions were again brought under review. Wanamaker had a much advertised Sunday School in Philadelphia to which he returned each week from Washington. President Harrison also had a piety which was outwardly displayed. Both were subjected to criticism which more than a few thought to be amply deserved. They had held themselves to be somewhat better than other men. They should be judged by their works rather than by their professions of morality and worth.[1] From March until August, 1889, 13,000 post offices had been taken out of the hands of Democrats and put in charge of Republicans, as compared with 4,000 changes in the same time four years since by Postmaster General Vilas, a rate of activity which promised soon to embrace the entire service, composed of 55,000 men.[2] Republicans who had held over were suspect. If they had continued to serve through Cleveland's time it was somehow taken to be proof that they were infirm of principle and undeserving of the confidence of a Republican administration.[3]

A test of Cleveland's sincerity had been found in the retention of Mr. Pearson as postmaster of New York City in the face of demands by Democratic spoilsmen for his place. This excellent public servant, who conducted a great office as a business establishment, was now dismissed, though he was a Republican, for the benefit of a "party worker" who "wanted the job." [4] Nothing could have been done, it was said, to attest so plainly to the want of interest on the part of the President and his advisers in civil service reform. In other branches of the government—the State Department, the Treasury, the Interior Department—heads were falling, not with a view to more efficient administration but to make places and give salaries and fees to Republicans instead of Democrats.[5] The changes were

[1] Cf. N. Y. Nation, Nov. 5, 1891.
[2] Ibid., Aug. 1, 1889.   [3] Ibid., March 14, 1889.
[4] Proceedings of Annual Meeting of the Civil Service Reform Association in New York, May 1, 1889. (N. Y. Times, May 3, 1889.) Cf. N. Y. Nation, March 21 and 28 and April 11 and 25, 1889.
[5] N. Y. Nation, April 18, 1889. For example note the removal of the Commissioner of Indian Affairs, John H. Oberly.—N. Y. Times, June 12 and July 3, 1889.

demanded by senators, representatives and local leaders in the old familiar way. The President refused to place the new Census Bureau, with some 2500 employees, under civil service rules.[1] He suspended the operation of the rules for the railway mail service, which Cleveland on January 4th ordered in effect on March 15, 1889, until May 1st, by which time, it was believed, that many of the Democrats in these offices could be replaced by Republicans.[2] Mr. Harrison, however, refused to revoke the order as politicians near him desired.[3]

Nowhere was there more reason for the expression of disappointment with the organization of the administration than on the subject of the management of the Pension Office. President Cleveland had made malfeasance in this field a great matter. The public conscience regarding the reckless payment of moneys to undeserving persons, under cover of gratitude and patriotism, had been aroused. In the campaign of 1888 the "old soldier vote" had been massed and put at Harrison's service, to the discomfiture of the Democratic party, which still labored under the memory of too little loyalty to the Union during the war, and, in a particular way, to the disadvantage of Cleveland whose many eloquent vetoes of pension bills were in the public mind. Now, under Harrison, a generous policy would be pursued. The Grand Army was increasing its political power. Its insistence upon offices and pensions grew with every passing year. A man who had suffered enough of the pains of war in all reason, for he had lost both legs in the service, without gaining higher rank than a corporal,[4] James Tanner of New York, was appointed commissioner of pensions. But the choice was a grievous mistake. The "corporal" was a prominent "Grand Army stump speaker."[5] He had made himself very voluble before his appointment on the subject of a free and easy giving out of pensions, and he con-

---

[1] Cf. N. Y. Nation, Dec. 26, 1889, Nov. 20 and Dec. 11, 1890.

[2] N. Y. Times, May 3 and 22, 1889; N. Y. Nation, March 14, 1889; Richardson, Messages and Papers, vol. ix, p. 27.

[3] For Harrison's reasons and his action see Richardson, Messages and Papers, vol. ix, p. 53.

[4] Cf. N. Y. Nation, Sep. 12, 1889.

[5] Ibid., May 30, 1889.

tinued in the way he had begun. His theories he early sought
to put into practice, and so large were his discretionary powers
that he was soon adding millions of dollars to the cost of the
administration of the bureau. Men said—"God help the
surplus!"[1] Tanner was the principal agent in the business of
"surplus busting" which became the motto, the Democrats
said, of the Harrison administration. Unaccustomed to the
management of a large public office, holding his place, as he
was too prone to say, for the purpose of getting money from
the government for his "old comrades" instead of in the general
interest, even the Republican press found it difficult to defend
him.[2] The "corporal's" dismissal was demanded. Tanner
must go. His raids on the Treasury must be checked.[3] His
continuance in office, it was clear, would embarrass the administration. Secretary of the Interior Noble said that many
of Tanner's reratings and increases of payments were "wholly
illegal and unwarranted." He was reproved and dismissed
for insubordination,[4] before he had been six months in office
and a man who would enjoy public confidence in greater degree,
General Green B. Raum, was named for the post.[5]

Whether the administration had any interest, or none, in
civil service reform the commission into whose charge the
subject was given had legally authorized duties to perform.
President Cleveland's nomination of Hugh S. Thompson to
take old Mr. Edgerton's place had been rejected by an unruly
Senate. President Harrison now again forwarded Mr. Thompson's name to that body, coupled with that of Theodore Roosevelt who was to be the chairman of the commission. That
Roosevelt would enliven the scene and enforce the law for his
own advertisement, if not because of a sincere interest in good
government, was certain. He could do no more than conditions would allow,[6] said those who saw in him a disturber of

[1] N. Y. Times, May 10 and July 16, 1889, and Feb. 20, 1890.
[2] Cf. N. Y. Nation, Aug. 1 and Sep. 12, 1889.
[3] Ibid., July 25, 1889.
[4] Report of Sec. of Int. for 1889, pp. clii–clxvii.
[5] N. Y. Nation, Oct. 24, 1889; cf. ibid., Jan. 16, 1890.
[6] Cf. ibid., July 25, 1889.

smug party schemes; he might be of distinct value to the reform, said the Mugwumps, in spite of a nature which was already famous for its erratic enthusiasms.[1]

The appointment was a sop to Cerberus; the wrangle for every accessible lucrative office went on. When the Civil Service Reform League met in Philadelphia in October, 1889, George William Curtis stated the case for the reformers. Public officers who were "conspicuously fitted by character, ability and experience," who had "absolutely and confessedly disregarded politics in their devotion to official duty and the public service," he said, had been summarily and brutally removed in violation of the "platform promise and the President's pledge." Mr. Curtis cited instances; "the ablest and most serviceable of experienced public officers," he declared, were being dismissed "like messenger boys." [2]

Harrison, like Garfield and others who were his predecessors in the Presidency, found that the more he yielded the greater was the dissatisfaction of the interests which he was making an effort to serve. When he gave to one leader or group he affronted some opposing leader or group, and he learned to understand, without having the bravery, however, to amend his methods, that he, from the first, might better have filled the offices solely with consideration for the public welfare, without regard to the attachment of appointees to party or faction, or for the men who, in cities and states, for services rendered and majorities rolled up for the ticket, arrogated to themselves a dangerous kind of extra-constitutional authority.

Platt was up in arms. Not enough had come to him. His bold demand that he be Secretary of the Treasury having been refused, he was offered the mission to Spain, which he was unwilling to accept.[3] Harrison was charged by Platt with ignoring those who had nominated him and elected him to the Presidency,[4] though it seemed to many that Platt was dispensing the patronage in New York and that the President accepted

[1] Cf. N. Y. Nation, May 9, 1889.
[2] Phila. Public Ledger, Oct. 2, 1889; N. Y. Nation, Oct. 10, 1889.
[3] Autobiography of Platt, pp. 207–9.
[4] Ibid., p. 210.

his leadership, leaving Warner Miller, at the head of a more respected faction of the party, without recognition or influence.[1] In Pennsylvania Harrison's personal liking for Wanamaker and the Philadelphia merchant's advantageous position at the President's right hand were counting against Quay and Cameron, the state's representatives in the Senate. Quay's discontent, in view of his rather well known services in the work of making Harrison President, was ill concealed. His friends openly denounced Harrison as an ingrate.[2] The offices in Virginia were put at the disposal of General Mahone, whose leadership could not be expected to increase confidence in the party in the South. In Illinois, in Michigan, in Indiana itself, the President's own state, where those who thought that they should be his advisers were ignored, complaint was open and the organization which was to be strengthened and improved by the removal of Democrats and the appointment of Republicans was, it was said, falling apart.[3]

Greater matters pressed for attention and received it. At last the "boomers" who so long had hung upon the borders of the Indian Territory, now and again raiding the fair country within,[4] to be as often expelled by Federal troops, were authorized to enter. When Cleveland's administration was near its end arrangements had been made with the Creeks and Seminoles for the transfer to the United States of a body of land comprising about five and a half million acres for a sum of money aggregating $4,193,000, which was made available by acts of Congress of March 1 and 2, 1889.[5] President Harrison, therefore, on March 23, by proclamation, set the hour of 12 o'clock noon on April 22, 1889, as the time when about 1,800,000 acres of the newly acquired Indian lands would be thrown open to settlement.[6]

The territory was known as Oklahoma and, if a bill in the last

---

[1] Cf. N. Y. Nation, April 11, Oct. 10 and Nov. 28, 1889.
[2] Autobiography of Platt, pp. 210–11.
[3] N. Y. Nation, Nov. 28, 1889.
[4] Cf. ibid., April 4, 1889.
[5] Richardson, Messages and Papers, vol. ix, pp. 46–7.
[6] Ibid., pp. 15–8.

Congress sponsored by Representative Springer of Illinois, had passed the Senate, as it had passed the House, the country would have had governmental organization.[1] Such bills had been before Congress for several years and were, for the most part, "killed in committee" on the ground that they violated "existing treaty stipulations" with reference to the Indians.[2] The area was traversed by the Atchison, Topeka and Santa Fé Railroad. Some of the land bordering streams promised to be productive; much of it, however, was sparingly watered, and when it had this advantage the water was alkaline and unpotable.

The tract lay in the heart of the Indian country. It was surrounded by the Cherokee Strip and other territory to which tribes of the aboriginal American race held title. The "boomers" had increased their numbers until, probably, 50,000 persons were ready to dash into the land of promise from selected vantage points. Those coming from Kansas, concentrated, for the most part, in Arkansas City, were permitted to cross the Cherokee Strip, a distance of about 60 miles, before the opening day so that when the rush began they should be on terms of equality with the "boomers" who were encamped at Purcell on the Canadian River in the south.[3] Federal infantry and cavalry were on duty to hold back the eager emigrants. A more picturesque and, at the same time, foolish spectacle has seldom been seen. At a bugle blast the race commenced, the horde pouring by rail, where it was possible, on horse, on foot and in their white covered wagons over the boundaries higgledy piggledy. Portable houses and other material for the instant creation of towns were included in the paraphernalia of the emigration.

In one place, called Guthrie, at least 10,000 persons gathered,

[1] Mr. Springer in N. Y. Tribune, April 22, 1889; House Reports, 50th Congress, 1st. sess., nos. 263 and 2857.

[2] Cf. House Reports, 43rd Cong. 2nd sess., no. 151; ibid., 44th Cong. 1st sess., no. 299; ibid., 44th Cong. 2nd sess., no. 82; ibid., 45th Cong. 3rd sess., no. 188; ibid., 49th Cong. 1st sess., no. 1684; Senate Mis. Doc., 45th Cong. 2nd sess., no. 82.

[3] N. Y. Tribune, April 18, 19 and 20, 1889.

mapped the city into blocks under the direction of an improvised land office, the officers of which were charged with favoritism in the distribution of lots,[1] opened a bank with a capital of $50,000 in a tent, and issued a newspaper—all between 12 o'clock noon and four P.M. In the same way other crowds of adventurers founded Kingfisher at the old King Fisher stage station, where another land office had been opened, and Oklahoma City. Smaller cities sprang into being though many of the settlers were sorely disappointed and as grievously swindled by the speculators who had led them on. Clouds of blinding and suffocating dust, cold nights and deficient supplies of water soon gave the country a bad name. Most of the roving spirits who had rushed in rushed out again. The wiser ones who came to farm and were willing to live by the plow profited by the opening of the territory, and thus soon the lands which the government had released were distributed to industrious families who laid the foundations for a prosperous commonwealth.[2]

Prior to December 1, 1889, 1,685,000 acres in Oklahoma had been covered by homestead entries. Secretary of the Interior Noble computed that the population at that time was about 60,000; 8,000 remained in and around Guthrie and 5,000 at Oklahoma City. There were 22 newspapers in Oklahoma of which four, all issuing daily editions, were in Guthrie.[3]

The four new states which were provided for by the enabling act, signed by President Cleveland on February 22, 1889, met the requirements laid down for them by Congress. Constitutions were adopted and capitals were selected. Each elected two citizens to act as United States senators. South Dakota was found to have a population large enough to entitle it to two members of the House of Representatives, while North Dakota, Montana and Washington would have one each. President Harrison proclaimed South Dakota and North Dakota on the 3rd, Montana on the 8th and Washington on the 11th of Novem-

[1] Senate Ex. Doc., 51st Cong. 1st sess., no. 33.
[2] Report of Sec. of Int. for 1889, pp. iii–viii; cf. N. Y. Nation, May 2, 1889; N. Y. Tribune, April 25 and 26, 1889.
[3] App. Ann. Cyclop for 1889, pp. 675–7; Richardson, vol. ix, pp. 46–8.

ber, 1889, to be states of the Union. All except Montana, as was foreseen, would have Republican management and would send Republican senators and representatives to Congress. The success of the Democratic party with reference to Montana extended to the governorship only, though an angry contest which was carried to Washington, ensued as to the choice of United States senators.[1]

Blaine's project for an all American conference which he had announced during his brief administration of the Secretary of State's office under Garfield was revived by his friends in Congress before his return to that post.[2] By act approved May 24, 1888, President Cleveland had been authorized to arrange such a meeting for the purpose of devising, if possible, "some plan of arbitration for the settlement of disagreements and disputes" which should arise between the governments on the American continent, for considering questions "relating to the improvement of business intercourse, and means of direct communication," for the encouragement of "such reciprocal commercial relations" as might be "beneficial to all," and might "secure more extensive markets" for the products of the countries concerned, and for forwarding other interests esteemed to be Pan-American. $75,000 were appropriated to meet the cost of the congress and Secretary Bayard issued the invitations, which were generally accepted. Delegates were appointed by Mexico and the various governments of Central and South America and by the United States.[3] They met in a large private house in Washington, which was made ready for their use, on October 2, 1889. Secretary of State Blaine delivered the address of welcome on behalf of the United States and he was appropriately elected president. The delegates were

---

[1] App. Ann. Cyclop, for 1889, pp. 571–2; McPherson's Handbook for 1890, p. 246; N. Y. Nation, Apr. 3, 17 and 24, 1890.

[2] Frye was the sponsor of the bill in the Senate.

[3] Those from the United States, were ten in number as follows: John B. Henderson of Missouri, Cornelius N. Bliss of New York, Clement Studebaker of Indiana, T. Jefferson Coolidge of Massachusetts, William Henry Trescot of South Carolina, Andrew Carnegie of Pennsylvania, Morris M. Estee of California, John F. Hanson of Georgia, Henry G. Davis of West Virginia and Charles R. Flint of New York.

formally received by President Harrison at the White House and they almost at once set forth in a special train for a tour of the East and Middle West which carried them a distance of 5825 miles. Manufactories and other industrial establishments were visited; the heads of municipalities, chambers of commerce and committees of citizens received them at the places at which they stopped, gave them escort and tendered them dinners. Good will was spoken of, healths were pledged, improved feeling and better understanding were promoted, it was believed, and the measure throughout, if born of a degree of platonic zeal which might not be sustained, would promote an harmonious interest among the governments of the Western hemisphere and cool the ardor of those of Latin temperament, who were so wont to convert their elections into revolutions and live in civil dispute rather than order and peace.[1]

It was November 18th before the delegates were at their tasks in Washington and the following year before they were making progress in their exchanges of opinion and their recommendations for action. Mr. Blaine, in his characteristically grandiose manner, found that the territorial extent of the countries represented was three times that of all Europe and but little less than a fourth part of that of the entire globe. The population of these American countries was about 120,000,000. If they were peopled as densely as Europe the total would exceed a billion.[2] There were but 28 delegates from 17 Latin American governments as compared with our 10 representatives, and some of these were members of the diplomatic corps at Washington, so that the meeting might easily be given unmerited consequence.[3]

The conference adjourned on April 19, 1890, after having made a number of proposals. It was determined to establish and maintain a permanent international American bureau of information at Washington. The representatives of all the governments assembled, Chile dissenting, prepared the articles

[1] Narrative of Tour in Int. Am. Conference, vol. iii.
[2] App. Ann. Cyclop, for 1889, pp. 440–2.
[3] Minutes of Int. Am. Conference, pp. 2–3.

of a treaty for submission to their respective governments whereunder all disputes arising among themselves should be settled by arbitration, which Blaine in his speech adjourning the congress called a "new Magna Charta." [1] An intercontinental railway was projected and there were suggestions as to the subsidization of steamship lines. An international American bank was proposed, as was a customs union in which there should be some degree of freedom of commercial exchange across boundaries, though with little prospect of advancing the idea. [2] From the meeting, too, came plans for an international monetary conference, which should meet in Washington in January, 1890, [3] for the adoption of the metric system and common systems of copyright, patents and trade marks, and the establishment in Washington of a Latin American Memorial Library. [4] Appropriations of money to give effect to the various resolves of the conference were requested of Congress by Blaine and contributions were expected from the other governments whose delegates had aided in the formulation of its extensive projects. [5] The New York Tribune said that the conference had been "one of the most notable events of contemporary history." [6] But the New York Times asked if any one knew what the congress had done. [7] The New York Evening Post spoke of the "small results achieved." [8] So long as we should build "impregnable tariff walls" to shut out the products of South American countries, in the opinion of the New York World, it was "nonsense" to discuss plans for increasing our commerce with them. [9] Those who had convened the congress had omitted representation from Canada which, Harper's Weekly said, was "the only cognate community with the United States upon the

[1] Proceedings of the Conference, p. 857.
[2] N. Y. Nation, April 24, 1890.
[3] App. Ann. Cyclop. for 1890, pp. 820–1; McPherson's Handbook for 1890, pp. 259–62.
[4] Cf. N. Y. Tribune, April 21, 1890.
[5] House Ex. Doc., 51st Cong. 1st sess., no. 407.
[6] Issue of April 21, 1890.
[7] Issue of April 23, 1890.
[8] N. Y. Nation, April 24, 1890.
[9] Issue of April 21, 1890.

continent." [1] There could be but little in common between
North and South America. There was, indeed, only one
analogy, the writer in Harper's Weekly continued, and this was
found in the more or less republican character of their institutions, in which particular it could be noted there was the
greatest divergence.[2]

The elections in 1889 were a reflection of the disappointment
which Harrison's administration had been to at least some of
those who had voted the Republican ticket in the preceding
year. They were a reminder, too, of the strength of an opposition which, as a matter of fact, had polled a larger popular vote
for its candidate for President than Harrison had received. The
Democrats carried New York, New Jersey, Ohio, Iowa and Virginia, where the demagogue, Mahone, with the support of
Federal patronage, was a threatening factor. The defeat of the
Republican ticket in Ohio had involved Foraker who was running again for governor. The result in Iowa, where, for the first
time, a Democrat had been elected to the governorship, was
taken to be a declaration of sympathy for tariff reform. Massachusetts was saved to the Republicans by a narrow plurality
through an alliance with the liquor dealers in Boston,[3] but the
leadership of the Democratic candidate for governor, William
E. Russell, gave happy promise for the future.

The Republicans, when Congress convened in December,
1889, had read the signs, though, probably, with little profit,
since power to them meant a return to the effort to develop
those constructive measures which they had recommended to
the country in the campaign of 1888. The President sent in
his message. While much was said about the tariff in its relation to the surplus, and about the currency, his declarations
were not very forceful or clear. He seemed to be at one with Mr.
Cleveland, and citizens generally, on the point that the collection of money "not needed for public uses," imposed "an unnecessary burden" upon the people. He recommended a

[1] Issue of Jan. 11, 1890; cf. ibid., March 8, 1890.
[2] Ibid., Feb. 1, 1890. For the results gained see M. Romero, in N. A.
Review for Sep. and Oct., 1890.
[3] N. Y. Nation, Nov. 7 and 14, 1889.

"revision of our tariff law." But he said that "the preparation of a new schedule of customs duties" was "a matter of great delicacy." Prompt action would produce a minimum of disturbance to business. "The protective principle should be maintained and fairly applied to the products of our farms as well as our shops." The "free list" could be extended, but there should be no impairment of "the just and reasonable protection of our home industries." As for the internal taxes they could be lifted from tobacco, which was "an important agricultural product," and from spirits used in the arts and in manufactures.

The President noted the disadvantages attendant upon the purchase of silver bullion and its coinage into dollars worth but 70 or 72 cents. On the other hand, to the silver men, he said that he had always been an advocate of "the use of silver in our currency." Being "large producers" of that metal we "should not discredit it." The Secretary of the Treasury had presented a plan for the issue of silver certificates against stored bullion "at its market value." The President had given the proposal "only a hasty examination, owing to the press of other matters," and could not endorse it. He might approve or disapprove and communicate his views to Congress at a later date. He was clear as to the propriety of attacking the surplus on another side, for he advocated postal subsidies for American ships, the Blair, or some similar, plan for giving Federal aid to education, a liberal policy as to soldiers' pensions, a large navy, coast defenses and further purchases of Indian lands. He expressed his party's indignation at the suppression of the suffrage among the negroes in the South, and advocated fuller control of Congressional elections by the Federal government so that the negro should be assured of, and guaranteed, a free exercise of his rights.[1]

The elections had returned to Washington a Congress which was Republican to a degree out of all proportion to the victory which Harrison had gained over Cleveland. In the Fiftieth Congress which ended its life in March, 1889, there had been in

[1] Richardson, Messages and Papers, vol. ix, pp. 32–58; N. Y. Nation, Dec. 5 and 12, 1889.

the Senate 39 Republicans and 37 Democrats, in the House
170 Democrats and 151 Republicans. In the new Fifty-first
Congress, meeting in December, 1889, there were in the Senate
47 Republicans, 8 of them from the new Western states, and
37 Democrats; in the House 173 Republicans and 154 Democrats. Both houses were clearly Republican. For the first time
since December, 1874, a period of 15 years, a President had at
his service a Congress which, in both branches, was in control
of his party. The ways were smooth and action might be
expected without delay. Thomas B. Reed of Maine, a bold and
forcible man, would be Speaker of the House of Representatives.
William McKinley of Ohio, whose name stood for a high tariff,
would be chairman of the Committee on Ways and Means.

The Congress, in so far as the House was concerned, would
answer the hand of its Speaker. This fact was made clear in
the first days of the session. In one branch of the law-making
assembly he would interpret the mandate of the people given
to the Republican party in the elections of 1888, and define the
policy upon which that party would go to the country in the
elections of 1890. His skill in debate and parliamentary inter-
change, his readiness in giving a witty or pert answer, his courage in any presence, albeit with a rather lofty and scornful air
toward those around him,[1] fitted him for the part which he chose
to play in the development of the program of the Harrison administration. The assertion of a moral and an intellectual
superiority by the Republicans was not new. They manifestly
felt that they occupied this position, and now that they had
wrested the control of the government from a detested enemy
they would brook none of the delays which come from frivolous
and obstructive argument.

The Democrats had not yet evidenced a purpose to filibuster
and put obstacles in the way of a development of the administration's policies.[2] Nor was Reed commissioned to represent
the President, though his plans were the subject of discussion
among some of the party leaders in Congress. It was a showy

[1] Cf. N. Y. Times, Jan. 24, 1890.
[2] Cf. Harper's Weekly, Feb. 15, 1890.

rôle which he himself preferred, an exhibition of his personal
nature. On the 29th of January, 1890, he surprised the Democrats, many of whom were lounging in the aisles and chose not
to answer to their names when the roll was called, by counting
them in attendance for the purpose of creating a quorum, amid
their most indignant and violent protests as soon as they could
recover from their surprise and gather breath for speech.[1]
Dilatory tactics on the part of members of the House who had
been sent to Washington to forward the public business would
be brought to an end.[2] It was no matter that Reed's schoolmasterly course was an innovation in parliamentary usage, or
that he himself, indeed, had expressed a different opinion as to
the power in this respect of a presiding officer of a deliberative
body.[3] It would now serve his purpose and the purpose of the
party to pursue another policy, particularly in reference to
contested seats in which it would be desirable to install Republicans to increase the party majority.[4] Reed made his own
rules for the government of the House, until the committee
which he had appointed should frame them, and, when its
report was received, he was confirmed in the exercise of his
assumed authority,[5] which had for its effect the easy and
expeditious carrying forward of a party program.[6] The Democratic and Independent press made a great ado about "Reed's
rules." They denounced him as a "Czar." He was "the
American Bismarck." He was an absolutist of the absolutists,
arbitrary, arrogant, tyrannical, revolutionary, a usurper, a
dictator, a despot. His action was equal to a *coup d'état.* He
was riding rough shod over minorities and was an enemy of
popular government, in spite of the fact that he was aiming a

[1] Cong. Record, 51st Cong. 1st sess., pp. 949–60.
[2] "Sixty millions of people in the republic join in the demand that, a
quorum of the House being present, the American House of Representatives
shall perform its function."—Representative Cannon in Cong. Record, 51st
Cong. 1st sess., p. 958.
[3] S. W. McCall, Life of T. B. Reed, p. 169; N. Y. Times, Feb. 1, 1890;
N. Y. Nation, Feb. 6, 1890.
[4] N. Y. Times, Feb. 1 and 2, 1890.
[5] App. Ann. Cyclop. for 1890, pp. 181–91; N. Y. Times, Feb. 7 and 15,
1890.
[6] S. W. McCall, Life of T. B. Reed, pp. 165–72.

blow at what had become in the House, and in parliamentary bodies generally, a silly abuse. Plainly there was no reason why men who were refractory, or often merely too indolent to perform their duties, should obstruct the transaction of public business. Nevertheless a large increase in the authority of the Speaker, if it were used unwisely, might have untoward consequences.[1]

And the opposition found cases in plenty in which the Speaker, under the new rules, misused his plaçe. The majority had now been given the power, it was complained by the New York Evening Post, "to push through all the wild schemes" which were "stewing in their brains, most of them simply undisguised attacks on the taxpayers." [2] "The caucus, the lash and the gag" had been "substituted for debate and deliberation"; all bills could be passed by "counting a quorum." [3] The only question on any Republican measure in the House was whether Speaker Reed wished it to pass.[4] Not even in the French Assembly was one man allowed to exercise such power.[5] The will of the Speaker was the action of the House. The other 329 members might as well return to their respective homes.[6] A "furious and reckless partisan" was exerting a power destructive of one of "the most valuable possessions" of the people under our system of government.[7]

Particularly valuable were the "Reed rules" in the enactment of the new tariff bill, called the "McKinley bill." Work upon it in the Ways and Means Committee, under the direction of its chairman, proceeded rapidly, amid all the furore which attended the discussion of this subject by manufacturers, wool growers and the interests affected by the fixing of rates of duty on imports, by the press and by the excited leaders of the opposing parties fresh from their contest over the "Mills bill"

[1] Cong. Record, 51st Cong. 1st sess., pp. 952–60, 979–95 and later.
[2] N. Y. Nation, Feb. 20, 1890.
[3] Ibid., June 12, 1890.
[4] Ibid., June 19, 1890.
[5] N. Y. Times, Feb. 7, 1890.
[6] N. Y. Nation, Sep. 18, 1890.
[7] Ibid., Oct. 2, 1890.

in the last Congress, during the heat of the Presidential campaign of 1888. As always the interests which were to be benefited by a higher or lower rate, or by one or another method of appraising values and administering the custom houses, made their wants known in no masked language. As was foreseen and prophesied those who had linked their fortunes to the party, and who had made contributions to its campaign funds in the nation at large and the Congressional districts were now to be served. They were in a position to enforce their demands and descended upon Washington in a truculent mood. This lobby was called by Carl Schurz "the third house," and it was, he said, "sometimes strongest of the three." [1] The tariff was held to have been the issue upon which Cleveland had been defeated and Harrison had been elected. A change in the law in the interest of a fuller protection of the country's industries was declared to be not less than a popular mandate, and rapid progress was made with the schedules. The hearings began immediately after the holidays in December, 1889,[2] and the first measure, an administrative customs bill, designed, New York commercial interests said, "to put the importing business in the category of crimes," was passed before the end of January.[3] The bill fixing the duties made its appearance after five months of consultation with those who conceived themselves to be concerned as to its terms. Again it was suggested that too much attention was being given to the wishes of manufacturers, whose interests called for higher rates, and too little to consumers, the masses of the people, who might prefer to have duties lowered or abolished.[4]

On May 7th McKinley opened the debate with a speech explanatory of the advantages of the measure, to which his name, by common consent, had been attached.[5] Mills very properly replied in behalf of the Democrats. It had been alleged, said the minority leader in his fervent and often humor-

[1] Writings of Schurz, vol. v, p. 45.
[2] N. Y. Nation, Jan. 2, 1890.
[3] Ibid., Jan. 30, 1890; N. Y. Times, Jan. 28, 1890.
[4] Cf. N. Y. Times, Jan. 1, 1890.
[5] Cong. Record, 51st Cong. 1st sess., pp. 4247–57.

ous speech, that the tariff question had been "settled at the last Presidential election." "Yes," he said, "Grover Cleveland had a majority of 100,000 votes of the American people." If there was a decision it was easy to discern what it had been. The Republicans spoke of a foreign trade. By their theory on this subject they would tax the people of the United States in order to sell cheap goods abroad. Mr. Mills had been under the impression that the Republicans were "afraid of foreigners." Every night when a Republican went to bed he looked under it to see if there was a "foreign pauper" there, and yet now the leaders of the party came into the House and declared that they would tax the people so that they might "go into the foreign markets and sell cheap goods to the foreign paupers." "I say to you, gentlemen," Mills continued, "we will meet you at Philippi on that." The Democrats would examine the bill; they would discuss it in so far as they were permitted to do so under the new Republican rules affecting debate, they would vote against it, and, Mills concluded, addressing the Republican side, "when you leave this House and Senate, with this enormous load of guilt upon your heads, and appear before the great tribunal for trial may 'the Lord have mercy on your souls.' " [1]

Discussion ended in a fortnight under the goad of the Speaker whose cynical taunt—"Thank Heaven, this House is no longer a deliberative body," was by this time famous.[2] The yeas and nays were taken on several points, for instance as to the rates on sugar, tin plate, jute and sisal yarns and various woolen and worsted manufactures, the bill being passed on May 21st by a vote of 164 to 142.[3] With changes it was reported by Mr. Morrill from the Senate Committee on Finance on June 18th,[4] and discussion continued in that body until September.

Blaine made a proposal which marked a turning point in his policy and that of his party on the subject of the tariff. An enlargement of his views had ensued upon the meeting of the Pan-American Conference. He had been brought to see the need

[1] Cong. Record, 51st Cong. 1st sess., pp. 4257–65.
[2] Writings of Schurz, vol. v, pp. 67–9.
[3] Cong. Record, 51st Cong. 1st sess., p. 5113.
[4] Ibid., p. 6207.

of commercial exchanges between nations, at any rate with reference to countries in the Western hemisphere, and he, by letters to members of Congress, by personal interview, by public speech used his energies actively in behalf of a bill which would be in the interest of reciprocal trade.[1] Hides, coffee and wool were matters of concern to him, if he were to realize his hopes, but the real crux of his plan was the retention of a duty on sugar which might be removed in return for tariff concessions to be secured by us from cane growing countries in the American tropics. It was said in the newspapers that one day in a committee room, in the presence of a number of United States senators, he grew so vehement while expounding his theory that he brought his clenched fist down on the tariff bill lying on the table before him and, by this motion, sent his hat whirling into the air. The arch protectionist had "smashed his hat," the Washington correspondents said, on the McKinley bill.[2] Blaine's idea gained support in the liberal Republican press; commercial organizations passed resolutions expressive of their approval.[3] The President was moved to action and, on June 19th, sent a message to Congress transmitting a letter from Blaine and endorsing the views expressed in it.[4]

As the response was not immediately reassuring Blaine, in July, put his views before Senator Frye in a letter which was widely published and discussed, and the agitation continued, Aldrich appearing in the Senate with an amendment to the bill not to Blaine's entire liking, though it had a similar end in view. There were only sugar and wool for the basis of a trade, and to let wool into the United States free of duty, even under a scheme of reciprocity in exchange for markets for our commodities, was not to be thought of in the presence of those ominous figures who stood in the way in Ohio.[5] No trade with South America could be developed at their expense; only sugar

[1] A. F. Tyler, Foreign Policy of J. G. Blaine, pp. 185–6.
[2] Gail Hamilton, Biography of Blaine, p. 685; Edward Stanwood, James G. Blaine, p. 331.
[3] A. F. Tyler, op. cit., p. 186.
[4] Cong. Record, 51st Cong. 1st sess., pp. 6256–9; Richardson, vol. ix, p. 74; App. Ann. Cyclop. for 1890, pp. 202–5.
[5] Cf. N. Y. Times, April 23, 1890.

remained. If it were to be free, Blaine and his friends declared,
reciprocity with the Latin countries in the South must be abandoned, the parleys already in progress with the new republic of
Brazil might better be brought to an end and the Pan-American
Conference itself would at once, and in the future, be seen as but
a small thing in the history of his administration of the Department of State.[1]

By the bill, as it was finally approved by the Republican
leaders in Congress, a bounty would be paid the Louisiana cane
and the Western American beet sugar growers.[2] If for free sugar,
molasses, coffee, tea and hides on our side foreign governments,
whose populations produced these articles, should not grant
us reciprocal privileges in the admission of our exports prior
to January 1, 1892, then the President of the United States
should, by proclamation, announce and enforce a retaliatory
policy.   Duties, which were specified, would be immediately
laid upon the articles named when these were presented from
the territory of the refractory governments for entry at our
custom houses.

The tariff reformers and the free traders expressed derisive
delight as they saw the heads of protectionism wavering in
adherence to the theory that the only valuable market was the
"home market." [3] Bringing men together for an exchange of
products was not so unseemly a proceeding after all.   Extremists
there still were who spoke jocularly of "reciprocity." Speaker
Reed asked what it was, and alluded without favor to trade with
"a lot of Dagoes." But Blaine and the administration had come
to the point at which they were willing to subscribe to the principle that it is good for a nation to engage in foreign trade.[4]

The Aldrich amendment, despite the opposition of Edmunds

[1] "The American government has already conceded nearly everything
which it has to offer." (N. Y. Tribune, April 22, 1890.) "If sugar is placed
upon the free list," said President Harrison, "practically every important
article exported from those states [the Latin American states] will be given
untaxed access to our markets except wool."—Richardson, vol. ix, p. 74.

[2] In Schedule E of the bill.

[3] N. Y. Nation, Sep. 4 and 11, 1890; Harper's Weekly, April 12, July 5
and Aug. 2, 1890.

[4] Cf. N. Y. Nation, Sep. 4, 1890.

and Evarts, whose objections were based upon legalistic grounds, became Section 3 of the bill,[1] which passed the Senate on September 10th by a vote of 40 to 29, all the Republicans voting for and all the Democrats against it.[2] The House non-concurred in the amendments "in gross," and the bill went to a conference committee which included such leaders as Senators Aldrich, Sherman and Allison and Representatives McKinley, Burrows and Dingley. Give and take and compromise were the result. The reciprocity amendment was accepted; the House and Senate passed the bill on September 27th and 30th respectively. It was approved by the President on October 1st, and it became a law of the land.[3]

The bill in general, though here and there rates in the law of 1883 had been lowered, or articles at that time made dutiable were now put upon the free list, effected a marked increase in customs duties. Henry W. Oliver, who had been a member of the Tariff Commission of 1882–3 which, in answer to opinion within the Republican party at that time, demanded a lower tariff, declared the McKinley bill to be the "most protective bill" that had ever been passed. Others were of the same view. It was frankly framed in this spirit. The leaders of the party who, a few years before, were advocates of a more liberal system of international commercial exchange had been overborne. Though disagreement among our industrial leaders themselves and the politicians who were aiming to serve them was little concealed, the voice of the tariff reformer within the Republican party was stilled. Those who had not received what they wanted from Congress, as well as those who were wholly pleased with the result, were persuaded that the country would prosper under the boon of a protection of which so much had been heard, and which had now come to expression under McKinley's name.[4]

With the progress of the tariff there was, concurrently, discussion among the Republicans of what should be done on the

[1] N. Y. Nation, Sep. 18 and 25, 1890.
[2] Cong. Record, 51st Cong. 1st sess., p. 9043.
[3] McPherson's Handbook for 1890, pp. 223–44; ibid. for 1892, pp. 4–23.
[4] But see N. Y. Nation, Aug. 14, 1890.

subject of great combinations of capital, with a view to meeting
the cry that the tariff was the "mother of trusts." "Combinations in restraint of trade," conspiracies of men and corporations
to monopolize production and to control the agencies of distribution must be checked by law.   Senator Sherman was the
sponsor of an "anti-trust bill," and it came to debate in 1890.
Referred to the Judiciary Committee Senator Edmunds made
changes in it and reported a substitute, which it was supposed
might reach the evil or, at any rate, satisfy the people that the
Republicans,while giving the country a high tariff, were not
unmindful of the dangers which, it was freely said, lurked behind
its walls.[1]   It passed the Senate and the House and was approved
by the President on July 2, 1890.[2]

On another question party leadership was not so sure. Silver,
which had been disturbing politics for a number of years and
which now was disorganizing trade and private and public
finance, called more and more insistently for courageous
statesmanship. If higgling with the standard of value were to
continue the country would soon face a crisis of grave dimensions. The silver miners were determined to increase the price
of their product. The prosperity of the Rocky Mountain
states was conditioned upon the profitable prosecution of this
industry. If tariffs should be laid to stimulate and support
business activity why should not the government give an encouraging hand to those who were taking silver from the bowels
of the earth, and who could get scarcely enough to pay them for
their toil? The government was taking two million dollars'
worth of bullion each month under the law of 1878 and continued
to do this, in spite of the protests of every President of the
United States whom we had had since that day, as well as of
all competent authorities on theoretical monetary science and
on practical banking. Yet the purchases were not large enough

---

[1] The anti-trust law, Carl Schurz said, was "a lightning rod to prevent
the popular feeling against the trusts from striking the tariff."—Writings
Schurz, vol. v, p. 62.

[2] McPherson's Handbook for 1890, pp. 112–9; John Sherman's Recollections, vol. ii, pp. 1071–6; App. Ann. Cyclop. for 1890, p. 235; N. Y.
Nation, March 27 and April 3, 1890.

to serve the ends of our Western miners and the communities supported by this business. What was simpler than an appeal to Congress and a demand that the government buy greater quantities of what deserving citizens in the Rocky Mountains had to sell to relieve the glut and raise the price?

With the growth of the idea that it was the function of government to improve the condition of whatever group of inhabitants needed its aid the miners were not loath to press their case. Already in evil plight it would be fortunate if the currency should escape further damage. Secretary Windom's plan for increased purchases of silver, as a support for silver certificates, which President Harrison had not found the time to consider up to the day of the sending to Congress of his message, and other schemes relating to the currency, made their appearance in the Senate and the House. The Secretary of the Treasury spoke of "the extraordinary concessions" which he had "offered to the silver sentiment of the country." [1] But the more he gave, the more these men wanted. He would, they said, "assassinate silver in the interest of the gold bugs." [2] Their object, and they dared to state it, was "free coinage" and no half way measures. The Republican caucus bill was a modification of the Windom bill and called for the purchase of 4,500,000 ounces of bullion per month to be paid for by a new kind of Treasury notes, receivable for all government dues and redeemable in silver dollars, which were to be coined from the purchases, as needed, to take care of redemptions. What remained above the amount coined would be stored. The existing two millions-per-month-law would be repealed. [3]

It was assumed that whatever bill should be passed would be in the direction of inflation, and Wall Street bought stocks in expectation of higher prices. [4] The Senate took the leadership in bringing the subject to debate because of the existence in that branch of Congress of a group of men who fully reflected the frenzy of the silver miners, led by Jones and Stewart of

[1] N. Y. Nation, April 24, 1890; cf. ibid., May 1, 1890.
[2] Ibid., March 27, 1890, quoting The Silver Dollar of Cleveland, O.
[3] Ibid., May 1, 1890.
[4] Ibid., May 8, 1890.

Nevada, and Teller and a younger advocate of the cause in Colorado, Wolcott, who had just come to the Senate for a trial of his oratorical powers.[1] The situation had been rendered the more menacing because of the admission of four new Western states, with eight senators who might be expected to hold similar views. Sherman, held to be the first authority on public finance, was wavering in his usual manner.[2] All that had been heard about the "crime of 73" and the stealthy demonetization of silver was repeated. Efforts to tamper with the $100,000,000 reserve which was kept in the Treasury for the redemption of greenbacks were renewed. The meaning of the currency plank in the Republican national platform was discussed and made a subject of dispute.[3]

The House under "Reed's rules," with little discussion, passed a silver bill based on the caucus plan, on June 7th, by a vote of 135 to 119. A motion of Bland, in the interest of the free coinage of silver, was defeated by a vote of 116 to 140.[4] The bill was amended by the Senate Committee on Finance and came to debate. It was seen from the first that the silverites were in control of the Senate. The "upper branch" of Congress, the house which was farthest removed from popular impulse, and which was looked to, therefore, as the repository of order and conservatism, was now completely radical. The free silver feature was attached to the bill at once, and it was passed on June 17th by a vote of 42 to 25, all the Democrats approving, except George Gray of Delaware, McPherson of New Jersey and Wilson of Maryland. The 14 Republicans who were pleased to vote for the measure were the twain from Kansas, from Colorado, from Nevada and from Nebraska, with these from the new states—one from Washington, one from North Dakota, one from South Dakota and two from Montana. To this company was joined "Don" Cameron of Pennsylvania who, misrepresenting the people of his state, allied himself with the

---

[1] N. Y. Nation, June 26, 1890.
[2] Ibid., May 22 and June 12, 1890.
[3] Cf. ibid., May 29, 1890.
[4] McPherson's Handbook for 1890, pp. 143–6.

silverites. Seventeen senators were absent or were paired with absentees.[1]

The House of Representatives, with the help of the Speaker and his "rules," saved the country from this outburst of folly,[2] and the free silver scheme was rejected by a vote of 152 to 135.[3] About 20 Republicans from the area swept by the fanaticism voted for it and as many Democrats against it.[4] The conference committee presented a "compromise bill" which Vest and Bland of Missouri, two of the six conferees, refused to accept, and it was passed. Finally, therefore, after the angriest argument, the bill, which the President signed, the Windom plan in its essential features, formulated with no conviction by its authors of what was proper or right, in answer to the rising fervor about silver, was incorporated into a law to supersede the purchase law of 1878.[5] Hereafter the government would buy four and a half million ounces of silver per month, if it were offered for sale, paying for it at the market price in new Treasury notes. Two million ounces of bullion should be coined monthly until July 1, 1891, and, thereafter, as much as might be necessary to provide for the redemption of the Treasury notes.[6]

The act requiring the Secretary of the Treasury to hold a reserve of $100,000,000 in gold to redeem the greenbacks was not repealed. It was stated that it would be the policy of the United States to maintain gold and silver "on a parity with each other," which was to say that silver would be supported by gold. The resumption act of 1875 which required the Secretary of the Treasury after January 1, 1879, to redeem greenbacks in coin and to sell bonds for that purpose remained in force. Plainly the gold standard would be maintained so long as the credit of the country should suffice for the purpose. The New

---

[1] Cong. Record, 51st Cong. 1st sess., pp. 6182–3; McPherson's Handbook for 1890, pp. 140–8.
[2] N. Y. Nation, July 3, 1890.
[3] Cong. Record, 51st Cong. 1st sess., p. 6503.
[4] McPherson's Handbook for 1890, pp. 148–55.
[5] App. Ann. Cyclop. for 1890, pp. 233–4.
[6] Ibid., pp. 155–7.

York Nation concluded that the law was "tremendously absurd," but the country could be "congratulated on not getting a worse measure." [1]

The silver men, however, gained a point in another direction, for, without any opposition worthy of note, two more Rocky Mountain states, Wyoming and Idaho, were informed that they might make their constitutions, elect United States senators and come into the Union. Wyoming, where women were voting, would bring female suffrage with it and introduce for the first time into our electoral practice this experiment, amid the exultation of the friends of the cause. [2]

The tariff and currency bills were closely bound up with another administration measure, a Federal elections bill, which came to be known at once as the "Force Bill." The President had spoken earnestly about the wrongs which negroes and other Republicans were suffering in the South in a restriction of their voting rights, clearly, as was said, in disregard of plain provision, added after the war to the Constitution of the United States. The Federal government might interfere and give supervision in the states to elections of representatives in Congress, a fact stated and restated, and confirmed by exercise, during the period of Reconstruction. But in the administration of President Hayes the practice had been abandoned. It was determined that the game was not worth the candle. More evil than good had come from such an assertion of Federal authority. Now, after an interval during which the South had been reborn industrially, and had accommodated itself to a new economic and social order, it was gravely proposed to revive measures which had so fired the anger of the people and disturbed the peace. Republican "Bourbons" wished to make "bloody shirt" speeches; radical Northern politicians thought that they saw in the issue which should be raised fresh opportunities to discredit the Democratic party and prevent it from again coming into power.

---

[1] N. Y. Nation, July 10 and 17, 1890.

[2] Ibid., April 10, July 10, 17, Sep. 4, 1890; McPherson's Handbook for 1890, pp. 134–42; App. Ann. Cyclop. for 1890, p. 235.

Sherman, early in the session, introduced a Federal elections bill in the Senate similar to that which he had sponsored in the last Congress.[1] Chandler of New Hampshire had another.[2] Both men had been conspicuously active in their unfriendliness to the South. In the House Henry Cabot Lodge, with a youthful eagerness for notoriety, was the advocate of a "Force Bill" which, as opportunity would allow, at intervals when the tariff and other subjects were not engaging attention, was advanced on the calendar.[3] With Reed's aid the idea was adopted in the House early in July,[4] and it passed to the Senate where Hoar, whose partisanship was of a rare order, had taken up the cudgels in its behalf.[5] It was predicted that it would be talked to death in that chamber if it were not disposed of by an adverse vote. The response of the country was most unfavorable. Well known Republicans in the South were fearful of the consequences,[6] and made their opinions known. The Independent press was unqualified in its condemnation of this attempt to revive sectional animosity. It was clearly a scheme to gain party advantage in the pending Congressional elections and in 1892. Shrewd Republican managers like Quay were beginning to understand that adoption and enforcement of the measure might react very unpleasantly, since it promised to interfere with the progress of the tariff bill in which Pennsylvania had an important stake.[7] In August he took the matter in hand and offered a resolution in the Republican caucus looking to the abandonment of this feature of the party program,[8] though senators like Hoar and Frye, and party organs like the New York Tribune and the Philadelphia Press, continued acridly to agitate the question and demand the passage of the bill.[9] The postponement of its further discussion until the next session was ominous and betokened its death.

[1] N. Y. Nation, Dec. 19, 1889.   [2] Ibid.
[3] Ibid., March 27, 1890.
[4] Ibid., July 10, 1890; McPherson's Handbook for 1890, pp. 201-19.
[5] N. Y. Nation, May 1, 1890.
[6] Writings of Schurz, vol. v, pp. 73-5.
[7] Cf. N. Y. Nation, July 17 and 24, and Aug. 14, 1890.
[8] Ibid., Aug. 21, 1890; Hoar, Autobiog. of 70 years, vol. ii, p. 155.
[9] N. Y. Nation, Aug. 28, 1890.

That the policy of pensioning the soldiers of the war would be extended in answer to the promises made to them during the campaign was foreordained. The fact that a Republican would be more generous to those who had saved the Union than a Democratic administration must be clearly established. The Dependent Pension bill which Cleveland had vetoed in 1887 appeared again, and was passed by the Senate on March 31, 1890.[1] Many advocated a still more liberal policy and the escape from further demands upon the Treasury was reckoned to be fortunate. A plan to remove the limitation as to arrears of pensions which was proposed would, it was computed, call for an outlay of not less than $600,000,000. Senator Blair said that it was a debt; it was time, he said, to call a halt on thinking about the "low and earthly and sensual and devilish things" which occupied the attention of Congress and to pay this debt. If it were a billion dollars it would be not too much. It had cost three billions to win the war and it was an "execrable shame" to do less than full justice to those who, on the day of rebellion, had risen for the nation's defence.[2]

The House on its side exceeded the Senate in the expression of its indebtedness to the "old soldier," and on April 30th passed a service pension bill granting a pension to every man who, having served for 90 days, had reached the age of 60, and to any enlisted man under that age who, from any cause, should be disabled.[3] The subject was referred to a conference committee. An agreement was reached. The "service pension" features of the House bill were eliminated and a bill was passed which, Gorman said in the Senate, would produce a Treasury deficit of $100,000,000 in 1892. But Ingalls of Kansas, with a heart as large and a hand as open as Blair's, said that he did not care whether the cost should be one hundred or a thousand millions. Every surviving Union soldier should have a pension.[4]

[1] McPherson's Handbook for 1890, pp. 119–21; N. Y. Nation, April 3, 1890.
[2] Cong. Record, 51st Cong. 1st sess., p. 2837.
[3] N. Y. Nation, May 8, 1890.
[4] Cong. Record, 51st Cong. 1st sess., pp. 6379–81; N. Y. Nation, June 26, 1890; McPherson's Handbook for 1890, pp. 123–7.

Private pension bills, which President Cleveland had examined and had vetoed, under Republican criticism, were generally approved by President Harrison. These grants, with bills to erect Federal buildings in towns and cities in all parts of the country, and a River and Harbor bill, which included an appropriation for the Hennepin Canal,[1] would convert a "surplus," of which so much had been said in the past few years, into a deficit,[2] a result which would be effected without the Blair bill for giving money to the states, with a particular view to the education of the people of the South, for that measure suffered in this Congress, to use the words of the New York Nation, "final and condign defeat." [3]

The further acquisition of Indian lands also increased the expenditures of the government. The President, in December, 1890, was able to say that, since March 4, 1889, agreements with various tribes had added to the national domain 14,726,000 acres of land, a total increased in another year to 23,000,000.[4] Oklahoma, which was opened with such a fanfare in 1889, was organized by act of Congress of May 2, 1890, into a territory and already its inhabitants were eager for statehood. The boundaries were made to include the Public Land Strip of 3,600,000 acres which contained, in 1889, about 15,000 inhabitants,[5] though it occupied an isolated position in the northwest and would be disconnected with the rest of Oklahoma until such time as the Cherokee Outlet should be acquired, an event which was in view, since provision was made for the inclusion in Oklahoma of this strip and other parts of the Indian Territory whenever the old tribal titles could be extinguished.[6]

A commission was diligently engaged in the endeavor to arrange terms of transfer with the Cherokees.[7] The Outlet

[1] McPherson's Handbook for 1892, p. 70; N. Y. Nation, March 13, 1890.
[2] Cf. N. Y. Nation, June 26, 1890, and April 30, 1891.
[3] Ibid., Jan. 9 and March 27, 1890. See McPherson's Handbook for 1890, p. 194.
[4] Richardson, vol. ix, pp. 117, 203.
[5] Report of Sec. of Int. for 1889, vol. i, pp. 62–3.
[6] App. Ann. Cyclop. for 1890, pp. 606 7.
[7] Report of Sec. of Int. for 1889, pp. xiii–xvi; ibid. for 1891, pp. vi–vii; cf. N. Y. Times, May 24, 1889.

was being used for grazing purposes by a cattle company, under lease from the tribe. The Attorney General as long ago as in 1885 had declared the contract to be invalid, and it was annulled now by President Harrison.[1] The land must be acquired and opened for settlement; it barred Oklahoma's communication with Kansas.[2] Remonstrances of the tribe, founded on distinct pledges in treaties, were entitled to more consideration than they would receive; though these protests made for delay.[3] More success was gained as a result of negotiations with the Sacs and Foxes, the Cheyennes and Arapahoes, the Pottawatomies and the absent Shawnees, the Wichitas and the Kickapoos, and other tribes.[4] These lands were thrown open for settlement by proclamation of the President. New "rushes" brought new "boomers" into the country for the location of farms and town lots.[5]

The aggressions of white settlers in the north among the Sioux led to complications which were unpleasant alike to the Indians and to the government, whose ineptitude in its relations with the native race was again widely advertised and impressively confirmed.[6] A commission, directed by the experienced hand of General Crook, after tedious and resolute effort, obtained their consent to a cession of a large part of their land in the new state of South Dakota where the reservation offered a barrier 250 miles long and 160 miles wide, thus preventing communication between its eastern and western portions, between the Missouri and the Black Hills.[7] As a result of this negotiation 11,000,000 acres were, by proclamation of the President, on

[1] Richardson, vol. ix, pp. 97–8; cf. Report of Sec. of Int. for 1889, vol. i, pp. cxl–cli; ibid. for 1890, vol. ii, pp. lxxi–lxxiii.

[2] N. Y. Times, Aug. 5, 1889.

[3] Cf. Senate Mis. Doc., 51st Cong. 1st sess., no. 109; Report of Gov. of Oklahoma for 1891, in House Ex. Doc., 52nd Cong. 1st sess., no. 1, pt. 5, pp. 452–3.

[4] Report of Sec. of Int. for 1891, pp. iii–viii.

[5] App. Ann. Cyclop. for 1891, p. 695; Richardson, vol. ix, pp. 156–60, 275–8.

[6] Cf. N. Y. Nation, Jan. 1 and 8, 1891; N. A. Miles in N. A. Review of Jan., 1891.

[7] N. Y. Times, May 24 and Aug. 7, 1889; App. Ann. Cyclop. for 1889, pp. 249, 775; Richardson, vol. ix, pp. 45–6.

February 10, 1890, thrown open to settlement and, at the sound of a shot from a cannon, a crowd of waiting "boomers," although the Missouri River was frozen over and cold winds blew across the prairies, rushed in to seize the coveted lands in the Sioux country.[1] The terms were more favorable to the Indians than those named in the plan which had been rejected in 1888, but, in spite of the appearance of satisfaction with the result among the groups gathered at the agencies, when they had been visited by the commissioners,[2] largely induced by promises that a new and more generous policy would be pursued in dealing with the tribe, assurance that all was well was not at hand.[3]

The Indian administration was still a pawn in "politics." Soldiers in contact with the subject on the plains had frequently made this charge, and they repeated it. Sagacious men everywhere who were acquainted with the Indian civil service knew that it was so, in spite of long agitation for reform. Delays attending the forwarding of food and other supplies to the tribes, their poor quality and the scant amounts issued made for discontent and recalled to the minds of the Indian race the long train of injuries done them by the white man.[4] The "annuities" were not being paid. The money of the Indians was invested in candle moulds, corn shellers and other articles which they could not use.[5] The crops on the plains had failed in 1889 and 1890 because of droughts. The shortage in the harvests affected whites and Indians alike, though many of the whites were able to migrate, returning to the East or passing on to the Pacific slope. The Indians must remain where they were at the mercy of civil agents "frequently changed and often inexperienced," [6] and also, too often, corrupt.

The Indians were told, and they knew, that they would be well fed if the United States government should keep faith with

---

[1] Richardson, vol. ix, pp. 94–7; N. Y. Times, Feb. 11, 1890; N. Y. Tribune, Feb. 13, 1890.
[2] Report of Sec. of Int. for 1889, pp. ix–xi.
[3] Ibid. for 1890, vol. ii, p. 49.
[4] Cf. ibid. for 1891, vol. ii, pp. 409–10.
[5] Ninth Ann. Report of Indian Rights Association.
[6] Report of Sec. of War for 1891, p. 133.

them. For want of the proper appropriations by Congress, and for other reasons, the Interior Department complied with the requirements of the treaties tardily or not at all, and disaffection was rife. The Cheyennes in Montana were suffering from hunger in the winter of 1890–91 and, to sustain life, they were killing cattle belonging to the whites.[1] In the case of a body of 1200 Indians it was complained that only $2,000 were available for their support, a sum, if apportioned, which would allow less than one cent a day to each person.[2] At the Pine Ridge Agency the Indians in 1886 had received 8,000,000 pounds of beef. This allowance had been reduced to 5,000,000 annually, and now, after the visit of the commission, to 4,000,000, though that body, to get the signatures of the Indians, had promised that the amount would be increased. The officers of the Indian Bureau at Washington said that they had no food and no money to buy it; they offered to send instead shoes, shawls, blankets, ticking and gingham.[3] Had the announcement of a reduction of the beef ration been made before the signatures had been obtained it was said at Pine Ridge that not any could have been secured at that agency. The signers were now called "fools and dupes" by the non-signers.[4]

In this situation the "Messiah craze" appeared. The Indians were performing "ghost dances." They would feast, sing, shout and go through weird gyrations until they swooned away from physical exhaustion, which was a kind of oblation to the Great Spirit. Many tribes were obsessed by a belief that a "Miracle Man" would come among them. There were some who had seen him. He was "like the white man's Christ."[5] He would deliver them from their accumulated difficulties. They would be endowed with perpetual youth. The buffalo would return to the plains. Their departed heroes, resurrected, would lead

---

[1] Report of Sec. of War for 1891, pp. 132–3.
[2] App. Ann. Cyclop, for 1890, p. 441; cf. T. A. Bland, A Brief Hist. of the Late Military Invasion of the Home of the Sioux, p. 20.
[3] Report of Sec. of Int. for 1891, p. 136.
[4] Ibid. for 1890, vol. ii, p. 49; cf. ibid. for 1891, vol. ii, pp. 133–4.
[5] T. A. Bland, op. cit., p. 8.

them in a triumphant battle against the whites, so that they would again be in undisputed possession of the American continent.[1]

This "Messiah craze" would be put to cunning use by leaders in whom the old war spirit persisted. Sitting Bull and Geronimo were the last in the long line of American Indian chiefs who could be made useful as heroes for juvenile romance. The curtain had fallen upon Geronimo and, but for mawkish sentiment in the East, Sitting Bull would have been kept under deserved restraint. As it was, after his flight to Canada, following the Custer massacre, he had been amnestied back into the United States. He was now said to be 56 years old. His hostility to the government, when he was afforded opportunity to display it, continued. He had broken up a conference, which had promised to be friendly in 1883. He appeared at another time and told the Indians that those who should sign a treaty laid before them would be shot in their tracks.[2] He was described as "the last great prophet of the Dacotahs." In him his race, it was said, "stood incarnate." He was "one of the historic characters of the continent." One, viewing his great frame, likened him to Gladstone, another to Daniel Webster.[3] Lately this old mountebank had been despatching couriers in all directions, even as far as into the British possessions, urging the chiefs of the tribes to collect arms and ammunition and to join the Sioux for battle upon the white race on some field near the Black Hills in the spring of 1891.[4]

The settlers on the frontier feared for their lives. The Indian agents were obliged to admit that they had lost control of the situation and appealed to the War Department, and the

[1] Report of Sec. of War for 1891, pp. 140–2.

[2] Cong. Record, 51st Cong. 2nd sess., pp. 69–70; cf. Report of Sec. of Int. for 1891, vol. ii, pp. 125–6. The Indian agent at Standing Rock described Sitting Bull at this time as a "polygamist, libertine, habitual liar, active obstructionist and a great obstacle in the civilization of these people." A woman in the East, representing some philanthropic association, had visited him, lavished money upon him and treated him as a martyr to his great disadvantage.—Report of Sec. of Int. for 1891, vol. ii, p. 329.

[3] T. A. Bland, op. cit., pp. 24–7.

[4] Report of Sec. of War for 1891, pp. 143–4.

President ordered it to act.[1] General Miles who had been in command of the Division of the Pacific was brought on in September, 1890, to the Division of the Missouri, with headquarters in Chicago. In a short time half of the infantry and cavalry of the United States were in motion, and were closing in on the Sioux reservations.[2]

The army officers on the scene were agreed that the promises of the government had not been kept. The Indians at the Rosebud Agency, it was said, had never received "the full treaty ration." [3] Their "grounds of complaint" at Pine Ridge, General Brooke said, were "reasonable." [4] General Ruger at Standing Rock said that, if there were to be peace, the provisions of the treaties should be "promptly and fully carried out"—promises must be "faithfully kept." [5] That the Sioux were without enough food to sustain life, in violation of plain agreement with the tribe, General Miles declared to be "beyond question." [6] Congress in one hour, he telegraphed General Schofield, could confirm the new treaties, appropriate the necessary funds and avert hostilities.[7]

From several agencies came suggestions that the chiefs who were fomenting war should be taken into custody and transported to military posts.[8] Sitting Bull's arrest and confinement were particularly recommended. He was plainly identified as a ringleader in the threatened rising and General Miles asked William F. Cody ("Buffalo Bill"), an experienced plainsman, who had had friendly relations with the chief to visit him in his camp, which consisted of two or three log cabins on Grand River, about 40 miles southwest of Standing Rock agency, and to induce him to come within military lines. If he should refuse he was to be taken into custody and carried to the nearest prison. This highly desirable movement was arrested

[1] Report of Sec. of War for 1891, pp. 144–5.
[2] Ibid., pp. 55–6.
[3] Ibid., p. 137.
[4] Ibid., pp. 136–7.
[5] Ibid., p. 135.
[6] Ibid., p. 133.
[7] Ibid., p. 149.
[8] Cf. ibid., p. 137.

by the President, on the advice of an Indian agent, and, as a propitiatory offering, additional rations were procured for the tribe from appropriations granted to the War Department,[1] a measure taken too late.[2]

The "ghost dancing" continued and, the Indian agent being now ready for action, the loyal Indian police were instructed to descend upon Sitting Bull, who was on the point of starting for the Bad Lands to join disaffected bands which had already assembled there.[3] The chief was found and arrested on December 15, 1890. This act was the signal for an outbreak. He called upon his friends to rescue him and, in the fight which ensued, before the arrival of the cavalry with a Hotchkiss gun, he was killed, together with a number of his following and several of the police.[4]

The warriors who escaped fled to join their friends in the South. Sitting Bull's death further exasperated them. The Seventh Cavalry, the military unit to which Custer and his unfortunate men had belonged, led in the pursuit. Troops of this command had surrounded the camp of a chief named Big Foot on Wounded Knee Creek and were disarming the hostiles when they turned and a deadly battle at close range followed. One officer and 24 enlisted men were killed, while 35 were wounded, some mortally. The Indians on their side lost 150.[5]

The excitement throughout the country was intense. Military organizations and individuals tendered their services to the government. General Miles himself advanced to give personal oversight to the operations of the troops. Rumors of disastrous impending battles filled the newspapers. But the hostiles, though desultory outrages continued, were con-

---

[1] Report of Sec. of War for 1891, pp. 129, 331–3.
[2] W. Fletcher Johnson, Life of Sitting Bull, p. 411.
[3] Report of Sec. of War for 1891, pp. 142–3.
[4] Report of Sec. of Int. for 1891, vol. ii, pp. 129, 325–38; Report of Sec. of War for 1891, pp. 146–7; App. Ann. Cyclop. for 1890, pp. 441, 666; N. Y. Tribune, Dec. 16 and 18, 1890.
[5] Report of Sec. of Interior for 1891, vol. i, pp. lii–lvii; ibid., vol. ii, pp. 123–35, 409–10, 411–2; Report of Sec. of War for 1891, particularly reports of Miles and Ruger, and accompanying dispatches and reports.

fined within a narrowing circle near the Pine Ridge Agency, where, under better counsel, seeing the hopelessness of resistance, even the more desperate were induced to come in and lay down their arms. The Interior Department relinquished the management of the agencies in the disturbed region and army officers took control which continued for some time at Pine Ridge with the usual protests from the civil authorities in the Interior Department.[1] The philanthropists again charged the soldiers with cruelty. The "battle of Wounded Knee Creek," the secretary of the "National Indian Defense Association" said, was "a deliberate massacre."[2] Sitting Bull had been "murdered."[3] Indian women and children had been brutally slain by the troops.[4] To allay criticism and, if possible, pacify the tribe they were invited again to send a delegation of chiefs to Washington to make a statement of their grievances.[5] This "battle" was to be the last considerable engagement in the history of the United States Army's long list of "Indian wars."

The elections in the September states in 1890 told of Democratic gains. Reed was reelected in Maine by a large majority which seemed, in so far as his own district was concerned, to be an endorsement of his rather dictatorial course as Speaker.[6] But it was certain that the Republican party in the nation at large would receive popular rebuke.[7] The civil service reformers were entirely displeased with Mr. Harrison. While the President had failed to meet the expectations of Quay, Platt and the politicians who had looked for larger rewards he continued to give but little proof of improvement upon Cleveland in keeping faith with those who had high ideals for the public service. After a year in office Assistant Post-

---

[1] Report of Sec. of Int. for 1891, vol. ii, pp. 143–5.

[2] T. A. Bland, op. cit., p. 19.

[3] Report of Sec. of Int. for 1891, vol. ii, p. 336; T. A. Bland, op. cit., pp. 24–5.

[4] T. A. Bland, op. cit., pp. 10–1, 15–8.

[5] Ibid., pp. 11–4; N. Y. Tribune, Jan. 2, 1891, and succeeding daily issues.

[6] N. Y. Nation, Sep. 11, 1890.

[7] Cf. ibid.

master General Clarkson was ready to retire. A few days before quitting his post he boasted that he had changed 31,000 out of 55,000 fourth class postmasters—he would remove 10,000 more and then leave the scene. At that time five-sixths of the post-offices would again be in the hands of Republicans, when he could paraphrase old Simeon and say to the President, "Let thy servant depart in peace." [1] The appointment of ex-Governor Warmoth of Louisiana to be collector of the port of New Orleans seemed to be an expression of complete contempt for the feelings of the Mugwumps and the principles which they had so steadfastly advocated.[2] At the end of the first year of the administration, it was alleged, that the changes in Federal offices had been nearly double the number of those made in the first year of Cleveland's term. Mr. Harrison was, said the New York Nation, "the most subservient disciple of the spoils doctrine" who had occupied the Presidential chair since the law on this subject had been passed.[3]

The McKinley tariff law had been enacted with an appearance of unanimity, and acquiescence in its provisions was at first the rule among Republicans. But the rates of duty, the result, as they were, of much log rolling and bargaining, when they were studied, had awakened no enthusiasm. The idea that rich men were seeking and had secured advantages in the law, that the manufacturing East was being served at the expense of the agricultural West was taking deep root. It was not clear that votes had been made by the McKinley bill.

The silver law also settled nothing and satisfied neither one element within the party nor the other. The miners had not got what they wanted, the bimetallists were not to see their theories accepted, the poor, with mortgages and other debts to pay, were not to enjoy the "relief" which they earnestly believed lay in a cheaper currency. The vehement debates over the "Force Bill," though it was not passed, made an unfavorable impression upon men of independent judgment

[1] N. Y. Nation, Feb. 27, 1890; Harper's Weekly, March 8 and April 5, 1890.

[2] N. Y. Nation, March 6, 1890.

[3] Ibid., March 13, 1890; cf. Harper's Weekly, March 8, 1890.

with higher political objects in view. The pension scandals attendant upon the administration of the bureau by Tanner, and the dissipation of the "surplus" by measures denounced by the opposition as extravagant were but a poor record for an appeal to the country. Meanwhile the administration of Cleveland was fresh in public memory. The leader under whom, for four years, national affairs had been conducted with economy, in protest against the too free use of public moneys, against onerous taxes, against governmental interference with private initiative, against socialistic schemes in their various forms and centralization of public authority resided in New York City. Admiration for him in many circles increased when the present order was contrasted with what had gone before it.

More significant than these movements in public feeling was the rising of the farmers, and the appearance in many states in the West and South of well organized, combative groups, with radical views. The frontier had been pressed out upon the dry plains. Crops had failed, prices of farm products had declined. Money lenders, some of them avaricious, if not cunning, offered the harassed tillers of the soil loans at high rates of interest. Not a small town in the East that had not held one or more agencies for the sale of Western farm mortgages. Widows and children, retired gentlemen and careful spinsters of small means, even the guardians of estates transferred their available capital to Kansas and other parts of the West where, by this time, land values were falling. The farmers could not sell their farms for the amount of the mortgages. They could no longer pay their six, seven and eight per cent. to the East. The agents of the lenders foreclosed. The late owners, if they remained on the soil, became tenants of Eastern landlords. Feeling grew wild and bitter. Causes were sought and they were discovered in strange places.[1] It was the same thing which we had had before, but it bade fair to attain more formidable proportions and such, indeed,

[1] Solon J. Buck, The Agrarian Crusade, pp. 102–10; F. E. Haynes, Third Party Movements, pp. 221–3; cf. N. Y. Nation, Jan. 29, 1891.

as had not yet been seen in the history of the Mississippi Valley. It was the "Ohio idea," Grangerism, Greenbackism, Blandism, free silverism. It was founded essentially on the fallacious notion that money was wealth. If money could be made "plenty" times would be better; the ease and comfort of the farming and laboring classes would be increased. The banker, the capitalist, the money lender of the East, summed up as "Wall Street," oppressed the poor man. If the people were not to have paper money it should be silver, or some form of currency cheaper and more abundant than gold, issued by the government and distributed for the relief of those who must support themselves and their families by the sweat of their face.[1]

The clamor of this *émeute* came out of the West. Likewise, in the South, groups of men who were burdened with debt incurred after the war and funded in mortgages were actively calling meetings, adopting resolutions and making demands upon the state and national governments.[2] The farmers were committed to principles which were neither Republican nor Democratic. They would influence and take control of old party organizations in communities where they might do this, and elsewhere would act separately. Their number was indeterminable, but the rumble of their discontent with existing measures and institutions betokened some social upheaval, and it was near at hand. Early in December, 1889, a meeting of representatives of the new farmers' clubs and associations was held in St. Louis. A union of the various sectional forces was attempted under the name of the National Farmers' Alliance, and a platform was adopted which was accepted by the Knights of Labor. They signed a pact. They would use their joint influences, though differences appeared to prevent complete union of purpose, upon the Fifty-first Congress which was assembling at Washington. They would support for office only such men as would give practical effect to certain "demands."

---

[1] Cf. Haynes, Third Party Movements, pp. 223–5.
[2] Haynes, Third Party Movements, pp. 225–6; N. Y. Nation, April 3, July 31, Aug. 14 and 21, 1890.

They called for—

The abolition of national banks and the issue of irredeemable paper money;

The prohibition by law of Congress of the dealing in "futures";

Free silver coinage;

The enactment of laws to prohibit "the alien ownership of land";

Taxation which would not "build up one interest or class at the expense of another";

Government ownership of railroads and telegraphs.[1]

The movement was fastening itself upon the Democratic rather than the Republican party in so far as it was not destined to find expression in a separate political organization. At every point, except in the statement about taxation, which might be taken to look toward tariff reform, the platform was contrary to the known views and policies of Mr. Cleveland. If such, or similar, ideas were to control the Democratic party that party would undergo extensive change, and it would cease to answer to the leadership which it had lately enjoyed.

So much seemed to be in prospect in the South where the intelligent old elements in the population, which had regained possession of their state and local governments upon the downfall of the negro-carpetbagger regime, were on the point of being overthrown by a new combination of poor and ignorant whites, hitherto inexperienced in public life. But it was clear that the whites of whatever class would not leave the Democratic party, lest by division, and as a result of a triangular contest, they should again come under the heel of the Republicans.

In the West considerations of this kind were no deterrent upon the farmers and their friends, and the campaign went forward with the enthusiasm of a religious revival. In Kansas, in particular, where the entire western part of the state was filled with men who could not make a living; where corn was

---

[1] McPherson's Handbook for 1890, pp. 265–6; Haynes, Third Party Movements, pp. 230–1; Buck, The Agrarian Crusade, pp. 122–3.

so low in price that the Alliance leaders said it was cheaper to burn it than to haul it to town and to buy coal for their fires, the canvass of 1890 was a moral crusade. Meetings were held in school houses, churches and public halls. Excited men and women denounced the East, the old parties and capitalistic civilization generally at all-day picnics which brought together thousands of people. A woman with a glib tongue who had studied law, Mary Elizabeth Lease, took the stump. This "Joan of the Dry Lands," speaking to the text, which she announced from time to time, that Kansas should "raise less corn and more hell," made no less than 160 harangues during the campaign. Land equal to a tract 30 miles wide and 90 miles long, she said, had been foreclosed in Kansas in a year. Eight cent corn, ten cent oats, two cent beef and no price at all for butter and eggs had ruined the farmers. The people were "at bay," and "the bloodhounds of money" could "beware." [1]

A luckless wight, whom every one knew as Jerry Simpson, was contesting a seat in Congress for a district comprising 37 counties in the western part of the state. He was a native of Canada. When a lad he had come down from New Brunswick into New York state. From the age of 14 onward, for 23 years, he had been a sailor, principally on the Great Lakes. He pointed to his opponent in the canvass, who, it was said, wore silk socks, and who, for this reason, it was plain to see, was an aristocrat. A newspaper reporter declared that Jerry wore no socks at all, so he became "Sockless Jerry," "Sockless Simpson" and, when irony was indulged in, "Sockless Socrates."

The elections in November, 1890, as was foreshadowed, were indicative of a sweeping revolution in public feeling. A Republican majority of 20 in the House of Representatives was converted into an overwhelming Democratic majority. In the lower branch of the next Congress there would be but 86 Republicans and 235 Democrats, while nine odd figures were returned by the People's party, as the farmers of the West were beginning to call their new organization. Two of these

[1] Solon J. Buck, The Agrarian Crusade, pp. 135-6.

came from Nebraska, the third representative from that state being William Jennings Bryan, a young lawyer with oratorical powers, who considered himself a Democrat and was elected as such; five from Kansas, including "Sockless Jerry"; one, Thomas E. Watson, from Georgia, and one from Minnesota.

McKinley himself was beaten in his contest with a Democrat, due to a gerrymander of his district in Ohio by a Democratic legislature. Cannon of Illinois and other prominent figures in the Fiftieth Congress would not be seen at Washington in the Fifty-first. In New England the Democrats elected 15 against only 11 Republicans; in the old Middle States of New York, New Jersey and Pennsylvania, the Democrats elected 38, the Republicans only 31.[1]

In Kansas where the separate party movement had reached the most impressive proportions the farmers gained a majority in the legislature and elected a picturesque bearded man, William A. Peffer, to succeed the rather notorious John James Ingalls in the United States Senate. A native of Pennsylvania, Peffer had lived in many places as a farmer, practised law in Tennessee and, as early as in 1870, had gone to Kansas where he edited an agricultural paper.[2] The radical faction in the legislature of South Dakota was strong enough to elect the Rev. James H. Kyle, a young Congregational minister, an adherent of the new order, as a United States senator from that state.[3] Both Peffer and Kyle had been Republicans; they were now clearly outside the party fold. But, with the aid of the new states—Wyoming and Idaho added four more Republicans to the membership of the body—the upper branch of Congress would remain in the hands of the friends of the administration by a plurality of six.

The Republicans, in addition to losing not less than 85 seats in the House, were beaten in contests for governorships and state offices. Young William E. Russell had been renominated by the Democrats of Massachusetts and, although defeated in

---

[1] McPherson's Handbook for 1892.
[2] Buck, The Agrarian Crusade, pp. 139–40; F. E. Haynes, Third Party Movements, pp. 239–40.
[3] Buck, The Agrarian Crusade, pp. 138–9.

1888 and 1889, was now successful by a plurality of 9,000.
In New England the Republicans carried only the states of
Maine and Vermont.[1] They failed in their efforts to elect
their state tickets in Pennsylvania, Indiana, Wisconsin, Nebraska, Michigan, Illinois and Montana. The Farmers'
Alliance had nearly elected their separate third party tickets
in Kansas and had endangered Republican success in Minnesota and South Dakota. They had made such inroads in the
South that, so it was said, three governors and 44 representatives in Congress who were elected nominally as Democrats
were Farmers' Alliance men. The farmers would control the
legislatures of five Southern states.[2]

What had occurred in Pennsylvania was a delayed expression
of popular resentment aimed at Quay. The movement gained
an added force because of national conditions, but it was
primarily a beating which most right-thinking persons held to
be due a man who had been exercising dictatorial powers in
the direction of the Republican party in that state. His
successful management of the Presidential campaign in 1888
had increased his assurance, and, having what he believed to
be absolute control of the machinery needed for nominating
and electing candidates in Pennsylvania, he had overstepped
the line. His convention had given him praise for his "match-
less" services and, in disregard of protests, he named his own
candidate for governor, a man with a vulnerable record, George
W. Delameter.[3] The opportunity was at hand. The Democrats
put forward Robert E. Pattison, who had occupied the office
before, as a result of a popular rising in 1882. Independent
Republicans rallied to his standard and "regulars" were in
affright. Those who made charges touching Quay's moral
rectitude in the management of the Harrison campaign had
not been silenced. The two years which had elapsed were

[1] The election in New Hampshire was the subject of a long dispute.
[2] Solon J. Buck, The Agrarian Crusade, p. 133.
[3] A banker who was an affiliate, it was said, of the Standard Oil Company. A. K. McClure, Old Time Notes of Pa., vol. ii, pp. 575 0; N. Y.
Times, June 26, 1890; N. Y. Nation, July 3, and Dec. 18, 1890, and Jan.
15, 1891.

marked by the constant reiteration by the Democratic and Mugwump press of these allegations. The New York World had made categorical statements concerning his earlier record in Pennsylvania politics, involving the misuse of public moneys, which could not be denied.[1] Henry C. Lea directed the attention of the President to the articles, saying that, if the charges were true, Quay should be in the penitentiary. Harrison's connection with the Pennsylvania "boss," Mr. Lea said, "rendered the scandal national."[2] In April the New York Evening Post recast the material and presented it in a still more impressive form.[3]

As the campaign of 1890 in Pennsylvania waxed warm the necessity for aid from the Harrison administration became more and more manifest. Wanamaker, it was observed, was loath to enter the contest and make common cause with the Quay party. Finally Blaine, who had been speaking in other parts of the country, was persuaded to come to Philadelphia. On the Saturday preceding election day, in the Academy of Music, Wanamaker and others being seated on the platform, he sang the benison of protection of American industry amid the enthusiasm that he imparted to admiring crowds. He also referred to campaigns of "slander and vituperation against honorable and reputable gentlemen" and expressed his "horror" of them. He spoke strongly for "party regularity," for he did not wish to see Pennsylvania "led by the free traders of New York City." If Pennsylvania should elect a Democratic governor on the following Tuesday there would be "no balm in Gilead" that could "heal the wound."[4]

Wanamaker followed Blaine. He had come home to vote.

[1] N. Y. World, Feb. 10 and March 3, 1890.

[2] N. Y. Nation, April 10, and 17, 1890; Harper's Weekly, April 26, May 3 and July 5, 1890.

[3] N. Y. Evening Post, April 16, 1890; cf. N. Y. Times, April 17, 1890; N. Y. Nation, July 3, 1890, and Feb. 19, 1891; Writings of Schurz, vol. v, pp. 78–9.

[4] A leading Republican newspaper in Philadelphia said that if Pattison were elected "the fires in the furnaces might as well be drawn and the great manufacturing industries of Pennsylvania might as well close their doors."—Quoted in N. Y. Nation, Nov. 13, 1890; cf. Phila. Inquirer, Nov. 6, 1890.

To have remained away would have been "cowardly," to be silent when George Wallace Delameter was attacked would have been "mean." He would support the whole ticket because he was a Republican and because, to act otherwise, would put him "outside of the Republican party." [1]

The People's party had gained triumphs which were not to be measured by the roll of names of their adherents in the new Congress. Bryan, for example, was in most respects as complete a "Populist" as his colleagues in the delegation from Nebraska, and as much might be said of other Democrats from the Western states. In the South where similar views had taken hold of groups of men these views would be reflected in the utterances of, and the votes upon measures by, its representatives. The Democratic convention in North Carolina had been controlled and the platform was a statement of the principles of the Farmers' Alliance.[2] Nowhere was there such striking evidence of the birth of a new order as in South Carolina. This was a state permeated with conservative, if not aristocratic, sentiments, both social and political. But in 1890 a complete overturn had occurred. An understratum had been raised, the lower classes of the people were organizing for battle at the polls under the leadership of a small farmer, Benjamin R. Tillman. The "Tillmanites" were clearly related to the Populists. The resulting party might have borne the name of the People's party. It was opposed in the election by a faction representing the principles of the Democratic party as these had been known and understood before. Tillman and his friends won. Better men, in South Carolina itself, confessed their inability to explain what had happened, but plainly Democracy had become Tillmanism.[3] The platform was described as an "unintelligible farrago of words"; Tillman, who had "caught up certain half truths," which he mixed plentifully with his own ignorance and conceit, was plainly a demagogue, but he had seized the Democratic

---

[1] Phila. Public Ledger, Nov. 3, 1890; N. Y. Nation, Nov. 13, 1890.
[2] Am. Ann. Cyclop. for 1890, p. 625.
[3] N. Y. Times, Oct. 27, 1890.

name and would hold it and use it as his own for many years to come.[1]

The New York Evening Post and the Nation spoke of the sweeping defeat of the Republicans as a "cyclone." It was a defeat which, by their "wicked and unprincipled measures," they had fairly earned.[2] The Democrats had won their victory, the Evening Post continued, on the issue made by Mr. Cleveland—the same issue would be referred to the people in 1892.[3] The "educational campaign" of 1888 had "borne fruit," said the New York Times. "It was a late crop but astonishingly abundant and the apples fell into Grover Cleveland's basket." [4] A "new period" opened, the Times continued, and "all Americans" had "reason for congratulation and high and confident hope of the future of their country." It was an "uprising of the true American spirit, a vindication of free representative government."[5]

The New York Tribune on the day after the election had been greatly deceived; it had told its readers that the result was "close," but that the Republicans would retain control of the House by two votes.[6] It was an "off year"; it was "a marvelous thing" that the new tariff had been "so far sustained by the people before its beneficial effects could be realized." [7] The next day the Tribune found that, because of misrepresentation of the tariff by the Democrats, its "workings" had been "honestly misunderstood" by many voters. If the "Force Bill" had been passed, as it should have been, the Democrats could not have carried by "improper methods" many districts in which their candidates for seats in the House of Representatives had been victorious.[8]

The Fifty-first Congress, upon convening for its second session in December, 1890, would add little to adorn the roll of

[1] Haynes, Third Party Movements, pp. 239, 244, 266.
[2] N. Y. Nation, Nov. 6, 1890.
[3] Ibid., Nov. 13 and 27, 1890.
[4] N. Y. Times, Nov. 5, 1890.
[5] Ibid., Nov. 6, 1890.
[6] N. Y. Tribune, Nov. 5, 1890.
[7] Ibid.
[8] Ibid., Nov. 6, 1890; cf. N. Y. Nation, Nov. 13, 1890.

its achievements. Its record had been made and the country, it appeared, had visited judgment upon it. President Harrison's message was a party manifesto penned in a quiet spirit. The tariff and silver bills were extolled. The President had no doubt, he said, that "more constant employment and better wages for our working people, and an increased supply of a safe currency for the transaction of business" would ensue upon the passage of these measures. If prices had increased it was due to the silver bill. The tariff act had been in force for less than 60 days. Criticism of the law "from foreign sources" could be "rejected for repugnancy." Of the plan for "reciprocity," the President spoke, as could have been anticipated, with favor. As a result of this measure he looked for an extension of commerce with countries producing coffee and sugar.

The depreciation in the price of silver was viewed with regret, though the Secretary of the Treasury had given to the market "such support" as the law contemplated. There was no present prospect of another international conference in silver's behalf. The "Force Bill" was again explained and defended. It was not "sectional." It did not look, the President said, to a revival of race animosities. The intent of the measure was merely to improve existing law in order "to secure to the citizen his constitutional rights." [1]

In the Senate the debate on the "Force Bill," led by Mr. Hoar, was resumed, but its fate had been plainly indicated at the last session. Several Republican senators openly opposed the measure and others were but lukewarm in their support. It was more than ever clear that opinion within the party on this subject was divided. Even threatened restrictions upon the suffrage of the negro through new provisions in Southern state constitutions were not sufficient incitement to more than a few of the Republican members of the Senate to give the bill enthusiastic approval. In the last session its progress would, it was believed, jeopardize the fate of the tariff bill —now in the short session it stood in the way of the silver

[1] Richardson, vol. ix, pp. 107–29.

man,[1] and it was set aside, not to be brought forward again. Mr. Hoar declared in his heat, so it was said, that such action meant "the death of the Republican party." But more moderate counsels prevailed. A day had come for other things. As the Supreme Court had declared in annulling Sumner's Civil Rights Bill there must be "some stage" in the "progress of elevation" of a man emerged from slavery, "when he takes the rank of a mere citizen and ceases to be a special favorite of the laws, and when his rights as a citizen, or a man, are to be protected in the ordinary modes by which other men's rights are protected." [2]

In his message to Congress the President had said that benefits were accruing to the country from the law which authorized large purchases of silver. Conditions of trade, and the state of opinion in commercial and financial circles generally, were not confirmatory of his judgment. The feeling of anxiety on this subject was intensified by the continued discussion of it in Congress, and proposals there indicated that even yet the concessions made to the silverites were not sufficiently propitiatory. To a bill offered in the Senate a free coinage amendment was attached. Stewart of Nevada said that "gold standard contractionists," "usurers" and "gamblers in money," profiting by the "outrage" which had been done silver in 1873, were robbing and enslaving the masses;[3] Reagan of Texas that he knew of no "crime" of a magnitude equal to "the crime of 1873," inspired as it had been by "a greedy class of money-holders and bondholders." [4] Others expressed not dissimilar views in the same irritable spirit, eliciting reply from Sherman who uttered truths that he sometimes obscured for partisan objects. It was not bimetallism that the silver men had in view but monometallism, he said. Free silver coinage would have for its effect the demonetization of gold. The proposal

[1] Hoar, Autobiog. of 70 Years, vol. ii, p. 156; N. Y. Tribune, Jan. 2, 1891.
[2] N. Y. Nation, Dec. 11, 1890, and Jan. 8 and 29, 1891; McPherson's Handbook for 1892, pp. 24–5.
[3] Cong. Record, 51st Cong. 2nd sess., pp. 913–4, 917; App. Ann. Cyclop. for 1891, p. 229.
[4] Cong. Record, 51st Cong. 2nd sess., pp. 918–9.

was for a change of the unit of value. Instead of enlarging
the volume of our currency, which was declared to be the
purpose of this new and much recommended legislation, it
would drive all gold out of use and decrease circulation. Gold
would be stricken from our money, our medium of exchange,
as clearly as wheat, cattle and horses. Whatever the end sought
the result would be the demonetization of nearly "one half of
all the money in our country," and the degradation of "all the
balance of it" to a "lower value." "What a wide reaching influence" that would have upon contracts, Sherman continued,
"God only knows." The "sudden revolution" caused by such
a change in the standard of value "could only be compared
with some of the great revolutions in the history of the past,"
when some "fool king" had reduced the quantity of precious
metal in a coin and continued to call it a pound, or a livre,
or a florin, though its market value had fallen by as much as
the real value which had been taken from it. The purchasing
power of a dollar would always be determined by its intrinsic
worth and all the laws of Congress "could not change this unalterable rule." [1]

Again no protest would avail. The free coinage bill was
passed by the Senate on January 14th by a vote of 39 to 27,
15 Republicans, including Cameron of Pennsylvania, voting
for, and one Democrat, Wilson of Maryland, against the
measure.[2] Fortunately it made no progress in the House.[3]
But what might come in the next Congress from men who were
the result of the new and latest draft upon the popular intelligence in the West and South was outside the range of confident
prophecy; at any rate the country would rest, with what content it could, under the laws which it already had until the
ensuing first Monday in December.

Some postal subsidies to steamship lines which won the
reprobation of those who opposed the making of grants for
the encouragement of private enterprise, though much more in

[1] Cong. Record, 51st Cong. 1st sess., pp. 914–7, 1228–43; N. Y. Nation,
Jan. 22, 1891.

[2] Cong. Record, 51st Cong. 2nd sess., p. 1323.

[3] McPherson's Handbook for 1892, pp. 25–30.

the interest of the enfeebled American merchant marine had been demanded of the party leaders by Republican ship owners and ship builders; [1] the passage of a Direct Tax Refunding bill, similar to that which Cleveland had vetoed in 1889, returning to the states the income tax collected during the war; [2] a new immigration law in answer to the increasing agitation concerning aliens arriving at our seaports; a bill creating a circuit court of appeals of nine judges to relieve the Supreme Court, and an international copyright bill nearly completed the legislation of the session. It had been a "billion dollar Congress." More than one thousand millions had been voted away for various uses during the two sessions of the Fifty-first, an increase of about $170,000,000 over the appropriations of the Fiftieth Congress. [3] If it were a "billion dollar Congress," said the Republicans, that sum was not more than the needs of the country required. The Secretary of the Treasury replied to the charge by the Democrats of Republican profligacy and extravagance. The United States, he said, was "a billion dollar country." [4]

Harrison had won the love of few men, not because of his indisposition to favor the party leaders with patronage, though many of them, as Quay and Platt, were estranged on these grounds, [5] but because of a want in him of the human qualities which tie one man to another. [6] Gresham's was an old feud in Indiana. His friends were being "punished," as they believed. Gresham himself should have been advanced to a justiceship in the Supreme Court. [7] It was clear that Harrison meant well, that he acted in accordance with his lights and his administration had been and would be respectable. He was

[1] Cf. N. Y. Nation, Jan. 8, March 5 and 12, 1891.
[2] McPherson's Handbook for 1892, pp. 44–8; App. Ann. Cyclop. for 1891, pp. 210–11.
[3] Cf. N. Y. Nation, March 26, 1891.
[4] Ibid., June 11, 1891.
[5] Cf. ibid., Aug. 27, 1891.
[6] Mrs. Blaine said a few days after meeting him in Washington—"Harrison is of such a nature that [in his presence] you do not feel at all at liberty to enjoy yourself."—Letters of Mrs. Blaine, vol. i, p. 257; cf. ibid., p. 263.
[7] Wellman to Gresham, March 20, 1889, in Gresham Papers.

loyal to the idea to which he had been bred that the Republican party had had a mission to perform, and that this mission remained still, in some degree, unfulfilled. He was, in this regard, a Bourbon, though his manner was mild and he would not greatly exert himself to make his views prevail. His conscience was active, but it kept him within a narrow lane. He would go with his party, which in quiet ways it was his desire to improve on its moral side. With thievery and corruption he had no sympathy, and, by example and precept, he would, as President, steer a course clear of such scandals as had marred the administration of Grant.

But it was undeniable that he warmed no man's heart. The party took delight in its return to power, but nearly none in Harrison himself, who, by the victory, had been placed in the White House. In the estimation of most Republicans he suffered by comparison with the "brilliant" and "magnetic" Blaine. To the Mugwumps and Democrats of discernment he was but a feeble magistrate beside Cleveland, whose strong, fearless and indomitable character made him, to them, a very citadel of strength for good government. To overcome some of the apathy which fell upon the President he projected a tour to begin soon after the adjournment of Congress. In a special train he started away to visit cities in the South. From Texas he proceeded to southern California and then up the Pacific coast to Seattle, making, as he progressed, pleasant and dignified speeches, returning to Washington, after four or five weeks absence, by way of the Union Pacific Railroad.[1] He remained, as was said without too much partisan exaggeration, the "nominal head" of his party, "but without the slightest hold upon its affection or enthusiasm." [2]

Whatever the next year might bring forth the campaign would go forward without the direction of Quay. He had been further discredited by a most unsavory banking scandal in Philadelphia. The treasurer of the city, one John Bardsley,

[1] N. Y. Tribune, April 14 to May 16, 1891.
[2] N. Y. Nation, May 21, 1891; N. Y. Tribune, May 16, 1891; A. K. McClure, Old Time Notes of Pa., vol. ii, p. 574.

who had been a friend of Wanamaker and others, enjoying
so much public confidence as to be dubbed "Honest John,"
had been guilty of criminal transactions which, in the summer
of 1891, were exposed.[1] The accounts of both the state and
the city were involved. The Democratic governor, Pattison,
was in no mind to let the state officials who were responsible
for the care of public funds escape the reprobation which their
connivance in wrong-doing deserved, and he called the state
senate in special session for a consideration of the question.
The treasurer and auditor-general of Pennsylvania, who rested
under the charges of complicity in the great embezzlements,
were Quay's puppets. But so were a controlling majority of
the senators and, for the sake of the party's reputation, the
fiduciary agents of the commonwealth, though their characters
were a good deal smirched, were not dismissed from their posts.
Further to whiten the picture the Republican state convention,
which soon met, adopted a platform, demanding criminal
prosecution of the guilty, whoever they might be, "without
regard to politics," and Quay caused men of a class which
he seldom drew upon to be nominated to the places of the
two unhappy officers whose terms were soon to expire.[2]

Such occurrences in Pennsylvania did nothing to improve
Quay's position in the nation and, being but little in the confidence of the President, and his friend, the Postmaster-General,
the Pennsylvania "boss" determined in August, 1891, to resign
from the Republican National Committee, of which he had
been the chairman. At the same time Dudley retired as
treasurer, clearing the way, it was hoped, for a more respected
leadership in the coming campaign.[3]

The state elections in 1891 were not indicative of that complete repudiation of the Republican party by the people which
the Democrats had pretended to think they had found in the
pollings in 1890. In Massachusetts Governor Russell was
reelected as a reward for the proof he had given of his capability

[1] Report of sub-committee of the Finance Committee of Councils of
Philadelphia upon the transactions of John Bardsley, March 31, 1892.
[2] A. K. McClure, Old Time Notes of Pa., vol. ii, pp. 580–82.
[3] N. Y. Nation, Aug. 6, 1891; cf. Schurz's Writings, vol. v, pp. 100–101.

and integrity, though the Republicans elected their candidates to the other state offices. On the other hand McKinley defeated Campbell and would be the next governor of Ohio. The Democrats elected Flower, their nominee for governor in New York, with the aid of Croker's reorganized Tammany machine, while Hill, entirely parochial in mind, to say naught of his moral attitude toward questions of government, was sent to the United States Senate to succeed Mr. Evarts.[1] If Pennsylvania had been reclaimed by the Republicans, it was only because Quay, seeing the danger of his position, allowed estimable men to be presented for the suffrages of the people. Iowa continued to be Democratic, to the point at least of reelecting Governor Boies, again largely for local reasons. The only state in which national questions were paramount, perhaps, was Ohio, and there the Republicans, under the leadership of McKinley and the tariff bill, won a pleasing victory.

Whatever else the campaign disclosed it was made clear that the silver question was rising in importance in the minds of an increasing number of men who, under new leaders, were intent upon putting it ahead of the tariff and other issues. Both parties were divided on the subject—the Republican party by the miners who wished to sell their product, the Democrats by the "debtor class," men who had borrowed money and wished to pay it back in a depreciated currency. The Populists in a new party were more extreme in their views than the old Bland faction in the Democratic party, and were so irreconcilable that they would, in all probability, greatly complicate the contest in 1892. The issue was distinctly sectional. The West and the South were arrayed against the East. The Democrats in New York and Massachusetts had elected their governors on platforms containing clear declarations in favor of the maintenance of the gold standard. The Republicans in states where it was not known whether more was to be gained by espousing one cause or the other were in great uncertainty as to the course which they should pursue. They had been in a particularly embarrassing situation in Ohio. That Mc-

[1] N. Y. Nation, Dec. 10, 1891.

Kinley should be elected governor was of the first importance
to the Republican party in the nation at large, as well as in the
state.

McKinley himself was a man of no deeply held convictions,
in some degree because what he said, and often very well, was
not founded upon information. He was on this account less
blameworthy than John Sherman who wavered, despite better
knowledge. McKinley would yield because he was uninstructed
in the principles of correct public action and he could be happy,
if the results for his friends and his party should, in his belief,
warrant tergiversation, to be on either side of a question.
McKinley had spoken at Toledo on February 12, 1891, as a
silverite. During all of Cleveland's years at the head of the
government, said McKinley, "he was dishonoring one of our
precious metals, one of our great products, discrediting silver
and enhancing the price of gold." Cleveland, McKinley
continued, would "contract the circulating medium and
demonetize one of the coins of commerce, limit the volume
of money among the people, make money scarce and therefore
dear." [1] On this occasion he was addressing the old Greenbackers and inflationists, who were now silver men. A statement on the money question which it was supposed might
catch votes was inserted in the Republican platform in Ohio.
"Thoroughly believing that gold and silver should form the
basis of all circulating medium," said the authors of this declaration, "we endorse the amended coinage act of the last Republican Congress by which the entire production of the silver
mines of the United States is added to the currency of the
people." The Democrats of Ohio, in their platform, went
farther, though a substantial minority in the party who respected Cleveland's leadership, as had been evidenced by a poll
of the delegates in the convention, held more conservative
views. The majority denounced "the demonetization of silver
in 1873" by the Republicans as "an iniquitous alteration of
the money standard in favor of creditors and against debtors,"
and demanded the "reinstatement of the constitutional standard

[1] N. Y. Nation, Aug. 27, 1891.

of both gold and silver," with "free and unlimited coinage" of both.

McKinley strove to keep the tariff issue in the foreground; his name stood for protection. But Governor Campbell who had been renominated passed, as the campaign proceeded, to a defense of silver; [1] McKinley, therefore, veered in the opposite direction. The appearance in the state during the campaign of Peffer and radical figures from the West [2] made no friends among the Cleveland Democrats and Mugwumps for Campbell, whose declared opinions seemed to be not essentially different from those of the prophets of Populism. McKinley saw the way clearing before him and, to draw, if possible, the Cleveland faction from Campbell, found it convenient to change the ground which he had occupied earlier in the year at Toledo and to point to the danger of "free silver." [3] In the midst of the campaign President Harrison spoke also. At Albany, in New York, he went so far as to say that he would disapprove a free silver bill if it should be sent him by the next Congress. It was now made quite certain that, whatever should be revealed concerning the new House, a two-thirds vote to override the Presidential veto could not be secured in the Senate,[4] a very reassuring fact, as was evidenced by a rise in prices in the stock markets.[5] It was as much for this reason, it would appear, as for any wish to reward McKinley for his services in connection with the enactment of the tariff law, which bore his name, that he was elected over Campbell by a plurality of 20,000 votes.

The phrases "honest money" and "sound money" and "cheap money" were hurled at the silverites. The impolicy of buying heavy ingots or, as the London Times called it, "pig silver," metal in pigs,[6] for storage was stated and restated. David A. Wells said that the amount of this metal held by the government at the end of 1891 was $400,000,000, and the hoard was increasing at the rate of seven tons a day. It would make

[1] N. Y. Nation, July 23, 1891.   [2] Ibid., Aug. 6, 1891.
[3] Cf. ibid., Aug. 27, 1891.   [4] Ibid., Aug. 27, 1891.
[5] Ibid., Sep. 24, 1891.   [6] Cf. ibid., April 14 and June 9, 1892.

a column one foot in diameter six and a half miles high; it would fill 1,000 freight cars. If one man were assigned the duty of counting all the silver dollars in the government's vaults it would require his constant application working eight hours a day for a period of eleven years.[1]

The tone of the President's message, his third, when the new Fifty-second Congress met in December, 1891, was unchanged. While he defended the silver purchase law because it increased the circulating medium, and because it created a market for the products of our mines, the absorption of which, it was gravely intimated, might be one of the functions of government, or at any rate a convenient corollary of currency legislation, Mr. Harrison definitely opposed free coinage. He likewise declared further international conferences to be useless. Putting business on a "silver basis," he said, "would mean a sudden and severe contraction of the currency." There would ensue "such an unsettling of values as would produce a commercial panic." He could not believe that "a people so strong and prosperous as ours" would "promote such a policy." Our currency system, as it had been established by the last Congress, was in the interest of the national well-being and should rest where it was. The tariff, likewise, was designed for the country's good; proof was at hand that the McKinley law had "disappointed the evil prophecies of its opponents, and, in a large measure, realized the hopeful predictions of its friends." The new tariff had "created," the President said, "several new industries," which in a few years would "give employment to several hundred thousand American working men and women." [2]

Such rather pleasing expositions of public affairs, with a preaching of goodness and repose as the means to happiness, if characteristic of Mr. Harrison and in the interest of party unity, were markedly out of key with the spirit of Congress as it would soon be displayed, and with the temper of the country. In the Treasury, in particular, grave disorders impended as a result of the studied efforts to compromise an issue which admitted of

[1] Harper's Weekly, Nov. 14, 1891.
[2] Richardson, vol. ix, pp. 180–211.

none.[1] The policy which Congress had adopted, and which the President had endorsed, was neither gold monometallism nor bimetallism. It had none of the safeguards which were required for the proper functioning of the gold standard, nor did it conform to the rules of the theorist who advocated the concurrent use of the two metals as a basis of value which, had it been attempted, would have assuredly led at once to silver monometallism. It was believed that the Congress would, after months of angry disputation, running through the period of the canvass for the election of another President, achieve but little. With a Republican Senate and an overwhelmingly Democratic House nothing of importance could ensue, barring passage of a free coinage bill which Harrison said that he would veto. So it was. A representative from Georgia, Charles F. Crisp, was elected Speaker to succeed Mr. Reed. Mr. Mills who was his competitor for the office should have been returned, it was said, as chairman of the Committee on Ways and Means, but the place was assigned to William M. Springer of Illinois with a view, it was freely declared, of preventing a renewal of the "tariff fight," or of recalling, indeed, that one which Mills had led and which had been followed by defeat in 1888. The party would not dare to renew the battle, the Republicans said, tauntingly. The setting aside of Mills meant, they declared again, a turning away from Cleveland, as in fact it was. His friends resented such a change of front. The party had set its face toward another candidate for 1892 and would wage the campaign on a new issue.[2]

There were changes in the Harrison cabinet. Windom died at the end of January, 1891,[3] and Charles Foster of Ohio followed him as Secretary of the Treasury.[4] Proctor's resignation as Secretary of War opened the way to the appointment of Stephen B. Elkins to that high post. He had been Mr. Blaine's campaign manager in 1884 and continued to be a lieutenant. All

---

[1] Cf. N. Y. Nation, March 10, 1892.
[2] Cf. N. Y. Tribune, Dec. 11, 15, 21, 22, 24, and 25, 1892; N. Y. Nation, Dec. 10 and 31, 1891, Jan. 14 and Feb. 18, 1892.
[3] N. Y. Nation, Feb. 5, 1891.
[4] Ibid., Feb. 26, 1891.

of his associations and objects in life had been commercial and the choice provoked surprise as well as criticism.[1] Though the President seems constantly to have been on his guard lest Blaine should advance to the centre of the stage, and color the administration, the Secretary of State, by one method or another, familiar to him, gained many points in Harrison's despite, and one of these was honorable recognition of a friend so unfitted for political preferment as "Steve" Elkins.

If Blaine's conduct of the State Department under Harrison had been far less sure and jaunty than when he had occupied the place under Garfield, due in part to his failing health and in part to the difference in the qualities of the two Presidents under whom he served, he had opened his administration with characteristic enthusiasm. The Pan-American congress, when the intoxicated elation which attended the visit of the representatives of so many of the governments of this hemisphere had subsided, was found to have led to no great result, though it served to turn the public mind in this country to the south and to increase our interest in the movements of peoples who, up to this time, were regarded as little worthy of our concern. The suggestions of the conference, even as to arbitration treaties, were not productive of consequence, since those that were prepared, except in the cases of two or three small equatorial states, were not ratified.[2] It is true that attention was given to the survey of routes for a railroad to run through Central and South America to the borders of Patagonia, and a bureau was established in Washington as a clearing house for information about the "American Republics," the number of which was increased by a revolution in Brazil in 1889, though the director of the bureau, of Blaine's appointment, was, it was asserted, unacceptable to the Latin peoples to whom we were offering an outstretched hand.[3] The reciprocity feature of the McKinley tariff law was rather clearly the outcome of the conference.[4]

[1] N. Y. Nation, Dec. 24 and 31, 1891; George W. Julian in N. Y. Times, Oct. 6, 1892.
[2] N. Y. Nation, March 19, 1891.
[3] Ibid., April 14, 1892; App. Ann. Cyclop. for 1890, pp. 819–20.
[4] App. Ann. Cyclop. for 1891, p. 832; cf. N. Y. Nation, Sep. 4, 1890.

Men had said that the President would never use the retaliatory power conferred upon him, and that, in any case, this provision of the act was "unconstitutional." [1] But John W. Foster who, while he had been minister to Spain, during Arthur's administration, had concerned himself with the extension of trade by treaty with the southern portions of the hemisphere, was assigned to the task in hand.[2] Under his guidance material progress was soon achieved, though, since the life of the McKinley tariff was to be brief, it could be a service of only fleeting value to us or to the Latin states.[3]

In February, 1891, a commercial agreement with Brazil was effected,[4] and similar arrangements were concluded before the end of 1891 with Spain (for Cuba and Porto Rico)[5] and the Dominican Republic.[6] Our advances in some quarters were not cordially met and, on January 7, 1892, Blaine informed the diplomatic representatives at Washington of Austria Hungary, Colombia, Hayti, Nicaragua, Honduras, Spain (for the Philippine Islands) and Venezuela that the President considered their tariff charges on products of the United States "reciprocally unequal and unreasonable," and that, unless these charges were reduced before the 15th of the ensuing March, we should proclaim section 3 of the McKinley law in effect against their sugar and other imports.[7] By persuasion and threat arrangements in the interest of free commercial exchange were concluded in 1892 with Guatemala, Salvador, the German Empire, Great Britain (for certain West Indian colonies and British Guiana) Nicaragua, Honduras and Austria Hungary.[8]

President Harrison heartily embraced the idea of opening foreign markets to our products, particularly those of the farm. In every case, he said, in December, 1892, in renewing the

[1] Cf. N. Y. Nation, Sep. 25, 1890, and March 24, 1892.
[2] Cf. ibid., July 31, 1890.
[3] J. W. Foster, Memoirs, vol. ii, pp. 6–19; A. F. Tyler, Foreign Policy of J. G. Blaine, pp. 187–9.
[4] Richardson, vol. ix, pp. 141–2; cf. N. Y. Nation, April 24, 1890.
[5] Richardson, vol. ix, pp. 148–52.
[6] Ibid., pp. 152–5.
[7] N. Y. Tribune, Jan. 8, 1892; N. Y. Nation, Jan. 14, 1892.
[8] Richardson, vol. ix, pp. 249–51, 253–8, 263–5, 279–81, 281–3, 283–4, 312, 365–7.

agreements which had been concluded, "a free or favored admission" had been secured for our "surplus." The "full benefits" of these arrangements were not to be "realized instantly." In 1885 we had had only 8 per cent. of the import trade of Central and South America; the President believed that one-third would be capturable "within a short period." [1]

With the extension of commerce with Canada the administration was not sincerely concerned, although some fruitless conferences were held, and, in the heat of the Presidential campaign of 1892, Congress drew attention to unreciprocal action on the side of the Canadian government in the collection of tolls on the canals over which trade proceeded on the Great Lakes. Contention was to proceed for some time to this text.[2] Tariffs should not be lowered for Canada. Blaine said that it should be made "hard" for her and "ultimately," he wrote President Harrison, she would, "seek admission to the Union." [3]

It is likely that interest in the Nicaragua canal was increased by the Pan-American Conference. This project was in the care of a group of men incorporated by Congress in February, 1889. The first expeditionary force of workmen carrying material for the prosecution of the work left New York for Greytown in the ensuing May.[4] A considerable sum of money was obtained from stock sales, but vastly more must be at hand if the canal were to be completed. President Harrison said in 1891 that the connection of the waters of the Atlantic and Pacific Oceans was "a matter of the highest concern to the United States," and he recommended a government guarantee of the bonds issued by the construction company and its completion under subvention of the United States.[5]

At least three other subjects of importance had claimed the

[1] Richardson, vol. ix, p. 312.
[2] Ibid., pp. 240–2, 290–2, 314–5, 335–46.
[3] Under date of Sep. 23, 1891, in Gail Hamilton, Biography of Blaine, p. 694.
[4] N. Y. Times, May 25, 1889; cf. ibid., Aug. 5, 1889.
[5] Richardson, vol. ix, pp. 188–9. For progress of work see N. Y. Tribune, letters of "I. N. F.," April 7, 1891, and subsequent dates; Report of Sec. of Int. for 1890, pp. cxxvi–cxxxvii; ibid. for 1891, cxlvii–cxlviii; Cong. Record, 52nd Cong. 1st sess., pp. 182–7.

State Department's attention while Blaine was at its head—
an exasperating event in New Orleans involving the lynching of
citizens of Italy; another in Chile where a revolution was in
progress; and differences with Great Britain as to the prosecu-·
tion of sealing in Bering Sea. For a long time in New Orleans,
as in other American cities, various bands of desperadoes, recent
immigrants from Sicily and southern Italy, had been involved in
bloody crimes. They brought with them their vendettas
resulting in assaults and murders which filled the newspapers.
On this account, and because of their competition in the labor
market, Italians generally came to be held in some disesteem by
the American masses who rather contemptuously dismissed
them as "dagoes." On the night of October 15, 1890, the chief
of police of New Orleans, Hennessy by name, was shot, apparently in revenge, because of efforts which he had made to
punish crimes among the Italians in the city, and great excitement ensued, the flames being fanned by the Irish and workingmen of other races. The "Mafia," a secret society in Sicily,
whose name had become identified with demand for tribute, and
with brigandage and assassination,[1] was said to have been
involved in the disorders. Suspects were put under arrest to
suffer maltreatment in the parish jail. The consul and other
Italians in New Orleans felt that they were in danger of their
lives. The grand jury indicted the prisoners and trial followed,
resulting in a verdict of acquittal for most of them. This was
not to the liking of many of the inhabitants of the city, some of
whom were influential in its government. Bribery of jurymen
was alleged, vengeance was spoken of, a "vigilance committee"
was formed and, on March 14, 1891, a mob broke into the prison
house and lynched eleven Sicilians, including some of those who
had been found "not guilty."

The news was carried to Italy; denunciation of the "atrocious
deed" was cabled to Washington by that government; protest
was lodged with the Secretary of State. Mr. Blaine, expressing
his horror at what had come to pass, telegraphed to the governor
of Louisiana urging the arrest and punishment of the leaders of

[1] N. Y. Nation, April 9 and 23, 1891.

the lynching party, who were well known and easy of identi-
fication. The governor, instead of pledging an exercise of his
powers in the interest of reparation, viewed the massacre
calmly, if not sympathetically.[1] The impatience of Marquis di
Rudini, minister of foreign affairs for Italy, and of Baron Fava,
the Italian minister in Washington, increased. The Federal
government should give them assurance of the punishment of
the lynchers and should recognize the principle that an indemnity be paid to the families of the murdered men. Receiving no
satisfaction on these points Fava, under instructions from
Rome, made a dramatic departure from his post. Our minister
to Italy was recalled.

It appeared, upon investigation, that only three or four of the
victims of the mob's vengeance were citizens of Italy—the
others were naturalized Americans; also that some of the men
who had been lynched had had but indirect, if any, part in the
murder of Hennessy; and also that, with proper precautionary
measures, since the attack was not unexpected, the local
magistracy, if this magistracy had been capable and honest,
could have prevented the shameful event. The consciousness
that nothing would be done locally to punish the guilty induced
comment very unfavorable to the state of human society in New
Orleans and Louisiana, and, by generalization, in the entire
American South. The part which the mayor of the city had
played in excusing and justifying such a breach of law and order,
and the attitude of the leaders of the mob who boasted of their
feat were irritating and incensed right thinking men in this
country as in Italy.[2] But with the departure of Baron Fava, so
hastily taken, which was the symbol of an international rupture,
a wave of national feeling swept the country and the advantage
was on Mr. Blaine's side. The Marquis di Rudini found it
difficult to comprehend—as indeed it was—our system of
federative government with its distribution of powers, and he
seemed to suspect that the Secretary of State was hiding behind
a form to escape a national obligation. After more than a year

[1] Foreign Relations of the U. S. for 1891, p. 672.
[2] Cf. N. Y. Tribune, March 17 and 18, 1891.

the sum of 125,000 francs was forwarded to Italy for distribution to the families of the victims of the mob, Blaine saying now that the payment was a "solemn duty." In April, 1892, the minister of each country returned to his place in the capital of the other, and the incident was at an end.[1]

The overthrow of Balmaceda, a dictator in Chile,[2] was accompanied by prolonged civil disturbance. Arms were taken out of the United States from San Diego in California and transferred at sea to a ship chartered by the insurgents called the *Itata*. She had been under surveillance while in port. A deputy marshal of the United States had been put on board her. She had broken her arrest. It was a case, it was held by our jingoes, similar to that of the *Alabama*.[3] The capture of the vessel, if possible, was resolved upon, and the *Charleston* set forth in chase, though our right of pursuit was not clear. A naval engagement seemed likely, and it would have delighted the excited readers of our newspapers, but the Chilean insurgents offered, through Paris, to surrender the *Itata* upon her arrival at Iquique, the seat of the new provisional government, where the *San Francisco* awaited her coming, and took possession of her and her cargo for a determination of fact as to her violation of the country's neutrality laws.[4]

Our minister to Chile was Patrick Egan, an Irish-American. He had come to the United States only recently. He was a fugitive from justice, having violated his country's laws. Here, in recent Presidential contests, he had been active in the work of marshalling the naturalized Irish for Blaine and the Republican ticket. For these reasons he was properly viewed with mistrust. He was, moreover, inexperienced in diplomacy,[5] at a time and a place where the greatest skill might not have

---

[1] Foreign Relations of the United States for 1891, pp. 658–728; App. Ann. Cyclop. for 1892, p. 362; N. Y. Nation, April 21, 1892.

[2] App. Ann. Cyclop. for 1891, pp. 123–36, 663–4; A. F. Tyler, Foreign Policy of J. G. Blaine, pp. 130–2.

[3] Cf. N. Y. Nation, May 21, 1891.

[4] Report of Sec. of Navy for 1891, pp. 25–6; App. Ann. Cyclop. for 1891, pp. 132–4; N. Y. Nation, June 11, Sep. 17 and Nov. 12, 1891.

[5] Cf. N. Y. Nation, Sept. 24, 1891; A. F. Tyler, Foreign Policy of J. G. Blaine, pp. 132–3.

sufficed to insure neutral conduct. Anti-American feeling in Chile, aroused by the chase of the *Itata*, was increased by his harboring in the legation, though he was acting within his right in this regard, some adherents of Balmaceda,[1] and by his supporting, as he could, the interests of that leader, on the ground that the revolution, if it were successful, would forward the interests of England, and in a belief, apparently, that it would fail.[2]

The animosity of the insurgents was from time to time felt by the officers and sailors on American ships, which were stationed in Chilean waters to watch the development of the war. On October 16, 1891, when two boats' crews from the *Baltimore*, in command of Captain Schley, went ashore at Valparaiso they got into an altercation with some native sailors in a grog shop. A mob collected. The "North Americans," who were without arms, and defenceless, were attacked in the street in front of the saloon, and in other parts of the city, and, before the riots were at an end, a boatswain's mate had been killed and various coal heavers and ship's carpenters in the shore party had been stabbed and otherwise wounded, one of whom subsequently died. American men-of-war's men were arrested wherever seen, and, while being taken to jail, and in their confinement afterward, were subjected to brutal treatment.[3] Captain Schley of the *Baltimore* telegraphed the facts to Washington. Great resentment was expressed in the United States. The State Department demanded immediate reparation. The *Boston* and *Yorktown* were ordered to the Pacific Ocean and the *Yorktown*, in command of "Fighting Bob" Evans, was soon at Valparaiso to take the position held by the *Baltimore* which returned to San Francisco. The revolutionists displayed a truculent spirit. They withheld expressions of regret for the outrage and spoke of municipal law, as we were doing in our exchanges with the Italian government on the subject of the lynchings in New Orleans. If the situation did not mend

[1] A. F. Tyler, Foreign Policy of J. G. Blaine, pp. 142-5.
[2] Cf. Foreign Relations of U. S. for 1891, pp. 107, 120, 163, 230-1; N. Y. Nation, Oct. 8 and 29 and Nov. 5, 1891, and Jan. 21, 1892.
[3] Report of Sec. of Navy for 1891, pp. 21-30.

President Harrison, in his message in December, 1891, announced a purpose to prepare a special message at an early day and to bring the matter to the attention of Congress.[1] Egan's legation was surrounded by spies; men going in and out were subjected to insult. The press spoke in an offensive tone. The government asked for Egan's recall. Mr. Blaine demanded the withdrawal of a despatch from the Chilean foreign office which had imputed untruth and insincerity to the President of the United States and the Secretary of the Navy, and an apology. He intimated that a termination of diplomatic relations was not far away. Congress was addressed by the President on January 25, 1892, in a statement couched in clear terms.[2] A new Chilean minister of foreign affairs was impelled to make, and at once, friendly statements which the President forwarded to Congress on January 28, 1892.[3] In the end Chile paid to the United States $75,000 in gold for distribution among the heirs of the two sailors who had been killed and to those who had been maimed in the riot.[4]

The seals in Alaska would involve us in relations with Great Britain as unpleasant as those from which we had just made escape on the subject of the fisheries off Newfoundland and on the Grand Banks. These acerbities Blaine's figure at the head of the State Department, supported by too much popular feeling, was well fitted to increase.

The destruction of seal life was moving on apace and it was in the interest of the Alaska Commercial Company which leased the rights, of the Treasury of the United States which received the attendant revenues, and the world generally, which admired and used the velvety skins, that the species should enjoy protection. A sudden and marked increase in demand for the fur had led to a rise in its price and the sea was scoured by seal hunters of many nationalities, who were as lawless as they were

[1] Richardson, vol. ix, pp. 185–0.

[2] Ibid., pp. 215–26; Cong. Record, 52nd Cong. 1st sess., pp. 514, 517–20.

[3] Richardson, vol. ix, p. 227; Cong. Record, 52nd Cong. 1st sess., pp. 610, 644–6. For the diplomatic correspondence see Foreign Relations of U. S. for 1891, pp. 90–313, and for a fuller record, with the Navy correspondence, see House Ex. Doc., 52nd Cong. 1st sess., no. 91.

[4] Cf. Report of Sec. of Navy for 1892, p. 42.

avaricious.[1] It had become a profitable pursuit. Fashion in
dress had made it so. Seal skin, like silks and satins and
diamonds and pearls, was the hall mark of wealth and elegance.
Capes, muffs and tippets were made of it. A woman who might
be coated from neck to heels in this soft fur was the envy of
beholders.[2] Men drew caps of seal skin over their ears to keep
out the bleak blasts of winter. If the animals should continue to
be shot and harassed on their way to the islands they would
certainly find other breeding grounds, and in no long time, in
all probability, they would be extinct. Prices of the fur rose
as the supply diminished. The Canadians whose ports were
near had a stake in the result, although it was said that in this
kind of adventure there were three boats flying the American
flag for one fitted out in British Columbia.[3] Our revenue cutters,
which, during the season, cruised in Bering Sea to deal with the
sealers which American newspapers were wont to call "poachers," now and again seizing a schooner from Victoria, or another
port in British America, might exercise some restrictive power,
but the depredations from boats which followed in the track of
the migrating herd in the north Pacific Ocean would not
readily yield to any system of patrol.[4]

Sackville-West, under instructions from the British Secretary
of State for Foreign Affairs, had commenced the correspondence
in 1886 after the seizure of three Canadian sealers by the
Corwin.[5] As the vessels were taken at a distance of more than
60 miles from land Great Britain desired to know the meaning of
our action. Did the United States lay claim to sole sovereignty
in Bering Sea? Little seemed to be known in Washington about
the movements of the *Corwin;* the captures were made, possibly, as was surmised, at the instigation of the Alaska Com-

----

[1] "There's never a law of God or man runs north of Fifty Three,"
Kipling wrote in his "Rhyme of the Three Sealers," which tells of the
altercations arising between sealing boats.

[2] "But since our women must walk gay and money buys their gear,
  The sealing boats they filch that way at hazard year by year."
                    —Kipling's "Rhyme of the Three Sealers."

[3] N. Y. Herald, Jan. 23, 1891; N. Y. Nation, Jan. 29, 1891.

[4] Cf. Senate Ex. Doc., 52nd Cong. 2nd sess., pp. 9, 10. Cf. vol. iv. of
this work, pp. 685–9.

[5] A. F. Tyler, Foreign Policy of J. G. Blaine, p. 305.

mercial Company.[1] The unpleasantness was allayed by an order to discharge the seized vessels.[2]

Inquiries as to our policy were renewed at the approach of the sealing season in 1887. New seizures were followed by new protests. Lord Salisbury took the subject in hand and reviewed it in the terms of international law. Neither the United States nor Great Britain had ever admitted the claim, which Russia had at one time put forward, to exclusive jurisdiction in Bering Sea.[3] The right, therefore, could not have been transferred to the United States by purchase. At this point in the controversy a suggestion was made on our side. Secretary Bayard, in August, 1887, addressed France, Germany, Great Britain, Russia, Sweden and Norway and Japan inviting their cooperation in the making of some international regulations on the subject.[4]

Russia and Japan, which, with Great Britain and the United States, were alone interested directly in the issue, replied affirmatively. Mr. Bayard, in the spring of 1888, promised that there should be no further seizures pending arrival at an international agreement, and the negotiations might have had a favorable issue. Canada, however, had its own view of the dispute. The people of the Dominion had been irritated by the course which we had pursued in the negotiations concerning the northeastern fisheries. The McKinley tariff was taken to be a further reflection of the feeling of the United States toward Canada. Truculence characterized many of our newspapers; a like spirit with reference to Canada, and Great Britain generally, marked our Presidential campaigns. It were impossible to believe that Blaine's frankly avowed policy of cultivating the friendship of all the peoples of the American hemisphere, except those who spoke our own tongue in the land lying north of us, would pass unnoticed; impossible to believe, too, that the

---

[1] Cf. J. W. Foster, Diplomatic Memoirs, vol. ii, p. 26; N. Y. Evening Post before and around March 28, 1891; N. Y. Nation, April 2 and 16, 1891; N. Y. Tribune, March 28, 1891.

[2] Correspondence in Senate Ex. Doc., 50th Cong. 2nd sess., no. 100.

[3] A. F. Tyler, Foreign Policy of J. G. Blaine, pp. 303, 304.

[4] Senate Ex. Doc., 50th Cong. 2nd sess., no. 106, pp. 84–117.

glib references in the United States to political annexation which, by our wealth and power, we were going to impose upon Canada should not increase the estrangement.[1]

Public feeling in Canada toward the United States, thus exasperated, blocked the British government, which, in pursuit of a fixed policy, declined to act in a Dominion matter without local concurrence, as sincerely as Lord Salisbury might have desired to prevent the destruction of a valuable industry. Our minister to London, Mr. Phelps, reported the difficulties which obstructed progress in the negotiation and recommended a resumption of activity in Bering Sea on the part of our marine police.[2]

Even yet diplomacy might have won a triumph but, in the last days of the Fiftieth Congress, a representative from Arkansas, Poindexter Dunn, attached an amendment in reference to sealing to a Senate bill affecting the salmon fisheries in Alaska. The lease of the Alaska Commercial Company had been made to run for twenty years; it would expire on May 1, 1890. Another, Mr. Dunn opined, would not be approved by this Congress. The situation was grave. No less than 150 vessels, he said, were being fitted out for unlawful seal hunting. The poachers shot and left in the water seven animals for one which they recovered for its pelt.[3] It was useless to protect the seals at the rookeries if they should be left to their fate while coming to and going from the islands. It should hereafter be the duty of the President of the United States, according to Mr. Dunn's amendment, which, after some verbal changes, with the help of the Alaska Commercial Company's lobby, received the approval of Congress,[4] to issue a proclamation each year, warning sealers not to enter the waters of Bering Sea over which jurisdiction had been obtained by the treaty with Russia in 1867. The President should cause one or more

[1] Cf. A. F. Tyler, Foreign Policy of J. G. Blaine, chap. xiv.

[2] Senate Ex. Doc., 52nd Cong. 1st sess., no. 52, pp. 93–5; Foreign Relations of the U. S. for 1891, p. 530; A. F. Tyler, Foreign Policy of J. G. Blaine, pp. 307–8.

[3] Cf. Senate Ex. Doc., 52nd Cong. 2nd sess., no. 107, pp. 9, 10.

[4] A. F. Tyler, Foreign Policy of J. G. Blaine, p. 310; Gresham, Life of Gresham, vol. ii, pp. 719–20.

vessels of the United States "to diligently cruise" in these waters, arrest all persons and seize all boats engaged in this illicit trade.[1]

At the expiration of the lease of the Alaska Commercial Company in 1890,[2] in spite of suggestions that the Treasury Department should assume direct control of the business,[3] the privilege was vested, after bids were taken, in the North American Commercial Company,[4] of which D. O. Mills was the president. Pelagic sealing, as the size of the herd was reduced, attracted greater attention. The agents of the Treasury Department in the islands repeatedly reported the facts, which were alarming.[5] 1888 was the last year in which the leasing company could take the full number allowed to them, 100,000 skins; in 1889 but 83,000 animals were at hand for slaughter. The scarcity in 1890 induced the Secretary of the Treasury to shorten the killing season for the company, in the face of its protests. It obtained but 21,000 skins.[6]

Congress had said that the President should warn away poachers and send cruisers north to make arrests. He had no choice and issued his proclamation on March 21, 1889.[7] Collisions soon ensued with a renewal of demand for explanation on the part of Great Britain, in answer to complaints from Canada.[8] Mr. Bayard had evaded the inquiry as to whether we were policing Bering Sea on the ground of sole jurisdiction. He had emphasized the danger of the extermination of the species, which he assumed might be a matter of general public interest.[9] But at the transfer of his post to

---

[1] Cong. Record, 50th Cong. 2nd sess., pp. 2448, 2614, 2672.

[2] This company underwent a Congressional investigation in 1888.— House Reports, 50th Cong. 2nd sess., no. 3883.

[3] Cf. Senate Mis. Doc., 51st Cong. 1st sess., no. 86.

[4] Report of Sec. of Treas. for 1890, p. lxxvii.

[5] Cf. Senate Ex. Doc., 50th Cong. 2nd sess., no. 30, p. 3.

[6] Senate Ex. Doc., 51st Cong. 2nd sess., no. 49, p. 27; Report of Gov. of Alaska for 1890 in Report of Sec. of Int. for that year, vol. iii, pp. 469–70; Report of Sec. of Int. for 1891, vol. i, pp. cxx–cxxl; Senate Ex. Doc., 52nd Cong. 2nd sess., no. 107, pp. 6–8; D. O. Mills in N. Am. Review for Sep., 1890.

[7] Richardson, vol. ix, pp. 14–5.

[8] Cf. Foreign Relations of U. S. for 1891, pp. 358–60.

[9] Cf. Senate Ex. Doc., 52nd Cong. 1st sess., no. 55, p. 94.

Blaine the correspondence, when it was renewed, took another
turn, for the new Secretary of State was willing, amid the
acclamation of his admirers, to accept the theory that Bering
Sea was *mare clausum* and he announced, practically, if not
in these words, that we were standing on that ground, at any
rate with reference to the seal "fisheries." [1] A proposal from
the Russian government, through its minister at Washington,
for a dual agreement, looking to control of the situation without
reference to Great Britain, was under consideration, and a
treaty was drafted for signature, though the negotiation came
to naught because of an indisposition at St. Petersburg to
proceed with it. [2] Of this nothing was publicly known. Not
so with the passage of notes between Mr. Blaine and Lord
Salisbury, which was prolonged. It is incontestable that Salisbury held a position much stronger than our own, though the
Canadian government's interposition, in answer to considerations which were peculiar to it, increased his difficulties.
Blaine's notes were rhetorical and jingoist. [3] The issues were
concealed in a cloud of words. As the head of the State Department he was still the politician, in the American sense,
that he had been; and, in writing, he had the fatal facility of
the journalist, from which place he had advanced into public
life. He was addressing a British statesman, as he would
attack an opponent in Congress, or on the hustings in an
ardently fought Presidential campaign. [4]

Salisbury's dignified statements of law and fact, Blaine's

[1] This subject is discussed in a Congressional report. See House Reports, 50th Cong. 2nd sess., no. 3883, pp. viii–xvii; Chas. B. Elliott in
Atlantic Monthly, Feb., 1890.

[2] A. F. Tyler, Foreign Policy of J. G. Blaine, pp. 310–4, 373–85; Baron
Rosen, Forty Years of Diplomacy, vol. i, pp. 78 et seq.; J. W. Foster
Dip. Memoirs, vol. ii, p. 25.

[3] It is said that there was more of Harrison than of Blaine in the notes
from Washington because of the President's unwillingness to leave the
negotiations to others, or because of the Secretary of State's accumulating
disabilities. (A. T. Volwiler in Am. Hist. Review for April, 1936.) Foster
credits Blaine with the management of the epistolary discussion.—Dip.
Memoirs, vol. ii, p. 25.

[4] See e.g. A. F. Tyler, Foreign Policy of Blaine, p. 344; cf. R. B. Mowat,
Dip. Relations of Great Britain and the U. S., chap. xxiii; J. B. Henderson,
Jr., Am. Dip. Questions, chap. i.

philippics,[1] and the proposals and counter proposals do not require particular remembrance. The sealing season of 1890 was marred by no clashes between the cruisers and the Canadian schooners.[2] The arbitration of the points raised by the disputants grew increasingly certain, and, lest there be outbreaks which might unpleasantly excite the popular sensibilities in both the United States and Canada, a *modus vivendi* was agreed to with reference to 1891. Great Britain would join the United States in enforcing existing regulations as to pelagic sealing, while we should limit the catch by the seal company upon the Pribylov Islands to 7,500 skins, a number merely sufficient to maintain the natives employed in the business.[3] This arrangement was of some advantage to the herd,[4] and the negotiations proceeded.[5]

An agreement between Secretary Blaine and Sir Julian Pauncefote in behalf of their respective governments to submit to arbitration the questions at issue was signed on December 18, 1891. At the same time both governments agreed each to appoint a joint commission of two members to investigate the facts regarding the life of the fur seal, the "physical data," to use the words of Lord Salisbury,[6] and submit them to the arbitrators.[7]

The treaty giving force to the agreement for arbitration was signed on February 29, 1892, to be promptly ratified by the Senate.[8] The arbitrators, numbering seven—"jurists of distinguished reputation in their respective countries"—were to

[1] The chief of these are dated Jan. 22, May 29, June 30 and Dec. 17, 1890. Foreign Relations of the U. S. for 1890, pp. 366–70, 425–9, 437–48, 477–501; cf. N. Y. Nation, July 31, 1890, and Jan. 8, 1891.

[2] For the reasons see those stated by Sir Charles Tupper in E. M. Saunders, Life and Letters of Tupper, vol, ii, pp. 138–9; Tupper, Recollections of Sixty Years, pp. 209–10; A. F. Tyler, Foreign Policy of J. G. Blaine, p. 328.

[3] Richardson, vol. ix, pp. 146–7; A. F. Tyler, Foreign Policy of J. G. Blaine, pp. 335–6. Secretary of the Treasury Foster had intended to allow the company to take 60,000 skins.—Senate Ex. Doc., 52nd Cong. 2nd sess. no. 107, p. 2; Report of Gov. of Alaska for 1892 in Report of Sec. of Int. for 1892, vol. iii, pp. 515–6.

[4] Senate Ex. Doc., 52nd Cong. 2nd sess., no. 107, pp. 6–11.

[5] Foreign Relations of U. S. for 1891, pp. 542 et seq.

[6] Ibid. for 1890, p. 361. [7] Ibid. for 1891, pp. 605–6. [8] Ibid., pp. 615–9.

be chosen—two by the President of the United States, two by
Queen Victoria, one by the President of France, one by the
King of Italy and one by the King of Sweden and Norway,
and to this board the case in its various aspects was referred.
Blaine's retirement from the State Department put the matter
into the hands of the new Secretary, John W. Foster, who
had drawn up the treaty and was familiar with the case. The
modus vivendi regarding the taking of seals pending the decision
of the points in dispute was continued during the summer of
1892,[1] and its provisions were enforced with earnestness and
effect. In spite of the activities of our cruisers it was believed
that in 1891 60,000 skins had been taken by the poachers
which our agent in the seal islands said meant the destruction
of at least 400,000 seals.[2] A large fleet of vessels under the single
command of "Fighting Bob" Evans was assembled. The
sealers numbered 105; 98 of these boats were boarded and
warned. Every one which entered Bering Sea in 1892, Secretary of the Navy Tracy said, had been captured. The British
navy cooperated to similar ends.[3] Though protected by the
naval forces of two great governments so few seals appeared
in the rookeries in 1892 that the Treasury agent in charge of the
islands said, in December of that year, that, in his opinion, the
business was "doomed." [4]

Incidents in Samoa had led to international misunderstanding
during the Cleveland administration. Great Britain, Germany
and the United States had a kind of tripartite agreement,
guaranteeing the autonomy of this group of islands in the
South Sea. But the natives, with or without fomentation by
European political agents, or by traders, had involved themselves in civil disturbance. The factions demanded protection.
There was danger that one power would act at the expense
of the others. Indeed, the American consul in May, 1886,

[1] Foreign Relations for 1891, pp. 630–8; Senate Ex. Doc., 52nd Cong.
1st sess., no. 55; House Ex. Doc., 51st Cong. 2nd sess., no. 144.
[2] Senate Ex. Doc., 52nd Cong. 2nd sess., no. 107, p. 11; Report of Gov.
of Alaska for 1892 in Report of Sec. of Int. for that year, vol. iii, pp. 517–8.
[3] Report of Sec. of Navy for 1892, pp. 39–40; Foreign Relations of U. S.
for 1891, pp. 638–42; Richardson, vol. ix, p. 313.
[4] Senate Ex. Doc., 52nd Cong. 2nd sess., no. 107, p. 53.

had made advances on behalf of the United States, and was recalled for his temerity.[1] Germany, it was plain, was closely watching events and, under Bismarck's leadership, quite favorably regarded the prospect of gaining control of the islands. England, it was believed, was furthering German plans for her own ends, and Mr. Cleveland's wish to protect Samoa for the Samoans, while keeping the United States out of international complications, would be, it was seen, difficult to fulfill. The other two treaty powers were invited by Secretary Bayard to authorize their ministers in Washington to confer with him. The meeting was held in the summer of 1887 to little purpose; it adjourned and the tension increased.[2] As Cleveland's term was nearing its end he laid the case before Congress.[3] Scarcely had Harrison entered upon his duties when a hurricane swept the islands. Our own and the German ships in the harbor of Apia broke their moorings. It was an "appalling calamity," President Harrison said;[4] all were damaged and some were sunk with loss of four officers and 47 seamen on the *Trenton* and the *Vandalia*. This devastating event was soon followed by a conference in Berlin, called at the invitation of Prince Bismarck, and attended by three representatives of the United States. They were ill assorted and their quarrels, which were carried to Blaine, increased his difficulties and, at the same time, little advanced the objects in view. A further trial of the tripartite system of control was agreed upon by the three governments,[5] though plotting and counter plotting went on until new plans were devised.[6]

[1] Cf. Richardson, vol. viii, pp. 503–4.
[2] Protocols in Foreign Relations of the U. S. for 1889, pp. 204–36; cf. House Ex. Doc., 50th Cong. 1st sess., no. 238.
[3] Richardson, vol. viii, pp. 804–5; cf. ibid., pp. 612, 800; Senate Ex. Doc., 50th Cong. 2nd sess., nos. 31, 68 and 102; House Ex. Doc., 50th Cong. 2nd sess., nos. 118 and 119.
[4] Richardson, vol. ix, pp. 44–5.
[5] Foreign Relations of U. S. for 1889, pp. 349–420; Senate Mis. Doc., 51st Cong. 1st sess., no. 81.
[6] A. F. Tyler, Foreign Policy of Blaine, chap. ix, based on studies of MS sources in State Department; cf. McElroy, Grover Cleveland, vol. i, chap. x; App. Ann. Cyclop. for 1889, pp. 757–9.

While the campaign of 1892 was taking form and direction Congress pursued a course as wayward as the popular mood. Advantage again, as in 1888, was to be gained, if possible, for the major parties, each at the expense of the other; but for the leader of neither of them was favor unanimously enthusiastic. Without firm control Republicans and Democrats alike drifted a rather rudderless course. The silverites though the bullion value of the silver dollar had fallen to 65 cents,[1] cast a dark shadow over the country. It was clear in March that obstinate opposition on the part of able and determined men in both parties in the House would obstruct progress of the "cheap money" idea in that body.[2] It would not be so in the Senate. The silver men had passed a free coinage bill in the last Congress; they would do this again. On July 1st, when the vote was taken, there were 29 yeas and 25 nays; 11 Republicans voted for the proposal, four more were paired in favor of it. The House, now Democratic, defeated the bill, as it had been defeated by the House in the last Congress, then Republican. The vote was 154 to 136.[3]

At the same time, as could have been foreseen, with the election pending, there would be a bringing forth again of the old scheme for an international monetary conference. Such conferences had been held in 1867, 1878 and 1881. A fourth had met in Paris as recently as in 1889.[4] Those who professed to believe that Europe was on the point of doing away with the gold standard, if we should lead the way, and those who knew that it could not be so, but would propitiate the silverites and quiet them, if possible, though it be for but a short time, with the hope of international action, were alike willing to talk about this fatuity.[5] President Harrison, sensing the need for the purposes of his campaign for reelection, called another

[1] Cf. N. Y. Nation, March 31, 1892.
[2] Ibid., March 31, 1892.
[3] McPherson's Handbook for 1892, pp. 219–20; cf. N. Y. Nation, March 31, June 2, July 7, 14 and 21, 1892.
[4] N. Y. Nation, Oct. 3, 1889.
[5] Ibid., Jan. 14, April 28, May 5, 1892; Richardson, vol. ix, pp. 238–9, 317.

such conference, and invited the nations of Europe to send delegates to a meeting at Brussels in the autumn of 1892.[1]

Attempts to repeal the McKinley law took the form of bills aimed at particular details,[2] as the duties upon wool and woolen goods, cotton bagging and cotton ties, tin plate and binding twine. But it was to no avail. Such bills as were passed by the House were smothered in the Senate.

Another venomous assault was made upon the Chinese. Both parties, to their shame, were agreed upon this subject and vied with each other in 1892 in the Geary bill, as they had in 1888 in the Scott bill, in their attention to the wishes of the anti-Chinese leaders on the Pacific Coast. Geary was an Irish-American from California. He was a fit successor of other politicians in that state who had played a part in framing our Chinese policy. His bill calling for a general registration of Chinamen living in the United States was agreed to by the House under suspension of the rules on April 4, 1892, by a vote of 179 to 43, several members of liberal and enlightened views opposing the measure. Hitt of Illinois reminded the House that to pass the bill would be a deliberate violation of "plighted faith." In adopting it we should emulate "barbarians." Its provisions, aimed as they were at all classes of Chinese, were "a revival of the darkest feature of the darkest ages in the history of man." [3]

Meantime the Senate had passed an anti-Chinese bill of its own. Action was hurried by the statement that the exclusion law of 1882 would soon expire, menacing the country with a new flood of Asiatic immigration.[4]

The Chinese government was a helpless onlooker as before.

---

[1] N. Y. Nation, July 7, 1892.

[2] "The monstrosities of the McKinley bill must be attacked in detail, one monstrosity at a time."—N. Y. Nation, Jan. 14, 1892.

[3] Cong. Record, 52nd Cong. 1st sess., pp. 2913-4. The bill, the New York Nation said, was "a deliberate sacrifice of self-respect and plighted faith at the behest of low demagogism." "It makes one wonder," this writer continued, "whether the teachings of Christ have produced any enduring effect whatever upon the hearts and consciences of men."—Issue of April 14, 1892.

[4] Cong. Record, 52nd Cong. 1st sess., pp. 3476, 3480

Protests were wasted effort. The Scott act had compelled
the officers of the United States government, the Chinese
minister at Washington observed in letters to Mr. Blaine,
who treated him with scant respect,[1] "to disregard and trample
upon solemn treaty stipulations." The measure had been
"rigidly enforced"—its "severities," indeed, had been added
to by executive action. The most respectable merchants in
Hong Kong had arrived at San Francisco. They were not
permitted to land; they remained as prisoners on their ship
until it sailed on its return voyage. Persecution of the Chinese
by the people of the Pacific coast states continued. Chinese
in San Francisco were driven from their homes and places of
business and were ordered to take up residence in a prescribed
district. The Chinese living in a town in Washington state
were notified to quit it at once. A mob burned the Chinese
quarter in Vallejo, California; the Chinese merchants had been
"repeatedly outraged, robbed and murdered." [2]

The government at Peking found the opportunity to express
a small part of its indignation by rejecting Blair, who, having
been defeated for reelection as a United States senator from
New Hampshire, was, as a *solatium*, appointed by the President
to be minister to China.[3]

When the Geary bill reached the Senate that body substituted its own,[4] though several Western senators expressed
their preferences for the more drastic measure, which had
been passed by the other branch of Congress.[5] John Sherman,
Platt of Connecticut, Dawes of Massachusetts, Gray of Delaware and a few others actively exerted themselves in behalf
of more liberal policies. But in conference the "worse than
Draconian code," as Sherman called the Geary bill,[6] was
fastened, in a number of particulars, upon the Senate bill and

---

[1] M. R. Coolidge, Chinese Immigration, p. 221.
[2] Foreign Relations of the United States for 1890, pp. 211–30; ibid. for
1891, pp. 461–7.
[3] Senate Ex. Doc., 52nd Cong. 1st sess., no. 98; cf. N. Y. Nation, April
14, 1892.
[4] Cong. Record, 52nd Cong. 1st sess., p. 3629.
[5] Ibid., p. 3624.
[6] Ibid., p. 3481.

the President signed the compound, which was to be called the Geary law.

The Geary law inflicted a number of new hardships upon a race which had been singled out already for so much special discriminative legislation. The Scott act, and all other laws for the regulation of Chinese immigration, were given continued life for ten more years. All Chinese found within the boundaries of the United States would now be required to appear before collectors of internal revenue within a year and prove that they were entitled to remain in the country. Descriptions of them were to be taken and they were to receive, if they were able to satisfy these officers, "certificates of residence" to be shown, in future, at demand. Those who could not prove their right to be in the United States were made liable to arrest, imprisonment at hard labor for as long as a year, and deportation at public expense. The burden of proof as to right to remain in the country rested in all cases with the Chinese. It was provided that at least one white witness should be at hand—the testimony of other Chinamen would not suffice. Bail would be denied in habeas corpus cases.[1]

Men in the Senate and the House said that such a law was virtually an order to all Chinese to quit the country within a year.[2] The collector might live 500 miles away. The Chinaman would need to make out a defence under conditions which were plainly almost impossible of fulfillment. Facing a term in jail and deportation he might better leave his home, employment or business, and other interests in the United States, whatever they might be, and return to China, which it was plain to see was the wish and purpose of those who had framed the law.

"Never before in a free country," said Representative Hitt, "was there such a system of tagging a man like a dog." Never before had it been "applied by a free people to a human being."[3]

---

[1] McPherson's Handbook for 1892, pp. 202–6; cf. M. R. Coolidge, Chinese Immigration, chap. xiii.

[2] Cf. Senator Platt, Cong. Record, 52nd Cong. 2nd sess., p. 3877.

[3] Cong. Record, 52nd Cong. 1st sess., p. 3923.

Two-thirds of the Senate [1] and all but 27 men in the House,[2] said the New York Nation, had given their approval to the principle that it was right "to trample upon a treaty" so long as it was a treaty with Chinamen.[3]

[1] The vote in the Senate on the conferee's report was 30 to 15.—Cong. Record, 52nd Cong. 1st sess., p. 3879.

[2] Ibid., p. 3925.

[3] N. Y. Nation, May 12, 1892.

CHAPTER XXXV

THE new and disturbing influence in the Presidential campaign of 1892 would be the Farmers' Alliance and its product, a third political party, the People's party. The tariff might have its uses for the managers of the coming quadrennial contest, but other ideas, the deflecting power of which could not certainly be calculated, were in the air and would play a larger or smaller part in determining the result.[1] The signs were seen in 1890 in such monitory figures as Jerry Simpson of Kansas in the House of Representatives, and William A. Peffer, whom the legislature of that state had elected to be a United States senator in the room of Ingalls. A half dozen or more of the Farmers' Alliance men in the Fifty-second Congress who appeared at Washington in December, 1891, together with a number of those who were ostensibly Democrats, but who owed their advancement in politics to the new farmers' movement were viewed with interest by their colleagues in Congress and by the Washington newspaper correspondents, eager to describe the mental quirks and the oddities of manner and dress of the newcomers. Peffer, made famous for a long, unkempt beard, and Simpson, of course, for his "sockless" campaign against an opponent, who stood, it was said, for wealth and privilege, were curiosities of the first rank. The Peoples' party men had been called "calamity howlers"—the East was prepared to find in them evidences of the yokel and the clown.

One of the number came from Red Cloud, another from Broken Bow, a third from Medicine Lodge—they were recruits from the agricultural frontier. All were of humble birth and

[1] Cf. N. Y. Nation, April 9, 1891.

with but little, if any, acquaintance with the colleges. Beginning in the East they had passed to the public lands of the West where they had unsuccessfully engaged in farming. Some had taught in country schools; a few had studied law. One or two had been lecturers and organizers for the Grange and similar farmers' organizations. Others were editors of local or "class" papers. They had gained office through campaigns which emphasized the poverty and distress of the people. Their own hard experiences, their capacity for sympathy for the poor, because they themselves had been dragged through bitter waters, they would widely advertise. The rich were to be abused, their motives and purposes misrepresented, their merits unfairly stated and a lower class in the population extolled, at the expense of an upper class, for political effect.[1] Conditions were bad enough. The foreclosure of mortgages and the loss of homes on lands made wet with tears, the burning of corn for fuel, because it could not be sold and exchanged for coal, were themes for oratory in Congress, as they had been on the Western stump.[2] But the attempt to fire the passions of groups of men who were in distress, largely because of the situation in which they had put themselves on infertile soils, far from the markets, against more favored bodies of citizens, brought upon the People's party leaders much ridicule and rather general condemnation.

The Farmers' Alliance had risen as a successor of the Grange,[3] but there were other farmers' organizations with similar names and like purposes. The meeting at St. Louis in December, 1889, to which reference has been made in an earlier place, tried to effect a fusion of the various groups, and a platform to their liking, was adopted.[4] Another statement of principles formulated at a meeting in Ocala, Florida, in December, 1890, and still another at Omaha, early in 1891,[5] were practically repetitions of that prepared at St. Louis. A plan for a national

---

[1] Cf. Forum for Oct., 1893.
[2] Cf. Cong. Record, 52nd Cong. 1st sess., pp. 605–6.
[3] Haynes, Third Party Movements, p. 228.
[4] Cf. Solon J. Buck, The Agrarian Crusade, chap. viii.
[5] N. Y. Nation, Feb. 5, 1891.

conference to be held at Cincinnati originated in Kansas. The meeting in that city on May 19, 1891, brought together more than 1400 delegates, three-fourths of whom came from the Middle Western states, and the "People's Party" of Kansas became the "People's Party of the United States of America." Another platform, which was called "progressive," was adopted.[1] The Prohibitionists, the woman suffragists and the apostles of other reforms presented themselves and put forward their causes in fervent words without, however, weaning the managers of the movement from their initial design, which was somehow to do away with poverty by power of the government. They had their various nostrums for the disorders of human society, but neither prohibition of the making and selling of intoxicating drink, nor its twin measure, woman suffrage, was destined to profit by this new third party.

The one proposal which distinguished the platform from other recent codes of proposals for the improvement of economic conditions related to the so-called sub-treasury system. This idea had been devised in the South and had been endorsed by the farmers at their meeting at Ocala.[2] Government offices would be established in agricultural districts. At them money should be lent at one or two per cent. per annum upon grain and other "non-perishable products" which should be delivered to, and held in, public warehouses. The farmer would thus be enabled to "pawn" his crops—if the pledge were not redeemed within a year they were to be sold at public auction for the satisfaction of the debt. As both fiat paper and silver in unlimited volume were to be the money of the country, if the "People's Party" could bring about these ends, no obstacle, it was believed, could lie in the way of the success of the plan.[3] "The hirsute Peffer," as the newspapers described the United States senator from Kansas, presided over the meeting in Cincinnati. General Weaver, the Greenbacker,

[1] Peffer's history of the Farmers' Alliance in Cong. Record, 53rd Cong. 1st sess., p. 1200.
[2] Cf. Solon J. Buck, The Agrarian Crusade, p. 130.
[3] Peffer's elucidation of the scheme is in Cong. Record, 52nd Cong. 1st sess., pp. 5232–45; N. Y. Tribune, May 21, 22 and 23, 1891.

and Ignatius Donnelly of Minnesota, who had gained fame by a "cipher" to prove that Bacon had written Shakespeare's plays and by strange economic theories, were prominent figures in attendance. Powderly of the Knights of Labor was at hand as an adviser, though he was nominally but an onlooker.[1]

The cave of Adullam, it seemed, had opened and its denizens came forth. They had resolved to form a new party to combat the old Republican and Democratic parties in the campaign of 1892. Political observers knew that the movement, if it should develop force, would in the West cross old party lines; results to be wrought in the South would be seen in changes in the internal organization of the Democratic party.

The Cincinnati conference had made provision for another conference at St. Louis on Washington's Birthday, 1892, where the farmers and representatives of divers clubs, unions and associations again discussed their course of action. Senator Kyle of South Dakota called it "the greatest labor convention of the age." [2] At this meeting it was made clearer than ever that the South would not support the movement, if it meant a secession from the Democratic party.[3] Nevertheless the third party forces announced that the People's party would meet at Omaha on July 4, 1892, and would nominate candidates for President and Vice-President.

The unrest among farmers was accompanied by a rising in industrial centres, and it was the hope of those who were directing the third party movement to bring the wage earners, who wanted shorter hours and more money for their work, into sympathetic relations with the agricultural population which was groaning under debt and low prices in the West and South. The conferences in the West for the formulation of a common platform were mainly for the purpose of harmonizing the discontented elements on the farms on the one side and in the mines and factories on the other. The groups

---

[1] Cf. N. Y. Nation, May 28, 1891.
[2] Cong. Record, 52nd Cong. 1st sess., p. 3868.
[3] Haynes, Third Party Movements, p. 259.

had one idea in common—that they had little, while others
had much, and that there should be some equalization of
opportunities, and a fairer distribution of wealth.

There was one difference between the farmer and the industrial worker, however, and it was wide. The farmers
of the West and South were, for the most part, of British
stock. Kansas, Nebraska and the frontier generally had been
settled by families from the East, who were of American interest
and feeling. A number of the Farmers' Alliance men in Congress had fought in the Union Army. The industrial workers
and the miners, on the other hand, were, to an increasing degree,
Continental European emigrants of the first generation,
"foreigners," as they were rather contemptuously called,
speaking alien tongues, and, in many instances, from eastern
Europe—Italy, Hungary, and Poland. They had been encouraged to come to America because it was known that
they would work for wages which, low as they were, would
be higher than any that they could ever hope to receive at
home.[1]

In April, 1891, soon after the Italian lynchings in New
Orleans, a disturbance occurred in the coke manufacturing
district which had its centre at Connellsville, Pa. This industry
had been developed by Henry C. Frick who gained such prominence in it that he was called the "Coke King." That he
might have unfailing and cheap supplies of a material indispensable in steel manufacture Andrew Carnegie, the richest
and best known of the iron masters in Pittsburgh, acquired
a controlling interest in the business which continued to go
forward under Frick's direction, not without friction between
the two men. A few years since the coal miners and coke
makers of this region were Welsh or Irish. Now they were
Slavic, and, at the command of the heads of labor unions.
Ever since 1887, when damaging concessions were made to
them, they now and again became intractable. Frick said that
there would be no further compromise. Another strike was
on and the employees of the company were threatening the

[1] Cf. N. Y. Nation, Feb. 5, 1891.

lives of men imported to take their places and the property of their employers, who had appealed to the public authorities for protection. A mob, numbering at least a thousand persons, came into collision on the night of April 1–2, 1891, with deputy sheriffs. Seven strikers were killed, others were mortally wounded. The leaders of the strike said that it was "unprovoked murder" and caused the arrest of some sheriff's deputies. Governor Pattison sent two regiments of state militia to the scene.[1] Public sympathy was generally withheld from the labor unions because they were so tactlessly led. The Knights of Labor had been discomfited in a recent struggle with the clothing manufacturers in Rochester, N. Y.[2] The mine workers' union lost its battle in the Connellsville district because of mistakes made by the managers of the strike. Business was unprofitable and greater demands upon employers at such a time were regarded as unreasonable, and little in the interest of the workingmen themselves,[3] though it must be thought that such conflicts with "capital" and with constables, sheriffs, and bodies of militia were, in the sight of the professional managers of the labor movement, a part of the martyrdom which must be suffered ere there could be liberty and justice in the world.

By their follies and excesses the labor leaders, who controlled some intelligent and worthy workingmen, but who had a foreign rabble in their train, were alienating public sympathy and it was clear that the farmers, if they were committed to separate political action in conjunction with such allies, had diminishing prospect of disturbing the balance of the old Republican and Democratic parties. Representatives of the new third party who had found their way into Congress, and there expounded its principles, had done little to increase confidence in the movement. Practically all the ills of the country, of which they told tirelessly, were ascribed to the "demonetization" of silver in 1873. "The Goths and Vandals swooping

[1] N. Y. Tribune, April 3 and 4, 1891.
[2] N. Y. Nation, April 2, 1891; N. Y. Tribune, April 3, 1891.
[3] N. Y. Tribune, April 3, 1891.

down upon ancient Rome," said Senator Kyle, one of the most discreet of those who presented the case of the People's party, "were not more ruthless or destructive than the organized moneyed forces" in the United States. The people were "long suffering" but, aroused now, they were not to be put down by those who were ignorant or heedless of their needs.[1] The people, Senator Peffer of Kansas said, were made to march "under the banner of a relentless despot, a conscienceless tyrant, whose God was gold." The "money power must be dethroned," he drooled, "that the republic may live." [2] Money was "a vital matter to the people," he said again—the "people," therefore, should determine of what material it should be made and the volume of it which should be issued for use.[3] Loans on mortgages to the farmers in Kansas would be paid, Jerry Simpson declared, but not in gold, of which there was not enough "to fill the old rotten teeth" of the people.[4]

The Republicans would hold their nominating convention before the Democrats should meet, and in Minneapolis, to propitiate, as well as to survey, the West. Nothing new concerning the Harrison administration would be disclosed. It was honest, efficient and moved forward in the course marked out for it. It was protectionist, modified in some degree by the new plan of reciprocity which operated principally with reference to Latin America. The device gave hope to the rising forces within the party identified with manufacturing, which were interested in the development of an export trade, and, in some degree, to the farmers of the West who were paying, as they considered, higher prices for what they must buy because of the tariff, while they received no more for their saleable products. The Republican policy under Harrison was progressive and constructive—it called for subsidies for shipping, the building of the Nicaragua canal, generous appropriations of money for rivers and harbors, and, in general, had in view a use of the government for the enlargement of

[1] Cong. Record, 52nd Cong. 1st sess., pp. 3861–9.
[2] Ibid., p. 4203.
[3] Ibid., p. 4211.
[4] Ibid., p. 606.

the opportunities of the people. Its tendencies were toward "paternalism," Democratic leaders alleged; the direction taken by their party under Mr. Cleveland was opposite and individualist. Never before, since the first years in the history of the republic, had the distinction between the principal parties been so clearly seen,—one asking for the strict construction of constitutional provisions, the other willing to interpret them loosely; one asking for the localization of power in the states, the other advocating centralization and an increase of Federal strength; one defending the citizen from government, the other prescribing the interposition of government for the public welfare. The development of the slavery question with its antipathies had clouded the old issues. After the war the Democrats were so thoroughly disorganized that they could take no certain course. But since Cleveland had appeared men again spoke of Hamilton and Jefferson.

President Harrison found his party still, in a measure, in the shackles of the corruptions which had come to afflict it by reason of its long and uninterrupted enjoyment of power, and the old forces in it which conceived of a political organization as an agency to be employed for private ends would try to defeat him for renomination. It was agreed that he was not a warm or very likable man. He had set out with the purpose of pleasing himself in the administration of his office; then, he is reputed to have said, at least one person would be satisfied.[1] When men called on him he was silent and apparently unconscious of what was going on around him. A United States senator, after coming out from a visit at the White House, said that it was "like talking to a hitching post."[2] John Sherman found the President "abrupt" as well as cold.[3] It would be folly again to put forward such a candidate; and it was so, said Senator W. D. Washburn of Minnesota, for two reasons. No one, in the first place, cared anything about him personally, and, in the second place, no one, so far

[1] N. Y. Times, March 13, 1890.
[2] Walter Wellman to Gresham, March 20, 1889, in Gresham Papers.
[3] Sherman's Recollections, p. 1160; cf. Cullom, Fifty Years of Public Service, p. 248; C. M. Depew, Memories of 80 Years, pp. 133–4.

as Washburn knew, thought that he could be elected, if he were nominated.[1] Thomas B. Reed spoke of the President as an "ice chest." The "Czar" had had two enemies in Maine, —"one of them Harrison pardoned out of the penitentiary and the other he appointed collector of Portland."[2] It would be too much to require the Republican party to "live four years more in a dripping cave."[3] If Harrison were nominated he "would be dead to start with."[4]

But Mr. Harrison had been chosen to the Presidency in 1888 for reasons which seemed good to the Republican masses, and it would be in answer to some influences not resident in them if he should not be their leader again. By whom could he be opposed? There were, as always, Blaine and John Sherman. The hope of the President's foes rested principally, as they thought, in Blaine, who had said in response to inquiry, in February, 1892, that he would not be a candidate.[5] Manifestly, as Secretary of State, he could not allow men to promote his interests in opposition to the President, unless he should wish to pronounce himself entirely unfriendly to the administration and should leave the cabinet. This he might do, in the view of some persons. For a long time the political gossips in Washington, many of them journalists, who sent the stories to their newspapers, had spoken of Blaine's uncordial relations with the President and his distemper, induced by a realization of the small part which he was permitted to play in the direction of affairs.[6] He had been "caged" by the President, said the New York Times, and deprived of the power of "doing anything that he very much wanted to do."[7] He was wont to remark to his friends that he had little influence in the administration.[8] He bowed to a superior will

[1] Washburn to Hay, May 20, 1891, in E. G. Hay Papers.
[2] S. W. McCall, Life of Reed, p. 188.
[3] Cortissoz, Life of Whitelaw Reid, vol. ii, p. 176.
[4] S. W. McCall, Life of Reed, p. 188; cf. Autobiog. of T. C. Platt, p. 213.
[5] N. Y. Nation, Feb. 11, 1892.
[6] Cf. N. Y. Times, June 21, 1889; N. Y. Nation, March 31, 1892.
[7] N. Y. Times, July 15, 1889.
[8] E. Stanwood, J. G. Blaine, pp. 335–6; T. H. Sherman, Twenty Years with Blaine, pp. 110–2.

with manifest hurt of his pride and worriment of his spirit, which was unused to discipline at the hands of other men.

However few believed that a real estrangement had arisen between the President and his Secretary of State as uncongenial by temperament as they were known to be. If Blaine should leave his post it would, probably, be on the ground of illness. His absence from the State Department after a breakdown in May, 1891, led to rumors of his retirement.[1] It was from both standpoints—on account of his close official relations with the President and the state of his health—not very conceivable that he would allow his name which had been before so many nominating conventions to be brought forward again.

Sherman was in different case. He was no part of the administration and was under no obligation to the President. He was seven years older than Blaine, therefore within one year of 70, but his vigor was apparently unimpaired. He had just begun another term in the Senate, where he was a force to be reckoned with and respected. The reputation of his brother had always mantled his shoulders also, in some degree, and his recent eulogy of the General in New York had recalled the services of both to the country during the war. His specific knowledge of financial questions, as well as his oratorical powers, had just been displayed in a fine and courageous speech in the Senate.[2] He stood unflinchingly for sound money. He had floundered now and again; he was at this time clear and firm. From many sides came requests for copies of his remarks. Chambers of commerce and other organizations of business men would reprint the speech and distribute it to the people. His old lieutenants rallied to his standard. He had been a candidate for the Presidential nomination as often as Blaine; might it not be that his hour had finally come? His managers conferred and commenced pulling wires. Many wrote to him filling him with the idea that he was not only a fitter man to be President than Harrison, which he knew, but also that he

[1] N. Y. Nation, Sep. 24 and Oct. 8, 1891; cf. ibid., March 3 and May 26, 1892; Gail Hamilton, Biography of Blaine, pp. 701-2.

[2] May 31 and June 1, 1892. See Cong. Record, 52nd Cong. 1st sess., pp. 4847-98 passim.

could be nominated and elected. Old internal revenue collectors in the South who had not faltered in their loyalty to him, wiseacres on farms and in hamlets in Ohio to whom his name was a household word, friends known and unknown, in all parts of the country, delegates who had been chosen to state conventions and who would sit in the national convention pledged him their support. When he spoke for the newspapers it was to say that he was not a candidate; he was inferentially, if not plainly, for the renomination of Mr. Harrison, though he made generous allusions to the eligibility of McKinley.[1] Those near him knew, however, that his ambition had never been quieted and that anything like an earnest call to leadership would have delighted his heart. He contented himself by saying that he would "neither seek nor decline the nomination,"[2] though he had very definitely put all visions of further political preferment behind him after his defeat in the convention in 1888.

The pundits of Republicanism who found so little to admire in Harrison and would do all things to put another in his place seem, at first, to have contemplated with favor the plan to bring Sherman forward. Agents who went to see Platt in New York found him, so they said, amenable. Quay in Pennsylvania exhibited a similar disposition, while Mahone in Virginia who had been an advocate in 1888 promised that 20 of the 24 delegates from that state would vote for Sherman. Senator Miller of California would bring the Pacific coast into line.[3]

Sherman referred his advocates to Mark Hanna, who had forwarded the movement in his behalf in 1888. Politicians abounded in Ohio and they were now arrayed in two camps. Foraker had not been a loyal friend in 1888 and no one could think that he would be faithful now. In his strife for ascendency he had allied himself with corrupt elements, including a thieving

---

[1] Sherman to Hanna, May 9, and Sherman to McDougall, May 9, 1892, in Sherman Papers.

[2] Sherman to Hanna, May 9, 1892, in ibid.

[3] H. G. Burleigh to Hanna, May 4, and to Sherman, May 5, 1892, in Sherman Papers.

ring in Cincinnati. To these base forces Hanna was ready to give battle and, as this forthright man became more and more active, he inspired jealousy and fear.[1] He was an admirer of Sherman but, after his experience in 1888, he was brought to understand the hopelessness of his exertions in that direction and he was transferring his devotion to McKinley whom he had helped to make governor of Ohio in 1891. At the same time members of the legislature were to be chosen in the interest of Sherman's return to the Senate against the opposition of Foraker who wanted the place for himself.[2] Hanna had freely contributed money for the prosecution of the state canvass in 1891 which involved the fate of both Sherman and Mc-Kinley, and he solicited it from others, a task made the easier because of the association of McKinley's name with a protective tariff law. Sherman's advances now were rather embarrassing. Hanna agreed that Harrison should be opposed. Republicans in Ohio regarded the President with scant favor; the campaign with him at the head of the ticket would be "lifeless," Hanna said.[3] Indeed it would be "the most lifeless campaign for a half century." Harrison could not "inspire" success.[4]

Thirty four of the 36 delegates in Ohio were friends of Sherman, but, if headway were to be made, "missionary work" must be done in the Southern states. The interest of Alger, Allison and Clarkson must be gained. Hanna would arrange to attend the convention with Judge Thompson, General Grosvenor and Ben Butterworth—they would be a "Big Four" who would be active "on the outside" for Sherman. But, continued Hanna, "there is McKinley. You know he has a feeling that lightning might strike him. I must be on the square with him." Harrison would be a "fool," Hanna said, to accept a nomination by a bare majority of votes from revenue agents

[1] Cf. J. B. Foraker, Notes of a Busy Life, vol. i, pp. 392 et seq.

[2] Herbert Croly, M. A. Hanna, pp. 140–1; H. H. Kohlsaat, From McKinley to Harding, pp. 1–3; Sherman's Recollections, pp. 1141–2; C. S. Olcott, Life of McKinley, vol. i, p. 272; J. B. Foraker, Notes of a Busy Life, vol. i, pp. 445–6.

[3] Hanna to Sherman, April 23, 1892, in Sherman Papers.

[4] Hanna to Sherman, May 11, 1892, in ibid.

and other Federal office holders sent to the convention from the Southern states.[1] As the days passed and as Harrison's nomination seemed to be increasingly certain, Hanna announced that he would not go to Minneapolis; going would simply mean a vote for the President and, this action being against his judgment, he would stay at home.[2] Foraker's unfriendliness to Harrison equalled Hanna's,[3] and when the Ohio delegates were chosen they were uninstructed—they would vote as they pleased when they reached the ground.

Meantime other forces were being organized. Platt and the leaders in the East, who were said to have been ready to concentrate their opposition to Harrison in a support of the claims of Sherman, turned to Blaine. The Republican convention in the President's own state of Indiana was the first to choose delegates to the national convention; they were for Harrison.[4] Iowa endorsed him—its delegates would vote for him.[5] In May all of the delegates, some 900, had been named and 328 were bound and committed to the renomination of the President, while 312, though uninstructed, were said to be favorable to his choice. A majority would suffice, but, if the calculations were correct, he had more than two-thirds of the whole number.[6] Only 50 delegates were for Blaine, though Clarkson, chairman of the Republican National Committee, Quay of Pennsylvania, Platt of New York and minor "bosses" in the states who would use the mantle of the "magnetic man from Maine" to cover their schemes, were still doing whatever they might to start a stampede in the direction of the Secretary of State,[7] rather than to Sherman, to whom it had been believed by the latter's friends that they might be inclined. Platt, in particular, was displaying insistent activity in the campaign of flattery which, it was surmised, would draw Blaine into the contest.[8]

[1] Hanna to Sherman, April 7, 1892, in Sherman Papers.
[2] Hanna to Sherman, April 29, 1892, in ibid.
[3] Grosvenor to Sherman, May 3, 1892, in ibid.
[4] N. Y. Nation, March 17, 1892.
[5] Ibid., March 24, 1892.   [6] Ibid., May 12, 1892.
[7] Ibid., May 26, 1892; cf. ibid. June 16, 1892.
[8] Cortissoz, Life of Whitelaw Reid, vol. ii, p. 177.

Always and again much was made of the President's unpopularity. Clarkson spoke of his "low temperature." [1] Platt called him the "White House iceberg"; [2] mere thought of him caused "a chattering of the teeth." [3] He was a "marble statue," "glacial," even in "torrid weather." Any one who met him, if he could "secure an interview," felt "like pulling on his winter flannels." [4]

Mr. Blaine's friends would draw a veil over this portion of their idol's life.[5] He was ill and his infirmities were increased by domestic sorrows. The manifestation of love, which in some groups in his party had amounted to worship, had not unnaturally given him a belief in the power of his name. At no time since entering the cabinet had he been happy to take less than the first place in the determination of the policies of the party. Now that it would serve their ends mischief makers busied themselves in causing him to think that he was being slightingly, if not curtly, treated by the President, and in telling Harrison, on the other side, that he was not being loyally served by his Secretary of State. Blaine was willing to hear it said that he was a wiser man than the President, and that he would be a stronger candidate in the convention and with the Republican masses in the campaign which should follow. The party required his leadership. He must subordinate his wishes, as he had stated them, and let his followers whoop and halloo him into a nomination. Clarkson, after reaching Minneapolis, was boasting of 600 delegates for Blaine on the first ballot against less than half that number for Harrison.[6]

Under such influences the Secretary of State capitulated.[7] In June, three days before the meeting of the convention, he,

---

[1] Autobiography of Platt, p. 219.
[2] Ibid., p. 215.　　　　[3] Ibid., p. 246.　　　　[4] Ibid., p. 252.
[5] Cf. Gail Hamilton, Biography of Blaine, pp. 704–6; E. Stanwood, A History of the Presidency, pp. 493–4; Stanwood, James G. Blaine, pp. 340–3.
[6] N. Y. Tribune, June 3, 1892.
[7] He was undoubtedly acting under the influence, in large degree, of the women in his household, particularly of Mrs. Blaine and Gail Hamilton. —Cf. N. Y. Tribune, June 11, 1892.

in brief and cold words, resigned his place in the cabinet and announced a schism between himself and the President which, it was confidently expected, would bring the country to his side.[1] It was as clearly an appeal to Caesar as Conkling's had been when he had left the United States Senate in 1881. The people, now as then, would decide the case. Newspapers which had been the most zealous in their admiration of Mr. Blaine were astounded—not a few openly criticized and deplored his course. Old friends were at a loss for words to explain such action, which a newspaper editor in the West described as "scandalous treachery to his chief." [2] To Chauncey M. Depew it was "nothing less than indecent"; he predicted that Blaine's "duplicity and insincerity" would "drive him out of the race and out of politics." [3] On the other hand "Tom" Platt, one of Blaine's new friends, was as certain of his nomination as of his election, should he be nominated,[4] while Foraker, Quay, Cameron and other Republican managers who were eager to beat Harrison spoke with equal confidence. Plumes were waved again for the "Knight" and a crowd of "boomers" appeared with their "Blaine, Blaine, James G. Blaine," their old rallying cry.

But it was said again, as it had been said before, that Blaine was the most popular man in the country every day of the year except on election day, when he seemed to be the most unpopular. This wise men in the convention knew. The very character of the support which was vouchsafed him attested eloquently to the impropriety of his choice at the expense of an Executive whose record was his party's for the three past years. Little of the favor extended to Blaine was honest; most of it masked evil objects on the part of men unfit to guide the destinies of a party which had been but too lately rescued from low control.[5]

[1] E. Stanwood, J. G. Blaine, pp. 337–40; N. Y. Nation, June 9, 1892.
[2] Edward Rosewater to Sherman, May 22, 1892, in Sherman Papers.
[3] N. Y. Nation, June 9, 1892.   [4] N. Y. Tribune, June 6, 1892.
[5] Blaine's action gave him "a very black eye," said ex-President Hayes. "He came into the fight when he was honorably bound to keep out. He had the support of almost all the unscrupulous bosses—Platt, Quay,

Hanna, though he had said that he would not go to the convention, could not remain away. He looked for "surprises." "I shall be a friend on the ground if you need me," he wrote to Sherman as the meeting day drew near.[1] Harrison and Blaine would "kill each other off," said General Miles. He would have Sherman confer with Blaine and make certain that, when the two contestants should "exhaust themselves," Sherman should be named as Blaine's "residuary legatee." The ticket should be Sherman and Gresham.[2] Others spoke of Sherman and Lincoln.[3] Sherman's friends, passing through Chicago on their way to Minneapolis, were "very hopeful of the result." They deceived themselves again. If the party were cold to Harrison, so was it cold to Sherman—he never had warmed more than a few men, though the more faithful in his retinue chose now to put the blame on Hanna, who telegraphed Sherman by private wire to Washington that the "situation was very unfortunate for the party." Hanna had had conversations in Minneapolis; Sherman was acceptable to the East, but the West, "particularly the silver states," disliked his views on the money question, and preferred McKinley.[4] The way was being

Foraker, Clarkson, etc. etc. Harrison represents the best elements of the party." (Diary and Letters of Hayes, vol. v, p. 90) "Quay, Platt and the silver contingent, without real love for the Plumed Knight, wanted to beat Harrison, and they have sadly ended the career of the one they claimed to be able to nominate and that by acclamation. They deceived both Mr. and Mrs. Blaine."—J. S. Morrill to Edmunds, July 5, 1892, in Morrill Papers

[1] Hanna to Sherman, May 30, 1892, in Sherman Papers.

[2] Miles to Sherman, June 1 and 2, 1892, in ibid.

[3] Both Sherman and Blaine should stand aside, wrote a Shermanite of a classical turn of mind. "If the Athenians were wise," Aristides the Just had said, when in a struggle with Themistocles, "they would cast both Themistocles and me into the barathrum"—a pit for the destruction of political offenders.—To Sherman, June 6, 1892, in ibid.

[4] Telegram of June 8 and letters of June 14, 1892, in Sherman Papers. Though McKinley seems to have been looked upon as a friend of silver Sherman's reputation in reference to this subject was such that a miner in Colorado could say to him that he had been "more of a curse" to America "than any traitor ever had been or ever could be in the future." In all our West and South, because of "the misery you have caused to millions of people you are detested and despised worse than Benedict Arnold ever was." If Sherman did not get his "just and deserved punishment while alive," there was a hell, etc. etc. Under date of July 12, 1892, in ibid.

prepared in the pre-convention conferences for a compromise. McKinley could be nominated "easily" was the report from Hanna on the following day, and "I think we should support him." Sherman was asked to see and talk to Allison.[1] "No satisfaction" was to be got from Hanna, a loyal friend telegraphed Sherman. "He talks McKinley." Was there not some one else with whom the faithful could confer? It may have been true that McKinley could have been chosen had that man, a more astute politician than Hanna, allowed himself to be considered as a possible nominee. But he knew that his hour had not struck and he, like Sherman, who also continued to make no mistakes in this regard, uniformly told inquirers that he was not a candidate.

The undercurrent of strength for the President was strong and the certainty of his renomination increased the more closely and dispassionately the situation was viewed. To have renounced and repudiated him would have been, of itself, an augury of division and defeat. McKinley was chosen as the permanent chairman of the convention. A ringing speech captivated the delegates. He let it be known that his sympathies were with Harrison.[2] At a conference on June 9th of the delegates who would vote for the renomination of the President Chauncey M. Depew was in the chair, and their strength was such as to leave no doubt of the result, when, on the morrow, the ballot should be taken.[3] Wolcott, the young senator from Colorado, whose reputation had been gained by his valiant advocacy of silver money, presented the name of Blaine, action which seemed to convey implication that the wing of the party interested in free coinage found more to admire in the retiring Secretary of State than in the President. The tumult which followed this speech and which accompanied every mention of Blaine's name, from a well organized claque,[4] might have

---

[1] Telegram of June 9, 1892, in Sherman Papers.
[2] Cf. C. S. Olcott, Life of McKinley, vol. i, p. 286.
[3] N. Y. Tribune, June 10, 1892.
[4] The N. Y. Tribune correspondent on the ground described the din when Wolcott named Blaine as "one universal howl."—N. Y. Tribune, June 11, 1892.

deceived any but the most experienced observers of the operations of our political machinery. The venerable R. W. Thompson of Indiana who had left Hayes's cabinet, in which he was Secretary of the Navy, on the promise of a large salary from the Panama Canal Company, nominated Harrison, a work which was completed in eloquent terms by Chauncey M. Depew. The first ballot disclosed 535⅙ votes for Harrison, more than a majority, 182⅙ for Blaine, including the entire delegation from Maine and a considerable number of votes which Platt held in the hollow of his hand in New York, and 182 for the governor of Ohio, a tribute to his engaging personality as well as the activity of Hanna, who did not allow his attachment to Sherman, as he had frankly said, or McKinley's protestations, to interfere with his movements.[1] Quay, seeing the hopelessness of Blaine's cause, had carried a large block of delegates from Pennsylvania to McKinley, while other substantial contributions to his total had come from Michigan, Connecticut and Massachusetts. All the contriving had been for naught. It might have had result if Harrison had not received a majority of the votes on the first ballot. His managers had, they said, "downed" the "toughest lot of political schemers in the United States." [2]

McKinley, whose want of loyalty to the President, if he felt disaffection, was not revealed, though he mustered a strength in friends as great as Blaine's, moved to make the nomination of Harrison unanimous, and the resolution was adopted "amid noise," said a correspondent of the New York Tribune, with the reportorial love of picturesque phrase, "that paralyzed the nerves of hearing." [3] "McKinley was superb and won new laurels," ex-President Hayes wrote in his Diary.[4] "His bearing and conduct and personal magnetism," Hanna wrote to Sherman, "won the hearts and respect of everybody." [5] Men said prophetically in greeting him as he left the convention hall—

[1] Cf. Wiborg to Sherman, June 19, 1892, in Sherman Papers.
[2] Letter to Hay, June 13, 1892, in E. G. Hay Papers.
[3] N. Y. Tribune, June 11, 1892.
[4] Diary and Letters of Hayes, vol. v, p. 92.
[5] Hanna to Sherman, June 14, 1892, in Sherman Papers; cf. Herbert Croly, M. A. Hanna, pp. 165–6; C. S. Olcott, Life of McKinley, vol. i, pp. 286–8.

"Well, you'll be nominated by acclamation in 1896 anyway." [1] It must be thought that Sherman's hopes had not been high. A friend offered him consolation. "The office of President," he wrote, "could not have added one thing to your high standing. You are greater than any President and the office would have been honored, not you." [2] As for Blaine he could indulge in like reflections—they had comforted him for many years.

The choice of some one to be put forward for the Vice Presidency whose name might close the breach in party lines, if any had been formed, resulted, not unnaturally perhaps, in the nomination of Whitelaw Reid. It was well known that no one in the country had done more by the agencies of journalism to elevate Blaine to eminence in the party, to defend him against animadversion and to celebrate his deeds than the owner and editor of the New York Tribune. Mr. Morton had been an entirely satisfactory presiding officer of the Senate. The Populists said that he was too rich, but he had won general respect. His renomination with Harrison might have been expected except on the theory, based on a historical fact, that Vice Presidents recently had never been renominated. Nothing was said to Morton on the point. The party flung him off like an old shoe.[3] Platt did not put himself to the trouble to enter protest against the proceeding. If Reid's name were joined to Harrison's the defeat of the ticket, he predicted, would be doubly sure.[4] Sherman disapproved of the nomination,[5] as did other men.

Foraker was chairman of the committee on resolutions. The platform reaffirmed "the American doctrine of protection," and directed attention to "its growth abroad." Prices, in spite of declarations by Democrats in a contrary sense, had not been increased under the "wise revenue legislation of the Republican Congress," which largely explained the present "prosperous

[1] N. Y. Tribune, June 11, 1892.
[2] Sherman Papers; cf. Sherman's Recollections, pp. 1160–1.
[3] R. McElroy, Life of Morton, pp. 196, 197–202.
[4] Autobiog. of Platt, p. 247.
[5] Sherman to Grosvenor, July 13, and to Willard Warner, June 15, 1892, in Sherman Papers.

condition" of the country. The Democrats were denounced for their endeavors to break down "our tariff laws." By the "Republican policy of reciprocity" we would eventually gain "control of the trade of the world." Outrages upon the negroes in the South were again noted and described and a "free and honest" popular ballot was demanded as "the foundation of our republican institutions." "Approval of the Monroe Doctrine," a restored mercantile marine, a larger navy to protect "the honor of our flag," "friendly relations with all foreign powers" and "entangling alliances with none," more restrictions upon foreign immigration, Home Rule for Ireland and freedom from persecution for the Jews of Russia, the construction of the Nicaragua Canal, the scotching of trusts and other capitalistic combinations, a "watchful care" of the veteran soldiers who had "saved the life of the nation," sympathy with "wise and legitimate efforts" to prevent "the evils of intemperance and promote morality," commendation of "the spirit and evidence of reform in the civil service" and protection of the life and limb of employees of railroads, miners and factory hands were among the bids for favor which the party, "assembled in general convention on the shores of the Mississippi River, the everlasting bond of an indestructible republic," made to various classes of men clothed with the franchise who would visit the polling places in November.

The silver "straddle" was a triumph in the evasive arts. The American people, it was said, "from tradition and interest," favored bimetallism. The Republican party demanded the use of "both gold and silver as standard money," under such restrictions as would "secure the maintenance of the parity of values of the two metals," so that "the debt-paying power of the dollar, whether of silver, gold or paper," should be "at all times equal." Every dollar issued by the government must be "as good as any other." "The wise and patriotic steps" taken in the interest of another international conference to fix "a parity of value between gold and silver for use as money throughout the world" was commended.[1] The *double entendre* in platform-

[1] McPherson's Handbook for 1892, pp. 261–3.

making could go no farther, for, while the plank satisfied the gold men in the East, it also awakened the enthusiasm of the silver miners. Senator Teller of Colorado said that it was "the most complete declaration in favor of the use of silver as money" yet made in any platform since the question had appeared in national politics.[1]

Cleveland's cause within the Democratic party had prospered more greatly than had Harrison's with reference to the Republican nomination. No figure larger than Hill's appeared in opposition. The governor of New York had caused himself to be elected by the legislature to a United States senatorship in January, 1891. His term would begin on March 4th, though, unless there should be an extra session, he would have no duties at Washington until Congress should meet in December. He should have resigned the governorship; he declined every suggestion of this kind in spite of criticism [2] levelled at a "double barrelled politician," drawing $10,000 a year from the state and $5,000 from the United States, and held to his resolution to remain at Albany.[3] His principal interest during the summer of 1891 was the election of a governor to succeed himself and he would have one who should be amenable and, as far as possible, removed from alliances with the Cleveland wing of the party. He selected Roswell P. Flower, a rich banker, an innocuous figure whose "barrel" would be opened in gratitude for the distinction.[4] "Billy" Sheehan, a shifty lawyer in Buffalo,[5] would be the candidate for lieutenant-governor. Flower was elected, after a warm contest, by a plurality of nearly 50,000 which strengthened Hill's hold upon the party machinery and magnified his hopes and pretenses with reference to the Presidency. On October 21st he had appeared in Atlanta as the orator of the day in connection with the unveiling of a

---

[1] N. Y. Nation, June 16, 1892.
[2] Cf. N. Y. Tribune, March 31, 1891.
[3] Ibid., Oct. 15 and 24, 1891.
[4] For his largesse see Flower to Lamont, Feb. 11, 1888, in Cleveland Papers.
[5] He never referred to Cleveland except as that "big beefhead" or by a worse name.—Shanahan, Feb. 5, 1888, in Cleveland Papers.

statue of Henry W. Grady, the editor of the Constitution. For
some time this newspaper had been forwarding Hill's interests
in that part of the South and they were to be further advanced
by personal acquaintance. He rode through the streets of the
city in a barouche behind four white horses, with the governor of
Georgia at his side, and spoke in his wooden way at the ceremony
which had drawn him southward, and at a dinner at night
before a young men's Democratic club, at which Senator
Voorhees of Indiana, who was giving encouragement to his
"boom," and others also spoke.[1]

That he might achieve his ends was sincerely believed by Hill
himself and by some of his political aides, while others, who were
promoting the movement were simply giving expression to their
antagonism to Mr. Cleveland. Men who were in control of the
Tammany organization and of the machine in New York state,
and Democrats generally to whom government was a congeries
of lucrative offices for the party "workers" knew that they had
nothing to gain from the election of the upright man who had
been President from 1885 to 1889.[2] He would, as before,
organize an administration in which they should have little, if
any, part and they would do all that lay in their way to defeat
the plan to renominate him. If, in 1884, Cleveland had been
loved for the enemies he had made it was true again now in 1892.
Opposition was an endorsement of his claims.

Since leaving Washington he had led a life entirely apart from
politics, but he had not been an idle onlooker. His utterances
were few, but when he spoke it was in the firm tone and with the
plain meaning which had characterized him during the four
years of his Presidency; when high minded men wrote to him his
replies were in defence of honest political principles and in the
interest of what he called and believed to be "genuine De-

[1] N. Y. Tribune, Oct. 22, 1891.
[2] Cf. McElroy, Grover Cleveland, vol. i, p. 321. A rhymster brought
the thought to expression—
    "O, Grover, dearest Grover, they used to think you hard,
    And so you were, dear Grover, for when did you regard
    The threats of statesmen who had jobs they wanted to get through;
    To these a rough stone wall was soft compared, old man, with you."
                        —Cleveland Papers.

mocracy." [1] He concealed no conviction and his bravery was an inspiration to other men. Wherever this vibrant moral leader had appeared at public gatherings he was greeted with prolonged applause which often expressed itself in men rising to their feet and cheering him. For ballot reform, civil service reform and tariff reform his favor was clear, and no one was allowed to think that he had surrendered any of his faith in them, or in his party, which must not "lag in the rear," as he declared in Boston, in December, 1889, "on any of those topics." [2]

He was painfully impressed by the progress of the Hill campaign. The candidacy for the Presidency of the United States of a man so meagerly endowed with moral and intellectual qualities was a disquieting phenomenon in our politics. Hill's design to capture the organization to which Cleveland and his friends had given a new purpose and to put it again to mean uses in the nation, as in New York state, met with their emphatic detestation. If the party were to achieve success there must be no trickery or evasion.

Some of the hostility to Cleveland's renomination, especially in the South, rested upon the knowledge that he would yield nothing on the financial question. Under the influence of the Farmers' Alliance movement the silver mania had come to affect the outlook of many Democratic leaders. Democratic conventions in twenty one states in 1890 had declared for "free silver." [3] Some men pretended to believe that Cleveland would let the party go its way on this question. He could and would not speak in protest against a movement which had so generally taken hold of the Democratic political organization, and which controlled the course of those who were gathered under its name in Congress to such a degree that only two or three adherents of the party in the United States Senate could be found to vote against free coinage. Mr. Cleveland's position would be not long in doubt. In February, 1891, while the subject was being

[1] R. W. Gilder, Grover Cleveland, pp. 27–8; N. Y. Nation, March 14, 1889.
[2] N. Y. Nation, Dec. 19, 1889; McElroy, Grover Cleveland, vol. i, pp. 311–2.
[3] A. Nevins, Grover Cleveland, p. 466.

hotly discussed in the Senate, he was invited to attend a meeting
of the Reform Club in New York. In declining he wrote to the
president of that organization saying that he was in agreement,
as every one must know, "with those who believe that the
greatest peril would be invited" by the adoption of the scheme
now pending at Washington. He deplored any attempt to
"enter upon the dangerous and reckless experiment of free,
unlimited and independent silver coinage." [1] His words were at
once a chief subject of public interest and comment.[2] Friends
interested in his political future admonished him in vain.
"D—— the nomination," he would exclaim, "I will say what I
think is right." [3] He made it clear on every occasion that no
dicker, deal, concession or compromise would move him from
his position.[4] There he stood—the only man whom the party
had been able to elect to the Presidency since the war, its
strong, respected leader, and feared because he was respected.
Democrats as well as Republicans could make of it what they
chose.

Abuse of him, such as had been indulged in for many years,
was continued in the dark alleys of our politics. Men, and
women, whispered old scandals. In his retirement he had
enjoyed no respite or freedom. The New York Sun, for the
common amusement, kept to its way, making a jest of good
government and the agencies through which such government
might be secured. That newspaper one day had said that
Cleveland was gaining fat at the rate of 25 pounds a month and
that he was about to undergo a kind of treatment by the use of a
"treadmill" which had "saved" Bismarck from the disastrous
consequences of obesity.[5] Upon the strength of this announcement the New York World "interviewed" Mr. Cleveland and
made him express unfavorable and resentful opinions concerning

[1] To E. Ellery Anderson, Feb. 10, 1891, in Nevins, Letters of Cleveland,
p. 245; Nevins, Grover Cleveland, pp. 467–8; McElroy, Grover Cleveland,
vol. i, pp. 319–20; N. Y. Nation, Feb. 19, 1891.

[2] N. Y. Nation, Feb. 19, 1891.

[3] McElroy, Grover Cleveland, vol. i, p. 310; cf. ibid., pp. 320–1, 328,
335.

[4] Ibid., p. 313; cf. Nevins, Grover Cleveland, pp. 468–9.

[5] N. Y. Sun, April 16, 1890.

Dana, the editor of the Sun.[1] Pleased by notice, the Sun called the ex-President a "cowardly liar," a "half drunken deputy sheriff" and a "selfish poltroon." [2] The "interview" was a forgery. Though the World published a retraction the Sun declared that, whether Cleveland had said what he had been quoted as saying or not, it was what he would have liked to say, and the paper, without expression of regret or apology, continued on its malicious course.[3]

To the Sun and its chuckling readers Cleveland, day after day, was "the Claimant" and "the Stuffed Prophet of William Street" (where the offices of his law firm were located.) Allusion to him emphasized his adiposity and was a signal to speak of his ambition. Having and holding the unconcealed esteem of the Mugwumps no effort was spared to make it appear that he was one of them, and that he, therefore, had forfeited his right to place in the party as a "regular." [4]

Already in January, 1892, unusual preparations were on foot in New York for the choice of delegates to the national convention. They would be "hand-picked," and for Hill. They would be chosen in bulk and would be his automata. His state committee called a convention to meet at Albany on Washington's Birthday to ratify his will. Cleveland's friends, Charles S. Fairchild, ex-Mayor William R. Grace, Frederick R. Coudert, E. Ellery Anderson and others convoked a mass meeting in Cooper Union. Other meetings were held to protest against this "snap" convention. Complaint was loud and angry, but vain.[5] The machinery was in Hill's hands and he was bent upon using it to forward his own ends. An admirer introduced him to the assemblage at Albany as "Young Hickory, the next President of the United States." He read from typewritten sheets a muddle-headed speech. A "solid" delegation from New York, with instructions to present his name and to vote for him as a unit at the national convention would confront other dele-

---

[1] N. Y. World, April 17, 1890.
[2] Issue of April 18, 1890.
[3] N. Y. Sun, April 21 and 22, 1890; cf. N. Y. Times, April 22, 1890.
[4] Cf. N. Y. Sun, Nov. 17, 18 and 24, 1890.
[5] N. Y. Nation, Feb. 4 and 11, 1892.

gations, which would thus be pointedly invited to come to his standard and give him the nomination.[1] Cleveland would be deprived of the support of as much as a single delegate from his own state, which would be telling the country in the plainest terms, Hill and his retinue believed, that the ex-President was without friendships counting for anything among that class of men who controlled the machinery for getting and recording votes in New York, now again to be, as it had been before, the ground on which the parties would win or lose the great prize.[2]

Hill's next maneuver carried him to the South with a view to taking further profit from the commendations of him as a public character which continued to appear from time to time in the Atlanta Constitution. In the previous October he had visited only that city and, presumably, to honor Grady. In March, 1892, he was travelling from town to town to receive the homage of such as saw in him the material for an American President. For public discourse he was not gifted and he made but an unhappy impression upon new groups of men. Plainly he did not understand large economic and political measures, but, being in high degree dexterous as a politician, it was his belief that he could repeat a speech on controversial subjects without inclining to either side. By "loose incoherencies"[3] and involved and foggy diction[4] he could draw support from all factions, he supposed, as did his advisers, and the scribes who prepared his statements for declamation. Thereby he might achieve his high ambition. He came back from his electioneering trip in the South of less consequence in the sight of the country than when he had gone away.[5] He was, the New York Nation said, a "self seeking shuffler," who worked for the Presidency, as a ward politician works for the place of an alderman.[6] To others who

[1] N. Y. Tribune, Feb. 23, 1892; N. Y. Nation, Feb. 25, 1892.

[2] In his enterprise Hill had the support of several anti-Cleveland leaders in other states who did not wish to show their hands. They were eager to see Hill try his fortune in the Presidential field, though they later left him to his fate.—McElroy, Grover Cleveland, vol. i, pp. 326–7; A. Nevins, Grover Cleveland, pp. 475–6.

[3] N. Y. Tribune, March 27, 1892.

[4] N. Y. Nation, Jan. 7, 1892.

[5] Ibid., March 10, 1892.

[6] Ibid., March 17, 1892.

sat in judgment he was an "adroit political rope dancer," and again a juggler whose ambition it was to be able to keep six balls in the air at once. The newspapers generally called his antics "peanut politics." During his trip he had successfully concealed his opinions about the tariff, silver and every other matter which, at the time, engaged the attention of the people.[1]

It was stated, and it was known, that he could command majorities in New York. He had been elected governor in 1888 when Cleveland had failed to carry the state under circumstances which it might not be well to recall. Hill with three or four ignorant men of foreign birth who controlled the Tammany machine and, through it, governed New York city, a coterie to whom politics was a predatory trade, were a unit in declaring that Cleveland should not be nominated in 1892; the people of the state did not want him and would not vote for him, they said, and, without New York, he could not be elected. There must be "unity." Victory was more to be valued than men; the welfare of the party demanded the nomination of one who would command party support. Hill's principles, policies and attainments as a public man had been summed up by him, and, for him, by others, in the sentence—"I am a Democrat."[2] On this

---

[1] N. Y. Nation, March 17 and 24, 1892. In illustration of Hill's manner of speech men pointed to such utterances as these in an address to the legislature of Mississippi:

"The South in her propinquity with Africans, whose type of civilization awaits historic record, has caused the only alteration thus far made in our governmental structure."

"I seek to make it clear that to repeal the McKinley laws, to wipe them off the statute books, reviving the lesser wrongs they superseded, is merely to take a first step toward living up to our unimpaired authoritative Constitution."

"Against united Democratic votes the Republican Congress passed the Sherman silver law, into which every Republican monetary heresy is crowded that has kept our finances in perpetual disorder for 30 years, [reviving] the most dangerous heresy which the Republican party once packed the bench of the Supreme Court to get a false judgment upon as constitutional."

"Permitted to make laws in order 'to promote the general welfare,' which can mean nothing else but what is for the welfare of all, they read into its magnanimity and breadth their own little rascally permissions to promote anybody's welfare that can bribe an appropriation from the people's taxes" etc. etc.—N. Y. Tribune, March 16, 1892.

[2] "I am a Democrat," with all the emphasis on the "I am," a correspondent wrote Cleveland.—Cleveland Papers.

platform he stood. It was at once an epitome of his record and a sling at Cleveland who, out of accord with Hill and Tammany, while holding the admiration of the Mugwumps, would be, if possible, detached from the party.

Coincidently a scandal was being exposed in New York state, where a politician, who had been improperly appointed to a high judicial position was under inquiry, and was being subjected to unsparing condemnation for the part he had taken in election frauds which had been perpetrated in connection with Hill's scheme to gain control of the New York state senate in the previous year.[1] The highly respectable New York Bar Association led this attack.

In New York City a campaign against Tammany which was destined to reach significance was being instituted by the brave preacher of a leading Presbyterian church, the Rev. Dr. C. H. Parkhurst. His first sermon, in which he declared "municipal life" to be "thoroughly rotten," was delivered on February 14, 1892. Every step looking to "moral betterment," he said, was "taken directly in the teeth of the damnable pack of administrative bloodhounds" who were "fattening themselves on the ethical flesh and blood of our citizenship." He found it of but little advantage to preach the Gospel to a young man on Sunday, if this young man were "to be sitting on the edge of a Tammany-maintained hell the rest of the week." The ire of the political gang and the ridicule of their newspapers (led by the New York Sun) availed nothing. Dr. Parkhurst was in possession of the facts and, by degrees, under his lash, the public was being aroused to the need of sweeping reforms.[2]

It was a fair deduction in many minds that the kind of government which was associated with Hill's name in his own state was the kind of government which he would give to the United States.[3] It was but little in proof of his statesmanship and, indeed, his sense of propriety that, having been elected to the United States Senate, he did not occupy his seat. He had

[1] N. Y. Tribune, March 23 and 24, 1892.
[2] C. H. Parkhurst, My Forty Years in New York, chap. vii.
[3] Cf. N. Y. Nation, Jan. 28, Feb. 11 and 18, March 30 and April 14 and 21, 1892; Harpers' Weekly, May 14, 1892.

been governor as well as senator since March. Upon the opening of Congress in December, 1891, he still remained in Albany. He would complete his term as governor, at the end organizing for himself a farewell dinner and making a muzzy speech in which he denounced "piebald legislation." [1] He was ready to take the oath in January and had returned at once to Albany where, for nearly two months, he was engaged in pulling wires to win support through the New York machine for his Presidential boom. After being in Washington again for a few days he had set off on his electioneering trip in the South. [2] By absenting himself from his place it would be the easier for him to follow the program which he had laid down for himself and escape taking sides on public questions. It was alleged that he was for silver, and again that he was for gold. When, a few days before the Democratic national convention should meet, he had had the opportunity to make his position clear, he had sat silent in-his chair while the roll was being called. [3]

Cleveland continued to make no movements in his own behalf. His enemies lashed his ample figure without drawing him from the quiet and dignified enjoyment of private life. The issues were tariff reform, sound money and the honest administration of public affairs, [4] and in him was seen, as in no other in view, a will to defend and give force to these principles.

Public sentiment throughout the country was drifting unmistakably toward him as the party candidate. He was its most distinguished leader and he grew in stature as the day for action approached. [5] Friendly voices were raised and the call grew clearer and stronger. Charles S. Hamlin was active in Boston; Charles S. Fairchild in New York. Mass meetings were organized and held in the states, Boston leading with one which brought forward such men as Moorfield Storey, John E. Russell, Dr. William Everett, Henry L. Pierce and Josiah Quincy. The object, Hamlin wrote to Cleveland, was to

[1] N. Y. Tribune, Jan. 1, 1892.
[2] N. Y. Nation, March 17, 1892.
[3] Ibid., June 2, 1892.
[4] Ibid., Feb. 25, 1892.
[5] Cf. ibid., April 7, 1892.

"reach the hearts of the people who earnestly desire your nomination, both as a personal tribute to yourself and as a coronation of the principles dear to us and represented by you as by no other living man." [1]

Cleveland had said, and he repeated, that he was not a candidate. Many wrote begging him not to decline. "The party ever since the war," said John P. Irish of California, had been "on the hunt for a herd of swine to run into and go with into the sea." Cleveland had lifted it up, set it on high ground "and the self seeking of a material age was shamed and rebuked." [2] He must accept the nomination and he should say now, in order to stop the movement to name such a man as Hill, that he would lead the party in the campaign of 1892. The "yeast was working from below." The masses were for him— 99 out of every 100 Democrats would vote for him—it was a rising of the people against the politicians.

On March 9, 1892, while Hill was in the South, Cleveland wrote a letter, in answer to one from General Bragg, expressing his preference for private life, but declaring his willingness to be the nominee, if the people, left to their free choice, should again wish him to head the ticket. His conception of the office was such that it would preclude the possibility of his "leading and pushing a self seeking canvass for the Presidential nomination." He was confident that success was still within reach of the party, if care were used in the selection of candidates, and on the point of "party action upon questions of immense interest to the patriotic and intelligent voters of the land." [3]

Cleveland wrote more freely to more intimate friends. The office, he said in a letter to Lamar, had not for him "a single allurement." But forces were at work which meant "the complete turning back of the hands on the dial of Democracy and the destruction of party hopes." He was acting from a "sense of duty to honest people and devoted friends." He would not have any one say that he had "refused to serve in time of

---

[1] Hamlin to Cleveland, Feb. 29, 1892, in Cleveland Papers.

[2] To Manton Marble, March 1, 1892, in ibid.

[3] McElroy, Grover Cleveland, vol. i, pp. 332–3; N. Y. Nation, March 17, 1892.

evil." [1] The rules which he had laid down for himself in political
life precluded the putting forth of exertions in his own behalf,
but in May appeared a volume of State Papers, embodying
speeches delivered and messages sent to Congress during his
first term. Copies of this book, autographed, were sent to
lawyers, editors, friends and prominent men of many kinds to be
acknowledged in letters of thanks which reached him in numbers
at Lakewood, N. J., where he was living prior to the family's
removal for the summer to Buzzards Bay.

Rhode Island, Minnesota and other states early took occasion
to choose delegates who were instructed to vote for him in the
national convention. In May it was computed that 300 out of a
total of 378 delegates thus far selected were favorable to his
renomination.[2] Western Democrats were practically unanimous
in his support; they were going so far, in deference to his opinion,
as to say little or nothing in their platforms concerning free
silver, about which they had made so much ado in 1890. In the
convention in Nebraska, where it was supposed that the
resolutions which had expressed party opinion two years since
would be reaffirmed, only one member of the committee appointed to prepare a platform favored a statement about free
coinage, and Bryan, who carried the contest to the delegates on
the floor of the hall, though he was regarded as "an exceedingly
forcible speaker," failed to win his case by a vote of 247 to 229.[3]
Sentiment in the South favorable to Cleveland had become
generally enthusiastic. Hill's boom there had almost entirely
collapsed,[4] though it was known that Cleveland would not, as
he wrote Lamar, lead the party, if it should adopt a muddy
policy on the financial question.[5] He would not "shuffle or
palter" on this point, he told his friend Bissell. The platform, if
he should be nominated, must be sound in the money plank.

---

[1] Under date of May 1, 1892, in Cleveland Papers; also in A. Nevins,
Letters of Cleveland, pp. 279–81.
[2] N. Y. Nation, May 12, 1892.
[3] McElroy, Grover Cleveland, vol. i, pp. 333–4; N. Y. Nation, April 21,
1892.
[4] N. Y. Nation, May 26, 1892.
[5] Cleveland to Lamar, May 1, 1892, in Cleveland Papers.

"I cannot forego my opinions," he said, "for the nomination or for anything else." [1] Even Georgia, in May, amid great enthusiasm, chose delegates all but a few of whom would support Cleveland in Chicago.[2]

Another convention in New York state, free from the influence of Hill and his machine, to be attended by delegates honestly chosen by caucuses, would be held in May in Syracuse. In this meeting the "Snap Convention" (also called the "Snowshoe Convention") of February was discredited. Hill was rebuked for his underhand and selfish leadership and a contesting delegation instructed to vote for Cleveland was authorized to lay claim to the seats of men who, it was alleged, would misrepresent the party at Chicago. Gentlemen whose names were known and respected were active in a demonstration which attracted thousands from all parts of the state.[3]

The national convention, in the huge, unpainted, box-like "Wigwam" on the lake front at Chicago, soon followed the renomination of Harrison at Minneapolis. It brought together Cleveland's friends, led more actively and resourcefully by William C. Whitney than by any other in the group,[4] and such figures hostile to Cleveland as Governor Flower of New York, Richard Croker and Bourke Cockran of Tammany Hall, Gorman of Maryland who was himself a candidate for the Presidency; Senator Calvin S. Brice of Ohio, Henry G. Davis of West Virginia, Senator Voorhees of Indiana, Senator Daniel of Virginia and Henry Watterson who had made himself into a prophet, declaring, in his picturesque way, that, if the convention should not choose another candidate, the party would "walk through a slaughter house into an open grave." [5]

All efforts, and they were many, to form anti-Cleveland combinations failed [6] and the sentiment in his favor grew as

[1] Cleveland to Bissell, June 11, 1892, in Cleveland Papers.
[2] Cf. A. Nevins, Grover Cleveland, p. 487.
[3] N. Y. Times, June 1, 1892; cf. N. Y. Nation, April 21, 1892.
[4] McElroy, Grover Cleveland, vol. i, pp. 336–7; A. Nevins, Grover Cleveland, pp. 489–90.
[5] Cf. A. Nevins, Grover Cleveland, p. 489.
[6] McElroy, Grover Cleveland, vol. i, pp. 338–9.

the delegates arrived and mingled preparatory to the organization of the convention, which was effected on June 21st. The
lusty shouting of the crowds in the hotels and in the streets
made it plain what the result would be before the meeting day,
namely the nomination of Cleveland on the first ballot.

William L. Wilson of West Virginia, lately president of the
university bearing the name of that state, described not in-
accurately as "a gentleman and a scholar," gave dignity to
the convention and its proceedings as permanent chairman.
He had stood up before "Czar" Reed while the contest over
the rules of the House was on and had delivered, to the Speaker's
face, what was said to have been one of the most satirical
speeches ever heard in Congress,[1] and for this, and other
services, had won title to party honors. Since his enemies
had preempted all of the 72 places assigned to delegates from
his own state Governor Abbett of New Jersey, the state of
Cleveland's birth, under instructions, since Abbett was but
a luke-warm friend, put the ex-President in nomination. A
"Snap Convention" delegate, DeWitt, eulogized the man who
found his highest boast in the sentiment "I am a Democrat."
Hill could carry New York—without that state, it was said
again, the battle would be lost before it had been fought. The
name of Governor Boies of Iowa, twice elected to the governorship of a Republican state on a platform demanding free
silver coinage, was presented as the first contestant for the
Presidency whose home was west of the Missouri River. In
the hope of moving the crowd, or at any rate of delaying a
result which was inevitable, Bourke Cockran turned on a
flood of his Irish oratory, and for an hour and a half developed
the theme that Cleveland's nomination would lead to certain
defeat. It was daybreak on the morning of June 23rd before
the speeches had ended, the shouting had subsided and the
ballot confirmed the prediction that Cleveland would again be
his party's leader in the campaign of 1892. It was announced
that 617⅓ votes were cast for Cleveland on the first ballot.

---

[1] Cong. Record, 51st Cong. 1st sess., pp. 1038–40; N. Y. Times, June 23,
1892.

Hill received 114, 72 of which were cast by "Snap Convention" delegates from New York. Since, to procure the result, it was unnecessary to bring the claims of the Syracuse contestants before the committee of credentials it was considered to be a more judicious measure for them to stand aside.[1] To these 72 were added 11 from Virginia, 6 from Ohio, 5 from Georgia and the votes of a few silver men to whom Cleveland's well known views on the currency question were unsavory. Boies of Iowa polled 103 votes, largely on the silver issue,[2] almost as many as Hill controlled, while 36 delegates found refuge under the name of Gorman and 14, rather than vote for Cleveland, expressed a preference for John G. Carlisle.

Ex-Governor Gray of Indiana was to have been the nominee for Vice-President. But he was unacceptable to elements in the party, not the least of which were the Hill following, and the Tammanyites, now somehow to be propitiated, and the choice fell upon Adlai E. Stevenson of Illinois. The crowds sang their own words to the refrain of the popular "Baby Song" from the current comic opera "Wang,"

> "Grover, Grover,
> Four more years of Grover,
> In he goes,
> Out they go,
> Then we'll be in clover,"

and made the accustomed demonstrations of enthusiasm for, and allegiance to, the party candidate. Cleveland and Stevenson were set before the country as the nominees of the Democrats who were to wrest the honors from Harrison and Reid upon the counting of the ballots in November next.

The Democratic, like the Republican, platform was a receptacle for much rhetorical claptrap. The "Force Bill" was condemned at length in the belief that references unfavorable to that measure would win votes. Sympathy for persecuted Lutherans (to outdo the Republicans), as well as maltreated Jews in Russia, and for the Irish in their struggle for Home

---

[1] McElroy, Grover Cleveland, vol. i, pp. 330, 336, 342–3.
[2] Cf. N. Y. Tribune, June 22, 1892.

Rule was expressed. The Chinese must be kept out of America. The United States must not be used as a "dumping ground" for paupers and criminals. Foreign workmen should be excluded at our ports lest American labor be "degraded." The platform denounced any attempts "to restrict the immigration of the industrious and worthy of foreign lands." Soldiers were to be pensioned, but not in the disgraceful and profligate manner of the Republicans. The Nicaragua canal should be completed and New Mexico and Arizona admitted to the Union. The free school system should be extended by the states. The lives and limbs of railway employees, held in mind by the Republicans, were not forgotten by the Democrats. Convicts should not make goods to compete with free labor.

Four planks concerning the tariff, the currency, the civil service and temperance would be discussed during the campaign. While the Republicans, fearing defections to the Prohibitionists, had expressed sympathy, as in 1888, with efforts to lessen "the evils of intemperance and promote mo- rality," the Democrats had summarily dismissed the subject by stating their opposition "to all sumptuary laws as an inter- erence with the individual rights of the citizen." The civil service plank opened with Cleveland's motto, "Public office is a public trust," and promised the country an "honest en- orcement" of all laws relating to the subject, an improvement pon the casual words contained in the Republican platform. ikewise the Democratic statement in regard to the currency as more candid and commendable than that of the Repub- cans, though marked by strange contradictions and much tentional ambiguity.[1] The Sherman silver purchase law of 390 was denounced as a "cowardly makeshift." It was aught with danger and should be repealed. Gold and silver ould be used as money, but it was specified that both metals ust be of "equal intrinsic and exchangeable value." "Paper rrency should always be kept at par with, and be redeemable , coin." The efforts of a delegate from Colorado to amend e resolution in the interest of free coinage failed and most of

[1] A. D. Noyes, Thirty Years of American Finance, pp. 177–8.

the delegates from that state, led by the editor of a newspaper in Denver, "bolted" the ticket.[1]

A tariff plank had been carefully framed by the committee on resolutions. It was a statement advocating a revision of duties to remove inequalities and lighten oppressions, without doing injury to domestic industries. It was essentially the party declaration on which the election had been won in 1884. Henry Watterson made an appeal to the delegates from the floor of the convention for a tariff "for the purpose of revenue only." More was unconstitutional. Taxes should be "limited to the necessities of the government." "Republican protection" was denounced "as a fraud, a robbery of the great majority of the American people for the benefit of the few." This was, to all intents and purposes, the plank in the Democratic platform of 1876. The anti-Cleveland delegation in New York, not averse to putting the candidate before the country as a free-trader, wildly shouted their approval, and the plank proposed from the floor was accepted as a substitute by a vote of 564 to 342.[2] Further declarations about the "atrocity" of the McKinley law, the "sham reciprocity" of the Republicans, and the need of legislation to restrain trusts and combinations completed the platform's contribution to the impending campaign on the subject of the tariff.[3]

A week later, on June 29th, the Prohibitionists met at Cincinnati. Clearly told in the Democratic platform that they could expect no favor from that party, and believing, as they said, that the "sympathy" of the Republicans for temperance and morality was hollow, they adopted resolutions upon the subject of the "liquor traffic." They expressed their interest in woman suffrage, voted down a free silver plank, asked for a tariff which should be retaliatory only, and with reference to governments which excluded our products from their markets and advocated public control of railroads and telegraphs, and restrictions upon foreign immigration. General John Bidwell

[1] N. Y. Times, June 24, 1892.
[2] Cf. A. Nevins, Grover Cleveland, pp. 491–2.
[3] McPherson's Handbook for 1892, pp. 264–7.

a California pioneer, the proprietor of extensive ranches in that state, was nominated for President, and the Rev. Dr. Cranfell of Texas for Vice-President.[1]

The People's party rising which had promised to be so discomfiting to the two old parties gave signs of waning, and the convention which met in Omaha the day before the 4th of July, with a view to synchronizing its action with the nation's celebration of the anniversary of the adoption of the Declaration of Independence found the Harrison-Cleveland campaign in progress, with little prospect of public interest in other candidates. The convention was a Western mass meeting which brought together men who had been prominent for years in radical political movements. Proof of this was found in the choice of a Presidential candidate, no other than General Weaver, the Greenbacker, who with, marked unsuccess, had led the cause of the fiat money men in 1880. His principal opponent for the nomination was James H. Kyle, the preacher who had been elected by the Farmers' Alliance as a United States senator from the new state of South Dakota.[2] The platform was written at a high tonal pitch; it was stridently extravagant in its statement and abusive of the old parties which were treated as one. Both together would "drown the outcries of a plundered people" and "sacrifice our homes, lives and children on the altar of Mammon." The nation, the makers of the People's party platform said, was on "the verge of moral, political and material ruin." Corruption dominated the ballot box, the people were "demoralized," the newspapers were muzzled, public opinion was silenced, business was prostrated, labor was impoverished and land was coming into the hands of the millionaires. The "fruits of the toil of millions" were "boldly stolen to build up colossal fortunes for a few, unprecedented in the history of mankind." Several suggestions were made—first with reference to the currency. Silver which had been "accepted as coin since the dawn of

---

[1] McPherson's Handbook for 1892, pp. 271–2.
[2] Cf. Solon J. Buck, The Agrarian Crusade, pp. 145–6; F. E. Haynes, Third Party Movements, pp. 261–4.

history" had been "demonetized." The money supply was "purposely abridged to fatten usurers, bankrupt enterprise and enslave industry." A "vast conspiracy against mankind had been organized on two continents." There should be free silver and gold coinage at the rate of 16 to 1. The amount of money in circulation should be "speedily increased to not less than $50 per capita." No banking corporation should issue national currency. The sub-treasury plan of the Farmers' Alliance was endorsed as a means of giving money to the people. The government should own and operate the railroad. and the telegraphs. "Alien ownership of land" should be prohibited, for the land, "including all the natural sources of wealth," was "the heritage of the people." The government should be supported by a "graduated income tax." "By imported pauperized labor" which was beating down American wages and a "hireling standing army," established to shoot down our working men, we were "rapidly degenerating into European conditions." Other questions might call for the attention of "a party of reform," but it must be determine whether we were to have a republic before we should present and dispute about, differing plans for the administration of our common affairs.[1]

Clearly the contest would be between the Republicans and the Democrats,—one led by the President, the other by him who had been President but little more than three years since and men entrusted with the franchise would see the issue and make their choice. Very fortunately both were leaders the better forces within their parties. The politicians who had been active in the management of Republican campaign had been shown to the rear. Clarkson, Quay, Platt, Dudle had wrapped themselves, as Platt said, "in overcoats and earmuffs" and left Minneapolis to take the first train out Chicago with predictions of defeat for the ticket.[2] Nor w

---

[1] McPherson's Handbook for 1892, pp. 269–71. The platform w largely a repetition of that one adopted by the convention which had m in St. Louis on Washington's Birthday.—Cong. Record, 52nd Cong. sess., pp. 3868–9.

[2] Autobiography of Platt, p. 247.

the result more pleasing to a new leader, Mark Hanna of Cleveland, of whom soon so much would be heard. The nomination, he told Sherman, fell "like a wet blanket" upon the convention. He found few signs of rejoicing among the people when he reached home. A "funereal sadness," had surrounded the bulletin boards when the nomination was announced. There was "utter indifference" and nothing, Hanna said, except a change of Harrison's "manner and policy toward the leaders of the party" would save him from defeat.[1] The men whose hearts were not in the contest, though it was their duty now to give outward pledges of their loyalty, would be set aside, and to find one to be chairman of the National Committee in 1892 was a difficult task.[2] Finally a quite unknown man from the new state of Montana, Thomas H. Carter, who had been in Washington at the head of the General Land Office was entrusted with the practical duty of directing the work of assembling enough votes to keep Harrison in the White House.

Apart from Harrison's inability to awaken enthusiasm the party, as well as its President, was in a not too fortunate position in reference to recent events. It had tried to enact a "Force Bill," or held before the country the measure bearing this name. If such a project for the control of Federal elections met with approval on some sides it clearly alienated other men who had the wish to support the Harrison administration. The rather high-handed management of the House of Representatives by Speaker Reed estranged voters who believed that his rules were not in the interest of fair play, although the influence of this incident was nearly exhausted in the Congressional elections of 1890. The scandals in the pension office and the free and liberal appropriation of public money were contrasted with the economies of Mr. Cleveland, and the interest in lower taxes which he so sincerely and frequently

[1] Hanna to Sherman, June 14, 1892, and Sherman to Grosvenor, June 13, 1892, in Sherman Papers. Whether the course which Hanna had taken at Minneapolis was approved by Harrison, and he, Hanna, had learned that his activities in behalf, first of Sherman and then of McKinley, had earned him Presidential disfavor, was, he declared, "not of much consequence" to him.—Hanna to Sherman, June 21, 1892, in ibid.

[2] N. Y. Nation, July 14, 1892.

expressed. The silver issue which had promised to loom so large would, for the time, fall into the background. The Republicans would look both ways in order to hold the West as well as the East and would stand, if they could, on the artfully contrived statement in their platform; and the Democrats, also divided, were clearly in no position to take the enemy to task for evasive treatment of the question, and to adopt measures which would bring it forward for open discussion.[1] Emphasis would be laid upon the tariff, as in earlier elections, and particularly the well remembered one of 1888, in which the Republicans had gained their victory, as it seemed, by calling the Democrats "free traders" and the friends of England, intent upon oversetting prosperity and sinking our manufacturing population to the level in wages and standards of living of the "pauper labor" of Europe.

This kind of campaigning had served its use once and might do so again. But there was a difference now in that the Republicans were on the defensive. They had attacked the Mills bill in 1888 until the welkin rang with their denunciations. In 1892 the Democrats were in a like advantageous situation— the target for their shafts was the McKinley bill which, unlike the Mills bill, had become a law; under it business was operating. The Republicans were the aggressors in 1888; the Democrats would lead the charge in 1892. The Harrison administration was an open book. The Republicans must stand or fall upon the record which they had made in the "Billion Dollar Congress." In their own behalf they pointed to "McKinley prosperity." They drew attention to fields of beet sugar, tin plate works and other industries which had been singled out for protective treatment and which were creating new employment. The hum of the spindles and looms of textile mills in many centres were said to be proof of "good times." The idleness of manufactories in England which had formerly supplied the American market and the grumbling of their owners and employees induced by "McKinleyism" were cited as sure omens of the practical merits of the Republican tariff.

[1] Cf. N. Y. Nation, Nov. 3, 1892.

A discovery had been made. In 1888 the Republican leaders in facing the Democrats, who declared that a high tariff would make living dear, had bravely attacked the whole idea of cheapness. Harrison had said four years ago that "cheaper coats necessarily," as it seemed to him, involved "a cheaper man and woman under the coats." Now, in 1892, among the arguments which he marshalled in defence of the McKinley law was "a reduction," which he asserted had taken place, in "the cost of articles of common necessity."

McKinley in 1890 had said that he had never liked the word "cheap." "Cheap and nasty" went together. The "whole system of cheap things" was a "badge of poverty; for cheap merchandise," he continued, "means cheap men, and cheap men mean a cheap country," etc. Now, in 1892, he declared that the "necessities of life" were cheaper than they had been eighteen months since, and he would be credited with having brought such a blessing to the country. While this beneficent movement had been in progress, both Harrison and McKinley averred that wages had risen.[1]

Tables to prove that the pay of industrial workers had advanced while the cost of living had declined, that more men were at work, that blessings of all kinds, indeed, had descended upon the country since McKinley's bill had been made into a law filled the newspapers, were sent out over all the country in pamphlet and hand bill by the campaign committees and were recited by the stump orators. The active and cohesive coterie of men in Philadelphia, largely engaged in the iron and steel and the textile industries, who interested themselves in high tariffs, were ready to argue, write and hire speakers and writers, as in previous campaigns. The Industrial League and the American Iron and Steel Association in Philadelphia, and the American Protective Tariff League in New York again issued their tariff tracts. Translations were made, particularly in the Scandinavian tongues, for the farmers in the northwest.[2]

[1] N. Y. Nation, Oct. 27 and Dec. 15, 1892.
[2] Cf. Sherman Papers and E. G. Hay Papers; also vol. iv of this work, pp. 143–4.

The unhappy farmers who were wont to complain that they were paying higher prices for the products of the protected industries of the East, and the old tariff reform element within the party generally, were referred to the reciprocal trade arrangements which had been effected with foreign countries. Manufacturers interested in the export trade, whose output was too large for the domestic market and whose processes were so highly perfected that they had no fear of the competition of the world, were similarly asked to look with grateful eyes upon reciprocity. The system by which duties were clapped upon sugar, hides, coffee and a few other articles, when other countries, especially those in the southern parts of the American hemisphere, would not open their ports to our commerce was the wheatsheaf on the top of the protectionist rick. The construction which had been in progress for many years was complete and the veriest wayfarer could see that it now answered every national need.

Nevertheless the old zest was not in anything. Rallies, torchlight parades, speaking by the spellbinders in hamlets and towns, the pen of the journalist did not betoken that heartiness, assurance and vim which had characterized the same activities in 1888 and in 1884. It were necessary to go no farther than the New York Tribune, the leader among Republican newspapers, for an illustration of the change which had come over the party mind. Its owner was his party's candidate for Vice-President, and he must choose his ways more carefully. There was in his newspaper less of that exuberant anti-British jingoism and immoderate enmity to Democrats, Mugwumps and all those who differed with it in politics which had distinguished it in earlier years.[1]

The Democrats, on their side, had facts which they brought forward to confound the Republican tabulators as to wages, prices and employment. It is easy to tell a man that he is prosperous, but, even if he be so, he may be convinced, without difficulty, that he is not so highly favored as he would like to be. It is feasible to mention for his pleased hearing

Cf. N. Y. Nation, Nov. 3, 1892.

courses which, if taken, would lead to his greater advantage. The New York Tribune spoke of the "unparalleled prosperity" of the country.[1] The farmers who had been drawn into a great alliance refused to believe that their welfare had been promoted by the McKinley law. Their views were recorded in no uncertain way in the platform of the People's party. The heads of various labor unions were not a unit in thinking that the Republican tariff had made all things right for the working man. They told the members of their associations that the common lot was no better than, if so good as, it had been; and they were speaking with more authority than the employers who had been wont, in Presidential campaigns, to instruct the men on their pay rolls how to vote if the mills were to remain open and wage earners were not to be thrown out of work. The labor leaders could point to facts in confirmation of their view and made it clear to large bodies of voting citizens that the "golden age" was not at hand. All the country knew, in the summer of 1892, of the stubborn strikes which, in general, were based on the idea that wages were too low, however smaller they might become under tariffs recommended by the Democrats. The chief of these occurred in iron mills at Homestead near Pittsburgh.

Henry C. Frick, with whom Andrew Carnegie had associated himself in the coke business, was admitted to partnership in the Carnegie firm and was soon invited to occupy a managerial position. He was made "chairman" of the Carnegie Steel Company, as the firm was called after July 1, 1892,[2] and exercised absolute directing powers. The profits under his management were greatly increased.[3] The company employed about 13,000 men, 3800 of whom were in the mills at Homestead on the banks of the Monongahela, which a few years since had been acquired from unsuccessful owners. Here, as elsewhere generally at the moment, supply exceeded demand.

[1] N. Y. Tribune, Nov. 11, 1892.

[2] Though called a company it remained a partnership.—House Ex. Doc., 52nd Cong. 1st sess., no. 335, p. 2; House Reports, 52nd Cong 2nd sess., no. 2447, p. 11.

[3] George Harvey, Henry C. Frick, pp. 93–4; B. J. Hendrick, Andrew Carnegie, vol. i, p. 378.

Prices were lower. Business was less profitable and the company—Frick in full understanding with Carnegie—resolved upon wage adjustments which affected, however, not more than 325 employees. These were skilled artisans; the others had but a sympathetic interest in the result.[1] The Amalgamated Association of Iron and Steel Workers, the union which had organized the men in this industry and had assumed authority to deal with the owners of manufactories as to the conditions under, and the prices at, which its members might work, would assert its power.[2] The "scale," a kind of treaty agreed upon and signed from time to time by the representatives of the men and their employers, would expire on July 1, 1892. When it should be renewed the association would demand wages even higher than those which were then being paid.[3] Mr. Frick, speaking for the company, declined such a suggestion and denied the right of a union to fix rates which it would be unprofitable to pay. He would hire and dismiss as he liked and go forward, under necessity, with new employees,[4] which led to a lockout. The men organized themselves on a "military basis," and guards to protect the property, even members of the firm, were denied access to the works [5] which were picketed for miles around, and the battle was on.

Many of the strikers, like the coke workers, were "foreigners." They hung an effigy of Frick in token of the contempt they entertained for him and the situation became so ominous that the company called upon the private Pinkerton agency [6] for a body of men to assist the sheriff of the county in protecting its property. This act was the signal for bloody strife. The "Pinkertons," who were engaged to act as "watchmen" or "guards," were assembled in New York and Chicago. They

[1] House Mis. Doc., 52nd Cong. 1st sess., no. 335, pp. 19–22, 163, 169, 175; House Reports, 52nd Cong. 2nd sess., no. 2447, pp. v, x; J. H. Bridge, Inside Hist. of Carnegie Steel Co., p. 209.
[2] Cf. Hendrick, Andrew Carnegie, vol. i, p. 384.
[3] House Mis. Doc., 52nd Cong. 1st sess., no. 335, p. 22.
[4] Ibid., p. 30.
[5] Cf. Cong. Record, 52nd Cong. 1st sess., p. 5899.
[6] For facts regarding this agency see House Mis. Doc., 52nd Cong. 1st sess., no. 335, pp. 189–92.

were conveyed to a point on the Ohio River where they were transferred to barges, upon which they were to live while in the service of the company, and were towed by a steamboat up the Monongahela to the works at Homestead. They were soon conscious that they would receive no pleasant welcome. A mob of infuriated people—men, women and children—were seen on the river bank when the barges drew near the mills. Whistles were blown and pistols were fired, at which sound the crowd increased. Abusive names were shouted at the men on the boats who were armed. Clinkers and pieces of iron were hurled at them and revolvers and rifles began a fusillade to which they replied in self defense. As the riot proceeded the strikers brought up one or more pieces of artillery. Oil was poured into the river in the hope that the "Pinkertons" could be burned alive. Some were killed or mortally wounded, and many suffered painful minor injuries before they were allowed to surrender. When they came ashore the mob set fire to, and destroyed, the barges. Though a truce had been declared foreign amazons and boys in the mob, whom the strikers themselves could not control, set upon the unfortunate men, and, before they could be escorted to a place of safety, they were compelled to suffer further brutal maltreatment.[1] The sturdy governor of Pennsylvania, Robert E. Pattison, was appealed to, as in the previous year, when trouble had occurred in the coke region, and the entire force of militia came to the scene at a cost to the state of more than $400,000. He himself visited Homestead to convince the strikers of his earnest purpose to keep the troops under arms until order should be restored.[2] Frick, while sitting in his office, was shot and stabbed by a Russian anarchist attracted to the scene from New York.

During these disturbances Carnegie himself was out of reach, enjoying his summer vacation in Scotland. He mixed with avidity for profit from his business enterprises, which was

[1] J. H. Bridge, Inside Hist. of Carnegie Steel Co., chap. xiv; House Reports, 52nd Cong. 2nd sess., no. 2447, p. ix.
[2] N. Y. Times, July 22, 1892; N. Y. Nation, July 14, 21, 28 and Aug. 11, 1892.

legend, a voluble interest in social reform of his own definition.
In book, magazine, letter and speech he had made himself a
public character. His advice to others was free; the theories
which he expounded, emanating from a man whose success
in the accumulation of wealth had been stupendous, came to
be widely known. Frick's want of sympathy for "labor,"
the friends of "labor" said, was unconcealed. His inflexible
temper had increased the disorder.[1] Although Carnegie outwardly seemed, during the struggle, to be supporting Frick,
he found occasion privately at the time, and openly afterward,
to say that if he had been on the ground, and had been in
control of the situation, more wisdom would have been displayed. He would not have brought in the "Pinkertons."
He would have closed his mills. But Carnegie, his critics
said, and they based their judgments on experience with him
in business, was in some degree a weathercock. What he
would do as an employer of labor had not been in the past,
and might not have been in this case, in conformity with the
philosophic aphorisms which fell from him as a literary man.[2]
In any case the arrest of strikers for assault, murder, conspiracy and high treason, retaliatory suits by the labor unions
and an aftermath of rancor, not diminished by the fact that a
bitterly contested Presidential campaign was in progress,
caused the outbreak to be described as the gravest of the
kind in the history of the country.[3]

In Idaho, at the Coeur d'Alêne mines, a similar situation
was created by a union which would fix the wages to be paid
its members. Non-union men in April, 1892, were met by mobs.
An appeal to the courts for an injunction was granted. More
non-union men were brought from Duluth, but the railway
trains on which they rode were attacked. A mill was destroyed by giant powder. Many on both sides were killed
before the governor during the summer called out the militia,

---

[1] George Harvey, Henry C. Frick, p. 127.
[2] J. H. Bridge, Inside Hist. of the Carnegie Steel Co., pp. 184, 201–6,
230–5; Hendrick, op. cit., vol. i, pp. 400–4, 407–13; George Harvey, op. cit.,
pp.158–9.
[3] App. Ann. Cyclop. for 1892, p. 626.

a body, it appears, of less than 200 men.[1] The President, who had been appealed to, declared the country roundabout under martial law and assembled regular troops.[2]

In August a large iron manufacturing company in Tennessee became involved in a dispute with its workmen; and the militia were called out to protect property and life. The switchmen on railways in western New York struck and grave disorders, interfering with the transportation of goods, passengers and the United States mails, made imperative the use of troops in that quarter.[3] At one time, in the summer of 1892, the militia of four states were under arms [4] facing mobs of workmen who, whatever the justice of their position, gave proof by their course of scant satisfaction with social and political conditions. The newspapers were filled each day with descriptions of strife between employers and employed in all parts of the land. These employers were "tariff barons" and it augured ill for Mr. Harrison and the administration which, though its responsibilities might be small, would be held to account on election day.

The two parties had been nicely balanced in 1884 and 1888 —a small weight would have turned the scale. In Congress in 1892 all parties—Democratic, Republican and Populistic— put forth the most diligent efforts to strengthen their hold upon the favorable opinion of the strikers. Each would be the workingman's friend; each would express sympathy for him and pledge itself to interest in his greater happiness. The "Pinkertons" who had been called in at Homestead would cast but few votes. Plainly they were engaged in an unusual business. They had been hired to guard property which was in imminent risk of destruction because of the want of legally established agencies for its protection. William Jennings Bryan spoke in Congress of the force of guards which Mr. Frick had brought to the scene as "a private and irresponsible

---

[1] N. Y. Nation, July 21, 1892.
[2] App. Ann. Cyclop. for 1892, p. 339; Richardson, vol. ix, pp. 288–9, 290; Report of Sec. of War for 1892, pp. 106–12.
[3] N. Y. Nation, Aug. 25 and Sep. 1, 1892.
[4] Ibid., Aug. 25, 1892.

soldiery"; their existence was an acknowledgement, he said, that government was a failure.[1] Jerry Simpson used still plainer speech; they were, he said, "a bloody band of assassins, organized for the protection of capitalists."[2] Peffer in stodgy oratory drew a distinction between "the owner of the works and the men who have builded the works,"[3] with a view to giving the Poles, Huns and other laborers, who had been hired by Carnegie and Frick, title to equal or superior consideration in any judgment of the merits of the controversy. Republican and Democratic leaders rushed to the discussion, Republicans to show that the strike had no bearing upon a protective tariff, Democrats to lay the blame at Harrison's and McKinley's door. Both were in a state of fright and together cried for an investigation that would bring the Pinkerton brothers, Frick and many other men, including the labor leaders, before Congressional committees for testimony which, it was surmised, might embarrass the opposite party.[4] Nothing came of the excitement but a meaningless resolution of Congress to employ no Pinkerton or other private detectives in the Federal government service, which was adopted and laid as an offering on the altar of the laboring man.[5]

Such maneuvers promising little, the managers of the Democratic House and the Republican Senate agreed to adjourn on August 5th instead of prolonging useless bickering and demagogic utterance into October, the policy which had been followed in 1888 and 1890. The cruel Geary Chinese exclusion bill had been approved on May 5th. The free silver bill had been passed by the Republican Senate on July 1st,[6] and de-

[1] Cong. Record, 52nd Cong. 1st sess., p. 4225.
[2] Ibid.   [3] Ibid., p. 5898.

[4] Majority and minority reports of the House committee in House Reports, 52nd Cong. 2nd sess., no. 2447; App. Ann. Cyclop. for 1892, pp. 208–11.

[5] McPherson's Handbook for 1892, p. 253.

[6] Hill was now ready to vote—he was for free coinage; so was Cameron of Pennsylvania, as before. (Cong. Record, 52nd Cong. 1st sess., p. 5719.) "I got Quay to put Cameron right, but, Quay being absent as usual, Cameron came out wrong as usual. How Hill, Cameron and Blodgett will adjust their differences with their constituents is a problem, as they voted for the worst bill the genius of Morgan could suggest."—Morrill to Edmunds, July 5, 1892, in Morrill Papers.

feated in the Democratic House on July 5th. The various bills to amend the tariff piecemeal were adopted by the House and sent to the Senate, not to be heard of again.

Proclamations of the President from time to time announced additions to the list of countries with which arrangements had been made for reciprocal trade under section 3 of the McKinley law. Canada was informed on August 18th, in accordance with Congressional action in July, that, in retaliation for discriminations against the United States in the use of the Welland Canal, we should, after September 1st, follow a like policy with reference to Canadian commerce on our St. Mary's Falls canal.

As the cooler days of autumn approached and the campaign called for an intensification of effort the Republican managers redoubled the energy of their defense. Blaine had said a few words in endorsement of the ticket soon after the adjournment of the nominating convention [1] and his following gave pledges of their loyalty to the party. Whitelaw Reid's name as the candidate for Vice-President met with little response. No journalist who was solely and preeminently a journalist, so far as could be remembered, except Greeley, another editor of the New York Tribune, had ever been nominated by a major political party for the Presidency or Vice-Presidency. The very volume of his utterance and the variety of it, printed and accessible for use against him, made a newspaper writer a weak candidate for elective office. Reid took the field which, in September and October, was crowded with orators. McKinley who was sought after by campaign committees in all parts of the country, John Sherman, Chauncey M. Depew, Foraker, Frye, Hale, Aldrich, Galusha A. Grow, Reed, Dingley, Julius Burrows, Roswell G. Horr, Sereno Payne, Warner Miller, Henry Cabot Lodge, John Dalzell, and all the men of light and leading in the party were enlisted in the work of addressing the people and asking them for their votes as a reward for deeds well done. The members of the cabinet appeared upon the stump in praise of their chief.

[1] N. Y. Tribune, June 11, 1892.

Harrison's letter accepting renomination was made public on September 6th. It came in "the first period of relief from public duties." By some inadvertence, it would seem, but plainly in answer to the prejudices expressed by the Populists of the West to a national banking system, a plank had been inserted in the Democratic platform demanding a repeal of the tax on state bank issues. The Republicans had discovered this declaration and, seeing in it an opportunity to charge their opponents with a wish to return to the unsecured and unregulated paper currency with which the country had been familiar, to its sorrow, prior to the Civil War, spoke in deprecation of the old "red dog" and "wild cat" bills and reproduced them in *fac simile* for use in the campaign with the rate of discount on each, together with samples of Thompson's Counterfeit Detector.[1] Harrison denounced this proposal which he found in the Democratic platform. He pointed with pride to a reviving mercantile marine, due to postal subsidies, and the policy of reciprocity which had increased foreign trade; accused those who opposed his election of a design to ruin American industry by a system of free trade, a subject which was discussed at length; defended the "Force Bill" as the means of securing honest elections in the South; congratulated himself and his party upon their contributions to civil service reform; advocated the construction of the Nicaragua ship canal; paid a tribute to the veterans of the Civil War; asked the farmer to consider what had been done for his good by the Department of Agriculture and, while demanding a money of one standard, and dollars which shall always be of equal value, gave his "cordial adherence and support" to the movement for free silver coinage and expressed his hope for a happy outcome of the new international conference in the work of finding a ratio of value for bimetallism. In conclusion he said that the Democratic party's program was one of "demolition" and the destruction was to be sudden—established institutions were not to be taken down gradually but "blown up." The policy of the Republicans on the other hand was

[1] N. Y. Nation, Oct. 27 and Nov. 17, 1892.

"a policy of safe progression and development of new factories, new markets and new ships." [1]

Harrison's letter which was inspired, the New York Tribune said, by "broad and lofty patriotism," [2] was followed by a letter from Blaine addressed to the chairman of. the Republican state committee in Maine. He said that there were three issues and he stated them:

(1) Protection, which the Democrats pronounced a "fraud" and anathematized generally. They had put a tariff plank in their platform which recalled Calhoun, South Carolina and the nullification scheme of 1833.

(2) Reciprocity which the Democrats had endorsed so long as the Republicans refused to accept it. They now would discredit it because "they did not originate it."

(3) The scheme which the Democrats advanced to break down the national currency and to put old state bank notes in circulation in its stead, the effect of which would be "to cheat the poor man out of his daily bread." [3]

More was not heard of Blaine until October 14th. The state of his health was sufficient excuse for his remaining in seclusion. His friends knew the force of his infirmities, though many to whom his name was dear importuned him to come hither and go thither to defend the citadels of Republicanism.

Our minister to England, Robert T. Lincoln, had come home to speak of the services which he and the party had rendered the country by arranging a conference of nations so that gold and silver might serve as money side by side. [4] But more was expected of Patrick Egan, the redoubtable Irishman who had been so wildly praised or blamed, according to the sympathies of those who judged him, for his conduct as our representative in Chile during the civil war in that country. He had returned opportunely to inject his figure into the canvass in New York. The "Blaine Irish" must not wander afield to join the greater body of their countrymen who were firmly attached to Tam-

[1] N. Y. Tribune, Sep. 6, 1892.
[2] Ibid.
[3] Ibid., Sep. 7, 1892; cf. N. Y. Nation, Sep. 15, 1892.
[4] N. Y. Tribune, Oct. 17, 1892.

many and the Democracy. Burchard with his "Rum, Roman-
ism and Rebellion" had nullified nearly all that had been done
to cement Irishmen to the Republican party in 1884. The
letter of Sackville-West was used to the fullest extent to keep
such Irishmen as were Republicans within the party fold
in 1888. Now, Egan, and the criticism which had been directed
against him, on the sole ground, as the Republican politicians
would have it appear, of his nativity and his anti-English
activities, would stir the souls of his countrymen and renew
their faith. "Ophir Farm" near White Plains, had been the
palatial home of Ben Holliday of the Overland Line of trans-
continental stage coaches. It had come into the hands of
John Roach from whom Whitelaw Reid acquired it. Partially
burnt, it had been rebuilt and enlarged. Mr. Reid dwelt
there in summer.[1] The campaign neared its end and a small
dinner in this house in Blaine's honor, attended by Chauncey
Depew, Egan, Garrett A. Hobart, later a Vice-President of
the United States, and eight or ten others, preceded the making
of speeches on the lawn. The torches of campaign marching
clubs lighted the scene. Blaine appeared on the piazza. A
lamp was held up at each side of his face so that he might
be seen. He received a stirring welcome. It was important
for the country to know that he was not sulking and that he
still wished the party well. He now named President Harrison
whose administration, he said, had improved the business of
the country. He doubted if, since the government of the
United States had been instituted, "prosperity" had been
spread so widely "throughout the whole domain of trade."
But he had come to speak about the "Irish vote." He could
not believe that the Irish in America would put themselves
"deliberately" on the side of "their former oppressors." They
should "defy all the machinations of the Democratic party
for free trade." They should be Republicans, throw their
influence "on the side of the home market of America against
the tide of the foreign markets of England." His "good friend"
Egan was present, "the brilliant and successful minister to

[1] Cortissoz, Life of Reid, vol. ii, p. 105.

Chile," and Blaine would rely on him "to intercede with his countrymen" not to aid the Democratic party by their votes "in lowering the standard and the wages of American labor."

Egan made a brief defence of his administration of the office which he had held in South America and the crowd called for Depew who, because of his talent in the use of jest and anecdote, had become one of the most popular speakers on the Republican stump. England had wanted Egan to be recalled; "the most distinguished of Secretaries of State" told the world, said Mr. Depew, that the United States selected her own diplomatic representatives "without consulting her enemies." "The whole Irish nation," Depew continued, was at "Ophir" in the person of Patrick Egan. He was named with, and stood by the side of, "a personality instinct with the best aspirations of his countrymen," one who "commanded, more of the attention and affection of his fellow citizens than any other American who ever lived, James G. Blaine." [1]

Now, said the Philadelphia Press, it was plain to the world that Blaine's "head and heart" were in the campaign, as they had been in every Republican campaign for 36 years; it was "a stirring war cry," said the New York Tribune. It was as true as ever that

> "One blast upon his bugle horn
> Is worth a thousand men." [2]

Meanwhile the other party was closing its lines in the effort to present a solid front against the Republicans. The task which lay before Cleveland's friends was formidable and much of the tact and energy necessary to gain the end in view were contributed by William C. Whitney, who tirelessly drew upon his powers to effect an organization which would command success. Cleveland had warmly acknowledged the value of Whitney's "generalship" at the convention. [3]

Having won the nomination Whitney's attitude was propitiatory. He would do much and go far to elect the candidate. No attempt had been made to seat the delegates of the Syracuse

[1] N. Y. Tribune, Oct. 15, 1892.   [2] Ibid., Oct. 17, 1892.
[3] N. Y. Times, June 24, 1892.

convention. The "Snap Convention" delegates had been allowed to occupy their seats. Elements antagonistic to Cleveland outside of the New York delegation were, in a number of cases, attached to his cause by his resourceful friends. It is true that Hill himself, who had remained in Washington while the national convention was in session; Murphy, a rich brewer in Troy; Sheehan, Bourke Cockran, Croker and the other leaders who controlled the machine in New York, were sullen and rebellious. They continued to say that they could not carry the state for the nominee, but the wiser of them, who were bred to "regularity," made public declarations indicating that they accepted the result, and would do whatever lay in their power to elect the ticket.[1]

Tammany and the "Snappers" had brought forward Watterson with his "tariff for revenue only" plank and it had been adopted by the convention in the place of one more clearly expressive of the interest of the party in "tariff reform." This, it was not to be forgotten, had been done for a reason. It was their wish, in the state of mind in which they then were, to give a disliked candidate the task of defending "free trade," a policy which the Republicans took delight in identifying with Mr. Cleveland's former administration and which, they averred, had been the issue on which he had been overthrown in 1888.[2] Surely blame for the nomination of the Vice-Presidential candidate could be laid at the door of the New York delegation. They were the ringleaders in the scheme to set aside Gray of Indiana, whose way had seemed to be clear, in favor of Adlai E. Stevenson. Stevenson came from a state habitually Republican rather than from a doubtful state, which Indiana was preeminently. He had been a Greenbacker and was fairly suspected of leanings toward free silver,—out of accord, therefore, with the head of the ticket on the money question.[3] He had been Assistant Postmaster General in the Cleveland administration. Like Clarkson, more recently in

---

[1] N. Y. Times and N. Y. Tribune, June 24 and 25, 1892.

[2] Cf. N. Y. Times, June 23, 1892; E. Stanwood, Am. Tariff Controversies. vol. ii, pp. 313-6.

[3] E. M. Shepard to Cleveland, Nov. 10, 1892, in Cleveland Papers.

the Harrison administration, he had been the "axeman" who removed the heads of the postmasters. Cleveland and his friends, the Mugwumps, were civil service reformers. Stevenson was openly recommended to the convention because he had proven himself a believer in the old doctrine that "to the victor belongs the spoils"; if he were elected, it was said on the floor of the convention, neither Mugwump nor Republican would enjoy favor at his hands.[1]

On the other hand the declaration in the platform on the currency question, if surprisingly at variance with the views which were entertained by a large body of voters of the party, was one, especially in its denunciation of the Sherman silver purchase law of 1890 and its insistence upon the maintenance of "equal power" in every dollar, whether of coin or paper, which Mr. Cleveland could whole-heartedly approve.

He had received neither congratulations nor proffers of help, he said, from "any state official in New York," or from the "Hill following."[2] They controlled the party machinery in the state, as they had so boastfully and repeatedly declared, and, though they now somewhat veiled their enmity, it was impossible for him to regard them with anything but suspicion and mistrust.

He would allow them to "dwell a while with their alleged reasons and consciences."[3] But an occasion for a statement soon presented itself. Tammany would celebrate the 4th of July. William J. Bryan had been chosen to be the orator of the day and there was much curiosity to see and hear the eloquent representative in Congress from Nebraska. Interest in his discourse, however, was secondary to a message from the regularly nominated candidate of the party for the Presidential office. It came in the form of a letter addressed to "Grand Sachem" Thomas F. Gilroy, which was read to the assembly.

---

[1] N. Y. Tribune, June 24, 1892. "We like Stevenson in New York," said Croker in Chicago, after he had been nominated. He was a "good Democrat" when he was in office; "he believed in turning the Republicans out."—Ibid., June 25, 1892; cf. Cortissoz, Life of Reid, vol. ii, p. 181.

[2] Cleveland to Bissell, June 30, 1892, in Cleveland Papers.

[3] To Bissell in McElroy, Grover Cleveland, vol. i, p. 344.

Mr. Cleveland's allusions to politics were veiled, but, in speaking of the Declaration of Independence, he ventured to express the confident belief that the Tammany Society would not lose the opportunity, on so auspicious an occasion, to draw attention to the fact that the patriotism which the Declaration inspired, enjoined "unselfish care for our country's welfare." "Political endeavor" was "only safe and useful," he observed, "when undertaken in the people's interest"; "political organization" could be "effective and successful" only when it was "approved and trusted by an intelligent popular judgment." It was "a queer kind of letter," Cleveland had told his friend Bissell; he would watch and see how it might be received. Apparently it was liked. The candidate's name evoked applause and cheers. Pledges were made then and there of loyalty to the ticket.[1]

While the Democrats were in convention in Chicago, McKinley and other officers of the Minneapolis convention had visited President Harrison at the White House to notify him of his renomination. Cleveland would be formally apprised of his selection as his party's candidate at a large ratification meeting in Madison Square Garden in New York on July 20th. He had gone to "Gray Gables," the house which he had recently purchased at Buzzards Bay. He and Mrs. Cleveland, with a daughter born since his retirement from the Presidency, found friendly contacts on this part of Cape Cod.[2] He came down to New York for the occasion and made a speech which breathed a spirit of honesty in political life and the need of high standards in government service. He had memorized it, as was his wont, and declaimed it with literal exactitude, with the gravity which characterized all of his utterances on public questions. The faces of at least 15,000 persons were before him. Many of those in the audience were, as he well knew, unfriendly and their words, if fair spoken, belied their feelings. But he was cool and imperturbable.

Congressman Wilson, the presiding officer of the Chicago

[1] N. Y. Times, July 5, 1892.
[2] Cf. R. W. Gilder, Grover Cleveland, pp. 53–4.

convention, brought "the message from the Democratic party," and put into Mr. Cleveland's hands the "commission," of which the chairman and those for whom he spoke were the "bearers." Mr. Cleveland, in his response, made some references to the "Force Bill" and "the saturnalia of theft and brutal control" which had followed an earlier attempt at "Federal regulation of state suffrage." But he addressed himself particularly to the tariff which he would make the issue of the campaign. No system, he said at one point, could be tolerated which had for "its object and purpose a forced contribution from the earnings and incomes of the mass of our citizens to swell directly the accumulations of a favored few." The Democracy was not a "destructive party." "We are," Mr. Cleveland said again, "not at enmity with the rights of any of our citizens. All are our countrymen." But consumers were to be relieved of a tariff system which "unjustly and relentlessly" demanded from them in "the purchase of the necessaries and comforts of life an amount scarcely met by the wages of hard and steady toil." [1] Outbursts of cheering greeted some of Mr. Cleveland's periods. "No Roman conqueror," a fulsome writer said, had ever had "a more notable triumph," yet there was no sense of pride or exultation in his face, only humility which was near to sadness, a sense of consecration for great impending duties and responsibilities.[2]

Outwardly all was well. Muttering was drowned in the cries of "Four, four, four years more of Grover." Then they would be "in clover," a glad prophecy of new raids upon the President for salaried offices. Tammany sachems took Mr. Cleveland's hand. Hill's "Snappers" sat beside "Anti-Snappers," Whitney, all the while, aiming to serve as the mediator who would bring about friendly understanding, though no one knew better than he how great were the obstacles which lay in his way. It was plain that the campaign should be conducted by men who were sincerely interested in the success

---

[1] N. Y. Times, July 21, 1892.
[2] Philadelphia Public Ledger, quoted in McElroy, Grover Cleveland, vol. i, pp. 345–6.

of the ticket. The Democratic National Committee must be reorganized. Calvin S. Brice had been its chairman, but he had used all his devices to prevent the ex-President's nomination and he would stand aside. Gorman who had directed the campaign in 1884 might return to the post. He had been late in coming under Cleveland's banners. He eliminated himself, as in 1888, and the responsibility was entrusted to William F. Harrity of Philadelphia who had been postmaster in that city, while Cleveland had been President in 1885–89, a member of the group of younger Democrats who had come forward in Pennsylvania under the leadership of Governor Pattison. Don M. Dickinson of Michigan, Postmaster General in the Cleveland cabinet, was made chairman of the campaign committee, a fact which assured the nominee not only loyal service but also an intelligent and active prosecution of the canvass in the northwestern states. Mr. Whitney, although unnamed as an executive officer, would have, it was known, the leading part in the management of the campaign.

The national machinery had been brought into the hands of friends, but it was not so in New York state where, as appeared, Tammany, Hill, Murphy and Sheehan held power in their firm control and would not yield it up, as they might have done in answer to some realization of their unfitness to direct a campaign for the election of a candidate whose nomination they had opposed, and whom they should vote for only grudgingly, if, indeed, they should support him at all. No trust in them was felt or expressed on any side. Their history was well known. Their objects were so openly stated as not to be mistaken. The newspapers which were supporting Cleveland, the Democrats who had called and attended the Syracuse convention to protest against the tactics of Hill and his following did not delude themselves on any point concerning the situation. Mr. Cleveland, although he was apart, at Buzzards Bay, from the factional commotions, as far as he could be, knew full well what treasons were being prepared for him in the city, county and state of New York. He wrote his friend Bissell that, if the complexion of things

were not changed, they should wake up on the morning after
the election and find that they had been "fooled by as base
a set of cutthroats as ever scuttled a ship." Whitney, though
he was "as true as steel," was bending all his efforts toward
"pacification." He was putting himself in the position of
begging the "gang" to vote the Democratic ticket. They,
meantime, were giving him nothing but unmeaning words.[1]
Sheehan actually, in August, was appointed chairman of the
campaign committee in New York state, while Murphy retained his place as chairman of the general state committee.

It was, in truth, a grotesque situation and one that was
full of the most unhappy possibilities. Whitney was a determined character, as well as a shrewd one. He had not that detestation of compromise which Cleveland felt, and, when intent
upon an object, he would not rest until he had gained it. He
could make assurances, he observed, but they must be enforced
by words from the candidate, and there was no doubt in any
one's mind as to what these should be. The Federal offices
in New York state were to be the price of a plurality for
Cleveland and the price, as the Tammanyites believed, knowing
the importance of the state's electoral votes, of his reelection
to the Presidency. Whitney, in August, asked Cleveland to
write a letter to Murphy, even drafting such a paper [2] which
he put before the Democratic nominee. Cleveland described
the letter. The tone, he wrote Bissell, must be "abject and
humble." It was to be, in effect, "a prayer" for Murphy's
support. Some one must be "crazy," Cleveland continued,
as he communicated his inmost feelings to his friend, and, he
added, with the vehemence which he knew how to express
when his ire was aroused, that he would "see the whole out-
fit to the devil" before he would accede to such a request.[3]
Many of Cleveland's friends were in the same state of mind

[1] Cleveland to Bissell, July 24, 1892, in Cleveland Papers; also in Nevins,
Letters of Cleveland, pp. 295–6.

[2] A. Nevins, Letters of Cleveland, pp. 299–300; Whitney to Cleveland,
Aug. 9, 1892, in Cleveland Papers.

[3] Nevins, Letters to Cleveland, p. 302; McElroy, Grover Cleveland,
vol. i, p. 349.

and their admiration for him increased as he girded himself
for resistance to such importunity. "Even a good politician
sometimes forgets the excellent popular effect of letting a
candidate live up to his own principles," Richard Watson
Gilder wrote Mr. Cleveland. "They would take away from a
man, sometimes, the very thing that makes him available even
in their own eyes." [1]

But Whitney was indefatigable and stoutly pressed his point.
So did other politicians. "Don't break by refusing to bend,"
counselled A. K. McClure.[2] Chairman Harrity offered similar
advice. Murphy had the votes, his faction had the "organization and the power." [3] Cleveland again stated his complete
dismay at the "whole policy of truckling conciliation," which
had thus far characterized the management of the campaign.
He had not "a particle of confidence" in Sheehan. The Presidential ticket was to be neglected, he knew, and the machine
would employ all of its energies to elect the candidates on its
local tickets. "Tickling these men" was not to his mind.
Conciliation meant from him "a promise of exclusive favor and
influence."

Whitney persisted. He wrote what Cleveland described to
Bissell as "a very petulant and unpleasant letter," [4] saying that
unless Cleveland should "get into personal relations" with the
"gang" he would be defeated.[5] Making little progress by letter
writing Whitney went to Buzzards Bay, when he seemed to be,
Cleveland complained, on the point of "exploding." [6] Finally,
although Cleveland wrote no letter he consented—and reluctantly enough—to come, early in September, to New York to
discuss the situation.

When Judge Herrick of Albany met Mr. Cleveland at the

---

[1] Gilder to Cleveland, Sep. 2, 1892, in Cleveland Papers.

[2] McClure to Cleveland, Sep. 2, 1892, in ibid.

[3] Whitney to Cleveland, Aug. 22, 1892, in A. Nevins, Letters of Cleveland, p. 303.

[4] Cleveland to Bissell, Sep. 4, 1892, in Cleveland Papers; also in Nevins,
Letters of Cleveland, pp. 305–6.

[5] Whitney's letter was dated Aug. 30, 1892, in Nevins, Letters of Cleveland, p. 304.

[6] Cleveland to Bissell, Sep. 4, 1892, in Cleveland Papers.

Victoria Hotel, soon after his arrival, he was in such a state of
moral and mental excitement, Herrick complained, that further
progress seemed to be scarcely feasible. Cleveland would not
ignore the men in the party in New York state who were his
friends. If it were required that he should do so and that he
should give his confidence to his and their enemies he would
withdraw from the ticket, and they could find another candidate.
He spoke, indeed, of calling mass meetings in all the counties of
the state at which he would address the people and make it
known to them that their committees had refused to support
the party's regularly nominated candidate for the Presidency.
Herrick argued for the taking of a middle way. The "gang"
could be given appointments in the foreign service; they could
have places at Washington where, under the President's own
eyes, their influence might be reduced to a nullity. Whitney
and Dickinson came in and all of them together persuaded Mr.
Cleveland to meet Murphy, Croker and Sheehan at a dinner in
the hotel.

If the leaders attended this dinner in a belief that the candidate had been delivered into their hands, and that they could
now make their own terms they were to suffer grievous dis-
illusionment. After the meal they were asked what they
wanted of him, to be told plainly by Sheehan that it was a
pledge that they should be "properly recognized" in case he
should be President again. He struck the table with his fist and,
with a "damn" or two, said deliberately and impressively that he
would make no "secret promises"; he would not go to the White
House under obligations to the men seated around him or to any
one else. Sheehan made a sneering inquiry as to the candidate's
immediate intentions with reference to the campaign, and
Cleveland, rising to his feet, replied unhesitatingly, and with
great earnestness, that he would address a letter to the people
telling them what had just been said to him and withdrawing
from the ticket. He would see whether the party in the nation
as a whole wanted a candidate who was under a pledge, or one
who should be, if he were elected, a free agent, and he added,
turning to Sheehan, "In my opinion public indignation will snow

you and your organization out of sight before the end of a week."

Richard Croker, who was wiser than some of those around him, interposed. He said that he was in agreement with Mr. Cleveland. Promises could not be exacted of the candidate and it was not right to ask for them.[1] The group parted company and the candidate returned to Buzzards Bay a free man for the consolations of fishing, life with his family and the companionship of his friends—Joseph Jefferson the actor; Governor Russell of Massachusetts, a young lion in the path of wrong-doers in politics, who was running for the governorship of that state for the fifth time; Richard Watson Gilder, Commodore Benedict upon whose yacht in these waters Cleveland was a welcome guest; L. Clarke Davis, editor of the Public Ledger in Philadelphia, together with the casual visitors who came to confer with him about the conduct of the campaign.

Hill, it was said, was still frankly unfriendly. He would not see Whitney, who asked for a conference. He was "thoroughly mad," as much so at his lieutenants for treating with the candidate as on other accounts.[2] But he made a speech at a political meeting in Brooklyn on September 19th in which he advocated "a solid front to a common enemy," and at the end, after an hour and a half of involved rhetoric, pronounced the words, "our honored standard bearers, Cleveland and Stevenson.[3]

Accretions of strength were announced. Walter Q. Gresham who had been a member of Arthur's cabinet and had reached the Federal bench through the favor of that President, had been rendering opinions as a Circuit Court judge on the subject of railroads which met the approval of those who were at war with wealth and "social privilege." He had been proffered a nomination for President by a faction in the People's party. He might

---

[1] The account of this meeting, given in McElroy, Grover Cleveland, vol. i, pp. 350–5, has been followed. A less dramatic and, probably, a more correct version of the incidents may be constructed from materials in Mr. Nevins' Life of Cleveland, pp. 496–8. Cf. R. W. Gilder, Grover Cleveland, vol. i, pp. 350–4. See also Brooklyn Eagle, Nov. 16, 1892; N. Y. Tribune, Nov. 18 and 19, 1892; N. Y. Nation, Nov. 24, 1892.

[2] Whitney to Cleveland, Sep. 15, 1892, in Cleveland Papers.

[3] N. Y. Tribune, Sep. 20, 1892.

have accepted it if it had been a unanimous call.[1] As it was he would vote for Cleveland.[2] So would Wayne MacVeagh,[3] Judge Thomas M. Cooley[4] and Seth Low. MacVeagh addressed public meetings in behalf of Cleveland. A large majority of the professors at Harvard, Yale and other New England colleges, the New York Nation said, would vote for him.[5] In the main the Independents were as strongly as ever on Cleveland's side, a fact that their press and Schurz and other leaders of the faction reaffirmed from day to day.

The hopes of the Republicans for a successful issue of the canvass rested upon the "free trade" bugaboo, though they were met by the not entirely satisfactory fruits of the McKinley law. It was an even greater matter with the party which was endeavoring to stay in power to undermine the Mugwumps and detach the ·independent voter from Mr. Cleveland. Reid's newspaper, the New York Tribune, had made pretense of welcoming the Democratic nomination—to beat Cleveland would be a simple task. But it was a bravery not founded on honest belief. The entire campaign on the Republican side was a reflection of doubt as to Cleveland's power to hold the affection and confidence of that part of the voting population which had been awakened to interest in "reform." The overtures of Whitney to the New York machine, Cleveland's coming to New York to dine with the Hill and Tammany men, and every other sign of a surrender of the high principles which the candidate had so frequently professed were described and magnified by the Republican campaign managers and their newspapers, with a view to planting distrust in the minds of those whose party ties were lightly held and who might be persuaded to believe that they were being made the victims of a great deceit.[6] The hope of the Republicans was in a crumbling of the Mugwump defenses

[1] Solon J. Buck, The Agrarian Crusade, p. 145; F. E. Haynes, Third Party Movements, pp. 261–2.
[2] N. Y. Nation, Oct. 13, 1892; N. Y. Times, Oct. 3 and Nov. 2, 1892.
[3] N. Y. Times, Oct. 5, 1892; N. Y. Nation, Oct. 13 and 20, 1892.
[4] N. Y. Nation, Oct. 27, 1892.
[5] Ibid., Oct. 20 and 27, 1892.
[6] After this dinner the New York Tribune called Cleveland "the fallen idol of the Mugwumps."—Issue of Sep. 10, 1892; cf. ibid., Sep. 29, 1892.

and of disaffection within the Democratic organization in New York. The predictions of Hill, Murphy and Sheehan and of Croker, Bourke Cockran and the Tammany leaders for months before the convention met, and at the convention, that Cleveland could not carry the state were recalled at every opportunity.

Evidences of their disloyalty were discovered and advertised. That they would not march their leashed legions to the polls and vote for one whom they loved so little was stated and restated with the assurance which is attached to a mathematical formula. The people were not allowed to forget that the candidate had been made by his enemies to stand on a tariff plank which was not of his choice, and to appear before the country in the canvass with a man named for Vice-President who was a spoilsman and a defender of "rag money." Mr. Cleveland was "watched," he complained, "like a suspected criminal." [1]. His enemies spied upon his movements and misrepresented his speech.

Following the Republican press, with the New York Tribune at its head, the masses in that party were persuaded that Cleveland could not defeat Harrison in the state which was pivotal, and would decide the result. If uncertainty were expressed in regard to Republican states in the West the possibility of departure from established traditions would be scouted rather bravely, though it was plain enough that rebellion in that section was planted in many breasts. The party overturn in the Congressional elections of 1890 and the continuing activity of the Populists in the Western states were proof of a discontent which the old devices of the Republican campaign managers would not allay. A wish among the people to strike at the rich, who were for the most part entrenched in the Republican party, and who were the patrons and defenders of its policies, a motion which to be effective could be better made through the Democratic than through any small new organization, was clearly observed, and men who were intelligent and candid judges of political currents were in real doubt as to the

---

[1] Cleveland to Vilas, July 24, 1892, in Nevins, Letters of Cleveland, p. 294.

outcome of the campaign. Indeed, in view of the fact that little enthusiasm could be aroused in behalf of the Republican candidates, or the principal measures of the party, which they offered as reasons for their continuation in office—the McKinley law which the people were ready to believe was responsible for many of their ills and the "Force Bill" which had been advertised until it bore a truly horrific mien—the prospect was dark.

Cleveland's letter of acceptance was delayed until the end of September. It was a re-statement of his principles, rather involved in literary form, as his state papers were likely to be when he gave them too much conscientious care. He had spoken at Madison Square Garden in July of other "objects and aims" besides tariff reform and resistance to the "Force Bill," then in his mind, which must add "inspiration" to the Democratic "mission." He now alluded to some of these "objects and aims"—to the pension roll which should be "a roll of honor, uncontaminated by ill desert and unvitiated by demagogic use"; to "honest adherence to the letter and spirit of civil service reform"; to a "hospitable sentiment" regarding immigrants, but no reception of that class among them whose presence here would be "a menace to peace and order"; to "vexatious sumptuary laws"—"paternalism in government" found "no approval in the creed of Democracy"; to "sound and honest money" which should be "so regulated and guarded by governmental action that no one can be deluded as to the certainty and stability of its value." [1]

Mr. Cleveland made another visit to New York in the first days of October to address a meeting of Democratic clubs and to confer with those who were directing his campaign. When he returned to "Gray Gables" on Mr. Benedict's yacht it was to close his summer home and to remove his wife and daughter to a house which he had recently leased in New York. Now and again in the last weeks of the campaign he attended receptions and meetings, which he briefly addressed, of "business men," "Buffalonians" and Germans, with visits to Brooklyn and

[1] McPherson's Handbook for 1894, pp. 34–7.

Jersey City. With the Germans he appeared on the arm of Carl
Schurz. At one of these meetings he spoke of the campaign.
No other he thought had been waged "with such a lack of noise
and excitement and in such an atmosphere of popular thought-
fulness." [1] There was, in truth, to the end, less of the cannon
and drum, of the shout and halloo, of flag waving and torchlight
parading than in 1884 and 1888. Whether thinking had taken
the place of boisterous outburst or not it was certain that the
spontaneity and zeal which had characterized the campaigns of
those years were not at hand,[2] and no artificial stimulant could
be applied by the Republicans, while the Democrats, always in
possession of less money for such demonstrations, made even
poorer progress in this direction.

Some quiet was lent the event because of the protracted and
dangerous illness of the President's wife. Cleveland had been
invited to Chicago. He would not make a "political tour," he
said, and seem to be taking advantage of an opponent when that
opponent was prevented from participation in the campaign.[3]
Mrs. Harrison died in the White House on October 24th, just a
fortnight before the pollings, amid expressions of sympathy and
respect which knew no party lines.

Some "business men's" parades in New York on the eve of the
election were reminiscent of the past, but the issue was taken to
the country with dispassionate persons gaining much less of a
sense of the nation reeling down the way to Bedlam, as one
foreign observer described our Presidential contests, than they
might have been justified in feeling had they been witnesses of
Cleveland's earlier campaigns.

Meanwhile the People's party leaders went forward with their
canvass with a zeal which indicated an honest belief in the
reality of public wrongs. Their remedies were radical and
socialistic. While, to Cleveland, a good government was that
one which laid its hand upon the citizen as lightly as possible, the

---

[1] N. Y. Times, Nov. 2, 1892. Ex-President Hayes spoke of it as "the
most lethargic canvass ever known in a Presidential contest."—Diary and
Letters of Hayes, vol. v, p. 122.

[2] N. Y. Nation, Sep. 22, 1892.

[3] McElroy, Grover Cleveland, vol. i, p. 355.

new forces released in the West and South would give the state
enlarged and drastic powers. Laws were to be multiplied;
public agencies were to be created to increase the public welfare;
difficulties were to be put in the way of the rich. Weaver
carried his message to Republicans in the West and to Democrats in the South in the hope of breaking up the old parties.
The story from his lips was not new—it had been told in many
campaigns. Now and again he was accompanied on his electioneering tours by Mary Elizabeth Lease, the flaming virago of
Kansas, or by some other one of the newer leaders of the cause.
In the South the "Force Bill" too vividly recalled the past for
expectation of defections from the Democratic party. But in the
West, in Kansas and two or three silver mining states, where the
ferment had attacked the Republican party, there might very
likely be significant results.[1]

The night of November 8th found the ex-President in his new
home in New York with a group of his friends, and the telegraph
wires, before the night was done, made his election certain. The
pluralities in 1884 and 1888 had been small, now they were
decisive. Cleveland had carried New York by 45,000, New
Jersey by nearly 15,000, Indiana by 7,000, Connecticut by
5,000. He had won all of these states in 1884, and two of
them in 1888. But it appeared that he had a plurality of
27,000 in Illinois, 6,000 in Wisconsin and, when the official count
was completed, that he led Harrison in California. It was
believed for some days that he would carry Ohio. Harrison's
plurality in that state was only 1072. By fusion with the
Democrats, and other arrangements suggested by local conditions in Colorado, Idaho, Kansas, Nevada and North Dakota,
those western states were taken from the Republicans by
General Weaver, by small pluralities. So close a vote gave
confused results in the electoral colleges. In California eight
electors would vote for Cleveland and one for Harrison; in Ohio
22 for Harrison and one for Cleveland; in Oregon three for
Harrison and one for Weaver; in North Dakota one for Harrison, one for Cleveland and one for Weaver. A new district

[1] F. E. Haynes, Third Party Movements, pp. 264–8.

system of choosing Presidential electors in Michigan gave five of that state's votes to Cleveland and nine to Harrison.

In the phrase of the day it was a "landslide." Cleveland would have 277 votes, Harrison 145 and Weaver 22, a majority of 110. Harrison, therefore, might have had New York's 36, Indiana's 15 and New Jersey's 10 votes—Cleveland would still have been elected and without the constitutional recourse to the House of Representatives where, with a great Democratic majority, his fate would have been safe.[1] Cleveland's plurality in the popular vote was 379,025, which would have been larger except for the fact that in localities in the West a compact had been sealed with the Populists in order to keep certain states from the Republicans.[2] Weaver's popular vote was beyond a million; Bidwell, the Prohibitionist's, nearly 300,000.[3] The House would be Democratic by a plurality of more than 90 and the Senate, very probably, would be lost to the Republicans also.

The explanations during the days following the election were as many as the points of view of those who engaged in the exercise. To the New York Tribune it was "the greatest surprise in recent political history." The vote was an expression of the "prevailing popular temper" regarding the tariff.[4] It was a victory for "free trade" which would bring "industrial and commercial disasters, widespread and vast." [5]

McKinley himself found reason for the party's defeat in the tariff law which bore his name. But no cause that was just, he said, was ever lost. All who loved their country must prepare for the next fight.[6]

Western Republicans, such as "Jerry" Rusk of Wisconsin and Senator Cullom of Illinois, whose states had voted for Cleveland were certain that the cause of their party's misfortune was the tariff. They said nothing of impending "disasters," or of new "fights." They believed, with many other persons in that portion of the country, that the Republican party had been

[1] N. Y. Nation, Nov. 3, 1892.
[2] Ibid., Dec. 29, 1892; E. Stanwood, History of the Presidency, pp. 516–7.
[3] McPherson's Handbook for 1894, p. 272.
[4] N. Y. Tribune, Nov. 10, 1892.   [5] Ibid., Nov. 11, 1892.
[6] Ibid., Nov. 18, 1892.

commissioned to revise the tariff law and reduce duties, which, however, had been mistakenly increased.[1]

Teller of Colorado also put the responsibility at the door of the Eastern wing of the party, though he had a different reason for its overthrow. Labor had been outraged and it was vindictive. The workingman who wanted relief by larger issues of currency had voted for Cleveland in order to punish the Republicans for their betrayal of the silver cause.[2]

Weaver, speaking for the People's party, found that it had had a hand in the result. The masses to whose wants the major parties had been so inattentive were in revolt. The "financial kings" and the "plutocrats" were at last being put under the heel of the people.[3] Weaver said that his party now held the balance of power in three-fourths of the states. They could compel the adoption of "an American currency system." The Republican party was as dead as the Whig party after the Frémont campaign of 1856.[4]

Henry Watterson, who was believed to know more than most other men about a "tariff for revenue only," drew back a few steps as the day of test approached. The Democrats intended "simply," he said, "to reverse the movement of the engines" that were driving the country to "ruin"; the "war tariff" was to be reduced "to a peace footing." But they would proceed with the work, he said, "like statesmen, not like mountebanks and revolutionists." Indeed the process would be "so gradual" that the transition would be "a pleasure to everybody." [5]

Many, if they had given free expression to their thoughts would have held the candidates, at least in some degree, responsible for the result.[6] Harrison's highly respectable administration had not appealed to the imagination of his party. He had alienated the Republican politicians who were dexterous in managing campaigns and in rolling up majorities. These men had deserted him and had tried to nominate Blaine, though they must have known that their leader was so ill as to preclude

[1] N. Y. Tribune, Nov. 11, 1892.   [2] N. Y. Times, Nov. 15, 1892.
[3] Cf. F. E. Haynes, Third Party Movements, pp. 266-7.
[4] N. Y. Tribune, Nov. 14, 1892.   [5] Ibid., Nov. 12, 1892.
[6] Cf. Diary and Letters of R. B. Hayes, vol. v, p. 122.

his taking part in another canvass, proof of which would be furnished by his death on January 27, 1893, but ten days after the death of ex-President Rutherford B. Hayes.

The Republican politicians were in a position now to say that neglect of their valuable counsel had brought about the great defeat. Their predictions as to Harrison's weakness as a candidate had been corroborated.[1] The canvass had not been and it could not be given into the conduct of the skilful, because these old and supremely sage campaigners did not very much care whether Harrison were elected or not. For his coldness to them "punishment" had been meted out to him.[2] Quay had visited the party headquarters in New York near the end of the canvass to give advice to one of his lieutenants, a ward politician in Philadelphia, who had been brought to New York to deal with Tammany on its own levels; but it was a futile and a not very earnest effort in the direction which had had more successful result in 1888.[3] Carter of Montana who had directed the proceedings, exculpating himself and the President, disposed of the matter by the oracular announcement that the result could "only be attributed to a reaction against the progressive policies of the Republican party."[4]

The President himself, in a letter to Whitelaw Reid, his companion in defeat, no less humorously than freely, expressed his view of what had befallen them. "The workingman," said Mr. Harrison, "declined to walk under the protective umbrella because it sheltered his employer also." He had "smashed it for the fun of seeing the silk stockings take the rain."[5]

To Mr. Cleveland the election was a solemn occasion. He had been oppressed by a sense of his small abilities in the face of great duties as he sat in his home on the night of November 7th awaiting the telegraphic reports of the counting of the votes in all parts of the republic.[6] At a dinner tendered him by Henry

---

[1] N. Y. Times, Nov. 19, 1892.   [2] Autobiography of Platt, p. 252.
[3] Cf. N. Y. Times, Sep. 23 and 28, 1892.
[4] N. Y. Tribune, Nov. 11, 1892.
[5] Cortissoz, Life of Whitelaw Reid, vol. 1, p. 188.
[6] McElroy, Grover Cleveland, vol. i, p. 356; R. W. Gilder, Grover Cleveland, pp. 105–6.

Villard, with Whitney, Schurz and honest political friends around him, on November 18th, he said that "every feeling of jubilation" within him was "so tempered as to be almost entirely obscured by a realization, nearly painful, of the responsibility" which he had "assumed in the sight of the American people." If nothing were seen in the victory but "a license to revel in partisan spoils" they should fail at every point. If they were to use the opportunity, Mr. Cleveland continued, merely as "a cover for seeking partisan advantage" they should "invite contempt and disgrace." [1] Such a man his friends knew that he had been, and they were now assured that he had undergone no change of character. Even the New York Tribune was willing, after the election, to speak of him as "a man of resolution" and of a "nature earnest and strong," [2] an appraisal not easily reconcilable with its frequent allusions to the "Victoria Hotel bargain," on the occasion when, in August, at the importunity of Whitney, he had sat down at dinner with Murphy, Sheehan, Croker and the "Snappers." A corrupt deal had been made, said the Tribune. Tammany and the Hill gang, after this dinner, had come to the support of a candidate whom they had declared that they would not support. Proof of the bargain, it was said by the Republicans, would soon appear.

But in only a few weeks evidence of an exactly opposite kind would be at hand. Hill had been elected to succeed Evarts as a United States senator from New York. The term of the other Republican senator, Frank Hiscock, was about to expire. His place would be filled by the legislature, which had just been elected and which would meet at Albany in January. The names of Schurz, Whitney and men, who could creditably represent in the Senate a rich, intelligent and populous state and who could be relied upon to support the new President, were suggested. They would be fit incumbents of the post. Another purpose was in view. The New York Democratic state machine was instantly greased and put in motion with the object of electing Edward Murphy, Jr., the brewer from Troy. [3] If there

[1] N. Y. Tribune, Nov. 19, 1892. [2] Ibid., Nov. 10, 1892.
[3] N. Y. Times, Nov. 21, 1892; N. Y. Nation, Nov. 24, 1892.

were more reason for choosing this man for a place in the United States Senate than Hill the fact was apparent to no intelligent observer.[1] Both were the embodiment and definition of the "peanut politician." They were wire-pullers in small towns who had been promoted in that business until their influence reached out over the state. Office to them was opportunity for private gain; party was an organization of office holders for deluding and mulcting honest citizens. They had been compelled to support Cleveland in the election, in view of the overwhelming evidences of his great personal popularity, after exhausting their power to nominate another in his place, though proof was at hand of a vindictive cutting of the ticket by Hill and his immediate following in some parts of the state where their sway was absolute.[2] Now this faction would openly exhibit their power. Cleveland might be President of the United States; they were the cocks of the lane in New York. Efforts on Cleveland's side to dissuade them from pursuing their headlong course were treated with no respect, and men who were still full of the bargain which the "Reform President" had struck with the rascals of his party at the hotel dinner-table [3] were suddenly estopped by not to be mistaken words of Mr. Cleveland himself.

But first he would state his course concerning the distribution of offices. He had been overwhelmed by letter-writers and visitors, and he told them finally that he would give no attention to appointments prior to his inauguration. Nothing, he assured applicants, would "so interfere with their chance of success" as their addressing him at this time, whereupon he closed his house in New York, boarded a special car which was attached to the Norfolk express, and, with his friends, Charles Jefferson, son of Joseph Jefferson, and L. Clarke Davis, proceeded to Hog Island, off the coast of Virginia. This refuge was owned by a group of gentlemen in Philadelphia who were fond of duck shooting. No one might land on its shores without their permission, so that the President-elect would be inaccessible for a fortnight. Mrs.

---

[1] N. Y. Nation, Dec. 8, 1892.   [2] Ibid.; N. Y. Times, Dec. 5, 1892.
[3] N. Y. Nation, Dec. 1, 1892.

Cleveland until his return would find seclusion among friends at Lakewood, N. J.[1]

Upon Mr. Cleveland's return from the South he made a clear statement about Murphy and gave it to the press. He saw no reason to repeat for the public what he had "so often expressed in private conversation" to many gentlemen, including Richard Croker and Murphy himself. The Democratic party, he said, was face to face with "a very hard task"; the people of the country expected much of it. A great deal must depend upon the state of New York and a senator should be chosen who could "not only defend the principles" of the party, but who could "originate and promote policies" which might come forward in Congress. The senator from New York should be "experienced in public affairs," with "a clear conception of the vital issues with which he must deal." It did not seem to Mr. Cleveland, he said, "that the selection of Mr. Murphy shows a desire or intention of placing in the Senate a man of such a type." [2]

Nevertheless the election soon ensued, with but one or two protesting voices in the party caucus and on the floor of the legislature when the vote was taken. In vain did a member declare that Murphy's choice was "dictated by himself and by three other individuals in defiance of public sentiment," that he was "not a statesman of high, or even low degree." [3] The project was originated and it was executed in malicious glee. Hill and Murphy would be, throughout Cleveland's second term, the United States senators from New York.[4]

President Harrison, when Congress met in December for the short session, which would precede the turning over of the government to the opposition, forwarded to it his final message. The tone of the paper was neither kindly nor conciliatory. The President viewed the scene from a lofty eyrie. The prosperity of the country, as he and other leaders of the party were wont to reiterate, was unexampled and, if ruin were now nigh, as seemed likely, the blame would attach to the party which should touch

---

[1] N. Y. Times, Nov. 23, 1892; N. Y. Nation, Dec. 1, 1892.
[2] N. Y. Times, Dec. 28, 1892; N. Y. Nation, Jan. 5, 1893.
[3] N. Y. Times, Jan. 18, 1893.   [4] Cf. N. Y. Nation, Jan. 19, 1893.

the tariff and introduce new policies. "There are no near frontiers to our possible development," said Mr. Harrison; "retrogression would be a crime." The message throughout breathed the smugness which the Republicans so well knew how to assume, and was at once a reproof to the country for entrusting its fate to the Democratic party and an attack, in advance, upon the evils which were certain to flow from its administration of public affairs.[1]

Both parties, one controlling the House and the other the Senate, were racked by a division of sentiment on the money question. If relatively little was said about it in the campaign the silver money scheme to help the farmer and the laboring man was not far in the background. No plank in a platform, no statement by the President or the President-elect could stop the mouths of the men who, for a generation, had been nursing this idea. They had a new sense of power gained by a realization that a million votes had been cast for the third party and that a leaven was at work within the old parties in the South, as well as in the West, such as had not been active before.

The international monetary conference convened in Brussels on November 22, 1892. It was an empty farce, as its predecessors had been, devised as they too, for the most part, had been to make the West think that the Republican party was "doing something for silver." A pleasure trip to Europe for a few delegates, including Senator Allison of Iowa, Senator Jones of Nevada and E. Benjamin Andrews, president of Brown University who had become a bimetallist, ended in adjournment under a promise which was not fulfilled to return to the work in the following May, the inconclusive course which had been adopted by the men who had attended the conference in Paris in 1881.[2]

Obviously the first duty of Congress when it met in December, 1892, would be to repeal the Sherman silver purchase law of 1890. It should never have been enacted, nor should the law on

---

[1] Richardson, vol. ix, pp. 306–32.
[2] Senate Ex. Doc., 52nd Cong. 2nd sess., no. 82; N. Y. Nation, May 11, 1893.

the same subject, which had preceded it, have been passed to menace our financial system. The scheme to buy pig silver at a cost, as was said at the end of 1892, of $125,000 in gold for each working day of the year,[1] was rapidly leading to dire consequences. Until recently the Treasury, for various causes, had escaped drafts upon it endangering the gold balance of $100,-000,000 which it was bound to maintain for the redemption of the old United States notes or greenbacks and, as was assumed, legal tenders of later issue. Soon, in all probability, it could do this no longer. Customs dues were being paid in paper currency and silver. Legal tenders were being presented in exchange for gold which was being exported; if the purchases of silver were not to cease only resort to unusual measures could save the credit of the government.[2]

The Democratic party in its national platform of 1892 had demanded the repeal of the Sherman law, and Sherman himself now recommended the adoption of this course. It had accomplished "long since" all he "wanted it to do," he said very honestly, and this use as well as that of the older law, though he was not so frank on this point, was to make a market for the product of the Republican silver miners and to hold up its price. At the same time he could not neglect the opportunity to cast suspicion upon the sincerity of the Democrats, when they had included a demand for repeal in their platform, and he declared that, if such a bill should pass the Senate under his leadership, it would meet its death in the House which that party controlled by so impressive a majority.[3] In a few weeks after Congress had convened Sherman expressed a different opinion; he could not make progress with his plan even in the Senate where the silver men would, he said, attach to his bill for repeal a provision calling for free coinage.[4] So much was as certain now as it had been before. The complexion of things in the Senate, which

[1] N. Y. Nation, Dec. 29, 1892.
[2] Cf. ibid., Feb. 9 and 16, 1893; A. D. Noyes, Thirty Years of American Finance, chap. vii.
[3] Phila. Press, Nov. 15, 1892; cf. N. Y. Nation, Nov. 17 and Dec. 1, 1892.
[4] N. Y. Nation, Dec. 29, 1892; cf. ibid., Jan. 19 and Feb. 9, 1893.

had not been improved by the admission to the Union of new states with a population engaged in silver mining, remained such that the outlook was wholly dark. The entire session, indeed, yielded nothing but frustrations as might have been foreseen,[1] and action must await the inauguration of the new President, and the assumption of power by the party to which the conduct of affairs had just been committed by the people in such decisive terms.

[1] N. Y. Nation, Jan. 26, Feb. 16 and March 9, 1893.

CHAPTER XXXVI

THE formation of a cabinet occupied Mr. Cleveland's thoughts while the 52nd Congress fruitlessly wrangled away its expiring days. He was his party's undisputed leader though it might prove to be a most unenviable post. The signs of rebellion in his own household were plain to see during the campaign and the enforcement of the program which he would outline for the party, now that he was President again, would very certainly lead to estrangement and divisions, the full gravity of which could not be reliably foretold. He would recognize, as he could, the forces which had contributed to his election, in so far as he believed that he could meld them and make them valuable in the development of his policies. A conference with Mr. Bayard who had ornamented Mr. Cleveland's first administration as Secretary of State led to his elimination as an active adviser.[1] He would become an acceptable ambassador of the United States to Great Britain,[2] while the President would reach out in an entirely new direction for a head of the State Department, no other than Walter Q. Gresham of Indiana.

In this appointment by Mr. Cleveland there was appreciation of the independent support which had come to him from the Middle West. Judge Gresham, it is said, had never before 1892 voted the Democratic ticket. He was not a Mug-

---

[1] McElroy, Grover Cleveland, vol. ii, p. 3; A. Nevins, Letters of Cleveland, p. 315.

[2] The minister became an ambassador in March, 1893. Sir Julian Pauncefote at Washington was raised to ambassadorial rank by the British government and, in accordance with provisions of the diplomatic and consular appropriation bill, passed at the end of the recent session of Congress, our representative at London would bear the same title. France, Germany and Austria followed.—See N. Y. Nation, April 6, 1893; also Gresham Papers.

wump in the true sense of the word—he had not left his party in 1884 in a revulsion of feeling induced by the nomination of Blaine. His dissatisfaction was ascribable to more recent happenings, particularly the enactment of the McKinley bill and the alliance of the party with industrialists who, he believed, had come to exercise too great a part in its management.[1] There were those in the Republican national convention of 1884 who would have made him the party's candidate for President. In 1888 he had been regarded by many as a more suitable nominee than Harrison, with whom he was not in cordial relations in Indiana. He polled many votes in the convention of that year and his friends in the party would have welcomed the opportunity to make him its "standard bearer" in 1892. His estrangement was increased when he understood that he was being ignored by the Harrison administration and he gave no encouragement to the suggestion. He declined the proffer of the People's party leaders to become their candidate and, as the campaign progressed, he had announced his intention of voting for Cleveland, whom he found to be "an honest, courageous and patriotic man," carrying with him out of the Republican party not a few of his friends, who also had been treated coldly by President Harrison.[2] A man of proven private worth, actuated by high motives, he, at first, declined the appointment of Secretary of State on the ground that he was not a Democrat, but yielded to the President-elect's solicitations.[3] His choice led, on many sides, to expressions of lively satisfaction.[4] One who had been Postmaster General and later, for a time, Secretary of the Treasury in the cabinet of a Republican President, Arthur, now came to the first place in the cabinet of a Democratic President.

[1] "I do not believe the Republican party to-day is animated by high aspirations. It is largely controlled by mere self seekers who are more anxious to promote the interest of classes than the public welfare."— Gresham to Martin Ross, Aug. 1, 1892, in Gresham Papers. Cf. J. W. Foster, Dip. Memoirs, vol. ii, p. 272.

[2] Gresham Papers, particularly letters to Gresham from Walter Wellman; M. Gresham, Life of Gresham, pp. 672-3.

[3] A. Nevins, Letters of Cleveland, pp. 316-7; Gresham Papers; M. Gresham, Life of Gresham, pp. 679-84.

[4] Cf. N. Y. Nation, Feb. 23, 1893

Gresham was a product of frontier life in Indiana. His origins had been humble. His youth had been one of barrenness and sacrifice. He had been an Abolitionist in his sympathies and he had been a soldier in the Union Army.

For Secretary of the Treasury Cleveland chose John G. Carlisle of Kentucky whose boyhood had been as dour as Gresham's. As a leader of the Democratic party in the House of Representatives, recently its Speaker, his growth had been rapid. The sanity of his outlook had increased under responsibility and experience and he had put himself in accord with the policies which Cleveland had made the foundation stones of Democracy. His competent statements on the money question in the House, and later in the Senate, to which the legislature of his state had advanced him, marked him for the direction of a Department which would bear the brunt of great labor,[1] and suffer the force almost instantly, as was clearly seen, of violent factional attack. By his training, as by his residence beyond the Allegheny Mountains, he could, by no feat of the imagination, be mistaken for a "tool of Wall Street."[2]

Daniel S. Lamont, Mr. Cleveland's faithful private secretary in the first administration, and Wilson S. Bissell of Buffalo, his old law partner, between whom and the President there were the closest personal relations, and who had been, during the first term, repeatedly besought to come to Washington to accept office, were selécted, respectively, to head the War and the Post Office Departments. The situation in Atlanta during the progress of the campaign for Hill in that city had brought into prominence the editor and owner of a newspaper which contested the ground with the Constitution. Hoke Smith held the Cleveland banner aloft and, for this service and as a representative of views and interests which the President regarded as progressive and sound,[3] he was appointed to be Secretary of the Interior. A comparatively young man who

[1] Cf. J. A. Barnes, John G. Carlisle, pp. 206–7.
[2] Cf. N. Y. Nation, Feb. 23, 1893.
[3] Cleveland described Smith as "a very able representative of the new and progressive South."—Cleveland Papers.

had known but little of the war, with family connections which were distinguished, he promised to strengthen the President's hold upon opinion in that part of the South.[1]

Mr. Cleveland sincerely wished George Gray of Delaware, who had been playing a useful part in the United States Senate, to become his Attorney General. But the arts of persuasion were unavailing,[2] and Richard Olney of Boston was commended, with the result that he was selected for the post.[3] Before Olney's appointment it was suggested that John Quincy Adams of Boston should enter the new cabinet as Secretary of the Navy. He had refused the post,[4] and, for an occupant of it, Cleveland again turned his eyes toward the South, where he found Hilary A. Herbert of Alabama, who had appeared in the House of Representatives soon after his state had freed itself of carpet bag rule. He had gained experience in the Naval Affairs committee with the tasks to be assigned to him. For the first time since the war a department having to do with the national defence would be entrusted to a man who had been engaged in secession.[5] The West would have the Secretaryship of Agriculture. After the place had been offered to Boies of Iowa, who declined it, J. Sterling Morton, an intelligent and sturdy Democrat in Nebraska, the very home of the farmers' defection, which so gravely threatened the integrity of the party, was tendered the position and accepted it. Not one man in the new cabinet, except Lamont, had been associated with the first administration of Mr. Cleveland who, with unchanged opinions, with the single purpose of trying to do what he believed to be right, with the high object of serving the country under the guidance of a "Supreme Being," to whose existence he so often referred, was now ready to set forth on the second season of his great adventure.

The day of his inauguration, unlike that one eight years

---

[1] N. Y. Nation, Feb. 23, 1893.

[2] Cf. Cleveland to Gresham, Jan. 25, 1893, in Cleveland Papers.

[3] McElroy, Grover Cleveland, vol. ii, p. 5; A. Nevins, Letters of Cleveland, pp. 317, 318.

[4] Henry James, Richard Olney, pp. 5–6.

[5] N. Y. Nation, March 2, 1893.

before which had the balmy warmth of opening spring, was stormy and cold—snow fell to whiten the streets and squares of Washington. He faced the elements unflinchingly, speaking without notes, as before, with the same courage, frankness and sincerity which had invigorated his friends and unsettled his enemies during his first term of office. The silver men and the inflationists heard what concerned them at once, for the President gave his attention in his opening passages to the symptoms of "insidious infirmity" which threatened the "national vigor." Nothing could be "more vital" than a "sound and stable currency." Its "exposure to degradation," he said, "should at once arouse to activity the most enlightened statesmanship." He spoke confidently of Congress, but meanwhile, until that body met, and, in its despite, if need be, he promised that none of the powers of the Executive branch of the government would be withheld when their exercise should be deemed necessary "to maintain our national credit or avert financial disaster."

He passed to the tariff. He abated nothing of his faith in the "injustice of maintaining protection for protection's sake," and denounced the evils which were the "unwholesome progeny of paternalism." This was "the bane," he said, "of republican institutions and the constant peril of our government by the people." "The lessons of paternalism," he continued, "ought to be unlearned and the better lesson taught that, while the people should patriotically and cheerfully support their government, its functions do not include the support of the people."

The waste of the money of the taxpayers should be checked—it was "a crime against the citizen." "Public expenditures should be limited by public necessity . . . measured by the rules of strict economy." One mode of misappropriating the public funds was rewarding inefficient men for partisan activity by appointing them to office. Civil service reform was removing "from political action the demoralizing madness for spoils." It was entitled to the hearty support and encouragement "of all who desired to see our public service well performed, and who hoped for the elevation of political sentiment."

This day, he said, the government came into the control of a party "pledged in the most positive terms" to tariff reform. No "vindictiveness" should be shown—"our mission," he declared, "is not punishment, but the rectification of wrong." The "necessity for revenue to support the government," he continued, following the statement in the party platform, furnished "the only justification for taxing the people." "By discrediting an abject dependence upon governmental favor" self confidence and business enterprise would again be put into our citizens—thus would be stimulated "those elements of American character which support the hope of American achievement." [1]

If, in such language, men found preachment, as many did, and the evidences of ethical standards which were rather consciously superior to those held by others it was, at the same time, necessary for the right thinking among them to feel a respect in their hearts for one who would keep such ideals before his countrymen. It were necessary to return to the state papers of the "Fathers" for the fearless presentation of so much sound public counsel. Its truth increased its force. Its author might be ridiculed, his right to read lessons to the people, when he was, by some conceptions of the Presidential office, a popular servant, might be denied. Criticism of his diction as stodgy, of his manner as severe and schoolmasterly, of his person as awkward and gross—and these exceptions to Mr. Cleveland were taken now, as they had been in his first term— might be indulged in. But the fact remained that he had been brought to his high place in his party over opponents by the plainly expressed wish of the party, and to the Presidency by decisive pluralities in the popular as in the electoral vote, as a result of clear discussion in a campaign covering the whole country. He had the right to believe himself a leader from whom leadership was expected, and to whom the Congress and the people would defer, especially as his character during the four years of another administration had been fully revealed, and his views, since that time and during the canvass,

[1] Richardson, Messages and Papers, vol. ix, pp. 389–93.

were the property of his fellow citizens. The attitude of the
Republican press, as he assumed office, had been lent toleration
by a consideration of all the facts attending his "restoration,"
as the New York Tribune named it, and quiet satisfaction was
felt in circles which eight years before were frankly hostile,
that a man had come to the direction of affairs in threatening
times who, as James Russell Lowell had said, on a memorable
occasion at Harvard College, quoting the pilot of Seneca,
would hold his "rudder true."

No member of the cabinet, overshadowed the President or
threatened his influence in the shaping of the administration,
or as a party guide. The strife for lucrative posts was keen,
but the very fact that he was returned to his great office,
tempered the demands of senators and representatives, and
city and district "bosses," who knew something of his standards for the public service. The reformers kept him under
their close observation and were ready, as in his first administration, to hold him strictly to account for deflections from the
narrow path of duty in respect of appointments and removals.
Carl Schurz was a "hard master," Mr. Cleveland told the
indomitable chief of the reformers, who, upon George William
Curtis's death, in 1892, had become president of the Civil
Service Reform League.[1] Some concessions for the appease-
ment of leaders in Congress seemed to be required to gain
large objects in the give and take of politics.[2] Nevertheless,
when he was not misled by friends and the dictates of expediency in the pursuit of important purposes did not call
for some compromise of views, the President brought to the
government, in its various departments, intelligent and high
minded men, imbued, as he was, with a sense of their public
responsibilities.

Still only 43,000 of some 180,000 persons in Federal employ
were included in the "classified service"; 65,000 of these were
the fourth class postmasters whose "execution *en masse*" had

[1] Writings of Schurz, vol. v, p. 134; Schurz to Cleveland, March 30,
1893, in Cleveland Papers; R. W. Gilder, Grover Cleveland, p. 163.
[2] A principle which the reformers, however, continued to denounce.—
N. Y. Nation, Feb. 16 and March 9 and 30, 1893.

so frequently caused "conspicuous scandal." [1] One-fourth, but only one-fourth, of those in the Federal civil service were safe from the quadrennial scramble for gainful place.[2] President Harrison's addition to the number, by including in the non-appointive classes new employees of the Post Office Department, near the end of his administration, the Democrats complained, had entrenched Republicans in these positions,[3] just as the Republicans had made objection to similar action by the Democrats when Mr. Harrison was ready to assume the Presidency. Comment of this kind was of little moment—the extension of such a reform would, very naturally, be accompanied by some expressions of dissatisfaction. It was an affirmation of Mr. Cleveland's true interest in its progress, its advocates believed, when he announced his resolution to retain Theodore Roosevelt as a member of the Civil Service Commission. Roosevelt's eager and restless nature had kept him prominently in view in that place during the Harrison administration and his continuance in it might ·be a guaranty of a watchful defence of the barriers in provisions of law which already had been raised to keep hungry politicians from preying upon the government.[4]

Outside of the classified list, as between a Republican and a Democrat, Cleveland, as a Democrat, preferred the Democrat, but with the requirement—in theory at least—that he be a man competent to perform his duties. The President was not averse to keeping a Republican in office so long as he was attentive to his tasks. If he had been appointed for a term he should not be removed, were he to be removed at all, until the expiration of that term. The fourth class postmasters made great demands upon the patience of the head of the Post Office Department, as well as of the President.[5] The pressure upon Mr. Cleveland's time by members of Congress

[1] Writings of Schurz, vol. v, p. 151. "The quadrennial St. Bartholomew's Day," Horace White called it. It was a "bloody spectacle."—To Cleveland, March 29, 1893, in Cleveland Papers.
[2] Writings of Schurz, vol. v, p. 150.   [3] N. Y. Nation, July 6, 1893.
[4] Cf. Writings of Schurz, vol. v, pp. 125–7.
[5] N. Y. Nation, April 6, June 1 and July 20, 1893.

who came to present candidates for place became so "bewildering in volume, perplexing and exhausting in their iteration, and impossible of remembrance," and Washington was so full of such persons, he said in May in an executive order, that he would, after that date, give no personal interviews on this subject except to those whom he, on his own motion, might invite into his presence. Applicants for office would only "prejudice their prospects by repeated importunities and by remaining in Washington to await results." [1]

The Republicans, aided by inflationists among the Democrats, had been laying sure foundations for a crisis which was fairly upon the country before the government had been transferred to Mr. Cleveland.[2] The magnificent gesture with which courtiers around the Republican throne, such as the New York Tribune, handed over the scroll and keys to the Democratic party would be difficult to surpass. "The measure of prosperity now enjoyed" by the republic, that newspaper said, in November, 1892, soon after the results of the election were known, was "unprecedented." [3] The "progress of the country" during the four years past had been "unexampled in history." [4] The Republicans delivered into Democratic control "a land of unparalleled prosperity." [5] The whole truth was, as men of judgment and candor knew, that Mr. Harrison had barely made his escape from overwhelming catastrophe induced by drafts upon the Treasury for purchases of silver to satisfy the Western miners and the free coinage men. The Bland-Allison act of 1878 had prepared the way for widespread future disaster, and the danger was brought measurably nearer by a further development of the same policy in the so-called Sherman silver purchase law of 1890.

[1] Richardson, vol. ix, pp. 399–400; McElroy, Grover Cleveland, vol. ii, p. 15; N. Y. Nation, May 11, 1893. Bayard, sympathizing with the President, wrote of "the exhausting warfare you are waging with the pestiferous foes of popular government."—Bayard to Cleveland, March 30, 1893, in Cleveland Papers.

[2] Cf. N. Y. Nation, June 22, 1893, quoting Public Ledger of Philadelphia.

[3] N. Y. Tribune, Nov. 10, 1892. [4] Ibid., Nov. 11, 1892.

[5] Ibid.; cf. ibid., March 8, 1893. For President Harrison's own view of the country's condition see his last message.—Richardson, vol. ix, pp. 306–11.

Large quantities of useless bullion were paid for month by month merely for storage. New Treasury notes were issued to make more difficult the task of keeping an already large paper currency in circulation at par in gold and the very solvency of the government was put in doubt as we pursued a career embarked upon and persisted in to placate interests which, even by so great a concession, were not placated, and to prevent party dissolution.

The Republican party, with correct leadership, might have coped successfully with the inflationists in the farming population in the West but for the silver miners, a body of men who, because of their wealth, were more potential figures than those who cultivated the soil. John Sherman and others were unwilling to cross the way of such influential personages, and the Rocky Mountain and Pacific Coast states were to be held in the Republican fold at the cost of a safe and sound currency system. Temporizing, born of a desire to reap party advantage, with much indifference and cowardice among Republicans of light and leading,[1] had brought the country to a place where a Democrat, as luck would have it, heading a party which, from the first, had been pursuing an opportunist and unintelligent course on the subject, must face the great issue. Meanwhile the difficulty of the task had increased. The rag money or silver "heresy," for one was like the other, had infected new classes of the people in the West, and it was sweeping the South.[2] The time, and the feat to be performed, called for a determined, a courageous and an unyielding leader, and such an one was at hand.

In 1890 the mortgages of several railroad companies were foreclosed and they were operating under receivers. The fall of the Barings and a crash in England[3] had increased the disquiet of careful investors, who sold their stocks and bonds as the prospect darkened. No experienced observer could fail to see that a panic would ensue if silver were still to be purchased for storage to support a languishing industry, and

[1] Cf. N. Y. Nation, July 6, 20 and 27 and Aug. 3, 1893.
[2] Cf. ibid., June 29 and July 6, 1893.   [3] Ibid., May 11, 1893.

if the circulation of depreciated coin and notes, which must one time be redeemed, was to be constantly increased. All that could be done by the government to vitalize business artificially had, probably, been done by the Congress which had passed the McKinley bill and had, by its generous expenditures, earned the name of the "Billion Dollar Congress." Nevertheless, prices of shares of prominent railroads and industrial companies were still, for the most part, at the end of 1892, at a level indicating profitable management, and speculation, if slower than it had been, was continued, with indifference to the outlook, or in the hope that, even with a currency which was "in politics," the country would survive its misfortunes. Charles Foster of Ohio, who had followed Mr. Windom as Secretary of the Treasury in the Harrison cabinet, had been but a poor financial adviser for the government, as he seemed to be but ill fitted for private business when his bankruptcy was announced, amid public comment, soon after his retirement from his high office.[1] His object was to leave his post without discredit to himself and his party, but, as the day of his departure from Washington drew near, it was clear that he could avert disaster only by arrangements with bankers in New York City. The gold balance in the Treasury was being lowered so rapidly that to maintain the reserve of $100,000,000 for the redemption of the greenbacks unusual measures must be taken. The assistance which he needed was secured. The banks would give him a limited amount of gold for legal tenders, though it was recognized that the measure could afford only temporary relief, and Foster was enabled on March 4, 1893, to turn over to his successor, Mr. Carlisle, about $103,000,000 in gold,[2] a balance which barely exceeded the legal limit.

The Reading Railway, which, after earlier reorganizations, had lately come into the hands of speculators, fell in February, 1893.[3] In the course of two or three days in May the securities

---

[1] N. Y. Nation, June 1 and July 13, 1893.
[2] Cf. ibid., Feb. 9 and 16, March 2 and 9, 1893.
[3] N. Y. Tribune, Feb. 21, 1893; N. Y. Nation, March 2, 1893.

of some industrial companies declined 30 or 40 per cent.[1] The
National Cordage Company failed, revealing unprincipled
operations which had been carried forward on a vast scale,
and taking with it several brokerage houses in New York.
Around July 1st money needed by borrowers in that city rose
to the exceptional rate of 73 per cent.,[2] and only by the use of
clearing house certificates by the banks was demoralization in
the stock market prevented. The number of failures for the
first half of 1893 exceeded that for any similar period since the
resumption of specie payments.[3] The Erie Railroad Company
could not meet its obligations and for the fourth time in its
history passed into the hands of receivers.[4] The Northern
Pacific Railroad Company followed in August [5] and the Union
Pacific in October, their reduced revenues testifying to the
almost complete collapse of business in the territory lying
west of the Missouri.[6]

Manufacturers dismissed their work-people and closed their
gates. Wholesale and retail business houses fell. Wages were
reduced and for many men there was no work. Large speculators spread terror as widely as possible. They had sold stocks in
expectation of a fall in prices. Their great profits increased
their courage,[7] while the public had diminished power or
inclination to buy, and panic was at hand. Twelve hundred
shares of Evansville and Terre Haute were sold on the New
York Stock Exchange on July 26th at 75; buyers on the preceding day had offered 126 without finding sellers. Nothing had
happened meanwhile to depress the price of the stock.[8] Money
commenced to be hoarded by the thoroughly frightened people.
For the first time since the panic of 1873 savings banks in the
New York financial district required sixty days' notice of the
intention of depositors to withdraw large sums, 30 days for
small sums of money.[9] In some places, as at Fall River, Mass.,
mill owners could not secure from the banks enough money

---

[1] N. Y. Tribune, May 4, 5 and 6, 1893; N. Y. Nation, May 11, 1893.
[2] N. Y. Nation, July 6, 1893.   [3] Ibid.   [4] Ibid., Aug. 3, 1893.
[5] Ibid., Aug. 24, 1893.   [6] Cf. ibid., Oct. 19, 1893.
[7] Cf. N. Y. World, May 4, 1893.   [8] N. Y. World, July 27, 1893.
[9] Ibid., July 29, 1893.

to pay their employees.[1] Some financial institutions suspended payments to increase the alarm; on one day, July 18th, five in Denver and five in Fort Scott and other places in Kansas closed their doors.[2] Three more Denver banks failed on the following day;[3] the streets of that city were filled with panic stricken people. By this time, throughout the country, mutual trust on which business is founded was completely destroyed.[4]

Men so prone to form opinions upon economic subjects and, in periods of business depression, to press their nostrums upon those in authority came forward with their peculiar schemes.[5] The President's mail, the newspaper press, conversation and debate bore testimony to the number of quacks who had remedies to propose and advice to bestow. To take fright at the seemingly preponderant force of those who spoke, many of them with so much violence and in so much rage, and to yield to importunity had been easy in the past and would have been so in this emergency. Carlisle, until recently, as his responsibility had increased as a party leader at Washington, had been quite ignorant concerning the principles of public finance, and had been numbered, indeed, not many years since as a "greenbacker"; he was at the parting of the ways. Without the President to guide him there is reason to fear that he would have made but a poor appearance at the head of the Treasury Department. There were outstanding $346,000,000 of the old United States notes or greenbacks; $334,000,000 in notes (silver certificates) had been issued under the Bland-Allison act, and $155,000,000 under the Sherman act of 1890.[6] All were legal tenders exchangeable for coin at the Treasury or sub-treasuries.[7] It was said now by the inflationists that Mr. Carlisle might pay out silver for notes issued under the terms of the Sherman act. Discretion was vested in him, a theory which might have been valid but for the

---

[1] N. Y. World, Aug. 3, 1893. [2] Ibid., July 19, 1893.
[3] Ibid., July 20, 1893. [4] Cf. N. Y. Nation, Aug. 3, 1893.
[5] Thomas A. Edison in closing his works, in Orange, N. J., said that the country had "resolved itself into a national lunatic asylum"—he would await its return to sanity.—N. Y. Tribune, Aug. 2, 1893.
[6] Report of Sec. of Treas. for 1893, pp. lxxi–lxxii.
[7] Cf. N. Y. Nation, April 20, 1893.

saving clause requiring the government to maintain gold and silver "on a parity with each other." Manifestly such parity would be destroyed if silver dollars, which at the time were worth but 50 to 60 cents in gold, were exchangeable for the new Treasury notes. Gold would be hoarded and exported, the reserve could, by no possibility, be maintained and the country would at once pass to the silver standard.

A crisis was at hand. Carlisle was wavering.[1] The President in his inaugural address, on March 4th, had said that none of the powers with which he was invested would be withheld when it was a question of supporting the national credit and he now, on April 23rd, in a public declaration made "emphatic contradiction" of reports that "any kind of Treasury notes" were to be redeemed by the government in any coin except gold. The President and his cabinet were "absolutely harmonious" on the point; they would "keep the public faith" and "preserve the parity between gold and silver and between all financial obligations of the government."[2] The business community, Carl Schurz said, had looked to the President to save it from financial ruin;[3] he had saved it. He had, by his definite declarations, said Horace White "snatched the country from the jaws of a great disaster."[4]

To hold the gold reserve at $100,000,000 Mr. Carlisle was continuing the plan devised by his predecessor, Mr. Foster. He was appealing to banks in different parts of the country to bring in gold coin in exchange for paper currency. On March 25th the reserve stood at $107,000,000, but, on April 22nd, for the first time since it had been established for the protection of the national credit, it fell below the minimum level, amounting on that day to about $97,000,000.[5]

[1] Cf. his statement of April 20, 1893, in N. Y. World, and in other newspapers of April 21; J. A. Barnes, John G. Carlisle, pp. 234, 236–8, 293.

[2] N. Y. Nation, April 27, 1893; McElroy, Grover Cleveland, vol. ii, pp. 22–5; J. A. Barnes, John G. Carlisle, pp. 238–9; N. Y. Tribune, April 24, 1893.

[3] Schurz to Cleveland, March 2, 1893, in Cleveland Papers.

[4] To Cleveland, April 24, 1893, in ibid.

[5] McElroy, Grover Cleveland, vol. ii, p. 21.

The assistance and cooperation of Congress were necessary and they must be obtained. Whatever else might be required of that body it was certain that its first step must be the repeal of the so-called Sherman law. Sherman himself had expressed this conviction and had made a motion in the last Congress to stop the purchase of silver,[1] though President Harrison in his last annual message in December, 1892, had omitted any recommendations on the subject.[2] The Republicans in their platform in 1892 evaded the question, and it was left to the Democrats to demand the law's repeal and to denounce it—more, however, as it would appear, because it was "Republican legislation" than because it was, as they rather boldly, for them, declared, "fraught with possibilities of danger in the future."

Importunate letters came to Mr. Cleveland at the White House; business men's organizations, mass meetings of citizens and other bodies passed resolutions and signed petitions urging him to act at once. Silver men, on the other hand, laid before him opposite views and arguments, predicting his political destruction and the ruin of the country if he should adopt the advice of men in the East who lived on their incomes and had money to lend. Cleveland knew that the law should be repealed. No man during the campaign now, or at any time, could doubt where he stood on this question. Repeatedly, beginning with his first message to Congress in 1885, he had condemned the purchases of silver under the Bland-Allison act and his approval of a worse law for the purchases of greater quantities of this metal was not to be expected.[3] When men urged upon him a message convening Congress in extra session, and many individually and through business organizations did so,[4] he made no premature statements regarding the course which he meant to adopt. But he intimated on June 4th that he would summon Congress to Washington to repeal the law, and, on the 30th, he issued his proclamation fixing August 7th,

[1] Sherman's Recollections, pp. 1175-6.
[2] Richardson, Messages and Papers of the Presidents, vol. ix, p. 319.
[3] Ibid., vol. viii, pp. 342-6, 512-3, 788.   [4] Cleveland Papers for 1893.

1893, as the date for the members to assemble to face the task in hand.[1]

At this conjuncture it was discovered that an ulcer which might prove to be malignant had developed in the roof of the President's mouth. It was agreed by medical men that it must be removed immediately and, lest public confidence be more severely shaken than it at the time was, secrecy was enjoined upon the attendant physicians. Dr. W. W. Keen, a skilful surgeon in Philadelphia, was called upon to perform the necessary operation. Commodore Benedict's yacht was put at Mr. Cleveland's disposal. As the President had travelled some 50,000 miles upon it no surprise would be expressed if he should board it now and should accompany its friendly owner on another cruise. The doctors, without exciting the curiosity of the newspaper reporters, were taken to the boat which lay at anchor in New York harbor and, as they proceeded at half speed up Long Island Sound in the early afternoon of a summer day, the President's left upper jaw was taken out. Five days later he was landed at "Gray Gables," his summer home on Buzzards Bay where he was provided with an artificial jaw of vulcanized rubber. The suffering was intense but the operation was successful and, though upon his return to Washington for the special session of Congress, whose opening day was so near at hand, he bore a weakened appearance the device in his mouth was so perfectly contrived that his voice was natural, and the secret would have been safe but for what Mr. Cleveland declared to be "a most astounding breach of professional duty" on the part of a dentist who had accompanied the physicians and had drawn some of his teeth.[2] The published reports of the operation met instant denial in order to allay public alarm;[3] he was suffering only from rheumatism. The whole truth was not revealed until more than thirty years had passed when Dr. Keen described the scene in which he had so usefully participated.[4]

[1] Richardson, vol. ix, p. 396.
[2] McElroy, op. cit., vol. ii, p. 41.   [3] Cf. N. Y. World, July 8, 1893.
[4] W. W. Keen, The Surgical Operations on Pres. Cleveland in 1893.

While he was convalescing the President, perforce, must give thought to the message which he would send to Congress. He had reason to know the temper of that body. He had been congratulated after the elections of the preceding November upon the prospect of a House of Representatives and a Senate which would be in control of his party. Both the executive and legislative branches of the government would be Democratic for the first time since March 4, 1861.[1] In the House there would be 216 Democrats, 125 Republicans and 11 Populists, a majority of 80. The elections of senators in the states had resulted in choice of 44 Democrats and 37 Republicans. Both of Wisconsin's senators, one of North Dakota's, one of California's, one from Kansas would be Democrats. The Populists would have four—Peffer of Kansas, Kyle of North Dakota, Stewart in Nevada, who was now clearly no longer a Republican, and a recruit named Allen from Nebraska. There were three vacancies from new Western states· which, on account of wrangling in their legislatures, would not immediately be filled. Here was a Democratic majority of three in the upper branch of Congress. But, as all competent political observers knew, it was only a nominal sympathy which Cleveland would receive at the hands of many of those who used the Democratic name. In the House, where, however, there was a large body of men who were frankly insurgent on the currency question as on other questions, he might count upon some show of party fealty. In the Senate it could be stated as a certainty that support would be withheld from him by silver men in the party, and, furthermore, on any convenient occasion, Hill and Murphy, the senators from his own state of New York, and other products of boss and machine politics, whom he could not please, would engage in bushwhacking if they did not give him open battle. Anyhow a message presenting the case would be forwarded to Congress and, in the state of his health, following such severe usage by the surgeons, the preparation of it was attended with great difficulty. His Attorney-General, Olney, gave him some aid.

[1] N. Y. Nation, March 9, 1893.

But that officer could lend only an untried hand, and his suggestions were subjected to extensive revision ere they satisfied the President, and he could make the paper his own.[1]

The message was a brief and clear explanation of the situation with one simple recommendation—the President called for the repeal of the Sherman law which was responsible for "present evils" and "dangers threatening the future." The monthly purchase by the government of 4,500,000 ounces of silver had not increased its price—never had the metal been cheaper. The great mass of bullion remained uncoined. It was paid for in notes; these being presented for redemption in gold there was a drain upon the Treasury, an operation which was trenching upon the gold reserve. The silver in the Treasury was increasing in volume; gold was being withdrawn to be exported to foreign countries. Unless government bonds were "to be constantly issued and sold to replenish our exhausted gold supply, only to be again exhausted," it was apparent, the President said, that government obligations would, in no long time, be paid in "depreciated silver." Gold and silver would "part company"—no longer could the government keep the metals "on a parity with each other," which had been declared by law to be "the established policy of the United States." We should then "no longer claim a place among nations of the first class." The people of this country, the President continued, "are entitled to a sound and stable currency and to money recognized as such on every exchange and in every market of the world." Their government had "no right to injure them by financial experiments opposed to the policy and practice of other civilized states." It was a matter rising "above the plane of party politics," and concerned "every business and calling," wage earners first of all, who, "because of their number and conditions," were "entitled to the most watchful care." Other reasons for the panic which prostrated the country there might be, but "one of the plain and principal causes of the present state of things" was to be

[1] McElroy, vol. ii, pp. 30–1; Henry James, Life of Olney, pp. 32–4.

found in the silver purchase law, and it should be repealed at once.[1]

Congress settled to its task, while the President returned to his home on the Massachusetts coast to recuperate from his distressing surgical operation. The work would not be soon done even under the lash of public opinion. The silver miners and the "cheap money" zealots called meetings, passed resolutions and put forth all the efforts of which they were capable in exhibition of their strength. In one breath in Colorado they spoke of a boycott—they would shut down their mines and let the "gold pirates of the East" see if they could do without silver;[2] in another of petitioning the Almighty. Ministers in their churches proposed a season of fasting and prayer.[3] At a mass meeting in Creede, a new silver mining camp in Colorado, resolutions were adopted calling for a division of the republic into a "Department of the West" and a "Department of the East" with separate Congresses and Presidents.[4] Some hotheads spoke of armed violence in defence of their hearths and firesides—a union should be sought with the silver using peoples in Mexico and South America.[5]

The inflationists were incensed the more by reason of the fact that at this very time the mints of India were being closed to silver. That market, therefore, was withdrawn from the miners,[6] and the hope of support for international bimetallism in this direction disappeared.[7] Such action, said Peffer of Kansas, was proof that "the millionaires and money lenders of the Old World" were in "copartnership with the money lenders and monopolists of Wall Street."[8] General Weaver put the blame at the door of "Britain." It was a part of her program for the "world-wide robbery of mankind." The people should "rise a second time and throw off the British yoke." "Let us have," said he, "a new Declaration of Inde-

---

[1] Richardson, vol. ix, pp. 401-5.
[2] N. Y. Nation, July 6, 1893; cf. ibid., July 13 and 27 and Aug. 3, 1893; N. Y. World, July 1, 1893.
[3] N. Y. Nation, Aug. 17, 1893.　　[4] N. Y. World, July 3, 1893.
[5] Ibid., July 13, 1893.　　[6] N. Y. Nation, June 29, 1893.
[7] Cf. ibid.　　[8] Ibid., July 6, 1893.

pendence and coin up our metals just when we please without asking further consent from crowned heads." [1] If the Sherman law were repealed and nothing "better" were put in its place it would mean, said Senator Stewart of Nevada, "the utter demonetization of silver and the permanent establishment of the commercial supremacy of England over this country." [2]

Fortunately such speech little impressed the minds of rational men. At a mass meeting in New York the silverites made a pitiful showing in numbers and in the quality of those who attended it,[3] while in Chicago, in what was dignified by the name of a national convention held in a Methodist church, though more were assembled to protest against the measure which the President had urged Congress to adopt, such folly was spoken in terms so violent and extreme that the intended effect of the demonstration against the "gold bugs" [4] and the "money power" was, in some degree, nullified. Carter H. Harrison, the mayor of the city, in welcoming the delegates from the West and South established his position as a silver man. They all might be "crazy men," said he, but it was "crazy men who marched the world forward." A. J. Warner of Ohio, the head of a Bimetallic League, called the convention to order and delivered an address on the "crime of 1873." Ex-Senator Thurman of Ohio was appointed permanent chairman, though he soon had reason to be ashamed of his connection with the meeting. Powderly of the Knights of Labor, Ignatius Donnelly, William Jennings Bryan, Thomas M. Patterson of Colorado, Senator Stewart of Nevada, "Cyclone" Davis of Texas and others spoke in insistent phrase.[5] For two days cries were raised for Waite whom the silver men and the Populists had elected governor of Colorado, and who had recently harangued himself into a national reputation in Denver. He was wildly cheered during a long tirade which

[1] N. Y. World, June 30, 1893; cf. his statement in ibid., July 3, 1893.
[2] Ibid., July 29, 1893.
[3] N. Y. Tribune, July 26, 1893; N. Y. Nation, Aug. 3, 1893.
[4] For "gold bugs" see N. Y. Nation, June 15, 1893.
[5] Their motto was "Liberty, Equality and Silver."—N. Y. World, Aug. 1, 1893.

he ended by repeating the words whereon his fame already rested. Rather than a destruction of the people's liberties "by the tyranny which is oppressing mankind all over the world," said he, it were "infinitely better" that we should "wade through seas of blood—yea, blood to the horses' bridles." Gross attacks were made upon President Cleveland and Mr. Carlisle. They were called Judases, amid loud cheering, and were read out of the Democratic party for their "betrayal of silver." Resolutions were adopted calling for free coinage at the rate of 16 to 1. The banks, not silver, had precipitated the economic crisis and the people's distress. Bankers were invited to "attend to their legitimate business," and to permit the people to run the government. Committees were appointed to carry on the fight, until "the voice of the people" should be "stronger than the voice of gold." [1]

As soon as the two houses of Congress were organized the same line of reasoning and similar language were employed in the debates on the repeal bill. The subject had been worn threadbare. The people's representatives in a legislative body were entrusted with power over the currency and for three or four decades the same intermittent demand for "cheap money," sometimes subdued in tone, sometimes loud and violent, had come out of the West. Uninformed men, far from the markets, with ambitions that ran ahead of their opportunities for gain, had turned to the government for aid. Demagogues who wished to ride into office which would take them to Washington encouraged the idea in their communities that if "more money" were issued by the mints and printing presses men should have plenty of it in their pockets, and so the folly throve. The source and character of the movement have been described at many places in this work—the rising in 1893 was but another in the series, strength and new significance being lent it because of a depression in business, at which times reasons for the dislocation of demand and supply are eagerly sought and remedies are insistently proposed.

[1] N. Y. Times, Aug. 1, 2 and 3, 1893; N. Y. Nation, Aug. 10, 1893; N. Y. World, Aug. 1, 1893.

The Congress was canvassed; the probable leanings of the members on the question of repeal were put before Mr. Cleveland.[1] Prophets and calculators were assisted by the New York Herald and New York Times and, with more advertisement of the feat, by the New York World which brought a peculiar enthusiasm to the task of putting in a newspaper not only reports of past events but also predictions of what might occur in the future, based upon requests by cable and telegraph of men in responsible positions to express their intention in advance of their action. The World said that there were enough votes in the House to repeal the Sherman law.[2] It was believed that the Senate, under the pressure of public opinion, would follow.

On August 11th William L. Wilson of West Virginia, the administration leader in the House, presented the bill. Immediately "Silver Dick" Bland of Missouri, gray in the service,[3] offered his familiar free coinage scheme as a substitute, and, while the heat of summer was still at its high point in Washington, the lines of battle were drawn. Bryan, "the sodhouse statesman" of Nebraska, rose on August 16th and for three hours, in persuasive voice, increased his fame for eloquence and advanced himself in position as a leader of the silver money men. He was a Populist in a Democratic mask. Like many others, particularly in the South, he would stay in the Democratic party and reorganize it, until it should be an expression of his opinion. While "spreading flowers of oratory like a heavenly carpet"[4] before the House, as a fellow Congressman described Bryan's appeal for "the dollar of our

---

[1] McElroy, Grover Cleveland, vol. ii, p. 31.

[2] N. Y. World, issues beginning June 8, 1893. The editor of the paper, who was reaching the heights of prosperity, having gained by his methods a circulation of 375,000 copies a day, described his feat as "a fresh instance" of his "enterprise in the procurement of news."—Ibid., June 8, 1893. Also issues beginning Aug. 8, 1893; N. Y. Times, June 12, 1893, and following issues; N. Y. Herald, Aug. 8, 1893; N. Y. Nation, June 15 and 22 and Aug. 10, 1893.

[3] Cf. Bayard's allusions to Bland's "attempts to create values by statute, to which he seems to have dedicated his powers."—Letter to Cleveland in Cleveland Papers, March 20, 1894.

[4] Cong. Record, 53rd Cong. 1st sess., p. 413.

daddies," he went far afield for lesson and illustration. Allusions indicative of a reading of the Scriptures, Greek, Roman and French history, the writings of Jefferson and some poetical quotations gave pomp to his uncommonly moving forensic discourse.

Cleveland might be honest, so were the mothers who threw their children into the Ganges. But was he right? Who was it that demanded unconditional repeal of the silver purchase law? The President had been deceived. He could no more judge the wishes of the "great mass" of the people by listening to the voices of the bankers of the Atlantic seaboard than he could "measure the ocean's silent depths by the foam upon its waves." There were "thousands, yes, tens of thousands, aye, even millions," who had not yet "bowed the knee to Baal." Could the Democrats go back to the people and tell them that, "after denouncing for 20 years the crime of 1873," they had "at last accepted it as a blessing"? Men said, "wait for international action, wait for England! Are we," Bryan inquired, "an English colony or an independent people?" Could England be conquered by waiting? The "Fabian policy" had been tried. She should be brought to terms by action. Out of 12 millions of voters more than 10 millions were watching for the signal which should announce "the financial independence of the United States." The present Congress could "not more surely win the approval of a grateful people than by declaring that this nation, the grandest which the world has ever seen," had "the right and the ability to legislate for its own people on every subject regardless of the wishes, the entreaties or the threats of foreign powers." One half of the "people's metallic money" was to be destroyed. You demand "unconditional surrender," do you? he exclaimed. "Why, sirs, we are the ones to grant terms. Standing by the pledges of all the parties in this country, backed by the history of a hundred years, sustained by the most sacred interests of humanity itself we demand an unconditional surrender of the principle of gold monometallism as the first condition of peace. You demand surrender! Aye, sirs, you may cry 'Peace, peace'

but there is no peace. Just so long as there are people here
who would chain this country to a single gold standard there
is war,—eternal war; and it might just as well be known now,"
and more in a like vein.[1]

At length, this course of argument being followed and re-
followed by one and another member, a day came when, by
the rules of the House, talk would end. Party lines were
broken. The Republicans would still say that the panic had
been brought on by Cleveland's election and the imminence of
a change in the tariff,[2] but many of them knew that the purchases of silver must cease, and that the currency had vitally
to do with a situation which occasioned nation-wide disquietude.
The vote was taken on August 28th, three weeks after Congress
had convened. It was decisive, as attentive observers knew
that it would be. Amendments providing for free coinage at
various ratios running as high as 20 to 1, and for reverting to
the provisions of the Bland-Allison act of 1878 preceded the
final roll call. All were defeated. The original repeal bill of
Mr. Wilson was then passed by 239 yeas to 108 nays.[3] In
the silverite minority were the Populists, 73 Democrats and
24 Republicans. For repeal there were 139 Democrats and
100 Republicans.[4]

Many congratulated Mr. Cleveland; he from Buzzards Bay
congratulated Carlisle, who was to receive for himself and
convey to "the rest of the Executive family" assurances of
the President's deep gratification.[5]

The senators, without rules of cloture,[6] with a presiding officer,
Stevenson, the Vice President, inexperienced and unskilful in
parliamentary matters, whose heart anyhow was with the
silverites,[7] were, meantime, making little progress with their

[1] Cong. Record, 53rd Cong. 1st sess., pp. 400–11.
[2] N. Y. Nation, July 27 and Aug. 24 and Nov. 9, 1893; Ida Tarbell, The
Tariff in Our Times, p. 217.
[3] Cong. Record, 53rd Cong. 1st sess., p. 1008.
[4] N. Y. Times, Aug. 29 and 30, 1893; McPherson's Handbook for 1894,
pp. 154–60.
[5] Cleveland to Carlisle, Aug. 28, 1893, in Cleveland Papers.
[6] Cong. Record, 53rd Cong. 1st sess., pp. 1637–8.
[7] Cf. N. Y. Nation, Oct. 19, 1893; J. F. Rhodes, From Hayes to McKinley, p. 398; A. Nevins, Letters of Cleveland, p. 370.

controversies over related phases of the money question. On August 29th Voorhees of Indiana for the Finance Committee reported the House repeal bill, framed in altered language,[1] and the debate continued through September and October. Public opinion had been expressed decisively in the House; it would be difficult to make out a case for the Senate as a repository of more correct knowledge regarding popular sentiment. That the opposition was merely selfish and obstructive and had no root in the principle of rule by majorities was clear when it was seen that much of it came from the new silver mining states.[2] The population of these states was small, their voting citizenry numbered but a few thousands of persons, yet each of them, with two senators, had power over the fate of repeal that was equal to that of a great state in which a million men exercised the franchise. Verbose and tedious speech, including reading from newspapers and public documents, repeated roll calls to determine whether a quorum was present, since members would not remain in their seats to hear such drivel, and dilatory strategy of many kinds prevented progress. Physical endurance was spoken of. The silverites threatened interminable locution. One likened himself and his friends to the Revolutionary army. Being in the minority they were asked to surrender. Had that been the course of Washington because he was outnumbered what would have been the result? They were fighting "the combined money power" of England and the United States which would "dethrone the people, overturn the Constitution and dishonor the flag." They would fight this "money power" as they would fight an enemy in the field, and give no quarter until the end.[3] Men spoke for two or three days. One, Senator Jones of Nevada, ran on for a fortnight. He began his speech on October 14th and ended it on October 30th.[4] When his voice failed, or he could stand on his feet no longer, a colleague took up the burden and the spate of words continued. The

[1] Cong. Record, 53rd Cong. 1st sess., p. 1009.
[2] Cf. ibid., p. 2079.   [3] Ibid., p. 2302.
[4] Ibid., p. 2955. Jones's speech filled 99 pages of the Record.—Ibid., app., pp. 606–705.

volume of utterance of Stewart, Peffer and Teller could be computed only by application of the yardstick to the Congressional Record. When they seemed to be done they started again. The sessions ran through the night—in the hope of compelling a vote one "legislative day" ended only on the third solar day. The galleries were packed with noisy silverites.

John Sherman, on the Republican side, had risen to one of his heights and made a vigorous plea for repeal.[1] The law bore his name—that he should now see its dangers and wish it to be swept away, coupled with the fact that he was, when frank and sincere, a valuable guide on financial questions, should have put weight in the scale. It might have been so under some circumstances. His influence now, as before, would have been vastly greater had he stood his ground, a feat which, though natural to some characters, seemed to be outside the range of his performance.[2]

The silverites in this conjuncture could not hope to gain their purpose which was the adoption of an amendment authorizing free coinage; they could scarcely hope to defeat repeal of the silver purchase law—they had high hope, however, of effecting a compromise. Sherman increased their confidence in such an eventual result and prolonged the fruitless contest. As the debate proceeded he told the newspapers that, while a majority favored the bill, it could not be passed and that concessions must be made to the silver men.[3] Even such friends of the administration as George Gray, who, as Gresham wrote to Bayard, was "able to see the path of duty" but "lacked the courage to travel in it," sought some middle way.[4]

Secretary Carlisle, by writing letters to the chairman of the Committee on Finance and giving out statements to the press, did valuable service. He had unusual gifts as a public speaker. He was earnest, direct and appealed to the reasoning powers

[1] Cong. Record, 53rd Cong. 1st sess., pp. 1049 et seq.
[2] Cf. Journal of Political Economy for June, 1893.
[3] N. Y. Nation, Oct. 12 and Nov. 9, 1893.
[4] Gresham to Bayard in letter book in Gresham Papers.

of his hearers.[1] How much more he could have done had he
had a voice upon the floor of Congress the advocates of cabinet
government repeatedly observed.[2] The combined powers of
the administration were used to gain the end in view. Appointments were delayed. When senators were "inclined to be mean"
the President told his secretary to hold up the nominations
which they "especially desired." We should "not incur too
much fatigue in our efforts to gratify at this time those who
bitterly oppose our patriotic attempts to help the country and
save the party."[3]

The Senate, Mr. Cleveland wrote to Bayard in London,
was making a "shameful display."[4] His response to those who
wavered was a laconic re-statement of his position—"that the
purchasing clause of the Sherman silver law should be uncon-
ditionally repealed."[5] The President would not "lower his
flag," said Gresham;[6] he "would not yield an inch" to the
enemies of sound money.[7] The iteration and reiteration of the
speakers—the threat and abuse heaped upon the bankers of
Wall Street and the "gold bugs" of the East, upon the mono-
metallists of Europe and particularly of England,[8] where
enmity to our institutions had abided, it was believed, since the
tea had been thrown overboard in Boston harbor, upon the
heads of the great moneyed aristocracy everywhere who were
conspiring to crush the common people—served at length to
surfeit even those who were half inclined to favor the silver
cause, and public opinion was having its effect. A number of
amendments of the silverites were rejected. The "gold kings

[1] N. Y. Nation, Nov. 30, 1893.   [2] Cf. ibid., Aug. 24, 1893.
[3] Cleveland to Thurber, Aug. 20, 1893, in Cleveland Papers, a mere
development of a policy which he had stated to Mr. Carlisle before beginning his second term—"One thing may as well be distinctly understood by
professing Democrats in Congress who are heedless of the burdens and
responsibilities of the incoming administration and of the duty our party
owes to the people. [He had the money question in mind.] They must
not expect me to turn the other cheek by rewarding their conduct with
patronage."—January 22, 1893, in Cleveland Papers.
[4] Sep. 11, 1893, in Cleveland Papers.   [5] N. Y. Nation, Oct. 26, 1893.
[6] Gresham to John W. Foster, Oct. 6, 1893, in Gresham Papers.
[7] Gresham to a correspondent, Oct. 4, 1893, in ibid.
[8] Cf. Cong. Record, 53rd Cong. 1st sess., pp. 1236, 1249-50, 1313, 1316,
1442, 1574, 1745, 1797-8, 2467.

are victorious," said Stewart, sensing defeat.[1] Peffer in a fine explosion called the bill "the crowning infamy of the century," [2] but finally, on October 30th, it was passed by 43 yeas to 32 nays.[3] Twenty three Republicans and 20 Democrats were numbered with the majority—9 Democrats, 4 Populists and 9 Republicans, including Cameron of Pennsylvania,[4] voted against repeal. On the list of those who wished to continue the purchase of silver were the senators from Idaho, Colorado, Nevada, South Dakota and Montana, one senator, the only one voting, from North Dakota, and one senator, the only one voting, from California. The two senators from Kansas and the Populist from Nebraska opposed repeal. The rest of the number, barring Cameron, came from those parts of the South in which the Populists had made conquest of the Democratic party.[5]

The victory was the nation's but it was, in every personal sense, Mr. Cleveland's,[6] and it was a sweet consolation to him, suffering as he was from an operation which, as he said, had come "very near putting a period to his public career," [7] costing him so much in "health and vigor" that he sometimes doubted whether he "could carry the burden to the end." [8] When Mr. Harrison had had the opportunity to bring the question to an issue he, and the leaders of the Republican party, had faltered. In fear of the result they had tried further to conciliate an interest which set little value on what was given them, and would not cease their demands until they should be soundly defeated in direct encounter. The glory that might have been Harrison's and his party's was now Cleveland's, and the Republicans, or such of them as had individually come to his support, were to be honored for rising above factionalism rather than for courageous leadership.

[1] Cong. Record, 53rd Cong. 1st sess., p. 2957.   [2] Ibid., p. 2955.
[3] Ibid., p. 2958.
[4] Cf. N. Y. Nation, Oct. 5, 1893. See Cameron's speech in Cong. Record, 53rd Cong. 1st sess., pp. 2930–1.
[5] Cong. Record, 53rd Cong. 1st sess., p. 2958.
[6] Cf. N. Y. Nation, Oct. 26, 1893.
[7] To Bayard, Sep. 11, 1893, in Cleveland Papers.
[8] To R. W. Gilder, Oct. 8, 1893, in ibid.

Letters and telegrams told of the general rejoicing. "Hail to the Chief who in triumph advances," said Don Dickinson from Detroit. "Your personal triumph blesses your country," said Ambassador Bayard in London. "Let me say thank you on behalf of this generation and many generations to come," wrote Ellery Anderson. Republicans dared to commend him. "If he will continue steadfastly in the same line of conduct until he shall have safely brought our country back to a sound financial basis," John W. Foster who had followed Blaine in Harrison's cabinet as Secretary of State wrote Gresham from Paris, "he will have rendered it a service unequalled by any President since the days of Lincoln." [1]

It was said, with too much confidence, that there would be "no more contests over free coinage." [2] But it was clear enough that the fight for the "money of our fathers" would hereafter be an open contest in which the participants could distinguish friend from foe. The unsettlement of the public mind as to money began with the legal tender act of 1862, passed from paper to silver and was now advancing to its last stage. When his message was sent to Congress in December, 1893, the President could say that "our currency affairs" wore an entirely different "complexion." Time must elapse before there could be a restoration of confidence in business, but hope for the future rested on better ground.[3]

"Tariff reform" now was directly before the country.[4] The President called for a reduction of duties upon "the necessaries of life" and for "free raw materials" for manufacturers in the interest of an enlarged foreign trade and lower costs to consumers at home. Congressman Wilson, who had been appointed by Speaker Crisp as chairman of the Committee on Ways and Means,[5] had been holding the inevitable hearings during

[1] To Gresham, Sep. 22, 1893, in Gresham Papers.
[2] N. Y. Nation, Nov. 2, 1893.
[3] Richardson, vol. ix, p. 444.   [4] Ibid., p. 458.
[5] To the marked distress of Mr. Springer who had proven himself an unreliable friend in Illinois. He had earlier held the post and was now, "against his wishes," put at the head of the Banking Committee. See letters of Springer and his wife, who called the removal a "base indignity," to Mr. and Mrs. Cleveland in Cleveland Papers; see also Gresham Papers for 1893.

the special session after the House had passed the bill repealing the Sherman act,[1] and the debates were near at hand. The Wilson bill for the revision of the tariff was, the President said in his message to Congress in December, 1893, "the result of much patriotic and unselfish work." He believed that it would produce sufficient revenue for the needs of the government and that it would, at the same time, conduce to the people's "prosperity and well being."[2] If public officers were really "the servants of the people," the President declared, and, if there were anything in "political promises and professions, failure to give them relief, so long awaited," would be "sheer recreancy." "Nothing should intervene," he continued, "to distract our attention or disturb our effort until this reform is accomplished." To act promptly was "both an opportunity and a duty."[3]

Here was battle again and Mr. Cleveland must count upon insurrection within his own party which his resoluteness in reference to the silver question had increased. He must now reckon without the support of the Republicans who had come to his aid on that subject. Democrats generally were tariff reformers, just as Republicans generally were protectionists. But human nature, under whatever party guise, is much the same, and Democrats who believed that their own interest, or that of the people who had sent them to Washington, would be forwarded by tariffs were ready to abandon principles founded on theories in order to gain practical personal ends. Such as these would not respect Mr. Cleveland's leadership, though the Populists and others who, in general, openly defied him and held him, they declared, in complete contempt, would vote for a revision of duties, because it was part of their creed to make life hard for the rich man, who, they believed, was favored by tariffs. The Republicans had just enacted the McKinley bill. They would stand upon it and defend it. Economic distress was in no way attributable, they said, to the law; quite the reverse—it was fear of the overthrow of the protective system

[1] Cf. N. Y. Nation, Sep. 17, 21 and 28, 1893.
[2] Richardson, vol. ix, p. 459. [3] Ibid.

which had precipitated panic and the resultant depression, now nation-wide.[1]

By the Wilson bill, as it was given to the House in December by him whose name it bore, and who commenced debate upon it on January 9, 1894,[2] lumber, coal, iron, wool and sugar, both raw and refined, were to be free. The duties on manufactured textile fabrics were to be lowered. An income tax of two per cent. to affect those who had more than $4,000 a year was subsequently attached to the bill to cover any insufficiency of revenues. Naturally this innovation excited angry comment, both because of the reluctance of the citizens concerned to pay it and because it appeared to be needless. No tax of this kind had been known except during the Civil War. At the restoration of peace it was reduced and, after being lowered again, it was abolished.[3] Since that time the more acceptable indirect tax, except for a few excise charges, had sufficed. The income tax "idea" was plainly an attempt on the part of the South and the West to lay a burden on the more opulent classes in the Eastern and Middle states,[4] and, as such, was supported by the Populists and silverites who had originated it and imposed it upon Mr. Wilson.[5] It was a raid upon property and was viewed in this light by both the raider and the raided— it was punitive and socialistic. There was a thought, therefore, that it would be a popular tax with the unpropertied classes.[6]

The proposal to put wool on the free list enraged not only the defenders of sheep husbandry in Ohio, past masters in raising the cry of "wolf" whenever the tariff was under discussion, but also men in other states who had become interested in this business. The prospect of free iron ore aroused the ire of American miners and of manufacturers who had purchased iron mines to feed their furnaces. It was so, too, with coal. But over sugar there would be the maddest fight. The refiners would have free raw sugar, a boon which they had gained in the McKinley law. The growers, on the other hand, both

[1] Cf. N. Y. Nation, July 27, 1893.
[2] Cong. Record, 53rd Cong. 2nd sess., p. 573.
[3] N. Y. Nation, Nov. 30, 1893. [4] Ibid., Feb. 1, 1894.
[5] Ibid., Feb. 8 and April 12, 1894. [6] Ibid., Jan. 11, 1894.

of cane in Louisiana and of beet in a number of Northern and Western states, who had been enjoying the encouragement of the bounty offered them by the law, were determined to secure protection from the cheap imported product of foreign countries. In spite of the revenges, cupidities and very obvious corruptions which were made to enter into tariff legislation, especially in such a time of perturbation, both economical and political, the House, on February 1, 1894, passed the Wilson bill with its main original features intact. The vote was 204 to 140, eight members being absent or not voting. Tariff reformers hailed it as the beginning of a beneficent "fiscal revolution." [1] The bill went to the Senate.

That body, as has been plainly indicated, was of a composition little calculated to reflect honor upon the country. The new Western states could be reproached for the election of unfit frontiersmen whose appearance might be grotesque and whose ideas might be the product of ignorance. But what basis of reason was there for an expression of loss of faith in our institutions, founded upon the admission of such men from yet uncivilized regions to what the newspapers were prone to describe as "the august upper house of Congress," when two of our commonwealths which led the others in population and wealth and, presumably, in intelligence, New York with "Dave" Hill and his âme damnée, Murphy, and Pennsylvania with "Don" Cameron and "Matt" Quay, were so unmindful of the value of example? With Gorman from Maryland, Brice from Ohio and "Bill" Chandler from New Hampshire, who shared with Cameron an interest in silver money,[2] the East could, with little propriety, point a reproving finger at the Rocky Mountains and the Pacific coast. Verification of this fact would soon be furnished in the Senate's prolonged torture of the Wilson bill. This measure, whatever might be thought of the tariff question in its relation to protection or free trade, was

---

[1] N. Y. Nation, Feb. 8, 1894.
[2] Cf. N. Y. Nation, Oct. 26, 1893; N. Y. Times, Feb. 21, 1895; Cong. Record, 53rd Cong. 1st sess., p. 2958; ibid., 53rd Cong. 3rd sess., pp. 2432-3. Mr. Cleveland on one occasion, feelingly described Chandler as a "pestiferous wasp."

an intelligent expression of the sentiment which was supposed to actuate the dominant political party, as judged by the platform and the statements of its leaders. Indeed many thought that the bill erred on the side of moderation, and that it was far from being an answer to the demand in the platform for a "tariff for revenue only." [1] It was fair to think, therefore, that it might receive respectful treatment in the Senate as well as in the House, since both were, nominally at least, in control of the same political organization.

It was not to be so; it was well enough foreseen that it could not be so, though no anticipation could have equalled the result. When Hill and Murphy had been sent to the Senate from New York it was made certain that effective management for administration policies would be wanting on that side in that branch of the national legislature. Hill, had, indeed, voted for repeal of the silver purchase bill under the pressure of a practically unanimous public sentiment in New York, and was, ostensibly, now an opponent of free coinage. At every available opportunity, however, he and Murphy were ready, in any feasible way, to embarrass the President whose political standards were so different from their own. The silver senators, their belief in their cause being so obstinately held, were, whether Republicans or Democrats, vengeful, and the discussion of the tariff bill, without party leadership or discipline, became a mere scramble of interested persons for their own and their friends' advantage. [2] Opposition by the Republicans on a basis of principle, opposition by Mills of Texas, now a senator, and Democrats who thought that the bill as it came from the House did not go far enough in the direction of free trade,[3] was abandoned in the general mêlée and gave place to a struggle to get whatever could be had. In the process of thus serving their own interests the Republicans would damage the President's party

---

[1] Tarbell, The Tariff in Our Times, pp. 218–20; Stanwood, American Tariff Controversies, vol. ii, p. 321; N. Y. Nation, Nov. 30, 1893.

[2] Called by Mr. Cleveland "the communism of pelf."—App. Ann. Cyclop. for 1894, p. 193. Cf. S. M. Cullom, Fifty Years of Public Service, p. 266.

[3] Tarbell, The Tariff in Our Times, pp. 221, 224–5; Stanwood, Am. Tariff Controversies, vol. ii, p. 328.

as much as possible for the Congressional elections of 1894. To
prove to the country that the Democrats were in hopeless dis-
unity, that they were paralyzing industry, that they were wholly
inept in statesmanship was a duty never out of mind. Hill
read stilted speeches,[1] openly or covertly assailing the President.
He opposed the income tax which he laid at the door of the White
House, but which Cleveland also looked upon coldly,[2] and which
was without bearing upon tariff reform, except as a method of
gaining revenue after the drying up of the sources at the custom
houses. Murphy who had acquired his skill as a politician in
Troy, N. Y., was interested in the duty on collars and cuffs, a
product of that place, said to equal 95 per cent. and to be
prohibitory.[3] Quay and others, who were speculating in shares
of the American Sugar Refining Company, the "Sugar Trust,"
which had active lobbyists on the ground and which had made
generous contributions to the campaign funds of both parties,[4]
were advocates of a duty on refined sugar, the Louisiana senators
of a duty on raw sugar.[5] Brice, who owned mines, interested
himself in a tax on iron ore and coal, being supported by Morgan
of Alabama, who was acting on behalf of industries in his state;[6]
Gorman in levies on the many products which came into his
life as a "practical politician." [7] Other men would have duties
to keep out foreign wool, lumber and a great variety of articles
in our import trade.[8] To gain their ends senators resorted to
filibustering. Quay had learned the lesson from the silverites

[1] Cf. that of April 9, 1894, in which occurred such phrases as "the
lovely cynosure of nations" and "the sea wall of our paradise."—Cong.
Record, 53rd Cong. 2nd sess., pp. 3557–68; N. Y. Nation, April 12, 1894.

[2] "You know how much I deprecated the incorporation in the proposed
bill of the income tax feature."—Cleveland to W. L. Wilson, App. Ann.
Cyclop. for 1894, p. 187.

[3] Letter of July 25, 1894, in Cleveland Papers; Ida Tarbell, The Tariff
in Our Times, p. 228; Stanwood, Am. Tariff Controversies, vol. ii, pp.
327, 337–8.

[4] Cf. N. Y. World, June 20, 1894; Tarbell, The Tariff in Our Times,
pp. 224–6. For Quay's admissions as to his speculation see Senate Reports, 53rd Cong. 2nd sess., no. 606, pp. v, xi, 497. Gresham to Wayne
MacVeagh, May 7, 1894, in Gresham Papers.

[5] Cf. Taussig, Tariff Hist. of the U. S., pp. 304–16.

[6] Cf. Gresham to Bayard, Jan. 21, 1894, in Gresham Papers.

[7] N. Y. Nation Aug. 2, 1894; Tarbell, The Tariff in Our Times, p. 221.

[8] Cf. N. Y. Nation, March 22, 1894.

in October. He would talk the bill to death, if he were not given what he wanted. His speech, or that which bears the name, began on April 14th, and did not end until June 16th. He would take the floor at need and read so long as he could articulate. The material fills 231 pages of the Congressional Record.[1]

The result, at length, was a completely changed bill which had lost its original purpose. It, in no way, satisfied the President, who, in a letter to Mr. Wilson,[2] freely and frankly stated his disappointment, or men generally who, following Mr. Cleveland's leadership, had made revision of the tariff on unselfish lines an issue before the country. It had been "Gormanized."[3] It was fairly called now the Wilson-Gorman bill, or the "Sugar Trust tariff bill," as Senator Hale named it,[4] but it was finally passed by the Senate on July 3, 1894, with only one Democratic vote recorded against it, that of Hill, who was accused by men of his own party of seeking an excuse in the income tax, which he opposed tooth and nail, to serve protectionism.[5]

The bill was returned to the House with such alterations, Mr. Wilson complained, that now only two of the various raw materials which it was the design of the Democratic party to make free—lumber and wool—were made free. The duties proposed by the House had been based on the *ad valorem* system; the Senate had returned to specific taxes. Not less than 634 amendments had been made in the bill.[6] In no way was the measure, as it came from the Senate, so great a disappointment in the sight of the people as in the surrender, which it seemed to be, to the Sugar Trust. Public excitement on this point, instigated by the press and an investigation by a committee of the Senate to determine to what degree senators were in-

[1] Cf. Tarbell, The Tariff in Our Times, p. 228; Stanwood, American Tariff Controversies, vol. ii, p. 329.
[2] Dated July 2, 1894, in App. Ann. Cyclop. for 1894, pp. 186–7.
[3] N. Y. World, June 13, 1894.
[4] Cong. Record, 53rd Cong. 2nd sess., p. 8499.
[5] The man who said "I am a Democrat" now had a new encyclical—I am a Democrat without the income tax."—Cong. Record, 53rd Cong. 2nd sess., p. 8416.
[6] App. Ann. Cyclop. for 1894, pp. 184–5; N. Y. Nation, July 12, 1894.

fluenced by the lobby sent to Washington by this monopoly, was at white heat.[1]

The House stood its ground and the subject went to a conference committee which was dominated by the representatives of the Senate. President Cleveland made a final appeal in a letter to Mr. Wilson. He knew the nature of the opposition and he, in his direct way, characterized it. The bill was an abandonment of tariff reform of the kind which could answer Democratic pledges. Such abandonment meant "party perfidy and party dishonor." "How can we face the people," Mr. Cleveland asked earnestly, "after indulging in such outrageous discriminations and violations of principles?" [2]

The guilty men, to cover their sinning, made a great ado about their honor and dignity. Gorman "hurled back" at the President the accusations of unworthy motives. It was not the part of a President to "join with the commune" in blackening the character of senators who were as honorable and patriotic as he, "to taunt and jeer" at fellow Democrats who had done as much to serve the party as he. The "limit of endurance" had been reached. They would be traduced no longer and more in a like strain.[3]

No counsel availed; the "sugar senators," as they were generally called, were immovable. The conferences were prolonged. The House had no recourse but to concur and finally in late summer, on August 13th, the Senate amendments were accepted. "It was a sorry fact," said Mr. Wilson, "that when a great fight had been won before the people at the polls" they must conduct a "further stand up and knock down fight with their own representatives." Bad as it was, and he made no

[1] Senate Reports, 53rd Cong. 2nd sess., nos. 436, 457, 485, 486, 487, 606; cf. Taussig, Hist. of the Tariff, p. 316; Tarbell, The Tariff in Our Times, pp. 226–8. The chairman of the Committee on Ways and Means, W. L. Wilson, said after the bill had been passed—"The gigantic power of that great organization [the Sugar Trust] has been felt from the beginning almost to the end of this great tariff controversy."—Cong. Record, 53rd Cong. 2nd sess., p. 8496.

[2] Cong. Record, 53rd Cong. 2nd sess., pp. 7712–3; App. Ann. Cyclo. for 1894, pp. 186–7; A. Nevins, Letters of Cleveland, pp. 354–7.

[3] Cong. Record, 53rd Cong. 2nd sess., p. 7805; N. Y. Nation, July 2, 1894.

concealment of his opinion of the measure, he still believed that it was "not as bad as the McKinley bill." [1] Men said that Mr. Cleveland would not sign it, even that he would veto the "monstrosity." He allowed it to become a law without his approval, for reasons which to him and his friends were good. Though he made no claim to being "better than the masses" in his party he would not, he wrote to Congressman Catchings of Mississippi, endorse what was "not in line with honest tariff reform." The people should be exhorted to continue the struggle. The question would not be settled until it should be "honestly and fairly settled in the interest and to the benefit of a patient and long suffering people." [2] The House returned to the charge and passed what Reed of Maine called the "popgun bills" for free coal, free iron ore, free barbed wire and free sugar, but they met death in the Senate and Mr. Cleveland's knight errantry in the interest of "tariff reform" was brought to a rather inglorious end.

The free coinage men, thwarted as they had been by the repeal of the Sherman law, had prepared a bill to coin the seignorage, the silver which remained in the Treasury as gain to the government by the purchase of bullion at a price lower than the value stamped upon the metal when coined, and when put into circulation as money. Bland saw in this scheme an opportunity to add about 50,000,000 silver dollars to the circulation and, on the familiar pleas that there was not enough currency for the uses of the people, that the "white metal" was confronted by a selfish and sordid enemy in New York and in England, and that, through gold, the poor were being robbed and oppressed, the bill was adopted by the House on March 1, by a vote of 168 to 129, and by the Senate, on March 5, 1894, by a vote of 44 to 31. Many "sound money" men said that it was a small matter—50 millions more of silver would not greatly alter the situation now that monthly purchases had been stopped, and to try to conciliate in some way a group,

[1] Cong. Record, 53rd Cong. 2nd sess., pp. 8468–84.
[2] A. Nevins, Letters of Cleveland, pp. 364–6; App. Ann. Cyclop. for 1894, p. 193.

which so madly pursued an idea, and were so plainly aggrieved by recent defeat, had in it elements of expediency. But Mr. Cleveland was still in no mind to allow the government to follow a paltering course if, by his interpositions, he could prevent it. He set his face against the proneness of members of Congress to pander to the illusions of the people, and, contrary to the advice of men of softer fibre, who added to their arguments the admonition that he was ruining the party and reading himself out of it, he, fully convinced that the scheme was "ill-advised and dangerous," vetoed the bill on March 29, 1894, amid the renewed clamor and recrimination of the silverites,[1] and the praise of other men.[2] The effort in the House to enact the bill, notwithstanding his objections, failed.[3]

The passage of the tariff bill and the repeal of provisions of law still in force concerning the supervision. of Federal elections so distasteful to the South,[4] were the principal fruits of a session of Congress which, for protractedness and futility, has had few equals in our parliamentary history.

Meanwhile, with lowered public revenues, the struggles of the Secretary of the Treasury to maintain the gold reserve of $100,000,000 for the redemption of the greenbacks and the upholding of the pledged faith of the government continued. The distressed condition of business reacted upon public finance; the fear of a breaking down of public credit, in turn disadvantageously affected industry and trade. The unsettlement which had distinguished the year 1893 ran on into 1894 and 1895, the irreconcilable differences between the President

[1] McPherson's Handbook for 1894, pp. 148–51; Richardson, vol. ix, pp. 483–9; McElroy, Grover Cleveland, vol. ii, pp. 79–82; N. Y. Nation, April 5, 1894.

[2] J. L. M. Curry expressed his gratification. The country now had a President who was a "beautiful illustration of the virtue of Aristides who once said, when a plausible proposition was submitted to him—'It is not expedient because it is not right.'" (To Cleveland, March 30, 1894, in Cleveland Papers.) If the Democratic party were damaged, as was asserted on many sides, "so much the worse for the Democratic party." The President was constantly "electrifying" right thinking men.—Cleveland Papers.

[3] McPherson's Handbook for 1894, p. 151.

[4] Ibid., pp. 131–42; N. Y. Nation, Oct. 12, 1893, and Feb. 15, 1894.

and Congress increasing the fright of employers of labor and of men with funds to invest in productive business enterprises. The spirit of riot on the part of the silverites, who found encouragement for their rebellion in other elements in Congress, particularly in the Senate, intent upon the humiliation of a chief magistrate whose movements they could in no way control for their own ends, was communicated to the already sorely disturbed economic and financial situation.

One course was open to the President, and only one, and he and Mr. Carlisle would resort to it, namely the sale of bonds for gold with which to replenish the reserve. The hoarding of gold by individuals and institutions, and the demand for it for exportation, were so alarming, and the destruction of the national credit was so imminent in January, 1894, that action was imperative immediately. Specific authorization, in such emergencies, to issue bonds running for two or three years at a low rate of interest, say 2 or 2½ per cent., had been asked of Congress at many times in past years. The request for such legislation for the protection of the Treasury had been renewed recently by John Sherman.[1] The necessity for a grant of authority of this kind was stated even more forcibly by Mr. Cleveland and Mr. Carlisle.[2] The present crisis had been foreseen. But the very mention of bond issues wildly inflamed the silverites, whose whole scheme—the taking of the country from a gold and putting it on a silver basis—would be thwarted by executive action under such a law. Fortunately an act nearly 20 years old, of January 14, 1875, the specie resumption act, continuing a provision of law of July 14, 1870, which had done service at need before,[3] was at hand and, although the bonds which might be issued, it was stated, were "payable in coin," conceivably, therefore, silver rather than gold, they would avail the Treasury if, on these terms, they could be sold. It depended upon the faith which those who had money to lend should repose in the fu-

[1] N. Y. Nation, Feb. 16 and 23, and March 9, 1893.
[2] Cf. Barnes, John G. Carlisle, pp. 290-1, 305-7, 310.
[3] N. Y. Nation, March 9 and 16, 1893, Jan. 25, Feb. 1 and 8 and March 1, 1894.

ture management of the government. Naturally a higher rate of interest must be paid for "coin" than for "gold" bonds.

For some time the reserve had been below $100,000,000. On January 17, 1894, it had fallen under $70,000,000 and the drain upon it, by reason of Treasury deficits and redemptions, was unceasing. Disaster seemed to impend. At this point the Secretary of the Treasury offered to the public $50,000,000 ten year 5 per cent. "coin" bonds;[1] they would be on sale until February 1st for 117, which thus would reduce the yield to the investor to 3 per cent. They were taken so slowly under Carlisle's rather awkward management of the operation[2] that he sent the Assistant Secretary of the Treasury to New York to confer with the bankers of that city. The Secretary himself, at the desire of the President, soon followed, not unmindful of the clamor which his visit would awaken among the silverites and his own aversion, as an old Kentucky soft money man, to association with the leaders of Wall Street.[3] Presently the bankers, led by John A. Stewart, president of the United States Trust Company, came to the rescue of the Treasury. The amount paid for the issue was in excess of $58,000,000, though the net gain to the government in gold was not so great, since some of the subscribers redeemed legal tenders to procure the coin with which to pay their subscriptions.[4]

The day was saved. The rage of the silver men was immense. They questioned the President's authority, impeached his patriotism and, indeed, his personal honesty, and poured the vials of their madness upon bankers, capital, gold, England and all men and things which, as they believed, stood in their way. After the veto of the seigniorage bill, though Mr. Cleveland addressed Congress on the subject of authority for bond issues to defend the reserve,[5] cooperation of the legislative

---

[1] Barnes, J. G. Carlisle, pp. 310–1.
[2] A. D. Noyes, Thirty Years of Am. Finance, pp. 213–5.
[3] Barnes, John G. Carlisle, pp. 315–6; A. D. Noyes, Thirty Years of Am. Finance, pp. 213–4.
[4] A. D. Noyes, Thirty Years of Am. Finance, pp. 215–6.
[5] Richardson, vol. ix, pp. 445, 489.

branch of the government in the solution of questions affecting the currency was the more unlikely to be accorded him. It was to be a stubborn battle in which he would not flinch. He pointed, in letters to, and in conversation with, his friends, to his oath of office and the responsibility of his position, revealing now, as on other occasions, a conscience which would admit of no compromises, while he still firmly expressed his faith in an overruling Providence for the guidance of men and governments.

But one bond issue called for other issues; while the source of the trouble should be untouched the same conditions would recur—the reserve which had been raised above the legal limit would again be attacked and would again fall. Once more Congressional and important state elections were at hand. The campaign of 1894 was in progress and its acrimony was intense. The tariff fell into a secondary place. In the sight of the President himself the greater issue was the money question. His gravity in regard to the duties on raw materials and the cost of the necessaries of life was in some degree displaced by a serious concern lest support should be taken away from the whole structure of price and value. It was an unfavorable hour for a change in the revenue system, especially in the direction of a policy likely to lead to a reduction in public income, a fact which the Republicans would emphasize, and they were supported in this opinion by many men engaged in banking and commerce who had earlier advocated tariff revision. The Wilson bill, as it had been mutilated by the Senate, was as unacceptable to the country as it had been to the President. Such an exhibition of irresponsibility and corruption in individuals sent to represent the people in a legislative assembly made a most unpleasant impression. The want of aptitude of the party which had been entrusted with the tasks and duties of government for the performance of these tasks and duties was so apparent that it could hope to gain no new friends.

The situation, bad as it was, was further complicated to the disadvantage of the Cleveland administration in the summer of 894 by strikes. One of these followed another. The labor unions were constantly rising in power under leaders of more skill and authority than those who had earlier been directing the affairs of these organizations. They had their speakers and their press, and distinct progress had been made in planting the idea in widening circles that "labor," as a class, had rights to protection from the impositions of "capital." The public generally was beginning to realize that there were certain well defined wrongs which were intolerable. A sense of justice was offended when in the strife of making a living men could not gain standards of comfort which we were coming to think were a common social heritage. It was equally clear in most minds that this movement to unite working men for a defence of their interests should proceed in an orderly manner without disturbance of the general peace of society. Too many of the leaders in the labor organizations were intent upon making themselves into heroes in the sight of their men and, through their advice, or in spite of it, as they generally averred when they were brought up for investigation before committees or courts, the destruction of property and life ensued.

The railroad riots of 1877 were put down by the military; so were the riots on the southwestern Gould railroads in 1886 which culminated in the bombing of the police by the anarchists in Chicago; so were the Connellsville and the Homestead riots in Pennsylvania in 1892, and so now again, in 1894, would a great strike call for decisive measures.

A World's Fair had been projected in celebration of the 400th anniversary of the discovery of America by Christopher Columbus. It would have been held in New York but the political factions in the legislature at Albany fell upon one another and threw away their chances of gaining the favor of Congress which was necessary, if it were to be a really national celebration.[1] Chicago, in this emergency, with some of the eager enterprise for which the city at the time was famous, came forward, seized the prize and carried it to the shores of Lake Michigan. The development of the "White City," built to shelter the exhibits which were sought in all quarters of the

[1] Cf. N. Y. Times, Feb. 4, 20, 25 and 26, 1890; N. Y. Tribune, Apr. 22, 1890.

globe, went forward amid many expressions of public interest. The project was the most considerable of the kind which the country had seen since the Centennial Exposition in Philadelphia in 1876. It was soon discovered, however, that the completion of the arrangements for so truly great an undertaking could not be compassed in 1892. Certain commemorative exercises of an impressive kind were held in the autumn of that year in the unfinished buildings and in New York, where there were naval and military "parades," [1] but the Fair itself must be postponed until 1893. One of the first official acts of President Cleveland's second term, in April, was the opening of the exposition in Chicago which attracted, even in the year of panic, millions of visitors from far and near, together with many adventurers who sought amusement, if not employment in the city and its environs at such a time. When the Fair was ended a large body of persons, many of them from foreign countries, were left on the ground without objects in life, or the means, indeed, of going elsewhere. Sooner or later they would breed mischief. They were a charge upon the city; they took to the roads to increase that body of vagrants who were called tramps; [2] they invaded and infested the smaller towns and cities of the West. This horde was added to the number of resident unemployed who, after a distressing winter, were, in the spring of 1894, in a desperate state of mind.

A picturesque torch bearer of this motley crowd of discontented people was found in a man named Coxey who quarried sand stone for making glass and bred and sold horses on a farm in Ohio. He had been a Greenbacker, now he was a Populist. He would be the Jack Cade of the out-of-works. With a reference which would have been profane, if it had not had some earnest meaning, he sought to bring the poor and needy together in the "Army of the Commonweal of Christ" and, under his fantastic generalship, they would set out for Washington on Easter Sunday, 1894, to advertise their woeful condition

---

[1] App. Ann. Cyclop. for 1892, pp. 523-4.
[2] Cf. D. L. McMurray, Coxey's Army, pp. 13-20, and authorities there cited.

and to demand of Congress [1] a great issue of inconvertible paper money to be given to the idle for building "good roads." [2] Coxey had said that he would have 100,000 men in his legion. Some lunatics, freaks and other draggle tail folk came to his side for the journey, and about fifty newspaper reporters. Three or four lieutenants rode horses and considered themselves marshals of the parade. The "general" himself sat comfortably in a phaeton, while Mrs. Coxey and their infant son, Legal Tender Coxey, occupied another vehicle. A few tramps made up the rank and file. Some fell away, while others joined the "army" as it proceeded east. The leaders gained courage from the publicity which their movements received through the industry of the reporters in their train. The arrival of Coxey and his men in a town drew crowds of curious spectators. They sought to exact food and shelter from the people of the country through which they passed. Work was offered them as they advanced, but this they had neither time nor wish to do. [3]

The alarm which the march of the "army" raised in the public mind was ludicrously out of proportion to any danger which lurked in its coming to Washington. Men wrote to the President to say that Coxey would cut the telegraph wires, stop the trains, attack the United States Treasury, blow up the White House, assassinate him, the Vice President, the Secretary of the Treasury and the justices of the Supreme Court. The rich were removing from the city and were taking their money with them. The President should order out 5,000 regulars at once. [4] Secret service men were sent out and, in disguise, enlisted in the "army" to watch its movements. [5]

As the "Coxeyites" advanced, the Populists in Congress, in defiance of the general feeling, expressed a wish to give them a

[1] He called his scheme to approach Congress through an "army" a "petition with boots on."—D. L. McMurray, op. cit., p. 33.

[2] No more or less than a return to Greenbackism, to a demand for money "cheap in material, easy of issue, worked by steam, signed by machinery."—J. H. Eckels in Forum, March, 1895.

[3] Cf. N. Y. Nation, April 12 and 19, 1894.

[4] Cleveland Papers for 1894.

[5] Reports to Secretary Carlisle under date of April 20 and 26, 1894, in Cleveland Papers.

public welcome. Allen of Nebraska, supported by Peffer, presented resolutions in the Senate insuring them entrance to the Capitol. They had the right of petition under the Constitution of the United States whatever their "rank or station in life." [1] They reached Washington in time for a parade on May Day, which ended in the arrest of Coxey and two or three of his companions for trespass on the grounds of the Capitol.[2] The Populists in the Senate called for an investigation of the "outrage." They would take testimony and know the facts in regard to the "remarkable and tragic scene." [3]

Organized bodies of tramps, loosely alluded to as "armies," were moving farther west. They overpowered the crews of trains to procure transportation from place to place, begging and stealing as they could.[4] Dumped by the railroads into one state they must be hurried over the border into another. They were an unwelcome burden to whatever community they came. Now and again the leaders harangued the people at the roadside and in town squares in the hope of inciting some kind of social revolt. Arrests were made by United States marshals at the direction of the Attorney-General, a movement which was facilitated by the fact that many of the Western railroads were in the hands of receivers appointed by the United States courts.[5] In a number of cases in Montana and on the Pacific coast Federal troops were used to keep the "Commonwealers" in order.[6] Primrose's "army" from Texas, Kelly's from San Francisco, Frye's and Galvin's from Los Angeles, the newspapers said, were coming east day by day with Washington as their goal.[7]

But the pilgrims from the far West, which for the most part on May Day were still on the way, were discouraged by the small

[1] Cong. Record, 53rd Cong. 2nd sess., pp. 3842–4, 4060, 4106, 4111, 4112; Senate Mis. Doc., 53rd Cong. 2nd sess., no. 151.

[2] Cf. McMurray, Coxey's Army, pp. 116–26; N. Y. Nation, April 12 and May 24, 1894.

[3] Cong. Record, 53rd Cong. 2nd sess., pp. 4511 et seq.

[4] Cf. Report of Sec. of Int. for 1894, vol. iii, pp. 466–73.

[5] Report of Attorney-General for 1894, pp. xxx–xxxi; James, Richard Olney, pp. 36–41.

[6] Report of Sec. of War for 1894, pp. 124–5, 152–5.

[7] Cf. N. A. Review for June, 1894, pp. 687 et seq.

success achieved by Coxey, and their followings melted away. Some of those who reached Washington lived for a time in squalid camps on the outskirts of the city. Others were sent to the work house. To be rid of a nuisance a few who remained were, late in the summer of 1894, provided with railway tickets to their homes by the commissioners of the District of Columbia.[1]

Harmless as the "armies" in themselves were, they were an expression of a condition in which danger was seen. Demagogues pressed forward to make use of the feeling of popular discontent and to increase it. They ostentatiously espoused the cause of the groundlings in their respective communities, flattered the leaders of the rising and, to gain applause from such sources, assailed in the familiar way, and denounced, men of property. The mayor of Chicago, Carter H. Harrison, rushed to the task of putting himself on the side of the oppressed, which did not save him from being shot and killed by an anarchist. The governors of five states entered into rivalry with the politicians who had been sent to Washington for places in a hall of doubtful fame—"Bloody Bridles" Waite in Colorado, Pennoyer in Oregon,[2] Lewelling in Kansas,[3] "Pitchfork" Tillman in South Carolina [4] and Altgeld of Illinois.

Altgeld was a German and he had been nominated for governor by the Democrats in 1892 to catch the foreign vote. He had conducted a campaign which emphasized the needs of the lower classes. He visited all parts of the state, entered factories, shook the horny hands of the sons of toil and generally made himself hail fellow, winning the election by a plurality of some 20,000 votes over the opposing Republican candidate, with the aid of separate People's party and Prohibition party nominations. On Sunday, June 26, 1894, a granite monument to the memory of the anarchists who had been hanged for the

---

[1] D. L. McMurray, op. cit., pp. 256–7.

[2] N. Y. Times, May 25, 1893.

[3] Cf. N. Y. Nation, Aug. 10 and Dec. 14, 1893, June 28, 1894.

[4] Called so because of his demagogic attacks upon Cleveland. "Send me to Washington," he said to cheering crowds of infatuated silverites in his state, "and I'll stick my pitchfork into his old ribs." He would hang the "gold bugs."—N. Y. Nation, Sep. 7, 1893.

bombing of the police in Chicago in 1887 was unveiled in a
cemetery of that city.[1] On the following day Altgeld pardoned
three men implicated in that crime who were languishing in the
state penitentiary at Joliet, two for life and the third for a term
of fifteen years. For seven years the attempt to make out a case
for them in the larger court of public opinion had been diligently
pursued not only in America but throughout the world. Judge
Gary, presiding in the criminal court in Cook county, who had
sentenced the men to punishment, had recently reviewed the
whole proceeding. They had been tried, he said, not for being
anarchists "but for procuring murder to be done, and being,
therefore, themselves guilty of murder." So much was charged
and this was proven; the offense had been one aimed at the whole
structure of society and the government set up by that society.[2]
The cases had been appealed to the supreme court of Illinois
where the judgment of the lower court had been unanimously
affirmed.[3] Nevertheless Altgeld said now that the trial had been
conducted with "malicious ferocity." His statement to the press
contained 17,000 words. Those whose admiration he desired
acclaimed his action. What he had done and his time and
manner of doing it produced consternation in the minds of other
men.[4]

It is clear that the ground was well prepared for a great strike
which would fix the eyes of the country on "organized labor" in
a contest with "capital." The Pullman Company had made
some progress with measures looking to the social welfare of their
working people. Near Chicago, in a place called Pullman, with
well-paved streets, parks, recreation centres, in neat and
sanitary houses, a certain number of the company's employees
could dwell.[5] This was the "Pullman experiment," a model

[1] N. Y. World, June 26, 1893.
[2] Joseph E. Gary in Century Magazine, April, 1893.
[3] Spies et al v. The People, 122 Ill., pp. 1 et seq.
[4] N. Y. World, June 27, 28 and 30, 1893; N. Y. Nation, June 29, 1893.
Altgeld delighted in the notoriety which he had suddenly achieved and
bade his critics "pitch in." They cannot, he said, "cut through my hide
in three weeks with an axe."—N. Y. World, June 28 and 29, 1893.
[5] Report of Strike Commission in 1894 in Senate Ex. Doc., 53rd Cong.
3rd sess., no. 7, pp. xxi–xxiii.

town, "happy Pullman town." No one was obliged to live there, but about a third of the men did so and, as would soon appear, without too much appreciation of their opportunities. They paid rents which they said were exorbitant.[1] Aesthetic surroundings were of no interest to them if they lacked bread. They felt themselves too much like villeins of an overlord who had once been a workingman like them, but who lived now in a palace in Chicago. It was, an observer on the ground said, "worse than Russia." He had never known a man who was "disliked by so many people as Pullman." [2]

Out of the welter of the depression had come a labor agitator, Eugene V. Debs. His father was a German who had kept a little shop in Terre Haute, Indiana. He was a glib talker. Averse to work and too fond of his dram he found congenial occupation in organizing and inciting men to make battle upon capital. To combat a General Managers' Association, a combination of the representatives of 24 railway companies, he had recently formed [3] the American Railway Union, of which he was president.[4] He invaded the Pullman village and enrolled some 4,000 car builders in the new organization. In a few months, in the country at large, he gained a membership of 150,000 for the union. It had lately, in April, 1894, won some prestige in strife with the officers of the Great Northern Railroad Company. Its agents were prepared for new action, when, in their opinion, a defense of their interests demanded it.[5]

The profits of railroads were no longer so large as they had been. The depression had very unfavorably affected freight and passenger car building in which Pullman was engaged.[6] The panic bore particularly hard upon the branch of the business having to do with the construction and operation of

---

[1] Report of Strike Commission, p. xxxv.

[2] Letter in Gresham Papers dated July 16, 1894; cf. Nico Bech-Meyer, A Story from Pullmantown.

[3] On June 20, 1893.

[4] For Debs see N. Y. Times, July 4, 1894; N. Y. Tribune, July 10, 1894; ibid., July 11, 1894, quoting Railway Age.

[5] Cf. Report of Strike Commission, pp. xxiii–xxviii. For General Managers' Association see ibid., pp. xxviii–xxxi.

[6] Ibid., p. xxxii.

the more sumptuous cars for riding in which extra charges were made, on which account the company in 1893 had laid off some of its employees, and reduced the wages of the others to the extent of 20 or 25 per cent., with a promise of better pay at a future day. Salaries of highly paid officials and dividends of stockholders were not cut. Why, the men argued, should they be the only sufferers from hard times? In May, 1894, they asked for a restoration of rates. Mr. Pullman met them in conference and gave them reasons why he could not accede to their demands. While, under necessity, he had reduced the number of employees from 4800 to about 1100, he had since, gradually, during the past winter, by strenuous effort, by underbidding for contracts, with the welfare of his working people in mind, increased the total to 3,300.[1] Wisely or not the men struck and Mr. Pullman, with or without wisdom, dropped the strikers from his pay rolls and sought non-union employees. He refused to arbitrate the issue. It was a subject which could not be arbitrated, he said—the company would itself decide whether it should continue to manufacture cars at a loss; it would not be told to do so by some third party.[2] The cause of the men became the cause of Debs and the other officers of his Railway Union who, in retaliation, ordered a "sympathetic" strike on the railroads of the country, an end the easier to gain since these companies had also recently reduced wages.[3] Trains containing Pullman cars, the labor leaders said, must not be moved out of stations and yards.

It was an expression of a praiseworthy desire, if it were an entirely impracticable ideal, when Debs issued an address to all the members of his organization on strike cautioning them against violations of law, municipal, state and national. No violence should be indulged in. The union "must triumph as law-abiding citizens, or not at all." If the companies could secure other men "to handle their trains" they had such a right.

---

[1] Report of Strike Commission, pp. 536–7, 573; cf. Pullman's statement in New York Times, June 29, 1894, and N. Y. Tribune, July 14, 1894.

[2] Report of Strike Commission, pp. xxxviii–xxxix, 552, 553.

[3] Ibid., p. 134.

The strikers should conduct themselves "as becomes men"; their cause then would be "crowned with success." [1]

This was well enough but Debs said much more. He undoubtedly incited his following to the turbulence which he seemed to deplore. He was misquoted and roughly used by the newspapers,[2] but it is not to be denied that in a manifesto, to which his name was attached, Pullman was declared to be in "the devilish work of starving his employees to death." The men were "mortgaging their bodies and souls as well as their children's" to a "heartless corporation." In a large sense it was a contest "between the producing classes and the money power of the country." [3] Peffer in the United States Senate spoke of Pullman as "heartless, soulless, conscienceless"; he was a "tyrant of tyrants." [4]

Violent men, augmented by the idle and vicious elements stranded in Chicago after the closing of the World's Fair, took control of the situation.[5] The object of the strikers, as soon appeared, was to "tie up and paralyze the operations of every railway in the United States and the business and industries dependent thereon." Riots were in progress at half a hundred places. The "labor men" gravely declared that the railway managers were employing "thugs and toughs" to create disturbances in order to prejudice the cause of the union. Excuse, if not justification for violence, was sought in this and other far fields, while conditions grew constantly worse. Debs spoke of extending the strike to the street railways, the Standard Oil Company and in other directions if settlement with him were not made "on a proper basis." [6] General Master Workman Sovereign, who had succeeded Powderly as head of the Knights of Labor, threatened the country with a "general strike," [7]

[1] McElroy, Grover Cleveland, vol. ii, pp. 144–5; cf. Report of Strike Commission, pp. xlv, 150, 408; N. Y. Times, June 30, 1894, and N. Y. Tribune, July 4, 1894.

[2] Report of Strike Commission, p. 158.

[3] N. Y. Nation, July 5, 1894; cf. statement in N. Y. Tribune, July 6, 1894.

[4] Cong. Record, 53rd Cong. 2nd sess., p. 7231; N. Y. Tribune, July 11, 1894.

[5] Report of Strike Commission, p. xliii.

[6] N. Y. Tribune, July 3, 1894.   [7] Ibid.

and later asked for such assistance from the various organized trades that "labor" might be emancipated from the "thraldom of greed," [1] though the call was ignored.[2]

Plunder and murder went on by day and by night. In the far West whole communities were cut off from the world. Mines and factories must be shut down, military posts could not be provisioned. The food supply of Chicago itself was threatened. The people faced famine.[3] Telegraph wires were cut. Boulders were rolled upon the tracks. Bridges were destroyed by dynamite. Railway station buildings were burned. Cars were derailed. Irons were torn from the sleepers. Non-union men were pulled out of engine cabs. Strikers stoned and fired pistols and guns at moving trains.

Mr. Cleveland's sympathy with the workingman was real and earnest. He, in practical ways, had shown only kind concern for the welfare of the plain and honest people of the country, of whom he was one, during his first administration of the Presidential office. But he was no man to be trifled with or bulldozed on the subject of the enforcement of law, which he had made equally clear in the course of his public career. When the mails were obstructed, as the Postmaster General said that they were, he was aroused. That their passage should be free was an injunction of the Constitution of the United States. It was a Federal power to protect postal communication from local interference. The President would perform his duty, and Attorney General Olney put the agencies of his department at the service of the Post Office. The situation was more serious at Chicago than elsewhere. Edwin Walker, a well known lawyer in that city,[4] was appointed to act as a special adviser of the government, and the judicial authorities, at the direction of the Attorney General, after conference, secured a "blanket injunction" from the United

[1] N. Y. Tribune, July 11, 1894. [2] Ibid., July 12, 1894.
[3] Report of Atty. Gen. for 1894, p. xxxi; N. Y. Tribune, July 4, 1894.
[4] "Recognized as the Nestor of the local bar, counsel for the World's Columbian Exposition and a corporation attorney of international repute." (Chicago corr. N. Y. Tribune, July 2, 1894.) However many in Chicago, like Judge Lambert Tree and Franklin MacVeagh, deplored the appointment and would have made some other choice.—Gresham Papers.

States District Court of Northern Illinois [1] forbidding acts of violence, which would do away with trial by jury, bringing offenders before judges for sentence,—in effect, a kind of substitute for martial law. [2] Similar restraining orders were obtained by United States attorneys in other railway centres in the area under disturbance. [3] These measures were taken not only because of the Federal obligation with respect to the forwarding of postal matter but also because of the Federal government's supervisory control of interstate commerce. To these authorizations was added the Sherman anti-trust law of July 2, 1890, relating to conspiracies in restraint of trade. Of this genus a great strike of this kind appeared to be a species. The injunction was called "a Gatling gun on paper." [4] If it should not prove to be effective the President, at need, could call upon the military power, and it was well understood that he would do so. [5]

On July 2nd the injunction was issued to restrain Debs and other men, whoever they might now or later be, from interfering with, and hindering and stopping trains which carried the mails. Three thousand special deputies were sworn in by the United States marshal at Chicago to enforce the orders of the court. They made an effort to perform their duties. Hoots and jeers greeted them. A mob of 25,000 in South Chicago overset cars upon the tracks, entirely closing the lines to traffic. The civil power was helpless. No mail train could leave Chicago. The marshal asked for military protection. [6] The Attorney General would be "surprised," Special Counsel Edwin Walker told Mr. Olney, "at the magnitude of the conspiracy." [7]

The mails into the White House were filled with protests. The President should stay Olney's "bloody hand." [8] The

[1] Cf. Henry James, Richard Olney, pp. 47–9.
[2] N. Y. Nation, April 4, 1895.
[3] Report of Attorney General for 1894, p. xxxii.
[4] N. Y. Tribune, July 3, 1894.
[5] McElroy, Grover Cleveland, vol. ii, pp. 146–7.
[6] Report of Attorney General for 1894, pp. xxxii–xxxiii.
[7] Under date of July 13, 1894, in Cleveland Papers. Cf. Edgar A. Bancroft, The Chicago Strike of 1894, pp. 67–8.
[8] John Swinton to Cleveland, July 3, 1894, in Cleveland Papers.

Knights of Labor told Mr. Cleveland that "indecent and malignant haste" was being shown in assisting "the railroad kings to coerce their striking employees." Olney was nothing but a "corporation lawyer"; he had no "respect for labor"; he should be dismissed as Attorney General. He was "toadying to monopoly." The injunction was "despotic usurpation." A prophet saw in what was taking place the end of the United States: the Mississippi would flow between two countries—"one the Cleveland monarchy, the other the republic of the West." [1]

No proper assistance being promised by Governor Altgeld— both the mayor of Chicago and the governor of the state were known to be on the side of the strikers,[2]—or, probably, from the volunteer militia, if it should be called to service, General Miles, in command of the Department of the Missouri, with headquarters in Chicago, was ordered, through the Secretary of War, to bring in from adjoining posts regular troops who were soon reinforced by infantry, cavalry and artillery from Michigan, Kansas, Nebraska, and New York. Miles told the people that the soldiers were not there "for display or for picnic purposes." They would not "stand too much nonsense," and would shoot.[3]

It was Altgeld's opportunity. He would openly espouse the cause of the strikers, being assured, as he was, of the support of a considerable body of socialistic and Populist opinion hostile to Mr. Cleveland, which was seeking expression in the Congressional campaign. Altgeld attacked the injunction and the judge who issued it, the President, Attorney General Olney, Special Counsel Walker, the United States marshals and the whole Federal system which, in a dispute, was being put at the service, as he expressed it, of "one of the combatants." [4]

He addressed a letter to the President. The Federal government, he said, had no authority to touch a situation in a state which was "able to take care of itself." [5] He even denied

[1] Cleveland Papers.
[2] Forum for August, 1894, p. 636; Henry James, Life of Olney, p. 204.
[3] N. Y. Tribune, July 6, 1894.
[4] McElroy, Grover Cleveland, vol. ii, p. 148.
     Ibid., p. 152.

the facts upon which military intervention was based. Where Federal officials saw trouble he found peace and good order. To "ignore the local government" in such a case, he said, was not only to insult the people of Illinois but to violate "a basic principle of our institutions." [1] He asked for "an immediate withdrawal" of the troops. President Cleveland replied. The action which had been taken, he said, had been "not only proper but necessary." [2] Altgeld returned to the charge, repeating his request that the troops be removed from the soil of Illinois, to be tersely told by the President that it was his (Altgeld's) duty, as well as the duty of all those in authority, to cease discussing the subject and to join in the general effort "to restore obedience to law and to protect life and property." [3]

In further proof that he was in good earnest the President, on July 8th, issued a proclamation warning all who were engaged in riotous proceedings in Illinois, and particularly in and around Chicago, to retire to their homes else they should be regarded as "public enemies" to be treated as such. The innocent would suffer with the guilty, if they did not get out of the way of the troops. [4] The country, Attorney General Olney said, had been "brought to the ragged edge of anarchy." [5] Cleveland declared that he would stamp out disorder if he had to mobilize the entire army of the United States and the militia of all the states. [6]

On July 9th the President, recognizing the riots as nation-wide, issued another and a similar proclamation with reference to the states of North Dakota, Montana, Idaho, Washington, Wyoming, Colorado and California and the territories of New Mexico and Utah. [7] "Regulars" on the Pacific coast under General Ruger were in the field and need was found for their services at Los Angeles and at Sacramento, and eastwardly to Truckee. At Oakland sailors and marines were landed to

[1] McElroy, op. cit., vol. ii, p. 155. [2] Ibid., p. 156.
[3] Ibid., p. 163; A. Nevins, Letters of Cleveland, pp. 357–62; N. Y. Nation, July 12, 1894.
[4] Richardson, vol. ix, pp. 499–500; Henry James, Life of Olney, p. 205.
[5] Washington corr. N. Y. Tribune, July 5, 1894.
[6] Barnes, John G. Carlisle, p. 332, quoting Curtis MSS.
[7] Richardson, vol. ix, pp. 500–1.

guard the mail trains.[1] General Merritt from his headquarters at St. Paul directed the operations of the troops on the Northern Pacific and the Great Northern lines.[2] General Brooke was active on the Union Pacific Railroad in the Department of the Platte.[3] General McCook dealt with the mobs on the Santa Fé system and on other roads in Colorado and New Mexico [4] which everywhere took to their heels at sight of sabres and bayonets.

Order was restored in a fortnight.[5] The troops saved the country from a "serious rebellion," said General Miles, who seems to have performed his full duty, despite the criticisms levelled at him by General Schofield, his superior officer.[6]

Many arrests were made both in Illinois and in the West. Debs himself was indicted by a grand jury in Chicago. He gave bail. Arrested again, with some of his confederates, he chose to enter the Cook county jail,[7] where he posed for a time as a martyr who had been crucified by capitalistic authority while crusading for a popular cause. In December, in the Circuit Court, he was sentenced to six months in prison.[8]

To soften the blow dealt to "labor" the President appointed a commission, headed by Carroll D. Wright, to investigate the causes of the troubles at Pullman town. Mr. Pullman and the officers of his company were annoyed by cross questioning and a report, which treated the strikers with more respect than they seemed to deserve, was printed at public expense.[9] Debs in January, 1895, carried his case to the Supreme Court. Before the highest judicial tribunal he was defended by enthusiastic friends, among them a young man practising at the Chicago bar, Clarence S. Darrow, who brought in as an associate the aged Lyman Trumbull whose sympathies had been excited to such a degree that he had volunteered

---

[1] Report of Sec. of War for 1894, pp. 111–6.
[2] Ibid., pp. 124–30.   [8] Ibid., p. 131.
[4] Ibid., pp. 138–40.   [5] Ibid., p. 109.
[6] J. M. Schofield, Forty Six Years in the Army, chap. xxviii.
[7] N. Y. Tribune, July 18, 1894.
[8] 64 Fed. Reporter, p. 724.
[9] Report of Strike Commission, 1894; N. Y. Nation, Nov. 22 and Dec. 6 and 13, 1894; Forum for January, 1895.

to proceed to Washington.[1] To no avail. The opinion of
the lower court as to the validity of Mr. Olney's injunction
was affirmed on the ground of the Federal interest in interstate commerce and the transmission of the mails, with the
elimination of the Sherman anti-trust law as a basis for the
action which had been a doubtful support for the proceeding
in the first instance.[2] The strike leaders were told that "the
means of redress of all wrongs" were "through the courts and
the ballot box." It was a lesson which could not be learned
too soon that, under the American system of government,
they had no right, in seeking remedy for grievances, either
"real or fancied," to invite "the cooperation of a mob with its
accompanying acts of violence."[3] Debs was now at the end of
his resources and he began his term of six months in prison,
residence which he improved by reading, whereby he converted
himself into a full-fledged socialist.

On such a background of events was set the biennial appeal
to the people on the subject of their representatives in Congress
and the governors and officers of various states, including legislatures which would elect United States senators. Public
feeling would be reflected in the result. The elections in 1893
had already indicated a revulsion of popular sentiment with
reference to the Democratic party. Maynard, who had been
arraigned by the Bar Association of New York City for corruptions in connection with elections, had been defiantly nominated by the Hill machine as judge of the court of appeals,
an officer who this year headed the Democratic ticket in New
York state, and he was defeated by more than 100,000 majority. [4]
A Republican legislature was elected which led to an investigation in New York City[5] by a committee under the chairmanship of Mr. Lexow, an obscure country lawyer, an adherent
of Republican Boss Platt. This was a pleasant opportunity
to expose the wicked alliances of Tammany with vice and crime,
and the gross thievery which went on in the name of govern-

---

[1] Horace White, Lyman Trumbull, p. 414.
[2] Cf. Henry James, Richard Olney, pp. 57–8.
[3] In re Debs, 158 U. S., pp. 564 et seq; N. Y. Nation, May 30, 1895.
[4] N. Y. Nation, Dec. 21, 1893.   [5] Ibid., Nov. 16, 1893.

ment under the eye of Richard Croker, who had exercised
paramount authority in New York after Hewitt was defeated
by Hugh Grant for mayor in 1888.[1]

Dr. Parkhurst had stirred the comfortable and stolid who
let evil thrive in democracies to avoid the labor of uprooting
it. He was aided by most of the newspapers, always under
the fearless and unfaltering leadership of the editor of the Evening Post,[2] and at last again the spirit which had unseated
Tweed was organized for effective action.[3] Croker's great
wealth was daily remarked by the newspapers. Of his houses
and carriages, his stock farm and racing stable, his trips in
private cars on railroads, the elegance and extravagance of
his life, without the performance of enough labor to win him
the meanest competence, everyone knew. Mr. Lexow, whose
name the committee bore, had little interest in the investigation,[4] but it was fortunate in having for counsel, John
W. Goff, who hauled up Croker's underlings for inquiry and
humiliation in the sight of the outraged community. They
sold offices; they "assessed" and took the gains of keepers of
dives, brothels, saloons and gaming houses; they blackmailed
honest business and industry. Croker himself was the subject
of cartoons which recalled Nast's pictorial attacks upon Tweed.
The pursuit of the man became so warm that he retired from
his place as Boss and fled to take a cure at one of the great
spas of Europe, although his return was not long postponed
when it was seen that he had little reason to fear the restraint
of his liberties. Tammany, Mr. Choate computed on the evidence adduced by the Lexow committee, had dishonest revenues of about $15,000,000 a year, while Tweed, it was said,
had stolen only about $6,000,000 in all.[5]

That the Tammany gang might be driven from place under
the pressure which was being put upon them seemed entirely

[1] N. Y. Nation, July 5, 1894.
[2] Life and Letters of E. L. Godkin, vol. ii, pp. 169–82; N. Y. Nation,
May 3, 1894.
[3] N. Y. Nation, Dec. 28, 1893.
[4] Cf. ibid., Feb. 7, 1895; N. Y. Times, Jan. 31, 1895.
[5] N. Y. Nation, Nov. 8, 1894. See Autobiography of Platt, chap. xiii.

probable. Hill would, of course, come to the defence of Croker in whatever way he could. He and his friends were conducting guerrilla warfare upon the President in both branches of Congress and on all fronts in New York state.[1] They found a new excuse for their enmity in the bond sale which they would condemn in an appeal to the prejudices of ignorant men, for the advantage of their "machine."[2] Whitney and others were suggested as candidates for governor, but Hill, who presided over the state nominating convention at Saratoga, on September 26, 1894, was shouted into the nomination by the Tammanyites, and, for his own and their purposes, he accepted it.[3] It was a dark day for the Democratic party in New York which had returned, Cleveland wrote to Daniel S. Lamont, to "wallowing in the mire."[4]

Hill when he had been elected to the United States Senate had not left the governorship until the expiration of his term; he would not resign his seat in the Senate now that he was to be engaged in a canvass for the governorship. The impudent and high-handed course of the managers of the machine, for the protection of unprincipled men who were misusing their powers, met with proper rebuke. Cleveland's friends nominated a separate ticket and for the governorship presented the name of a respected figure, Everett P. Wheeler,[5] while the Republicans, seeing their opportunity, nominated no less a personage than the late Vice-President of the United States, Levi P. Morton, who was elected over Hill by a plurality of more than 150,000, together with a Republican legislature, a movement which, unless there should be a sudden

---

[1] Cf. N. Y. Nation, April 12, 1894.

[2] Cf. McElroy, Grover Cleveland, vol. ii, pp. 82–3.

[3] Cf. Carl Schurz in N. Y. Times, Oct. 30, 1894; Writings of Schurz, vol. v, pp. 234–5.

[4] Cleveland Papers under date of Sep. 28, 1894; A. Nevins, Letters of Cleveland, p. 369.

[5] N. Y. Times, Oct. 10, 1894; N. Y. Nation, Oct. 18, 1894. Of Hill Cleveland at this time wrote to Lamont—"I don't see how anybody who knows what Democratic principles are, or cares to see them prevail, can support the man the Democratic organization of New York state has definitely and impudently attempted to cram down Democratic throats."— Letter from Buzzards Bay, Oct. 12, 1894, in Cleveland Papers.

change in popular sentiment, would send Hill back to private life.[1]

In New York City Croker's entirely arrogant management of the city for the profit of himself and his friends in Tammany Hall[2] had become insupportable. In the Parkhurst crusade and the Lexow investigation the Republicans saw their way to victory in the city as in the state, and, bidding for the aid of the awakened reformers, they nominated for mayor William L. Strong, a business man of high reputation.[3] He was elected amid expressions of satisfaction and reorganized the city government in the interest of honest service. His appointment of Theodore Roosevelt as police commissioner, who left the Civil Service Commission at Washington to accept the post; George E. Waring, Jr., a competent engineer and sanitarian, disconnected with politics, to clean the streets, and of other men with good purposes promised, with the proper cooperation of the legislature at Albany, should this be gained, to make an end of Tammany's venalities[4] which, however, with Platt directing that body, was rendered doubtful, indeed, as was seen by the sudden ending of the investigation and the character of the committee's report.[5] As it was, for three years, a number of genuine reforms would be effected in the government of America's greatest city.[6]

In the country at large many Republican leaders, such as Lodge, Reed, McKinley and even John Sherman, for the occasion, displayed leanings toward "free silver" in order to attract votes to their party tickets.[7] Silver planks found their way into Republican state platforms.[8] The elections resulted in astounding gains for the Republican party. It was a "land-

[1] Cf. N. Y. Nation, Oct. 4 and 11, and Nov. 15, 1894.
[2] Cf. ibid., Oct. 19, 1893.   [3] Ibid., Oct. 11, 1894.
[4] Cf. ibid., Nov. 29, 1894 and May 2, 1895.
[5] Platt's vindictiveness as a result of his failure to dictate Strong's appointments to office is displayed in Autobiog. of Platt, pp. 268 et seq. Cf. N. Y. Nation, May 16 and June 27, 1895.
[6] N. Y. Nation, June 27, 1895.
[7] Cf. ibid., June 7, 14 and 28, 1894; N. Y. Times, Oct. 10, 1894.
[8] Even in New York the platform contained a declaration in favor of "the use of both gold and silver as a circulating medium."—N. Y. Times, Sep. 19, 1894; cf. N. Y. Nation, June 14 and 28, 1894.

slide" of another kind. The Democrats had been tried; they
had been found wanting in unity, efficiency and good sense
in the sight of the country, and they would be retired in another
of those fits of emotion which so frequently overtake the people.
Only five Populists under that name would sit in the House
of Representatives of the next Congress and only 117 Democrats. Opposing them they would find 234 Republicans, a
majority for that party of about 110. It was noted by the
leaders of the triumphant political organization that even
the "Solid South" had been broken, for in the 54th Congress,
which would convene in 1895, there would be three Republicans
from North Carolina, four from Tennessee, seven from Missouri,
two from Virginia, one from Texas, four from Kentucky,
not counting members from districts in West Virginia, Maryland
and Delaware, control of which had been wrested from the
Democrats.

The disturbances attending such a campaign made further
havoc with the gold reserve. On November 14, 1894, eight
days after the Congressional elections, the Secretary of the
Treasury announced a second issue of $50,000,000 in 5 per
cent. bonds to protect the credit of the government. Public
bidding was reluctant and at low prices. It was important
that gold payments for the bonds should not involve withdrawals from the Treasury—that the gold should come from
other sources. The best offer "for all or none" was made by a
syndicate of 33 individuals and banking institutions in New
York City, again under the leadership of John A. Stewart.
They received the award at a rate which brought into the
Treasury more than $58,000,000 in gold, a sum nearly equal to
the proceeds of the first sale. The President's and the Secretary of the Treasury's course had been impelled by patriotic
feeling, and in the banker who had had the principal part in
forming the groups which purchased the two issues such motives
were not absent, since the risk was large and, instead of the
profit which it was assumed that he and his associates might
reap, they had suffered loss.[1] A part of the gold which the

---

[1] Barnes, John G. Carlisle, pp. 357-9; McElroy, Grover Cleveland, vol.
ii, p. 84.

bankers in the "syndicate" had turned into the Treasury was withdrawn in a little while by these same bankers who must redeem legal tenders to pay their subscriptions.[1] The greenbacks were paid out again to meet the daily expenses of the government, the falling off of estimated revenues being increased by the action of the Supreme Court, which, by a close vote of its members, in May, 1895, declared the income tax, devised and put into the tariff law by the Populists, to be a direct tax and, therefore, unconstitutional.[2] The operation of exchanging United States notes for gold was repeated and again repeated. The President called the process an "endless chain"; more than $300,000,000 in gold had been paid out for greenbacks which were still outstanding and at hand for further visits to the Treasury.[3] They should be retired. The President and Secretary Carlisle appealed to Congress and raised an issue which had been quiet for many years. The plea at an earlier time had gone unheeded and the danger had been forgotten.[4] Again the greenbacks were seen to be a menace to the credit of the country. The President in his message in December, 1894, called for "the absolute divorcement of the government from the business of banking." Plans for a more "elastic currency" were presented.[5] That paper or silver might become the currency of the country and that all payments might be made in cheaper money created general alarm.[6]

Congress was again in session and made no response to the President's earnest presentation of the case which, on Jan-

[1] A. D. Noyes, Thirty Years of Am. Finance, p. 231.

[2] Pollock vs. Farmers' Loan and Trust Co., 158 U. S., pp. 601 et seq.; Henry James, Richard Olney, chap. vii; A. D. Noyes, Thirty Years of Am. Finance, pp. 227–9; Cong. Record, 54th Cong. 1st sess., p. 492; N. Y. Nation, April 11, 1895.

[3] Richardson, vol. ix, p. 562.

[4] Thomas F. Bayard, in the Senate with John Sherman in 1878, told Sherman then that the demand Treasury notes when they came in should not be reissued; they should be cancelled. Remonstrance was in vain. Redemption with reissue, said Bayard, was "like bailing water with a sieve."— Bayard to Cleveland, Dec. 4, 1895, in Cleveland Papers.

[5] Richardson, vol. ix, pp. 553–6; Report of Sec. of Treasury for 1894, pp. lxxv–lxxvii. Cf. ibid. for 1893, p. lxxiii; N. Y. Nation, Dec. 13, 1894.

[6] The situation was plainly and competently, as well as briefly, stated by the Comptroller of the Treasury, James H. Eckels, in Forum for March, 1895.

uary 28, 1895, he repeated in a special message to that body.[1]
The absurdity of the system he stated in terms which it seemed
that everyone must comprehend. If other measures were not
taken to protect the Treasury he must renew his request for
authority to issue bonds on terms more favorable than any
which he could hope to obtain, while he must act under the
provisions of the old law of 1875. But the silverites would
withdraw even this power from him in order that their object
might be the more speedily attained,[2] though he assured them
that, if Congress should still fail in its duty, he would continue to exercise the authority with which he was already
vested "whenever, and as often" as, it should be "necessary to
maintain a sufficient gold reserve"; and he added, with the
bravery for which he gave so many proofs, that he would do
this "in abundant time to save the credit of our country and
make good the financial declarations of our government." [3]

Enemies whom Mr. Cleveland gained because of his refusal
to cooperate with the spoilsmen in his party, and to give them
free access to lucrative offices, joined the Republican politicians
who sought to embarrass and discredit him and who were
pleased to say that the situation had been brought on by the
reduced revenues coming from a "free trade" tariff bill instead
of from a foolish currency system. Their abuse of him they all
together believed would overwhelm him and bury him under an
avalanche of popular reprobation.[4]

In January, 1895, but two months after the second sale of
bonds, the reserve fell so rapidly that, on February 8th, it
was below $50,000,000. The popular madness on the money
question was not to be stopped. "I am sure I never was more
completely in the right path of duty than I am now," the
President said to Richard Watson Gilder, "but it is depressing
enough to have no encouragement from any quarter." [5] So

[1] Richardson, vol. ix, pp. 561–5; N. Y. Nation, Jan. 31, 1895.
[2] Cf. Barnes, J. G. Carlisle, pp. 367–8.
[3] Richardson, vol. ix, p. 554.
[4] How far the revenues affected the general troubles of the Treasury
is competently discussed in A. D. Noyes, Thirty Years of Am. Finance
chap. ix.
[5] Dec. 26, 1894, in Cleveland Papers.

terrific was the proscription as a result of the sentiment which had been aroused, that there was, he wrote to Mr. Bayard at the embassy in London, not one man in the Senate with whom he could be on terms of "absolute confidence." Even Vilas of Wisconsin, one of his fondest friends during the first administration, and Gray of Delaware, whose infirmities were frequently displayed, were, in some degree, estranged in the face of the tirade of unthinking opinion. They did not come to him; when he sent for them they were "full of reservations and doubts"; all seemed to have abandoned the effort to "stem the tide" except the President himself and the loyal men in his cabinet,[1] particularly Carlisle who had mastered the principles governing public finance. The Secretary of the Treasury, who had commenced with little knowledge of the subject now engaging his attention, had displayed a capacity to learn and he had the power of exposition which was evidenced in his reports, his official statements and the speeches which he was frequently called upon to make.[2]

It was not Cleveland's wish to go with his trouble to J. Pierpont Morgan of New York who, at the time, was regarded as the most powerful financier in the country. His character was such as to make even appearance of an admixture of public and private finance repellent to him. His political sense was sufficient to protect him from tactical errors. He would not do that which he knew to be damaging to his party to which he was faithfully attached, unless action in another direction should involve an important principle and the performance of a duty. He had plainly enough indicated his views on the question in connection with the two former bond sales. These sales had failed in that the bankers in the syndicate, who paid gold into the Treasury, at once, or soon, withdrew the greater part of it to make good their subscriptions.[3] Manifestly the foreign gold supply must be reached for the replenishment of the reserve and the services of the international banking

[1] Cleveland Papers, Feb. 13, 1895; A. Nevins, Letters of Cleveland, pp. 376–8; McElroy, Grover Cleveland, vol. ii, pp. 89–90.
[2] N. Y. Nation, Dec. 19, 1895.
[3] Noyes, Thirty Years of Am. Finance, p. 234.

houses must be sought.[1] No time now was to be lost; a run
on the Treasury which was imminent would lead to a general
crash.[2] A few days or a few hours would settle the question.[3]
Visits of August Belmont and other financial leaders to Washington, inquiries cabled by bankers to Europe as to the aid
which might be available in that quarter, anxious conferences
of members of the cabinet at the White House told of the
tensity of the crisis.[4] Curtis, the Assistant Secretary of the
Treasury, whose official errands carried him so frequently to
New York was again in Wall Street to gain information for
Carlisle. At this juncture, on the last day of January, 1895,
Morgan's talents were brought into requisition. He and
Belmont made proposals which Curtis bore back to Wash-
ington.[5]

A few days passed before the President's and Mr. Carlisle's
reluctance to resort to the more or less secret methods inevitable in private negotiation could be overcome. The bankers
were convinced that a popular loan could not be arranged
in such an emergency as the existing one, and this view was
powerfully enforced on the morning of February 5th when
Morgan and Belmont called at the White House to tell the
President of the desperate dangers confronting the country.
The Secretary of the Treasury and Attorney General Olney,
Morgan's partner, Robert Bacon, and his counsel, Francis
Lynde Stetson, a member of the President's old law firm in
New York, participated in the discussion. For four hours,
it is said, the consultations continued; they ended with no
decision on the part of the President. New and additional
authority for the contemplated action which had been discovered by Mr. Curtis in an old law of 1862 [6] was cited to break
down opposition to the signing of the contract. When Morgan
again came to Washington, on the 7th, he was met at the station

[1] Noyes, Thirty Years of Am. Finance, p. 234.
[2] N. Y. Nation, Feb. 28 and April 4, 1895; N. Y. Times, Feb. 18, 1895
[3] Noyes, Thirty Years of Am. Finance, p. 233. The country, Carl
Schurz said, was "within a hair's breadth of bankruptcy."—McClure's
Magazine, vol. ix, p. 638.
[4] Barnes, John G. Carlisle, pp. 371–2.   [5] Ibid., pp. 372–5.
[6] Sec. 3700 Revised Statutes.

by Secretary Lamont, but he was told that the President would not see him. He waited until morning. Meanwhile arrangements had been made for a conference, though it soon appeared, when the banker came to the White House, that Cleveland was still committed in his own mind to a public sale. At length, fully realizing that no other way opened and that instant action was requisite, Morgan and his legal adviser, the Secretary of the Treasury and the Attorney General agreed upon the terms of a contract which was signed and the momentous step was taken.[1]

An issue of $100,000,000 was suggested. But the President would hear of nothing in excess of $60,000,000, the present need of the Treasury in order to restore the reserve to its lowest limit, hoping that the gold, when it should be gained, could be held, or that Congress might, in the face of such startling conditions, come to the aid of the government for whose safe management they had joint responsibility. For the furnishing of this amount of gold Morgan was bound. He would accept 3 per cent. bonds to run for thirty years, if they were made payable in gold. If they were still to be payable in coin he would make the rate 4 per cent. For thirty years, at the price of sale agreed upon, which yielded the Treasury $65,116,244.62, the interest rate, taking account of the premium, was about 3¾ per cent. This meant a loss to the government of more than $16,000,000 which would be fairly chargeable to the obstinacy of the silver men and those who wished spitefully to serve the President. They were allowed ten days in which to consider the matter and undergo a change of heart.

The associates, the Morgan firms in New York and London and the Rothschilds, acting through their representatives, August Belmont & Company, in New York, were to deliver to the government from time to time 3,500,000 ounces of standard gold coin of the United States in return for United States bonds. At least one-half of the amount was to be obtained in Europe. The bankers rendering this service obligated them-

[1] This account follows that in the biography of Carlisle by James A. Barnes who has made careful investigations. See his chap. xv.

selves to exert their influence, in whatever way they could, to protect the Treasury against withdrawals of gold "pending the complete performance of the contract." [1]

Nothing was to be expected of Congress. The discussion of bills in the House and Senate which would have loosed the President's hands in relation to bond issues gave no promise of result, though members were hearing from chambers of commerce and individual business men in all parts of the country. The shadow of "repudiation," the impending "suspension of specie payments," topics which daily occupied the editorial pages of competently edited newspapers had no effect on what the New York Evening Post called the most "brutish" Congress in American history.[2] At the moment the "Springer bill," designed to bring gold into the Treasury and to afford the President relief, was under discussion in the House. On February 7th, the day preceding that one on which Mr. Cleveland and Mr. Morgan were so gravely engaged at the White House in formulating their plans to save the Treasury, this bill was defeated, with many expressions of bitterness, by a vote of 162 to 135.[3] The temper of the House could not be mistaken. A Populist from Georgia would horsewhip the "money changers" out of Congress—that is what Washington or Jackson, if either of those saintly men were alive, would do to "Grover" and the "goldites." [4] The gold bond that Cleveland wanted to issue, a Populist from South Carolina averred, would "enslave the country" for the next fifty years, a declaration which was received by the House with "prolonged cheers." No vote of his would be cast for a bill whose "whole purpose" was "to crush the people."

> "Princes and lords may flourish or may fade,
> A breath can make them as a breath has made;
> But a bold peasantry, their country's pride,
> When once destroy'd, can never be supplied." [5]

[1] Richardson, vol. ix, pp. 567–8; cf. statement of Sec. of Treas. in N. Y. Times, Feb. 19, 1895.
[2] N. Y. Nation, Feb. 21, 1895; cf. N. Y. Times, Jan. 30, 1895.
[3] Cong. Record, 53rd Cong. 3rd sess., p. 1926; N. Y. Times, Feb. 8, 1895; Barnes, J. G. Carlisle, pp. 369–70.
[4] Cong. Record, 53rd Cong. 3rd sess., p. 1905.   [5] Ibid.

The President, with certain knowledge of what the two houses would do, had gone forward without reckoning on their cooperation. A few hours after the conference with Mr. Morgan, on February 8, 1895, he communicated to Congress the details of the contract with the bankers. Mr. Wilson, chairman of the Committee on Ways and Means, presented a joint resolution in the House authorizing a promise by the government to pay the bonds in gold. The Populists made their speeches again. Jerry Simpson said that "Shylocks" had the country by the beard—it was a war "between man and the dollar."[1] A rustic who represented a disturbed community in Nebraska declared that the English language was not adequate to express his detestation of the President.[2] Another from the South caused the clerk to read lines from Thomas Hood which seemed greatly to amuse the members who were holding themselves as cheap as a party of naughty street gamins—

> "Gold! Gold! Gold! Gold!
> Bright and yellow, hard and cold,
> Molten, graven, hammered and rolled;·
> Heavy to get and light to hold,
> Price of many a crime untold," etc. etc.[3]

Bryan, the greatest Populist of them all, who, however, would not detach himself from the Democratic organization and was reading and laboring with the writings of Jefferson to prove that he, and not Cleveland, had a correct understanding of party principles, savagely attacked the contract. The President was the "trainman who had opened a switch and precipitated a wreck." He had made a deal with the "magnates of Wall Street" and "foreign money lenders." He could as little expect to come unharmed from such association as one could expect to escape asphyxiation if he locked himself up in a room and turned on the gas. The bankers had virtually offered us 16 millions of dollars as a bribe, if we would change our financial policy and deliver ourselves into their hands. The United

---

[1] Cong. Record, 53rd Cong. 3rd sess., p. 2188. [2] Ibid., p. 2195.
[3] Ibid., p. 2188. Lines concluding a humorous poem entitled "Miss Kilmansegg and her Precious Leg."

States could take care of itself without calling upon "foreigners."
The issue had come—it was the East against the West and
South—the East which was building up a "plutocracy" and
would make "servants of the rest of the people." [1]

Republicans in their anxiety to reap partisan advantage
spoke in the same mad way. Cannon opposed the resolution
in bitter words. If Carlisle were a Republican and he had made
such a contract the Democratic House would have impeached
him.[2] Grosvenor of Ohio denounced the contract as "monstrous." The Rothschilds had the Old World by the throat—
they were now putting their hands on the United States.
What a scheme! What an outrage! There was nothing the
matter with the credit of the United States until Cleveland
had "assailed" it in his messages, and these bankers had said
that it had gone down.[3]

The resolution reached a vote on February 14th—94 Democrats, 63 Republicans and 10 Populists, in all 167 members
of the House, voted to condemn the Morgan-Belmont-Roths-
child contract and the President's entire method of dealing
with the money question, and only 120 were willing to extend
to him the authority which would have reduced the interest
rate to 3 per cent.[4]

In the Senate, now as before, sympathy was still more impressively withheld from the President, though Gray and Vilas,
with the support, for the moment, of Hill,[5] were trying to defend
the administration. The announcement of the contract with
the bankers found that body engaged in another attempt
to pass a free coinage bill. The familiar drool from Stewart,
Peffer and the Populists about the "gold corner" and the "gold
pool," about buying peace from our rulers—the "gold kings"—
about the relations of the few who are very rich to the impoverished mass which pointed to the end of republican institutions
and would soon, and certainly, lead to a repetition of the French
Revolution was heard again.[6]

[1] Cong. Record, 53rd Cong. 3rd sess., app., pp. 284–7.   [2] Ibid., p. 2183.
[3] Ibid., pp. 2184–5.   [4] Ibid., p. 2201; N. Y. Nation, Feb. 21, 1895.
[5] Cong. Record, 53rd Cong. 3rd sess., p. 2282.
[6] Ibid., pp. 2069, 2070, 2321.

The "Silver Republicans" in the Senate looked at the subject from their quite as familiar standpoint. Wolcott declared the President's message a "wanton, cruel and deliberate attack" upon the credit of the country.[1] Its terms were "degrading to American manhood."[2] Teller said that the contract was "part and parcel of a great conspiracy to put the country on a gold basis and keep it there."[3] It was "the most scandalous transaction" which he had witnessed since his entry upon public life.[4]

Republicans who should have supported the President here, as in the House, were not far behind the Populists and the attorneys for the silver miners. Their hatred of Democrats exceeded their patriotism, and many of them lived to see a day when they were not glad to be reminded of their attitude at this time toward a great public issue. Henry Cabot Lodge disappointed his friends by calling the contract "the blackest" ever known in the history of the republic.[5] Sherman, Aldrich and Hoar declared that Cleveland had been a victim of the bankers. Men whose "services were not necessary" had driven a "hard bargain" with the government.[6]

Meantime the operations of the syndicate with which the agreement for the purchase of gold had been concluded were progressing favorably. Confidence was restored, though but a few days since disaster had seemed to be immediately at hand. If the investment were good for Morgan and the Rothschilds it would be good for others. A veritable stampede ensued. Those who had been unwilling to make subscriptions directly in aid of the government crowded one another to secure the issue. Bonds which the President had been obliged to distribute to a syndicate for 104½ were sold in a few minutes for 112¼. The issue was oversubscribed ten times. The prices for re-sale shortly ran up to 118 to 120.[7] At Rothschilds' office in London, before the lists for the loan had been open for two

---

[1] Cong. Record, 53rd Cong. 3rd sess., p. 2279. [2] Ibid., p. 2280.
[3] Ibid., p. 2287. [4] Ibid., p. 2286. [5] Ibid.
[6] Ibid., pp. 2327–8, 2381, 2383, 2385; N. Y. Times, Feb. 19 and 20, 1895.
[7] Cf. N. Y. Times, Feb. 22, 1895.

hours, applications were received for fifteen times as many bonds as were offered.[1]

Well informed men of affairs throughout the country made no question of the terms by which this invaluable protection for the Treasury had been obtained. It was clear enough to those who knew the facts and who cared for the result that the President had acted with wisdom and courage at a critical hour.[2] "Your unflinching steadfastness is the one encouraging thing in the present gloomy political situation," wrote ex-Governor Russell of Massachusetts. "Heaven only knows where we should have drifted without you."[3] He had been, another said, "the rudder and anchor of our ship of state."[4]

Not so with Mr. Cleveland's diligent foes. The bankers had made money in the operation and, eager to find new cause for assailing him, the outcry became louder. The scandal was so great that the contract should be thoroughly investigated by Congress.[5] The New York World called it "dark lantern financiering." The people would have subscribed for the bonds at a low rate of interest. It was "blood money"; the tax payers must pay the bill. Cleveland had been "worked," "mulcted," "buncoed" by a lot of money jobbers.[6]

He had thrown away the revenues of the government, said the New York Tribune, and had put the Treasury where it was— "at the mercy of all the world." For 30 years the United States had dictated terms to the bankers; the policy of the country now was that of the Rothschilds and Belmonts—it was an English rather than an American policy. "International wreckers" had been called in, the Tribune continued, to haul the ship off the rocks where the Democrats had put it. Cleveland could have made the rescue himself if he had trusted the people instead of posing before the world as the champion of gold bonds.[7] Old Mr. Chittenden, who had been Register of

---

[1] N. Y. Nation, Feb. 28, 1895; N. Y. Times, Feb. 21, 1895; McElroy, Grover Cleveland, vol. ii, p. 94.
[2] Cf. N. Y. Times, Feb. 18 and 21, 1895; Barnes, J. G. Carlisle, p. 398.
[3] Feb. 25, 1895, in Cleveland Papers. [4] Cleveland Papers.
[5] Cong. Record, 53rd Cong. 3rd sess., p. 2447.
[6] N. Y. World, Feb. 13, 18, 19, 20 and 21, 1895.
[7] N. Y. Tribune, Feb. 12, 13, 15 and 21, 1895.

the Treasury during the war, said that Carlisle should be impeached.[1] Others spoke even more plainly and intimated, when they did not allege, that the President had acted corruptly. He and the bankers together had robbed the government. He had opened the doors of the Treasury to some of the first malefactors in the land; they had put in their hands and they had taken out millions of the people's money.

Though the immediate outlook with reference to the reserve was reassuring, the bond sale was a temporary device as every one of competent knowledge knew. The greenbacks, so long as they were uncancelled, would appear again; gold would be demanded in exchange for them. In his third message to Congress, in December, 1895, the President made a fresh appeal for treatment of the currency question which would remove the cause of the disorder and apply a permanent remedy. The last Congress which had been nominally Democratic had failed in its duty; the new, the Fifty-fourth, was predominantly Republican. Reed was again Speaker of the House. More support than had been vouchsafed the President by his own party could not be expected of the opposing one. In less than a year the country would be disturbed by another election and already the way was being prepared for the great quadrennial contest.

The sound money men among the Republicans still held aloof. They were careful to say that they were "bimetallists" lest they fling away their political chances. They as diligently evaded statements in favor of the retirement of the greenbacks and appeared to be as muddle-headed on the financial question as they presumed the masses of the people to be.[2] Many of them manifested unconcealed glee in seeing a President who had been elected by another party in such a plight. Their favorite and reiterated explanation of the drain upon the government's gold supply was the Democratic tariff law. It had disturbed business; it had reduced the revenues; it had started a run upon the Treasury; its presence on the statute books prevented return to confidence in the solvency of the

---

[1] N. Y. Tribune, Feb. 16, 1895.
[2] Cf. Cong. Record, 54th Cong. 1st sess., pp. 349, 350.

government; "free trade" was responsible for the "endless chain." It was as well known by intelligent and sincere Republicans who were not silverites as by the President and his friends in the Democratic party that the currency system was unsound and that it should be reorganized.

Mr. Cleveland now in his message at the convening of Congress in December, 1895, called for the retirement and cancellation of the greenbacks and the Treasury notes issued against silver purchases in accordance with the terms of the Sherman law of 1890. They could be exchanged for United States bonds, bearing a low rate of interest and they could be put out of the way. The stringency which might result from a measure, the mere suggestion of which was so inflaming to the inflationists, could be averted by the use of gold obtained by their retirement, by an increase in the note circulation of the national banks and the conversion into coin from time to time of silver owned by the government, when this could safely be done.[1]

The President combined with these suggestions the plainest statements yet uttered in a state paper regarding the dangers of free silver coinage. His bravery set him apart from most men at the time in public position and presented the issue between him and the Populist wing of his own party; between sound and cheap money men whatever their party allegiance; between men who were mere politicians hunting for votes in the oncoming election and those whose statesmanship rested on personal character and high moral principles.

The gold reserve at the date of the President's message had fallen to less than $80,000,000.[2] Another bond issue might not have been avoidable in any case.[3] But a startling communication to the new Congress soon after it had convened in regard to the old boundary question in Venezuela led to sudden further demands upon the Treasury for gold. Europe sold our stocks and bonds. There were sharp recessions in quoted prices in Wall Street. Several brokerage houses failed.[4] In this conjunc-

---

[1] Richardson, vol. ix, pp. 641–8.   [2] Ibid., p. 645.
[3] Barnes, J. G. Carlisle, p. 410.
[4] N. Y. World, Dec. 21, 1895; Barnes, J. G. Carlisle, p. 409.

ture the President addressed another message to Congress asking for legislation to protect the gold reserve,[1] with as little hope of respectful hearing as before.

A visit of Mr. Morgan to Washington gave rise to rumors of a fourth bond issue. The situation was alarming enough to suggest the necessity of another contract with the bankers and, while there were consultations between Mr. Morgan and his partner, Robert Bacon, on the one side, and the President and the Secretary of the Treasury on the other, no assurances were given. Mr. Morgan, nevertheless, believed that a call upon him might be imminent and he went forward with his arrangements. He addressed other bankers and formed a syndicate which should sell the government $200,000,000 worth of gold.[2] The news of this action led to the publication of statements that the President had concluded a secret agreement with "money changers in the market place."

The New York World was eagerly seeking to distance all its competitors as the "people's friend." The owner, Joseph Pulitzer, saw the opportunity for again putting its name before the country and increasing its circulation among the unthinking masses from which it had, from the beginning, recruited its readers. Morgan had "cornered" the gold which the government must have for its reserve, said the World.[3] There should not be another "deal" like that which had "discredited" the nation in the previous February.[4] The bankers were ready for a "second hold up" of the government.[5] The President was about to give "princely millions of the people's money" to his "near friends." They formed a "ring"; he should "smash" it. If he should fail to do so the inference would be plain. His honor as a public officer was at stake. The people would take the loan. Mr. Pulitzer, who had found his new kind of journalism very profitable, would himself subscribe for $1,000,000 worth of the bonds to bear interest at 3 per cent. The whole country would respond "with alacrity." It would

[1] Richardson, vol. ix, pp. 659–660; N. Y. World, Dec. 26, 1895.
[2] McElroy, Grover Cleveland, vol. ii, pp. 96–8.
[3] N. Y. World, Jan. 1, 1896.
[4] Ibid., Dec. 27 and 28, 1895.   [5] Ibid., Jan. 1 and 2, 1896.

"hardly require a day," the World said, to sell the entire issue to the people.[1]

The members of Congress had made an appearance of remaining in session during the Christmas holidays, fearful of the President's reproofs were they, in such a conjuncture, to vote themselves a long recess. They met and adjourned and met again. When they were at work the tone of debate and speech was critical and angry. The House, with its overwhelming Republican majority, passed a tariff bill, at the dictation of.the growers and shearers of sheep in Ohio, restoring the duty on wool. Such a bill, they said, would increase the revenues of the government whose troubles, they continued to assert, were solely attributable to an impaired income. The Republican leaders were striving timidly and factiously, without doing affront to cheap money elements whose strength in the coming Presidential election would be great, to find some middle way in regard to the greenbacks and issues of bonds to protect the gold reserve. In the Senate, with an increase in the Populist strength, and with Silver Republicans and Silver Democrats who were utterly unruly on the money question and filled with bitter hate for all who rose in defense of sound financial principles, the most indecent attacks were made upon the President.

Democrats in Congress who dared to raise their voices for the administration were "cuckoos." The last sale of bonds to the syndicate was recalled. That transaction, Teller of Colorado said, was marked either by "dishonesty or imbecility." [2] Strangely enough Cleveland's leading defender now in the Senate was Hill, who skillfully parried the incessant attacks upon "Wall Street" and the city and state of New York.

As soon as the World entered the field the motley opposition took hold of the idea which that newspaper was developing, ornamenting and commending day by day, the while it pointed a long finger to its own wisdom in the field of public finance. Pictorial caricature of the President, Mr. Morgan and Secretary Carlisle were freely used to enforce its argument. Senators and representatives, silverites and other men, seeking

[1] N. Y. World, Jan. 3, 1896.   [2] Cong. Record, 54th Cong. 1st sess., p. 471.

some new hook upon which to hang their words, called for a popular loan. Even senators who had been graduated from colleges found it a kind of forensic sport to pillory a President who would not trust the people. The silver men had marshalled their forces; the jingoes must be stirred, too, and brought in to swell the volume of popular indignation. The American people had never been appealed to in vain, said Lodge.[1] They would subscribe, said Senator Hawley, as soon as they could telegraph to the Treasury Department.[2]

No facts were at hand, nor were they asked for. It was admitted that the whole basis for the outburst was "newspaper talk."[3] Intelligent men who were honest with themselves knew that no certain line of action had been resolved upon by the President. Attack, Mr. Cleveland said in a letter to Senator Caffery, after he had read the report of the debate, was based upon the "accusations and assertions of a maliciously mendacious and sensational newspaper." No banker had been invited to Washington, the President continued. No arrangement for the sale of bonds had been concluded. No assurance that such an agreement would be made had been given to any one either directly or indirectly. The administration had always, and still now, expressed decided favor for popular loans. Senators could know, if they would inquire, that, if bonds were issued, every means would be used to dispose of them by popular subscription after public advertisement. The President indicated an early announcement by the Secretary of the Treasury.[4]

Mr. Morgan, reasoning from his own standpoint, in view of the state of the gold reserve, was acting entirely within his right and the President and the Secretary of the Treasury were committing no imprudence on their side. It was one thing to sell bonds, another, as experience had shown, to sell them for gold, and gold which should not be drawn out of the Treasury by the subscriber to make good his subscription. Only power-

---

[1] Cong. Record, 54th Cong. 1st sess., p. 470. [2] Ibid., p. 473.
[3] Ibid., p. 463; cf. Barnes, J. G. Carlisle, pp. 410, 411.
[4] McElroy, Grover Cleveland, vol. ii, pp. 102 4; A. Novins, Letters of Cleveland, pp. 422–3; cf. Mr. Morgan's testimony in Senate Doc., 54th Cong. 2nd sess., no. 187, pp. 301–2.

ful financiers capable of controlling the situation could be useful in forwarding such a financial operation.[1]

At once, on January 6, 1896, Mr. Carlisle announced a new 30 year 4 per cent. loan to the amount of $100,000,000. The conditions eliminated Mr. Morgan and his syndicate which he dissolved, though not before he had addressed its members asking them as individuals to subscribe for themselves and to induce others to aid in making the loan a success.[2]

Meantime the World informed the country that it had averted a great scandal and, lest it lose the advantage which it had gained from so much advertisement, inquired by telegraph of 10,000 bankers in all parts of the country, whether they would give gold for bonds. The replies, though many of them were, if not evasive, plainly negative, were spread before its readers as an evidence of its amazing "enterprise." [3]

Only 827 out of 4635 of those making tenders named higher rates than J. P. Morgan and Company. Many of the bids came from irresponsible persons. Others who had subscribed could not secure gold to pay their subscriptions. The 827 persons and firms whose bids were accepted received $62,321,150 in bonds. The rest, nearly $40,000,000, were awarded to J. P. Morgan and Company.[4] Of the $111,000,000 realized by the government from the sale $97,000,000 had come from New York, nearly all of which amount had been subscribed by Mr. Morgan and other men who, from the beginning, had been supplying gold to the Treasury.[5] Thus, while it was a public subscription, the people again expressed but a cool interest in the sale about which there had been so much ignorant clamor.[6]

---

[1] Cf. N. Y. Nation, Jan. 9, 1896.

[2] McElroy, Grover Cleveland, vol. ii, p. 104; A. Nevins, Letters of Cleveland, pp. 425–6.

[3] N. Y. World, Jan. 7, 1896, and following issues.

[4] Senate Doc., 54th Cong. 2nd sess., no. 187.

[5] Barnes, John G. Carlisle, p. 422; N. Y. Nation, Jan. 23, 1896.

[6] The excuse for the failure of the loan as a popular loan offered by the World and the advocates of its theories in and out of Congress was that the Secretary of the Treasury had not reached the people. The people would not make bids at a few large money centres. The loan should have been carried to them in small amounts.—Cf. Cong. Record, 54th Cong. 1st sess., pp. 488–9, 532–3.

On the last day of January, 1896, the gold reserve had fallen below $50,000,000. At the end of February, as a result of the bond issue, it was $124,000,000 and, by good fortune, no further sales were necessary. In two years, by the creation of a debt of $262,000,000, $293,000,000 in gold were brought into the Treasury to support the reserve.[1]

In the midst of this uproar the Republicans increased their number in the United States Senate by two; both were silverites. At the end of January a pair of newcomers from Utah presented themselves at the bar to take the oath.[2] One was a Mormon. The sudden bringing into the Union of a territory which was filled, as it was so freely said, with a dangerous people who could on no account, certainly at no early day, be entrusted with the self determination implied by statehood, is difficult to explain. But the Republicans were seeking an increase of strength. It was a small matter if the new state should be for the free coinage of silver—the managers of the party were still striving to conciliate the insurgent element in the West. As for the Democrats many were content to see two more men in the Senate who would combat the President on the currency question.[3]

The Federal law, it was said, had made an end of polygamy. The ecclesiastical organization of the sect which had practised it had undergone complete change under the punishment meted out by Congress. The pledges of the leaders lately distrusted were now found to be worthy of respect. President Harrison in 1893 pardoned and amnestied a large number of polygamists, and in 1894 President Cleveland had completed the work.[4] The Mormon and anti-Mormon political parties in the territory had been dissolved; men now were Republicans or Democrats.[5] The enabling act was passed by the House and the Senate. The President was asked to veto it. A friend wrote him, what he well knew, that experience with new states had been unsatisfactory. They "diluted the Senate." Constituencies composed of less than one-tenth of the population

[1] Cf. McElroy, Grover Cleveland, vol. ii, p. 105.
[2] Cf. N. Y. Nation, Jan. 9 and 27, 1896. [3] Cf. ibid., July 19, 1894.
[4] Report of Sec. of Int. for 1894, vol. iii, p. 481. [5] Ibid., p. 481.

of the country and much less than one-tenth of the intelligence were represented by a third of the senators, and these senators opposed every measure which the President commended and defended.[1] But any other course could not well be taken and he approved the bill on July 16, 1894, in the midst of the excitement attending the railway riots in Chicago. A constitution was framed breathing religious toleration and prohibiting plural marriages, and it was adopted by popular vote in November, 1895. On January 4, 1896, Utah was proclaimed a state—the 45th state—of the Union,[2] and the officers of the Mormon church, with more politeness than propriety, perhaps, wrote to the President thanking him for permitting the territory to emerge "from the clouds" that had "obscured her true lustre before the nation," and to shine as "one of the bright stars upon our country's flag." [3]

Another sage brush and mining camp community with a population of about 200,000 was given a voice in the determination of public matters in the upper branch of Congress equal to that of New York or Pennsylvania or Massachusetts. The House of Representatives had voted to admit Arizona and New Mexico. If these, too, were brought in, seven thinly settled states—Arizona, Idaho, Montana, Nevada, New Mexico, Utah and Wyoming—with less than 750,000 inhabitants, would have 14 out of 94 senators, one-seventh of the whole number, all, as was pointed out, with a common interest in silver mining and in the sale of that metal to the government for use as money.[4]

So much was in view without taking account of Oklahoma. Its importance in wealth and population was increased, when, in September, 1893, in accordance with a provision of an act of Congress approved on the last day of Harrison's administration, satisfying the claims of the Indians to the Cherokee Outlet, that strip of land was opened to settlement. President Cleveland's proclamation set the day for the "rush." [5] More

---

[1] Everett P. Wheeler to Cleveland, July 13, 1894, in Cleveland Papers.
[2] Richardson, vol. ix, pp. 688–9; N. Y. Nation, Nov. 14, 1895.
[3] Jan. 4, 1895, in Cleveland Papers. [4] N. Y. Nation, July 5, 1894.
[5] Richardson, vol. ix, pp. 406–24.

than 100,000 "boomers" were assembled at Arkansas City and other places on the border awaiting a firing of the signal gun. They poured into the country seeking farms near water courses. Many in disgust, meeting dust storms and "sooners" with six shooters already on the ground, trailed out again.[1] The 9400 square miles in the strip were divided into seven counties, towns were built and, when the strife with the "sooners" was ended, peace reigned under the mistletoe which the legislature had designated as the "floral emblem" of Oklahoma. The adjoining Indian Territory, containing about 31,000 square miles, was regarded enviously; it might be annexed. Memorials began to appear in Congress which, if statehood should be achieved, would bring two more frontiersmen into the United States Senate, four, if the Indian Territory were separately organized, an end which some men had in view.

The troubles prepared for the government by the Geary law which had been passed by Congress during the campaign of 1892 were the inheritance of Mr. Cleveland. The Chinese in the United States, one and all, were to register before May 5, 1893. Those who should not do so were to be deported. Under advice of the Six Companies they were taking no note of the singularly brutal statute,[2] and anti-Chinese officers of the Treasury Department in San Francisco were boasting that they would arrest the "pigtails" in a body and clear the Pacific coast of them at a swoop.[3]

The President was appealed to for a statement of his intentions with reference to the enforcement of the law and the question of its constitutionality had been taken to the Supreme Court.[4] Secretary Carlisle in a circular practically suspended enforcement pending a decision from that body. It was hoped, said the New York Nation, that the court would permit the country "to retreat gracefully from a position worthy only of barbarians."[5] But the court's judgment of the act,

[1] N. Y. Tribune, Sep. 19, 1893.   [2] Cf. Forum for June, 1893, p. 413.
[3] N. Y. Nation, Feb. 23, 1893.   [4] Ibid., March 30 and April 6, 1893.
[5] Ibid., May 11, 1893.

which was rendered on May 15, 1893, was, to everyone's surprise, favorable, though with powerful dissenting opinions, and it supported deportation.[1] Therefore some other line of action must be devised. It was not so certain as before, even in California, that it would be well to be rid of all the Chinese. Employers, especially land owners, were still not convinced that they could do without the labor of this useful people.[2] Everywhere, Secretary Gresham thought, opinion with reference to the Chinese was more tolerant than it had been.[3] The immigration of the Italians with their Mafia, and of hordes which were beginning to arrive from Hungary and from eastern Europe, were turning the attention of the country from the Chinese to other classes of undesirable aliens.[4]

It now appeared that there was no money to enforce the provisions of the law without further action by Congress.[5] Seven millions of dollars would be required to deport a hundred thousand people. This lacking, the Chinese, upon arrest, which the law required, must remain in American prisons until the means were at hand to send them out of the country,[6] and a few suffered this cruel treatment at the hands of vindictive authorities in California.[7]

McCreary, a representative in the House from Kentucky, led a movement to amend the Geary law, extending the time allowed for registration for six months and introducing a few other liberalities. Though all by the Geary law were to be tagged and photographed, only about one-eighth of the whole number, if so many, had presented themselves to the proper

[1] Fong Yue Ting v. U. S., 149 U. S., p. 698; N. Y. Nation, May 18, 1893; Coolidge, Chinese Immigration, p. 225.

[2] N. Y. Nation, May 18, 1893; Coolidge, Chinese Immigration, p. 227; Cong. Record, 53rd Cong. 1st sess., pp. 2565, 3085. "The people of California are but dimly aware that all the great industries here are founded on the patient and reliable labor of the Chinese, a labor that is constant without a taskmaster and faithful to contract without threat of the law."— John P. Irish to Cleveland from San Francisco, May 16, 1893, in Cleveland Papers.

[3] Foreign Relations for 1893, p. 255.

[4] Cf. Coolidge, Chinese Immigration, pp. 232, 235–6.

[5] N. Y. Nation, May 25 and June 1, 1893; Cong. Record, 53rd Cong. 1st. sess., p. 2565; Foreign Relations, 1893, pp. 234–5.

[6] Cf. Foreign Relations for 1893, p. 246.   [7] Cf. ibid., pp. 256–9.

officers.[1] The Chinese had been invited to the United States, said Mr. McCreary; they had been encouraged to come by our treaties and laws. Some of them had been living here for 25 years. They must have the opportunity to "prove their residence." Banishment without a hearing could not be thought of in "this Christian and civilized age."[2] The amendment was adopted by the Congress which Mr. Cleveland had called to repeal the silver purchase act against the mad opposition of Geary and other members from California and the Pacific coast who owed their seats, as they thought, to the labor unions,[3] and it was signed by the President in November, 1893.[4] This amendment and a new treaty in 1894 marked at last the beginning of a reaction,[5] though it was yet slight and promised to be slow, against one of the most discreditable displays of race prejudice in the history of the republic.[6]

President Cleveland's ideals for the civil service had suffered some damage by the necessity under which he labored of making terms with leaders of his party in order to secure support in Congress for his policies. He thereby met the criticism of the reformers. They would have had him be unyielding under such temptations and they never ceased to give him such advice.[7] His appointments may have aided him at the special

[1] Cong. Record, 53rd Cong. 1st sess., p. 2565.   [2] Ibid., p. 2564.
[3] McCreary said of the opponents of the measure—"Indeed I have sometimes wondered whether they were masquerading or in earnest."— Ibid., p. 2565.
[4] Ibid., pp. 2567, 3092.
[5] Ascribable in some degree to a much admired and enlightening Chinese exhibit at the Chicago World's Fair. (M. R. Coolidge, Chinese Immigration, p. 234.) On our side a correspondent of the N. Y. Tribune suggested that we should put in the exposition two companion pictures—one the emancipation of the slaves, the other the expulsion of the Chinese. He had formed some verses—
    "Here's the land of the free and the home of the brave,
    Knight errants are we to succor and save;
    In the civilized world are we not in the van?
    The slave we have freed. As for this yellow man
    We'll hoot him and loot him, and so, by degrees,
    We'll worry the life out o'these horrid Chinese," etc. etc.
                —N. Y. Tribune, Feb. 13, 1893.
[6] Cf. A. C. Coolidge, The United States as a World Power, p. 336.
[7] N. Y. Nation, Feb. 16 and Nov. 9, 1893, and Jan. 25, 1894; Writings of Schurz, vol. v, pp. 179–80.

session in securing a majority for the repeal of the Sherman silver purchase act.[1] But he received no credit from the Mugwumps for dealing with men who had low standards for the public service. Nor can he himself have thought that he was in any way rewarded for breaking his own admirable rules in view of the rebellion which, as his administration advanced, broke out within his own party over the tariff and currency questions.[2] He was again, in his second as in his first term, surrounded by heads of departments and bureaus who did not share his views in regard to office-holding, and acted, when they could, without regard to his enunciated principles.[3] He earned reproof for appointing, at W. C. Whitney's request, as minister to Italy a gentleman from Rhode Island, J. J. Van Alen, who had contributed a large sum to the party campaign 'fund and, when, under criticism, Mr. Van Alen declined the appointment, for urging that he accept it,[4] a flurry which ended only when Wayne MacVeagh was named for the post.[5]

On the other hand the President was warmly praised for his stout defence of a high purpose in regard to the Supreme Court. Hill in the Senate vengefully awaited nominations of men from New York state who were not in his retinue. With the aid of spiteful Republicans he managed to prevent the confirmation of William B. Hornblower.[6] This excellent appointment, commended by the leaders of the New York bar,[7] having met with opposition, was followed by the nomination of

---

[1] As, for instance, from Voorhees who was "wobbly," as Gresham said, (Gresham Papers) in return for patronage in Indiana. Voorhees was plainly bought for service and almost immediately after repeal resumed his place in the ranks of the silverites.—N. Y. Nation, Dec. 21, 1893; cf. ibid., March 30, 1893; J. F. Rhodes, From Hayes to McKinley, p. 403; Writings of Schurz, vol. v, pp. 134–8; R. W. Gilder, Grover Cleveland, pp. 111–2; A. Nevins, Letters of Cleveland, p. 321; Schurz to Cleveland, March 30, 1893, in Cleveland Papers; M. Gresham, Life of Gresham, p. 670.

[2] R. W. Gilder, op. cit., pp. 114, 204.

[3] J. F. Rhodes, From Hayes to McKinley, pp. 411–3.

[4] N. Y. World, Dec. 4, 1893.

[5] The correspondence between Cleveland, Whitney and Van Alen, and various protests on this subject, are in the Cleveland Papers. Some letters bearing on the incident are printed in A. Nevins, Letters of Cleveland, pp. 333, 336–7, 338–41. See also N. Y. Nation, Oct. 5, 12 and 26 and Dec. 7, 1893; N. Y. Times, Sep. 28 and 29 and Oct. 5, 1893.

[6] N. Y. Nation, Jan. 11 and 18, 1894.   [7] Cleveland Papers.

Wheeler H. Peckham, president of the New York Bar Association,[1] confirmation of whom Hill, by mischievous activity, was also able to defeat,[2] compelling the *coup* which placed Senator White of Louisiana on the high Federal bench.[3]

The independence of the President's action increased as his party crumbled around him and he was left to himself.[4] As he could he extended the classified service, which, when his second term began, included about 43,000 employees of the government, to about 84,000. During his second term, therefore, he doubled the number of office holders under protection and put them permanently out of the reach of the spoilsmen.[5]

The American mind on subjects pertaining to international relations remained uninformed. The summation of our foreign policy comprised little more than two ideas, first, the undesirability of making "entangling alliances," especially with the governments of Europe, or of adopting courses which might, in future, involve us in such alliances, a tenet founded on the counsel of George Washington; and secondly, the Monroe Doctrine, which was made to mean more or less as the words left the lips of the politician, or the pen of the writer for the press. Our State Department concerned itself largely with these two principles which lay at the foundation of our interest in foreign affairs and with "insults" which were done sailors on our ships and citizens, frequently filibusters, poachers and refugees from justice, meted out to them by other governments. Commotion in regard to such small questions which were magnified into provocation for *ultimata*, naval movements and wars

---

[1] N. Y. Nation, Jan. 25, 1894.

[2] In spite of the highest recommendations of James C. Carter, Joseph H. Choate, Elihu Root and others. His merits, Choate said, were "universally recognized."—To Cleveland, Jan. 30, 1894, in Cleveland Papers. Cf. N. Y. Nation, Feb. 22, 1894; A. Nevins, Letters of Grover Cleveland, pp. 345, 346-7.

[3] McElroy, Grover Cleveland, vol. ii, pp. 131-7.

[4] N. Y. Nation, Jan. 25, 1894; S. M. Cullom, Fifty Years of Public Service, p. 269.

[5] McElroy, Grover Cleveland, vol. ii, p. 16; cf. J. F. Rhodes, From Hayes to McKinley, pp. 456-7; Theodore Roosevelt in Atlantic Monthly for Feb., 1895; Forum for July, 1896, pp. 555-6; N. Y. Nation, May 14, 1896.

by the new sensational journals, and by demagogues who gained their knowledge of international matters through such newspapers, gave little dignity to our foreign policy. An outlook so provincial served but to increase our reputation for jaunty "Yankeeism" which the untravelled and inexperienced men who were appointed to take charge of our consulates and legations in other countries could do little to correct.

The indifference with which we viewed representation of the government in foreign lands was exasperating to judicious Americans residing abroad. One said that the incompetency of our representatives was such as to make them "the laughing stock of their colleagues"; they were ignorant in many cases of the "ordinary usages of refined society." [1] The failure of the appointing powers to understand the dignity, tact and intelligence required of a minister or a consul at a foreign capital was mortifying to right thinking men.[2]

Though conditions were remarked they were not changed. And they were not changed because the diplomatic and consular services were bound up with the spoils system. Country editors wanted "bridal tours" at public expense. Boors in all parts of the country, with political influence, looking upon a consulship as an opportunity for a junket, might, and often did, persuade their Congressmen, who would persuade the President to send their names to the Senate. Such persons were soon at their posts where they did not even understand the spoken language of the country to which they had come.[3]

Practically the entire body of men in the foreign service were dismissed at each change of the administration.[4] In a peculiar way foreign posts were regarded as perquisites for favorites. The revolution was particularly thorough when a Republican President succeeded a Democrat, or vice versa. Of 263 consuls-general and consuls in place in 1889 when Harrison assumed office but 66 remained in February, 1893, and 43 of these were

[1] Cf. Italian corr. N. Y. Nation, April 6, 1893; Forum for April, 1893, pp. 163 et seq.
[2] N. Y. Nation, Nov. 30, 1893; N. A. Review for May, 1895, p. 572.
[3] Cf. N. Y. Nation, Aug. 3 and 10, Nov. 30, 1893, and Sep. 26, 1895.
[4] Ibid., April 5, 1894; W. F. Wharton in N. A. Review for April, 1894.

Republicans whom Cleveland had not removed during his first term and had suffered to remain at their posts.[1]

Now again there were unjustified and brutal dismissals of useful men.[2] It was not better under Cleveland, the New York Evening Post said, than it had been before, when we had Presidents who made no profession of interest in reform.[3] Josiah Quincy in the State Department, with or without Mr. Cleveland's approval, was making a "clean sweep." If there were any men of experience in the service soon none would remain.[4] However better things were in view. A step toward the introduction of the "merit principle" in the consular service would be taken by President Cleveland in 1895.[5]

A few fine figures were put at prominent posts and the appreciation of them was the greater because of the contrast which their names and lives afforded when set against the general scene. The appointment by the President of his former Secretary of State, Thomas F. Bayard, as ambassador to England was warmly appreciated by the British people. The Queen expressed her personal satisfaction when his appointment was announced.[6] His being assailed by Republicans in Congress and in the anti-Cleveland press for effusively complimentary allusions to England at the expense of our manners made him no less acceptable, though to the discreet it may have been an indication of his inexperience as a diplomatic officer.[7]

Mr. Cleveland's understanding of foreign affairs was equal to that of the average American public man of his day. He was far above any suspicion of wish to use the State Department to aid private commercial undertakings. He could be cleared, too, of any desire to pursue a roistering, swashbuckling or jingoist course for political effect, a charge made too often, and with too

[1] N. Y. Nation, Mch. 23 and Aug. 3, 1893.   [2] Ibid., Nov. 2 and 9, 1893.
[3] Ibid., Oct. 5 and 12, 1893; cf. May 10, 1894 and Sep. 26, 1895.
[4] Cf. ibid., Oct. 12 and 26, 1893; M. A. D. Howe, Moorfield Storey, pp. 181-2.
[5] W. G. Rice in N. A. Review for November, 1895, p. 000.
[6] Bayard to Gresham, May 19, 1893, in Gresham Papers.   Cf. N. Y. Nation, April 6, 1893.
[7] Cf. N. Y. Nation, Nov. 14 and Dec. 19, 1895, and March 26, 1896; Foreign Relations for 1895-6, pp. 580-4; also House Ex. Doc., 54th Cong. 1st sess., no. 152.

much basis of truth, against Blaine, a man of more contacts with other countries, who put better knowledge behind him with the object of holding the allegiance of his Irish and other anti-English friends in the American voting body. Mr. Cleveland, when he entered office in 1885, had withdrawn a treaty with Nicaragua on the ground that it contemplated the acquisition of new and distant territory which might lead to entangling alliances with foreign states.[1] Upon entering the Presidency a second time he was confronted with a situation in Hawaii created by his predecessor in office. In addition to possible foreign involvements he found facing him, in this case, a question of "international morality." Any attempt on the part of a strong nation to bully a weaker one awakened resentment in him. Such had been his reaction in his first administration with reference to Germany's advances in Samoa and he would continue, in his second administration, in so far as he could act alone, without the cooperation of Congress, to check Germany's advances in that distant insular post.[2] The same rule for doing impartial justice to native peoples which marked his Samoan policy was now to be extended to Hawaii. The stage had been set at the end of the Harrison administration for the annexation of the Sandwich Islands. Since 1875 a reciprocity treaty, the terms of which were extended in 1887,[3] had governed our commercial relations with Hawaii and a provision in it specified that the king should not alienate any of his territory to nations other than the United States.

In 1884 a supplementary convention, granting us the sole use of Pearl Harbor as a naval and commercial base, was concluded and ratified. We had, therefore, all that could be reasonably required—free trade with the islands, a "coaling station" and protection from foreign intrusion. Others, however, held a different view. The islands were rapidly coming under the influence of Americans, many of them sons and grandsons of missionaries who were interested in the growth of sugar cane

[1] Richardson, vol. viii, pp. 303, 327; cf. vol. iv of this work, pp. 351–2.
[2] McElroy, Grover Cleveland, vol. i, pp. 261–3.
[3] Richardson, vol. viii, pp. 500 and 783; House Ex. Doc., 53rd Cong. 2nd sess., no. 48, pp. 411–3; N. Y. Nation, Feb. 9, 1893.

and its manufacture for the market in the United States. Such a government as they found there was entirely preposterous to men familiar with the British and American political systems and, in a short time, the monarchy would be overthrown. It was generally conceded that annexation in due course would ensue. The movement was hastened by a change in our tariff policy. The reciprocity treaty had permitted Hawaiian sugar to come into the United States free of duty and it reached San Francisco at the rate of 200,000,000 or 250,000,000 pounds per annum to be refined principally by Claus Spreckels, who enjoyed an advantage over the refiners on the Atlantic seaboard. When the McKinley law was passed and sugar was made free the advantage disappeared; favors were reserved for the Louisiana cane growers and the beet sugar men who were to have a bounty. If Hawaii could make her way into the Union she, too, could collect from the United States Treasury two cents a pound for her raw sugar.[1]

The minister to Hawaii, John L. Stevens, had been the owner and editor of Blaine's old newspaper in Maine. He was an associate and had been a friend for many years of the Secretary of State. Arriving in Honolulu on September 20, 1889,[2] he actively interested himself in the movement for annexation, apparently with the favor of Blaine and our State Department.[3] When the king died in 1891 his sister, the Princess Liliuokalani, had come to the throne. She had but little sympathy for the white men in her country who were regarded as intruders and she inadvisedly attempted to withdraw from the people rights which had been wrung from her brother. She thus prepared her doom. A revolution ensued in January, 1893. Stevens, who had just returned from a trip around the

---

[1] Cf. N. Y. Nation, Feb. 2 and March 2, 16, 23 and 30, 1893; N. Y. Times, Nov. 16, 1893; article by L. A. Thurston in N. A. Review for March, 1893.

[2] House Ex. Doc., 53rd Cong. 2nd sess., no. 48, p. 25.

[3] Richardson, vol. ix, pp. 463–4; corr. of Stevens with Blaine and Foster, House Ex. Doc., 53rd Cong. 2nd sess., no. 48. For Blaine's interest in annexation see ibid., pp. 410–11. For Secretary of the Treasury Tracy's interest see ibid., p. 10; cf. N. Y. Nation, Feb. 23, Nov. 16 and 23 and Dec. 7, 1893.

islands on the *Boston*, was appealed to by his friends at the head of the junta which was managing the *coup*, and, that they might the more readily gain their ends, he authorized the landing of a body of marines who came ashore with two Gatling guns. The American minister recognized the new provisional government which the annexationists had established under the presidency of a man named Dole who, abetted by Stevens, ran up the stars and stripes on the Government house.[1] The islands were as much as annexed already, though Dole sent a commission, composed of four Americans and one Englishman, to Washington[2] to make a formal request of President Harrison for ratification of so much rash action. The Queen, protesting against the landing of our forces as "an unwarranted invasion of Hawaiian soil," also started envoys away to Washington to present her side of the case. Though Stevens was plainly told by Secretary Foster that, in raising the flag and establishing a protectorate, he had exceeded his authority and overstepped the limits set for a diplomatic officer in such a case,[3] the whole program was developed and unfolded rapidly. Eleven days after the arrival of Dole's delegation at Washington, on February 15, 1893, President Harrison sent to the Senate a treaty which the commissioners and the new Secretary of State, John W. Foster, had signed,[4] and a great debate in Congress and in the press was begun. "The key to the Pacific," "manifest destiny," the "ripe pear" ready to be plucked, "watchful waiting," "Americanism," "expansion," "the white man's burden," "getting ahead of England" and like words and phrases filled the air.[5]

President Harrison said that the overthrow of the monarchy had been in no way "promoted" by the government of the

---

[1] House Ex. Doc., 53rd Cong. 2nd sess., no. 48, pp. 120–2, 139.

[2] Ibid., pp. 199, 202, 204.   [3] Ibid., pp. 220–2.

[4] Richardson, vol. ix, pp. 348–9. For historical basis for the annexation of Hawaii see Secretary Foster's letter to President Harrison of Feb. 15, 1893, in Foreign Relations, 1894, app. ii, pp. 5–6. Cf. Senate Reports, 53rd Cong. 2nd sess., no. 227; House Ex. Doc., 53rd Cong. 2nd sess., no. 47.

[5] Cf. N. A. Review for March, 1893, pp. 265–86; Carl Schurz in Harper's Mag. for Oct., 1893.

United States,[1] although it became plain, upon inquiry, that
American agents had been long and actively laboring to this
end. The idea that England wanted the islands was shrewdly
injected into the argument by the annexationists.[2] The
Queen, it was said, was acting under British influence.[3] Harrison himself saw and feared the grasping, outstretched hand
of Great Britain. Should she acquire Hawaii she, in Canada
at the north, and in Bermuda and Jamaica, from which points
she could watch the Caribbean, would surround us.[4] It was
a disappointment to the annexationists that England did
not actively protest, so that they might have had an issue
to inflame the American mind.[5] Without this spur public
opinion might not be such as to drive the Senate to prompt
confirmation of the treaty, and their cause, in all likelihood,
would be lost.[6]

Day by day the New York Tribune told its readers that
"patriotism" required action. Any other advice was "un-
American." England would steal in and take the islands.
Delay was dangerous. Annexation had the unanimous approval
of the people.[7] The New York Sun called for the confirmation
of the treaty in the interest of a lofty national destiny. Opposition to it on the part of any one interested in the "welfare
and progress" of the country was "incredible." [8]

The annexationists rightly guessed that haste was imperative
if they were to realize their hopes. Public opinion, which the
New York Tribune had declared to be unanimous, was not so
favorable as might have appeared upon the first announcement
of the scheme. On many sides the Senate was urged not to
give it headlong approval. No cable yet connected the United

[1] Richardson, vol. ix, p. 348.

[2] House Ex. Doc., 53rd Cong. 2nd sess., no. 48, pp. 138, 144, 145, 147–8,
149–50, 152.

[3] Cf. N. Y. Nation, Nov. 16, 1893.

[4] Ibid., Nov. 23, 1893; a view expressed by A. T. Mahan in Forum,
March, 1893, p. 3.

[5] N. Y. Nation, Feb. 8, 1893; N. Y. Tribune, Jan. 31 and Feb. 1, 1893,
and succeeding issues.

[6] N. Y. Nation, March 2 and 18, 1893.

[7] Cf. issues of Feb. 17, 21 and 25, 1893.

[8] Issues of Feb. 18 and March 1, 1893.

States with the islands. The facts were unknown. The treaty could wait.[1]

Cleveland would soon reenter the President's office. Diligent efforts had been made to involve him in the discussion and to extract from him some statement of his attitude toward the treaty. He withheld all comment, but promptly after his inauguration asked the Senate for the return of the document for "reexamination."[2] He would see whether officers of the government of the United States had promoted the revolution. Not one Polynesian native of the islands had been included in the membership of the commission appointed to visit Washington; there was no evidence that annexation was desired by the people to whom the islands had always belonged. Mr. Cleveland's principle in foreign politics that a weak and helpless nation should not suffer subversion of its government at the hands of a powerful one may have been violated. He would determine whether this were true at his leisure, and after proper and thorough investigation of the facts, a resolution in which he was heartily supported by his Secretary of State.

Mr. Gresham set about the task with zeal.[3] Attorney General Olney was asked for his opinion. He said that a "great wrong" had been done "under the auspices of United States Minister Stevens." There was no question that "this great wrong should be rectified by the restoration of the *status quo* at the time of its perpetration."[4] "Our country is too great

[1] Cf. N. Y. Times, Feb. 17 and 18, 1893; W. S. Holt, Treaties Defeated by the Senate, pp. 152–3.

[2] Cleveland wrote to Carl Schurz, March 19, 1893—"I do not now say that I should hold annexation in all circumstances and at any time unwise, but I am sure that we ought to stop and look and think."—Writings of Schurz, vol. v, pp. 133–4.

[3] Gresham's interest in the subject is attributed by John W. Foster to his well known dislike of Harrison and a wish to discredit that President's administration. (Foster, Dip. Memoirs, vol. ii, p. 168.) This was also the view of Senator Cullom, quoted in Gresham Papers. Harrison had not appointed Gresham to a vacant seat on the bench of the Supreme Court which healed no breaches. Gresham's friends chose to say that he had been refused advancement because of his unfriendliness to large corporations as evidenced by his decisions in the Circuit Court.—M. Gresham, Life of Gresham; cf. E. G. Hay Papers.

[4] Olney to Gresham, Oct. 9, 1893, in Gresham Papers.

and aspires to too high a place in civilization," Thomas F.
Bayard wrote Mr. Gresham from the embassy in London,
"to stoop to the small arts of tricking or bullying a scanty and
feeble set of islanders out of their rights—whatever those rights
may be." [1] The way was being prepared for what soon followed.

Seeing the opportunity for activity the dethroned Queen
Liliuokalani addressed the President and asked "redress for a
wrong" done "under color of the assistance of the naval forces
of the United States." [2] Another claimant to the throne, should
Liliuokalani be deprived of it, the Princess Kaiulani, the
Queen's niece, a young woman who had been living for some
time in England, appeared at Washington to present her side
of the case. [3]

James H. Blount of Georgia, an intelligent man, chairman
until recently of the Committee of Foreign Affairs in the House
of Representatives, was asked by Mr. Cleveland to visit Hawaii
as "Special Commissioner" with "paramount" powers. Without
any expression of opinion on the part of the President to bias
him he should investigate the facts and make a report. [4]

Stevens, meanwhile, rather too ardently pleaded his own cause
and that of the annexationists, which still further unsettled the
President's confidence in him as a diplomatic officer. [5] Upon
Blount's arrival in Honolulu on the United States revenue
steamer *Rush* both parties sought to propitiate him and gain
his ear. [6] He had surveyed the scene for only a few hours when
he ordered the marines back to their ship which was riding at
anchor in the harbor, and hauled down the American flag
which, since January, had been flying over the Government
building. [7] Stevens, confronted by an officer whose authority
was "paramount," prepared to depart for his home in Maine.
Gresham, taking advantage of a letter of resignation on file
in the State Department, told him to quit his post at his "early

[1] Bayard to Gresham, Nov. 25, 1893, in Gresham Papers.
[2] McElroy, Grover Cleveland, vol. ii, p. 54.
[3] North Am. Review for May, 1893, pp. 605–10.
[4] House Ex. Doc., 53rd Cong. 2nd sess., no. 47, pp. 1–3.
[5] Cf. ibid., pp. 7, 15–6; ibid., no 48, pp. 147, 153.
[6] Ibid., no 47, pp. 4–5. [7] Ibid., pp. 6, 8–9.

convenience."[1] Mr. Blount, entirely against his own wishes, was put in the place [2] and remained until July. The nature of his report to the Secretary of State did not occasion surprise. He found that a group of Americans had stealthily made the arrangements to overset the Hawaiian government. They projected a revolution with the express object of annexing the islands to the United States. On a vote of the Hawaiian people, excluding American and foreign residents, Mr. Blount said, annexation would be defeated by more than five to one.[3]

This was such a statement as was expected and it amply confirmed the suspicions which the President and the Secretary of State had entertained. Mr. Cleveland, who was recovering from his secret surgical operation, waited until the silver purchase law had been repealed and the elections were done with. Then the main points of Mr. Blount's report were incorporated by Mr. Gresham in a letter to the President.[4] The Secretary of State reviewed the case. The treaty which had been withdrawn from the Senate, he said, should not be resubmitted for action. A "great wrong" had been done "a feeble but independent state by an abuse of the authority of the United States." Nothing short of a restoration of "the legitimate government" would "satisfy the demands of justice."[5]

Mr. Gresham's letter created a great pother. Minister Stevens, the New York Times said, had given countenance and aid to a "foul conspiracy." Intent of wrong by this government had now been "officially and publicly renounced."[6] The New York World declared the record of events as they were disclosed, to be "one of the most scandalous and shameful in the whole history of the foreign relations of the country.[7] The New York Herald characterized it as "the darkest chapter" in our diplomatic annals.[8] To the New York Evening Post the

[1] House Ex. Doc., 53rd Cong. 2nd sess., no. 48, pp. 154, 155.
[2] Ibid., pp. 155, 163.
[3] Ibid., no. 47, pp. 101–39; McElroy, Grover Cleveland, vol. ii, p. 57; N. Y. Nation, April 20 and Nov. 23, 1893.
[4] Dated Oct. 16 and made public on Nov. 10, 1893.
[5] House Ex. Doc., 53rd Cong. 2nd sess., no. 47, pp. xvii–xxi.
[6] N. Y. Times, Nov. 21, 1893.   [7] N. Y. World, Nov. 21, 1893.
[8] N. Y. Herald, Nov. 22, 1893.

various episodes in what it called a "most un-American proceeding" were disgraceful.[1] The annexation of the islands, the Evening Post continued, was "the last conception" of Blaine's "disordered and reckless ambition."[2]

On the other side language was passionate also. The American flag had been hauled down,[3] an unpopular movement in the sight of empire builders. The way had been prepared for a bitter attack upon "Paramount" Commissioner Blount. His motives, as well as his facts, were impeached. The Democratic administration by a narrow, un-American policy had undone what had been effected by the far-sighted, patriotic administration which had preceded it. Cleveland had countered Harrison and Blaine and had set back the hands of the clock of national progress. Stevens, who was a redoubtable controversialist, soon after leaving Honolulu in May, had denounced "the semi-heathen and grossly spurious mechanism called the Hawaiian monarchy." Statesmen who would not "accept this valuable prize," he had said, would be brought "to the bar of history with an indictment of blundering criminality."[4] He now resumed his outbursts. Blount's report, he said, was "calumnious,"[5] and a "shameless perversion of facts."[6]

The New York Tribune, the particular custodian of the Blaine tradition, led the tirade which filled the Republican press. Could it be, this newspaper asked, that American guns would be used to "set up the rule of vice and ignorance" and "to surround a half civilized Kanaka woman with the monkey show of a preposterous monarchy"?[7] Gresham had been made by the President to don cap and bells to go forth in the name of the United States as "the knight errant of the dusky virgin of the Pacific" and subject the intelligent people of Hawaii "to the rule of a corrupt, idolatrous and barbarous despotism."[8]

---

[1] N. Y. Nation, Nov. 16, 1893.
[2] Ibid., Nov. 23 and Dec. 21, 1893; cf. N. Y. Times, Nov. 22, 1893.
[3] N. Y. Nation, April 20 and 27 and May 11, 1893.
[4] N. Y. Tribune, Nov. 13, 1893.   [5] N. Y. Times, Nov. 21, 1893.
[6] N. Y. World, Nov. 21, 1893. A long and detailed answer to Blount by Stevens was made public on November 30, 1893—See N. Y. Tribune for that date. See also his article in N. A. Review for Dec., 1893.
[7] N. Y. Tribune, Nov. 13, 1893.   [8] Ibid., Nov. 14, 1893.

Cleveland was preparing himself for the severest indictment that public opinion had formed against any President since it had finished with James Buchanan and Andrew Johnson.[1]

Blount having retired, Albert S. Willis, for several years a member of Congress from Kentucky, had been appointed minister to Hawaii. He had just reached his post to be "serenaded," in turn, by brass bands of the rival "governments." The people, white and native, were madly excited. Every word and action of the new representative of the United States was watched, reported and discussed. Admiral Irwin had arrived in Hawaiian waters to command our naval forces. His movements and those of his flagship, the *Philadelphia*, were also the subject of close observation and of anxious rumor.

The annexationists were beside themselves with rage when, in a few days, advices concerning the Gresham letter reached them by steamship from San Francisco. They called meetings, they adopted resolutions. They had overthrown, they said, a "corrupt and rotten monarchy." [2] They indignantly repelled the suggestion that the Queen should be restored to her throne and that the liberties which they had gained by their revolution should be taken away from them. Cleveland had been elected in 1884 by three R's—he now stood impeached before the American colony in Hawaii by three R's—"the Restoration of a Rotten Royalty." [3]

"Queen Lil" was the toy of the journalists. Her ancestors who had eaten missionaries, her palace intrigues which indicated her unchastity, the color of her skin, her paganism, her "rings" of favorites who got from her concessions to traffic in opium and manage lotteries converted her into a figure fit for comic opera from which, in truth, she was not far removed.

Secretary Gresham held his ground. He was "unalterably opposed to stealing territory or to annexing a people against their consent." He spoke of "force and fraud." There was "no pretense that the provisional government was an outgrowth of a revolution of the people or that it is at all republican in form,"

[1] N. Y. Tribune, Nov. 17, 1893.
[2] House Ex. Doc., 53rd Cong. 2nd sess., no. 70, p. 8.   [3] Ibid., p. 15.

he said. Only "selfishness and greed" were at the bottom of the scheme. A "free government" like ours could not pursue "an imperial policy." [1]

Mr. Willis's instructions were clear. He should present his respects to the Queen and express the regret of the United States for the late Minister Stevens's "reprehensible conduct." She had suffered a "flagrant wrong" which the government of the United States would redress.[2] Steps would be taken to secure her reinstatement, if she would enter into an agreement to treat her enemies, the revolutionists, with magnanimity and manifest a spirit of forgiveness. So much she declined to do, saying that they should be beheaded and their property should be confiscated, as the laws of the kingdom required.[3] But she shortly relented and, under advice, expressed to the American minister a willingness to accede to the terms imposed upon her,[4] whereupon Mr. Willis addressed Mr. Dole, the head of the provisional government, who, throughout the ten or eleven months which had elapsed since the revolution, held the Government building, and whose attitude was very hostile. He and the group of Americans around him fortified the palace grounds and made preparations for defence. They put a thousand men under arms.[5] Dole, when he was requested to "relinquish" to Liliuokalani her "constitutional authority," [6] instantly declined—under no circumstances would power be surrendered to the Queen.[7] Willis, by course of steamship to San Francisco, asked for instructions. From this point how should he proceed? Justice, strictly considered, might favor the cause of Liliuokalani, but it would be an unnatural rôle for us to assume, were we to endeavor to re-establish an overthrown monarchy and to put a semi-civilized people in control of a government which, in our own interest, and for the protection of our citizens residing there, should have enlightened management. Abstract right

---

[1] Gresham to correspondents, Nov. 23, 1893, and July 25, 1894, in Gresham Papers.
[2] House Ex. Doc., 53rd Cong. 2nd sess., no. 47, pp. xxi–xxiii.
[3] Ibid., no. 70, pp. 1–3.
[4] Ibid., pp. 29, 43–4.
[5] Ibid., no. 140, p. 5; ibid., no. 76, pp. 6–7; ibid., no. 70, p. 6
[6] Ibid., no. 70, p. 35.   [7] Ibid., pp. 36–42.

might call for one policy, practical considerations for an opposite one.

The President was made by his enemies, supported by sensational newspapers, to seem to be an advocate of the restoration of the Queen by force. But no preparations for the landing of troops from the American ships at Honolulu were in progress—no war-like activities were instituted at Washington.[1] The President was disillusioned, in some degree, possibly, by the Queen's refusal to show magnanimity to her enemies. The press generally in the United States was averse to "putting the old girl back." Even newspapers which emphatically condemned the conduct of Stevens with reference to the revolution deplored any suggestion of the restoration of the royalists.[2] Attorney-General Olney may have given expression to the sentiment of discreet men when he said that there was no right to redress the original wrong by the commission of a still greater wrong, "namely the imposition upon Hawaii of a government not wanted by its people."[3]

Little light was thrown upon the confused problem in the President's message of December 4, 1893. But a fortnight later, having worked himself into an awkward situation,[4] he laid the whole question before Congress.[5] He denounced the selfish intrigue which had deprived a sovereign people of their liberties. There was such a thing, he said, as "international morality." It was an "odious doctrine" that strong powers might, with impunity, despoil the territory of feeble peoples. In a message which the New York Evening Post found to be "the finest expression of real Americanism which this century has heard,"[6] the President committed the subject to the judgment of the Senate and the House of Representatives, where the annexationists and the anti-annexationists, and the

[1] Cf. House Ex. Doc., 53rd Cong. 2nd sess., no. 76, pp. 6–7.
[2] As, for example, the N. Y. World. For Attorney-General Olney's views see James, Life of Olney, app. iii.
[3] Olney to Gresham. Oct, 9, 1893, in Gresham Papers.
[4] Cf. James, Life of Olney, chap. ix.
[5] Richardson, vol. ix, pp. 460–72; House Ex. Doc., 53rd Cong. 2nd sess., no 47, iii–xvi.   [6] N. Y. Nation, Dec. 21, 1893.

Queen's friends, if there were any to espouse her cause, and
the friends of the provisional government could balance their
views and work out a plan of national procedure.

They, however, developed none. Long debate was fruitless.
The House on February 7, 1894, passed a resolution condemning
Stevens.[1] The Senate conducted an investigation, the committee reaching diverse conclusions.[2] Finally, on May 31,
1894, a resolution was passed by that body, making an empty
statement that interference with the local political affairs of
Hawaii by any other government would be regarded as an act
"unfriendly to the United States."[3]

A natural development of events was the stabilization of
the revolutionary government as a republic,[4] which was formally
proclaimed on July 4, 1894.[5] Our war vessels were withdrawn
from the harbor of Honolulu where they had seen duty for
many months, and, on August 7th, President Cleveland definitely recognized Hawaii under its new government as a member of the family of nations. The colored royalists did not
cease to plead with the President for their hopeless cause and
instituted a rising in 1895 which the republicans suppressed.[6]
The white annexationists would renew their agitation which
would continue, they said, until their object should be gained
and one of them, Thurston, ostensibly the minister of the
republic in the United States, so "grossly violated his privileges," in the opinion of Mr. Gresham, that he should have
been given his passports.[7] There the matter rested until the
end of Mr. Cleveland's term.

The necessity, as it seemed, of possessing for political uses
a standing disagreement of some kind with Great Britain
had been met during Cleveland's first term by the northeastern
fisheries question. Mr. Bayard had arranged for the settlement

---

[1] McPherson's Handbook for 1894, pp. 119–22.
[2] Senate Reports, 53rd Cong. 2nd sess., no. 227.
[3] Cong. Record, 53rd Cong. 2nd sess., pp. 5499–5500.
[4] Cf. N. Y. Nation, Dec. 28, 1893.
[5] House Ex. Doc., 53rd Cong. 2nd sess., no. 256, p. 8.
[6] App. Ann. Cyclop. for 1895, pp. 345–6.
[7] Gresham to Willis, Feb. 20, 1895, in Gresham Papers.

of this difficulty by treaty which he had framed in conjunction with Mr. Chamberlain who visited Washington for the purpose, and the English minister to Washington, Lord Sackville, then Sir Lionel Sackville-West. The Senate in a partisan rage would have none of it, and the "Blaine Irishmen" and those who were using anti-English prejudices to gain votes in the Presidential campaign of 1888 had given characteristic culmination to this outburst of feeling in the demand for Sackville's recall.

The excitement over sealing in Bering Sea during the Harrison administration furnished the public mind with new and continuing basis for the enjoyment of its suspicion and mistrust of Great Britain. Mr. Blaine's theories as to international law bearing upon the conflict of interests in the waters of Alaska had fortunately gone to arbitrators. These were Justice Harlan of the United States Supreme Court and Senator John T. Morgan, chairman of the Senate Committee on Foreign Relations, for the United States; Lord Hannen and the Prime Minister of Canada, Sir John S. D. Thompson, for Great Britain; Baron de Courcel for France; the Marquis Visconti-Venosta for Italy and Judge Gram for Sweden and Norway. The tribunal met in Paris in March, 1893. Ex-Secretary of State John W. Foster prepared the case for the United States and the British agent, Charles H. Tupper of Canada, son of Sir Charles Tupper, for Great Britain. Among our counsel were E. J. Phelps, American minister to England in Cleveland's first term, James C. Carter, Frederick R. Coudert and Robert Lansing. After full argument decisions were rendered on August 15, 1893, which disposed rather completely of the structure upon which Mr. Blaine had built his theories.[1] It was denied that Russia had ever had exclusive jurisdiction in Bering Sea; therefore no such monopoly of authority in

[1] N. Y. Nation, Aug. 17 and Sep. 7, 1893, and April 12, 1894. The New York Tribune, Blaine's organ, said that "that sagacious statesman's prudent forecast of possible defeat on questions of technical right" had enabled the United States "to achieve a substantial victory." England had the "letter of the decision," but the United States had "saved the seal," etc. etc.—N. Y. Tribune, Aug. 16, 1893.

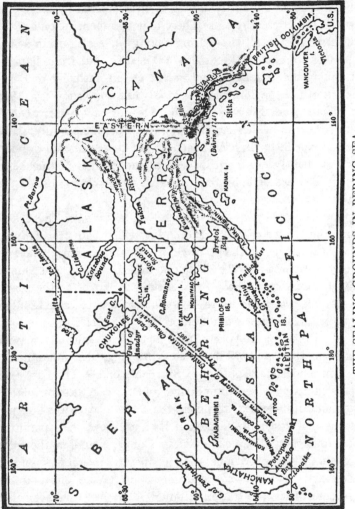

THE SEALING GROUNDS IN BERING SEA

these waters could have passed by cession to the United States. We could, on this account, have no property in seals when in waters outside the usual three mile limit. Regulations, nevertheless, should be jointly agreed to and enforced by the United States and Great Britain. The two governments should forbid their citizens at all times from taking fur seals within a zone of 60 miles around the Pribylov Islands and from pursuing or killing the animals in the Pacific Ocean, inclusive of Bering Sea, north of the 35th parallel of latitude and east of the 180th meridian, from May 1st to July 31st, of each year. During the season in which sealing would be permitted only sailing vessels should be used and each one of these must be provided with a British or American license, and carry a distinguishing flag. The use of nets, firearms and explosives would be prohibited.

It was furthermore recommended, in view of the critical condition to which the "race of fur seals" had been reduced, that the taking of them, whether on land or sea, should entirely cease for a period of from one to three years. The amount of indemnity to be paid by the United States for the seizure of British vessels by its revenue cutters was to be determined by other agencies.[1] An act enforcing the articles was approved by the President on April 6, 1894, and he proclaimed the award and the law on April 9th, thus bringing this unhappy and rather ridiculous dispute to a peaceable end.[2] The San Francisco company whose monopoly, and its eagerness to get the most out of its lease, had precipitated the quarrel was informed of the new restraints put upon its activities.[3] Complaints of bad faith would be continued in Congress and in the newspapers. It was obvious that cooperative action would be necessary by the two governments in giving effect to the decisions of the arbitration tribunal. The Anglophobes denied

[1] Proceedings of the Paris Tribunal, Senate Ex. Doc., 53rd Cong. 2nd sess., no. 177; App. Ann. Cyclop. for 1893, pp. 79–86; N. Y. Nation, Jan. 10, 1895.

[2] J. W. Foster, Diplomatic Memoirs, chap. xxvii; McPherson's Handbook for 1894; cf. N. Y. Nation, April 12, 1894.

[3] Cf. N. Y. Nation, Aug. 24, 1893; J. W. Foster, Diplomatic Memoirs, vol. ii, pp. 26–7.

that Great Britain was passing an enforcing act equal to ours in its probable efficiency in restraint of "poaching." England was overreaching Cleveland—nothing so weak-kneed in the face of British "bluff" could have marred our polity under Harrison and Blaine.[1] The subject should never have been submitted to arbitration anyhow, said Theodore Roosevelt— this course had been taken under the influence of "peace-at-any-price men." [2] The seal herds were still at the mercy of pelagic hunters. The species would be exterminated.[3] Commissioners must again be despatched to Alaska by the United States and Great Britain to consider the case.[4]

A sum of $425,000 was offered in settlement of the damages sustained by the Canadian sealers, accepted and submitted to Congress.[5] President Cleveland urged "prompt payment." [6] Congress refused. The bargain had been made, but we would not keep it. Some of the "poachers," it was said, were Americans who had masqueraded as British subjects and were entitled, therefore, to no indemnities, a new discovery on the part of our jingoes, since the foundation of the controversy was mischief making by the Canadians.[7] Inquiry must be made as to the nationality of the claimants.[8] Another treaty was necessary. It was ratified by the Senate in 1896 and a commission of two members, one British (a Canadian) and one American, Judge William L. Putnam of Maine, was appointed to reconsider the question of claims.[9]

[1] N. Y. Nation, April 12, 1894.

[2] J. W. Foster, Diplomatic Memoirs, vol. ii, p. 30.

[3] Richardson, vol. ix, p. 630; Senate Ex. Doc., 53rd Cong. 3rd sess., no. 67; Foreign Relations, 1894, app. 1, pp. 107–223; ibid. for 1895, pp. 585 et seq.; ibid. for 1896, pp. 255 et seq.; ibid. for 1897, pp. 258 et seq.

[4] Richardson, vol. ix, p. 723.

[5] App. Ann. Cyclop. for 1894, p. 749; Senate Ex. Doc., 53rd Cong. 3rd sess., no. 67, pp. 156–7. Sir Julian Pauncefote had computed damages amounting to $542,000.—Ibid., pp. 136–43.

[6] Richardson, vol. ix, p. 526.

[7] N. Y. Nation, Feb. 28 and March 7, 1895.

[8] Ibid., Nov. 21, 1895. Senator Morgan, chairman of the Committee on Foreign Relations, and an arbitrator, said that they were "rascally and recalcitrant Americans who hired themselves out to the British flag to rob the government of the United States, violate its laws and dishonor the country."—Ibid., Dec. 12, 1895.

[9] Foreign Relations for 1896, pp. 281–5; N. Y. Nation, April 23, 1896.

More might follow in an atmosphere which was so surcharged with anti-British sentiment. Many attempts have been made to explain, and to apply a measure to, this hostility of feeling. That the text books used in the common schools fostered it is demonstrable. The newspapers promoted it.[1] The knowledge of American history in possession of the masses began with some main incidents of the Revolutionary war, all of them derogatory of England, and ended with the burning of the Capitol at Washington during the War of 1812, the battle of New Orleans and a conviction that the British nation had been on the side of the Confederacy during our Civil War and had earnestly desired the disruption of the Union. The anti-English influence of the Irish who had immigrated to the United States in large numbers and who, upon their arrival, almost at once got into our politics, has been frequently adverted to in this work. Free trade was British; in every tariff campaign the notion that England was, in some way, secretly, if not openly, conspiring to close our mills and ruin all that we had succeeded in doing to upbuild native industry was sedulously propagated. Some men actually had such a belief, many others spread it for political advantage. The silverites, with similar objects, would follow the example of the protectionists. In their campaign to discredit gold and change the standard of value they were putting the onus of the country's and the world's economic misfortunes upon England. If an old sound it would be a welcome one in ears ready to receive it. England would overawe and subvert weak peoples in the development of a great scheme of imperialism. One of her weapons was gold. She lent money throughout the world and demanded that it be returned to her in a metal, or its

---

[1] North Am. Review for May, 1895, pp. 570–9. The English people themselves, as such, upon visiting the United States did not escape unpleasant judgments. Cf. N. Y. Tribune, the first newspaper in the first city of the United States whose editor was a candidate for appointment as ambassador to England. "The people there [in England] are firmly convinced that everything alien is necessarily bad, that, when dealing with foreigners, they are under no obligation to observe the conventional rules of life which govern their intercourse with their fellow countrymen. . . . The result of all this is that no people are more justly abhorred abroad than the ordinary Briton," etc. etc.—Issue of June 2, 1893.

equivalent, which was all the while becoming scarcer and dearer. Bankers everywhere were her body servants. It was England which had defeated the objects of international monetary conferences, made exchanges in gold necessary, enchained the poor and laughed at human distress. Violent abuse of Great Britain was the stock in trade of every silver money demagogue in the West and South. The more he thought of the wrong which had been done the world by gold the more he raved about the hereditary enemy of our institutions.[1]

Cleveland wrote to his friend Don Dickinson that troubles followed him "thick and fast." "We are out of one perplexity," he said, "to immediately face another." [2] He would now prove the truth of these words in impressive fashion. Soon he would face a trouble which had not come to him, but which he actively sought. At an hour when the air was filled with the strangest extravagances concerning England he left his moorings and went with his enemies out into the storm. For many years the various governments of a South American state, Venezuela, had taken their turns in trying to determine the boundary line between its territory and that of British Guiana. Since the end of the eighteenth century, prior, therefore, to the revolt of the Spanish colonies and the creation of Venezuela as a separate state, Great Britain had had this foothold, its only one, on the mainland of South America. The resources of British Guiana, principally a soil on which sugar could be grown, were negligible, and its importance to the empire was inconsiderable until gold had been discovered about 1886. The significance of the bordering state of Venezuela with reference to the United States, or the world generally, was not large. Our interest in the affairs of that republic was supported by the popular understanding of the meaning of the Monroe Doctrine. The public concern for the progress of South American matters was increased, in some degree, by

---

[1] Cf. Edward Atkinson in North Am. Review for Nov., 1895; James Bryce in ibid. for Feb., 1896, pp. 149–51.

[2] March 20, 1895, in Cleveland Papers.

Blaine's Pan-American congress, but the potentialities for
the United States of a boundary controversy between two
governments in the southern hemisphere would not have been
great except for the fact that one of them was England. That
Great Britain should have a lodgment of any kind upon this
continent was disliked by a part of our ignorant masses, led
by artful and demagogic politicians and newspapers. It was
presumed that her presence anywhere was but for an enlargement and extension of power. If England were not watched
and checked she would overstep her limits and crush the
small republican states which, since the Monroe Doctrine had
been enunciated, stood under our protection against the avarice
for territory and the political ambitions of the European powers.
It further inflamed prejudices of such anti-British elements as
were silverites when they were told that England's interest
in the Venezuelan frontier was founded upon gold mining.

It is certain that Mr. Cleveland, as enlightened as was his
outlook respecting domestic affairs, shared the popular feeling,
in some degree, concerning England. His horizons were narrow.
His mind had not been enlarged by travel. His knowledge
of international questions was based upon a reading of our
political writers of the Revolutionary period and a reference
to maps. He had the most correct standards of morality in
domestic, and it was his wish to extend them to foreign, politics. If any one were robbing, intimidating or brow-beating
the poor and the weak at home his reprobation was prompt
and emphatic. He naturally carried this idea into international
relations and it was only necessary to implant in his mind the
notion that Germany was encroaching upon native rights in
Samoa, that Americans were dealing unjustly with Polynesians
in Hawaii, or that England was trying to seize a portion of
Venezuela to stir him to moral fury.

Mr. Gresham was an upright man ready to defend his
convictions. He also had no intimate understanding of foreign
questions.[1] But he had been an admirable judge in the Federal
courts and he carried the judicial spirit into the State Depart-

[1] Cf. J. W. Foster, Dip. Memoirs, vol. ii, pp. 273–4.

ment. Cleveland found "comfort" in association with him and valued him for "his hard sense, his patriotism and loyalty." [1] In the performance of his duties he was dignified and courteous. He reversed the policy of Blaine who, as the New York Nation rather picturesquely said, was prone to take "the hated foreigner by the beard." [2] He was praised by the diplomatic corps for his "lofty and unswerving spirit of honor, justice and conciliation." [3] and returned American diplomacy to quieter paths. At his death, in May, 1895, he was succeeded by Richard Olney, the Attorney-General, whose place, in turn, in the Department of Justice was supplied by Judson Harmon of Ohio. [4] It is likely that Olney brought to the office more outward signs of gentility than Gresham had lent the position. He had formality and reserve; he was an observer of official proprieties. [5] A solitary man, he had found in Boston little pleasure in social contacts, though his geniality was somewhat extended in Washington. He was noted in his family circle and among his friends chiefly for the tenacity with which he would hold to his opinions, come what might. A stern face told of his obstinacy of spirit which was, indeed, so marked a characteristic of him that it has seemed to warrant his biographer in alluding to it as "lockjaw of the will." [6]

His life had been that of a corporation lawyer and he was prepared to regard a government as, in a sense, an analogue of a great private company. Of practical knowledge of official life and of statesmanship he had hitherto had none, and his treatment of international questions was legalistic. As a successful lawyer in large fields Mr. Olney seems to have won the admiration of Mr. Cleveland who had gained less distinction in the profession. As a gentleman radiating some of the

---

[1] Cleveland to Don Dickinson in A. Nevins, Letters of Cleveland, p. 382; cf. ibid., p. 397; "His companionship and constant loyalty," the President said again, "largely constituted all the comfort that came to my official life." (Cleveland to Benedict, June 9, 1895, in Cleveland Papers.) Bayard shared the President's admiration of Gresham.—Letter to Cleveland of May 28, 1895, in ibid.

[2] N. Y. Nation, May 30, 1895.   [3] Ibid., June 6, 1895.

[4] A. Nevins, Letters of Cleveland, p. 396.

[5] Henry James, Life of Olney, pp. 78–9.   Cf. ibid., pp. 11, 20.

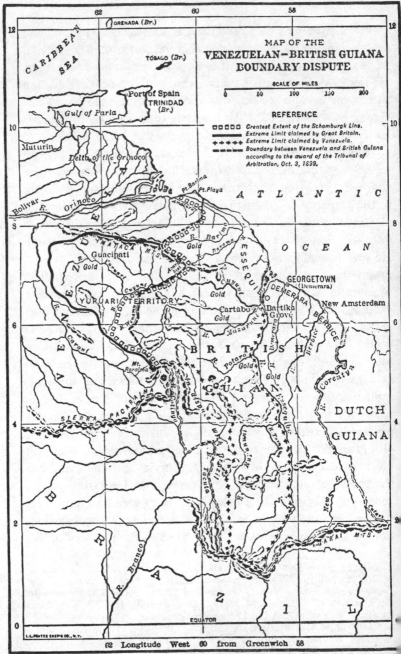

social graces he claimed the attention of one who had less acquaintance with the drawing room, and he was regarded with deference by the President. Though Mr. Cleveland, like Mr. Olney, was a man difficult to lead it is certain that no other in the cabinet in his second term enjoyed a more enviable position in the President's esteem than the gentleman who was now his Secretary of State. The place which Mr. Gresham had held in his confidence with respect to foreign affairs seems to have been more than filled after a period of association with Mr. Olney.

Ever since about 1840, therefore for more than 50 years, the Venezuela boundary line had been a subject of discussion. What ground had England received from the Dutch, how much had the revolution against Spain given to the newly established republic? Diplomatic exchanges had built up a body of documentary material bearing upon the controversy. Plans of settlement which were proposed on one side or the other were rejected. Now and again the United States was brought into the negotiations and we proffered our good offices in the interest of friendly agreement. The Venezuelans repeatedly put forth efforts to involve us in the discussion with advantage to their side of the cause.[1] The banks of the Essequibo River, the Schomburgk line, the Aberdeen line, the Granville line and other suggested frontiers of earlier years seemed now, in the light of discoveries of gold, to have been discarded, and the British holders of valuable mining claims and empire-builders, who had gone well up the streams and into the mountains on ground which had earlier been Venezuela's indisputably, were unwilling to subject themselves to the uncertainties of native politics. There had been a long series of revolutions and civil wars in Venezuela, and foreigners of Nordic stock settled on the frontier eagerly pressed the British government to maintain a firm policy.[2]

[1] Cf. N. Y. Nation, Oct. 24, 1895; McElroy, Grover Cleveland, vol. ii, p. 185; Senate Ex. Doc., 50th Cong. 1st sess., no. 226; Senate Doc., 54th Cong. 1st sess., no. 31, p. 10; Cleveland, Presidential Problems, p. 247.
[2] Cf. N. Y. Nation, Dec. 12, 1895.

Diplomatic relations with Great Britain had been broken off by Venezuela in 1887 and were not resumed. Secretary Bayard, during President Cleveland's first term, had more than once given expression in official correspondence to the grave concern felt by the United States over the delay in the settlement of the questions in controversy, and suggested arbitration,[1] to which Great Britain gave an indication of acceding with reference to a part of the country in dispute. She would not, however, admit to the contest ground which had long been held and administered as, and lay by right of long possession within the limits of, a colony of the British crown. Congress had called for the papers bearing upon the case[2] without losing sight of the fact that there might be two sides of the question. Even Blaine, though he expressed his sympathies in a robust manner, finding that "the volume of evidence in favor of Venezuela was overwhelming," did not advance the dispute to the point of intervention.[3]

It was said now with insistency that the boundary claim of Great Britain was being moved constantly further west. Some authorities were cited to show that the line had been so far extended between the years 1884 and 1886 as to produce an area for British Guiana of 109,000 instead of 76,000 square miles.[4] President Cleveland adverted to the subject in his first message to Congress in December, 1893.[5] All quiet efforts to compose the dispute failed and Mr. Gresham, in 1894, recurred to the idea of mediation. Cleveland again in his second message in December, 1894, called attention to the need of an "early settlement."[6] Congress by joint resolution of February 22, 1895, earnestly recommended arbitration to the disputants.[7] The anti-British press added fillip to the controversy and inflamed, as it could, the public mind in this

[1] Cf. Henry James, Richard Olney, pp. 22–4.

[2] Senate Ex. Doc., 50th Cong. 1st sess., no. 226.

[3] N. Y. Nation, Oct. 24 and 31, 1895; Beckles Willson, America's Ambassadors to England, pp. 399–401.

[4] Senate Doc., 54th Cong. 1st sess., no. 31, pp. 5–6, 18, 21–2; James, Richard Olney, p. 225.

[5] Richardson, vol. ix, p. 444.   [6] Ibid., p. 527.

[7] App. Ann. Cyclop. for 1895, p. 746.

country.[1] Henry Cabot Lodge, whose nationalism was of an unusually ardent kind,[2] Theodore Roosevelt,[3] for whom the police department in New York was too narrow a field, and other political leaders, in newspaper interview, magazine article and public speech suggested *ultimata* and war if Great Britain should not come from her high horse.[4] Such truculence might have been laughed at had it not been known that, in the state of public opinion, it was fraught with the gravest possibilities.[5]

Upon Gresham's death the new Secretary of State interested himself in the question. That quality of mind, which his biographer has described as "quarrelsome independence," [6] would soon be exhibited. Mr. Olney would not mince matters. England should understand what he meant and, after some study of the facts as they were presented to him, he visited Cleveland at "Gray Gables" on Buzzards Bay in the summer of 1895 with a draft of a note to Bayard, which our ambassador at London should put into the hands of the Marquis of Salisbury. The writing was left with the President for consideration and emendation. The changes which he suggested were of a minor kind. The paper was shown, it is said, to other members of the cabinet who still remained in Washington, to be disapproved by at least one of the number, Mr. Carlisle, the Secretary of the Treasury.[7] It was Olney's work and, under date of July 20, 1895, it was posted for London.[8]

[1] Cf. N. Y. Nation, March 28, 1895.

[2] For Lodge's condemnation of the "hauling down of the American flag" in Hawaii see Forum for March, 1895.

[3] Cf. his articles on "Americanism" in Forum for April and July, 1894, and February, 1895; Corr. of Roosevelt and Lodge, vol. i, pp. 145, 148, 195, 204–5, 214, 215, 218; N. Y. Nation, Oct. 31, 1895.

[4] N. Y. Nation, Oct 31, 1895. "I don't care whether our sea coast cities are bombarded or not," Roosevelt said. "We would take Canada." (Corr. of Roosevelt and Lodge, vol. i, p. 200.) The country needed a war.—Ibid., pp. 205, 206.

[5] See H. C. Lodge in North Am. Review for June, 1895, pp. 651–8; E. L. Godkin in ibid., May, 1895, pp. 570–9.

[6] James, Richard Olney, p. 60.

[7] Cf. Barnes, John G. Carlisle, p. 409.

[8] Foreign Relations for 1895, pp. 545 et seq; James, Richard Olney pp. 110–1; R. B. Mowat, Life of Pauncefote, pp. 177–8.

Mr. Bayard was associating with leaders of thought in England on terms of pleasant intimacy, cementing, as it was believed, the bonds of friendly racial feeling. He knew the question by contact with it as Secretary of State in Cleveland's first administration. He had earlier stated the case with reference to Latin America to Mr. Gresham. "The English view of law and of international administration," he said, "are nearer to our own than those of any other nation, and it is to be regretted that a class or a party in the United States are so addicted to irresponsible abuse of everything British and to seeking any occasion to testify hostility to Great Britain, because it does much color the public view in both countries." It would be "impossible," he continued, for the United States to extend over the hemisphere south of us the "guarantee of a republican government" which our Constitution secures to each state of the Union, and yet there really seemed to be "such a wild idea in the minds of some of our people." [1]

Mr. Bayard gave the President his advice in this particular conjuncture. He would not, he said, allow the "interests and welfare of our country" to be "imperilled or complicated by such a government and people as those of Venezuela." [2] As could have been foreseen he was grievously pained to receive Mr. Olney's despatch for transmission to the British Foreign Office. [3]

It was more than an unfriendly statement of the case. Olney had assumed that Great Britain had been an aggressor—she was striving to increase the area under her control on this continent by imposing her will upon a feeble people. But it soon appeared, as the argument proceeded, that it was less on Venezuela's account than on our own that we were involving ourselves in the dispute. England's action was a serious and direct menace to the United States. The "moral and material interests" of

---

[1] Bayard to Gresham, Dec. 28, 1893, in Gresham Papers.
[2] Cleveland Papers under date of Dec. 18, 1895; McElroy, Grover Cleveland, vol. ii, p. 191; cf. James, Life of Olney, pp. 112–3.
[3] Cf. A. Nevins, Henry White, p. 112. Cleveland made an explanation and defence of his action to Bayard on Dec. 29, 1895.—A. Nevins, Letters of Cleveland, pp. 417–20.

the European powers were "irreconcilably diverse" from those familiar to this hemisphere. This idea was developed at length. Monarchical government was contrasted with "self government" founded on "inalienable right." The United States had furnished the world "the most conspicuous and conclusive example and proof of the excellence of free institutions." These institutions had brought us to a position "unexampled in point of national greatness or individual felicity." Our position was one of "superiority," not only because of our "high character as a civilized state," but also because of our "isolated position" and our "infinite resources." We must consider "any attempt on the part of the European powers" to extend their objectionable systems to whatever portion of the Western World as "incongruous and injurious," and not to be "tolerated." Under the Monroe Doctrine of 1823 a movement to oppress any one of the independent states in America had been, and must continue to be, regarded as a manifestation of an unfriendly disposition toward the United States itself. Our fiat was law on this continent. Great Britain was called upon to arbitrate the question as to the Venezuela boundary at once.[1]

A more sophomoric deliverance has, probably, never found its way into the literature of the State Department.[2] A lawyer who could state a case for a railroad or a gas company in an American court of law was employing experience gained in that field in correspondence with the masters of European statecraft. The allusions to the republics of Latin America as similar in character to the government of the United States, and the assumption of a common virtue in them which, in mass, could be set off against and contrasted with the governments of England, France and the "European powers" indicated no very profound knowledge of comparative politics. The dictum that the United States stood on elevated ground on the subject of government was supported by a rather general belief among our people in our excellent traits, and the admiration for our own

---

[1] Senate Doc., 54th Cong. 1st sess., no. 31, pp. 4–21.
[2] Nearly so much Olney lived to recognize and admit.—James, Richard Olney, p. 140.

institutions had latterly led us to attribute like moral superiority to the "sister republics" of Ecuador, Bolivia and the rest; but so uninstructed and superficial a view of political matters could not well befit the grave papers which were exchanged between foreign offices. As for his history of the dispute Mr. Olney's argument was taken over bodily from the Venezuelans.[1]

Blaine was jingoist and could make a diplomatic note ring with the dogma and shibboleth so dear to those who wear their patriotism upon their sleeves. But he could not have stated the old case for the Monroe Doctrine so crudely and, at the same time, in language so bumptious and irritating as Mr. Olney. Of the impossibility of Bayard, no mean master of international law, of which there was proof while he had been Secretary of State, and a practised parliamentarian, taking the President on such a course something has already been said, and it is unthinkable that Mr. Gresham who conducted the negotiations with reference to Hawaii with so much quiet judgment would have indulged in such rhodomontade. He would likely have described the outburst as "twisting the lion's tail." [2]

The Secretary of State had written and forwarded the note in official course, after a full understanding with the President, and nothing remained to Mr. Bayard, but to take it to Lord Salisbury, a very veteran in diplomacy, read it to him and await the outcome.[3] Our action was so sudden and bewildering, the paper was couched in terms so commanding and peremptory that the answer was a good while delayed.[4] The case was referred to the law officers of the crown and it was November before a communication was received through Sir Julian Pauncefote, the British ambassador in Washington, from the British Secretary of State for Foreign Affairs. Lord Salisbury was not wrong in saying that no such doctrine as Secretary Olney had

[1] N. Y. Nation, Dec. 26, 1895.

[2] Thus did he comment on Bayard's reference to anti-British sentiment in the United States.—See Bayard to Gresham, Dec. 28, 1893, in Gresham Papers; cf. M. Gresham, Life of Gresham, pp. 794–7.

[3] R. B. Mowat, Life of Pauncefote, p. 179.

[4] Cf. A. C. Coolidge, The U. S. as a World Power, p. 104.

evolved from a reading of the message of President Monroe
had ever before been incorporated in a state paper.[1] The
dangers of which Monroe had spoken 70 or more years ago,
he said, bore no relation to the conditions under which we were
living at the present day. Great Britain was imposing no
"system" upon Venezuela. They were neighbors and they had
a difference in regard to a boundary line. The issue was "the
determination of a British possession which belonged to the
throne of England long before the republic of Venezuela came
into existence." Moreover the British government must generally deny the validity of the Monroe Doctrine as a part of
international law. The announcement of Mr. Olney that a permanent political union between a European and an American
state was inexpedient and unnatural must meet with protest
from a government whose jurisdiction extended on the American continent to Canada, Jamaica, Trinidad, Honduras and
Guiana.

In a second note the subject of the Venezuela line itself was
discussed. The pretensions of Venezuela, founded on claims
going back to another century, were inadmissible. Great
Britain had always been willing to arbitrate the case with reference to territory lying west of the Schomburgk line. The
British government, in a larger area, where its rights were not
open to question, would not jeopardize its interests by a submission to the will of foreign jurists, no matter what their
eminence, involving as it did "the transfer of large numbers
of British subjects who have for many years enjoyed the settled
rule of a British colony to a nation of different race and language, whose political system is subject to frequent disturb-

---

[1] "The most pronounced and advanced exposition ever enunciated by
an American statesman." (J. W. Foster, Diplomatic Memoirs, vol. ii,
p. 274) Rhodes agrees that the Monroe Doctrine was inapplicable to such
a question as the Venezuelan boundary. (From Hayes to McKinley,
p. 446) E. J. Phelps, John Bassett Moore, Theodore S. Woolsey, J. W.
Burgess and others held similar views. (Beckles Willson, America's
Ambassadors to England, p. 407; J. F. Rhodes, From Hayes to McKinley,
p. 454; Theodore S. Woolsey, America's Foreign Policy, pp. 223 et seq;
Political Science Quart. for March, 1896; N. Y. Nation, March 19, 1896;
Forum for February, 1896). McMaster was of a different opinion.—
With the Fathers, pp. 44–6.

ance and whose institutions, as yet, too often offered very inadequate protection to life and property." [1]

President Cleveland had alluded to the dispute in his third annual message on December 2, 1895, reported the substance of the dispatch of July 20th, and hinted at a special message to Congress on the topic, which was not long in making its appearance. In a fortnight, on December 17th, the bomb fell. The suggestion of Lord Salisbury that the Monroe Doctrine was obsolete irritated the President, as it had done affront to many other Americans, who may have known little enough about the subject, but who had been taught to repeat the words. Salisbury, on his side, had been provoked by the tone of Olney's dispatch and had reason to write as he did. [2] Mr. Cleveland declared that the "Doctrine" was as applicable to existing conditions as to those of another day. The acquisition of territory by a European government by the arbitrary extension of a boundary, against the will of an American government, was in derogation of the "Doctrine" and called for the active intervention of the United States. Our "safety and welfare" were involved and we must act. We had proposed arbitration; Great Britain had refused the suggestion; we should now determine for ourselves the "true divisional line" between Venezuela and British Guiana. We should appoint a commission to make such an inquiry and report without delay. If it should then be shown that Great Britain were attempting the exercise of governmental jurisdiction over lands belonging to Venezuela such exercise of power should be resisted, in the President's opinion, by "every means" as "a wilful aggression" upon the "rights and interests" of the United States.

Mr. Cleveland said that he keenly realized the consequences; he was "fully alive" to the "responsibility" which he had assumed. It would be a "grievous thing to contemplate the two great English-speaking peoples of the world as being otherwise than friendly competitors in the onward march of civilization,"

---

[1] Cf. Senate Doc., 54th Cong. 1st sess., no. 31, pp. 22–35.
[2] Cf. Andrew Carnegie in North Am. Review for Feb., 1896, pp. 135–6.

but, he said in conclusion, "there is no calamity which a great
nation can invite which equals that which follows a supine
submission to wrong and injustice and the consequent loss
of national self respect and honor beneath which are shielded
and defended a people's safety and greatness."[1]

The Irish who disliked England, the silverites who held
her responsible for oppressions which they suffered by reason
of the gold standard, the protectionists who, in so many political campaigns, had charged her with wish and design to destroy
our struggling industries that she might deluge our markets
with her cheap goods, and the jingoes everywhere whose patriotism consisted of waving the flag and speaking of war, though
none of them knew or cared a tittle about Venezuela, hailed
the President's message with loud approval.   A wave of pride
in country, right or wrong, surged across the continent.[2]   The
people were for Venezuela, as James Bryce said, simply because
it was a "republic," while British Guiana was a colony of a kingdom.   Venezuela, however, was and had been for many years
a military tyranny, while the government of England, as
informed men knew, if nominally a "monarchy," was the most
enlightened of modern democracies.[3]   Even men who had
actively hated Cleveland found in his statement of the national
aim and purpose an evidence of his vigorous statesmanship.
There are now living those, then young, who were so pleasantly
excited by a prospect of war with England that they still
speak of Mr. Cleveland's Venezuelan message as the proudest
achievement of his Presidency.

Congress leapt at the task before it.   The people should
not think its devotion to the interests of the country in international affairs smaller than the President's.[4]   Without
opposition, and unanimously, they authorized the appointment
of the commission which Mr. Cleveland had asked for.   He
named as members of the body Justice David J. Brewer of

[1] Richardson, vol. ix, pp. 655–8.
[2] Cf. A. C. Coolidge, The U. S. as a World Power, p. 104; D. A. Wells
in North Am. Review for April, 1896.
[3] North Am. Review for Feb., 1896, pp. 147–8.
[4] Cf. N. Y. Nation, Dec. 19, 1895.

the United States Supreme Court, Andrew D. White, president of Cornell University, Frederic R. Coudert of New York and Daniel C. Gilman, president of Johns Hopkins University. The President's message created complete bewilderment in England. It was like this, as the lines ran under a cartoon in Punch—"The Compliments of the Season," since Christmas was at hand—"Wall, Salisbury, Sir, whether you like it or not, We propose to arbitrate on this matter Ourselves and, in that event, We shall abide by Our Own decision." [1]

Intelligent Englishmen could "scarcely credit their eyes and ears." Why, they said, should they be so regarded as it seemed by the tone of the communications of the President and his Secretary of State that they must be regarded by their own kinsfolk.[2]

It was an "absurdly trivial pretext" for a statement of "readiness to go to instant war." The British people remained "calm"—they were "rather amused than otherwise" by an outbreak which had in it, whatever the final outcome, aspects bordering on the ridiculous. Its most dangerous feature lay in the effect which such a statement of policy might have on other South American states. Claims of all kinds affecting Europe might be presented on the presumption that, however unjust their causes, these causes would be espoused and supported by the United States.[3]

There were not a few in the United States who held themselves aloof from the popular frenzy. They said, at the risk of seeming to be pro-British, that an old boundary dispute in South America was too small a matter about which to make so much pother. An incident in which we could, as a people, have no real interest had been magnified and was not seen in its correct proportions. Such an interpretation of the Monroe Doctrine as that on which Mr. Cleveland rested his action was unhistorical and indefensible. To hold the motives of another government, especially of a government like England's as dis-

---

[1] Issue of Dec. 28, 1895.
[2] James Bryce in North Am. Review for Feb., 1896, p. 150.
[3] A gentleman writing from London, Dec. 25, 1895, in Cleveland Papers.

tinguished from Venezuela's, to be evil and to say frankly, through the highest official agencies, that they were such was ungenerous; it was conduct not in accord with polite international usage. England was not averse to arbitration—her view was simply that she would not arbitrate the question of "right to territory long settled and governed as a part of a British colony." [1] The difficulties attending the management of our public finances were still great and a fright induced by a threat of war would certainly increase the tension. The President's message, it was observed, had started a new run upon the gold reserve which he had lately replenished with such cost of personal criticism. The public debt had been increased. Bonds which must later be repaid were sold. Now more must be issued if the credit of the government were to be sustained. What had come over Mr. Cleveland? Whatever his convictions concerning Venezuela how could he now, at so critical an hour, make an international issue of a boundary line which concerned a few hundreds of thousands of persons not included in our body of citizens? What to many appeared to be in the highest degree patriotic was in reality unpatriotic. The President was in the midst of a contest in which he held the respect of at least a few of his countrymen; now, in announcing a Quixotic policy in South America, he left these friends aghast, none more so than E. L. Godkin who was "thunderstruck," but instantly sprang to service in the cause of rational behaviour and international peace.[2]

As ignorant in the field of foreign politics as the President in the sight of his critics had proven himself to be he had been still more tactless, as they remarked, in the choice of a time for the assault upon England. Moreover, if, by resisting Great Britain "by every means" in our power and taking "all the consequences that may follow," the President meant war he was rash beyond belief. The United States had been engaged in building a "new navy," but only one modern battleship

[1] Memorandum of conversations between Lord Kimberley and Bayard in Feb., 1895, in Cleveland Papers.
[2] Ogden, Life and Letters of E. L. Godkin, vol. ii, pp. 187-90, 202; N. Y. Nation, Dec. 26, 1895.

had yet been completed and was in the water ready to face
the powerful British fleet.[1] For armed conflict on land we
were in still more ludicrous plight. The whole regular army
of the republic amounted to only 25,000 men. Even the com-
monest precautions regarding our "safety and welfare," which
the President said were at stake in Venezuela, should have
stayed his hand.

The Chamber of Commerce of New York passed resolutions
deploring the "war craze." Carl Schurz made his thrust at
men who advocated war to save civilization from effeminacy,[2]
a theory which he said was "as preposterous" as it was "disgraceful and abominable." [3]   Bishop Potter called such men
"pinchbeck patriots." [4]   E. L. Godkin unceasingly ridiculed
the patriotism which was "entirely bellicose," the "warrior
press" which boasted that we could whip England with one
hand tied behind our back, the "wild fellows" who wanted
war "to educate the boys and encourage trade," the furious
non-combatants who would not be caught within 500 miles of
a battle field. The New York Evening Post was "overwhelmed"
with letters commending its course, and for a time its circulation rose at the rate of 1,000 copies a day.[5]

It may have been known, at least by some men, that England
in such outbreaks of popular temper in this country would indulge us as in some way errant children of a parent race, and
that war which was in many mouths was not so near as it
seemed. Salisbury said to an American who expressed amaze-
ment at the calm in England in the face of our fulminations—
"Would you remember forever, and would you let it be known
as widely as possible that Great Britain will bear at the hands
of America what she will bear from no other quarter." Dr.
Jameson had just led a raid into the South African Republic

[1] Cf. J. F. Rhodes, From Hayes to McKinley, pp. 438–42.
[2] With such in view as Theodore Roosevelt who was speaking contemptuously of the "futile sentimentalist of the international arbitration type"
whose legitimate fruit was "a flabby, timid type of character" which
was eating away "the great fighting features of our race."—Corr. of
Roosevelt and Lodge, vol. i, p. 218.
[3] Writings of Schurz, vol. v, p. 250.   [4] N. Y. Nation, Dec. 26, 1895.
[5] Ogden, Life and Letters of Godkin, vol. ii, p. 202.

to overthrow an oligarchy which vexed with oppressive laws a large body of Englishmen and Americans residing there. The German Emperor found it an occasion to express his sympathy for the Boers. The British fleet was ordered to sea bound for South Africa, not for the American coast.[1]

Mr. Cleveland himself, it must be thought, was not consciously blustering, though so much seems not to have been true of his mentor, Mr. Olney.[2] History also acquits the President of any wish to make votes by proclaiming his Americanism.[3] His political career, as he knew, was nearing its end. Neither he nor his party had anything to win by what he might do in fomenting anti-English feeling. He, largely through the influence of his Secretary of State, had gained the idea that the Venezuelans were being unjustly dealt with by a strong government.[4] He firmly believed that it was so, and he would endeavor to correct the wrong at any cost. It must be believed that Mr. Cleveland's message was but another expression of a frank, open, blunt and rather stubborn personality. He applied himself conscientiously to all his duties and he found one of these in a far place, to which it was then, and remains, the opinion of many men his knowledge and understanding did not extend.

[1] The Landmark for Jan., 1933, p. 4, on the authority of Dr. John A. Hutton of the British Weekly.

[2] James, Life of Olney, p. 140.

[3] Another view in N. Y. Nation, Dec. 19 and 26, 1895. Also, in N. Y. World, Dec. 23, 1895. The World strangely enough resisted the "war craze." The New York Times, under new direction, (N. Y. Nation, May 7, 1896) approved the President's course.

[4] Cf. McElroy, Grover Cleveland, vol. ii, pp. 181–2, 188–9.

CHAPTER XXXVII

BRYAN

As the day of another Presidential election drew nigh it was increasingly apparent that new forces were stirring. For many months the persistent and fanatical spread of the idea that the gold standard was impoverishing and oppressing the lower classes of the population had controlled Congress. The West and South kept up a clamor which interfered with the proper conduct of the government. Wrangling in the newspaper press, in party conventions, at local elections, in legislatures indicated that an hour was at hand when the issue must be faced. The air could not be cleared until there should be a direct appeal to the people of the country on the plain question as to whether we were to have the currency which was money in the rest of the world, whether debts were to be paid in the dollars which had been lent, or whether we were to pass over to some new, unstable and depreciated standard of value.[1]

The appearance of a little book by a man named Harvey, called "Coin's Financial School," attracted an immense amount of attention. Probably nothing in pamphletary literature in this country, barring Tom Paine's "Common Sense" and Hinton Rowan Helper's "Impending Crisis" took so quick and successful a hold of the popular mind. Harvey had been publishing a weekly periodical called "Coin." He was the secretary of a Bimetallic League and he put together in his booklet the statement and argument which had been serving the silver men and the greenbackers for two or three decades in their attacks upon gold as a basis for money. It was confirmatory of what the poor man wished to believe—that his lot was not due to his own errors and shortcomings, nor yet to

[1] Cf. McElroy, Grover Cleveland, vol. ii, p. 204.

the misfortune which is vaguely ascribed to Providence, but to one definitely assignable wrong—a money standard which was making the lender rich and was robbing the debtor. It was a reiteration of the doctrine of all the silver men that gold was scarce and "dear," that its "price" with reference to commodities was increasing. We must coin both metals at some ratio to be agreed upon. In no other way could the gold "corner" be broken. In no other way could the prices of what the people produced by their toil be raised. In no other way could debts be brought down to a level approximating that at which they had been contracted.

"Coin" was a sleek little fellow who had an imaginary school. He lived in Chicago. He stood on a platform in front of a blackboard. Newspaper editors, bankers and other men who were named—Joseph Medill, Lyman J. Gage, H. H. Kohlsaat, Professor Laughlin—came in and in six lessons they were told all that there was to know of the monetary science. When they questioned "Coin" he answered them fluently and at once. He floored all his interrogators. The greatest thinkers left him wiser and better men. The young schoolmaster made the whole subject as clear as crystal It was a new and an arresting way in which to dress up the old fustian about money, and the boys who peddled reading matter in railway trains, the vendors at newsstands and in book stalls sold hundreds of thousands of copies of the "lectures" in a few weeks. Harvey said that the reception of his work had been "unprecedented in the history of literature." [1] His text was interspersed with wood cuts of men standing on one leg and eating with one arm over the words "Single Standard"; of the capitalist milking a great cow and running off toward New York and New England with the pail, while farmers in the West were feeding the animal; of a cube representing all the gold in the world standing in the centre of the Chicago wheat pit; of John Bull throttling a female figure labelled "Prosperity," while "Silver," a fine, lusty looking young man chained to a pillar, was trying to break his bonds to unhand the villain; of industry manacled

[1] Coin's Financial School Up to Date, 1895, p. 3.

to a rock in full sight of a sumptuously laden table, while
vultures, marked Cleveland and Carlisle, and other birds bearing the three balls of the pawn shop, hovered over the man's
emaciated body awaiting his death. At the end of the book
was the mouth of a cave strewn with skulls, marked "Gold
Standard" and the words—"All ye who enter here leave hope
behind."

Harvey's unexpected success as an author led to his publishing other primers and handbooks. He also sold silver
badges with "16 to 1" on them and he organized a lecture
bureau: "Coin" and his like could be hired through Harvey
for appropriate fees to instruct the people about public finance.
The pamphlet drew forth much similar writing by other men,
a deal of it aimed at "Coin" and in reply to that worthy who,
by this time, had gained great fame.[1]

Neither group of advocates of a monetary policy being in
a frame of mind to yield to the other the campaign of 1896
would be a grand trial of strength. It were, perhaps, worth
months of the newspaper printing and reading, the pamphlet-
eering, the stump speaking, the organization of the voters
by money which politicians should extract from the rich,
the hopes and fears and wild alarums which accompany a
Presidential contest in America, if we could rid ourselves of
a heresy which had got into the minds of the people to such
a degree that it had quite corrupted their political sense.

It was manifest that the infection was most deeply affecting
the Democratic party, though, under Cleveland, that party
had had leadership in resistance to the cheap money doctrines
stronger and more inspiring than had been offered by any
Republican who had attained eminence in our politics. The
members of his cabinet were a unit in supporting him and their
influence in their states delayed the complete capture by the
silver men of the Democratic organization in those states.
Carlisle and Hoke Smith, both of whom had been infirm on

[1] Coin's Financial School; Rhodes, The McKinley and Roosevelt Ad-
ministrations, pp. 22–3; Haynes, Third Party Movements, pp. 295, 369;
H. H. Kohlsaat, From McKinley to Harding, pp. 51–2; N. Y. Nation,
April 25, May 16, and June 6, 1895.

the currency question, valiantly, in 1895, defended the gold standard in Kentucky and Georgia,[1] while the influence of Secretary of Agriculture Morton had been used to prevent Bryan from seizing control of the party machinery in Nebraska. Vilas in Wisconsin and Dickinson in Michigan, members of the cabinet during Cleveland's first term of office, were sturdily withstanding silverism in the Northwest. "Sound money" conventions which were attended by eminent citizens, intent upon the education of the people concerning the principles of finance without regard to party sympathies, were held in various cities and the attention of the Democratic managers was particularly directed to the South. There all men were Democrats. From that section of the country the party received unthinking strength. The South was counted for the candidates without an enumeration of the votes on election day, and in states so overwhelmingly Democratic it was a disturbing sight to witness the estrangement of the people from their President and their old leaders. The movement must be checked. The farmers in the South, as in the West, were poor. They were told that they were bestridden by the rich and that silver would save them from destruction. The idea was burning its way through the country like fire in stubble. If the South were lost to the gold standard men it was practically certain that the silverites would control the nominating convention in 1896 and determine the course of the party in the campaign of that year.

A Sound Money convention, organized by Southern men on Southern ground, meeting in Memphis in May, 1895, promised to arrest the progress of the flames. Carlisle, as Secretary of the Treasury and as a Southern man whose leadership had earlier won the respect of the people, would address the convention. It was his own and other men's lively hope to meet by education the error which had come to control the public mind. He spoke in his own state of Kentucky on his way to and from Tennessee, explaining the rudiments of public finance in terms which, it was believed, the most

[1] N. Y. Nation, July 18 and Aug. 1, 1895.

ignorant could understand. Nearly 1,000 delegates attended the meeting, more than 5,000 listened to the speeches. The resolutions endorsed President Cleveland's "unflagging courage" and squarely opposed the free coinage idea.[1]

William Jennings Bryan, by correspondence and speech, was making himself a national leader. He had lost his seat in Congress and was returned to Nebraska which was quite too small a theatre for his activities. He had tasted the sweets of eminence and he must have more. He was seeking and finding men in all parts of the country who were ready to subscribe to his doctrine that "gold monometallism" was the curse of the country and of the world. Bryan followed Carlisle into the South. The work done in the Sound Money convention in Memphis must be undone, and men in great variety who had gained prominence in writing and speaking about the sins of the "gold bugs" were asked to attend a silver convention in the same city. They held their meeting in June and sent their resolutions over the country as proof that the South was not as Cleveland and Carlisle would like it to be.

But Bryan was going too far. He had been pressed and he had said at Jackson, the capital of Mississippi, that, if the Democratic convention in 1896 should adopt a single gold standard platform, he would "die in his tracks" before he should vote for the ticket.[2] This was too much for many of his hearers among the Bourbons who could not think a Democrat a Democrat if he, under any circumstances, would leave the party. The Gold Democrats in the summer of 1895 were encouraged to believe that some obstacles had been reared to check a movement which a little while since had seemed to forebode a complete undermining of the foundations of sound opinion.[3]

Bryan who, after earlier contests with the gold men in Nebraska, made conquest in 1895 of the Democratic convention in that state, dictating the nominations and writing the platform, had met complete defeat on election day. Although

---

[1] N. Y. Nation, April 25, May 30 and June 20, 1895; N. Y. Times, May 24, June 13 and 14, 1895.
[2] N. Y. Times, June 13, 1896. [3] Cf. N. Y. Nation, July 18, 1895.

the Republicans were victorious, the sound money Democrats who had bolted the Bryan ticket polled more votes than the "regulars." Men said that Bryan had been "shelved." [1] It was too confident a prediction. His reverse seemed but to increase his pertinacity. He and his wife inaugurated an epistolary campaign which embraced the whole country. He had suggestions for the calling of conferences, the election of delegates, trading and trucking by which conventions could be captured and fusions effected and, in general, for relentless attack upon the walls of the old Democratic party until they should crumble and the silverites could enter. [2]

The elections of 1895 indicated throughout the country, as had those of 1894, an unmistakable movement of the people entirely away from the Democratic party, whether it be led by Mr. Cleveland or by the silver men. It was plain that the "landslide" of 1894 had not run its course and in the wreckage of the following year it was not displeasing to see the figures of Hill, Brice and Gorman. No one of the three disturbers in the Democratic household would be returned to the Senate unless there should be a change in the political currents before the expiration of their terms. The Republicans would control the legislatures of New York, Ohio and Maryland. Brice would go at once. The Democratic candidate for governor in Ohio, whose boast it had been that the British lion could not put its paws on him, was defeated. The candidate for governor in Kentucky, who had defied the statements concerning money in the Democratic platform of Kentucky, and who had made his campaign as a silverite, met a deserved fate. The state elected a Republican governor. [3]

The exultation which followed the elections in 1895 in such a newspaper as the New York Tribune was unconcealed. Nothing could arise, as it seemed, to prevent the choice of a Republican President in 1896 and the return of the party to power. It only remained for the leaders to close their ranks and present a can-

---

[1] N. Y. Nation, Nov. 14, 1895.   [2] Barnes, J. G. Carlisle, pp. 443–8.
[3] N. Y. Tribune, Nov. 6 and 7, 1895; N. Y. Nation, Aug. 29 and Nov. 7, 1895.

didate who, having the united support of the various elements within the organization, could command the good will of the voters generally. Whether, in the end, the opposing party be for gold or for silver the Republicans were certain, barring some unforeseen obstacle, of no doubtful victory.

It was agreed that the tariff should be the issue of the campaign. It had served the Republicans well before. The manufacturers were protectionists. The workingmen had been instructed to believe that they could be employed at good wages only during Republican administrations of the government. Periods of panic and depression were coterminous with Democratic rule. The Wilson tariff law of 1894 could be made to carry the whole load of the people's troubles. It was free trade—Cleveland was a free trader. The Democratic party was a free trade party. Once again the story would be told. There were silver Republicans, as well as silver Democrats. It was not clear how many votes could be had by standing up for sound money. Cleveland had made but few friends by such means. The Republicans would tread softly on the money question, stay on familiar ground and, with protection on the party banners, recapture the national government.

This program met the favor of those who saw in William McKinley the figure to lead the Republican ticket. In a tariff campaign what more could be asked for than a leader who had given his name to the law which the Democrats had so ruthlessly overthrown? Under it there had been "prosperity." The depression came after the Democrats had taken office on a platform demanding its repeal. The Wilson law, with free wool and other abominations which inflamed the minds of the farmers as well as the manufacturers, could be made into the bugaboo of the day and McKinley could be furnished forth as the knight on the white steed to go out to recover the holy treasure in the shape of large profits, high wages and that return of "good times" which was every man's hope.

McKinley had, indeed, much to commend him for the part in the sight of the politicians. He was not greatly troubled by scruples and convictions in the sense that Mr. Cleveland was. Conscience did not prick him to stubbornness. Education had not closed his mind. He could be turned from side to side. Protection was a fixed idea to be sure, but he pursued that light as a politician rather than an economist. He was for a high tariff as a party measure rather than a principle in some system of social and political philosophy. No man could certainly say from a study of his public declarations what were his views on the money question, and nothing could so well serve the conveniences of the Republican party at this time as one who scarcely knew what he thought in reference to a matter which so sorely divided the country. He could be commended and voted for in the West as a bimetallist, in the East as a protectionist who, whatever his past record, would not dare to go far astray in relation to the currency.)

Ohio was a state which had been notoriously unsound on the subject of money. John Sherman had picked his way for a period of years and had negotiated the hazards which beset his course not without a good deal of manipulation and trickery. The state was as likely to have a greenbacker or a free silver man in the Senate, or in the governor's office, as a man with opposite views. McKinley had been elected governor in 1891; he was reelected in 1893. In the campaigns of both years he had evaded the money question. In 1891 he and the platform on which he stood endorsed the silver purchase law of 1890.

In 1893 he stuck to the platitudes about the "financial honor" of the country and made no point as to the necessity for repeal of the law of 1890. He said on one occasion during that campaign that the "silver product of the country" should not be "discriminated against." Some plan should be devised to utilize silver because mining and milling it was an important American industry. Our policy should be to "insure, not the displacement of gold, but the safe and full use of both metals." [1] Such utterances could be fairly characterized, as they were, as "twaddle"; they were not meant to be frank; they were not the reflections of a settled mind; they were not intended for the instruction of men, but to get their votes.

[1] N. Y. Nation, Sep. 21, 1893, and May 7, 1896.

The movement to nominate McKinley for the Presidency on the Republican ticket went forward steadily under the pressure of a group of politicians in Ohio responsive to the touch of Mark Hanna who had risen to eminence in the retinue of John Sherman. A representative of the enterprising, uncritical manhood of the Middle West, as his biographer has observed, he firmly believed that prosperity was diffused by Republican tariffs and it is certain that he looked upon his design to bring McKinley to the Presidency as, in some degree, a patriotic mission.[1]

Hanna, as has been seen, was not a warm admirer of Harrison, nor had McKinley been eager for Harrison's renomination in the convention at Minneapolis in 1892.[2] Though McKinley presented the name of the President for a second term there was, as has been related, not a little fear in the minds of Harrison's friends that the delegates might see in the orator standing before them a better candidate, as they had done in Garfield's case when he spoke for John Sherman in 1880. But McKinley's claims, which others emphasized, he had himself suppressed. His loyalty to Harrison's interests were not visibly shaken at sight of the demonstrations which his own personality evoked. Harrison was renominated and was defeated. Men had said that McKinley would be the nominee in 1896. The time, as he and other astute men knew, had not come for a campaign to be led by the advocate of a high tariff. The West was wavering in its admiration of the law which bore his name and which was his principal title to popular fame. He should wait until there was some revulsion of feeling regarding the measure which his candidacy would have recalled so forcibly to the public mind. But as the months wore on and Cleveland was taking the brunt of the blame for the state of the times McKinley's position would improve. The probability of his coming forward with irresistible force in 1896 was increased by his triumphant reelection to the governorship of

[1] Croly, M. A. Hanna, p. 188; Rhodes, The McKinley and Roosevelt Administrations, p. 13.
[2] Cf. J. B. Foraker, Notes of a Busy Life, vol. i, pp. 447–50; H. H. Kohlsaat, From McKinley to Harding, pp. 4–9.

Ohio in 1893 and the assurance of the earnest management of his campaign, should he be chosen to lead the party in the nation at large, by a business man of such resources and such unbending purpose as Mark Hanna.

But the plans were nearly overset by McKinley's awkward conduct of his personal affairs. He had endorsed the notes of a man named Walker in Youngstown, Ohio. Friendship actuated him, and it was one of the ironies of life that the money was to be invested in the manufacture of tin plate, the chief of the "infant industries" which were to be bottle-nursed and set on their feet by the McKinley tariff law. The business failed. McKinley thought that his indebtedness was about $5,000. As a matter of fact—he gave so little attention, it appears, to his affairs—there was $130,000 of Walker's paper bearing McKinley's endorsement in bankers' hands.[1] If the aims of those who were resting their hopes in him as a figure through whom they might advance were not to be frustrated they must come to his rescue. Hanna, Myron T. Herrick, H. H. Kohlsaat, the owner of a newspaper in Chicago; W. R. Day, A. A. Pope, a bicycle manufacturer; Andrew Carnegie, Henry C. Frick and Philander C. Knox of Pittsburgh; John Hay, Charles Taft, Mr. and Mrs. Bellamy Storer of Cincinnati and others discharged McKinley's debts and his political bark was again sailing on propitious seas.[2] He himself, as a business man, or the lender of money to a business man, had been brought down in the panic of 1893. He had not done very well by himself, but it was made to appear in the Republican newspapers that he was the genius who could save the country in the day of general disaster. The large vote by which he had been re-elected governor of his state deeply impressed the public mind and, in a time of economic dejection, hope was seen in his high tariff which the Democrats were engaged in repealing in the interest of free wool and an in-

[1] T. B. Mott, Myron T. Herrick, p. 48; J. F. Rhodes, The McKinley and Roosevelt Administrations, p. 11.

[2] Herbert Croly, M. A. Hanna, p. 170; C. S. Olcott, Life of McKinley, vol. i, pp. 288–92; H. H. Kohlsaat, From McKinley to Harding, pp. 10–17.

vasion of foreign products. What shrewd men in 1892 had foreseen had occurred. The opportunity had come. McKinley was announced as "the advance agent of prosperity" who would give the workingman a "full dinner pail." He had been elected to the governorship, he would be nominated for and elected to the Presidency on the "prosperity" issue. All men could see that times were hard. All men would have them better and the way to this end led to McKinley. Such a to-do can be created about one man's personality in our democracy and it was in victorious progress. Nothing could withstand it, as those who put their figures in the way would soon learn to their grief.

Not anything that Hanna had done for his friend was likely to be so useful as the meetings with Republican politicians in the South in the spring of 1895. McKinley was a guest at Hanna's winter home in Georgia. He declined invitations to make speeches on his way to or from the South,[1] but scores of men from that and adjoining states were invited to luncheon, to dinner, to stay over night. McKinley was a particularly affable and in some degree fascinating companion. His manners were fairly described as "winning." A short, sturdy figure, with a radiant, smooth-shaven face, men found in him a resemblance to Napoleon. The "little Corporal" smiled upon his Southern visitors, talked to them in a cordial way with great advantage to his political prospects, and the old collectors of the port, revenue agents and postmasters who had been so faithful to Sherman in national nominating conventions, were transferred, almost in a body, to the new prophet of Republicanism.[2]

There were leaders who had other objects in view. Their purposes would not be served through the "Ohio crowd" who seemed to be on the point of taking control of the party in national matters. First of all there was Thomas B. Reed

[1] He would not, he said, be put in the position of seeking office, or be seen in the light of "disporting" himself in his trip through the South.— McKinley to Hanson, Feb. 27, 1895, in McKinley Papers.
[2] Croly, M. A. Hanna, pp. 175–6; H. H. Kohlsaat, From McKinley to Harding, pp. 23–6.

of Maine, now again Speaker of the House of Representatives. He had his friends, especially in New England. Those young aspirants for high honors, Lodge and Roosevelt, were ardent Reed men.[1] Reed was a brilliant parliamentarian. No one questioned his talents in the give and take of a legislative body. His wit was sharp and his thrust was feared. But he was far from being of a fibre suitable for a Presidential candidate. He was arbitrary by nature, an uncompromising partisan, contemptuous of the rights of those who differed with him. Not long since he had been generally denounced as a "Czar." In no sense, however much men might admire his quick and acute understanding, was his name one to put before his fellow citizens in a bid for votes. The shrewd and experienced in our politics knew this well and, outside of New England, Reed's boom made little progress.

Harrison was a candidate, though few stopped to consider his claims. He had been renominated in 1892 against the will of most of the party leaders. They had found his nature ungrateful and cold; they had given him indifferent support in the campaign. He had been defeated. Why draw him from the private life to which he had been returned? But Harrison himself and his friends in Indiana were not convinced of his unavailability. He might anyhow, if he remained in the field, interpose obstacles to the progress of McKinley,[2] who, Harrison believed, had been far from sincere and single-minded in the words that were spoken in the re-nominating speech at Minneapolis in 1892. No love was lost between the two men and Harrison's antipathy extended to Hanna who in 1892 had opened "headquarters" for McKinley in Minneapolis in the hope that his protegé might, by some chance, profit from the dislike which Harrison knew how to engender in others, and who, on the first ballot, had received the votes of no less than 182 delegates.[3] Cullom in Illinois was a candidate. He

[1] S. W. McCall, Life of T. B. Reed, pp. 223, 225, 228; Corr. of Roosevelt and Lodge, vol. i, pp. 203–4, 219, 223.

[2] N. Y. Nation, Oct. 3, 1895.

[3] Croly, M. A. Hanna, pp. 165–6; J. B. Foraker, Notes of a Busy Life, vol. i, pp. 447–8; H. H. Kohlsaat, From McKinley to Harding, pp. 4–5; cf. N. Y. Nation, Oct. 3 and Dec. 19, 1895.

defended himself and refused to withdraw. "We were twice beaten," said he, by the bill bearing McKinley's name, "and we would be in danger again with McKinley as the standard bearer" since to choose him as the party candidate must be "regarded as nominating the bill as well as the man for whom it was named." [1]

Platt in New York saw the opportunity to hold his delegates in leash through the prestige of the large majority which Levi P. Morton had gained in the election for governor in 1894.[2] He had been Vice President with Harrison. But there was little reason to think that his name would awaken popular enthusiasm in a Presidential campaign. Allison of Iowa might meet approval in the trans-Mississippi states and was the hope of elements which were endeavoring to stop McKinley. Quay, in absolute control of the party organization in Pennsylvania, with sufficient audacity, caused himself to be put forward as that state's choice for the nomination.[3]

But Hanna and his friend were far ahead in the race. They established contacts with, and enlisted the services of, local managers in all parts of the country. Unquestionably promises were made, though McKinley himself properly disclaimed responsibility for bargains looking to support for his nomination.[4] Money, nearly all of it Mr. Hanna's, was provided. The canvass cost him more than $100,000. It is not averred that delegates were purchased, else larger sums would have been expended,[5] but the practical business of organization, especially in states in which the opposition was active, called for remittances which Hanna personally made, often from stores much depleted by the prolonged industrial depression.[6]

Early in February, 1896, Harrison withdrew from the contest. He could not consent that his name be presented to the con-

---

[1] Letter of April 4, 1896, in McKinley Papers.
[2] Cf. Cortissoz, Life of Whitelaw Reid, vol. ii, p. 205; McElroy, Levi P. Morton, chap. x.
[3] Cf. A. K. McClure, Old Time Notes of Pa., vol. ii, pp. 600–1.
[4] Cf. T. B. Mott, Myron T. Herrick, pp. 60–1; S. M. Cullom, Fifty Years of Public Service, p. 273.
[5] Cf. S. W. McCall, Life of T. B. Reed, p. 223.
[6] Croly, M. A. Hanna, pp. 183–6.

vention and he begged that his statement be taken "as a sincere and final expression upon the subject." [1] Indiana was now released for other candidates and the opportunity for McKinley's friends to capture delegates in that state was at hand.

Though the Foraker faction, at the expiration of McKinley's two terms as governor, had taken control of the party in Ohio [2] no obstruction was put in the way of an endorsement of McKinley when the state convention met in March. Wisconsin, Oregon, Nebraska and North Dakota soon followed. All were for McKinley. Vermont, at the end of April, proclaimed him its choice, a significant event as it marked a movement away from Reed in New England.[3] A decisive victory over Senator Cullom was won in Illinois,[4] and the impression, which it was the hope of the McKinley managers to create, that their candidate was irresistible was becoming widespread.

The nominating convention of the Republican party would be held in St. Louis in June. In the meantime the outlook for the Democrats was dark. That this organization was disintegrating was clear. No one supposed that Mr. Cleveland was a candidate to succeed himself. It was not necessary for him to state his views concerning a third term, which would have been definite enough had the situation called for a declaration on his side as to his renomination.[5] Everywhere support for the principles which he had announced as the reason for the existence of the party was being withdrawn. He had given it a mission which had warmed the pulse of the nation and written his name high on the scroll of its statesmen. Now all was on the point of being undone. What would, probably, be the party's immediate fate was not difficult to predict. The signs had been seen for two or three years in state conventions, in legislatures and in Congress. Bryan was industriously at work carrying on a pre-convention campaign. It is believed that he personally addressed, by post, every silver delegate

[1] N. Y. Tribune, Feb. 5, 1896.
[2] J. B. Foraker, Notes of a Busy Life, vol. i, pp. 452-6.
[3] S. W. McCall, Life of T. B. Reed, p. 233.
[4] S. M. Cullom, Fifty Years of Pub. Service, pp. 273-4.
[5] Cf. McElroy, Grover Cleveland, vol. ii., p. 215.

to the convention.[1] Other men were talking, writing and
organizing. The Populists had made no progress with their
third party. The capture of the machinery of an old party
was a simpler way to their ends and in the Democratic
party the sapping and mining proceeded without effective
hindrance from any side. Times were hard, the masses were
ready to listen to any explanation of poverty and to embrace any plan which promised relief from unemployment and
economic distress.[2] Politicians without principles, intent upon
holding place and power, left Cleveland, especially now when
his term was near its end, and professed views entirely at
variance with those which they had held before, thus increasing
the force of the movement. In some parts of the country the
new system of democracy, in which the individualistic philosophy and *laissez faire* economy of Mr. Cleveland were discarded in favor of socialistic schemes, was sweeping everything
before it. As well put breath against a hurricane as this in-
fatuation.

The Democratic national convention would be held in Chicago
on July 7th. One Southern and Western state followed another
with declarations in favor of the free coinage of silver, which
was the idea first and foremost in the minds of the new Democrats. In Illinois they renominated Altgeld for governor
and called for the "remonetization" of silver at the ratio of
16 to 1, "without waiting or depending on any other nation
on earth." In Ohio they expressed their unalterable opposition
to the "single gold standard" and demanded "immediate
return to the constitutional money of gold and silver." In
Indiana, Missouri, Iowa, Kentucky the conventions adopted
similar resolutions. Missouri put forward, and instructed its
delegates in the national convention to vote for, the arch
prophet of silverism, Richard P. Bland. There had been "gold
men" in the conventions. Factional wrangling had preceded
the adoption of platforms and the naming of candidates for
state offices, but the silverites drove all before them. Commendation of Mr. Cleveland was omitted, when he was not

[1] Barnes, J. G. Carlisle, pp. 456–7.   [2] Cf. ibid., pp. 448–53.

singled out for detraction and abuse.[1] When the Democrats in a block of states in the centre of the country, such as these, were lost to reason the end could be seen. The party, said the New York Nation, was "worm-eaten" by Populism. Tillman, Altgeld, Boies of Iowa, Morgan of Alabama, Harris of Tennessee and Bryan were Populists with hardly any disguise. If they were to control the convention the party might as well haul down its flag and hoist that of Weaver and Peffer in its stead.[2]

All the while President Cleveland viewed the scene with the most painful sensations. He wrote letters to his friends urging them to action. They wrote to him reporting the spread of the craze and the disruption of the party. The people must be educated. "If reckless discontent and wild experiment should sweep our currency from its safe support," the President said, "the most defenceless of all who suffer in that time of distress and national discredit will be the poor."[3] The Democratic party, "our party" as the President called it, was "the party of the people." With a campaign on foot to add to the circulation of the country "unrestrained millions of so-called dollars, intrinsically worth but half the amount they purported to represent," a time had come for Democrats to "realize their responsibility."[4] He was up in arms against the "ingrates and traitors" who had stolen the livery of Democracy and were wickedly duping the people.[5]

"I am having a dreadful time here," he wrote to a friend in March, 1896.[6] He would "patiently wait for the final verdict" of his countrymen, he told Don Dickinson—this verdict would "certainly in due time be returned."[7] He was "longing" for "two things—the adjournment of Congress and the 4th of March, 1897."[8] "I believe, I am, by nature, an undismayed and persistent fighter," he said in June, again to Dickinson, "and I do not believe in giving an inch until we are obliged to,

[1] Cf. McElroy, Grover Cleveland, vol. ii, p. 213.
[2] N. Y. Nation, May 28, 1896.
[3] McElroy, Grover Cleveland, vol. ii, p. 206; A. Nevins, Letters of Cleveland, pp. 429–30, 432–3, 438, 439–42.
[4] McElroy, Grover Cleveland, vol. ii, p. 211. [5] Ibid., p. 213.
[6] Cleveland to Rev. W. M. Smith, March 26, 1896, in Cleveland Papers.
[7] Feb. 18, 1896, in ibid. [8] March 19, 1895, in ibid.

and yet it is hard to call on friends to maintain a struggle which seems so hopeless." Of course he had not seen anything like this before, but his faith in the American people was so great that he could not believe they would cast themselves over the precipice. Was the party with "all its glorious traditions" to founder on the rocks? "Will not sanity return before we reach the final plunge?" [1] The President "honestly believed" that the present Congress was "a menace to the good of the country, if not its actual safety, every day developing their wildness and recklessness," their "seeming desperation and wickedness." If the Democratic party were "inclined to half behave itself it could profit from the situation." [2] But "the brood of liars and fools" were having their "carnival." [3]

The Democrats in New York spoke of compromise, though they were held in place by the most vigorous assertion of public opinion. Pennsylvania and New Jersey would support the President. Massachusetts and all the New England states were faithful. Massachusetts offered its young leader for three terms governor of the state, the much admired William E. Russell, as its candidate for President. Mr. Cleveland's friends in Michigan, Minnesota, Wisconsin and South Dakota withstood the storm and held their ground on the money question. But these delegates, it was plain, would be outnumbered in the national convention. Carlisle, who was still speaking effectively, was suggested as a candidate whose name might be brought before the convention. "Carlisle Clubs" were formed. They would secure a million letters endorsing him, and nearly so many were secured in a short time. Campaign buttons were made with his face and name upon them.[4] Governor Pattison of Pennsylvania, Secretary of State Olney and Whitney were among those who, it was thought, might lead the battle, if it were not too late. The two-thirds rule might yet prevent the silver men from controlling the nomination.[5]

---

[1] Cleveland to Dickinson, June 10, 1896, in Cleveland Papers.
[2] March 19, 1896, in ibid.
[3] McElroy, Grover Cleveland, vol. ii, p. 217.
[4] Barnes, J. G. Carlisle, pp. 454–5.   [5] Cf. ibid., p. 453.

Those who viewed the progress of McKinley's cause with disfavor taunted him increasingly. Was he for or against free coinage? He was silent. His record was studied for an indication of his convictions in regard to a subject around which the canvass was certain to be waged. It was pointed out that he had spoken equivocally, when not plainly, for silver in his campaigns for the governorship of Ohio in 1891 and 1893. The Congressional Record and the reports of his stump speaking were explored for further statements in a like sense, and they were found. He had voted repeatedly in the House of Representatives some years since not with the sound money men, but with their opponents.[1] Contrariwise the silver men attacked him and would know his views. He was under suspicion on that side also. Senator Stewart of Nevada asked him direct questions and demanded answer at once.[2]

The new Republican House of which Thomas B. Reed was the Speaker and in which Nelson Dingley, Jr. of Maine was chairman of the Committee on Ways and Means had thrown together a bill to repeal the Wilson law, which was called an "Emergency Revenue Bill," or more often the "Dingley Bill." It was built around a tariff on wool. It would mark a return from "free trade" to protective duties. If it were passed it would, its advocates said, reassure manufacturers who would employ the workingmen and start the wheels of industry; while bringing in needed revenue it would end business depression. The measure was hurried through the House on December 26, 1895, but progress was obstructed in the Senate by Teller and the Western senators who had made it their business for a number of years to hold up tariff legislation unless, at the same time, something should be "done" for silver.[3] The bill, therefore, was a mere campaign document, a statement of what the Republican leaders would do if they could—a further assertion of McKinley's theory that the issue was the tariff.

[1] N. Y. Nation, April 16, May 21, June 4, 11 and 18, 1896; H. Croly, M. A. Hanna, pp. 192–3; Rhodes, The McKinley and Roosevelt Administrations, pp. 13–4.
[2] See his letter of April 29, 1896, in McKinley Papers.
[3] Cf. N. Y. Nation, May 7, 1896.

Reed, after a long delay, stated his views about the currency. With his Presidential candidacy in mind he had been conducting himself in the speakership more amiably than when he had earlier held the office. His friends bade him make clear his position as to gold and silver and, with the hope of reaping benefits at the expense of the sphinx-like McKinley, from whom no utterances came, he acceded.[1] However, if this were the manlier course to pursue, it but little aided his canvass.

It was stated and the inference, the more McKinley was studied, was plain that he was a man of an untrained and a superficial intellect. He was commended as an orator. A volume of his speeches had been published. A reading of them raised him but little in the esteem of discriminating persons. An allusion to the Chicago exposition as "the hallelujah of the universe for the triumph of civil liberty and Christian civilization," another to General John A. Logan as one, the success of whose careers, both military and political, was "almost unrivalled in the history of men" made the effort to reward the author of such judgments by an election to the Presidency of the United States seem rather audacious.[2] But his unconsidered eulogies, his love of the trite and obvious,[3] his wavering to suit the need to the hour were excused. It was proof of a wish to be "in close touch with the people." It was his policy as a public man to study popular currents and, in an obliging way, to follow their directions.[4] It was a quality which politicians viewed as almost a talent and, in his case, came to be described as "keeping his ear to the ground."[5]

Cleveland's forthright nature had set up new and fine standards of leadership for our public men. It was the more difficult, in the face of such example, for those who admired sincerity and courage to brook the evasive and rather sly attitude of

[1] N. Y. Nation, April 23 and June 11, 1896. McKinley, Reed said, "does not want to be called a gold-bug or a silver-bug, so he has compromised on a straddle-bug."—Ibid., May 14, 1896.

[2] N. Y. Nation, March 19 and June 18, 1896; Speeches and Addresses of Wm. McKinley, pp. 276, 631.

[3] Cf. N. Y. Nation, Jan. 31, 1895.   [4] Ibid., April 16, 1896.

[5] The American Indian thus would listen for the sound of thunder afar off and of approaching storm.

McKinley with reference to the question which was uppermost in every mind. His friends simply said that he would be a fool to state his views now, while delegates were still to be chosen in the silver states.[1] In the West the impression that he was a bimetallist must be nursed. John Sherman made speeches which gave comfort to the silverites. Those who had found reason to praise him in earlier years were now bound to conclude that he was laboring under the impairments of age,[2] proof of which would soon be given. Foraker pursued an uncertain course. The money "plank" in the platform adopted by the Ohio Republican state convention was taken to be an expression of McKinley's mind. Mention was made of "honest money," a "currency of gold, silver and paper . . . as sound as the government and as untarnished as its honor"; of "bi-metallism," the use of "both gold and silver as standard money," either by international agreement or by such legislation as would "secure the parities of value of the two metals, so that the purchasing and debt-paying power of the dollar, either of silver, gold or paper, shall be at all times equal."[3] Such a jumble of words regarding a question which called for plain speech had but one object in view. Republican state conventions in the East made direct demands for the maintenance of the gold standard. Not a few in the Mississippi Valley, following the example of Ohio, looked both ways and the Rocky Mountain states definitely declared for free coinage. In many of the silver states McKinley was endorsed. Some delegates threatened to bolt if the national platform should commit the party to the gold standard. Teller in Colorado and Dubois in Idaho who led the silverites in the Senate on the Republican side spoke openly of walking out of the convention at St. Louis if their demands were not met.

McKinley, and those who were managing his canvass for the nomination, had gone a long way to conciliate the silver

---

[1] N. Y. Nation, May 14 and 21 and June 4, 1896; cf. T. B. Mott, Myron T. Herrick, pp. 67–70.

[2] Cf. N. Y. Nation, Oct. 24 and 31, 1895, and Jan. 9, 1896. J. B. Foraker, Notes of a Busy Life, vol. i, pp. 499–500.

[3] N. Y. Nation, March 19, 1896.

men. They had put much suspicion and mistrust into the minds of those who could in any case feel but little admiration for the candidate. He would come to the nomination, they freely observed, and to the Presidency, if he should be elected, (a very probable event) under obligations to the rich men who had paid his debts in 1893, to the manufacturers who were to contribute large sums to the Republican campaign fund, so that they might have another "McKinley law" and, in particular to one Midas, his friend, Hanna, who would always be standing at his side. Such liens upon the future conduct of a rather yielding figure were enough, without possible bargainings with the silver men, who had been so successful in recent Congresses in blocking ordinary legislative progress and disturbing the public welfare.

At least a month before the convention met the result was assured. Mr. Reed's friends, Platt who was hiding behind Morton, Quay and others who, with the honest conviction that a better nomination might be made, or merely with a view to securing in return for their support promises of offices and other favors within a President's gift and, therefore, withheld their enthusiasm,[1] saw clearly what the outcome would be.[2] Platt was confronted by a formidable revolt as a result of his despotic course. McKinley's admirers in New York had formed a McKinley League. They had collected the signatures of more than 100,000 men which were wound upon a wheel. This impressive contrivance they placed in an observation car at the end of a special train filled with a shouting claque for a trip to St. Louis. The coaches were garlanded and festooned. Flags flew from the locomotive. Pictures of McKinley and streamers proclaimed the purpose of the zealots who rode within. So well organized was the movement that, in spite of Platt, who treated all opposition to his will as a kind of treason, a group of delegates from the state, led by

---

[1] For the attitude of Platt and Quay cf. H. H. Kohlsaat, From McKinley to Harding, pp. 30–1; T. B. Mott, Myron T. Herrick, p. 61. Platt said that McKinley was "mortgaged up to his eyes."—Whitelaw Reid to McKinley, Dec. 5, 1896, in McKinley Papers.

[2] Cf. N. Y. Tribune, June 11 and 12, 1896.

Warner Miller, would disregard the instructions of the "Boss" and his machine. They would have none of Morton. They would vote in the convention for McKinley.[1]

Congress adjourned on June 11th; the convention would meet on the 16th in a great auditorium in St. Louis hastily reared for the use, capable of seating more than 15,000 people.[2] Charles W. Fairbanks of Indiana was chosen to be the temporary chairman of the meeting; John M. Thurston of Nebraska, an eloquent man, who had recently won election to the United States Senate over William Jennings Bryan, the Democratic candidate for the office, the permanent chairman. Both made their speeches and the committees, the chief of which was that one appointed to construct a platform for the party, were set at their tasks. Nothing was in doubt, indeed, but the nature of the money plank and the name of the man who should join McKinley on the ticket as the candidate for Vice President. The third day of the convention began with Foraker's reading of the report of the committee on resolutions, a piece of writing which was a match for most platforms made to attract votes to a party during a Presidential campaign. It began by pointing to "the calamitous consequences of full and unrestricted Democratic control of the government," and to the Democratic party's "record of unparalleled incapacity, dishonor and disaster." The government must be "restored to the party which for thirty years administered it with unequalled success and prosperity." The "Democratic tariff" was denounced. The "American policy" of protection was the "bulwark of American industrial independence and the foundation of American development and prosperity." The repeal by the Democrats of Blaine's reciprocity arrangements with other countries was declared to be "a national calamity." "Protection and reciprocity" were "twin measures of Republican policy" and should go hand in hand. "Democratic rule" had "recklessly struck down both, and both must be reestablished."

---

[1] N. Y. Tribune, June 13 and 14, 1896; R. McElroy, L. P. Morton, pp. 296–300.

[2] N. Y. Tribune, June 15, 1896.

Growers of sugar, wool and hemp—all were to have "ample protection," while reciprocity would afford an outlet for our surplus products.

"Discriminating duties," that is to say higher duties on goods imported in foreign bottoms than in American bottoms, were recommended as a means of building up the nation's merchant marine. Old soldiers were to be generously pensioned. One plank spoke of an enlarged navy and better seacoast defenses, another of a policy in regard to foreign immigration which would exclude those who could "neither read nor write." The "fatal competition" of low-priced foreign labor was deplored. The negro delegates were in the mind of the committee when it offered a statement expressing "unqualified condemnation of the uncivilized and barbarous practice" known as lynching; the labor union, when favor was expressed for a "national board of arbitration" to settle wage disputes; the Prohibitionists when sympathy was extended to "wise and legitimate efforts to lessen and prevent the evils of intemperance and promote morality"; the woman suffragists when the cooperation of women was welcomed "in rescuing the country from Democratic and Populistic mismanagement and misrule."

The platform advocated "a firm, vigorous and dignified" foreign policy "at all times." Hawaii should be "controlled" by the United States—nothing was said about annexation. The Nicaragua canal should be "built, owned and operated by the United States"; the Danish islands should be secured by purchase as a "naval station" in the West Indies. The Monroe Doctrine was reasserted "in its full extent" and made applicable to every case of "European encroachment," and the Republican party, through its spokesmen at St. Louis, would "hopefully look forward to the eventual withdrawal of the European powers" from the American hemisphere and to "the ultimate union of all the English-speaking part of the continent," which seemed to point to the annexation of Canada. The Cuban "patriots" in their contest with Spain, which was coming to occupy so much attention in Congress and the press, were pledged Republican sympathy in their "heroic battle" for freedom from Spanish "cruelty and oppression." The United States should "actively" use its influence "to restore peace and give independence to the island."

The money plank was made ready only by dint of much debate and revision in and out of committee. Whether the word gold should be used or should not be used, whether the statement regarding party policy should be clear, as a rising public sentiment in the East and, in only reduced measure, in the Middle West wished it to be, or should remain vague, as McKinley and Hanna would have preferred,[1] had been tediously discussed by the pundits of Republicanism. Knowledge and conviction, high and honorable purpose, the public weal seem to have been entirely out of mind. The question to be considered was what influence the declaration would have, in the first place, on McKinley's nomination and then, in the second place, on the successful management and triumphant issue of the campaign. When these interests were pondered and balanced the plank was presented and adopted.[2]

The form of the statement finally agreed upon was clearer than many had supposed that it might be. The Republican party, it was said, was "unreservedly for sound money." The law for the resumption of specie payments had been passed by the party and the party was "unalterably opposed" to every measure calculated to debase the currency or impair the credit of the country. All silver and paper outstanding must be "maintained at parity with gold" which was "the present standard, the standard of the most enlightened nations of the earth." The obeisance of the party before its old Mumbo

[1] Cf. N. Y. Nation, Dec. 31, 1896.
[2] This subject is discussed at length in H. Croly, M. A. Hanna, pp. 192–204 and H. H. Kohlsaat, From McKinley to Harding, pp. 33–48. See also T. C. Platt, Autobiography, p. 310; J. B. Foraker, Notes of a Busy Life, vol. i, pp. 463–82; T. B. Mott, Myron T. Herrick, chap. ix.; Cortissoz, Life of Whitelaw Reid, vol. ii, pp. 205–8; Charles Emory Smith in Phila. Press, June 24, 1896; J. F. Rhodes, The McKinley and Roosevelt Administrations, pp. 14–6; Corr. of Roosevelt and Lodge, vol. i, pp. 222–3, 246; C. S. Olcott, Life of McKinley, vol. i, pp. 311–4; Walter Wellman in Review of Reviews for Jan., 1897. Whitelaw Reid's draft of a plank incorporating suggestions of J. Pierpont Morgan and others is in the McKinley Papers.

Jumbo—an "international agreement" on the subject of bimetallism—was repeated; until then the "existing gold standard" must be preserved.

The reading of the plank touching the currency was interrupted by loud applause and cheering, except for a group of
delegates from the Rocky Mountains who made preparations
to leave the hall. Teller of Colorado presented a minority
report from the platform committee and delivered a long
address, in which he dramatically stated his reasons for saying
farewell to the Republican party which had nurtured him
and raised him up to his eminent place in public life. He
described the distress which he felt in the face of such a sever-
ance of old relations. But it was a great moral crisis. He must
decide whether to take the side of the people or the side of
those who were oppressing and robbing them, whether to
stand with those who would destroy the government and
attend the funeral of human liberty or with God and right.
His course might mean for him his retirement from political
life, the end of his political career. But he would follow the
leadings of his conscience and accept whatever fate lay in
store for him. Foraker moved to lay Teller's report on the
table. Lodge seconded the motion and it was disposed of
in this manner by a vote of 818½ to 105½. All the delegates
of Colorado, Idaho, Montana, Nevada, Utah, Wyoming and
Arizona voted for silver, as did 15 out of 18 of the California
delegates and some men standing under Populistic influence
in Kansas, South Dakota and the old South. Cannon, a fiery
young senator from the new state of Utah, was given the
floor to read a long protest which had been signed by Teller
and the other seceders, restating their reasons for their self
immolation on the altar of popular freedom, and to which
the convention listened with marked impatience. The martyrs
then took up their banners and other paraphernalia and marched
down the main aisle of the hall to music by the band, amid yelling and waving of flags by the delegates who remained behind.
Teller of Colorado carried his entire delegation with him, as
did Senator Dubois of Idaho. These groups with Senator

Pettigrew of South Dakota, Cannon of Utah, a representative
in Congress from Montana and a few others, totalling 22 in
all, made up the party. As they went out of the door the chairman announced dryly that enough delegates remained in the
hall to transact business; they would, therefore, proceed with
it, which in a short while, after several silverites were allowed
to explain why they had not followed their friends into exile,
brought on the names of the candidates for President.

If the McKinleyites enjoyed an overwhelming advantage
the opposition was in no mood to run away and leave them
in full control of the field. Allison of Iowa was named by a
delegate from that state in a speech which had a cool welcome.
Lodge spoke for Reed, for whom there were more marks of
friendship; Chauncey M. Depew for Levi P. Morton. Foraker
rose in behalf of McKinley. He was frequently interrupted.
Uncontrollable outbreaks by the delegates, and by the masses
put into the galleries for this purpose, prevented continuance of
the speech. One period of uproar lasted for 12 minutes, another
for 25 minutes. Thurston of Nebraska, the chairman, left
his place to second McKinley. "On behalf of that dismantled
chimney and the deserted factory at its base, that the furnaces
may once more flame, the mighty wheels revolve, the whistles
scream, the anvils ring, the spindles hum . . . that the firesides again may glow, the women sing, the children laugh,
yes, and on behalf of that American flag and all it stands
for and represents, for the honor of every stripe, for the glory
of every star that its power may fill the earth and its splendor
fill the sky," he asked for the nomination of "that loyal American, that Christian gentleman, soldier, statesman, patriot,
William McKinley." After so much as this Governor Hastings
of Pennsylvania had the task of nominating "Matt" Quay.
Only one ballot was necessary. There were 924 delegates—
463 would make the nomination. When the call of states
had been completed it was found that 661½ had voted for
McKinley; 84½, nearly all from New England, for Reed;
61½ for Quay (who had held all his delegates but 6, who
voted for McKinley); 58 for Morton (Platt having kept all but

17 in the New York delegation from voting for McKinley); 35½ for Allison. One Montana silverite had voted for "Don" Cameron.[1] Hanna had captured all but 26 of the white and black delegates from the South and had made throughout the country an almost complete sweep except in New York, Pennsylvania, Iowa and New England where McKinley had Vermont and 7 of the 12 votes cast by Connecticut.

Morton positively forbade the presentation of his name as a candidate for the nomination for the Vice Presidency[2] and the second place on the ticket was given to Garret A. Hobart of New Jersey, who had early allied himself with Hanna in the interest of McKinley.[3] Hobart's principal opponent was Henry Clay Evans of Tennessee who, however, fell far behind in the balloting. The convention's work had been done and it adjourned *sine die*.

McKinley remained at his home in Canton, Ohio, enjoying an, at that time, unprecedented experience. A long distance telephone had been installed in the room in which he sat. Six hundred miles separated him from St. Louis yet he could hear over the wire sounds of the turmoil which attended his nomination.[4] Newspaper correspondents and friends surrounded him. Cannon boomed and the town gave itself up to noisy celebration of the honor done its foremost citizen. Throughout the country bonfires and fireworks, street parades and flag raisings, blaring bands and bell ringing, cannonading, the blowing of factory whistles and of sirens on steamboats, ratification meetings at which village orators eulogized the nominees and the platform to crowds of shouting men told of the resolution of the rank and file of the party to work for victory.

The New York Tribune, which had been giving its support to McKinley,[5] viewed the result as a triumph of the people

---

[1] Official Proceedings of Convention, p. 123.
[2] R. McElroy, L. P. Morton, pp. 301–2.
[3] H. Croly, M. A. Hanna, p. 191.
[4] N. Y. Tribune, June 15 and 19, 1896; J. B. Foraker, Notes of a Busy Life, vol. i, pp. 486–8.
[5] Cf. N. Y. Nation, April 2, 1896.

over the "bosses," with particular reference to Platt, of whom, at the moment, it was pleased to speak in terms of complete disparagement.[1] That Platt had been influential in making changes in the money plank of the platform in the interest of a plainer declaration for the gold standard, as he was free to own, the Tribune denied. He came home in his private car a disappointed man. All his boasts of power were seen to be empty.[2] He and Quay, and Manley of Maine, who had directed Reed's canvass, and Clarkson of Iowa, who had been promoting Allison's cause, had pooled their talents with a view to defeating McKinley. They had been out-generalled by one whom they must consider an amateur in politics. On this genius was imposed at once the task of directing the campaign. Hanna was elected chairman of the Republican National Committee.

The defeated aspirants for the nomination congratulated the victor, and, but for Teller and his group of insurgents in the far West, the party presented a united front to the. foe. The platform, the New York Tribune said, was "magnificent." McKinley was a man who had "made himself, by years of patient labor in the people's cause, the foremost champion of sound ideas." Hanna was a "prince of organizers" and was to be supported as a Republican who believed, "with his whole soul, in Republicanism."[3] No previous Republican "standard bearer," said the Philadelphia Press, "more visibly represented the broad desire of the great body of voters."[4] The convention, in the declared opinion of the Boston Advertiser, had nominated "the most popular man in the United States."[5] Success was assured, Republicans everywhere declared; "prosperity" would follow.

The prospect of a clear declaration at the Democratic convention at Chicago in favor of free silver coinage had strengthened the hands of the gold standard men at St. Louis. It was as certain as anything could be that irreconcilable differences

---

[1] Cf. Cortissoz, Life of Whitelaw Reid, vol. ii, pp. 204–5.
[2] N. Y. Tribune, June 20, 1896
[3] Ibid., June 19 and 20, 1896.
[4] Phila. Press, June 19, 1896.   [5] Issue of June 19, 1896.

would separate the Cleveland wing of the party from the numerous, and, as it appeared, preponderant, faction which had embraced the principles of the Populists. The President now and again, at every opportunity, called upon the Democracy to set value upon its patrimony, to defend its ideals, to resist attacks upon the faith which had made it great.[1] But the party organization, in one state following another, was seized by the silverites.

They were on a mad career and it was fortunate that there was a party, inviting popular trust, with a different object in view. If the Republican leaders, before the meeting in St. Louis, had mistakenly supposed that the tariff could be made to be the issue, they must now, after that event, as they looked about them, comprehend how their wishes had impaired their judgment. An overwhelming majority of the delegates who would assemble at Chicago to nominate candidates for President and Vice-President bearing the Democratic name would have but one idea in their heads—the breaking down of the gold standard and the setting up of a new and a lower standard in its stead as a means of punishing the rich and giving advantages, as they believed, to the common people.

The handful of Western Republicans who had seceded from the St. Louis convention were joined, after the adjournment of the great meeting which had nominated McKinley and Hobart, by a few other delegates from the same part of the country. They continued to be actuated by impulses not in the minds of the Populistic Democrats, or, as they were now frequently called, the Popocrats, who were assembling in Chicago. The impelling motive of the Silver Republicans continued to be an enlarged market for the product of their mines. Their central figure was Teller of Colorado. He was an orator. He had occupied a seat in the Senate of the United States since his state's admission to the Union in 1876, except for the period during which he had been Secretary of the Interior in the cabinet of President Arthur, and he had enjoyed other honors at the hands of the Republican party. The

[1] Cf. N. Y. Nation, June 25, 1896.

faction would make him the nominee for President on a separate ticket. He represented, said United States Senator Lee Mantle of Montana, "the true principles and purposes of the Republican party as advocated by Lincoln, Grant and Blaine." [1] The insurgents, before they returned home, issued addresses to the people which, however, made them few new friends. They turned their eyes to Chicago; alliances might be arranged with the Democrats.

The silver wing of the Democratic party would be in control of the convention which was about to meet in that city—there was no doubt about this. Michigan and Nebraska, on the face of the returns, were entitled to seat gold standard delegates, but these delegates might be unseated by a majority vote. Nebraska's contestants were led by Bryan. Ex-Secretary of the Navy William C. Whitney postponed a trip to Europe in order to accompany the New York delegation to Chicago. He read the signs of the times and he had contrived a compromise. He would straddle the money question in the manner which the Republican party had so long followed with a measure of success.[2] But the silverites were at hand in such numbers and under such madly excited leaders, bent upon their ends, that suggestions for a middle way to be taken by the divergent factions were incontinently rejected. The gold men would make David B. Hill temporary chairman of the convention. Strategy dictated this determination. Hill in 1892 had been, so far as could be told, a silver man. At any rate he had been able, up to that time, to conceal his opinions to such a degree that he had been the choice of the silverites in the party as their candidate for President in opposition to Cleveland.[3] Now, in the convention of 1896, he was put forward as the hope of the gold standard men. Whitney, William F. Harrity of Pennsylvania, the chairman of the National Committee, which had directed the Cleveland campaign in 1892; Senator Gray of Delaware, Don M. Dickinson of Michigan; the President's friend, ex-Postmaster General Wilson S. Bis-

[1] N. Y. Tribune, June 20, 1896. [2] N. Y. Nation, July 2, 1896.
[3] Cf. J. W. Daniel in N. Y. Tribune, July 8, 1896.

sell; ex-Governor William E. Russell of Massachusetts and other men who, until now, had been weighty in the counsels of the party conferred but without prospect of influencing the result in the slightest degree. When the convention met on July 7th Hill's name was rejected by a vote of 556 to 349 and Senator John W. Daniel of Virginia was put in the chair. It was a majority—620 delegates, or two-thirds, would control the nomination. The radicals knew where to find these and it was patent to everyone that the platform would contain a declaration in favor of the coinage of silver at the ratio of 16 to 1, and that Bland, or some other free silver man, would be named as the party candidate for President. This old and tried champion of the silver dollar seemed to be the most likely choice. He was Missouri's "favorite son." Other delegations were instructed to give him their support. It was admitted that he had more than 200 delegates in his following—his managers who had established headquarters in all the Chicago hotels said 400. He was far and away ahead of any other who was in mind as a possible nominee.

The convention hall was a great new frame building called a Coliseum in the southern part of Chicago. It would hold more than 15,000 people,[1] and it was crowded to the doors with the delegates, the alternates and a noisy mob. Daniel soon relinquished the gavel to Senator White of California whom the free coinage men had selected for the permanent chairmanship.

The third day, Friday, July 10th, brought the proceedings to a climax. The Committee on Resolutions, as every one had for some time foreseen, presented a platform, the principal feature of which was a demand for free and unlimited silver and gold coinage at the ratio of 16 to 1, without regard to the action of any other nation. It was the money plank in the platform of the People's party in 1892, reiterated in many state platforms, the basic scheme of the silverites, so baldly expressed that it became the plain issue before the convention, as it would be before the country in the campaign.

[1] N. Y. Tribune, July 8, 1896.

"Gold monometallism," the platform makers declared, had "locked fast the prosperity of an industrial people in the paralysis of hard times." It was a "British policy"; it had "brought other nations into financial servitude to London." It was "not only un-American, but anti-American," and it could be fastened on the United States only after "stifling" that "indomitable spirit and love of liberty which proclaimed our political independence in 1776 and won it in the Revolution."

Furthermore, the Democratic party was opposed, so the resolutions presented by its new leaders said, to the issue of interest-bearing bonds in time of peace; it condemned "the trafficking with banking syndicates which, in exchange for bonds and at an enormous profit to themselves," supplied the Treasury with gold "to maintain the policy of gold monometallism." The further issue of currency by the national banks should be suspended; such money issues were "in derogation of the Constitution." The decision of the Supreme Court denying the validity of an income tax was denounced. Rich men should not be allowed to escape the burdens of taxation. The "arbitrary interference" by Federal authorities in local affairs was deemed to be "a crime against free institutions." "Government by injustice was in contempt of the laws of the states and rights of citizens." Cleveland's method of dealing with Altgeld and the mobs in Chicago was "a new and highly dangerous form of oppression."

Opposition which was expressed to "life tenure in the public service" was, in effect, a demand for an overthrow of what had been gained in the long and hard struggle for reform in this field. The railroads were to be put under further restriction to protect the people from "robbery and oppression." The platform, in effect, denounced all the important achievements of Mr. Cleveland's administration. That resistance which his strong figure offered to the repudiation of debts, in the interest of the stable progress of business, his resistance to the assaults upon public and private property by mobs, his resistance to the destruction of the sound virtues lying at the basis of our society, as it had been developed by the slow

processes of time, were decried and condemned. Contrary
to every precedent no word of praise was given to the man
whom the party had named and elected to the Presidency
four years before, whom it had nearly elected in 1888, by whom
it had been led in 1884 to its first victory since the Civil War.
He was cast aside in the most openly and deliberately in-
sulting way by the adoption of the platform which enunciated
principles wholly at variance with his known views; he was
also denied an expression suggesting his personal honesty
or good purposes, when his friends presented a resolution
in appreciation of his services as a public magistrate.

The crowds in the convention hall shouted for Altgeld and
Tillman. These two men who were famous as the most scur-
rilous of the President's foes were the favorites of the silverites
gathered in the great arena. Altgeld was on his own ground.
He had been renominated as the Democratic candidate for
governor of Illinois. He headed the state delegation. His
bold defiances amused a convention which was little more
than a crazy mob. It laughed at and applauded his attacks
upon gold as the instrument of tyranny, upon capitalists
as the authors of "moneyed terrorism," upon the English who
had governed the Republican convention in St. Louis and whose
pleasure consisted in "getting more blood and sweat out of
the American people." We had conquered them at arms and
would now deal with them as conscienceless money lenders.
The "hand of compromise" had never run up "the flag of
freedom." [1]

"Pitch-fork" Tillman's Cyclopean eye opened upon the convention; his notorious vulgarities, his extravagant vilifications
and blasphemies met with some protests which seemed but
to increase the vigor of his expression. In the Senate he had
been calling the President a "besotted tyrant," [2] Carlisle,
the "Judas from Kentucky." [3] Cleveland should be impeached.[4]
He rose again to the charge in the convention. The President,

[1] N. Y. Tribune, July 9, 1896.
[2] Cong. Record, 54th Cong. 1st. sess., p. 1076.
[3] Ibid.   [4] Ibid., p. 1079.

he said, had been trying to establish a "plutocratic despotism" on the ruins of the republic. He again suggested the impeachment of Cleveland for his "usurpations of authority," and offered a resolution to forward the end in view.[1]

Hill was seen in the most heroic rôle which he had yet played in public life. He was put forward to lead those who were defending the President and the policies of the administration. He accepted the task and delivered a cogent speech deprecating and protesting against the headlong surrender of the party to the Populists. He repeated his shibboleth—"I am a Democrat," but he was not, he added, a "revolutionist." The party must stand by its principles. He spoke "more in sorrow than in anger." His manner was propitiatory. He addressed the delegates as "friends." They should "keep in the good old paths of the party." Then they would win; if they should depart from the old ways they would be "lost."[2] Senator Vilas and ex-Governor William E. Russell, the young leader in whom so much hope reposed, and whose career was now near a deplored end, followed Hill. All were listened to impatiently. The silver men were not to be turned from their course, and Bryan, the "young Demosthenes from the West," found his opportunity to rise for speech. He had been seated with his contesting delegation from Nebraska. His views about silver had been stated and re-stated with oratorical power in Congress. He had spoken fervently on various occasions from platforms in Eastern cities, and had been heard by limited groups of people in the West and South with admiration and even marvel for the fluency of his utterance. He had been carrying on an untiring correspondence with silver leaders in the states, the heads of silver delegations in the convention and the delegates themselves for weeks and months, and his leadership, if it had yet been unacknowledged, was to have recognition now.[3] He eagerly stepped to the platform to close the debate. It was the hour for the elation which

[1] N. Y. Tribune, July 9 and 10, 1896.
[2] Ibid., July 10, 1896.
[3] Barnes, J. G. Carlisle, pp. 458–9.

comes from tropes and metaphors, from words spoken with assurance without regard to reason.

Bryan in appearance was not much more than a youth. Tall, lean, with a smoothly shaven face, marked by a wide mouth, he stood before the auditory to do more successfully, through his finer command of language and by his dramatic talents, that which Altgeld and Tillman had essayed to achieve.[1] The thousands who crowded the hall sensed the swell of an emotion which would lift them from their seats. Because of the uproar with which the sight of the "Boy Orator of the Platte" was welcomed he could, for a time, utter scarce a word. When the cheering, clapping, stamping and waving of all objects capable of being brandished had subsided he went with the confidence of some moral crusader into the silver subject, the subject of the man who was poor, who had been, and was being, robbed by the "money power." Not a new thought had been or could be presented by the speaker whose spirit was exalted for the duty which, according to his understanding, lay before him. He was one of the people—he spoke for those who were carrying the burdens. "We beg no longer," he said, "we petition no more, we defy them." In his usual way he turned to the Bible; he drew upon Roman history; he introduced the names of Jefferson and Jackson. The platform and all its demands were defended as if they were the expression of his own creed, as they seem to have been, without need of subtraction or addition. More, it was alleged, by the Cleveland Democrats, should have been made of the tariff question—that, indeed, was but casually referred to. But there was a reason, the young orator said—if protection had slain its thousands, the gold standard had slain its tens of thousands. In the currency was the issue for McKinley, for the Republicans. Any man who would "surrender the right of self government" and "place legislative control in the hands of foreign potentates and powers" could not hope to be elected to the Presidency of the United States. Bryan had been told that the great cities were in favor of the gold standard. "Burn

[1] N. Y. Sun, July 11, 1896.

down your cities," he cried, "and leave our farms, and your cities will grow up again. But destroy our farms and the grass will grow in every city of the Union." The Democratic party was not afraid to declare that the nation could "legislate for its people upon every question without waiting for the consent of any other nation on earth." It was the "issue of 1776 over again." When we were but 3,000,000 we declared our independence; could it be, now since we had grown to 70,000,000, that we had less courage? We should stand up to the gold standard men and say—"you shall not press down upon the brow of labor this crown of thorns. You shall not crucify mankind upon a cross of gold."

"Tremendous cheering" followed each peroration and at the end, when the figure, likening the treatment of the poor of the land to the crucifixion of Christ, was completed, a figure which Bryan had used repeatedly before in oratorical flights,[1] there was a furore which, after all the noise-making contrivances of a convention had done their duty, included a parade of the excited silverites, with their guidons in hand, up and down the aisles. The crowds in the galleries, as well as the delegates, barring the stolidest of the gold men, were electrified by the actor-like grace, the facile phrase and the melodious voice of the young champion of silver money. The convention, when quiet had been restored, passed at once to a roll call of the states. Hill's minority report from the Committee on Resolutions was voted down and the platform, with the free silver plank and its other Populistic declarations, was adopted by a majority of 628 to 301. New York, Pennsylvania, New Jersey, Wisconsin, South Dakota, all the delegates in New England except 3 in Massachusetts and 2 in Maine, all but 4 in Maryland, all but 1 in Delaware, all but 6 in Minnesota, stood firm— nearly all the rest deserted the beaten ways of Democracy and embraced Populism. Only 357 votes could be mustered

---

[1] N. Y. Times, July 15, 1896; N. Y. Nation, July 16, 1896. "Launched as an impromptu fomentation but really an old speech warmed over."— E. F. Uhl in Lamont Papers, dated August 17, 1896, quoted in Barnes, J. G. Carlisle, p. 474.

for the resolution commending Mr. Cleveland's administration
—564 delegates shouted "No."

The next day, the 10th, the convention would choose its
candidates. The feeling was now tense. Those who had been
the leaders of the party in the past had been shown no honor.
Their places had been usurped by inferior Western and Southern
men, most of them upstarts obsessed with the idea that they
were designated by the grace of a sovereign people to overthrow
existing social and political institutions. Wilson S. Bissell,
resenting the indignities which were being prepared for his
friend Cleveland, left his seat in the convention after the first
day and returned to Buffalo.[1] The adoption of the platform
was the signal for others to depart. Many of the gold standard
men were convinced that it would be inappropriate, as well
as futile, for them to assist in the selection of candidates,
if the party were to go before the country with such a statement
of principles as the convention had just approved. Others
were of a different opinion and, as a matter of record, would vote
for Robert E. Pattison, the governor of Pennsylvania, for whom
that state's delegates were instructed, or William E. Russell
of Massachusetts. "Silver Dick" Bland was still in a leading
position, with Teller as a possibility in the background. Senator
Dubois of Idaho and other "bolters" from the Republican
convention were early on the ground. Populists pleaded
Teller's cause [2] and, though the reception of his name had been
cold, since the strength of the silverites of Democratic ante-
cedents was so overwhelming as to make alliances unnecessary,
there were not a few who recommended a union of all the free
silver interests, without regard to party, under his leadership.

Altgeld and the Illinois delegation were supporting Bland.
Other states had for some weeks given assurance of being in
the following of the unyielding champion of the silver dollar
from Missouri. Vice-President Stevenson, who was seen to be
wanting in sympathy for the President, was regarded as a
candidate, though few stopped to consider his claims. Blackburn of Kentucky, John R. McLean of Ohio, Horace Boies

[1] N. Y. Tribune, July 10, 1896.   [2] Ibid., July 8, 1896.

of Iowa, for whom there was a frantic demonstration;[1] Tillman of South Carolina and others were the subjects of complimentary allusion, principally within the delegations of their respective states. Bryan's figure, especially now since his oratory had cast its spell upon the convention, loomed over the scene.

The first ballot revealed 233 votes for Bland, 105 for Bryan, 95 for Pattison, 86 for Boies and 83 for Blackburn, with smaller totals for 9 or 10 other men. As the states were called chairmen announced that their entire delegations would refrain from voting. Ex-Governor Roswell P. Flower of New York said that, in view of the platform and the acts and proceedings of the convention, the 72 votes of that state would not be cast for any candidate. Connecticut, New Jersey and some other states made similar declarations. It appeared that many of the delegates from Massachusetts had gone home. Most of those who remained declined to vote, as did gold standard men in several other delegations amid shouts of "Put them out," "You don't belong to this convention," an obvious truth, and other incivilities and impertinences not designed to heal the widening breach between the factions. The second and third ballots indicated a gain of 48 for Bland and 92 for Bryan, who now had 197 delegates in his following. On the third ballot Colorado, which had been voting for Teller, turned to Bryan whose strength was now nearly equal to that of Bland. The fourth ballot was taken amid perceptibly increasing commotion, which betokened a stampede. Alabama, Kansas and Idaho deserted Bland who fell into second place. Illinois and other states were on the point of taking similar action and it was plain that the next, or fifth, ballot would be the last. Illinois, Tennessee, Ohio—nearly all were ready, amid the turbulence and confusion which was vastly increased by the unruly thousands of spectators, to swell the chorus for the "Boy Orator." The names of "favorite sons" were withdrawn and Bryan in a little while was declared to be the nominee of the Democratic party for President by a two-thirds majority vote of the delegates. A member of the Nebraska delegation moved that the

[1] Haynes, Third Party Movements, p. 362.

nomination be made unanimous. There were loud cries of
"No" from the New York, Pennsylvania and other Eastern
delegations who were still in the hall and who laughed deri-
sively when the chairman audaciously announced—"The
nomination is made unanimous." [1]

The next day, with a view to conceding something to the
East,[2] the convention conferred the honor of running as a
candidate for Vice-President on Arthur Sewall of Maine
who had recently declared his faith in free silver,[3] for which
reason he had been removed from the Democratic National
Committee. This martyrdom was gratefully remembered.
He had striven "for liberty," said the man who presented
his name to the convention, "when God himself was dumb."
A number of contestants for the honor appeared, among
them George Fred Williams of Massachusetts, who was now
a silverite, Joseph C. Sibley of Pennsylvania and John R.
McLean of Ohio. Several attempts were made to stampede
the delegates for Bland, but, after he, McLean and others
withdrew, Sewall, on the fifth ballot, was chosen for the
second place on the ticket. He and members of his family
were well known as builders of wooden ships in Bath, where
they had resided for several generations. The sails of their
schooners and square-rigged three and four masters were
bellied by the winds in the seven seas, a business in which
they had accumulated a fortune. Mr. Sewall was a strange
companion at arms for the young people's man who had just
been belted and horsed to go forth to goad the flanks of wealth.

The Populists and free coinage men who had crowded the
tried, intelligent and substantial elements of an old party
out of it, and had captured it for adventure in new paths
expressed joy in their great victory. More than a few of them,
however, upon reflection, when they were at leisure to consider
what had been done, were brought to wonder whether their

---

[1] N. Y. Tribune, July 11, 1896.

[2] Cf. Haynes, Third Party Movements, p. 290.

[3] Sewall so lately as in January, 1896, had been an enthusiastic sup-
porter of President Cleveland who, he said, should be renominated for
a third term.—N. Y. Tribune, Jan. 15, 1896.

wisdom had been as great as the heat of their enthusiasm.[1]
They might well indulge such reflections. The New York,
Pennsylvania, New Jersey and other Eastern delegations
went home in silence, when not in open complaint. Leaders
whose names had been written high on the banners of the party
had been read out of it. They could not endorse the platform
or vote for the candidates. Many would openly bolt the ticket
and use all their influences to bring about its defeat. The
administration, of which not a few of them were a part, had
been accused of a great corruption when, as a result of stupendous effort, it had saved the nation's credit. The President
was charged with gross usurpation, though he had, by the only
feasible method, quelled riots and put down mobs which
were taking life, destroying property and terrorizing the nation.
Intelligence was called stupidity, courage an arrogant use of
power, honesty the robbery of the poor, patriotism love of
self and a few men in Wall Street by a risen commune which
was now, as it appeared, the Democratic party.

The country spoke and it used words the meaning of which
was in no kind of doubt. The New York Evening Post said
that "no such collection of inflammatory and reckless men
ever put themselves on exhibition in a national convention."
It denounced the "Populistic, Anarchistic" platform. Nearly
all those who gave character to the party would repudiate
the ticket, as well as the platform, "as they would the pest." [2]
To the New York Tribune the convention was "an assembly
of lunatics." The platform was an "anarchist manifesto."
Never before had a great political party made itself "the avowed
champion of the right of pillage, riot and train wrecking." [3]
The New York Times described the platform as "incendiary";
it was framed by "repudiators." An "open fight" was now
possible. The right would win.[4] The New York Herald
declared the issue to be "patriotism against silverism, the
country against Populism." A shot "as dangerous and treason-

[1] Cf. W. F. Vilas in N. Y. Tribune, July 11, 1896.
[2] N. Y. Nation, July 16, 1896.
[3] N. Y. Tribune, July 9, 10 and 11, 1896.
[4] N. Y. Times, July 10 and 11, 1896.

able as that fired on Sumter in '61" reverberated over the land.
It was every one's duty to vote for McKinley as a "protest
against the iniquity consummated at Chicago," said the New
York Sun. A "wild horde" was preparing to attack and destroy
American institutions.[2] The New York World declared that
"lunacy" had dictated the platform, "hysteria" had evolved
the candidate. The party was doomed to defeat. The only
doubt remaining was as to the size of McKinley's popular
and electoral majorities.[3]

The newspapers in Philadelphia, Boston, Baltimore and in the
smaller Eastern cities, as well as the country press, were not
far behind those in New York—they were practically a unit
in condemning the platform and in expressing their indisposition
to support the ticket, if not their unalterable determination
to aid in bringing about its defeat. Leading Democratic
newspapers in the Mississippi valley and in the South stood
firm in protest against such a betrayal of what the Louisville
Courier-Journal described as "the very life principles of Democracy." [4] Bankers and business men generally were shocked,
though their expectations in reference to the convention
had not been high. They had supported Cleveland; they
would not vote for Bryan. The leaders of the Cleveland Democrats, as distinguished from the Hill-Tammany element in
New York state, and the old Mugwump faction everywhere,
came forth at once in speech, statement and newspaper interview. Their minds were made up. Over all the country
men of light and leading, who had been Democrats by birth
as well as by conviction, declared that they would not vote
for Bryan. Many who set a high price on organization and
would not surrender local advantage to elements which were
eager to press in and steal the party machinery, as it had been
seized in the West and South, were slow to sever their relations
with the party. But even in Tammany there were leaders
who thought that the organization should bolt. Croker's

[1] N. Y. Herald, July 10 and 11, 1896.
[2] N. Y. Sun, July 11, 1896.   [3] N. Y. World, July 11, 1896.
[4] N. Y. Tribune, July 11, 13, 14 and 15, 1896; N. Y. World, July 15,
1896; Haynes, Third Party Movements, p. 293.

mayor of New York, Hugh J. Grant; the comptroller of the city, Ashbel P. Fitch; Tammany's principal orator, Bourke Cockran, and many others said that they would never vote for free silver. William C. Whitney would support the ticket "under no possible conditions or circumstances."

As for the President he said that he, and the members of his cabinet, had "a right to be quiet." Indeed he felt that he had been "invited to that course." The men who controlled the convention had "displayed their hatred" of him and "wholly repudiated" him. Having been "pushed so much aside" he had "an idea, quite fixed and definite, that, for the present at least, we should none of us say anything." Secretary Herbert had declared at once that he would not support the ticket, so had Mr. Eckels, the Comptroller of the Currency. The President was sorry that they had broken silence.[1]

On July 22nd the Populists would hold their convention in St. Louis. Some of them were in favor of endorsing Bryan and making him their candidate since he so fully represented their principles, while another faction, the "Middle of the Road" element, which advocated no alliances with any one of the old parties, preferred separate nominations. At any rate no one of them could or would vote for the millionaire shipbuilder whom the silverites had put on the ticket as Bryan's "running mate." The two groups of cranks fell upon one another in the angriest way.

It soon appeared that Bryan's friends were in control of the convention which was, in effect, not more than a great mass meeting. For him there was trust and sympathy. They would fuse with the Democrats with reference to the Presidency, but, to rid themselves of Sewall, they would follow the extraordinary plan of naming the candidate for Vice-President first. The chairman of the Democratic National Committee was Senator Jones of Arkansas. He urged Bryan to decline the nomination of the Populists unless they would accept the whole ticket. Bryan said that his name must be withdrawn, if they would not take Sewall also. No attention was paid to this

[1] Cleveland to Lamont, July 15, 1896, in Cleveland Papers.

injunction. For Vice-President the convention, amid much disrespectful allusion to bankers, railway officers, millionaires and "worshippers of the golden calf," nominated Thomas E. Watson of Georgia, a Populist, who had presented his peculiar views to Congress, while for a short time, three or four years ago, he had been in the House of Representatives. Bryan was then named with a rush as the People's party candidate for President. His peremptory inhibition having not been respected by the convention he, in turn, gave his earlier words on the subject but little notice. He preferred silence, though what he did say contained an implication that he would run on the ticket of one party with Sewall and on the ticket of the other with Watson. He would do nothing to "endanger the success of bimetallism." Simultaneously another party, meeting in St. Louis, not too respectfully described as a "side show," the Silver Party, less squeamish in taste as to shipbuilders, while nominating Bryan, endorsed Sewall.

To the unusual and startling declarations set forth in the Democratic platform for Bryan's exposition and defence during the campaign the Populists added others. They advocated government ownership and management of railroads and telegraphs, the initiative and referendum, two words borrowed from Switzerland, new fangled instruments of what was called "direct legislation," and the election of United States senators by popular vote.

The Sound Money Democrats in Chicago, meantime, were hearing from leaders in other states. It was hoped to bring Hill into the movement for separate and protesting action. But his canniness, like Gorman's,[1] prevented him from following to a logical conclusion the sympathies which he had expressed at Chicago. He had spoken for sound money and stated his objections to changes in party policy which he called revolutionist, but he would stop there. He now sought quiet and practised silence. Democrats from a number of states who were ready, as Senator Palmer expressed it, "to fight Anarchy and Populism" held a conference at a hotel in Chicago on July

[1] N. Y. Times, July 15, 1896.

23rd. General Bragg and Senator Vilas came from Wisconsin, James O. Broadhead from Missouri, W. D. Bynum from Indiana, James H. Eckels, the Comptroller of the Currency, from Washington. Men who could not attend telegraphed, pledging their support if a third ticket would "help defeat Bryan." It was resolved to organize meetings in the states and, after progress was achieved in various communities, to issue a call for a national convention which would put an Honest Money Democratic ticket in the field.[1] Some thought that Mr. Cleveland could be persuaded to accept the nomination with Mr. Carlisle as the candidate for Vice-President.[2]

The Republicans were making it increasingly difficult to bring about such a union as there should have been between sound money men in both parties, which, Mr. Whitney said, was a mistake.[3] As many as 254 delegates in the convention at Chicago had refrained from voting for candidates.[4] It was assumed that they and their followings at home would support McKinley. Instead of a welcome Democrats were denounced *en masse* by such an organ of the party as the New York Tribune, and by the leading Republican politicians. All together, indiscriminately, were treated as ignoramuses, lunatics and Anarchists. It was persistently stated that the issue was the tariff and not sound money. The free trade Democratic party it was alleged and re-alleged had brought upon the country the ills from which it suffered; a protective tariff law would make everything right again. Such words spoken with heat and in a derisive tone could draw no Democrat to McKinley and strongly encouraged the making of separate nominations.[5]

It is true that McKinley took courage in some measure at sight of what had been done at Chicago and Hanna, and the other long-headed men in charge of his campaign, loosened the candidate's tongue. He lived in a brick house with what the newspaper correspondents, who took up their abode for

---

[1] N. Y. Tribune and N. Y. Times, July 24 and 25, 1896.
[2] N. Y. Tribune, July 25, 1896.   [3] Ibid., July 24, 1896.
[4] There were 162 who did not vote on the fifth and last ballot for President; 252 who did not vote for Vice-President.
[5] N. Y. Tribune, July 24, 1896.

the summer in Canton, called a "piazza" and a "lawn." The scroll saw had been used, after the manner of the age, to decorate the building. Visitors found McKinley in his "library" on a swivel chair in front of a "roll top" desk. His debts had been paid by his friends. He was a poor man and but little provided with the means to support a campaign conducted even on such simple lines. A small company of friends in Pittsburgh in February had sent him $6,000 to meet personal demands which should be made upon him, Philander C. Knox subscribing one half of the amount,[1] and, beginning in August, when John Hay returned from Europe, McKinley received $1,000 a month from that source.[2]

Delegations were constantly arriving on the railway trains at Canton to pay their respects to the candidate and to hear him expound party issues. These visits in the interest of a happy result were the subject of pre-arrangement. The speeches made by the leaders of the pilgrims as well as by the candidate were not unconsidered, for they were to be carried by telegraph to all parts of the country.[3] It was a new kind of a campaign for the Presidency. Thousands of hands were shaken. Tens of thousands of ears heard McKinley's voice and were made acquainted with an ingratiating personality as he told them, while they stood on the "lawn," of the healing power of Republican tariffs.[4]

Every Republican President before him since the Civil War had been a general—Grant, Hayes, Garfield, Arthur and Harrison. McKinley had been in the Union army and he had left it as a major. Men gave him his title. The war was moving farther and farther into the distance and less and less was being thought or said about it and the angry issues which it had evoked. Thirty years had thinned the ranks of the Grand Army of the Republic. The last of the Federal election laws for the regulation of affairs

---

[1] Memorandum dated Feb. 26, 1896, in McKinley Papers.
[2] Letter dated Aug. 3, 1896, in ibid.
[3] Cf. H. Croly, M. A. Hanna, pp. 215–6; Rhodes, The McKinley and Roosevelt Administrations, p. 25. The drafts of many of these speeches are to be found in the McKinley Papers.
[4] Cf. Haynes, Third Party Movements, pp. 296–7.

in the South had been swept from the statute books and in 1896, for the first time in a national Republican platform, nothing was said of the villainy of Democrats on the subject of the negro.[1] The intimidation of the blacks, the suppression of their votes and the stealing of states, which on a fair polling of the population would be unquestionably Republican, had been under bitter discussion for three decades and nothing had come of it. Now there was an issue of immediate general concern, and it must be faced. The convention in Chicago had stated it, Bryan's active campaign on the stump would keep it before the country and no evasions would avail.

McKinley's speech at Canton on June 30th, in response to the committee which had notified him of his nomination, was a mere rigmarole of platitudes about the flag, the tariff and prosperity. The most that he said of money was that, "whether of paper, silver or gold," it should be "as good as the best in the world."[2] He had spoken of a "full dollar" for a "full day's work."[3] He had said that a dollar must be "good for a dollar, not only at home, but in every mart and market place of the world."[4] He was, all the while, telling his visitors about the tariff; with a tariff the government would have revenues; with revenues the currency would be safe. In the sight of Hanna, and the other Republican leaders, too, the tariff was the only issue.[5] In late July, after Bryan's nomination, Hanna was willing to say that the two issues, the tariff and the currency, should go hand in hand.[6] McKinley, at the same time, was advancing;[7] he screwed his courage to the sticking point and pronounced the word "gold."[8] On July 30th a delegation of admirers from Pennsylvania crowded his lawn which by now was quite bare of grass, and, standing upon a chair, he told them in plainer words than he had yet used

---

[1] Cf. N. Y. Nation, May 21, 1896.

[2] N. Y. Tribune, June 30, 1896.

[3] N. Y. Nation, June 25, 1890. [4] Ibid., July 2, 1806. [5] Ibid.

[6] N. Y. Tribune, July 29, 1896; cf. N. Y. Nation, July 9, 1896; Rhodes, The McKinley and Roosevelt Administrations, p. 19.

[7] The man who J. Pierpont Morgan said had "a backbone of jelly."— T. B. Mott, Myron T. Herrick, p. 69.

[8] N. Y. Nation, Aug. 6, 1896.

of the disasters which could flow from a depreciated currency. The measure of value "must be as true as the bushel which measures the grain of the farmer," he said, "and as honest as the hours of labor which the man who toils is required to give." The currency of the country to-day, he continued, is "as good— all of it is as good as gold, and it is the unfaltering determination of the Republican party to so keep and maintain it forever"; [1] and the next day, July 31st, addressing a crowd made up of Grand Army men and tin plate workers, he spoke in the same strain with still more emphasis. The old soldiers, McKinley said, wanted every dollar of the debt incurred in the war by the United States paid in gold. "Up to this hour" it had been paid in gold or its equivalent, the best money known to the commercial world" and "every dollar of that debt yet to be paid, my comrades," he continued, "will be paid in the same unquestioned coin." The old soldiers, the Republican candidate declared, as he rose to his subject, would this year, as before, "stand by the financial honor of the government," and would "no more permit our nation's integrity to be questioned than they would permit that flag [he pointed to the stars and stripes] to be assailed." [2]

These utterances evoked expressions of satisfaction. There was cheering which was described as "tremendous" on the lawn at Canton and the telegraph wires bore the words to the newspapers, by which they were carried to the people. It was clear enough that McKinley was the sound money candidate; the gold standard men in both parties in all sections of the country must, it seemed, vote for him. He, and he alone, stood between them and the election of a 16 to 1 Populist, campaigning on a platform of "free silver and free riots."

The more that was seen and heard of Bryan the more menacing was he accounted to be. Men of informed and responsible minds, grounded in the theory and practice of government and the history of our institutions, whatever their party, shuddered at the very possibility of his success in his appeal for votes. Much abuse of him in these weeks was unwarranted and

[1] N. Y. Tribune, July 31, 1896. [2] Ibid., Aug. 1, 1896.

needless, though it was an unavoidable part of the canvass. A few truths were lost to sight. He was a man who, in his 36 years in our Western states, had led a clean and respectable life. He was honest in that he believed in his preachment—he believed in it with the faith of some evangelist. Nature had given him oratorical powers, and human sympathy and fearlessness in the face of opposing forces, no matter what their strength. Accuracy in historical statement will acquit him of charges of unworthy ambitions. He was truly concerned about the condition of the "common people," as he called them, from whom, it was plain, that he was not far removed, and, with such light as was given him, he would improve their situation. That rich men were dangerous to a well ordered society, that Wall Street, a haunt of rich men, was an iniquity, that England as a heartless money-lender was an enemy of mankind was arrant tosh which had been in the air for many years. Not a few of the elder politicians were more or less ashamed of themselves when they pronounced such judgments. It was a part of the demagogism which they thought was necessary if they were to get and hold elective office at the hands of the people settled in many parts of the United States. But Bryan's belief in such ideas would seem to have been no pretence. He was a rare bigot. A man who, as a final gesture in life, could publicly defend the position of a group of rustics who had enacted a law interdicting the teaching of the theory of evolution in the schools and were prosecuting an instructor for denying, in violation of this law, in the presence of youth put under his charge, that the earth had been swung into space and finished for human habitation in six days and that the Creator had then set two beings, male and female, Adam and Eve, upon it to people it, seems to have had a simplicity of mind excelling that of any one who ever gained eminence in our public life.[1] The supposition that he failed to learn more than he knew in his childhood, either by contact with other men, or by reading, alone saves him from assignment to a place as a mountebank. Phrases captivated him and he was so intoxicated with the

[1] Cf. Memoirs of Bryan, pp. 480–4, 529–56.

sound of them and his sense of power over those to whom he spoke that he made no drafts on his reason, which, remained, it must be believed, in an undeveloped state.

But it is not enough to say that he was uninstructed—so were most of those who followed him for so many years. He was persuasive; he was adroit in controversy; he won the confidence of some kinds of men. Undeniably he had powers of leadership. He was a lawyer but made no progress in the practise of the law, the laborious details of which irked so shallow a character. When the political platform failed him, and he held no office from the time that he left Congress in 1895, after two terms in the House of Representatives, until 1913, when he was appointed Secretary of State, he did not return to the bar. He wrote for a journal in Omaha, he founded and edited a weekly paper for the promulgation of his views and offered himself as a lecturer on various topics in which rôle he, for years, would visit hamlets as well as great cities in all parts of the republic. By these means a considerable fortune was amassed and his name as a "great commoner" was kept in the popular mind. In the correctness of his conduct on all occasions and the infallibility of his advice on subjects, political, economical, social, religious and historical, there is no reason to think that he had the least personal doubt, and it was this elation of the ego in the man, coupled with his power to fire the hearts of the poor, who felt that as a class they were suffering a grievance, which may explain his retention until his death of a prominent position in the nation.

While McKinley was resolved to remain on his own front porch Bryan would take the stump and make a tour of the states. First he was to be formally notified of his nomination and a theatrical advance would be made upon New York for this ceremony. Mr. Sewall, the candidate for Vice-President, would be present. He, too, was to be told of his nomination by the committee to whom this duty was assigned by the Chicago convention. Bryan left his home at Lincoln on August 7th. To the crowd which assembled to see him start away he stated, amid "great applause and cheering," that he was going to New York to present his cause in the heart of what now seemed to be the "enemy's country," but which he hoped "to occupy" before the campaign was over. He spoke from the railway train as he passed through Nebraska, Iowa and Illinois. In Chicago, on August 8th, thousands of people filled the streets to give him a welcome. The tumult was deafening. He could not make himself heard for the din as he stood on a hotel veranda. With all the newspapers of the city against him (the mention of them was hissed) he was reminded, he said, as he looked at the mob of beings massed before him, of the words of one of his friends—"Nobody is on our side except the people."

While much of the noisy acclamation which attended the sight of his person and the hearing of his voice was ascribed, properly enough, to curiosity the effect was disquieting to business men everywhere. Bryan said that he represented the "toiling masses." If he were elected he would be their "hired man." [1] Just as the farmer had a "hired man" to milk a cow or harvest a crop he would do the people's will in case they should entrust him with the great office for which he was a candidate, though it was rather plain that he would serve them in his own way, on the theory that his will was theirs. [2] If McKinley were the "advance agent of prosperity" Bryan meant panic and crash. Holders of stocks sold them; prices fell.

After rest in Chicago on Sunday and attendance at service in a Presbyterian church the journey to New York was resumed. The meeting would be held in Madison Square Garden on the night of August 12th. Tammany, in spite of the defection of some of its leaders, had braved the storm which the nomination of such a man had awakened in the East and proclaimed itself "regular." It would take whatever came under the party name, so that its hold on the treasury of New York city should not be shaken in the interest of rivals who, if they could, would gain access to such rich stores. Here sponsorship, and a background for the candidate's reception, would be found.

Bryan, full of the grandeur of his mission, was coming east,

[1] In a speech delivered in Iowa.—N. Y. Herald, Aug. 9, 1896.
[2] Cf. N. Y. Nation, Aug. 13, 1896.

as he declared quite airily, "to make war on the corporations" and help the people "to save themselves from the domination of European bondage." [1] It was a repetition of the "campaign of 1776"—Americans could again prove whether they were "patriots or Tories." [2] When the new George Washington, or Thomas Jefferson, as he preferred to envisage himself, should have had his day in New York he would invade New England. Not a newspaper, bar one, which, however, scarcely deserved the name of newspaper, that did not fill the air with ridicule and detraction as the prophet of silver money and the advocate of rule by the populace approached the scene. He was clapper-clawed wherever east of the Allegheny Mountains his name was spoken. The New York Tribune greeted him with lines adapted from Oliver Wendell Holmes—

> "The comet, he is on his way,
> And spouting like a whale,
> Ten million cubic miles of head
> Ten billion leagues of tail." [3]

A mob waited to receive him at Jersey City for the ferry ride over the river to New York and followed him through the streets to the home of William P. St. John, a financier, who had seen a light and had resigned the presidency of his bank to become the treasurer of the Democratic National Committee. The next day, August 12th, the candidate was in seclusion nursing his bruised hand and taking remedies for laryngitis, so that in the evening he could deliver the address that would make Wall Street quake.

Such heat as fell upon New York at this time is seldom experienced. The crowds which came to greet the "Boy Orator" and to ratify the ticket underwent an unusual test of faith. The inhabitants of the city were being prostrated by the score; many died in the sultry atmosphere the oppression of which did not abate for eight days. [4] The great hall was filled by a sweat-

---

[1] N. Y. Times, Aug. 10, 1890.   [2] Ibid., Aug. 11, 1896.

[3] Issue of Aug. 14, 1896; cf. one of Holmes's earlier poems entitled "The Comet."

[4] The recorded toll on the day of Bryan's arrival in New York was more than 230 prostrations and 89 deaths. There were scores more in

ing mass, determined either to honor the people's friend or
enjoy a raree show, as the case may have been. The orator was
not at his best. The task of appearing in a great Eastern city
where, as he knew, he was viewed with complete unfriendliness,
if not contempt, caused him to try to draw upon resources which
he did not possess. He would gravely discuss the issues,
particularly free coinage, which his candidacy presented, and
establish his reputation as a social economist. Lest he be
carried away by his rhetoric he had carefully prepared his
speech [1] which it took him nearly two hours to read. The crowd,
which, for the most part, was coatless, stewing in the torrid air,
began to depart before he had fairly commenced his tedious
defence of himself and the Chicago platform. Ere he was done
the hall, it was said, was less than half full.[2] Sewall who had
come down from Maine and who followed Bryan could not be
heard for the feet of those who were tramping out, except by
a few seated near the platform.

That Bryan's speech had disappointed those who had come to
hear a flamboyant oration, that the meeting altogether had done
nothing to aid the silver cause in the East was plain. He was
"in over his head." For the serious work of economic exposition
he was declared to be incompetent. "Every paragraph in
his dull speech," said the New York Times, "was a nail in
his political coffin." Men thought of the visit to New York
of another Western man—it was in 1860.[3] There was a difference. Lincoln had "a righteous and patriotic," the other
"a mean and dishonest cause." The speech, the Times continued, was "the flattest fizzle ever made by a candidate for
the Presidency." [4]

Bryan had exhibited himself, said the New York Tribune, in
"all his mental nakedness." From opening to end the speech

Brooklyn. Horses died in the streets and lay for hours where they fell.
On the following day there were 171 deaths resulting from the heat in
the "metropolitan district."—N. Y. Tribune and Times, Aug. 12, and
13, 1896.
[1] N. Y. Times, Aug. 14, 1896. [2] N. Y. Tribune, Aug. 13, 1896.
[3] It was a favorite comparison among Bryan's friends. They likened
him to Lincoln.—Cf. Barnes, J. G. Carlisle, pp. 461, 463.
[4] N. Y. Times, Aug. 13 and 14, 1896.

was a "maze of sophistries" without a new argument in it.[1] He had failed, said the New York Evening Post. The people had been led to expect "a sort of Buffalo Bill show," but they were "tricked." Instead of the "sallies and audacities" which they had come to hear they found a "Professor Dryasdust prosing through two mortal hours." He had made himself an "object of mirth," and "American humor," the Post continued, "casts an enormous vote."[2] "There never was a more disheartening, humiliating failure on the part of a mimetic politician," said the Sun. The reception of the speech was "a deserved rebuke to the Chicago revolutionists" who had tried "to steal the good name of the Democracy."[3]

Bryan's plans were changed. It was announced now that he would not visit New England, though he was entertained for some days by friends and sympathizers in and around New York —among them John Brisben Walker, a rich silverite from Colorado, the owner of the Cosmopolitan Magazine, a singularly enthusiastic admirer of the candidate, who found the reorganized Democracy to be "the party of humanity," the party which stood "for the principles of Jesus Christ."[4] The candidate was not far away from the city on August 17th when Bourke Cockran, in the same Madison Square Garden, made a rejoinder. The meeting was organized by the recently established Honest Money Democratic League of America. The hall was again filled and by an audience of intelligent people rather than a curious mob. Perry Belmont presided. The list of vice-presidents was long and it included well known and respected names. The crowd remained in their seats to enjoy the fluent discourse of the Tammany leader who had bolted the Democratic ticket and who was now presenting the reasons for his action. Being a meeting organized by men who, until this time, had been Democrats faithfully attached to the party, it was prophetic. Ranks were broken. Tammany, Hill who still kept silence, leaders who were holding the organization

[1] N. Y. Tribune, Aug. 13 and 14, 1896.
[2] N. Y. Nation, Aug. 20, 1896.   [3] N. Y. Sun, Aug. 13 and 14, 1896.
[4] N. Y. Times, Sep. 24, 1896.

together might vote for Bryan. Other Democrats would not do so and they were giving reasons why their friends should desert the standard of a man who was using the good name of the party while he trampled on its creed.

With two tails to his kite Bryan was in an awkward situation. Sewall would not retire. His corporate connections being extensive he continued to be an object of suspicion by many of Bryan's friends. His interest in the construction and sailing of ships led him to favor governmental subventions for that business; he was the president of an association formed to demand and obtain protection by discriminating tariffs on goods which were not imported in American bottoms.[1] This was an entirely obsolescent idea with reference to the upbuilding of a merchant marine and, were it adopted, must lead to international entanglements. It was out of harmony with the spirit of the Cleveland Democracy, was similarly difficult to place in the political system which was called Bryanism and, when attention was publicly directed to the fact, Sewall resigned the office, though a resolution endorsing the scheme had also been lobbied into the Republican platform.[2]

Bryan had said that he would not take the nomination of the People's party unless Sewall were accepted also. His words were not forgotten. His companion on that ticket, "Tom" Watson, was no quiet politician. He prodded Sewall, the rich shipbuilder; he ran his blade into the managers of the Populist, as well as the Democratic campaign.[3] The neglect shown him as a candidate nettled him and he moved about the country voicing his bitterness, to the manifest discomfiture of Bryan, who, not knowing what to do, said nothing. Lines from "The Beggar's Opera," under newspaper cartoons depicting him with Sewall and Watson, may have correctly represented the state of his mind—

> "How happy I could be with either
> Were t'other dear charmer away."

[1] N. Y. Times, Aug. 13, 1896; N. Y. Nation, Aug. 13, 1896.
[2] Cf. N. Y. Tribune, June 13, 1896.
[3] Cf. N. Y. Nation, Oct. 1, 1896.

As for them, unlike the two kings of Brentford, they very certainly would not smell at the same nosegay. On its face it was an impossible situation. It served, however, to confirm the assertion of Cleveland's friends that Bryan had no right to bear the banners of the party. If he were acceptable to the Populists, if they endorsed him and if they would vote for him he was not a fit man to receive the suffrages of true Democrats.

The arrangements for naming separate Honest Money Democratic candidates, instituted at Chicago soon after the adjournment of the convention which had nominated Bryan, progressed. The movement was favored by Democrats who themselves would vote for McKinley as the most direct and certain way to "save the country." There were many in the party who knew and cared nothing about the money question. They would vote the Republican ticket in no case. They would soon drift into the Bryan camp where the Democratic flag was flown, if measures were not taken to hold them back. For this reason it was reckoned advisable to go forward with the suggested plan, though the task of putting the old state Democratic organizations behind it was soon seen to be hopeless.[1] The Bryanites as "regulars" were in command. As the summer wore on the party organizations in the states reversed action which they had bravely enough taken in April and May, and put themselves on the side of the Chicago platform.[2] The party was being rapidly and thoroughly Bryanized, even in sound money strongholds in the East.

The movement of gold standard Democrats for separate nominations for the Presidency and Vice-Presidency had been advanced by a conference at Indianapolis on August 7th. A number of men of high purposes there and then assembled determined to issue a call for a convention of the "National Democratic Party," the name chosen for their organization, to be held in Indianapolis on September 2nd. Meetings in all parts of the country were largely attended. Ringing resolutions were adopted. Bryan was set forth as a Populist candidate, pure and

[1] N. Y. Nation, July 23, 1896; N. Y. Times, July 24, 1896.
[2] N. Y. Nation, Sep. 17, 1896.

simple. Delegates were elected to the convention and, on the
appointed day, a thousand estimable Democrats, moved to
action by the strongest personal convictions, made their ways to
Indianapolis. After an effort to draft Cleveland, a suggestion
which he peremptorily declined,[1] though he at one time seems
to have thought that circumstances might make it necessary for
him to lead the ticket,[2] they nominated General John M.
Palmer of Illinois for President and General Simon Bolivar
Buckner of Kentucky for Vice-President. Palmer had been a
Union, Buckner a Confederate soldier. Palmer had been
governor of Illinois and was now a United States senator from
that state. Buckner had been governor of Kentucky. He had
been in private life when the silver craze swept his state, whereupon he emerged from retirement and took the field for honest
money. A platform was adopted. In the clearest and most
direct terms it stated the case for sound money, for the withdrawal of the greenbacks, for an elastic currency system and the
payment in gold of public and private debts. Planks on the
tariff, on government economies, on civil service reform were
in accord with the views of the President and his friends.

The Republicans on their side, in most of the Western states in
which the money question divided the party, were passing
through similar adjustments. The conventions, early in the
year, had adopted resolutions which were entirely out of accord
with the St. Louis platform. The twenty or more delegates who
had followed Teller out of the hall were, at first, full of the idea
of nominating him on a new Republican ticket. Seeing the
futility of such action they had resolved to vote for Bryan and
issued a statement to this effect,[3] just as the Gold Democrats
would, in general, support McKinley. Teller early offered his
services to Bryan in the "cause of the people," [4] and made an
extensive tour of the country in the interest of the young
prophet of silverism from Nebraska. But the local party
machinery was worth fighting for and the "regulars," where

[1] McElroy, Grover Cleveland, vol. ii, p. 232; A. Nevins, Letters of
Cleveland, pp. 455–6; N. Y. Times, Sep. 4, 1896.
[2] Cf. Barnes, J. G. Carlisle, p. 470.   [3] N. Y. Times, July 21, 1896.
[4] Barnes, J. G. Carlisle, pp. 461–2, quoting Bryan MSS.

any could be found, were determined not to give it up without a struggle. Bitter factional contests ensued. In Colorado, Idaho, Montana, Nevada and Utah, where practically all Republicans were silverites, groups of men who would vote for McKinley formulated plans for approving the St. Louis platform with the exception of the money plank, and for taking the party's nominees for President and Vice-President, with emphasis on the promise in the platform of bimetallism after international agreement. Thus did Senator Wolcott in Colorado, and others, try to hold the madly excited Republican voters in the Rocky Mountain states so that the local party machinery should not be rendered entirely unavailable for future use.

The campaign raged with intensity from ocean to ocean. Hanna's powers of organization were put to a severe test. He surrounded himself with efficient aides. Offices were opened in New York and Chicago, while the Congressional committee at Washington played its usual part in the canvass. Money must be collected from the rich and there were reasons not before in their minds why they should contribute generously. The manufacturers were appealed to in tariff campaigns—now banking and all business had a stake in the result. New York was the principal field for the activity of the solicitors who, under Hanna's direction, assembled about $3,000,000 in and around that city and $500,000 more in Chicago and its vicinity. The total sum, three millions and a half, is said to have met the disbursements of the National Republican Committee, though other lesser funds were amassed for expenditure in the states. Hanna's friends in the Standard Oil Company made a contribution of $250,000 in the name of that corporation.[1] It was often far from plain how sufficient amounts could be obtained to print and circulate pamphlets, hire halls, organize meetings, move hundreds of speakers from place to place and bring the necessary powers to bear upon our great gigmanity. The whole country was converted into an elementary school.[2] It was

[1] H. Croly, M. A. Hanna, pp. 220–1; Rhodes, The McKinley and Roosevelt Administrations, pp. 23–4.
[2] Cf. H. Croly, M. A. Hanna, pp. 211–2.

assumed, not without reason, that the voters as a mass knew nothing about public finance. They were to be taught their a b c's. New tables of weights and measures were suggested—

> Six inches make one foot;
> Eight ounces make one pound;
> Sixteen quarts make one bushel;
> Fifty cents make one dollar.

The Bible, which was being so freely used by Bryan, was explored for a contribution to the sound money campaign. It was found in Proverbs, the eleventh chapter and the first verse, "A false balance is an abomination to the Lord, but a just weight is his delight." [1] Monetary catechisms, questions and answers in simple words, cartoons were distributed far and wide, as were the speeches of John Sherman, Secretary Carlisle, Carl Schurz and others for higher classes of readers. Posters showing McKinley's face above the line, in great letters,—"The Advance Agent of Prosperity" were glued to hoardings. Newspapers in cities were supplied with articles to be set up and printed, the country press, with plate matter ready for use without expense for typographical composition. Over 100,000,-000 copies of campaign documents, many of them in foreign tongues for foreign language speaking voters, were sent out from the Republican headquarters in Chicago near the seat of the silver heresy, 20,000,000 from New York.[2] Badges, buttons, streamers and other campaign devices were manufactured in great quantities to forward McKinley's cause, while Bryan went galumphing over the country trying to incite the populace, by flatteries and bribes in promise of comforts and new liberties, to give the government into his hands so that he might overthrow the institutions of the land. It was, some one said, a grand rally of all the malcontents. We at last had reached the climax of the long conflict with silver which for weary years had infested our politics and blocked so many movements in Congress for the public welfare.

[1] Cf. N. Y. Times, Aug. 8, 1896.
[2] H. Croly, M. A. Hanna, pp. 217–8; cf. Rhodes, The McKinley and Roosevelt Administrations, p. 24; H. H. Kohlsaat, From McKinley to Harding, pp. 51–2.

Mr. Cleveland had up to this time deplored declarations. Now he was ready for utterance. "The quicker and stronger you, or any other member of the cabinet, speaks the better I shall like it," he wrote to Lamont on September 6th. As for himself his inclination was, of course, "to join the chorus of denunciation," though he was "doubtful" as to the wisdom of such action. "My position," he observed, "cannot be misunderstood by any man, woman or child in the country. I am President of all the people, good, bad and indifferent, and as long as my opinions are known I ought, perhaps, to keep myself out of their squabbles. I must attempt to cooperate with Congress during another session," he continued after further reflection, and, "perhaps, ought not to unnecessarily further alienate that body and increase its hatred of me." But, he added, addressing Lamont, "if you say anything I do not care how plainly you present the inference that I am in accord with your views." [1]

Accordingly what must have been, in the ordinary case, an overwhelming blow to Bryan's cause, if it had not been fully anticipated, came soon. All the members of the cabinet, a Democratic administration through and through by every definition of Democracy until a new one had been found in the convention at Chicago, repudiated the party candidate and his platform. Their principles had found expression in the conference at Indianapolis which had nominated Palmer and Buckner. There had been, it is true, one seceder in Mr. Cleveland's household, Hoke Smith, the editor of a newspaper in the principal city of Georgia. He had been closely pressed by a rival, the editor of the Constitution, who was a Bryanite, and Mr. Smith, frankly telling the President that he could no longer follow the administration, or his own conscience either, for he had been doing useful and, as it seemed, sincere service for the gold standard in his state, returned silverized to Atlanta.[2] The

---

[1] Cleveland to Lamont, Sep. 6, 1896, in Cleveland papers.

[2] McElroy, Grover Cleveland, vol. ii, pp. 227–31; Hoke Smith to Cleveland, July 20, Aug. 5 and 6, 1896, in Cleveland Papers. Smith, perhaps without improving his position, said that in 1860 he would have gone with his state and he must stand by it now.

President put David R. Francis of Missouri in the place and the cabinet was again a unit in its defence of conservative Democratic principles. J. Sterling Morton, the Secretary of Agriculture, who had so long combated Bryan in his own state of Nebraska; the Secretary of the Navy, Hilary Herbert of Alabama, who had been prompt to express his dissent; the Postmaster General, William L. Wilson; Attorney General Harmon and others published their views actively. Mr. Wilson said that he would not "leap into the foul pit of repudiation, Socialism, Anarchy et cetera. Much as I love my party," he continued, "I put duty to my country higher." [1] Carlisle spoke effectively and with the authority of his high office. Eckels, the Comptroller of the Currency, and the Assistant Secretaries of the Treasury also took the stump.

The President himself still maintained a dignified restraint. He had been invited to attend the meeting to notify Palmer and Buckner of their nomination. He had declined but not without saying to Mr. Bynum, the chairman of the convention, that he should be delighted to "mingle," if he could, "with those who are determined that the voice of true Democracy shall not be smothered and who insist that its glorious standard shall still be borne aloft, as of old, by faithful hands." [2] More was to follow. The President found opportunity on October 22nd when the election was but a fortnight away to attend a celebration at Princeton on the 150th anniversary of the foundation of the college. His speech on this occasion rang with but little veiled allusions to the issues of the campaign. It was a call to all men, and to those in the colleges and universities in particular, to protect the republic from "the cankering rust of national dishonesty" and "the meanness of national bad faith." When attempts were made "to delude the people into the belief that their suffrages can change the operation of natural laws" it would be a duty of educated men, he said, to proclaim those laws "inexorable and far removed from political control." [3]

[1] W. C. P. Breckinridge Papers, quoted in Barnes, J. G. Carlisle, p. 466.

[2] Under date of Sep. 10, 1896, in Cleveland Papers.

[3] N. Y. Times, Oct. 23, 1896.

McKinley, meanwhile, was busy with his canvass on his lawn
at Canton. On one day it is said that no less than 30,000
persons came to his door. During the campaign he made 300
speeches to more than three quarters of a million pilgrims
drawn from at least 30 states of the Union.[1]

Every available effective speaker in the Republican party,
including ex-President Harrison, was put into the field,[2] and,
while references to the tariff were not omitted, especially on
McKinley's side,[3] the money question was uppermost in speech,
in the press and in the minds of the whole voting citizenry.
Bryan had made the issue and from it there was no escape.

It has been said that he believed in his creed. If he were a
demagogue, he was a "convinced demagogue." No education
in the schools restrained him, for from these he had gleaned little.
No sense of humor of which his character was devoid served to
make his rôle seem to him in any manner comic, or his following
the rag-tag and bobtail which it was. He kept away from the
East after his elaborate discourse on the nature of money in
New York City in August. His managers would have had him
remain in friendly territory. They knew that he could not
hope to make votes for his cause on the Atlantic seaboard. But
he would not rest under a taunt that he was afraid to discuss his
favorite theme in New York, and at the end of September he
came to the city again during a trip projected ostensibly to visit
Sewall in Maine in order to dispel the idea that he was not on
congenial relations with the shipbuilder, who was his companion
on the Chicago ticket. A few speeches in Boston and in other
places in New England brought him on the night of September
29th to Tammany Hall for an address which was more successful
than that one, still remembered, on a hot August night in
Madison Square Garden. He was no mean antagonist. He was

---

[1] Haynes, Third Party Movements, pp. 296–7; Rhodes, The McKinley
and Roosevelt Administrations, p. 25.

[2] It was in a speech in Carnegie Hall in New York on August 27th
that Mr. Harrison coined a phrase which travelled the length and breadth
of the country—"The first dirty errand that a dirty dollar does is to cheat
the workingman."

[3] Cf. Haynes, Third Party Movements, p. 299.

not without shrewd political sense. He could feather his oar.[1]
He knew where, in the West, to assail property and raise class
and sectional issues, and where to say less of that which had led
to his being regarded as a firebrand. With abundant black locks
that fell over his ears he in the East was shorn of his hair. He
left off wearing a long, shiny, black tail coat and appeared in a
new "cutaway," looking less like a frontier revivalist or an
Indian doctor, to both of whom he had been likened by ob-
servant reporters for the newspapers.

His speeches in the West were transcribed for general reading.
They were set before the people. The Creator, Bryan said from
time to time, had made man—He had not used "any superior
kind of mud when He made financiers." The "great common
people" could think for themselves—they did not need to be told
what they should do by "a particular class." He (Bryan)
would "rather have a foreign general in command of our army,
a foreign admiral in command of our navy, than to have the
Treasury of the United States run upon the European plan."
The "common people" were the only people who had "ever
supported a reform that had for its object the benefit of the
human race." A carpenter at work at his bench could better
determine what was an honest dollar than a man who represented a syndicate and bowed "to the dictation of Lombard
Street." If the government were not "greater than the bankers
of Wall Street" it was "no government at all." [2] There was
"not a law, human or divine," that the financiers would respect
"because they think," Bryan said, that they are "bigger than
the government and greater than the Almighty." [3] "Look at the
people who are at the head of the gold standard propaganda in
the United States," he would exclaim: 1800 years ago "the meek
and lowly Saviour threw the same kind of people out of His
temple because they had made His house a den of thieves." [4]

The issue everywhere was found in the 16 to 1 cure-all. In the
West the proposal was linked with much statement about giving
direct power to the masses as against banks, railroads, corpora-

[1] Cf. N. Y. Times, Aug. 28, 1896.   [2] N. Y. Times, Aug. 29, 1896.
[3] Ibid., Sep. 5, 1896.   [4] Ibid., Sep. 18, 1896.

tions, syndicates, capitalists, Wall Street and England. Bryan's appeal was distinctly to the poor man who had gotten nowhere with his life, who was probably in debt, who was ready to lay the blame on the well-to-do classes and the government, controlled hitherto, he said, with possible interruptions in Jefferson's and Jackson's periods in the Presidency, by the rich.

It was easier, as it would be more effective, in a popular political campaign, to designate such a course of argument than to examine it and make answer. It seemed to deserve no patient consideration. It was not new in this country or to the world. It had been heard in one form or another from the lips of the Jacobins of the French Revolution; it had appeared in books, newspapers, party resolutions and speeches of Socialists, Communists, Anarchists and other radical bodies. It was convenient to associate Bryan's proposals with discredited and disliked men who had been given a rather horrific mien in the sight of most Americans. His name was linked with Altgeld's, Tillman's, Peffer's, Debs's,[1] and other Toms of Bedlam.[2] He was "revolutionary and Anarchistic," and he was to be dismissed in short measure as such. He was seen, in the best case, in the East as an impracticable and very inexperienced young man. He was looked at and listened to at all because of his audaciousness in thinking himself fit for the Presidency. He was not really to be feared as a candidate for so great a post.

The effort to inject religious prejudices into the campaign failed.[3] A revival of the old Know Nothing movement against the Catholics had led to the formation so long since as in 1887 of the A.P.A., letters standing for the American Protective Association, interpreted also by the unfriendly as the American Protestant Association and the American Proscriptive Association. Its founder lived in Iowa, its "Supreme President," now at this time, in Michigan. Its activities were stealthy and

---

[1] Debs, of course, was enthusiastically for Bryan as "the people's standard bearer in the great uprising of the masses against the classes"; Bryan was "the hope of the republic, the central figure of the civilized world."—Bryan Papers quoted in Barnes, J. G. Carlisle, pp. 463–4.

[2] N. Y. Nation, Oct. 15, 1896.

[3] Described in H. J. Desmond, The A.P.A. Movement, pp. 75–92.

mysterious, but it was said to be powerful. It published papers and sent out lecturers. From "Songsters" men, women and children sang to popular tunes lines aimed at the Catholic Church.[1] The growth of the order had been forwarded by an increasing concern respecting immigration.[2] The "Irish conquest" of our cities was alarming. It was alleged in 1894 that they ruled New York, Brooklyn, Jersey City, Hoboken, Boston, Chicago, Buffalo, Albany, Troy, Pittsburgh, St. Paul, St. Louis, Kansas City, Omaha, New Orleans and San Francisco. They had made themselves a factor in the administration of the affairs of many other municipalities.[3] The Irish who had pressed into politics were Catholics and they were admittedly far from single-minded in their interest in the honest and efficient government of the older American elements among whom they had recently come to dwell. This fact made simple the stirring of anti-Popery prejudices and hatreds. The A.P.A. required its members to take oaths that they would vote for no Catholic for political office, that they would employ no Catholics in their homes as servants, and none in business, if Protestants could be found to do the same work.[4] When they were finished with the Papists they would advance upon the Jews.

In five years, therefore up to 1893, the order had gained only 70,000 members in the entire United States, principally in the Mississippi Valley.[5] In that year it grew rapidly. The Supreme

---

[1] To the tune of "John Brown's Body"—

"A throng of foreign paupers are swarming to our shore,
Who seek to serve the Romish church and papacy restore;
They must learn that in America his power can be no more.
Our country must be free," etc. etc.

And to the air, "Dare to be a Daniel"—

"Dare to be an A.P.A.,
Dare to stand alone,
Dare to work for Freedom's cause,
Dare to make it known," etc. etc.
—H. R. Howe, The Patriotic Campaign Songster.

[2] J. H. Jackson, The Am. Protective Ass'n. What it is. Its Platform.
[3] J. P. Bocock in Forum for April, 1894.
[4] Cf. F. R. Coudert in Forum for July, 1894.
[5] W. J. H. Traynor in North Am. Review for June, 1896; cf. ibid., July, 1894, and Aug., 1895.

President said in June, 1894, that it had 2,000,000 members and that it was "travelling at the rate of a cyclone"; it was enrolling 10,000 men weekly.[1] There were 80 "Councils" in New York City alone, some of which had more than 30 members each,[2] though the order was more powerful in the West where the Supreme President spoke of "Councils" with 3,000 members. The leaders had newspapers, they distributed inflammatory literature which, it was complained, they put in public places, even leaving it in the pews of churches, though the ministers, except of some of the fanatical sects, expressed their disapproval of the society and its proscriptive doctrines. Forged encyclicals of the Popes designed to arouse anti-Papist enmities were printed and given wide circulation. Stories most extravagantly false were whispered about—one that rifles and other military supplies were being stored in the basements of cathedrals, convents, churches and Catholic schools ready for use against the Protestants. The buildings were thrown open for inspection and search. Even the denials of Protestant clergymen who visited suspected places were not accepted by the half mad zealots who were repeating the tale.

In most cases the A.P.A. cooperated with the Republican party,[3] since the Irish, as a rule, were Democrats. In local communities, especially in the West, it influenced elections. The politicians feared to nominate Catholics for office; if they were nominated they were defeated on the religious issue. The society determined the fate of members of Congress who were unacceptable to it. The Supreme President said that there were 100 members of the 54th Congress who, before the election, had pledged themselves to the principles of the order, though it was complained that they afterward, when installed in place in Washington, renounced some of their enthusiasm for its aims.[4]

Catholics who were candidates for nomination as governors of states were objects of attack. In New York in 1894 a man,

---

[1] N. Y. Times, June 19, 1894.   [2] Ibid., June 28, 1894.
[3] H. J. Desmond, The A.P.A. Movement, pp. 30–1, 32–3, 65.
[4] W. J. H. Traynor in North Am. Review for June, 1896.

whose wife was a Catholic, was the subject of a threat else he
would have been nominated by Hill's Democratic organization
as lieutenant-governor. The Republicans in New York, it was
noted, refused to denounce the A.P.A., while Hill improved
his opportunity to make the most violent attack upon the order
and carried denunciation of the proscription of men for their
religious beliefs into the party platform.[1] Elsewhere, as in
Massachusetts, where the governor feared the loss of the
Irish vote, Republicans, like the Democrats, ostentatiously
defended "religious freedom." [2]

In 1896 there were 2,500,000 members and the Supreme
President said that the A.P.A. controlled 4,000,000 votes,[3]
which was manifestly much too free a boast.[4] In the Democratic national platform in 1896, "religious liberty," as one of
the guarantees of the Constitution, was declared to be a cherished doctrine of the party. The Republican platform was
silent on the subject. But the tacticians in charge of the
national convention in St. Louis, wishing not to offend the
A.P.A. by employing a Catholic, or the Catholics by employing
a Protestant, opened the meeting with prayer by a Jewish
rabbi.[5] It was said during the campaign that the order would
support Bryan,[6] and again that it would support McKinley.
Charges that McKinley was a Catholic, that Hanna was a
Catholic, that McKinley's secretary while he had been governor
in Ohio, a man named Boyle, was a Catholic, that in this
office he had unduly favored Catholics in making appointments called for frequent and categorical denials, especially
in the early weeks of the campaign.[7] The A.P.A. put fear
into the heart of every politician of the day. All the nominees
were Protestants—McKinley was a Methodist and Bryan a
Presbyterian; Hobart was a Presbyterian and Sewall a Sweden-
borgian. It is likely in the end that Bryan with Irish ancestry

[1] New York Times, Sep. 10 and 21, 1894.
[2] N. Y. Nation, Oct. 3, 1896.
[3] W. J. H. Traynor in North Am. Review for June, 1896.
[4] Cf. N. Y. Nation, April 4, 1895.   [5] N. Y. Nation, June 25, 1896.
[6] Cf. Corr. of Roosevelt and Lodge, vol. i, p. 224.
[7] See McKinley papers.

and an Irish name repelled some of the A.P.A. men. Tammany's support of him forfeited his right to expect the enthusiastic endorsement of such an organization. It was a great ado about nothing and such campaigning fell flat. The order and its objects were soon lost in the 16 to 1 maelstrom into which the whole body of the people plunged headlong.[1]

During the campaign not much was developed relating to Bryan's private life. Fortunately, for which fact Hanna's sensible direction may have been in some degree responsible, the personalities which had marred so many of our Presidential canvasses were but little stressed. Alienists were heard on the case and it was observed that Bryan had "errabund tendencies"—he was a "political mattoid." There were inferences that high scientific authorities entertained doubt of his sanity.[2] It was said that he was a paid agent of a Bimetallic League and of the silver miners. That he had spoken at times for silver, that he had received money for his speeches, and in communities in which mining was the principal industry of the people, could not be denied. But the "silver kings" were not at the time an affluent class and Bryan's statement that he had done nothing which was open to criticism, when charges were aimed at him on this point, were accepted at their face value.[3]

The amount of silver in a dollar fell in value during the campaign to less than 50 cents. Bryan said that, under free coinage, bullion, selling at the time for 66 cents, would reach a price of $1.29 an ounce.[4] The mine owners were told, and it was plain, that they would reap additional profits if he were elected. They subscribed to his campaign fund and assessed their employees without bringing it, with the aid of Sewall, St. John, the New York banker, who was treasurer of the National Committee, and the very few Eastern men of means who had

[1] Cf. Rhodes, The McKinley and Roosevelt Administrations, p. 27; G. F. Hoar, Autobiog. of 70 Years, vol. ii, pp. 292–3.
[2] Cf. N. Y. Times, Sep. 29, 1896.
[3] Cf. N. Y. Tribune and N. Y. Times, Aug. 17, 18 and 19, 1896; N. Y. World, Oct. 20, 1896.
[4] Cf. N. Y. Nation, Aug. 27 and Sep. 24, 1896.

espoused the silver cause, to a sum in any degree comparable to that which Hanna was assembling to accomplish the election of McKinley.[1] No one but the New York World considered the connection of the "silver kings" with the campaign to be a great scandal.

Nor was the shock profound or the excitement long-lived when men were found to say that Bryan, and at a recent time, had been under consideration for employment as a press agent for a travelling theatrical company. It was well enough known that he was an adventurer, that he was trying to live by writing and lecturing, when the fees for such services were not large, until he had been elevated by "man hysteria" at Chicago to the rank of a Presidential candidate of a great political party. He might not be defeated by reiterating stories about his impecuniosity—he could be, perhaps, by making it clear that he was an incendiary whose objects, if he could gain them, were to overthrow the republic.

On the Republican side Hanna suffered more than McKinley. He was the butt for the most malicious of the personalities in which the Democrats indulged at the expense of their opponents. The rags of journals which espoused the cause of Bryan in the East, led by one in New York whose new owner derived an income from silver mining, made rude sport of the manager of the Republican campaign. Hanna's rotund figure was covered with dollar marks. He was set in a barrel with bulging staves in token of his riches. It was suggested by the Bryan press everywhere that he and the gold bugs who were bursting with money were corrupting the electorate and purchasing the Presidency so that they could clamp the press the harder on the poor. Barbs of this kind daily aimed in lampoon and pictorial caricature at a man who had higher standards of honor than any one who had recently directed a Republican campaign were the unpleasant but inevitable features of a party battle as angry as this one must be.[2]

[1] Cf. N. Y. World, Oct. 1, 1896, and following days, particularly Nov. 2, 1896; N. Y. Nation, Oct. 22, 1896.
[2] Cf. Rhodes, The McKinley and Roosevelt Administrations, pp. 6–7; H. Croly, M. A. Hanna.

The stock markets throughout the summer and autumn reflected the state of the public mind. Some men, for safety, sent their money abroad.[1] Many withdrew gold from the banks and hid it in fear of the result.[2] At one time bankers in New York were compelled to give their support to the Treasury in order to hold up the reserve.[3] The far West and the lower South were Bryan's without a question. Nothing could be done to save them from the craze. Gorman of Maryland, as was expected, supported the ticket that he might continue to be the party "boss" in his state. Hill invited Bryan to dine at his home in Albany of which meeting neither of the principals said anything.[4] The whole New York state Democratic organization, following Tammany, attested its "regularity" by pledging its support to the candidate. At a convention in Buffalo in September, Hill's men (he himself still maintained his silence) in defiance of general sentiment and in complete disregard of the course which he and the New York delegation had taken at Chicago, ratified the platform and declared for the free coinage of silver.[5] A leader in New Jersey who had been prominently active in behalf of the gold standard at Chicago was concerned about his political future and abandoned his principles. Confidence was shaken by such betrayals of the cause and there were not a few men of careful judgment who were in honest doubt about the ability of the country to throw off the disease which had so dangerously darkened the public mind. In his persistent campaigning up and down the country Bryan travelled 18,000 miles and made 592 speeches in 477 towns and cities in 27

---

[1] N. Y. Times, July 21, 1896; N. Y. Nation, Oct. 22, 1896.

[2] N. Y. Nation, Nov. 5, 1896.

[3] Barnes, J. G. Carlisle, pp. 477–8; N. Y. Times, July 21, 22, 23, 24 and 25, 1896.

[4] N. Y. Times, Aug. 26, 1896.

[5] Cf. N. Y. Nation, Sep. 24, 1896. Hill privately explained his position to Secretary Lamont as follows: "There are many reasons why it is desirable to control or, at least, keep in touch with the regular organization of our state, which, of course, represents three-fifths or four-fifths of the party's voters. If I withdraw the organization will go into the hands of adventurers and the blatherskites. Will I not be serving the country better to remain passive and at the same time virtually control the organization?"—Sep. 14, 1896, in Lamont Papers, quoted in Barnes, J. G. Carlisle, p. 467.

states.[1] It was impossible to believe that such an onslaught on established institutions could succeed. But hopes rose, and fell again, until the end.[2]

The early elections in Vermont and Maine were a promise of great Republican majorities, but these states lay outside the area under the influence of the craze. The issues had reached all classes of the people and there was bitterness in those who had put their whole souls into the campaign to elect Bryan which they had persuaded themselves meant life or death to them and their like as a social class. They had been told that their betterment lay only in the direction of the overthrow of a wicked enemy and, as they saw in the closing days of the campaign the signs of defeat, they lost control of themselves. Carlisle was pelted with rotten eggs and other offal in his own city of Covington in Kentucky where he dared to raise his voice for sound money.[3] General Palmer, General Buckner and other men who were on the platform were confronted by angry mobs who hooted and jeered them and tried to disperse their meetings.[4]

Except in the South, where apathy, induced by overwhelming strength, prevailed,[5] the people, on both sides, came to the voting places to deposit their ballots with a firm step. In Pennsylvania 190,000 more men voted in 1896 than had done so in 1892, in Ohio 158,000, in Illinois 217,000, in Indiana 83,000, in Kentucky 105,000, in Missouri 133,000.

In Kentucky, South Dakota and California the result was at first in doubt and the final count was necessary to determine the result. Four border states, usually accounted, up to this time, a part of the "Solid South"—Delaware, Maryland, West Virginia and Kentucky (except for one out of 13 electors)—were Republican and for McKinley. The whole northern part of the Mississippi Valley—Ohio, Illinois, Indiana, Iowa, Mich-

[1] Cf. N. Y. World, Nov. 3, 1896; Haynes, Third Party Movements, p. 296.
[2] Cf. N. Y. Nation, Oct. 29, 1896.
[3] Barnes, J. G. Carlisle, pp. 483-4.
[4] Cf. N. Y. World, Oct. 31, 1896.
[5] Cf. N. Y. Nation, Nov. 19, 1896.

igan, Wisconsin, Minnesota and North Dakota voted for sound money. Kansas, following Missouri, South Dakota and his own state of Nebraska, were Bryan's. On the Pacific coast 8 of the 9 electors in California were Republicans. Oregon was Republican by a small majority. In the Rocky Mountains Bryan carried Colorado, Idaho, Montana, Nevada, Utah, Wyoming and Washington. McKinley had 271 electoral votes compared with Bryan's 176, and he was elected by what appeared to be a substantial popular majority. McKinley's plurality in New York state was 268,000; he carried the city by 20,000, the first time that it had ever given a plurality for a Republican candidate for President. The plurality in Brooklyn was 32,000. In Pennsylvania, McKinley's plurality was 300,000, in Massachusetts 173,000, in New Jersey nearly 90,000.

But the results beyond the Allegheny Mountains were an indication of the hold on the people which free coinage had gained. Illinois, it is true, gave McKinley a plurality of 143,000 (of which 60,000 came from Chicago) and Altgeld was defeated for re-election as governor. In the Republican nominee's own state of Ohio his plurality was only about 50,000; in Iowa it was 66,000, in Michigan 57,000, in Wisconsin, where better conditions prevailed, 102,000. In Indiana the Republican plurality was only about 18,000.

The rejoicing in the Eastern cities was unbounded. A hundred thousand men, borne along, without thought of party had marched through New York in a great demonstration for McKinley and sound money on the Saturday preceding the election. For seven and a half hours the procession had moved up Broadway and Fifth Avenue with steady tread under flags, banners and other decorations, suspended over the streets and hanging from the windows of houses and shops; election day might afford a still greater spectacle. Early in the evening of Tuesday, November 3rd, the streets were literally filled with people anxiously awaiting the returns and later, as the result was assured, a storm of sound broke forth and the lords of misrule took command until dawn.[1]

[1] N. Y. Tribune, Nov. 4, 1896.

All Europe had solicitously watched the course of the campaign. The press in England, France, Germany and other countries instantly congratulated us on our happy awakening after a nightmare which had lasted for so many weeks and months. The release was marked by more than a sentimental elation; it led instantly to practical displays of confidence in the future. Brokers' offices in New York and London were open all night. Orders to buy stocks and bonds were received from speculators and investors anticipating higher prices upon the opening of the American exchanges, and were cabled to England, where, the sun rising earlier, business would begin a full five hours before it should do so in Wall Street. Europe also bought our securities. Soon after daybreak the financial district in New York was packed with excited men eager to participate in the "boom." Gold which had been hoarded was brought from its hiding places. Millions of dollars were released for profitable investment. Employers of labor lighted fires in their mills, hired labor, set idle machinery in motion. On all sides business felt the impulse, as certainty that debts would not be repudiated and our institutions would not be overturned sank into the consciousness of the people. Men said and believed that "the corner had been turned"; trade and commerce would revive; prosperity would come again; capital which had been under attack by the ignorant and the malicious would be put to work for the advantage of all classes of the people.

In the past thirty years there had been a party of inflation in the United States, said the New York Times. A chance had been given the people to vote "Yes" or "No" on the question. They had said "No," and had "utterly annihilated" Bryan. Now everyone could "pluck up courage and get to work." [1] "The anxiety of all patriotic hearts," the New York Tribune said, gave place to "a joy too profound for expression." There had been "few grander moments in the history of self government." [2] Not since the fall of Richmond had patriotic Americans had such cause for rejoicing, said the New York

---

[1] N. Y. Times, Nov. 4, 1896.   [2] N. Y. Tribune, Nov. 4, 1896.

World. The integrity of the Union had been secured—its honor was preserved.[1] Hard times were at an end, confidence had returned.[2] The country had been saved, said the New York Herald,—"No nation on the earth breathes more freely than we Americans do to-day." [3]

If McKinley was to be congratulated, so, too, was Mr. Cleveland. Many wrote and telegraphed him. The fight had been fought and he had been the leader. Victory lay not in the election of McKinley, but in the defeat of Bryan, and the President had won.[4] "When the history of the present time comes to be seriously written," the Baltimore Evening News remarked, "the name of the hero of this campaign will be that of a man who was not a candidate. The fight which has just been won was made possible by the noble service of one steadfast and heroic citizen; the victory which was achieved must be set down as the crowning achievement of his great record of public duty." [5]

But McKinley's election was not effected by that overwhelming majority which it had been hoped that he might receive were the result to serve, as it was ardently hoped that it might, to put a complete quietus upon the silver agitation and clear the Democratic party of those who followed Bryan's Quixotic fortunes. The popular vote for McKinley throughout the country was 7,104,244, while for Bryan, including the Populist and Silver party votes—he was at the head of both these tickets as well as the Democratic ticket—it was 6,506,835. Only 134,652 Gold Democrats had been willing to run the risk of nullifying their influence by voting for Palmer and Buckner rather than the Republican nominees.[6]

It was pointed out that if a few thousand more votes had been cast for Bryan in a few states which were named he would have been elected.[7] It was disquieting to realize that so large a portion of the people of the country could be caught by such

---

[1] N. Y. World, Nov. 4, 1896.   [2] Ibid., Nov. 5, 1896.
[3] N. Y. Herald, Nov. 5, 1896.
[4] Cf. Cleveland Papers for Nov., 1896.   [5] Issue of Nov. 4, 1896.
[6] Cf. Barnes, J. G. Carlisle, pp. 478-9.
[7] Cf. N. Y. Nation, Nov. 19, 1896.

baited hooks as he had dangled before them. The whole conservative part of the country had strained every resource for months to reveal the man and his isms to the voters, and he had nearly gained his end in their despite. He had been, and might very likely remain, a danger, since he was as earnest as some religious fanatic in the pursuit of his ideas and a skilful political strategist. He had addressed himself to the discontent of the country and he had increased that discontent. He had fastened himself on an old and well organized political party. Apparently he was its undisputed leader, supplanting other men of widely different views. So long as his ambition should impel him to use his adroit abilities in directing the movements of the party he would keep the place he had so lately won until another competent to exert a like or greater influence upon the electorate should appear. He congratulated McKinley, but he abated nothing with reference to free silver. The result was due, he and his friends said, to the "money power." The opposition had subsidized the press. They had bought the Presidency. The bimetallists had been beaten, but they were eternally right and they would continue the fight for the happiness of mankind. The battle would never cease until the gold standard had been "driven back to England." Truth crushed to earth would rise again, and so on.[1]

Bryan was solaced by the sympathy of those who believed in him as he believed in himself. The post was filled with letters full of gratitude to him for having preached "the gospel of righteousness." He had fought "the great battle for humanity." He had battered the fortified strongholds of plutarchy. Women and children, it was said, had shed tears upon receipt of the news of his defeat. They wanted plenty of money; now they must wait for four more long years. They already now put him in nomination for 1900 when, they said, he would certainly drive the enemy from the land.[2]

It was consoling to reflect that Congress would continue to be Republican in both branches—in the House of Representa-

---

[1] Cf. N. Y. Times, Sep. 23 and Nov. 7, 1896.
[2] Barnes, J. G. Carlisle, pp. 486–9, quoting Bryan Papers.

tives by a majority of more than 60, not greater, however than
it had been. In the Senate the Western silverites still, very
probably, would hold the balance of power.[1] But now that
the country had been definitely polled it was believed that the
Republican party would find its mandate clear on the money
question, and the utterances of McKinley and the Republican
leaders would certainly not be muddy henceforth on this point.

That great matter of a year ago, the boundary of Venezuela
soon faded from the popular consciousness. The commission
to determine the "true" line which Cleveland had authorized,
President Gilman of Johns Hopkins University, Andrew D.
White of Cornell University, Justice Brewer, Frederick R.
Coudert and R. H. Alvey of the Court of Appeals of the District
of Columbia, called for maps and documents and made some
progress with a difficult investigation. Just why such men
should have assumed such duties it was difficult to surmise
except in the belief that it would be a public service if they
could take the whole subject into a quiet place until the outburst of dangerous jingoism should subside. Precisely this
end was gained and, while they were hiring clerks and amanu-
enses, reading books and studying charts, the popular enthusiasm was being mustered for display on the question of Cuba
and in other fields. The large comprehension of international
affairs which distinguished Lord Salisbury and the indulgence
with which the advances and retreats of public opinion in our
American democracy could be viewed by such a man spoke of
the early accommodation of the dispute. That grave complications should result from a difference of opinion on such a matter
it was impossible to believe. Lord Playfair, an unofficial
delegate of the British Foreign Office, whose wife was an
American woman, visited Mr. Bayard in London [2] and a plan
of arbitration, a method of settlement to which Great Britain
in point of fact was at no time averse, was proposed. Other
peacemakers appeared, among them the opposition leader,
Sir William Harcourt, whose wife, like Playfair's, was an

---

[1] N. Y. Nation, Dec. 17, 1896.
[2] Wemyss Reid, Memoirs of Playfair, pp. 414–26.

American,[1] and Joseph Chamberlain, Salisbury's Colonial
Secretary who stood behind Playfair. Chamberlain, too, had
married a lady from America, and he at this conjuncture
visited the United States, where he met Olney and reduced
the asperity of that not too mellow man's tone.[2] These English
friends of America would, if possible, extricate the two countries
from what has been properly designated an "absurd impasse."[3]

By this time Bayard had been pretty completely superseded
as a factor in the settlement. Olney was turning the negotiation into other channels.[4] The disturbance which the gross
violation of diplomatic amenities had occasioned in our ambassador's mind unfitted him for the service. A secretary,
James A. Roosevelt, who through Mr. Whitney and the Van
Alen bargain had been imposed upon Mr. Bayard,[5] wrote
confidentially to Olney disparaging the Ambassador's competency.[6] Olney needed no spur—there was by this time
entire estrangement between the man who had been Secretary
of State during Cleveland's first term and him who now directed
the affairs of the American "Foreign Office," and the aliena-
tion, to Mr. Bayard's grief, was extended to the President who
had so whole-heartedly espoused the Venezuelan cause.[7]

Only the most discreet utterances escaped Lord Salisbury
and Mr. Balfour and a plan was duly agreed upon and put
into effect before the President's commission had completed
its, what now seemed to be, quite gratuitous inquiry. Mr.
Cleveland in his final message to Congress, in December,
1896, could announce that the question had "ceased to be a
matter of difference" between the two countries. A treaty

---

[1] A. G. Gardiner, Life of Harcourt, vol. ii, pp. 395–404.

[2] J. L. Garvin, Life of Chamberlain, vol. iii, pp. 159–65.

[3] R. B. Mowat, Life of Pauncefote, p. 196.

[4] For Henry White's part as Olney's agent in England in explaining
the American position to Salisbury and others see A. Nevins, Henry
White, pp. 111–9.

[5] Roosevelt was a brother-in-law of Van Alen. He had "never in any
way," Gresham wrote Bayard, "demonstrated that he possessed ability
of any kind."—Gresham's Letter Book in Gresham Papers in Library
of Congress.

[6] Under date of Feb. 28, 1896, in Cleveland Papers.

[7] Cf. Olney to Cleveland, March 25, 1896, in Cleveland Papers.

had been drafted. If Venezuela would agree, which she soon did, the whole controversy would be referred to arbitration. Her Majesty's Privy Council, in behalf of Great Britain, would name two members of the court, Venezuela two, one to be chosen by the President of Venezuela and the other by the justices of the Supreme Court of the United States, while a fifth arbitrator was to be selected by these four. If within a period of three months they should not be able to agree upon this fifth man he should be nominated by the King of Sweden and Norway. The treaty which was signed in the State Department on February 2, 1897, by Sir Julian Pauncefote for Great Britain and the Venezuelan minister to the United States for Venezuela, named Chief Justice Fuller and Justice Brewer of the United States Supreme Court as the representatives of Venezuela. Lord Herschell (who died to be succeeded by Lord Russell of Killowen) and Sir Richard H. Collins would represent Great Britain. In due time Frederic de Martens, a Russian publicist, was selected as the fifth member of the tribunal and, as was specified, became the presiding officer. The court, thus constituted, would "determine the boundary line between the colony of British Guiana and the United States of Venezuela."

The material which the President's commission had assembled was transferred to the arbitrators and finally, on October 3, 1899, nearly four years after Mr. Cleveland's stirring message, the line was fixed and the dispute was brought to an end.[1] Almost nothing was gained by the republic whose cause we, as the guardian of the states of the Western hemisphere against the encroachments of the governments of Europe, had espoused with such a flourish of outraged dignity.[2] To all intents and purposes the boundary declared to be the rightful

---

[1] The effort of Venezuela to draft Mr. Cleveland, after his retirement from office, as counsel in the arbitration and his declination is described in Am. Hist. Review, vol. xxxix, pp. 78–81.

[2] Cf. R. B. Mowat, Diplomatic Relations of Great Britain and the U. S. p. 267. The ingratitude of the Venezuelans, indeed the open disrespect shown by them for the United States in answer to our Quixotic interest in their affairs, is referred to in R. B. Mowat, Life of Pauncefote, p. 202.

one, delimiting British and Venezuelan influence on the Guiana frontier, was the Schomburgk line. Great Britain never gravely claimed more, and the mountain which had been in labor brought forth only a mouse.[1]

What was regarded as a very noteworthy evidence of advancement in friendliness of feeling between England and the United States grew out of the Venezuelan excitement. This dispute, the open question of the boundary between Canada and Alaska, the unsettled damages for the sealing vessel captures in Bering Sea and further measures proposed and declared to be necessary to prevent the extermination of the herd were prolific of ill feeling.[2] Why could not all these and like differences affecting the two peoples be submitted to an arbitration tribunal without the outbursts of acerbity which every slight incident induced? If a rule could be established which would send controversies to a court for adjustment by argument, and discountenance "war scares," in which the newspapers, and so large a part of the population, led by hotheads in Congress, found so much delight, it would be an obvious gain for civilization. Sir Julian Pauncefote and Secretary Gresham had given their attention to a general treaty of arbitration. The negotiations were continued by Sir Julian and Mr. Olney who were successful in having their work approved by the Foreign Office in London and by the President. The treaty must still have ratification by a two-thirds vote in the Senate. It was predictable that recalcitrancy in that body might prevent action, but only good was promised by recourse to such a mode of settlement of international disputes and public opinion, it was believed, might be awakened in such a degree as to make rejection by the upper branch of Congress very improbable. It was a particularly satisfactory victory for

[1] Mr. Cleveland, however, never ceased to justify the firing of Olney's "20 inch gun" with a zest born, perhaps, of a conviction of mistaken judgment.—A. Nevins, Letters of Cleveland, p. 547. Cf. J. F. Rhodes, From Hayes to McKinley, pp. 451–6; Henry James, Richard Olney, chap. xi and app. iv; R. McElroy, Grover Cleveland, vol. ii, chap. vi; R. B. Mowat, Diplomatic Relations of Great Britain and U. S., p. 272; ibid., Life of Pauncefote, chaps. xviii and xix.

[2] Cf. App. Ann. Cyclop. for 1897, pp. 789–90.

diplomacy, since Lord Salisbury gave it as his opinion that England would enter into arrangements for general arbitration with no other country. The negotiation had been based on a belief in good faith and a recognition of the fact that there could be fuller understanding and a better friendship between peoples of a common origin than between those of alien sympathies and foreign tongues.

Conversations between Mr. Olney and Sir Julian Pauncefote and correspondence between the State Department and Lord Salisbury had led to agreement on several points which, at first, were the subject of doubt. It was agreed in the treaty which was signed that "pecuniary claims" not involving an amount in excess of £100,000 should be referred to a court made up of two "jurists of repute," one nominated by each government. They together should choose an umpire who would be the presiding officer. In case of their failure to make this choice within two months, the umpire should be appointed by agreement between members of the Supreme Court of the United States and the members of the Judicial Committee of the Privy Council in Great Britain. This method failing the umpire should be chosen by the King of Sweden and Norway. A majority, two votes, should decide questions at issue.

Claims in excess of £100,000 and all other matters in difference, except "territorial claims," were to be submitted to the same tribunal of three members, in which cases there should be unanimous judgment. If the award should not be unanimous the subject was to be referred to another tribunal of five members, two to be appointed by each contracting party. The four thus named should select an umpire and, if they should fail to act, he should be chosen, as in the case of the umpire in the court of three members. Controversies involving "territorial claims" should be submitted to a court of six members, three of them justices of the Supreme Court of the United States or judges of the Circuit Courts to be nominated by the President of the United States, and three to be British judges nominated by the British crown. The award, if it were agreed to by five of the six, should be final. In the event of no result satisfactory to five members being reached it was stipulated that hostile measures should not be taken on either side until resort were had to the expedient of mediation by a friendly power. The treaty was signed on January 11, 1897, and Mr. Cleveland forwarded it to the Senate with his benison and a hope that it would be ratified. It was hailed in England and in the United States with deserved acclamation.[1] Responsible newspapers, influential bodies of business men, leaders in churches, colleges and schools, all citizens of correct views and good purposes commended an achievement which seemed to mark the beginning of a new epoch in civilization.[2] Mass meetings were held. They were addressed by men highly esteemed in the communities in which they dwelt and in the nation. Resolutions were adopted. Petitions signed by tens of thousands of persons were forwarded to the Senate. Letters, telegrams, visits of individuals and delegations to Washington, if they were evidences of the small trust reposed in the members of the upper house of Congress, were, at the same time, an expression of public opinion in regard to the treaty.[3] Carl Schurz called it "a masterpiece." It shed, he said, "the brightest lustre upon the close of the nineteenth century." It was "a triumph of human civilization." Robert Treat Paine gave the President's message a place beside Magna Charta and the Declaration of Independence.[4]

Chandler of New Hampshire, whose blathering extended to international, no less than to domestic, topics; Morgan of Alabama whose conceit of himself was joined with the amplest powers of utterance on foreign questions;[5] Lodge who was acting in this stage of his career like a mischievous school boy; all the silver senators who would hector Great Britain until she should "do something" for money made from the

---

[1] Cf. N. Y. Times, Jan. 13, 1897; A. Nevins, Henry White, p. 124.
[2] N. Y. Nation, Jan. 13, 1897.
[3] Cf. W. S. Holt, Treaties Defeated by the Senate, p. 157.
[4] Cleveland Papers.
[5] "The most wholly and dangerously unreliable person I ever knew in public life."—T. F. Bayard to Gresham, March 9, 1895, in Gresham Papers; cf. Bayard to Gresham under date of Feb. 6, and May 29, 1894; also Gresham to Bayard, Jan. 21, 1894, in ibid.

metal which came from their mines were devising excuses, more or less plausible to themselves and their political friends, for raising objection to that which it seemed that no man could oppose. Hoar, who was a bimetallist,[1] stood upon his great dignity and would not be hurried to a judgment. John Sherman, who was chairman of the Committee on Foreign Relations, to which the treaty was referred, could, in the state of his faculties, give no proper leadership to the movement for ratification.

It was soon made plain that the influences of the enlightened part of the country would go for naught. The treaty was to meet the fate of most of that which bore the recommendation of the President, except his message suggesting an imbroglio with England over Venezuela. The treaty was too rapid a change of ground for the jingoes in the Senate. It was not arbitration, they said, but surrender. The nature of the differences between the countries could not be foretold. To refer disputes automatically to a court was to sign away the national honor. England had some concealed and interested motive else she never would have entered into the negotiation. Cleveland and Olney were unpatriotic and they, too, on their side, could have had no honorable ends in view.[2] The senators were jealous of their share in the exercise of the treaty making power; they had not been taken into counsel—they were asked to ratify what they had had no part, even consultatively, in formulating. Here was a plan, indeed, for eliminating them in the future from a determination of national rights and wrongs, from a determination of the importance or unimportance of grievances—all were to be thrown into a peaceful court.[3]

One had one amendment and one had another—if the treaty should be ratified at all it must be radically changed. The stamp of the Senate rather than Olney's, or Cleveland's, or England's must be placed upon it. Cleveland's administration

---

[1] Hoar, Autobiog. of 70 Years, vol. ii, chap. xxii.
[2] Cf. N. Y. Times, Feb. 19 and 20, 1897.
[3] For Olney's explanation of the opposition to the treaty see Olney Papers, cited by W. S. Holt, Treaties Defeated by the Senate, pp. 158–60.

ended without action. Olney's pride in his lineage had reasserted itself after his lapses on the subject of Venezuela. It was the destiny of "the great English-speaking family," he said, to "lead and control the world." The course of the Senate he described as a calamity of "world wide proportions." [1] The subject was passed on to McKinley who warmly espoused the cause, but with no more avail. The articles were mutilated and distorted until the treaty entirely failed to express the enlightened sentiment which it had been devised to proclaim. The Senate had taken all the meaning out of it, the English newspapers said. The exhibition of anti-British feeling evoked by the discussion was making a travesty of the friendship which the event was meant to celebrate. Finally, on May 5th, what the New York Times called "the miserable remnant of the treaty" [2] was rejected; 43 senators voted for it and 26 against it. There were for it four less than the necessary two-thirds. Twenty-five of the 31 senators who were still opposed to the treaty, after divers and sundry jingoes had amended it to please their tastes, were silverites. [3]

Bound up with the general treaty of arbitration was the Monroe Doctrine, which had lately had such an airing during the Venezuela furore, as it might affect the question of constructing the Nicaragua Canal. The collapse of the French enterprise at Panama had put new life into the plan for utilizing a route farther north by way of the San Juan River and Lake Nicaragua. Men who knew little enough about such matters believed this way to be the one marked out by nature for the passage of ships from sea to sea. Engineers favored it and fixed prices for which it could be successfully built.

When Cleveland, upon entering the Presidency in 1885,

[1] Olney to White, May 8, 1897, in A. Nevins, Henry White, p. 125.
[2] N. Y. Times, April 22, 1897.
[3] Senate Ex. Journal, vol. xxxi, p. 104; Henry James, Richard Olney, chap. xii and app. v; Foreign Relations for 1896, pp. 222–40; A. Nevins, Henry White, pp. 124–5; J. F. Rhodes, The McKinley and Roosevelt Administrations, pp. 40–1; R. B. Mowat, Life of Lord Pauncefote, pp. 164–71; McElroy, Grover Cleveland, vol. ii, pp. 243–5; N. Y. Nation, May 13, 1897; cf. ibid., Jan. 21 and 28, Feb. 4 and 11, March 25 and April 1, 1897.

withdrew the treaty which would have made the canal a national undertaking concessions were obtained from the government of Nicaragua by a group of private individuals, and these rights were transferred to the Maritime Canal Company, of which Hiram Hitchcock was the president, and a construction company of which Warner Miller was the president. A. G. Menocal who for years had given much study to the scheme became chief engineer.[1] Stock was sold, largely through Warner Miller's efforts, and some progress was made, not only with the surveys, but with the building of jetties, docks and a railroad, and the assembling of material.[2] The panic of 1893 rendered fruitless further appeals for money. The construction company passed into the hands of a receiver and the works were falling into decay.[3] The scheme was laid at the door of Congress, but always the old Clayton-Bulwer treaty with Great Britain, which had been in mind in 1885, lay in the way.[4]

The canal was described as a great national improvement; it must have national support. In no other way could a hundred millions or more be obtained to open this new transoceanic trade route.[5] Morgan of Alabama, the chief opponent of the arbitration treaty, and of all measures which spoke of anything but war upon England, was the foremost advocate of the canal in the United States Senate. He was a Democrat. Its principal proponents, however, were Republicans, since they were not averse, in theory, to government subventions for the advantage of commerce, and hope rested in them. The Re-

[1] Am. Ann. Cyclop. for 1888, pp. 614–7.
[2] Cf. Senate Reports, 51st Cong. 2nd sess., no. 1944; ibid., 52nd Cong. 2nd sess., no. 1262; Senate Doc., 54th Cong. 1st sess., no. 315; Senate Reports, 54th Cong. 1st sess., no. 1109; Report of Sec. of Int. for 1890, pp. cxxvi–cxxvii; ibid. for 1891, pp. cxlvii–cxlviii; ibid. for 1892, pp. cxliv–cxlvi.
[3] Report of Sec. of Int. for 1894, p. liv.; letter from Greytown to N. Y. World, May 2, 1894.
[4] Reprinted in Senate Doc., 54th Cong. 1st sess., no. 133.
[5] The latest estimates came from a board of engineers appointed by President Cleveland, in answer to an act of Congress of 1895. They said that the cost at the lowest calculation would be $133,000,000.— House Doc., 54th Cong. 1st sess., no. 279.

THE NICARAGUA CANAL

publican platform in 1892 had contained a plank expressive of interest in the construction of the work which, in 1896, became a clear declaration—the canal should be "built, owned and operated by the United States."

The election of McKinley gave new zest to the friends of the project and they were proceeding with their oratory when a disconcerting fact was brought to their attention. A new minister arrived in Washington from Nicaragua and, while the debate was at its height, Secretary of State Olney was informed that the concession of the company to which money was to be voted had expired. Anyhow the agreement with the company specified that control of the canal should not pass to the United States, or to any government, without Nicaragua's consent. The contract fell and was forfeit, because the holders of the concession had not fulfilled its provisions.[1] Congress was to guaranty the bonds of a group of men who seemed to have no right of way. The subject, it was agreed, must now be treated *de novo;* and it was passed on with other problems to the new President.

[1] Preliminary Report of Isthmian Canal Commission, 1900, pp. 12, 39; N. Y. Nation, Jan. 28 and Feb. 4, 1897.

CHAPTER XXXVIII

THE WAR WITH SPAIN

THE election of McKinley made the composition of his cabinet a subject of immediate importance to the politicians and the press. The adjustment of the claims of the various elements which had contributed to the new President's nomination and election would be shrewdly managed. McKinley's skill as a party leader was an assurance of such a result. Hanna's large share in shaping the policies of the administration was not absent from any reckoning. He would be a power behind the throne, as every one knew, and those who had crossed his way viewed the outlook less happily than those who had stood loyally at his side. It was assumed that he could have for himself any appointment within the gift of the President-elect. And it was so. McKinley wrote Hanna a few days after the victory: "I turn to you irresistibly. I want you as one of my chief associates in the conduct of the government." Hanna's disinclination to take a cabinet post was known, but acceptance, he was told, should be a "patriotic duty." [1] The Postmaster-Generalship was in the President's mind, a department of administration whose direction might properly be entrusted to a business man. But other places were at the disposal of Mr. Hanna who declined all proffers and it was only a fortnight before the inauguration that the President-elect abandoned any further thought of gratifying his "dearest wish." [2] Hanna had another object in view—he would be a United States senator, and, if he were to realize this ambition, John Sherman must be dispossessed of a post to which, by right of long occupancy, he would, probably, be

[1] H. Croly, Mark Hanna, p. 229.
[2] Ibid., p. 230; cf. H. H. Kohlsaat, From McKinley to Harding, pp. 56, 60–1.

448

returned upon the expiration of his term two years hence. Foraker's faction had elected the governor of the state in 1895 and for some time he had looked upon himself as the party "boss" in Ohio; it was discomfiting to him in the highest degree to see Hanna's figure looming behind the man who would be President and who would reward the loyal and punish the faithless in the dispensation of Federal patronage in Ohio for the next four years.

Hanna's need was urgent; he must go to the Senate at once. John Sherman could be asked to take a place in the cabinet; the vacancy thereby created would be filled by appointment of Foraker's governor. Only negotiation and some kind of a pact between the factions could bring the fondly desired result. Sherman, in whom the signs of senility were quite apparent, though he himself was unaware of the impairment of his faculties, was invited to be Secretary of State by the new President, who may or may not have been fully sensible of the increasing incapacities of his appointee.[1] Sherman was not very eager to exchange one office for the other.[2] But he played his part like a true politician. He told Hanna, after a conversation on the subject, that he would yield his seat in the Senate and pass to the State Department.[3] When he wrote McKinley stating his willingness to accede to the plan he expressed a wish that Hanna should be his successor in the Senate.[4] In forwarding his resignation to Governor Bushnell of Ohio he "naturally" felt, he said, that he "should be consulted in filling the vacancy." He had not conferred with Mr. Hanna, he averred, and did not know whether that personage would accept the office, but he was certain that such a disposition of it would gratify the new President.[5]

This flummery done with, Foraker, seeing the necessity for

[1] When informed by Joseph Medill of Sherman's "mental decay" the President replied that such reports were "without foundation and the cheap inventions of sensational writers, or other evil disposed or mistaken people."—McKinley to Medill, Feb. 8, 1897, in McKinley Papers.
[2] Sherman to Richard Smith, Feb. 9, 1897, and Sherman to W. S. Ward, April 28, 1898, in ibid.
[3] Dec. 15, 1896, in ibid. [4] Jan. 7, 1897, in ibid.
[5] Sherman to Bushnell, Jan. 16, 1897, in ibid.

it, instructed his governor to let bygones be bygones, and, in
the hope, indeed with the assurance, that his action would not
go unrewarded when favors were to be bestowed by the new
administration at Washington, Hanna was given Sherman's
place in the Senate.[1] This barter and sale of a great office could
be viewed with little approbation by scrupulous men. But
Sherman had a name which was still held in some degree of
veneration by large bodies of the people, so that his appointment to the leading post in the cabinet might be regarded, on
his side, as an opportunity for him to "round out" his career,
and, on McKinley's side, as an opportunity to secure the counsel of one who, in point of service at least, was preeminent
among the leaders of the Republican party. Hanna, in turn,
was seen, except by those who had tried and were still trying
to fasten upon him corruption, based upon his wealth, as a
very astute and capable personage. He was inexperienced in
political office; he might not add oratory or even quiet wisdom
to the United States Senate. But it was a body, at the moment,
in much disrepute and his business-like methods, especially
now when he was so attached a friend of the new President,
might very greatly facilitate the operations of government.[2]

For the head of the Treasury Department Mr. McKinley
turned to Dingley who had been directing tariff legislation in
the House. But his health forbade his accepting the appointment and he could be more useful, he believed, if he were to
hold his place as chairman of the Committee on Ways and
Means.[3] The post was offered also to Cornelius N. Bliss who
had been treasurer of the Republican National Committee in
1896, as he had been in 1892. He, too, declined. Greater
success was had in another field. If there were misgivings

---

[1] "The fact is they are ugly and do not intend to appoint me if they
can possibly avoid it." (Hanna to Sherman, Feb. 6, 1897, in Sherman
Papers.) Bushnell made the appointment on February 21, 1897.—Bushnell to Hanna on that date in ibid.

[2] Cf. J. B. Foraker, Notes of a Busy Life, vol. i, pp. 496–506; H. Croly,
M. A. Hanna, pp. 231–41; N. Y. Nation, Feb. 25, 1897; N. Y. Times,
Feb. 22, 1897.

[3] Dingley to McKinley, Dec. 22, 1896, in McKinley Papers; E. N.
Dingley, Life and Times of Nelson Dingley, Jr., pp. 410–4.

with reference to Sherman they were more than offset by the very deep satisfaction which was felt when it was announced that Lyman J. Gage,[1] after carefully considering the tender of the appointment,[2] would be Secretary of the Treasury. Here was a man who was in no sense a politician. His position as a banker in Chicago had won for him the esteem and confidence of the "sound money" forces in the East, no less than in the Mississippi Valley. His opinions were frankly stated and widely known. The Treasury, under his management, would be in no danger of falling into the hands of those who wished to pay public and private debt in paper or silver money. He would be the safest of advisers for the new President who had given signs of too little knowledge of banking and finance, and who, under bad counsel, even after the notable victory in November, might slip away from the post to which he had been hitched during the campaign.[3] Mugwumps gladly noted that Gage was sound on the principle, so dear to them, of civil service reform.[4] These were the key positions in the cabinet—the Department of State and the Treasury.

A very unhappy impression was produced by the choice of General Russell A. Alger, a rich lumberman of Michigan, to be Secretary of War. He had been using his money freely to purchase delegates to recent Republican national conventions who would forward his ambitions to be President of the United States. His ineligibility for the Presidency was only exceeded by his temerity in offering himself for so eminent a post. His fitness for the place was in "inverse ratio to his anxiety to get it." [5] He had been the commander-in-chief at one time of the Grand Army of the Republic in which McKinley also played a prominent part. He was "in touch" with the veterans

---

[1] H. H. Kohlsaat, From McKinley to Harding, p. 56. Platt's efforts to make a bargain which would have given him the appointment was repelled prior to McKinley's nomination.—Ibid., p. 30.

[2] C. G. Dawes to McKinley Jan. 21, 1897, in McKinley Papers.

[3] Kohlsaat, op. cit., pp. 56–9.

[4] N. Y. Nation, Jan. 28 and Feb. 4, 1897; cf. N. Y. Tribune, Jan. 30, 1897.

[5] N. Y. Times, March 6, 1897; cf. N. Y. Nation, Feb. 4, 1897; John Sherman's Recollections, vol. ii, p. 1029.

of the Civil War so potential in politics,[1] and he had contributed his money as well as his oratorical talents to the campaign, after his own prospects of a nomination were dimmed.[2]

Platt must be considered in New York. He had used all his influences to prevent McKinley's advancement, but he now stood in the way of the appointment of those who had not been friendly to him and his political organization. He was on terms of amity with Levi P. Morton and Chauncey M. Depew. Morton was offered a place in the cabinet, but declined it.[3] John J. McCook and General Stewart L. Woodford were acceptable to Platt. McCook, youngest of an Ohio family known as "the fighting McCooks," consisting of a father and his eight sons all of whom, with five cousins, served in the Civil War, a prominent corporation lawyer in New York, was invited to become Secretary of the Interior, but he wanted the Attorney Generalship or the Navy Department, and refused the proffered honor.[4] An *impasse* in New York was averted by Cornelius N. Bliss. To his name Platt could not actively object and, after having been vainly invited to be Secretary of the Treasury, he was made Secretary of the Interior, a post which, at the last moment, he had reluctantly accepted.[5] Another business

[1] Redfield Proctor to McKinley, Jan. 12, 1897, in McKinley Papers.
[2] He was endorsed and commended to McKinley by T. C. Platt, (Platt to Alger, Jan. 31, 1897, in McKinley Papers.) W. E. Chandler (Chandler to McKinley, Jan. 12, 1897, in ibid.) and by Hanna (Alger to McKinley, Jan. 11, 1897, in ibid.) Sherman had written of Alger in 1888 when he was striving for the nomination for the Presidency. Alger's canvass, said Sherman, "will always be stained with dishonor and bribery. This was open and flagrant and, if he had been nominated, I do not believe he would have carried a single state in the Union in the face of the facts that would have then been made public. The purchase of votes in a convention is morally as great a crime as the bribing of members of a legislature." (Sherman to C. F. Martin, June 28, 1888, in Sherman Papers.) It was well known that opposition to Alger's appointment would be expressed and effort was made to allay it. Charles A. Dana's vitriolic pen was feared. Platt visited him and McKinley was assured that the New York Sun would not be unfriendly.—Burrows to McKinley, Jan. 20, 1897, in McKinley Papers.
[3] Morton to McKinley, Jan. 26, 1897, in McKinley Papers.
[4] McCook to McKinley, Feb. 27, 1897, in ibid. Cf. "The Fighting McCooks" in The Scotch Irish in America, Proceedings of Sixth Congress, pp. 161–71.
[5] Cf. Bliss to McKinley, Jan. 11, 1897, in ibid.

man, James A. Gary of Baltimore, who had been prompt in Maryland to further McKinley's cause as a candidate,[1] became Postmaster General. John D. Long, an ex-governor of Massachusetts, held in high regard, was to be Secretary of the Navy; Joseph McKenna, a native of Pennsylvania who had lived long in California, Attorney General, after Philander C. Knox of Pittsburgh had declined the post,[2] and James Wilson of Iowa, a Scot who had come to this country as a lad, Secretary of Agriculture. Long, McKenna and Wilson had been McKinley's friends and associates in Congress, and were, in a sense, personal appointees.

The cabinet was completed without account having been taken of Whitelaw Reid and Theodore Roosevelt, who diligently strove for posts. Reid was determined to get a place for himself, preferably the Secretaryship of the Navy.[3] He had actively combated Platt, and persisted in his opposition, reminding the President of a fact, of which he was quite cognizant, that the New York Tribune had done more to bring about his nomination for the Presidency than the Republican organization in New York state. Another appointment which Reid fondly wished for and had long sought was the ambassadorship to England. Platt would not hear of his selection for either office. Importunity continued, chiefly through John Hay, who was at the President-elect's right hand, and to whom Reid was attached by friendship and association as one of his writers on the Tribune, and who, at length, wrote to McKinley— "I have ceased thinking about Reid; he thinks about himself enough for two." [4] But Reid was not to be put aside. He was in Arizona whither he had gone for his health. Hay finally prepared two letters—McKinley could autograph and forward one or the other as he chose. A messenger was despatched to the Southwest to cushion the refusal. The letter of Hay which

---

[1] McKinley to Gary, April 13, 1895, in McKinley Papers.
[2] George Harvey, Henry C. Frick, pp. 290–1.
[3] Hay to Hanna, Jan. 15, 1897, in ibid.; cf. Hay to McKinley, Feb. 13 and 16, 1897, in ibid. Reid telegraphed that he would like to be Secretary of the Navy.—Hay to Hanna, Jan. 15, 1897, in ibid.
[4] Hay to McKinley, Feb. 16, 1897, in ibid.

McKinley selected breathed undying friendship. It spoke of obligation and gratitude. It promised future rewards. But now, under the circumstances, in Reid's state of health, the President-elect would not wish to impose the burdens of a cabinet post on him, or send him away into the "harsh climate" which he would encounter during a residence in London.[1]

Roosevelt was viewed by McKinley, and, indeed, by most of the President's advisers, as too restless a spirit for executive office.[2] Henry Cabot Lodge was his most active friend, but Thomas B. Reed and Senator Wolcott who pleaded with Hanna [3] were diligent advocates also. It was stated to be the foremost and preeminent desire of these three men that Roosevelt be given at least an assistant secretaryship.[4] Other friends were Bellamy Storer and Mrs. Storer of Cincinnati.[5] They had contributed to the fund which was raised to relieve McKinley of his debts, though the $10,000 which they paid for this end was accepted with misgivings in the anticipation that their gift would probably lead to unwelcome demands.[6] Roosevelt in his anxiety for preferment brought himself to the point of discussing the matter with Platt; his friends also spoke to the New York state "boss" without whose, at least, passive attitude toward the nomination little could be achieved. Roosevelt promised not to be a "marplot or agitator." [7] While

[1] McKinley to Reid, Feb. 19, 1897, in McKinley Papers. These facts are made clear in letters and telegrams from John Hay in McKinley Papers.

[2] Cf. Corr. of Roosevelt and Lodge, vol. i, pp. 241-2; Archie Butt, Taft and Roosevelt, vol. ii, p. 441; H. F. Pringle, Theodore Roosevelt, pp. 165, 168; M. L. Storer, Theodore Roosevelt the Child, pp. 20, 23-4; ibid., In Memoriam, pp. 21 et seq.

[3] Cf. Corr. of Roosevelt and Lodge, vol. i, pp. 243, 244-5, 247, 261-2

[4] John Hay to McKinley, Feb. 23, 1897, in McKinley Papers.

[5] Bellamy Storer was the son of a lawyer of the same name. His wife was Maria Longworth, a granddaughter of Nicholas Longworth, a founder of Cincinnati. She was an artist and established potteries, the products of which gained wide esteem. They were friends of Roosevelt who wrote to Cleveland recommending Storer for his (Roosevelt's) place on the United States Civil Service Commission—"He is a man of great ability and of singular sweetness and strength of character," etc. etc.—April 20. 1895, in Cleveland Papers. Cf. A. Nevins, Letters of Cleveland, p. 387.

[6] T. B. Mott, Myron T. Herrick, p. 73.

[7] Corr. of Roosevelt and Lodge, vol. i, pp. 242, 244; M. L. Storer, Theodore Roosevelt the Child, p. 56; ibid., In Memoriam, pp. 18-9.

Platt would have welcomed the opportunity to be rid of Roosevelt, who for some months had been making the welkin ring as police commissioner in New York City,[1] neither he nor other men, barring a very few, could view with equanimity the experiment of bringing such a disturber of the peace of living into a great post at Washington. Platt was called to the White House and was told by the President that the appointment must be made and, though it was a most ungrateful communication to the "boss," the step was acquiesced in with the hope, born of assurance, that action which would give him greater satisfaction was near at hand.[2] Roosevelt who had been speaking brashly about war and larger navies was, to his intense joy and to the discomfiture of Mr. Long,[3] named to be Assistant Secretary of the Navy. Storer was to have been Assistant Secretary of State,[4] but he was turned aside and appointed minister to Belgium.

The inauguration of the new President on the 4th of March brought with it an expression of enthusiasm which had marked the hours and days following his election. It was in large degree thanksgiving for deliverance from Bryan, and the attack, which his candidacy for the Presidency had been upon national integrity and private credit, and the sound foundations of industry and trade. It was furthermore a pean of victory on the part of the Republicans, who were, undeniably, however great their errors when given too free a rein in the direction of political affairs, the custodians of a greater portion of the intelligence and competency of the country. They would again control the Presidency and Congress, and guide the destinies of the republic. Campaign clubs from all parts of the country, military bodies from the various states, led in a number of instances by the governors of those states, the representatives of organizations of many kinds, as well as individual citizens, visited Washington to see McKinley inducted into office. The

---

[1] Cf. Corr. of Roosevelt and Lodge, vol. i, p. 263.
[2] T. B. Mott, Myron T. Herrick, pp. 72–4.
[3] H. F. Pringle, Theodore Roosevelt, p. 170.
[4] Corr. of Roosevelt and Lodge, vol. i, p. 254; N. Y. Times, March 6, 1897.

crowds upon the streets, the general festooning and beflagging of the city, the parades of soldiery and of civic societies, and the inaugural ball prospered under a cloudless sky and in warm airs. The picture of President Cleveland working until the last moment to dispatch the business before him and of President-elect McKinley arriving at the White House, their going together to the Capitol, the administering of the oath of office by the Chief Justice and the delivery of the inaugural address was spread before the eyes of the delighted onlookers, and, upon the following day, the readers of our newspapers.

McKinley's statement of his policies was clear and confident; his ringing voice and his easy oratory stirred his hearers, and the sentiments contained in the speech were calculated to meet general approval. His declarations in favor of preserving the national credit, in favor of the ratification of the arbitration treaty with Great Britain, and in support of civil service reform, which were unmistakable in their meaning, were warmly commended by intelligent citizens regardless of party predilections. The allusions to another international conference in the interest of bimetallism, to the restriction of trusts and combinations in industry, to better immigration laws to obviate "a grave peril to the republic," and the upbuilding of an American merchant marine were a phrasing of popular tenets proclaimed during the campaign, and now meant little more than they had then. The announcement of the new President's policy on the tariff was also what could have been reasonably looked for in his opening address. He expressed his favor for indirect rather than direct taxation, for a tariff on imports to protect domestic industry as well as to increase the revenues, which manifestly, as had been said so often by Republicans in Congress, in their newspapers and on the stump, must be increased to obviate public loans and to strengthen the Treasury. Congress should, "at the earliest practicable moment," obey "the voice of the people" as it had been expressed in the recent election, and enact "protective legislation." Reciprocity treaties, similar to those provided for by the tariff law of 1890, were demanded that there might be foreign markets for "surplus agricultural and manufactured products." An extra session of Congress would be called at once "to put the government upon a sound financial and economic basis."

It could be said that the attitude of the President, as it was displayed in his address, was smug—he had uttered only platitudes. But it was such a man, ready to translate its platform into action, that the party demanded at this hour. Mr. Cleveland had been at daggers drawn with Congress. The party system had gone to wreck during the four years past. It would be possible now to restore some degree of harmony between the executive and legislative branches of the government. The quiet, accommodating spirit of the new President, the attitude of a leader being led, might make the House a more orderly body, and could, conceivably, reduce the singular egotism and subdue the wild tempers of those men who had been bringing so much contempt upon the Senate.

Mr. Cleveland's disappearance from view, after he had, with dignity, assisted in the customary way in the transfer of the chief magistracy of the nation to the hands of another, was accompanied by little of the exacerbating language with which he had been assailed during his administration, at any rate from the Republican side. A bond of sympathy at the end had been established between the more estimable elements in the two parties. It is pleasant to recall an exchange of amenities which occurred upon inauguration day when the retiring Democratic President rode with the Republican President-elect to the Capitol. "Now, Mr. Cleveland, is there not something that I may do for you"? Mr. McKinley inquired of the man at his side. "No," replied Mr. Cleveland. "There is nothing that I want personally, but I hope you will remember that the time again may come when there must be another union of the forces which supported honest money against this accursed heresy, for which reason I ask you to use your influence to prevent extreme action calculated to make such a union difficult or impossible." [1]

[1] McElroy, Grover Cleveland, vol. ii, p. 254. A paraphrased conversation, source not given.

Only the slanderous, malignant men in his own party who had abandoned his leadership and gone away to defeat under other banners spoke ill of him. The Atlanta Constitution, in a heated editorial, said that Mr. Cleveland was leaving office "under a greater burden of popular contempt" than had ever been "excited by a public man since the foundation of the government."[1] The Salt Lake City Tribune said that until his name should perish from the earth it would be the "wonder of the world" how he had come to be President of the United States. He had proven himself "all that was brutal in American business and politics." He had used all the power of his office "to give the wealth of the country to a few and make beggars or slaves of the rest."[2] No one, the Irish World declared, would regret his "outgoing" except "the circle of money lenders and trust magnates in whose pockets" he had placed "millions of dollars."[3] The Kansas City Times was of opinion, and asserted, that he had "deceived, betrayed and humiliated" the Democratic party which long since had "stamped him as a political leper and cast him out as one unclean. The reproaches and contumely of the entire American people," the newspaper said, "would accompany him in his retirement."[4]

On the other hand independent newspapers like the New York Times[5] and the New York Evening Post[6] judiciously and appreciatively reviewed the signal personal achievements of his Presidency. Mrs. Cleveland and the children proceeded at once to a new home which he had bought in Princeton, N. J., where he joined them after a fortnight's recreation with friends, fishing and shooting in the South.[7]

The call for an extraordinary session of Congress was issued by Mr. McKinley within 48 hours after his installation in office. It would meet on the 15th of March, at which time the position of the President and his party was plainly restated. The old ground was traversed. The receipts of the government were not

---

[1] Issue of March 4, 1897.
[2] Quoted in N. Y. Literary Digest, March 13, 1897.
[3] Ibid. [4] Quoted in McElroy, op. cit., vol. ii, p. 253.
[5] Issue of March 2, 1897. [6] N. Y. Nation, March 4, 1897.
[7] Public Ledger, Phila., March 5, 1897.

equal to its expenditures. It should not be necessary to increase the public debt in time of peace. A higher tariff law, designed to protect the home market, as well as to afford larger revenues, was immediately imperative. Nothing was said in the message about other legislation. Indeed it was clear that the silver group in the Senate, which was unbroken, would prevent any satisfactory approach to a solution of the money question. If a tariff bill were not confused with other issues it might pass. Nothing was said either about the difficulty of increasing the income from duties on imports when these were to be raised to such a height for the advantage of our own trade and industry as to ward foreign products away from our customs frontiers. The message met the approbation of the protectionists; it was a mad tariff harangue in the sight of the free traders. Mr. McKinley, the New York Times said, had "learned nothing since 1890." [1]

The Republicans were forewarned and forearmed. Reed was again chosen to be Speaker of the House. He again appointed Dingley chairman of the Committee on Ways and Means which had occupied itself during the short session of the last Congress with "tariff hearings" and the compilation of a bill.[2] The several schedules of this measure "to provide revenue for the government and to encourage the industries of the United States" were instantly reported by the committee, and the subject was before the House of Representatives.[3]

There were 357 members in the House, 132 of whom, it appeared, had never sat in Congress before. Two hundred and six were Republicans, 122 Democrats and 29 were classified as Populists and other kinds of independent Radicals.[4] The prospect of early action was favorable. The discussions were perfunctory and brief; the result was in no kind of doubt and no obstruction on the part of the Democrats would avail.[5]

[1] N. Y. Times, March 16, 1897.
[2] House Doc., 54th Cong. 2nd sess., no. 338; E. N. Dingley, Life and Times of Nelson Dingley, Jr., pp. 417–20; N. Y. Nation, April 8, 1897.
[3] The purpose of the Wilson Law of 1894, expressed in its title, was "to reduce taxation" and "to provide revenue for the government."
[4] N. Y. Times, March 16, 1897.
[5] Cf. Stanwood, American Tariff Controversies, vol. ii, p. 379.

Indeed opposition, under the leadership of Bailey, a young firebrand from Texas, was scarcely organized for expression. On the last day of March, in a fortnight, the bill was passed by a vote of 205 to 122. The Republicans rose *en masse* and cheered, the galleries joining in the celebration of an event which, to those who were certain that a protective tariff was the remedy for the people's economic ails, as well as for the fiscal disorders of the state, could be fairly regarded as one calling for jubilant outburst.

The Senate had undergone but little improvement in its complexion. The two parties were deadlocked as in the previous Congress on any money question, however it might be in reference to the tariff. The Silver Republicans remained a force to be reckoned with when proposals for legislation not to their liking appeared. They could defeat any administration measures, as their moods and interests inclined.

Platt succeeded Hill in New York—the boss of one party took the place of the boss of the other without honor to the state or gain to the nation. The "Me Too" man of Conkling, the man who had followed his master out of the Senate when Garfield and Blaine in 1881 would not recognize their right to name all Federal officers in New York state, was now again, after 17 years, returned by his faithful minions in the legislature at Albany to the scene of his exploit. For Ohio Foraker, Republican demagogue and "boss," succeeded Brice, a Democrat whose loss no discriminating citizen mourned, and Hanna occupied John Sherman's vacated chair. "Don" Cameron retired from his place beside Quay as a senator from Pennsylvania and Boies Penrose, a young man who had abandoned the rôle of a "reformer" to embrace "machine" politics, a pupil of Quay, entered in Cameron's stead. A Republican succeeded a Democrat in Indiana—Voorhees made way for Charles W. Fairbanks. In the same manner in Wisconsin a Democrat who had made an enviable name for himself, William F. Vilas, was displaced by a Republican. Republicans succeeded General Palmer in Illinois, Blackburn in Kentucky and Gibson in Maryland.

Nominally there were 49 Republicans, 34 Democrats and 8 Populists. But numbered with the Republicans were such men as Teller, who had bolted the ticket in 1896 and stumped the country for Bryan, and senators from Idaho, Montana, Utah and the Dakotas who would support party policies when and as they wished to do so. There was so much confusion as to allegiance that it was impossible to organize the Senate from a party standpoint.[1] It was the wish, as well as the study of the President, to conciliate divergent interests and bring them into some degree of harmony. The distribution of patronage would await the adjournment of the extra session of Congress. The President when Whitelaw Reid was out of the way had sent John Hay to London,[2] Horace Porter to Paris and Andrew D. White to Berlin, entirely acceptable diplomatic appointments, a promise of high standards for the public service. But, in general, the offices at his disposal were still unbestowed. He would be, for a while, in the advantageous position of all new Presidents. Expectancy and hope of favors to be received would make the senators more compliant. They would, in the nature of the case, be more obliging now than at a later day when the President had been tried and, for one reason or another, had passed over their requests for the salaried posts in their states with which controlling politicians oil their "machines" and maintain their leadership in local areas in our democracy.

But apart from this element of strength, which even Cleveland had had with his party at the extra session of four years ago, when the silver purchase law had been repealed, McKinley had qualities that made for mutual happiness. Though he was a man of decision and was not wanting in the powers of guidance his convictions did not deeply trouble him and he would confer and listen, compose differences, please rather than antagonize state leaders in appointments, just as he preferred to be the advocate of legislative policies to which there was little resistance. His nature led him to take the easy ways. Instead

---

[1] N. Y. Nation, April 22, 1897.
[2] Cf. Tyler Dennett, John Hay, p. 79.

of denying the right of the senators of a state to control the appointments to Federal office within that state, as President Hayes had done in a memorable way, he called these senators to him, sought their advice and recognized the right.[1] When he deviated from the rule it was with an apologetic air which kept him in pleasant relations with those around him. He harbored no resentments, smote no one in answer to grudges. His refusals were kindly and made him few enemies.[2] There was reason to think that the senators, in due time, after they should amend and discuss his tariff bill, perhaps at considerable length, would pass it, especially if some of their demands for offices for their henchmen should be satisfied. Many ignorant and incompetent men were appointed to Federal posts during this period with a view to gaining the favor of Platt, Quay and other "bosses" who had come into the United States Senate that they might be in a position to dicker and deal—in no two cases more unworthily perhaps than when John Russell Young, a journalist in Grub Street, was made Librarian of Congress and the notorious Powderly was named as Commissioner-General of Immigration.[3]

The changes in the bill, before the Senate was done with it, were material—the action of the House had been entirely precipitate and improvement of the measure was generally demanded.[4] But improvement was not given it. The changes, some 872 in number, were compromises and adjustments, now with a purpose of satisfying interested persons, again in the mere haphazard way in which a bill is given form in a popular

[1] N. Y. Nation, March 18 and April 29, 1897.

[2] Cf. H. H. Kohlsaat, From McKinley to Harding, p. 5; J. W. Foster, Dip. Memoirs, vol. ii, pp. 256–7.

[3] Henry Watterson and Alexander K. McClure, Democratic editors who had aided McKinley in the campaign, wished Young to have a place in the cabinet. Quay was enlisted in behalf of an appointment for Young who had taken up residence in Canton during the canvass and sent out to the newspapers flattering accounts of the Republican candidate. (N. Y. Nation, July 8, 1897.) Hanna thought that Powderly's appointment would forward his arrangements in Ohio.—Letters of Watterson and McClure, Jan. 24 and 25, 1897, in McKinley Papers; Hanna to McKinley, July 15, 1897, in ibid.

[4] Cf. N. Y. Times, April 2, 1897; N. Y. Nation, May 13, 1897.

legislative assembly. Senator Aldrich of Rhode Island took charge of the measure and guided it on its way until illness prevented him from remaining in Washington, when the task fell to Allison of Iowa.[1] Many of the familiar charges that manufacturers and other beneficiaries had dictated duties and, indeed, framed entire schedules were bandied about, and there was too much ground for the suspicion of such interferences.[2] Finally, on the 7th of July, more than three months after the bill had been received from the other branch of Congress, it was adopted by a vote of 38 yeas to 28 nays. One Democrat of Louisiana, who was befriending the sugar industry of his state, and four or five silverites, including Jones of Nevada, voted for the bill. Seven Populists refrained from voting.[3] Conferees completed the work in the familiar star chamber fashion, and the President signed it on July 24, 1897. As it left the House the New York Evening Post called it the "most extraordinary measure of the kind ever heard of";[4] it was to the New York Times "a congeries of abominations."[5] Later when it was finally passed it was not much more acceptable to the tariff reformers. It was not made for the people, said the Times, but for the trusts, which would "take its benefits with the most swinish greed."[6] It was "a fresh instance," said the New York Evening Post, of "the recklessness with which the problem of the exchequer" was handled by our statesmen.[7]

The duty on wool which had been repealed in the Wilson-Gorman bill of 1894, as was to have been expected, was restored. This was the principal point which had been won by President Cleveland in his contest with the Senate for free raw materials. The rates in the McKinley law of 1890 were now reimposed; indeed, on some kinds of cheap fleeces for carpet making and

[1] Cf. Stanwood, American Tariff Controversies, vol. ii, pp. 386–7; N. W. Stephenson, N. W. Aldrich, p. 112.

[2] Cf. N. Y. Nation, July 1, 1897.

[3] Cong. Record, 55th Cong. 1st sess., p. 2477; E. N. Dingley, Life and Times of Nelson Dingley, Jr., pp. 423–40.

[4] N. Y. Nation, April 12, 1897. [5] Issues of March 18 and 19, 1897.

[6] Issue of July 26, 1897. [7] N. Y. Nation, July 29, 1897.

similar uses, they now were higher than in 1890. The manufacturers, being compelled to pay the resultant greater price for their material, to which they still made not unnatural objection, were again given compensating duties on their products.

Rates in excess of those in the McKinley law were imposed on linens and silks. A duty of three cents a pound, the same as in 1890, was levied on flax. On cotton goods the level was about as high as, at points slightly lower than, in 1890. A proposal by the Senate to tax raw cotton disappeared in the conference committee.

Hides were made the subject of a duty—they had been on the free list since 1872. The duties of 1890 on china and glassware were restored. In the metal schedules, iron and steel, since that industry had reached a point where the manufacturers themselves said that they had little to fear from foreign competition, the lower rates of 1894 were, in general, retained without important change. On manufactured iron, however, the duties of 1894 were increased. The duties on lead and lead ore were raised to the level at which they had stood in the McKinley law. That "infant industry," tin plate manufacture, which had been the subject of so much solicitous regard by the protectionists in 1890, was now, it seemed, a matter of no moment to any one, and the duty on this article was increased only a small fraction of one cent per pound. Copper was allowed still to come in free; a large export trade made the government's fostering care of this business of no interest to the owners of our extensive copper mines. Coal, which Mr. Cleveland and his friends had wished to put upon the free list, but on which the refractory men in his party had placed a duty of 40 cents a ton in 1894, would now, by the Dingley law, meet a tax of 65 cents; the rate in 1890 had been 75 cents.

Lumber and salt which had been freed from tariff charges in 1894 were again made dutiable. Cotton bagging and cotton ties which were the subjects of heated discussion among Southern planters were once more to be taxed, though at rates below those fixed by the McKinley law. Works of art, except those intended for exhibition, were dutiable.[1] Books and maps, more than 20 years old, and books in foreign languages were to have been taxed, but the protests of colleges, learned societies and men of cultivation generally were so loud that this design was abandoned.[2] No traveller in foreign lands could reenter the country with more than $100 worth of new purchases in his luggage. The exemption in the Wilson, as in the McKinley law, covered apparel which had been worn and personal effects appropriate for use and designed for the traveller's comfort and convenience while on his journey, without naming a limit of value.[3]

The duty on sugar which had been the bone of contention in 1894 and which, it was said, had been fixed by the "Trust," must still be made satisfactory to the "members from Havemeyer." Raw sugar by the McKinley law had come in free— by the Wilson-Gorman law in 1894 it was subject to a duty of 40 per cent. *ad valorem*. A new scheme for the levy was now devised and the duty was practically doubled. This arrangement satisfied the cane planters of Louisiana and the beet farmers. On refined sugar there was a differential for the "Trust" of one-eighth of one cent a pound, a rate which extended to that group of American business men nearly as much favor as they had enjoyed at the hands of Mr. Gorman and his friends, who had been active in that behalf in the Senate in 1894, and who still stood at their accustomed posts.[4]

A still clearer view of the manner in which the bill, generally, had been compiled was afforded by a reference to the provision regarding an additional tax on imports in other than American bottoms.[5] This scheme for building up a national mercantile

---

[1] Paintings and sculpture were taxed 20 per cent. ad valorem under the classification, "Miscellaneous Manufactures."

[2] N. Y. Nation, March 25, April, 1 and July 22, 1897.

[3] Sec. 2 of act, item no. 697; cf. Tarbell, The Tariff in Our Times, p. 243; N. Y. Nation, March 25, 1897.

[4] F. W. Taussig, Tariff Hist. of the U. S., pp. 350-2. What the tariff meant to the "Trust" is supposed to have been represented by an increase in the price of the common stock of the American Sugar Refining Company—between March and July the price rose from 110 to 146.—N. Y. Nation, July 22, 1897.

[5] Sec. 22 of the act.

marine at the expense of the foreign trade of the country had been flourishing in dark places, and, on this occasion, it was surreptitiously inserted in the bill by a clerk at the behest of Stephen B. Elkins, a politician of national notoriety, who was now a United States senator from West Virginia. He openly spoke of the part he had played, pointing with satisfaction, indeed, to the success of the trick. By good fortune the provision was soon held to be invalid by the Attorney-General.[1]

"Reciprocity" appeared again in the Dingley law, as in the McKinley law, in answer to the promise of the national Republican platform of 1896. Clauses authorized the President to suspend the permissive provisions of the free list with reference to tea, coffee and tonka and vanilla beans in case any country with which we traded should impose duties "reciprocally unequal and unreasonable," at their customs frontiers, on our products. The privilege was rather empty of meaning. Sugar and hides which had been free in 1890 were, by Blaine's "reciprocity" scheme, the basis of international tariff negotiations. But these articles were now dutiable and could not be used in exacting concessions from the governments in Latin America.

With reference to other countries of higher rank in civilization the President, by the Dingley law, was entrusted with power, after securing "reciprocal and equivalent concessions" in favor of products and manufactures of the United States, to reduce, to rates named by Congress, duties on crude tartar, brandies, champagnes, wines, paintings and statuary. It was hoped by this provision to make bargains with France and, perhaps, other European countries.

Furthermore, a section of the law authorized the negotiation of commercial treaties by means of which duties, generally, might be reduced. The President might, within two years, make a change, to continue for a period of five years, in the tariff rate on any article, if this change should be not in excess of

[1] N. Y. Nation, Sep. 30, 1897.

20 per cent. But all such treaties must be ratified by the Senate, and be "approved" as well by the House, insuperable obstacles to any progress in the direction of tariff reform.[1]

It had been clear enough from the first that very little could come from the extra session on the subject of the currency.[2] So much was foreordained, though those who had voted for McKinley because of the menace of Bryan's theories about money, aimed to keep the President on firm ground on the question which had been the issue in the campaign and upon which the election had been won. The gold standard as a basis of value should be affirmed, the greenbacks must be retired, the currency must be rationally reformed to afford security in the future from the scaling and repudiation of debt. In January, 1897, a meeting of representatives of commercial bodies in all parts of the country had been held in Indianapolis. Delegates were present from 29 states and territories. Definite recommendations were made, in line with the best opinion of the country, for the guidance of the new administration. Congress would be asked to authorize the President to appoint a commission to report a plan of reform. Failing in this the chairman of the conference, H. H. Hanna, should select the members of such a body.[3] The Honest Money Leagues of the campaign continued their activities; new organizations committed to sound money principles were formed.[4]

Mr. McKinley's remarks on the currency question in his inaugural address had been satisfactory.[5] But when, in his message to the assembled Congress, less than a fortnight later, he omitted all allusion to that topic there was mistrust, and reason for it.[6] Now and again, as the weeks passed, while

[1] Sec. 4 of the act; Taussig, Tariff Hist. of the U. S., p. 354; N. Y. Nation, July 8, 1897.

[2] Cf. N. Y. Tribune, May 1, 1897.

[3] The commission should "make a thorough investigation of the monetary affairs and needs of the country in all relations and aspects and make proper suggestions as to any evils found to exist and the remedies therefor."—Cong. Record, 55th Cong. 1st sess., p. 2948. Cf. N. Y. Nation, Jan. 21, Feb. 11 and 25, 1897.

[4] N. Y. Nation, March 4 and 18, 1897. [5] Ibid., March 11, 1897

[6] Ibid., March 18, 1897.

the House awaited the determination of the Senate on the tariff bill, action was urged upon the President. He could, at least, appoint the suggested commission to start an investigation and recommend legislation. Now and again it was thought that he was on the eve of taking such a course. But his counsellors told him that he would thereby imperil the tariff—the silver Republicans in the Senate whose votes were needed, if the tariff were to receive the approval of that body, must undergo no laceration of feeling. To the end the hope of a message from the President was not abandoned. Finally Quay, it was said, had put the project entirely out of the President's mind and Congress would adjourn without hearing from the White House.[1] At the last moment, however, a few hours before adjournment, Mr. McKinley rather languidly suggested the appointment of the much discussed commission. He had not acted before, since he believed, he said, that the tariff for providing the government with "adequate" revenues was the "most pressing subject for settlement." He now reverted to the words in his inaugural address concerning the currency which the people at the late national election had clearly said should be kept "stable in value and equal to that of the most advanced nations of the world." There should be "early action" by Congress, and he urged that authority be given him to name a number of "well informed citizens of different parties" who should arrive at conclusions, to be made the subject of a report on or before the 1st day of November next.[2]

The House, "under whip and spur,"[3] passed the bill to give effect to the plan,[4] knowing that it would meet with no attention in the Senate which, after some brief "pollyfoxing" as to its reference to the Committee on Finance, was its fate.[5]

Nothing remained now but for Mr. Hanna, the chairman of the Indianapolis conference, to appoint the commission. He did so.[6] Ex-Senator Edmunds of Vermont was chosen to be its chairman and, at the end of the year 1897, it presented

[1] Cf. Cong. Record, 55th Cong. 1st sess., p. 2952.
[2] Cong. Record, 55th Cong. 1st sess., p. 2948.   [3] Ibid., p. 2949.
[4] Ibid., pp. 2962-3.   [5] N. Y. Nation, July 29, 1897.
[6] Ibid., July 29 and Oct. 7, 1897.

a report; it proposed "a consistent, straightforward, deliberately planned monetary system," which it commended to the attention of Congress.[1] The completion of the work was, said the New York Times, "the most important event in the history of the long struggle of the country with the errors, disorder and peril originating in the currency measures of the Civil War." [2]

The price of the McKinley tariff had been the Sherman silver purchase law—the silver men in 1897 were conciliated by duties on lead, hides, coarse wools and some other products of the ranches, highlands and mountain slopes of the states whose interests they were sent to Washington to defend,[3] and by inaction on the subject of the currency. They got more, though it was a bribe which no longer beguiled the older heads among them—another international monetary commission. Senator Wolcott of Colorado was a dapper young lawyer of Denver who had been unwilling to follow Teller out of the party in 1896. He led and kept the Republican organization in the field in his state, though it was overwhelmed at the polls. He had taken occasion, if at a late day, since he had a turn for oratory, to rise in the Senate and to hold a brief for England in reference to the Venezuela boundary, thereby causing his name to be mentioned in the press, and to be pronounced by the people, of Great Britain. He had thus prepared the way for a trip to Europe. McKinley, before he had yet taken office, invited Wolcott to confer, during his absence, with the heads of governments, and to canvass the prospects of international bimetallism. The unofficial legate passed from one capital to another, and was received, dined and otherwise entertained by statesmen and the bigwigs of silverism of which each country had a few, whose names were household words in the mouths of our own silverites. He timed his return so that it would synchronize with McKinley's inauguration and was on the ground

---

[1] N. Y. Nation, Jan. 6, and July 28, 1898; J. L. Laughlin, Report of the Monetary Commission.

[2] Issue of Jan. 3, 1898.

[3] Cf. Stanwood, American Tariff Controversies, vol. ii, pp. 386 and 388.

for the extraordinary session of the new Congress, having found out nothing that was not known before.[1]

Meantime the dying Congress had provided for a new international conference which the Republicans had held before the eyes of the silver men in the campaign of 1896, and which the latter, in the Senate and the House, though they recognized that it was no more than a political trick, did not oppose. Nor did President Cleveland think the scheme worth his active opposition, and the bill authorizing the new President to appoint, and the Treasury to pay the passage to Europe of, a commission of five or more members, to secure by "international agreement a fixity of relative value' between gold and silver as money, by means of a common ratio between these metals, with free mintage at such ratio," was approved. He might appoint one or more persons to prepare the way for such a conference.[2]

In April, 1897, McKinley selected three men to pursue, as the New York Evening Post called it, the *ignis bimetallicus:* [3] Wolcott; Adlai E. Stevenson, the Vice-President of the last administration, whose desertion of Cleveland on the money question was well remembered, and General Charles J. Paine, a rich man in Boston, who had been Wolcott's travelling companion in 1896, and whose fame as a national figure rested upon the building and sailing of yachts in defense of the "American cup." [4] The envoys spent six months in Europe, making extraordinary proposals to England, with or without the authority of President McKinley,[5] receiving pleasant social attentions, largely because of Ambassador Hay's finesse and Wolcott's attractive personality,[6] and returning in November,

---

[1] N. Y. Nation, Jan. 7, Feb. 18 and 25, 1897; N. Y. Times, March 5, 1897.

[2] App. Ann. Cyclop. for 1897, pp. 188–9.

[3] N. Y. Nation, April 15, 1897.   [4] N. Y. Times, April 13, 1897.

[5] N. Y. Nation, Oct. 28, 1897.

[6] Hay to McKinley in McKinley Papers. They were given an audience by the Queen, Hay looking on with his unfailing sense of humor at Adlai Stevenson in knee breeches who was now and again surveying his legs furtively, and wondering what they would think of it all in Bloomington, Ill.—Ibid.

1897, with the information that, the government of India being unwilling to cooperate, Great Britain could give no encouragement to our emissaries.[1]

Anyhow the entire foundation of the silver cause was on the point of crumbling away. The demand for gold was leading to a rapid increase in the supply. Exploration, discovery and improved processes for recovering it from its ores were swelling the world's annual output. The contention of the silver miners, and of the farmers of the West, who owed money on mortgages or were otherwise in debt, that there was not enough gold in existence to qualify the metal to serve as a standard of value was falling to the ground. Bryan and his party were advocates of inflation by the introduction of silver into the currency of the country—something of the same nature by a slower and surer process might be gained by an augmentation of the gold supply.

In Colorado itself, which complained so bitterly of the injustice done its silver interests by the "gold bugs," the production of gold was increasing by leaps and bounds. In 1897 that state led all the states of the Union with an output of about $20,000,000.[2] By the intensive treatment of low grade ores the Leadville district was producing nearly as much gold as silver, and at Cripple Creek where a "boom" had followed discoveries and developments in 1892, 1893, and 1894, comparable to the Leadville excitement of 15 years before, the output was in excess of $1,000,000 a month.[3] It was said that a tract four miles square in Cripple Creek was the richest gold-yielding ground in the world.[4] An international gold mining convention met in Denver, in July, 1897.[5]

In South Africa, in the Kaffir country, in and around Johannesburg, the strife for the wealth which comes from the uncovering of auriferous deposits was attracting great numbers

---

[1] Report of Director of Mint for 1898, pp. 535–53 in House Doc., 55th Cong. 3rd sess., no. 8; N. Y. Nation, Oct. 28, 1897; A. Nevins, Henry White, p. 128.
[2] Report of Director of Mint for 1898, p. 451.
[3] App. Ann. Cyclop. for 1898, p. 135.
[4] Ibid. for 1895, p. 146. [5] Ibid. for 1897, p. 142.

of men. But of yet more importance was the news from a land under the Arctic Circle penetrated by tributaries of the Yukon River, one of which, the Klondike, gave its name to the region.[1] Title to it rested partly with Great Britain and partly with us, through our stake in Alaska. The country was mountainous and covered with timber. For a considerable part of the year, the water courses were bound with ice and the earth was frozen solid. Only by toiling through the snow and working excitedly in the short summer could the frantic adventurers, who soon crowded the trails into the new El Dorado, recover the coveted wealth from the placers. Geologists said that the quartz had been ground down by glacial action—the gold rested in and about the beds of the streams. Those who had reached this wilderness returned with accounts of fabulous treasure obtained in a few weeks.[2] In August, 1896, three men on Bonanza Creek washed out $14,200 in eight days, and, in the summer of 1897, the country was aswarm with fortune hunters. Claims were staked and changed hands at swiftly rising prices. The hardships suffered by the gold diggers and their great gains were told about in each day's newspapers to start more men away to the north. A town called Dawson City, in which the first house was built at the approach of winter in 1896, had a population the following summer of 5,000, with four or five kinds of churches, saw mills, an opera house and a hospital. Food which must be brought through Chilkoot Pass in southern Alaska, over a long and difficult route, cost a dollar a pound.[3]

The output of gold for the entire United States in 1897 was $57,363,000—$4,000,000 more than in the previous year. It had been only about $36,000,000 in 1893.[4] The production of the world in 1897 had risen to $237,000,000—it had been $202,000,000 in 1896.[5] Australia in a year had increased its

[1] From the Indian name of the river—Throndink.
[2] N. Y. Nation, July 29, 1897.
[3] Cf. App. Ann. Cyclop. for 1897, pp. 443–5.
[4] Report of Director of Mint in Report of Sec. of Treas. for 1898, pp. 627, 631.
[5] Ibid., p. 453.

output from $45,000,000 to more than $55,000,000; South Africa from $44,000,000 to $58,000,000, and Canada, due to the activity in the Klondike, from $2,800,000 to $6,000,000.[1]

In another year, during the calendar year 1898, our gold mines yielded $64,000,000, of which $23,000,000 came from Colorado,[2] and the production in the world had increased from $239,000,000 to $287,000,000, South Africa bounding forward to $80,000,000 and Canada to about $14,000,000,[3] an amount for the Klondike which in two years more would be doubled.[4] The Director of the Mint said that the stock of gold in the world was being increased at a greater rate annually than in the period from 1850 to 1860 during the excitement which attended the discoveries in California and Australia. He thought that the yield would soon exceed $400,000,000 a year.[5]

That the white population of the Sandwich Islands would again seek annexation was certain, now that the political party which had befriended their cause at the time of the oversetting of the old Polynesian native government had returned to power. They had been living for three or four years under a republican system of government, fashioned after that of the United States, the president being Sanford B. Dole, the annexationist who had been active in the management of the revolution. He had sought connection by cable with the United States and various efforts were made to obtain the construction of such a convenience at our expense. The agitation in behalf of annexion at no time ceased, either in Hawaii itself or in this country, based as it was on commercial interest and the feeling in the United States of men who were usually called jingoes that we should enlarge our influence, as well as our national limits, whenever opportunity knocked at the door. The people, or such part of them as were civilized, were mainly of American origin; the islands "belonged" geographically and commercially to the United States; "manifest destiny" was

[1] Report of Director of Mint for 1898, pp. 630–1.
[2] Ibid for 1898, pp. 236–7.
[3] Ibid., p. 334.   [4] Ibid for 1901, p. 441.
[5] Ibid for 1899, p. 192. In separate reprint, p. 6.

still in the air.[1] The obese, much ridiculed and, perhaps, defamed ex-Queen Liliuokalani, the Queen "Lil" of our newspapers, had been put in prison for five years in connection with a plot to restore her dynasty and, upon being pardoned by the Dole government, made her way to our shores.[2] She resided for a time in Brookline in the suburbs of Boston, and was one of the witnesses of McKinley's inauguration from a comfortable seat for which she had applied to Secretary of State Olney, and which was procured for her by his valetudinarian successor, John Sherman.[3] The scheme which had been thwarted by Cleveland in 1893 was not long in coming to light. Two or three of the annexationists, who had been hovering about Washington, appeared at the State Department and, on June 16, 1897, Mr. Sherman signed the treaty. Hawaii was to be ceded to us and the islands were to have the status of a territory in our Federal system.

Sherman made a report to the President, explaining and justifying his course, which was given to the press, and McKinley at once transmitted the treaty to the Senate with a message advocating its ratification. Annexation, the President said, was "a necessary and fitting sequel to the chain of events" which had, "from a very early period in our history, controlled the intercourse and prescribed the association of the United States and the Hawaiian Islands." Under such circumstances what the treaty would effect was "not a change," it was "a consummation," and so on. There were senators who said that they would remain in Washington all summer, if it were necessary to do so, in order to defeat the project.[4] The newspapers which had opposed it in 1893 resumed their assaults. Annexation was a "job," a "plot," said the New York Times; only that could have kept "the vicious scheme alive all these years." Did the American people wish "to add to the Union an Asiatic state lying 2,000 miles from the mainland and twice as far from the national capital"? The President did not realize

---

[1] Cf. App. Ann. Cyclop. for 1896, p. 341; N. Y. Nation, Jan. 13, 1898.
[2] N. Y. Nation, Dec. 17, 1896.   [3] N. Y. Times, March 6, 1897.
[4] N. Y. Times, June 17, 1897.

what he was doing. On the other hand it was said that he very well knew what he was about; he had felt the force which was behind the movement—he was the puppet of the Senate Committee on Foreign Relations. He was registering the will of the clique which had been fostering the enterprise from the first day.[1]

The authorities of the Hawaiian republic at Honolulu ratified the treaty at once as a matter of course. A protest filed at a mass meeting in that city was feeble, though it undoubtedly voiced the sentiments of a great body of the native islanders and it served to nerve the old opposition to the scheme in this country. The ex-Queen Liliuokalani in Washington issued a statement expressive of her dissent.[2] To forward action by this government Dole came to the United States and visited President McKinley.[3] A publicity bureau directed an agitation in the press.[4]

The annexationists again circulated reports that Great Britain would be ill served if we should take Hawaii. Her hands, it was said, were outstretched for the capture of outlying islets in the Pacific which had been brought under Hawaiian influence, and her agents were seeking an opportunity to foment a new movement for the restoration of the monarchy, a charge which her ambassador at Washington, Sir Julian Pauncefote, was put to the trouble to deny.[5] The scheme was again to sleep. It was not possible, in spite of a great body of public sentiment which was awakened in favor of annexation and which was violently expressed by some of the senators, to secure for ratification the votes of a number of them equal to two-thirds of the membership.

The President's message to Congress when it met for its regular session in December, 1897, congratulated the country

[1] N. Y. Times, June 16, 17, and 18, and N. Y. Nation, June 24, 1897.
[2] N. Y. Times, June 18, 1897.
[3] Described as "the first president of a republic known to history who travelled round the world trying to sell his own country to a foreign power."—N. Y. Nation, Feb. 17, 1898; N. Y. Times, Feb. 9, 1898.
[4] N. Y. Nation, Jan. 20 and 27, 1898.
[5] Cf. App. Ann. Cyclop. for 1897, p. 388; ibid., for 1898, p. 323; N. Y. Nation, Feb. 3 and March 24, 1898.

upon the "timeliness and wisdom" of the passage of the tariff act, although it was not yet certain that the measure would greatly increase the public revenues. Time would determine its "permanent value." No one would wish to withhold from it a "fair trial." Secretary of the Treasury Gage presented much commended suggestions concerning the currency. These were incorporated in the President's message, forming a clear statement of the need of action which should withdraw the greenbacks, take the government out of the banking business and hold all the country's money at par with gold. Some allusions were made to Mr. Wolcott and the "special envoys" who had gone to Europe to talk about silver. The cause of the Nicaragua Canal, the President said, had been committed on July 24th, upon the adjournment of the extra session of Congress, to a commission which was to continue the surveys and examinations authorized by act of March 2, 1895. John A. Kasson of Iowa, whom the President had appointed a "special commissioner plenipotentiary" to negotiate reciprocity treaties with foreign countries in the interest of an increase in "the volume of our commercial exchanges," was conducting negotiations with governments in Europe and America. The inferiority of our merchant marine was "justly humiliating to the national pride"—it should be "improved and enlarged," though no definite suggestion as to a policy on this head was proposed. New docks to accommodate naval vessels which were in commission and were under construction should be built on the Atlantic and Pacific coasts. The naval force of the United States was "formidable"—it should be enlarged, especially in the interest of coast defense.

If the impression created by Mr. McKinley's official papers, as by his speech, was one of graceful fluency rather than, as in Mr. Cleveland's messages, of sincerity, conviction and earnest understanding there was, at the same time, a knowledge that he was the mouthpiece of his party. He was giving expression to a body of feeling which he controlled and which he, in greater degree than any President in recent times, could translate into effective action. But all orderly progress of policy would soon be violently interfered with by a war which, if it were to be one of the most ludicrous of the national disturbances bearing this name, barring our hostilities with the Indians, would be fraught with consequences of influence upon the very nature of the republic and would greatly alter the American outlook. New issues would be injected into our politics. Whether the Dingley law could and would produce sufficient income to support the government, a question upon which so much heated argument had been spent, was destined to take its place in the limbo of forgotten things. New tax laws, other interests and problems would soon possess the minds of the people and carry the country away from the tariff and the currency around which at least five Presidential contests had revolved.

Cuba was a fair island, almost within hailing distance of the Florida Keys. It was the "pearl of the Antilles." With "the Havana" we had long carried on a lucrative trade. Our ships from the earliest days sailed to and departed from the harbor. We sold our products to the people of Spanish blood who lived in the city and tilled the land of which it was the capital town, and took away sugar, tobacco and tropical fruits. Spain found here and in the island of Porto Rico, a few miles to the south and east, a last foothold in the American hemisphere. She had lost a great colonial empire which had been hers by right of discovery in the heydey of her power. Nearly all of it had gone as the civilization of the rest of the world had advanced and she rested where she had been, or fell backward, and she deserves no sympathy at the hands of history. Her capacity in civil administration diminished even as she declined in her skill at arms. The heritage she had left us on this continent was merely a people of her own stock, degenerated by mixture with native races and the negro slaves from Africa, who, while they had gained their political liberty distinguished themselves little by the use of it. Henry Clay and James G. Blaine had expended much sentiment upon the Latin republics. But there was a full realization by well informed men that it was, in considerable degree, misplaced. Their progress in government was slow and the population was ignorant, unquiet and wanting in the moral fibre which had given value to the Northern races of men. The note of brotherhood which politicians aimed to inject into our relationships with the peoples living to the south never rang true in the ears of North Americans and would not do so now in reference to Cuba and the Cubans.

Whatever our view of the republics which had risen on the ruins of Spain's old colonial empire she, where her sway continued, could have no friends. Her political system could only be regarded as effete. A long record of injustices and cruelties could be cited against her. Bull fighting, in which the shedding of the blood of poor beasts was a popular joy, was a verification of something uncivilized in the national character. Repeated risings of the inhabitants of Cuba, repeated efforts, attended with undoubted barbarity, to put down the "revolutions," one of which within memory had lasted for ten years, from 1868 until 1878, attested to the existence of conditions of which we could not be forever unmindful. Adventurers shouting "Cuba Libre" coming from the island to the cities of our Eastern seaboard, and striving to involve us in their rebellions, selling bonds of mythical "republics," collecting arms, enlisting soldiers and sending out filibustering parties in violation of the law of nations had brought trouble throughout many years upon our State Department. It was particularly exasperating to know that much of their activity was actuated entirely by a desire to entangle us in their domestic affairs. They maintained a revolutionary bureau in New York, they organized mass meetings, they wrote for the American press. Spanish military authorities were dealing harshly with the rebels in an effort to restore order. Many of the stories of atrocity, however, were inventions to feed the minds of classes, especially on our Atlantic coast, who, it was hoped, might be so inflamed by the outrages done a small liberty-loving people, that we should be compelled to intercede in their behalf. It was not difficult to fan those hates which one nation must feel before it is ready to make war upon another.

The Spanish immigration to this country was small; that element in our population was negligible, and, of all the national groups of Europeans, this one, barring the Turks, was, probably, in the mind of the American masses, the least likely to find sympathy and meet defense.

The situation in Cuba in 1893 and 1894 again grew ominous. Markets—including our own, due to our dispositions as to sugar in the Wilson-Gorman tariff law—were closed to the products of the island—even Spain imposed high duties upon them. With low prices came crushing taxes for the support of corrupt officials and the soldiers which were imported to subdue popular aspirations for self government.[1] With the aid of the revolutionists who were exiles in North and South America the rebels at home, at the instigation of a New York Cuban, José Marti, an orator as well as a soldier, rose in February, 1895, in a new insurrection. Some of the provinces are wooded and mountainous. Here bands of men roved for a guerrilla war upon Spanish troops sent out from the garrisoned towns to capture them. Pursuit was difficult. The Captain-General, with such facilities as were accorded him from Madrid, could not guard the entire coast line. War material for the rebels was landed from small boats at little harbors. Fresh troops were despatched from Spain; martial law was proclaimed; arrests were made; Morro Castle at Havana was filled with political prisoners. A new Captain-General, Field Marshal Martinez Campos, who had brought the long revolution to an end in 1878, arrived as soon as the gravity of the rising was understood. He was promised an army of 40,000 men. Meantime the insurgents had been reinforced by Antonio Maceo, a mulatto who had come with an expedition from Costa Rica, and Maximo Gomez, a native of San Domingo. Both had played prominent parts in the insurrection of 1868–78. A new Cuban republic was proclaimed, a president was elected, General Gomez became commander-in-chief of the revolutionary forces and a campaign

---

[1] F. E. Chadwick, Relations of the U. S. and Spain, Diplomacy, pp. 403–5.

was begun to secure foreign and, particularly, American sympathy for the insurgent cause. Diplomatic agents were sent to Washington and other capitals. The Junta in New York was supplied with new issues of Cuban bonds for distribution to politicians and journalists. They cost the price of the paper and the printing and could be issued in any desired amount.[1]

The troops from Spain at first were mere boys, unqualified in every way for combat with the hardy negroids who had been born on the island. They could not fight with the insurgents who pursued the methods of bandits, lying in ambush and shooting from swamps and from behind trees. They died in swarms from the fevers which were virulent during the rainy season. The situation was desperate. Spain increased her force to 80,000 men and now brought forward her best soldiery, the flower of her army, built and purchased new naval vessels the better to protect the insular coast line against filibusters, and prepared for a determined effort to put down the rebellion.[2] One skirmish, one massacre, one barbarity followed another. Revolutionists who were captured were shot or sent to prisons in Africa. The insurgents knew every foot of their terrain. Their constitutions were proof against disease germs and the weather. They hung on the heels of the soldiers and the police, always avoiding pitched battles. It was made plain to Madrid that the revolution was as formidable as the ten years' rebellion of 1868-78. Estates were ravished, isolated garrisons captured, railroads destroyed, towns burned and the larger cities threatened. A veritable reign of terror, directed by Gomez and Maceo, prevailed in practically all the provinces.[3] Campos had had a reputation for humane strategy.[4] He was called the "pacificator" because of his earlier successes in winning the Cubans back to the crown. Plainly this time he had failed. He would make way for General

---

[1] N. Y. Nation, April 7 and 14, 1898; E. F. Atkins, Sixty Years in Cuba, p. 212.

[2] Chadwick, Relations of the U. S. and Spain, Diplomacy, pp. 431-2.

[3] H. H. Sargent, Campaign of Santiago, vol. i, p. 18 and app. B.

[4] Chadwick, Relations of the U. S. and Spain, Diplomacy, p. 430.

Weyler, a man whose name stood for harsh and relentless measures. Now another policy would be adopted. The new Captain-General signalized his arrival by proclamations which spoke of rigorous action at once. The methods of the insurgents were barbarous; they must be met, if anything were to be achieved, by warfare in kind. The death penalty was prescribed for all who should aid or abet the rebellion. Weyler was called the "Butcher," though it was a name which could as well have been given to Gomez.

The insurgents had gathered the non-combatants into concentration camps that crops might not be grown and that there should be no food for the Spanish troops, or for the people who sympathized with them in the garrison towns. Weyler would adopt similar measures on a greater scale. He would form camps to serve his purposes in his war upon the guerrillas who haunted the hills. If they would starve him and his troops they would be made to see that he could starve them also. The entire civilian population—women, children and old men—in extensive sections of the island were drawn in from the fields, their lands laid waste and their dwellings burned.[1] The year ended without Weyler's gaining any of the objects which he boastfully had said that he would soon achieve. In 13 months, ending in April, 1896, Spain had sent an army of 120,000 men to the island.[2] More were soon on shipboard for transport thither and the war was costing her $6,000,000 a month, a huge sum for a government so impoverished as hers.[3] Raids, murder by dynamite guns, the plunder of towns, the destruction of fair estates, the burning of sugar mills, assassination, massacre with the deadly machete, arrest, imprisonment, went on month after month, with no credit either to Spain or to her rebels, and with increasing resentment of feeling on the part of the people of the United States as they contemplated the tragic scene.

Filibustering could not be controlled. Manufacturers eager

---

[1] Richardson, vol. x, p. 141; N. Y. Nation, Nov. 18, 1897; G. C. Musgrave, Under Three Flags in Cuba, chap. ii.
[2] N. Y. Nation, July 9, 1896.   [3] Ibid., May 21, 1896.

to sell rifles, cartridges, gunpowder, dynamite, revolvers and knives, owners glad to hire their ships to carry out the cargoes, seamen ready for any adventure kept the waters between our coast and the shores of Cuba filled with suspicious craft. As a neutral it was the duty of our navy to prevent this trade; it was Spain's task, with revenue cutters and other boats with which she had surrounded the island, to capture the blockade runners.

The propaganda in behalf of the Cuban insurgents was promoted by two New York newspapers. With zeal they embraced the opportunity which the situation seemed to afford. The debauchery of the entire idea of journalism in this country was begun in the New York Herald under the elder Bennett and then under his son, who for many years breathed the pleasant atmosphere of Paris, while still owning and editing, at arm's length, the paper which came to him by the law of descent. Its conduct was flighty, it delighted in exciting feats. It departed entirely from the standards set by a press which was dignified and responsible. It dealt in rumor and falsehood. It printed offensive references to the entirely private affairs of men and women made prominent by their wealth, their achievements, or their social position. To "interview" a king, a president, a prime minister, a general leading an army, a high functionary of the church, likely on some wholly inconsequent topic, or to make pretense of doing so, and to lay the result before the public at some great real or presumptive outlay of money, or to perform some similar deed of distinction, was each day's task of the unfortunate wights whom Bennett hired to do his will.

But this paper faded in rivalry with those who could do the same thing in still more sensational ways. It was the ambition of Mr. Pulitzer when he acquired control of the New York World to plumb our mixed society, especially in a great city which was being fed each year by practically unrestricted immigration, and introduce the newspaper to lower and lower popular strata. Plainly this was the task of the man who wished to gain an immense circulation for his journal, secure advertisements and make the greatest possible amount of money out of his property. The World, under the Pulitzer control, was at first, a rather rugged organ of democratic opinion. It advocated what it believed to be popular causes in an outspoken and independent spirit, though its news columns were marred by great "headlines" announcing its discoveries and exposures, and its attention to crime and scandal and impertinences aimed at individuals were proof of the material end which the owner had in view. He averred in 1888 that his average daily circulation had risen to 285,000 which was twice that of the New York Herald, his nearest competitor, that it was more than five times the circulation of the Times or the Tribune.[1] He was timidly illustrating his pages with small wood cuts from drawings by a new kind of "journalist," the "newspaper artist." These were indifferent likenesses of men, with now and again a cartoon breathing rough humor or impudence. Gains came rapidly. In 1893 the World was boasting of a circulation of more than 400,000. But such progress was slow compared to that which immediately ensued. Mr. Pulitzer had projected an evening edition of his newspaper. At the end of 1896 the World averred that it printed 820,000 copies in a day which, of course, included both morning and evening editions. It had doubled its circulation in four years and it was the "largest circulation," so its owner and promoter said, "ever reached by any newspaper printed in any language." This result had been achieved by the increase of the amount of silly and sordid matter published in the journal. It seemed, indeed, as any student of the subject may learn by comparison of the files of our American gazettes, that the fall of the newspaper from its place as an organ of opinion and an agency of public instruction could reach no greater depth.

By such means was the World making itself of interest to ever widening circles of uninformed people, though still more was done by the editor to attach it to the illiterate by the astounding development of the picture which the buyer could enjoy without spelling out the printed line. This picture came

[1] N. Y. World, April 1, 1889.

from a cut made from a crude drawing, often of so great a size as to occupy half a page. Entirely imaginative illustrations of shipwrecks,[1] railway disasters, murders, and human disorders generally so filled some of the pages that not a column was left for reading matter. In one week in December, 1896, in addition to the pictorial treatment of subjects of the classes already indicated there were great portrayals of women felling trees in the hills of New York state, of a Cherokee Indian being married to a white woman in the New York city hall, of the shooting and killing of camels which had contracted an incurable malady at Coney Island, of a fat man squeezing through a gate in a magistrate's court, of an old man embracing his young wife on their honeymoon, of an architect who had starved himself and gone insane in order to "save" his wife, who was shown at his bedside, together with a quantity of caricatures of well known citizens larger and more insolent in tone than ever before. Everything which it was conceived could be set before the ignorant in pictures for their easy use was treated in this way, and in the most inflaming manner, day after day and year after year, to excite wonder that men could be found with the gift of so shrewdly sensing the crass tastes of the masses and the willingness to devote their energies to such ends.[2]

A spur to the World's activity was found in the determination of the son of a very rich man in the West, one of the California "pioneers," to outmaneuver Mr. Pulitzer in his chosen field. An old and unworthy sheet called the Journal was purchased in September, 1895, by William Randolph Hearst.[3] This young man—he was 28 at the time of his father's death in 1891—already for some time in control of a newspaper in California, seemed to be unaffected by a social sense; his obligations to the public—if he felt them—were suppressed; all his ambitions appeared to be personal. He took from Mr. Pulitzer many of the writers and "artists" who had been developed into their

[1] For the World's picture of the explosion of the Maine see issue of Feb. 17, 1898.
[2] Cf. N. Y. World, Dec. 7-12, 1896. The issues for any other week would be as useful for illustration.
[3] Walter Millis, The Martial Spirit, pp. 37, 42-3.

strange proficiency in the World's offices and attached them to his staff, while he reached out to gain buyers for the sheets which fell from his printing presses among classes of the people already captivated by Mr. Pulitzer, or yet free of any knowledge of reading.[1] The race between these two lusty contestants for the honors of what came to be called "yellow" journalism was fast. Money was spent in wild ventures. Scruples kept the rivals from no deed which they conceived might enable them to gain their objects. The Century Club in New York, the Union League, libraries in all parts of the country barred both papers from their reading rooms.[2] Together Pulitzer and Hearst saw in Cuba a chance to play an heroic role. They would "free" the oppressed inhabitants of the island from the heel of a hated monarchy. We should actively take the part of the liberty-loving Cubans, drive out Weyler, the "Butcher," release the poor people from the concentration camps, the concentrados or, as they were more generally called, the reconcentrados, set up a republic, with Havana as its capital, or annex the country and make it a part of the United States. The search for and description of Spanish "outrages" in the World and the Journal, to be copied day by day in the press in other parts of the country, always distorted and often wholly false, brought us measurably nearer to grave international complications.[3]

President Cleveland, already in his message to Congress in December, 1895, drew attention to the flagrant conditions which prevailed. Whatever our sympathies, said he, we must "honestly fulfil every international obligation." Nor should individuals violate the laws of neutrality by which we, as a people, were bound.[4]

Of our failure to exercise a proper restraint upon the movements of our filibusters Spain informed us repeatedly through

[1] Cf. N. Y. Nation, May 7, 1896.
[2] Ibid., March 11 and April 1, 1897; N. Y. Times, March 3, 8, 18 and 22, 1897.
[3] Cf. N. Y. Nation, March 3 and 17 and May 5, 1898; Walter Millis, The Martial Spirit, pp. 68, 108.
[4] Richardson, Messages and Papers, vol. ix, p. 636.

diplomatic channels. We had at least one cause of grievance against her when, in March, 1895, the *Allianca*, a steamship carrying the United States mails, which was beyond the specified three miles from the Cuban shore, was assailed by blank shots from a Spanish gunboat. The *Allianca* continued on her way even when solid shots, which, however, fell short of the mark, were fired by the chasing Spaniards. It was said that the boat contained munitions of war for the insurgents, and that she had dropped recruits for the insurgent army into fishing boats on the high seas. These charges our authorities, after inquiry, denied, demanding disavowal and apology, which were duly received. A new Spanish minister arrived at Washington, Senor Dupuy de Lome.[1] On June 12, 1895, filibustering was proceeding so actively that President Cleveland issued a proclamation invoking the cooperation of the people in observing the neutrality laws.[2] He repeated the warning on July 27, 1896,[3] shortly after the capture by the Spaniards of the *Competitor* and its crew, who had just landed in Cuba a cargo of war material for the use of the insurgents. With one exception, in this case, it appeared that the men were American citizens. They were tried by a military tribunal and ordered to be shot. It was only after ardent effort that our State Department, appealing to provisions of treaty, on the ground that the men were not captured with arms in their hands, secured commutation of the sentences they had been doomed to suffer to long prison terms.[4]

In Mr. Cleveland's final message to Congress in December, 1896, he said that, so far as he could discern, no progress had been made toward the restoration of order in Cuba. Spain held Havana and the seaports but the rebels roamed at will over at least two-thirds of the inland country. He drew attention to the large sum in capital which Americans had invested in the island,—between $30,000,000 and $50,000,000; to the

---

[1] Richardson, vol. ix, p. 636; Foreign Relations for 1895, pp. 1184–5; App. Ann. Cyclop. for 1895, p. 224; Walter Millis, op. cit., pp. 27–30.

[2] Richardson, vol. ix, pp. 591–2.　　　[3] Ibid., pp. 694–5.

[4] Walter Millis, op. cit., pp. 53–4; cf. Senate Doc., 54th Cong. 2nd sess., no. 79, pp. 146 and 377.

trade which, before the commencement of the latest insurrection, had amounted to $100,000,000 annually; to the expense of guarding our coast line in order to prevent the outfitting and departure of filibustering parties; to the entanglements arising from the residence in this country of Cubans who were doing what they could to promote the rebellion, and to the naturalization of some of these men who, when they were caught in Cuba, or on the high seas, pleaded their American citizenship and their right to the protection of our laws.

Mr. Cleveland reviewed the plans which had been recommended—in the first place for accordance to the insurgents of belligerent rights, a course which was so blatantly advocated by politicians with overheated brains and the yellow journalists, and which, incorporated in a concurrent resolution of Congress, had been the product of the anti-Spanish excitement in the spring of 1896; [1] in the second place, for a recognition of the independence of the insurgents based upon their establishment of a "republic," shadowy and impotent as it was known to be; [2] thirdly, for the purchase of the island and its cession by Spain to us; and, fourthly and finally, for armed intervention with a view to terminating the persistent strife.

Our "ample and diversified domains," the President said, satisfied all our longings for territory. Nevertheless it must be recognized by Spain and by the world that we were manifesting "restraint" and "patient endurance." The people of Cuba had grievances which should be redressed. Spain should offer them autonomy, "a measure of home rule," which, while preserving her "sovereignty," would meet all the "rational requirements" of her subjects. "Pacification" might then be expected to ensue. Instead of this she prescribed "unconditional surrender" of those in arms against her ere there could be discussion of reform.

Sincerely desirous of a happy and an early settlement the United States had tendered its good offices to this end. Secretary Olney, at the wish of the President, had suggested to Spain

[1] Summarized in App. Ann. Cyclop. for 1896, pp. 203–10.
[2] Henry James, Richard Olney, pp. 155–6.

a statement of her willingness to do away with abuses which, it was alleged, had provoked the rebellion, whereupon we should urge the insurgents to accept the proposal with our "guaranty" that the agreement would be faithfully executed. No result had yet been attained and Spain was informed by the President in December, 1896, that, because of our "inevitably close relations" to the conflict, it might be possible, "by the course of events," for us to be "drawn into such an unusual and unprecedented condition as will fix a limit to our patient waiting." A time might come when "a correct policy, and care for our interest," joined by "considerations of humanity, and a desire to see a rich and fertile country intimately related to us saved from complete devastation," would constrain us to such action as would "subserve the interests thus involved," while at the same time promising to Cuba and its inhabitants "an opportunity to enjoy the blessings of peace." [1]

The President's suggestions deserved a more respectful hearing than they would receive. His term was nearly at an end. The eyes of the country were set upon his successor and what McKinley should see fit to propose with reference to Cuba. The jingoes in Congress, driven on by the "yellow journals," with their tales of sorrow and ruth, were constantly asking the State Department for correspondence and reports concerning "outrages" committed by Spain upon our citizens. Each day's record of the banditry of the insurgents and the revenges of the terrible Weyler was scoured for attacks upon the honor of the American name. Insults done our seamen and their ships, suspected, often quite justly, of filibustering operations,[2] the arrest, imprisonment and execution of Cubans who said that they were naturalized Americans, the destruction of property belonging to such citizens were monotonously reiterated.[3] The case of one Jules Sanguily who, for his activity

---

[1] Richardson, vol. ix, pp. 716–22; Henry James, Richard Olney, pp. 158–66 and app. v; Foreign Relations for 1897, pp. 540–8.

[2] For a summary of this activity see Am. Ann. Cyclop. for 1897, pp. 263–4; also Chadwick, Relations of U. S. and Spain, Diplomacy, p. 418.

[3] Richardson, vol. ix, pp. 746–52 passim; Henry James, Richard Olney, pp. 157–8.

in behalf of the rebels, was tried, found guilty and condemned to "perpetual imprisonment in chains" raised loud protest.[1] The Senate Committee on Foreign Relations, which a little earlier had approved a resolution recognizing the independence of Cuba, to be told by Secretary Olney that, if it were passed by Congress, it would be of no effect, since recognition of governments rested exclusively with the President,[2] called for the immediate release of the man who was a citizen of the United States.[3] Such fury, which our "Cuba Libre" press shared, seemed to be based on no knowledge of the facts. However, Spain preferred to free the culprit in spite of the charges against him, in answer to Secretary Olney's expert handling of the case, and another crisis was passed in the train of events leading up to the war, which firebrands at Washington were so diligently endeavoring to foment.[4] The capture, imprisonment and expulsion of correspondents of the New York World and Journal who were in the island seeking and inventing "outrages" increased the war lust of the newspapers and still further involved our diplomacy.[5] The intemperate language used by our politicians, as well as by our press, exasperated the government and people of Spain, excited the insurgents in Cuba and interfered with the proper management of the subject in the State Department.[6] When the mulatto Maceo was ambushed, as it was said, and killed (Marti had been slain earlier) there was a veritable convulsion in the ranks of our fireeaters. War must be declared at once.[7]

In vain did the Spanish minister in Washington, Dupuy de Lome, protest. He wrote a "strictly personal and confidential" letter to Secretary Olney. Repeatedly he had been urged to induce his government to make this concession and that concession in the interest of peaceful relationships, to

[1] Richardson, vol. ix, p. 749.   [2] James, op. cit., p. 168.
[3] Cf. Cong. Record, 54th Cong. 1st sess., pp. 216 et seq.
[4] Cf. N. Y. Nation, March 4 and 11, 1897.
[5] Cf. Senate Doc., 54th Cong. 2nd sess., no. 84, p. 247.
[6] Cf. James, op. cit., p. 155.
[7] N. Y. Nation, Dec. 17, 1890, and Dec. 23, 1897. Many of the "outrages" are described in Senate Reports, 55th Cong. 2nd sess., no. 885.

overlook the escape of filibustering expeditions, to forgive trespass and violation of the rules of international neighborliness. Olney had expressed a wish that the struggle be brought to an end, but it was maintained, Dupuy de Lome said, only "by the help coming from this country." So long as the insurgents had evidence of our sympathy for their cause in the tone of articles in our press and in the unhindered departure from our coast of boats laden with arms and men the rebellion would continue. Dupuy de Lome was acting as "a second minister of the United States, not as the minister of Spain." It could be so no longer. He could not go on "asking favors for the United States" at Madrid when "equal proofs of friendship" were not given in return. How could he, "with honor, remain here in these circumstances?" He had better resign and go home. Spain "could and would end the insurrection," he said in conclusion, "but to do this soon it was necessary that the rebels be deprived of the hope of aid from this country."[1]

The problems to which McKinley fell heir in connection with the island would have taxed any President's ingenuity. There was nothing in his composition to induce a thought that he would, on his own initiative, forward movements to make our relations with Spain more menacing than they had been. He let it be known, even before his inauguration, that he was no lover of international brawling and that he viewed the Cuban agitation with disfavor.[2] But already war, with the temper of the people irritated as it had been by the systematic and prolonged making of propaganda in this country favorable to the insurgents, could have been said to be inescapable. While avoiding, upon his accession to office, any open reference to the Cuban question the new President, after some allusions to "a firm and dignified foreign policy," sounded a peaceful

[1] Dupuy de Lome to Olney, May 11, 1896, in Cleveland Papers; cf. Dupuy de Lome to Olney, June 25, 1896, in ibid.
[2] N. Y. Nation, Feb. 11 and May 13, 1897; Herbert Croly, M. A. Hanna, pp. 276, 277–8, 294; A. D. White, Autobiography, vol. ii, pp. 161, 165; S. M. Cullom, Fifty Years of Public Service, p. 283; J. F. Rhodes, The McKinley and Roosevelt Administrations, pp. 49, 59–60; H. Hagedorn, Leonard Wood, p. 141; H. H. Kohlsaat, From McKinley to Harding, p. 67; A. Nevins, Henry White, p. 133.

note. "We want no wars of conquest," he said; "we must avoid the temptation of territorial aggression. War," he continued, "should never be entered upon until every agency of peace has failed." [1]

The hotheads in Congress, during the extra session which was convened to deal with the tariff, had much to say about Cuba. But some of the pot valiant who were attached to the Republican party had been brought to a degree of harmlessness by Speaker Reed, whose influences were distinctly pacific. One Congressman, Sulzer of New York, presented a "monster" petition which contained, he said, hundreds of thousands of signatures, praying for intervention. He called Weyler "the greatest thief, the greatest coward, the greatest brute, the greatest liar, the greatest murderer, the greatest enemy of humanity that the world had ever known." [2] His petition was "pigeonholed." Others beat the air around them with no more effect.

But Reed's control of the situation did not extend to the Senate, nor did the President's. That body, on May 20th, had passed a joint resolution recognizing a state of belligerency in Cuba similar to that which had been so exuberantly adopted by both branches of the Congress in the spring of 1896, though that had been a "concurrent resolution." [3] On that occasion the spitfires could be told that their fulmination was vain unless the Executive branch of the government should be disposed to take note of it. But the present joint resolution called for the approval or disapproval of the President; if he should disapprove his veto might be overridden. It was fraught with dire consequences had the powerful Speaker not taken his stand against it in the House.[4] The adoption of the measure by both chambers could have led directly to war which was the hope of those who had under their care the entire subject of belligerent rights.

One step was taken at the extra session which had its bearing

[1] From the inaugural address, App. Ann. Cyclop. for 1897, p. 203.
[2] Cong. Record, 55th Cong. 1st sess., p. 181; N. Y. Times, June 18, 1897.
[3] Cf. Richardson, vol. x, p. 131; N. Y. Nation, March 12, 1896.
[4] Cf. N. Y. Nation, May 27, 1897.

on events and which was a definite expression of the national sympathies. The cruelties which Weyler practised on the country people by confining them in camps, though he had only turned the tables on the insurgents and was pursuing a policy well known in war, were the theme of every sensational newspaper. Fitzhugh Lee who had been Mr. Cleveland's consul-general at Havana, though his course greatly disturbed the President,[1] was still at his post. He had, it was averred, openly taken the side of the rebels; his house and the consulate, it was said, were centres of sympathy for the insurrection,[2] and the bluster of his mien gave great delight to our jingoes and, at the same time, offense to Spain.[3] He said that many Americans in Cuba were starving. Congress, on May 24, 1897, on the recommendation of President McKinley, voted $50,000 to relieve their wants and to transport them, at their desire, to the United States.[4] This was a very unusual expenditure of public money and met with criticism.[5] That a part of the sum was distributed to impostors admits of no question.[6] It was meant by the President, in whom the spirit of conciliation was so active as to be a fault, to be a propitiatory offering to the "Cuba Libre" party which, however, gaining so much, was not likely to rest until we should have adopted their entire program and followed it to its bitter end.

If Lee "rattled the sabre" in Havana so also did Roosevelt in the Navy Department. He fulfilled all the prophecies made by those who had looked with misgivings upon the plan to admit him to a part in the national administration. He spoke and wrote about a "big navy." Soon after coming to his office he visited the Naval War College at Newport, where he made a bellicose speech and then went to the West where he addressed the naval militia, pointing to Japan as a menace to our national

---

[1] Lee's conduct in connection with one international "outrage" induced a rebuke from Secretary Olney which seemed to invite his resignation.— Cleveland Papers, February, 1897.

[2] Foreign Relations for 1898, p. 674.

[3] Cf. McElroy, Grover Cleveland, vol. ii, pp. 273–4; Walter Millis, The Martial Spirit, pp. 53, 97; A. Nevins, Henry White, p. 133.

[4] Richardson, vol. x, pp. 217, 129.   [5] N. Y. Nation, June 10, 1897.

[6] Ibid., June 24 and Aug. 19, 1897.

liberties and urging instant action in Cuba. When he returned to Washington Secretary Long gave him a "heavy wigging." [1] To no purpose, for during the Secretary's absence later in the summer of 1897 Roosevelt called upon the President, outlining a plan of campaign in the event of war with Spain, which he confidently anticipated, and tendering his services as a fighting man in the approaching contest.[2] He visited the fleet, carried on conversations with naval officers and members of Congress [3] and, before the return of Long, upon whom he had been laboring in behalf of his rash schemes, he had succeeded in widely advertising himself.[4] To content him in some degree he was appointed to head a naval war board which should serve the use of a general staff.

But the Assistant Secretary would not have a wholly free rein. His capers were regarded merely as such by the President and more responsible men.[5] Nothing would be done precipitately. The State Department resumed the efforts which had been made by Secretary Olney to effect mediation. Protests against the harsh and unfair treatment of American citizens continued. General Stewart L. Woodford of New York would succeed Hannis Taylor [6] as our minister to Spain. He enjoyed the favor of Platt who had wished him to have a place in the cabinet. He might have gone to Paris but Spain promised to provide opportunities for the exercise of good sense and diplomatic skill, and he, not too willingly, accepted the appointment [7] after it had been put within the reach, probably

[1] Corr. of Roosevelt and Lodge, vol. i, p. 268; H. F. Pringle, Theodore Roosevelt, pp. 172-3.

[2] Corr. of Roosevelt and Lodge, vol. i, pp. 276-9; cf. A. Nevins, Henry White, pp. 131-2.

[3] Roosevelt, The Rough Riders, pp. 2-3.

[4] Corr. of Roosevelt and Lodge, vol. i, pp. 274-5, 279-80. For Lodge's sympathies see E. F. Atkins, Sixty Years in Cuba, p. 212.

[5] Cf. H. Hagedorn, Leonard Wood, p. 141. Roosevelt recognized that the President was "jollying" him.—Corr. of Roosevelt and Lodge, vol. i, p. 277.

[6] Described by Woodford as "a wise, brave and faithful representative of our government."—Woodford to McKinley, Sep. 14, 1897, in McKinley Papers.

[7] Woodford to McKinley, June 21, 1897, in ibid.

without his knowledge, of Henry White [1] and John W. Foster.[2] The choice, it was complained, was not the best that could have been made, though it was a better one than some men had conjectured might come from the new Republican administration. Woodford was charged with the task of making the most urgent representations to the Spanish government, based upon our profound concern, material and otherwise, for the fate of Cuba.[3] Spain was informed that we had a direct interest in the issue. Yellow fever swept Cuba because of the unsanitary conditions which were aggravated by misgovernment—the epidemic was brought to the United States. Our people were dependent upon Cuba for cheap sugar—the supply was meagre so long as war raged. We received tobacco and iron ore from the island; we shipped it food and manufactured goods in return.[4] The tender of our friendly offices in bringing the rebellion to an end was renewed.[5]

It was officially stated by the Spanish Minister of War that from November, 1895, to May, 1897, 181,738 men, 6,261 officers and 40 generals had been sent to Cuba. With the force on garrison duty and already in the island the troops engaged in Weyler's campaign, counting irregulars, must have numbered near to a quarter of a million.[6] In the same length of time it is believed that no nation ever transported so many soldiers overseas.[7] It was a display of energy, but it had not brought peace.

A change of conditions was imminent without effort on our side. A new government at Madrid headed by Sagasta, following the assassination by an anarchist of the Prime Minister, Canovas, who was a man of rigor, described as "a Spaniard of the past," [8] opened the way for a recall of the stern Captain-

[1] A. Nevins, Henry White, p. 22.

[2] John W. Foster, Dip. Memoirs, vol. ii, p. 255.

[3] Foreign Relations for 1898, pp. 558–61.

[4] Ibid., pp. 562–3, 573–4.   [5] Cf. ibid., pp. 568–73.

[6] H. H. Sargent, The Campaign of Santiago, vol. i, pp. 20–1, and app. A and B in vol. iii. Chadwick, Span. Am. War, vol. i, p. 5; N. Y. Nation, Oct. 14, 1897.

[7] Cf. N. Y. Nation, July 9 and Sep. 17, 1896; Foreign Relations for 1898, p. 578.

[8] Cf. Chadwick, Relations of the U. S. and Spain, Diplomacy, p. 406.

General whose name was held so generally in the United States to be synonymous with inhumanity. Weyler's place was taken in the autumn of 1897 by General Blanco who had received instructions to adopt softer ways. Men confined in prisons were to be released, the starving were to be fed, devastation was to cease, damage done in the name of war was to be repaired, burdens were to be lifted, native Cubans were to be installed as magistrates. Minister Woodford at Madrid was officially told of the resolves of the new government with not improper renewal of references to our responsibilities as a neutral. Was it true that we were doing all in our power to suppress filibustering expeditions? The Junta in New York, "in the sight of all men," continued to make the boast that it was aiding and abetting the rebels.[1] The "Home Rule" of which President Cleveland had spoken, though it is doubtful whether Spain comprehended the meaning of the words,[2] was now a promise which, if the men in the hills had been willing to lay down their arms and take up peaceful pursuits, might have borne fruit.

It was very plainly the hope of McKinley in December, 1897, when he addressed Congress at its regular session, that so much would be gained. He spoke most considerately of the new Spanish government and its announced policy of reform, though he resented the implication in a recent note from Madrid that we had failed in the performance of our international duties in allowing the "insurrectos" to recruit men and purchase munitions in the United States.[3] He went so far as to say, with a chauvinistic fervor not in full accord with the facts, that we had "successfully prevented the departure of a single military expedition, or armed vessel," from our shores, and, in further confirmation of the perfection of our system of government, especially since it had come into

[1] Foreign Relations for 1898, pp. 585–6.
[2] N. Y. Nation, Nov. 4 and Dec. 30, 1897; Hannis Taylor in N. A. Review, for Nov., 1897.
[3] How little we had done to prevent filibustering, in the opinion of Spain, may be learned from the notes of the Spanish minister, de Lome, to the State Department in Foreign Relations for 1897, pp. 529 et seq.

the hands of the Republican party, he averred that "not a single American citizen" was now under arrest or in confinement in Cuba. He effectively disposed of the demand for the recognition of the belligerency of the rebels. They had set up no government which could be recognized—to adopt such a course would be to increase vastly and dangerously our international obligations. Patience was called for. The new Spanish government and its policies were on trial. It was "honestly due to Spain, and to our friendly relations with Spain," that she should be given "a reasonable chance to realize her expectations." If a "righteous peace" could not be attained, and it should hereafter appear to be our duty, "imposed by obligations to ourselves, to civilization and humanity, to intervene with force," it would be "without fault on our part," and only because the necessity of action was "so clear as to command the support and approval of the civilized world." The President would not speak of "forcible annexation" which could "not be thought of." That, "by our code of morality," he said, "would be criminal aggression." [1]

The "reconcentrados" were the object of a national appeal on the day before Christmas, 1897.[2] President McKinley asked for contributions in money or kind for the succor of the poor and starving, subscribing to the fund himself, and a fortnight later a Central Cuban Relief Committee was formed with headquarters in New York which, cooperating with the Red Cross, should superintend the collection of donations, transport them to Cuba and distribute them to the sufferers. Through this agency the President a few weeks later said that thousands of lives had been saved.[3]

The conduct of the negotiations with Spain, as with other foreign governments, indeed the entire management of the State Department, was embarrassed by the mental condition of the man whom the President had put at its head. A place

[1] Richardson, vol. x, pp. 127–36; cf. Foreign Relations for 1898, pp. 646–54.

[2] N. Y. Times, Dec. 25, 1897.

[3] Richardson, vol. x, pp. 142–3; Foreign Relations for 1897, pp. 507 et seq.; ibid., for 1898, pp. 655–6.

must be found for Mark Hanna and it was his ambition to be a United States senator. He had been appointed by the governor of Ohio in the room of John Sherman, who had resigned to become Secretary of State, but he had the greatest difficulty in keeping his post when, in the winter of 1897-8, he must gain election at the hands of his state legislature, where his enemies abounded.[1] Mr. McKinley and Mr. Hanna, in spite of their manifest wish to excuse themselves in the case, were not successful in most men's sight in doing so. They might have known that Sherman was borne down by his years.[2] He had always trimmed his sails to the winds—he now seemed to have no certain principles. What he did one day he forgot the next. He had been told before his appointment to the cabinet that the course which he had chosen to take as a senator, expressive of sympathy for the Cuban insurgents, was unseemly if he were to be at the head of the State Department—he renounced his views and prepared himself to wear the mantle of a minister of foreign affairs.[3] Already, in June, 1897, three months after he had taken office, the incompetency which his speeches for two or three years past had evidenced was advertised to the world to the embarrassment of the administration. His statements and explanations concerning the treaty of annexation which was arranged with the representatives of Hawaii, involving good faith with reference to Japan, were the subjects of criticism,[4] as was a note to Great Britain on the sealing question in Bering Sea,[5] written by John W. Foster [6] but in a tone which Mr. Foster might not have chosen had he signed it and had he been made personally answerable for it. This piece of writing created a new pother in England, causing Joseph Chamberlain to say to Hay that it was another example of our "peculiar" diplomacy. "You

[1] H. Croly, M. A. Hanna, chap. xviii.
[2] Cf. J. B. Foraker, Notes of a Busy Life, vol. i, pp. 499–500; N. Y. Times, Feb. 21, 1898; J. D. Long, America of Yesterday, pp. 153, 187.
[3] Chadwick, Relations of the U. S. and Spain, Diplomacy, pp. 437–8; N. Y. Nation, Jan. 21, 1897.
[4] N. Y. Nation, June 24, July 1 and 8, 1897.
[5] First published in N. Y. Tribune, July 14, 1897.
[6] Tyler Dennett, John Hay, p. 185.

will carry it too far some day," he remarked, "and get hurt." [1]

Shortly after the reorganization of the Department of State by the new President he had chosen a friend, a fellow lawyer at the bar in the town of Canton, William R. Day, to be Assistant Secretary.[2] Mr. Day had headed the company of gentlemen who had defrayed the indebtedness which arose from Mr. McKinley's putting his name on bank paper to secure loans of money in support of an old friend's adventures in tin plate manufacture. Without experience in public life, except as a judge in courts in Ohio, he, as Sherman's condition developed, became the virtual head of the Department.[3] The President relied upon his judgment in regard to Spanish and other international questions and henceforward Sherman was, to all intents and purposes, ignored, to his great irritation, for the vanity which a long life in the public eye and four or five approaches to the nomination for the Presidency had developed in him was undiminished. He was unable to appreciate the declension of the sharpness of his faculties and found a plot in his being taken out of the United States Senate, to accommodate Hanna, for appointment to a post in which he was almost immediately to be shorn of his powers. His bitterness was unconcealed, though he remained nominally in office as Secretary of State until after the declaration of war,[4] when he resigned and Day was named in his stead.[5]

[1] Hay to McKinley, July 16, 1897, in McKinley Papers.

[2] N. Y. Nation, April 29, 1897.

[3] "I greatly hesitate to allude to a matter which is the subject of public and general comment, Mr. Sherman's failing memory," John W. Foster wrote to the President's private secretary on August 11, 1897. "Even the lowest servant in the State Department knows and talks about it. It is pitiable in the extreme." (Foster to J. A. Porter in McKinley Papers.) "State Department en deshabille" was the Baltimore Sun's description of Sherman's administration of the office.—Cleveland Papers. Cf. N. Y. Nation, June 24, July 22 and 29, 1897; J. W. Foster, Dip. Memoirs, vol. ii, p. 173; Tyler Dennett, John Hay, p. 185.

[4] N. Y. Times, April 26, 1898; cf. W. R. Thayer, Life of Hay, vol. ii, p. 173.

[5] J. W. Foster. Dip. Memoirs, vol. ii, pp. 275-6; cf. J. B. Foraker, Notes of a Busy Life, vol. i, pp. 507-9. His continuance in office, Sherman wrote to W. S. Ward, on April 28, 1898, was made "intolerable" by "the conduct of the President." He had not been long in the Department when McKinley showed a disposition to assume all of its functions. One

Sherman's name is linked with Blaine's; the two men were, probably, the most prominent figures in our public life in the two or three decades following the Civil War. Both can be named among the majestic failures of our history. With native talents they combined a certain want of moral solidity. They sacrificed convictions and principles in a belief that, to attain their ambitions for office, which were of the highest, they must practise upon the populace cajoleries consonant with its changing moods. They thereby forfeited the respect of those who had the finest purposes, and were not sufficiently successful in winning the trust of the masses to gain their too obvious ends.

The Cuban insurgents, by the time Spain was ready to offer them a certain limited autonomy, which a few years since the sagacious among them must have regarded as a generous boon, were in no mind to be conciliated by any proffer of reform. The new system was formally inaugurated with the commencement of the year 1898. But the rebels would not lay down their arms. Like brigands they were ravaging the country and slaughtering unoffending citizens as well as Spanish soldiers. They blew up railroad trains and killed the passengers.[1] All agricultural operations were interfered with and in large areas entirely stopped. The "reconcentrados" were afforded no relief. Our consul at Santiago said in February, 1898, that he did not believe the western continent had "ever witnessed death and starvation equal" to that which then existed in eastern Cuba.[2] Conditions throughout the island continued to shock public sensibilities in the United States.[3] Conciliation became increasingly difficult. Indeed so much had been done toward bringing our people into a frame of mind for a war of liberation that they would not listen to

of the causes of his annoyance was the circulation of repeated talk about his impaired health which was really "very good." There was, Sherman complained, no "free exchange of opinion" in the cabinet. The President's mandates were those of a "paramount ruler," etc.—Sherman Papers.

[1] N. Y. Nation, Dec. 27, 1897; Foreign Relations for 1898, p. 667; Senate Doc., 55th Cong. 2nd sess., no. 230. pp. 40–1.

[2] Senate Doc., 55th Cong. 2nd sess., no. 230. p. 41.

[3] Foreign Relations for 1898, p. 704.

suggestions of compromise. Nor did such suggestions meet with unanimous favor on the side of Spain. Weyler and his friends at home, and many persons in Cuba, opposed the more liberal policy which had been announced by the new government at Madrid. A faction bent upon the complete conquest of the rebels indulged in riots in Havana in expression of their dissent.[1] The lives of Americans, Consul-General Lee said, were in danger and a war vessel, the *Maine*, at his urgent request,[2] was ordered to Havana, after a conference with the Spanish minister who was constrained to say that the "visit" would not be unwelcome.[3] Such a step did, and was intended to, convey threat;[4] it should not have been taken.[5] Lee himself, after the ship had left Key West, therefore when it was too late, asked that the "visit" be deferred. President McKinley and others, whose hopes and wishes spoke of patient endurance while Spain was making her experiment with her new colonial policy, were being overborne. It was now said that the Spanish government had moved to the island in the three years during which the insurrection had been in progress nearly 250,000 men; 52,000 it was stated in January, 1898, had been killed or had died of wounds or disease, while 47,000, unable to cope with the climate, had been invalided back to Spain and 42,000 were resting in Cuban hospitals.[6] Immense loans had been floated in the long struggle to hold the island for the crown. Munitions had been purchased, the navy had been increased in strength—all still, as it seemed, to no avail.[7]

The inevitable end was hastened by two events. The Spanish minister to the United States, Depuy de Lome, had unfor-

[1] Foreign Relations for 1898, pp. 1024–5; Senate Doc., 55th Cong. 2nd sess., no. 230, pp. 15, 19, 83.

[2] The sending of a war ship to Cuba was no new scheme with Lee. He had commended it to Cleveland who, writing to Olney on July 16, 1896, said that Lee had "fallen into the style of rolling intervention like a sweet morsel under his tongue."—Cleveland Papers.

[3] Richardson, vol. x, p. 137; J. D. Long, America of Yesterday, p. 155.

[4] N. Y. Nation, Jan. 27, 1898.   [5] Miles, Serving the Republic, p. 269.

[6] App. Ann. Cyclop. for 1898, p. 736; cf. Chadwick, Span. Am. War, vol. i, p. 52; N. Y. Nation, Aug. 25, 1898.

[7] Cf. Foreign Relations for 1898, pp. 564, 575.

tunately, in January, 1898, or somewhat earlier, written a "private" letter. It was addressed to a Spanish journalist, a friend whom he had reason to trust, and who was at the time in Havana. It was somehow stolen from the post-office in transit and put into the hands of agents of the insurgents who forwarded it to the Junta in New York. Hearst's Journal reproduced it in facsimile,[1] and it passed at once to every newspaper in the country. President McKinley was referred to as a vacillating and shifty politician.[2] The minister, seeing the position in which he had been placed, resigned at once to have his resignation immediately accepted, which somewhat took the point from our cabled demand for disavowals and for his recall.[3]

This incident increased the popular pother and fed the war spirit of the country, though it was of small import compared with another happening. The *Maine* had been at anchor in the harbor at Havana for three weeks. Her presence there was not liked by the Spaniards in the city.[4] The sailors, indeed Captain Sigsbee himself, when they went ashore were not viewed with friendliness. Even the ship, some thought, might be in danger.[5] It was so, for at 20 minutes to 10 on the evening of February 15, 1898, after the crew had gone below for the night, a terrific explosion, followed shortly by a second, lifted the vessel out of the water and split it wide open from side to side. The wreckage sank in six fathoms of water. Of 355 men on board 2 officers and 258 sailors were killed or drowned, while many were taken away wounded, 8 of whom died of their injuries.[6] The excitement in the United States following

[1] Feb. 8, 1898.

[2] Letter in Foreign Relations for 1898, pp. 1007–8; Walter Millis, The Martial Spirit, pp. 97–8.

[3] Foreign Relations for 1898, pp. 1008–21; cf. N. Y. Nation, Feb. 17, 1898.

[4] Foreign Relations for 1898, p. 1026.

[5] "We were reviled on the streets of Havana," said a survivor of the wreck, "sneered at until our blood boiled and found out, for our own safety, that it was necessary to make our visits to the city in force."— N. Y. Times, Feb. 22, 1898; cf. ibid., Feb. 18, 1898; C. D. Sigsbee, The Maine, chap. i, and p. 186.

[6] Senate Doc., 55th Cong. 2nd sess., no. 231.

this event was mad. The "yellow press" now had a *casus belli* for certain,[1] and the leaders of the pack in New York made the most of the occasion. They stormed about as never before.[2] As a result of his antics Hearst was now able to boast that his circulation was in excess of one million copies daily.[3] The World said on April 26th that it was selling 1,300,000 copies a day.[4] The country must go to war at once to avenge a horrible international crime.

Captain Sigsbee who commanded the ship, in reporting the disaster, asked for a suspension of judgment until there could be an investigation.[5] Captain-General Blanco cabled to Madrid. The explosions, he said, were undoubtedly internal. Spain expressed her regret in appropriate terms and the authorities in Havana, in the collection of the bodies of the dead and the care of the survivors, rendered the assistance which was dictated by the sentiments of humanity.[6] To allay, if possible, the rising fury of the American people the Spanish government proposed a joint inquiry to ascertain the cause of the catastrophe. There were various theories about it. The Spanish preferred to think, and repeated, that the explosion had originated in the magazines of the vessel; others connected it with renegades who were cooperating with the Cuban Junta —they had somehow planted a mine under the ship in order to bring on a war; still others, and their number was by far the greater, said that Spanish agents had deliberately set a trap for the *Maine*—she had been sent to a spot which had been mined with a wish for her destruction.[7] Some who were

[1] Cf. N. Y. Nation, Feb. 24 and March 3 and 10, 1898; N. Y. Times, Feb. 18, 1898.

[2] In response to W. R. Hearst of the New York Journal for a contribution to a fund to be used to raise a monument to the memory of the men who went down on the Maine ex-President Cleveland at Princeton replied: "I decline to allow my sorrow for those who died on the Maine to be perverted to an advertising scheme for the New York Journal."— McElroy, Grover Cleveland, vol. ii, p. 272; A. Nevins, Letters of Grover Cleveland, p. 495.

[3] Walter Millis, The Martial Spirit, pp. 108, 110. [4] Ibid., p. 163.

[5] Report of Sec. of Navy for 1898, p. 4.

[6] Richardson, vol. x, p. 137; Foreign Relations for 1898, pp. 1029–35.

[7] Cf. C. D. Sigsbee, The Maine, pp. 180 et seq.

calmer considered the possibility of an explosive having been sunk in the harbor for other uses, its presence or location having been overlooked by the authorities.

To the suggestion of a joint investigation we replied that we would make our own inquiry and a board of American naval officers, composed of Captain William T. Sampson, Captain French E. Chadwick and two others were appointed for the task. Their report, on March 21st, six weeks after the disaster, based upon an examination of the wreck by divers, led them to the conclusion that the destruction of the *Maine* was in no way due to fault or negligence of the officers or the crew of the ship. A mine had caused the initial explosion; the second explosion, presumably, had involved two or more of the forward magazines.[1] The Spanish government, making an independent investigation in which they complained that we had not cooperated for the establishment of the facts, repeated their original announcement that the ship had not been destroyed by a mine. There had been but a single explosion and the cause was internal.[2]

Only in President McKinley, now for some time, had the intelligent minority in the United States, who fervently desired peace, rested their hopes.[3] Six powers of Europe through their representatives at Washington—Great Britain, France, Germany, Austria-Hungary, Russia and Italy—addressed the President in a "pressing appeal" to his "feelings of humanity and moderation." He returned with references to "a duty to humanity by ending a situation the indefinite prolongation" of which had become "insufferable." [4]

Only a few of the leading newspapers of the country, notably the New York Evening Post, used their influences in so un-

[1] Richardson, vol. x, pp. 136–9; Senate Doc., 55th Cong. 2nd sess., no. 207, with photographs of the wreck.

[2] Senate Report, 55th Cong. 2nd sess., no. 885, pp. 625–9; cf. Foreign Relations for 1898, pp. 1036–46. For an English view see H. W. Wilson, The Downfall of Spain, chap. i. For a discussion based on later examinations of the wreck see House Doc., 62nd Cong. 2nd sess., no. 310; J. F. Rhodes, The McKinley and Roosevelt Administrations, p. 51; Walter Millis, The Martial Spirit, pp. 128–9.

[3] N. Y. Nation, April 7, 1898.

[4] Foreign Relations for 1898, pp. 740–1.

popular a cause; only a few men in Congress stood erect to
repel the powerful wave of enthusiasm with which the prospect
of a resort to arms was contemplated. Senators and representatives visited the President and, to drive him into action,
intimated to him a doubt as to his patriotism.[1] Roosevelt boiled
with rage at the suggestion of anything less than an immediate
declaration of hostilities.[2] His friend Lodge more diplomatically
argued the case with the President. He had been in New
England attending his town meeting in Nahant. He had seen
all kinds of people. The demand for a recognition of Cuban
independence was unanimous. If McKinley should not act in
this sense the Republican party would "go down in the greatest
defeat ever known before the cry 'Why have you not settled
the Cuban question?'" To ignore the duty would be "deadly."
Lodge would not have the President go to war "for political
reasons," but to "sacrifice a great party and bring free silver
upon the country for a wrong policy," he averred, would be
"hardly less odious."[3] Other men, in letters and telegrams,
urged the President to say the word which would lead to war.[4]
Senator Proctor of Vermont who had visited Cuba, in this
conjuncture, returned, painting conditions in the island, in a
speech in the Senate and in conversation with Mr. McKinley,
in the darkest hues.[5] He had been Secretary of War in the
cabinet of President Harrison. While his visit was brief and
his information was of little honest value[6] his sensational
utterances had a wide influence. American consuls, naval

[1] C. S. Olcott, Life of McKinley, vol. ii, pp. 28–9; also ibid., pp. 52–3,
citing Cortelyou's Diary; J. D. Long, America of Yesterday, pp. 176–7;
J. F. Rhodes, The McKinley and Roosevelt Administrations, pp. 59–60;
N. Y. Nation, Nov. 24, 1898.

[2] Walter Millis, The Martial Spirit, p. 130.

[3] Lodge to McKinley, March 21, 1898. Here was nearly a realization
of the prophecy of the London Spectator—"Some day or other we shall
see a war waged, not for its avowed object, but in order to consolidate
the hold of a party upon office."—Issue of Nov. 3, 1888.

[4] S. H. Acheson, Joe Bailey, pp. 92–3. They will not be so eager for
war, McKinley said to John W. Foster, "when their sons are dying in
Cuba of yellow fever."—Foster, Dip. Memoirs, vol. ii, p. 256.

[5] Cong. Record, 55th Cong. 2nd sess., pp. 2916 et seq.; C. S. Olcott,
Life of McKinley, vol. ii, pp. 14–5; N. Y. Times, March 18 and 19, 1898.

[6] L. P. Morton to McKinley, March 20, 1898, in McKinley Papers.

officers in Cuba and others made their observations—all of
them emphasizing the frightful sufferings of the non-combatants,
especially the "reconcentrados," the prevalence of hunger and
the decimation of the innocent population by death.[1] The
popular temper was wildly disturbed. The President was
supported—some commended him for standing fast in the face of
clamor, among them the late Vice President, Levi P. Morton,[2]
and William H. Taft. Taft from his judge's chambers, in
Cincinnati, thanked McKinley for his bravery in resisting
"the thoughtless jingoism of some and the blatant demagoguery
of others in and out of Congress." The "froth of public sentiment," he observed, "was often its greatest impurity." The
President should take heart—there were voices which he may
not have heard. "The shallows murmur while the deeps
are dumb." [3] But the President deceived those who may have
thought that he could withstand the forces raging around him
and men acquainted with his character knew that he would
take the easy way.[4]

The result of our inquiry as to the cause of the destruction
of the *Maine* had been immediately communicated to the
Spanish government. Minister Woodford was assured in
Madrid that there would be full and satisfactory redress.
Spain asked that the question of responsibility might be submitted to arbitration, a proposal to which we would not give
ear. We demanded reparation and, coupled with it, a guaranty
of improved conditions in Cuba. Spain should take her hand
off the island and pacify the inhabitants. They were starving.
One hundred and fifty thousand persons in the concentration
camps, at least, had died, according to President McKinley; [5]

---

[1] Cf. N. Y. Times, April 12, 1898.
[2] Morton to McKinley, April 1, 1898, in McKinley Papers.
[3] Taft to McKinley, March 30, 1898, in ibid.
[4] He was not "a victim of ignorance but of amiable weakness not un-
mixed with political ambition," said his predecessor in office, Grover
Cleveland. (McElroy, Grover Cleveland, vol. ii, p. 273.) Rhodes made
and recorded a like estimate of McKinley. If Mark Hanna had been
President, Rhodes said, there would have been no war with Spain.—The
McKinley and Roosevelt Administrations, p. 64.
[5] Richardson, vol. x, p. 141.

Congress said 200,000; [1] other estimates were as high as 400,000 and 500,000.[2] Two hundred thousand more were in such desperate straits that they soon would perish if they were not afforded relief. Spain made some evasive reply, though there were evidences that the government was genuinely alarmed and begged that the report concerning the *Maine* be withheld from Congress.[3] No promise of this kind would be made. General Woodford proposed an armistice until October 1st, until the end of the rainy season, during which period negotiations under our offices might proceed between Cuba and the mother country; the immediate revocation of the order by which the people were herded in camps where they were unable to procure food, and the opening of a way for their relief by shipments of supplies from the United States.[4] As compliance was tardy and qualified [5] the President, on March 28th, transmitted to Congress the report regarding the *Maine*. The sinking of the ship had been an "appalling calamity," he said; a community of men less well accustomed to self control could have been "incited to acts of blind resentment." The President summarized the facts as they were presented by the court of inquiry, as well as the conclusions of the court, which were simply that the ship had been sunk as a result of an explosion of a submarine mine causing internal explosions of the magazines, and that no evidence was obtainable fixing the responsibility upon any person or persons. He awaited the announcement of a "course of action" on Spain's side, "suggested by honor and the friendly relations of the two governments." [6]

Events in this country now moved rapidly. On April 11th the President forwarded to Congress a message in which he reviewed the progress of the negotiation with Spain in the interest of a restoration of order. The destruction of the

[1] App. Ann. Cyclop. for 1898, p. 159; cf. Chadwick, Relations of U. S. and Spain, Diplomacy, p. 493.
[2] Captain Sigsbee to Sec. Long, Foreign Relations for 1898, pp. 671–3.
[3] Foreign Relations for 1898, p. 701.
[4] Richardson, vol. x, p. 143; Foreign Relations for 1898, pp. 711–2
[5] Foreign Relations for 1898, pp. 727–8, 732–3, 735–7.
[6] Richardson, vol. x, pp. 136–9.

Maine was "a patent and impressive proof of a state of things" which was "intolerable." It was plain, he said, that peace could not come "by present methods"; the "only hope" of repose in the island rested in "enforced pacification." His mind was made up. "In the name of humanity, in the name of civilization, in behalf of endangered American interests which give us the right and the duty to speak and act," he said, "the war in Cuba must stop." He asked the Congress for power to take measures looking to "a full and final termination of hostilities," to secure in the island "the establishment of a stable government" and "to use the military and naval forces of the United States for the attainment of these ends." He had "exhausted every effort to relieve the intolerable condition of affairs" which was "at our doors." The issue was now with the Congress.[1]

Meantime Spain asked that merchantmen should be substituted for naval vessels in transporting supplies to the "reconcentrados." She would have us remove from Havana disreputable American correspondents who were doing their utmost to bring on a war [2] and suggested the recall of Consul-General Fitzhugh Lee, whose sympathies with the insurgents were so unmistakable that he was no longer an acceptable representative, though he was vigilant and tactful enough still to hold his uncomfortable post. Compliance with these requests was declined.[3] An American squadron was sent to Key West. Ordnance factories were feverishly manufacturing war material. Work on uncompleted naval vessels went forward at accelerated pace. Harbor forts and coast batteries were strengthened, and $50,000,000 were voted unanimously by Congress to the President for use, at his discretion, for national defence.[4] The Spanish ministry, and intelligent men generally in Spain, Minister Woodford said, were "stunned." [5] Only a miracle

---

[1] Richardson, vol. x, pp. 139–50.   [2] Foreign Relations for 1898, p. 675.
[3] Ibid., p. 676. "As to the objectionable newspapers," Day wrote to Woodford, "their sensational and unfounded reports are the cause of as much embarrassment at home as they can be abroad."—Ibid., p. 681.
[4] Cf. Richardson, vol. x, p. 162; N. Y. Nation, March 10 and 17, 1898.
[5] Foreign Relations for 1898, p. 686.

now could avert war. The Pope offered his mediation,[1] and the
Queen of Spain, at the request of "the Holy Father of all
Christendom," in "Passion Week," ordered a suspension of
hostilities for a period of six months.[2]

It was too late. The galleries in Congress were crammed
with noisy jingoes.[3] Bailey, the Democratic minority leader,
who found in the situation an opportunity to magnify himself
and to gain advantage for his party, amused the eager onlookers
with his parliamentary agilities, while Speaker Reed stood firm
in his opposition to a declaration of war.[4]

The use of new tools of destruction on land and sea interested
military and naval experts.[5] An entire generation had grown to
manhood since the country's last war. They had heard their
elders, in mellow reminiscence, boast of feats on the battle
fields of Virginia, on the Mississippi, while "marching through
Georgia." Roosevelt, Lodge and the young "war hawks" of the
day could scarcely keep in their beds as they dreamed each
night of Mausers and Krag-Jorgensens and serried legions of
marching men. As for the masses, in love with excitement, in
which they might not participate, but, which could be communicated to them by the pictorial newspapers, bombardment
and battle filled their imaginations. What they were about to
see was a great play. Men declared that we could "blow the
Spanish navy out of the water" in ten, some said three days.
We could drive Spain out of Cuba and out of the American
hemisphere in thirty days.

One benefit was visible—jingoism would now spend itself on
a country and a people with whom we had no common history or
racial alliances. Our enmities would be transferred from
England to the inhabitants of the Iberian peninsula. The
change was sudden and noteworthy. Through four or five
Presidential canvasses we had fought, in the newspaper and in

---

[1] A form of intervention not fitted to pacify those members of the
A. P. A. in the United States in whom the martial spirit dwelt.—Walter
Millis, op. cit., pp. 132–3, 136.

[2] Foreign Relations for 1898, pp. 741–50.

[3] E. N. Dingley, Life and Times of Nelson Dingley, Jr., p. 457.

[4] S. W. McCall, Life of Reed, pp. 233–4.

[5] N. Y. Nation, Feb. 24, 1898.

stump oratory, wars with Great Britain. So long as Blaine and his following, in which the chief, among journals, was the New York Tribune, discerned success in the propitiation of the Irish vote, with particular reference to the pivotal state of New York, the sowing of hate of England would not cease. This exercise could be conveniently joined with tariff campaigns. In 1896, with Bryan leading an attack upon the gold standard, which the Populists confused with British "tyranny," the Republicans must retire from their favorite ground and leave the field to the Democrats. Since this party was to be combated as ignorant and revolutionist the politicians and newspapers of the Republican party changed their tone. Whitelaw Reid, the owner of the Tribune, though he had stood by approvingly while his writers for many years multiplied their insinuations about England, still nourished an ambition to represent the United States at the Court of St. James. It was made clear to him in 1889 by President Harrison that he could not well be named to such a post.[1] Reid, actively antagonized by Platt, had been set aside again, not without difficulty, when, in 1897, John Hay, who had not allowed the President to be long out of his sight,[2] was preferred for the appointment.[3] Even casual reference to the files of the Tribune would justify objection to such an ambassador should the British government seek an excuse for not receiving him, though it is quite probable that his daily missiles in ink were not remembered, if they ever were dignified by particular notice. Anyhow President McKinley, in compliance with earlier promises, making his peace with Platt, was ready in the summer of 1897 to appoint Mr. Reid, to that gentleman's intense satisfaction,[4] a special envoy

[1] Cf. Tyler Dennett, John Hay, p. 173.

[2] Hay sent a ring containing a few hairs from the head of Washington or the President to wear as a kind of mascot on the day of the inauguration. It had come down from Mrs. Alexander Hamilton to whom Washington had presented it. The initials G. W. and W. M. were engraved by Hay on each side of the setting.—Hay to McKinley, Dec. 28, 1896, in McKinley Papers.

[3] A. Nevins, Henry White, p. 120; Tyler Dennett, John Hay, p. 79; Autobiog. of T. C. Platt, pp. 258–64.

[4] He is "the delight of the nobility and the gentry," Hay wrote to McKinley on July 16, 1897, "and is going to stay over another week to

to represent the United States in England on the occasion of the celebration of the 60th anniversary of Queen Victoria's accession to the throne when, during the "Diamond Jubilee," in one of the fine houses in London which he leased for the summer of 1897, he fitly enough testified to his own affluence and the magnitude and wealth of the United States.[1]

It was a happy circumstance now, clearly forwarding better feeling, when it was announced that the British government would not join in negotiations proposed on the Continent of Europe to fetter the United States in dealing with the Cuban question.[2] John Hay in Great Britain, following Bayard, whose warm sympathies with England had cost him favor at home, and Lord Pauncefote at Washington were, in their own ways, in their respective positions, sweetening relationships which would bear happy fruits.[3]

Upon receiving the President's message of April 11th, Congress leapt at the task before it. The House, under Speaker Reed's firm hand, passed a resolution granting Mr. McKinley the authority for which he asked. It was still not the recognition of Cuban independence which the yellow journals had been demanding with so much insistency. The President had said, the administration leaders in the House supporting him, that it were not well to ally ourselves with such a government as the insurgents pretended to have established, or any other the

give a dinner for the Prince of Wales. You have been the cause of great happiness to a worthy fellow being. I only wonder whether this experience may not whet his appetite for further grandeurs."—McKinley Papers.

[1] R. Cortissoz, Life of Reid, vol. ii, pp. 215–7; A. Nevins, Henry White, p. 126; Foreign Relations for 1897, pp. 249–52; A. Carnegie to McKinley, April 27, 1898 in McKinley Papers; Tyler Dennett, John Hay, pp. 192–4; unpublished correspondence relating to Reid's embassy in Hay Papers cited by Mr. Dennett in ibid.

[2] Cf. N. Y. Nation, May 19, 1898; cf. John Hay's letter to McKinley, in Olcott, Life of McKinley, vol. ii, pp. 129–36; A. Nevins, Henry White, pp. 129–35; B. A. Reuter, Anglo-American Relations during the Span. Am. War.

[3] R. B. Mowat, Life of Pauncefote, pp. 204–5; ibid., Relations of Great Brit. and the U. S., p. 274; N. Y. Nation, June 17, 1897. Hay and Henry White were unable to admire Mr. Bayard. Hay found Bayard's speeches in England "vapid flattery." He was "slobbering over the British," and they were sick of it.—Hay to McKinley, May 9, 1897, in McKinley Papers. Cf. A. Nevins, Henry White, pp. 97, 112; Dennett, John Hay, p. 82.

character of which we were in no position to appraise. We would "intervene to stop the war in Cuba to the end and with the purpose of securing permanent peace and order." The President was empowered "to use the land and naval forces of the United States" with this object in view.

The Democratic minority returned with a resolution recognizing the "republic" which the rebels said that they had formed, assailed the Republicans for their delays and eagerly sought to take the credit for being the "war party." The substitute of the Democrats was defeated by a vote of 190 to 150 and the administration's plan for intervention was approved by the House with practical unanimity, barring a few members who voiced the conservative feeling of the country, which still drew back at the prospect of an appeal to arms.[1]

The Senate, long controlled by the "Cuba Libre" party and still unmanageable, would have nothing but "recognition." Fairbanks of Indiana would not vote for such a resolution as was brought forward by the hotspurs—the "republic" which it was proposed to sponsor was "too nebulous, too mythical to be invited into the family of nations." Hoar opposed the measure —it was a discourtesy to the President who had asked for a resolution in another form; it would put our army and navy, if we should enter Cuba, under the command of the insurgent Gomez, else we should be making war on him as well as Spain; it would be a violation of international law. Nevertheless the resolution was passed by a vote of 67 to 21, a number of the more intelligent men in the Senate being included in the minority.[2]

The House, when the resolution was returned to it, added amendments which, in conference, through influences emanating from the White House, made the measure agreeable to the President to the point, at least, of omitting the recognition of the revolutionary government. In a provision, inserted upon motion of Senator Teller, "any disposition or intention to

[1] The vote was 325 to 19.—Cong. Record, 55th Cong. 2nd sess., pp. 3819–21.
[2] Ibid., p. 3993.

exercise sovereignty, jurisdiction or control" over Cuba, except for "pacification," was expressly disclaimed—when this end should be gained the United States would "leave the government and control of the island to its people." [1] After conference the final vote on the measure (which still included the Teller amendment) was 42 to 35 in the Senate [2] and 311 to 6 in the House of Representatives. [3]

The President approved the resolution on the 20th of April. To Spain its contents were at once communicated by the State Department; she could but regard it as a declaration of war and so informed us. Her minister who had succeeded the unfortunate Dupuy de Lome, Senor Polo de Bernabé, asked for his passports and withdrew to Canada. General Woodford, whose bearing had been dignified and above criticism, [4] was notified that diplomatic relations were terminated and he left Madrid, committing American interests there to the care of the British embassy. He made his escape without unhappy incident, though mobs were incited to attack his house, [5] his train was stoned at Valladolid, and there were at other places on his way to Paris hostile demonstrations. [6] All our consular officers in Spain who had been performing their duties amid difficulties withdrew, some amid violent scenes, and left American interests in charge of the British consuls. Fitzhugh Lee and the other consuls of the United States in Cuba and Porto Rico also retired. The sending of the President's message to Congress had been delayed in order that they and American residents might have the opportunity for safe return to this country.

On April 22nd the President proclaimed a blockade of a number of ports in Cuba. [7] He asked for 125,000 men to serve for two years. War upon Spain was formally declared by an act of Congress of April 25th—it had existed since the 21st of that month— [8] and, on the following day, the 26th, the President

---

[1] Richardson, vol. x, p. 155.
[2] Cong. Record, 55th Cong. 2nd sess., pp. 4040–1.
[3] Ibid., pp. 4063–4; Richardson, vol. x, pp. 161–4.
[4] Cf. N. Y. Nation, April 28, 1898.
[5] Foreign Relations for 1898, p. 745.　　[6] N. Y. Times, April 23, 1898.
[7] Richardson, vol. x, pp. 154, 202–3.　　[8] Ibid., pp. 201, 204.

called upon the states for 75,000 more troops.[1] The ranks of the regular army were filled. No trouble impended on this point. Public excitement was intense. The streets of cities, North and South, were filled with people. Old Confederate as well as Union soldiers volunteered their services. Companies of young men were formed and were engaged in military drill. Helen Gould offered the President a check for $100,000 to show "her affection for the country and her loyalty to it"; she was willing to double the amount if her gift should be accepted.[2] Others pledged smaller sums. Various foreign governments issued proclamations of neutrality, Great Britain, it was gratifying to observe, being the first among the number. Our ambassador, John Hay, was loudly acclaimed at an official dinner in London.[3] Crowds assembled before the embassy and cheered. Evidences of the heartiest sympathy and friendship were displayed on every side.[4] The American flag was unfurled in all parts of England.[5]

The poet laureate, Alfred Austin, felt the new surge of kinship and gave it expression in verse—

> "Now fling them out to the breeze,
>   Shamrock, Thistle and Rose,
> And the Star Spangled Banner unfurl with these,
>   A message to friends and foes,
> Wherever the sails of peace are seen and wherever the
>   war wind blows;
> A message to bond and thrall to wake,
>   For wherever we come, we twain,
> The throne of the tyrant shall rock and quake
>   And this menace be void and vain,
> For you are the lords of a strong land and we are
>   lords of the main." [6]

[1] Richardson, vol. x, pp. 205–6.
[2] McKinley replied coolly, saying that "the voluntary offering of private wealth for the public welfare" was not without precedent and suggested that she deposit her check with the Assistant Treasurer in New York, or send it to the Treasury in Washington.—Miss Gould to McKinley, April 23, 1898, and McKinley to Miss Gould, May 5, 1898, in McKinley Papers.
[3] N. Y. Times, April 21, 1898.
[4] W. R. Thayer, Life of Hay, vol ii, pp. 168–9.
[5] Cf. McElroy, Grover Cleveland, vol. ii, p. 273.
[6] London Times, March 29, 1898.

Congress made haste with its plans to finance the struggle. New taxes must be laid,—these finally, after the Senate had taken a prominent hand in the work, being made to apply to liquors and tobacco, chewing gum, mineral waters, cosmetics and perfumery, proprietary medicines, stock transfers, bank checks, bills of lading, telegrams and telephone messages, instruments, papers and documents of a hundred kinds, tea, sugar and petroleum, berths in sleeping cars and seats in parlor cars, with occupational taxes for bankers and brokers, the owners of theatres, bowling alleys and billiard rooms, and inheritance taxes. The government then would sell $400,-000,000 of 3 per cent. bonds, "ten twenties," payable in 10 years, if it be convenient, and in 20 years in any event, an operation which, it was surmised, might be forwarded through popular subscription at the post offices; also $100,000,000 of temporary certificates of indebtedness bearing interest at 3 per cent., payable in one year to meet the immediate costs of the war. In all, therefore, Congress gave the government a borrowing power of $500,000,000,[1] in addition to the $50,-000,000 which had been taken out of current regular income in March for preliminary uses and new taxes which would yield, it was believed, $100,000,000 more. Two hundred millions of the authorized loan were offered to the public—the amount was oversubscribed seven and a half times and the bonds rose to a premium of 6 per cent. within three months.[2]

After the Populists had made their speeches advocating income taxes, and the greenbackers and silver men had stated their well known theories as to public finance the silver men succeeded in the mêlée in fastening upon the measure a provision authorizing the coinage of the "silver seigniorage" in the Treasury,[3] a design in the execution of which they had been checked by President Cleveland. The finished bill, because of the Senate's obstructions, was not ready for McKinley's signature until June 13th.

[1] Richardson, vol. x, pp. 167–8.
[2] Noyes, Forty Years of Am. Finance, p. 279.
[3] Cf. N. Y. Nation, May 5, 1898.

Meantime the war was nearly fought and won. Spain had exhausted her poor military resources in her protracted efforts to subdue the Cuban rebels. For more than two years she had poured troops into the malarial swamps of the island and there were but few reserves. She had on the ground at the time an army of about 200,000 men of whom upwards of 155,000 were regulars.[1] Marshal Blanco organized such additional volunteers as he could collect to support his seasoned troops and made other arrangements to meet the expected onset. The Spanish navy was small and but ill conditioned for war with a navy such as ours, which in the past two or three years had been raised in rank by the addition of powerful new battle ships. The pundits, nevertheless, bade us put not too mean an estimate on the power of the antagonist. Large sums must be appropriated —it would be a long war.[2] There was fight in a Spaniard. The navy of Spain was one to be feared. Such statements were made in order to increase the interest in the approaching spectacle, to fan the war flame, to justify the free expenditure of money and to prepare the way for the claim to glory in the day of victory. Naval officers were sent to Europe to buy additional war vessels; passenger and freight boats were taken over by the government, some of which were plated with metal and mounted with guns.[3] Vessels that could not be put to other use entered the service as colliers, transports and hospital ships. Sailors were enlisted in the principal cities at high pay. The naval militia was mobilized for auxiliary service. The cadets were taken out of the academy at Annapolis and ordered to sea to officer the recruits.

When war was declared the new battle ships, the *Iowa* and the *Indiana*, with a number of cruisers, monitors and despatch boats, a torpedo flotilla, and four gunboats were at Key West. Captain William T. Sampson was ordered to take command of the squadron in the room of Admiral Montgomery Sicard who

[1] Chadwick, Span. Am. War, vol. i, pp. 51–4; Sargent, Campaign of Santiago, vol. iii, p. 158.
[2] Cf. Dingley's statement when he presented the war revenue bill.— App. Ann. Cyclop. for 1898, p. 167.
[3] Cf. Report of Sec. of Navy for 1898, pp. 21–3.

had been "condemned by medical survey." Sampson was raised to the rank of commodore, and shortly to that of rear admiral. He had the confidence and admiration of men in the service. His simplicity of mind, his reserves, his decision, his courage gave promise of wise command.[1] He was respected by naval authorities abroad.[2] His flag ship was the steel cruiser *New York*. The *Oregon*, a new battle ship which was at San Francisco, was ordered to the Atlantic at once and set forth on the long journey around the Horn.

A flying squadron under the command of Captain, since February, Commodore Winfield S. Schley, made up of his flag ship, the *Brooklyn*, with the battle ships *Massachusetts* and *Texas*, and a few other units, was stationed at Hampton Roads, so that it might be available for quick movements north or south in case of a raid upon the coast. A third squadron, consisting of four cruisers and a gunboat, was at Hong Kong. Commodore Dewey had been in command of this fleet since January. Seeking an assignment and, knowing that there would be a vacancy at the Asiatic station, he, in the summer of 1897, had visited Assistant Secretary of the Navy Roosevelt whose office was the meeting place for the leaders of the war party in Washington.[3] Dewey did not enjoy the confidences of a clique in the Department to which much power in the making of appointments was ascribed. Roosevelt advised him to take his case to Senator Proctor of Vermont, his native state. Proctor's friendliness to McKinley, when all the rest of New England was supporting Reed for the Presidential nomination in 1896, was well known. The use of such political methods was to meet with the disapproval of Secretary Long, but the object was gained. Dewey got the coveted post and, before sailing for the East, he was well instructed by Roosevelt and the jingoes who surrounded that young man. The Commodore studied maps and read descriptions of the Philippines, a group of islands off

[1] F. E. Chadwick, The Spanish American War, vol. i, p. 21. See also J. D. Long, The New Am. Navy, vol. i, pp. 210–2; ibid., Am. of Yesterday, p. 207.

[2] Cf. H. W. Wilson, The Downfall of Spain, pp. 373–4.

[3] Cf. H. Hagedorn, Leonard Wood, pp. 140–1.

the coast of Asia which had not yet come within the consciousness of the American people, and his tutors led him to understand that, in the event of the expected war, it would be his duty to advance upon and seize this distant appanage of Spain.[1]

But the chief of Roosevelt's audacities was yet to come. On February 25th, ten days, therefore, after the destruction of the *Maine*, in Long's absence from the Department, he sent a "secret and confidential" telegram to Dewey at Hong Kong, who was ordered to hold the *Olympia*, which there had been an intention of calling home for repairs; he should keep his bunkers full; and when he should receive word of a declaration of war he should make certain that the Spanish squadron did not leave the Asiatic coast, and begin "offensive operations in the Philippine Islands." In the short space of an afternoon Roosevelt flung out other orders right and left with, he has said, Lodge's abettance. "Do not take any such step involving the policy of the administration without consulting the President or me," Mr. Long wrote to his assistant when he learned of the order for an attack upon the Philippines.[2] "The very devil seemed to possess him," said Long, who had left the office merely for a few hours' rest. Nothing was required of Roosevelt during his chief's absence except the performance of "routine" duties. He went at things "like a bull in a china shop." Because of his "natural nervousness," accentuated by recent events, the Secretary was bound to conclude that his young assistant was not fit to be "entrusted with the responsibility of the Department," and he dragged himself back to his desk.[3]

[1] Autobiog. of Roosevelt, pp. 231–2; Autobiog. of Dewey, pp. 167–70; Walter Millis, The Martial Spirit, pp. 85–6; Corr. of Roosevelt and Lodge, vol. i, p. 278.

[2] Millis, The Martial Spirit, p. 112.

[3] Report of Bur. of Nav. for 1898, app., p. 65; J. D. Long, America of Yesterday, pp. 169–70; ibid., The New Am. Navy, vol. i, pp. 147, 172; Autobiog. of Roosevelt, pp. 3–4; Autobiog. of Dewey, p. 170; Millis, The Martial Spirit, pp. 85–6, 111–2. The singular fatuities of Roosevelt, with reference to the war with Spain, springing from his perpetual adolescence, are stated with documentation in H. F. Pringle, Theodore Roosevelt, chap. xiii. A classmate of Roosevelt's at Harvard, a Philadelphian, recalls a night soon after they had entered college. They were rollicking

Nelson A. Miles had come to the highest command in the army in 1895, upon the retirement of General Schofield.[1] He had not been trained at West Point. He had been a volunteer in the Civil War and since that time had been fighting Indians and writing and talking about his vigor and celerity as a soldier. He had spent the summer of 1897 in Europe, observing military operations in the war between Turkey and Greece, attending Queen Victoria's "Diamond Jubilee" and witnessing army maneuvers in Russia, Germany and France.[2] His relationship by marriage with General Sherman and John Sherman had not retarded his advancement in the service. A rather obstreperous character he was clearly not a perfect figure for the management of the war [3] in which work, however, he was to be given a part much smaller than his position would have seemed to warrant. He was overruled by the War Department and snubbed by its head from the first day. He was of opinion that the campaign should be left to the navy until the sickly season had passed. It were rash, he said to ears that were deaf, to send soldiers into the tropics at once—they should be trained,

through a part of the town in which poor men dwelt to the annoyance of the inhabitants. Some Irish women at a second story window threatened to pour hot water on the boys. A voice was heard above the din: "Let's go up and clean them out." The young man from Philadelphia, not yet acquainted with all the members of his class, asked who it was that had shouted out that suggestion. "That fellow," said a bystander, "is Theodore Roosevelt."

"Roosevelt came down here," Thomas S. Butler of Pennsylvania, long a member of the House Committee on Naval Affairs, told H. F. Pringle, in recalling the events of 1897, "looking for war. He did not care whom we fought so long as there was a scrap." (Pringle, Theodore Roosevelt, p. 171.) Secretary Long in his Diary made these entries regarding Roosevelt while he was Assistant Secretary of the Navy: "He shouts at the top of his voice and wanders all over creation—His forte is his push—He lacks the serenity of discussion—The best fellow in the world is worse than no use if he lack a cool head—He raised the devil in his impetuosity—In his precipitate way he came very near causing more of an explosion than happened to the Maine." (America of Yesterday, pp. 169, 170, 188, 212.) Roosevelt in conversation, was calling the President, when Mr. McKinley prolonged his efforts to avert war, a "chocolate eclair" and a "white-livered cur."—Pringle, Theodore Roosevelt, pp. 114, 130; H. H. Kohlsaat, From McKinley to Roosevelt, p. 77.

[1] Miles, Serving the Republic, p. 260. [2] Ibid., p. 262.
[3] Cf. H. H. Kohlsaat, From McKinley to Harding, pp. 107–8.

equipped and kept in camp at home until a movement southward should be safe.[1]

The land forces for the war would number in all about 275,000 men. Seven corps on the Atlantic coast were commanded by Major-Generals John R. Brooke, William M. Graham, James F. Wade, John J. Coppinger, William R. Shafter, James H. Wilson and Fitzhugh Lee, who, upon leaving the consulate in Cuba, immediately offered to take up arms.[2] Lee being a Southerner, with a name which was associated with the highest command on the Confederate side in the Civil War, (he was a nephew of Robert E. Lee and had been himself a doughty cavalry captain in our great sectional conflict) his enlistment signalized a reunited country and led to expressions of the liveliest satisfaction. His forwardness at Havana had put him in the war before the war had been declared. On his return from Cuba he had enjoyed ovations all the way from Key West to Washington where he arrived on April 12th. Crowds met him and cheered him. Ladies presented him with bouquets and it was with difficulty that he could pass through the streets.[3] He had become "the idol of the populace."[4] Joseph Wheeler, another Confederate soldier, generally known during the Civil War, and since, as "Fighting Joe" Wheeler, a member of the House of Representatives from Alabama, who had tendered his services to the country, was put in command of a cavalry division. Lee was an obese Virginia politician, Wheeler a small wizened man with a gray beard. Both were figures for Gilbert and Sullivan rather than the battle field. It had been more than 30 years since the war in which they had shone had ended and its soldiers were now short-winded old men. The various units

---

[1] Report of Maj. Gen. Commanding, pp. 5-8; N. Y. Nation, Nov. 17, 1898.

[2] The President offered an appointment as Major-General of volunteers to Minister Woodford when he came home from Spain, but he declined, saying that war was for younger men. (Woodford to McKinley, May 9, 1898, and McKinley to Woodford, May 11, 1898, in McKinley Papers.) General Lew Wallace had a different feeling; he was done great affront when his application for service was denied on the ground of age.— Wallace to Dick, Sep. 13, 1900, in ibid.

[3] N. Y. Times, April 13, 1898.

[4] McElroy, Grover Cleveland, vol. ii, p. 274.

were assembled at Tampa, Jacksonville, New Orleans, Chick-amauga Park in Georgia, a few miles from Chattanooga, Falls Church in Virginia (Camp Alger), about seven miles from Washington, and other places.

We had learned little on the subject of army practice since the Civil War. Now again country squires, eager to gain some glory in their communities by rushing to the defence of the flag, farmers, storekeepers and lawyers, with an eye to their future in politics, young hotspurs intent on adventure, not a few of them from the colleges and universities, flew forward at the President's word and competed for the chance to fight Spain. They were given courage for their tasks by the cry—"Remember the Maine." They offered their own services and formed companies and regiments which they would command. The militia units in the various states, which were social rather than military organizations, were the principal source from which the volunteer army would be drawn.

An amusing display of forwardness as the tocsin was sounded was Roosevelt's. Having done what he could as Assistant Secretary of the Navy to involve us in the war,[1] he now laid down his office and gathered a group of men around him who went through the newspapers and into the field as "Roosevelt's Rough Riders." One of the passions of his life was amateur ranching; his vacations were spent astride a horse in association with cowboys in the West. Plainsmen, policemen from Eastern cities and other blunt characters from all parts of the country, together with some gentlemen's sons whose skill in horsemanship had been gained on the polo field or in fox hunting, were dramatically welded into a volunteer cavalry regiment at San Antonio, Texas.[2] As Roosevelt knew nothing about the practical side of war he took a commission as lieutenant-colonel. Leonard Wood, an army surgeon, who had accompanied Miles on some expeditions against the Indians and who had recently been transferred from the plains to Washington, where he was administering medicines to old army officers and acting as

[1] Theodore Roosevelt, The Rough Riders, chap. i.
[2] Corr. of Roosevelt and Lodge, vol. i, pp. 298, 300–1.

White House physician,[1] was the first in command of this motley company. Wood and Roosevelt, since Roosevelt's arrival in Washington to be Assistant Secretary of the Navy, had become "playmates."[2] They now got for themselves the best uniforms, the best rifles and smokeless powder. One, a "human tumult,"[3] the other cool and self controlled, no stickler for formality in the War Department could withstand their importunities.[4] At least one other group of this kind was enlisted for the service, though it could not gain that notoriety for its movements which Roosevelt brought to his band.[5] Bryan, not yet done, as he thought, with politics, fearing loss of advantage were he to remain quietly at home, offered his services to the President. When they were not accepted he enlisted in a company in Nebraska and subsequently organized a regiment, of which, by appointment of the governor of his state, he became colonel,[6] though he knew as little of war as of the monetary science and though his interest in the event was far from earnest, a fact which his later course confirmed.[7] More than the number of men asked for by the President presented themselves for enrollment at the recruiting stations and were sent to the camps and to ports of embarkation for a campaign in the tropics, which, knowing that they could meet with little opposition, they contemplated with high zest.

The earliest activities of the army were directed to the relief of the Cuban rebels for whom the newspapers had developed a considerable amount of public sympathy, though these same

[1] In this capacity he established confidential relations first with President Cleveland and later with McKinley to whom he endeared himself by his devoted attentions to Mrs. McKinley, who was a pathetic invalid.

[2] Corr. of Roosevelt and Lodge, vol. i, p. 285; Theodore Roosevelt, The Rough Riders, pp. 3–4; J. H. Sears, The Career of Leonard Wood, pp. 60–7; H. Hagedorn, Leonard Wood, pp. 133, 138–9.

[3] Described by one of his Rough Riders as a "Biff-bang-do-it-right-now-can-not-put-it-off-another-minute" sort of man.—Hagedorn, op. cit., p. 152.

[4] Ibid., pp. 146–7.

[5] Roosevelt would have "his share of strut and sensation," said ex-President Cleveland.—McElroy, Grover Cleveland, vol. ii, p. 274.

[6] Memoirs of W. J. Bryan, pp. 119–20.

[7] Cf. N. Y. Nation, May 26 and June 26, 1898; S. H. Acheson, Joe Bailey, p. 125.

newspapers would frustrate some quixotic efforts in this field by their betrayal of demands for secrecy in the sending out of such expeditions.[1]

The throb of humanitarianism was not a principal basis for the war, but it played a part in bringing the country to hostilities and some of the men in our expeditionary forces may have been animated by a wish to liberate a down-trodden people. It was understood, however, that the insurgents were a poor mark for our chivalry. Those in arms numbered few more than 15,000 and were but little above banditti.[2] Many of the innocent peasants were starving—this was clearly the truth— and interest in them was not misspent, but the portion of the male population under arms which would have us regard them as soldiers, fighting for freedom, could awaken but little enthusiasm in the breasts of well informed and discriminating men. To gain the ends in view, now that we were in the war, arms, ammunition and supplies, which unauthorized persons had been surreptitiously forwarding to the rebels, were to be officially delivered to them—so that they, from the interior, could increase the trouble which they had been giving to the Spaniards in garrison on the coast, while we should apply naval force from the outside.

A Cuban leader, Calixto Garcia, a veteran of the revolt of 1868-78, seemed to be making some progress with a campaign in the eastern part of the island around Santiago, and it was deemed advisable to land troops within his reach. Gomez, the generalissimo of the rebel army, however, opposed our coming ashore anywhere, in the belief that we would never leave the country once we had set foot upon it. He himself could compel the Spaniards to evacuate. He asked of the United States only arms and cartridges, and an effective blockade, so that Spain could have no accretions in man power or in military supplies. Such boasts were made, though Gomez seems to have had not

[1] R. A. Alger, The Span. Am. War, p. 42.
[2] Chadwick, Spanish American War, vol. i, p. 51. Ex-President Cleveland before we were yet in the war described them as "the most inhuman and barbarous cutthroats in the world."—McElroy, Grover Cleveland, vol. ii, p. 274.

more than 3,000 men in his command.[1] His resources were so low that, while waiting for American expeditions which were promised him, he was obliged to kill his horses for food. The rebels even despatched an envoy to Washington to inform the authorities that an army of invasion would be viewed with extreme disfavor.[2] It was plain now, if it had not been before, that little could be done with such "patriots." Leaders who were so suspicious of our motives and so jealous of their own glory as to deny us the opportunity to render them useful aid would be but poor allies.

Admiral Sampson, in response to orders based on the proclamation of the President, established a blockade of Havana and the ports connected by railway with the city, and here Captain-General Blanco was confined, in so far as egress by water was concerned, with a garrison of, perhaps, 30,000 men. The line up and down which Sampson's vessels cruised from Cardenas to Bahia Honda was about 140 miles in length. From time to time targets were made of batteries, when attacks were directed at his ships, and of firing squads on shore. It was his wish to reduce Havana by bombardment, a purpose from which he was dissuaded by definite orders from the Navy Department.[3] A number of Spanish merchantmen and fishing boats were captured and boarded with prize crews. A few weeks later, in June, the blockade was extended to cover the entire coast of Cuba, a distance of about 1200 miles, and also the port of San Juan in Porto Rico.[4]

General Miles, as has been said, was clearly of the opinion that the recruits should undergo intensive training before there should be any movement upon Cuba. This work could go on in the states. Until the rainy season should be at an end and the danger of infectious fevers had passed the new army could well spend its time in preparation.[5] Doughty young

[1] Cf. N. Y. Nation, May 12, 1898; Spanish American War, Described by Eye Witnesses, pp. 24–6.
[2] N. Y. Nation, May 12, 1898.
[3] Chadwick, Spanish American War, vol. i, pp. 70–7; R. D. Evans, A Sailor's Log, p. 406.
[4] Richardson, vol. x, p. 200.
Cf. Report of Comm. to Investigate the War, vol. vii, p. 3249.

messengers were set ashore in both Cuba and Porto Rico to
gain and bring back correct and useful information in regard to
the country preparatory to the formulation of plans for the
campaign. We should aid the insurgents as we could, and
watchfully await the failure or success of their operations.

But the popular eagerness to win the war at once was uncontrollable. The cry was "On to Havana" and the pressure for
action put upon the Department at Washington led to the
formulation of many schemes. Untrained men were crowded
into Tampa for embarkation, material was forwarded—all
was confusion because of the zeal that was demanded by the
politicians, goaded by a heedless and excitable press, and because
of the incompetency in Washington which General Miles, when
he arrived upon the scene, warmly denounced.[1]

Troops were to be landed on the south coast for a recon-
noissance in the country over which Garcia's forces roamed,
or, as Miles suggested, to be marched up through the centre
of the island, thus dividing the Spanish forces. Then, at the
end of the sickly season, infantry and horses could move west-
wardly upon Havana which, it was believed, with the cooperation of the navy, could be rapidly reduced. Again the army
was to land on the north coast. All the while there were plans
for an invasion of Porto Rico.[2]

The Cuban expeditionary force would be directed by Major-
General William R. Shafter. He was the son of a frontier
farmer—a native of Kalamazoo, in Michigan. He had had
some experience with soldiering as a volunteer during the Civil
War and, after an interval, reentered the service. At the outbreak of hostilities with Spain he was stationed at San Francisco.
Secretary Alger, also of Michigan, was a friend at Washington
who would make certain that Shafter should have a chance
to gain renown, and he was sent to Tampa. He weighed
more than 300 pounds and could mount a horse only with

---

[1] Cf. W. H. Carter, Life of General Chaffee, pp. 129, 130; Corr. of
Roosevelt and Lodge, vol. i, pp. 303–9; N. Y. Times, June 10, 11 and 14,
1898.

[2] Report of Comm. to Investigate the War, vol. ii, pp. 1341–3; ibid.,
vol. vii, pp. 3285–7; R. A. Alger, The Span. Am. War, chap v.

difficulty. As a figure for active military duty in the tropics he gave promise of being far from an appropriate choice,[1] but it seemed to be certain that he would lead the first body of troops to leave the country and he awaited in Florida the word that should release him for the campaign.[2]

Early plans were changed perforce. This was to be a naval war—the army would play minor parts, a fact which was soon to be established in theatrical fashion in the China Sea. When Great Britain issued her proclamation of neutrality, Commodore Dewey and his Asiatic squadron, now reinforced by the *Baltimore* from Honolulu, with Roosevelt's and Lodge's words in his ears, set sail from Hong Kong for the Philippines.[3] Secretary Long now issued the order—Dewey was to capture or destroy the Spanish vessels, rather splendidly called a "fleet," known to be assembled at this point.[4]

A number of men in our consular service in that part of the world had been quite officiously concerning themselves with the political situation in the Philippines, where Spain was confronted with an insurrection not unlike that which was in progress for her damage in Cuba.[5] The war for the suppression of the rebellion had been attended by many of the cruelties which the readers of our newspapers were taught to associate with the profession of arms in Spain and our consuls, as the hatred for the oppressor in Cuba took possession of the American people, were quite clear in their sympathies for the Filipinos, small brown-skinned Malays of an unfamiliar race, who were struggling for freedom and independence.

A young native, Emilio Aguinaldo, was the principal leader of the insurgents and, to be rid of him, the Spaniards, at the end of the year 1897, offered him a sum of money if he would

[1] F. E. Chadwick, The Spanish American War, vol. ii, p. 110; J. C. Hemment, Cannon and Camera, pp. 76–7.

[2] Report of Sec. of War for 1898, pp. 82–3; N. Y. Nation, Dec. 1 and 8, 1898.

[3] Autobiog. of Dewey, p. 193.

[4] Report of Sec. of Navy for 1898, p. 6; Richardson, vol. x, p. 155; Autobiog. of Dewey, p. 195.

[5] "Conditions here and in Cuba are practically alike."—O. F. Williams, Am. Consul in Manila, Feb. 22, 1898, in Senate Doc., 55th Cong. 3rd sess., no. 62, pt. 1, p. 319.

leave the country. He had taken the bribe and had departed for Siam,[1] since which time a degree of quiet had reigned in the land. Lately he had appeared in Singapore, where our consul was cooperating with the American consul at Hong Kong and a very active jingo who had lately come out as our representative at Manila. Commodore Dewey was persuaded to give Aguinaldo an audience if he would repair to Hong Kong, which he did, and arrangements were made for transporting him in a revenue cutter to Manila at an appropriate early day so that he might resume his war upon Spain.[2]

The Captain-General was, on many accounts, in no position to meet the attack of the American squadron which arrived on April 30th at Subig Bay on the west coast of Luzon, the largest island of the group. Dewey, not finding his quarry there, steamed on to Manila Bay. Batteries on shore, mines in the harbor and power not possessed by the boats and their ineffective commanders and crews were emphasized to make his task seem arduous. As a matter of fact the entire engagement which was to follow was of a very simple nature and the glory which his action brought him reached important proportions because of the zest of the country for some war-like feat after more than 30 years of peace. Dewey, it may be said for his credit as a fighter, prepared for the battle intelligently, maneuvered his vessels skillfully and kept them out of the range of the shore batteries and the Spanish ships, and his conduct after his victory was chivalrous and humane. The entire enemy "fleet," seven ships, two of them called cruisers, at least three of the whole number disabled by broken machinery, and some smaller craft, on May 1, 1898, faced the disastrous and well directed fire of our gunners. In less than two hours all were burned, sunk or captured, except a few of the light gunboats which were not in the battle, and which escaped by running up the lagoons. The batteries on shore were silenced. On our side not one ship was damaged, not a man was killed.

[1] R. A. Alger, The Span. Am. War, pp. 344–5.
[2] Senate Doc., 55th Cong. 3rd sess., no. 62, pt. 1, pp. 319 et seq., N. Y. Nation, Jan. 19, 1899.

The only casualties were on the *Baltimore* when a shot exploded a case of ammunition, slightly wounding eight men. The Spaniards were abominable marksmen and, in general, made but stupid use of such facilities as they had at hand for defence.[1] They, on their side, lost 167 men killed, while 214 more were wounded, including the Spanish Admiral, Montojo. Dewey now established a blockade of Manila. The waters of the bay were under his complete control.[2] He cabled the Secretary of the Navy that he could "take the city at any time." But he could not hold it without troops.[3] He would await the progress of the campaign to be opened by Aguinaldo.

Bringing this leader back was to the Spaniards like releasing the pest among them. He was nothing loath again to raise the standards of rebellion with a view, as he soon stated, of securing the support of the United States in his design to found a republic of which he might be the president. It was understood that we had no territorial aims in Cuba; Aguinaldo sought the same assurances in reference to the Philippines, which our representatives said that they had been discreet enough to withhold, though they certainly took little trouble to disabuse him of the hope which he may have cherished in the direction of self government.

The news of what "Dewey did" reached the United States in the form of a garbled relation of the event from Madrid for the newspapers of May 2nd. The cable to Hong Kong had been cut, but a press boat raced thither from the battle scene with the news. On the 3rd confirmation of the feat

[1] Autobiog. of Dewey, pp. 232-3.

[2] The great inferiority of the Spanish squadron is indicated in the Spanish official report, where it is stated that the tonnage of the Spanish fleet was but half that of Dewey's and the horse power less than one fourth as great. The Spanish had 76 to Dewey's 163 guns and these were not "rapid fire." (Report of Bur. of Nav. for 1898, app., pp. 89–92). Dewey to emphasize his difficulties makes a different comparison (Autobiog., p. 203). In the Philippines Admiral Cervera said in a letter to the Ministry of Marine at Madrid on March 7, 1898, that the Americans would have "not even a shadow of a resistance to oppose them." (Cervera's Docs. Translated for the Office of Naval Intelligence, p. 35.) Both sides had this measure of equality—that neither had any armored ships and both fought with the old brown powder.—Autobiog. of Dewey, p. 203.

[3] Report of Bur. of Nav. for 1898, p. 68.

was at hand in a despatch received by at least one New York newspaper and, on the 7th, word came from Dewey himself in the form of an official report, which had been carried to Hong Kong by the *McCulloch*.[1] The news electrified the nation. Dewey was the toast of the country. The President thanked him, congratulated him and made him a rear admiral. "The magnitude of this victory," the President said, could "hardly be measured by the ordinary standard of naval warfare." The "great heart of the nation" throbbed "at this unsurpassed achievement." The country owed Dewey and his men "an incalculable debt." Congress sent him its thanks in the name of the American people.[2] The Secretary of the Navy was ordered to present "a sword of honor" to the distinguished commander-in-chief of our forces on the Asiatic station, and to distribute bronze medals commemorating the battle of Manila Bay to the officers and men on the ships.[3]

The naval experts compared horse power, diameters, weight of metal, muzzle energy and other points of interest to them. Many theories about the utility of the ships which had been recently added to the navies of the various maritime powers had been tried and tested and, if of more interest to the professional than to the lay mind, the results would have their influence in the war offices of the world. All danger of raids upon our Pacific coast was now removed [4] and the effect of the event upon the military morale of Spain was profound.[5]

Fear still reigned on the Atlantic coast; ports had been mined, navigation in and out of them at night had been forbidden, the naval militia on converted yachts, tugs and ferry boats cruised outside on the watch for the main Spanish fleet.[6] The exaggerated power attributed to the vessels composing it and the cunning of its commander, Admiral Cervera, in the light of events, was not short of comic. He left Cadiz on April 8th with two armored cruisers bearing the names *Infanta Maria*

---

[1] Report Bureau of Nav. for 1898, app., pp. 68–72.
[2] Ibid., p. 98; Richardson, vol. x, pp. 155–6.
[3] Richardson, vol. x, pp. 155–7, 208.
  Report of Sec. of Navy for 1898, p. 6.
[5] N. Y. Nation, May 12, 1898.   [6] Cf. Richardson, vol. x, pp. 166–7.

Teresa and *Cristobal Colon*. They were to rendezvous at the Cape Verde Islands, and join a few torpedo destroyers there and two more cruisers, the *Vizcaya* and the *Almiranta Oquendo* which had been in American waters (the *Vizcaya* for a few tense days after the destruction of the *Maine* in New York harbor), and which, for safety, had been sent to meet him.[1] A well organized intelligence service should have been able to discover the number of the ships and to have given true information as to their potentiality. Anyhow those who were managing the war for us preferred to think that the squadron was of great size and strength.[2] That the ships were on the Atlantic and would bombard New York or any one of a hundred places on our seaboard with destructive effect was implicitly believed. Now and again, like the old sea serpent, the fleet was seen and the news in the sensational journals struck intended terror into the hearts of women and children, and the naval militia. Owners of cottages on the seashore could not let them for the summer because of the popular fright.[3] Gentlemen in Boston took their bonds and mortgages inland to Worcester and Springfield.[4] Cities, towns, even individuals with homes, hotels, fisheries or other business interests on the coast, urged their Congressmen to visit the Navy Department, or addressed it directly, asking for war ships and batteries to ward off attacks of the dreaded foe.[5] The most vociferous of the jingoes, Frye and Chandler, loud and long in their cries for war, must have vessels to protect the coast of Maine and New Hampshire's precious outlet to the sea at Portsmouth.[6] Nothing less than a monitor would allay the fears of the people settled on the banks

[1] He said when he received the *Vizcaya* that she was "nothing more than a buoy"; she had not had her bottom cleaned for nine months; she was "only a boil in the body of the fleet." (Cervera's Docs., pp. 57, 65). The *Colon*, recently built at Genoa, had sailed without her heavy guns.— Concas, The Squadron of Admiral Cervera, pp. 16, 42.

[2] Cf. C. S. Olcott, Life of McKinley, vol. ii, pp. 41–2; F. E. Chadwick, Span. Am. War, vol. i, pp. 70, 222; Walter Millis, The Martial Spirit, p. 119.

[3] N. Y. Times, March 11 and 23, 1898.

[4] J. F. Rhodes, The McKinley and Roosevelt Administrations, p. 76.

[5] Autobiog. of Roosevelt, pp. 235–6.

[6] J. D. Long, America of Yesterday, p. 185.

of the Kennebec River.[1] It was May 11th before it was authentically reported that the Spanish squadron had reached Martinique.

Sampson had abandoned blockade duty and, with his fleet, accompanied by a flotilla of boats bearing the newspaper correspondents,[2] set sail for the harbor of San Juan in Porto Rico into which it was surmised that the enemy might advance. Cervera, however, halted at Curaçao, took on a small quantity of coal [3] and, strangely enough, though because of dirty engines, disabled machinery and foul bottoms he could proceed no faster than about seven knots an hour,[4] he eluded the eyes of Sampson and other naval commanders who were patrolling the channels leading to Spain's Caribbean ports. On the morning of May 19th he drew safely into Santiago de Cuba,[5] under the shelter of the old Morro and other shore batteries, which rose high and commanded a wide spread of water. His triumph was to be a hollow one, but he, at any rate, had brought his ships to port in Cuba which it was not expected that he could do in view of the vigilance of the American navy, which had every advantage on its side.

While Cervera was limping along from Curaçao to Santiago Sampson was returning to Key West from San Juan in Porto Rico which he had shelled. This was a rather fruitless exercise of marksmanship upon a number of forts and unoffending parts of the adjacent city. The black powder which our navy was still using in gunnery prevented the taking of effective aim. One man was killed and another died of the heat; a few were wounded. The casualties were not much greater on the Spanish side. A score or more civilians were injured, and damage was inflicted on the cathedral, the palace, the town hall, a school and a number of dwelling houses.[6]

[1] E. N. Dingley, Life and Times of Nelson Dingley, Jr., p. 455.
[2] Chadwick, Spanish Am. War, vol. i, p. 221.
[3] Tejeiro, Battles and Capitulation of Santiago, p. 108.
[4] He left one of his three destroyers at Martinique—she could proceed no farther.—Ibid., p. 30; cf. Chadwick, Relations of the U. S. and Spain, vol. i, p. 244.
[5] Cervera's Docs., p. 80.
[6] Cf. H. H. Sargent, The Campaign of Santiago, vol. i, pp. 197-8.

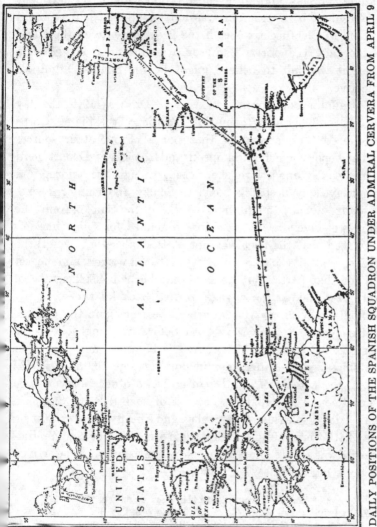

DAILY POSITIONS OF THE SPANISH SQUADRON UNDER ADMIRAL CERVERA FROM APRIL 9
TO JULY 3, 1898

(Taken from the log book of the Cristobal Colon.)

Again at Key West Sampson conferred with Schley who commanded the flying squadron which had been ordered hither from Hampton Roads, and, after consultation with the Department at Washington, a program was agreed upon. Schley would proceed to Cienfuegos to see if the fleet had entered there and to blockade the port. Sampson would remain off Havana which it was fair to believe might be the Spanish admiral's objective.

But affairs soon wore a new aspect. On May 19th, the day Cervera and his ships came into Santiago, the Signal Corps announced their arrival at that port.[1] From other sources similar reports reached Sampson and the Navy Department, to be looked upon with skepticism, though the information was relayed by despatch boats to Schley at Cienfuegos who, standing outside the harbor, watching the smoke from the funnels of divers merchant ships,[2] remained for some time unconvinced that the fleet was not at that place. At length he received positive orders to proceed to Santiago [3] and he set sail for that port. But he said that he had insufficient coal and, after making the voyage, turned back for a new supply without really discovering anything bearing upon the purpose of his quest. It was May 28th before, meeting colliers, he was enabled to retrace his course.[4] The next morning, after the ships had been ten days in port, he sighted the *Cristobal Colon*, the *Infanta Maria Teresa* and two other vessels.[5] The Department was impatient because of such delays. Sampson shared its displeasure and Schley and the flying squadron on May 24th were put under Sampson's orders.[6] The commander-in-chief was sent to join Schley before Santiago, where he arrived on June 1st.

---

[1] Report of Comm. to Investigate the War, vol. .vi, p. 2935.
[2] Chadwick, Span. Am. War, vol. i, pp. 267–8, 288–90.
[3] Report of Sec. of Navy for 1898, p. 9; Chadwick, op. cit., vol. i, p. 291.
[4] This beating back and forth is described in Report of Sec. of Navy for 1898, pp. 8–11; F. E. Chadwick, op. cit., vol. i, pp. 262 et seq.; R. D. Evans, A Sailor's Log, pp. 428–9. Also in R. A. Alger, The Spanish American War, pp. 222–4, and at length, and in great detail, in the Report of the Schley Court of Inquiry of 1901.
[5] Report of Bur. of Nav. for 1898, app., pp. 400, 404.   [6] Ibid., p. 394.

Even yet the intelligence system and the methods of communication between branches of the service were so imperfect that a young lieutenant, Victor Blue, of the U. S. S. *Suwanee* was set on land for two long trips, on mule back, one of 73 and another of 60 miles, round the harbor, which he was enabled to complete with the aid of the Cuban insurgents, before it could be certainly known whether the entire Spanish fleet were inside.[1] There they were—"bottled up," as the phrase went. Dazzling search lights played on the harbor entrance to prevent escape during the night.[2] A plan was laid for sinking the weighted hulk of a collier in the channel. Then the ships could stay where they were until they should rot—surrender would be necessary in no long time without battle. A young man from Alabama, an assistant naval constructor, educated at Annapolis, and subsequently at marine engineering schools abroad, Richmond Pearson Hobson, was chosen for the service from among many who were eager for the dangerous adventure. Seven men accompanied him (hundreds volunteered)[3] and, before dawn, on June 3rd they entered the harbor through a fusillade, sank the collier with torpedoes in the center of the channel at its narrowest point, as they thought, taking refuge themselves on a catamaran which they threw overboard. They could not reach a launch which was to have effected their rescue. All, two of the number slightly wounded, fell into the hands of the Spaniards.[4] It was a gallant deed, entirely futile as it proved, since the wreck, by ill fortune, had not been sunk in the right place and the shipway out of the harbor was as free to Cervera as before. But the acclamation of the people, excited with the war fervor, was boundless. Hobson was named with Dewey. Sampson in his official report said that "a more brave and daring thing" had not been done "since Cushing blew up the *Albemarle*."[5] The President addressed

[1] Report of Bureau of Navigation for 1898, pp. 443–6.
[2] F. E. Chadwick, Span. Am. War, vol. i, pp. 362–4; Cervera's Docs., p. 145.
[3] Cf. R. D. Evans, A Sailor's Log, pp. 433–4.
[4] Cf. R. P. Hobson, The Sinking of the Merrimac.
[5] Report of Bur. of Nav. for 1898, pp. 437–8, 481.

Congress on the subject and asked that the young man be advanced in rank, and be thanked by them for his heroism.[1] When he came back to America to receive the myrtle from grateful hands young women fell upon him and kissed him. He reigned as an idol until other great persons appeared on the horizon and his figure could be seen in quieter lights.

Meantime the navy stood outside and watched Cervera's fleet. The plan of campaign for the army took definite form. Though Miles was in command he found himself entirely overborne by the Secretary of War and others in Washington who, operating through the President as commander-in-chief, were conducting the war in their own way. Admiral Sampson advocated a land movement in support of the navy.[2] Major-General Shafter had been waiting in Florida for the opportunity to embark and he now got away at the head of an expedition which was to go ashore near Santiago. On May 30th he was ordered to put his troops in transports at Tampa. General Miles wished to accompany this expedition; 30 or 40 per cent. of the men, he said, were undrilled—in one regiment there were no less than 300 men who had never fired a gun.[3] His request was denied—he was asked if he would go to Porto Rico instead, and some days later he was ordered to report to Washington where his advice, it was said, was required at once. On the 26th of June he was told to organize an expedition to operate against the enemy "in Cuba and Porto Rico," which, it was intended, should take him to Porto Rico, while Shafter, his superior absent, should be enjoying the honors at Santiago.

Guantanamo Bay, about 40 miles east of Santiago, was seized as a base for the fleet. At that place, after it had been shelled, a few hundred marines landed and drove out the Spaniards. A half dozen of our men were killed in this work. Shafter's troops would go ashore still nearer the objective, a part of the expedition at Daiquiri, about 18 miles away, and the rest at Siboney, seven or eight miles still nearer the entrance

---

[1] Richardson, vol. x, pp. 158–60.
[2] Report of Sec. of War for 1898, p. 89. [3] Ibid., p. 24.

to Santiago Bay. The expeditionary force included about 17,000 men—infantry, cavalry and artillery—and a large body of newspaper correspondents.

Tampa for some weeks had been thronged with sightseers. Conditions there had not improved during the period of waiting. The railroads were congested with passengers and material. Commands competed with one another for places on the ships which were not suited to the use they were now to enjoy, and were overcrowded.[1] Disorder reigned as the transports, 28 in number, with a few lighters, one of which was lost in transit, with all the advertisement which journalism could give to the movement, started, after incredible mismanagement and much delay, for Cuba.[2]

The water which the men were to drink on their voyage had come from New York. The tanks were foul. Fortunately the sea was as smooth as glass and the men were able to live in the open air. Had they been confined in the "unventilated holds" the chief surgeon of the expeditionary corps said that the suffering would have been "intolerable."[3] In eight days the ships reached their destination.[4] Confusion again ruled at disembarkation which commenced on June 22nd. The facilities for lighterage were so inadequate that two men and many horses and mules were drowned. It was a miracle that more were not lost in view of the conditions under which the landing was made.[5] General Henry W. Lawton commanded one division, General J. Ford Kent another; Wheeler had charge of the cavalry, most of whom had been obliged to come without their horses. Officers who were better supplied, because of the difficult character of the country, could make but limited use of their animals. The men went ashore with only such

[1] Report of Sec. of War for 1898, pp. 778–9.
[2] For conditions at Tampa see Stephen Bonsal, The Fight for Santiago, pp. 44–64; Theodore Roosevelt, The Rough Riders, chap. ii; Roosevelt's Autobiography, pp. 253 5; J. Bigelow, Jr., Reminiscences of the Santiago Campaign; F. E. Chadwick, op. cit., vol. ii, pp. 14 et seq.; J. D. Miley, In Cuba with Shafter, chaps. i, ii, and iii.
[3] Report of Sec. of War for 1898, p. 780.   [4] Ibid.
[5] Ibid.; Stephen Bonsal, The Fight for Santiago, pp. 80–3; J. D. Miley, In Cuba with Shafter, chaps. iv and v.

rations, tentage and cooking utensils as they were able to bear on their backs. The little which they took with them they, in the insufferable heat of midday, threw aside. Even first-aid packets were cast away.[1] Medical officers landed with only such supplies as they could carry in their hands.[2]

In this situation some of the volunteers, in their haste to get into action, pushed into the jungle. No time was to be lost by such cock-a-hoop warriors. "Fighting Joe" Wheeler, whose reputation as a son of Mars was at stake, and Roosevelt with his "Rough Riders" who must fire the first shot, kill the first Spaniard and gain a place on the front page of the American newspapers could not be restrained. Lawton of the regular army had been put in command of the advance. But no account was made by the volunteers of this disposition and they were in the "battle of Las Guanimas" before any one knew what they were about. Without necessary equipment, heedless of their own safety and inviting dreadful miseries for their wounded,[3] they, nevertheless, escaped disaster and, because of this good fortune, and the impossibility of reproving an "ex-rebel brigadier" who was now fighting for his country at the head of Northern troops, and a like impossibility with reference to Roosevelt, the movement was advertised as a great feat at arms.[4] In spite of such disrespect for discipline and common

[1] Report of Sec. of War for 1898, p. 780; Report of Major-General Commanding for 1898, p. 148; R. A. Alger, The Span. Am. War, pp. 95–8; J. Bigelow, Jr., Reminiscences of the Santiago Campaign, p. 46.

[2] Report of Sec. of War for 1898, p. 780.

[3] Cf. Report of Sec. of War for 1898, p. 786; J. D. Miley, In Cuba with Shafter, p. 95. Roosevelt's version is in his Rough Riders, pp. 76–104.

[4] Report of Comm. to Investigate the Conduct of the War, vol. vii, p. 3251. General Wheeler in justifying his departure without supplies said: "There was an impression that we ought to get ashore and go right at the enemy. I took that view myself. We came there for business and it was necessary to move upon the enemy with rapidity." Wheeler kept "going on to the front." For a week he did not see General Shafter "or anybody else from the ships." (Ibid., vol. iii, p. 16; cf. W. H. Carter, Life of General Chaffee, pp. 136–9; J. Bigelow, Jr., Reminiscences of the Santiago Campaign, chap. ix; George Kennan, Campaigning in Cuba, pp. 105–6.) Roosevelt, writing to Lodge of the first skirmish into which he rushed with his cowboys, said boastfully, as if there were merit in such action, "Shafter was not even ashore."—Corr. of Roosevelt and Lodge, vol. i, p. 315; cf. Roosevelt, Autobiog., pp. 255–60.

recklessness, passing over difficult trails, mere mule tracks, which were choked by rank tropical vegetation, the whole expedition was, in a few days, within sight of Santiago. Now there was some heavy fighting much of which, it is believed, might have been obviated.[1] The fortified village of El Caney and San Juan hill were desperately defended and only impetuous attack dislodged the Spaniards, a result which was effected in as awkwardly and foolishly managed an engagement as, probably, ever was seen in modern warfare. Our troops, after their costly success, strengthened their positions—they now were very near the city, but, on July 2nd, the Spaniards renewing battle, Shafter, as he contemplated the number of his killed and wounded, cabled the War Department to ask if he might withdraw from the line which he occupied to await the arrival of reinforcements. Supplies were running low; the loss of life in the face of Santiago's defences might be too great.[2] The Secretary of War bade the commander of the expedition hold his ground; reinforcements would be despatched at once.[3]

Suddenly Shafter took courage. He turned to Admiral Sampson, asking for an active forward movement by the navy to remove the pressure on his lines. He would demand the surrender of Santiago under threat of immediate shell fire, while the admiral should be running into the harbor and attacking the city from his side with the naval guns.[4] Shafter in his urgency lost his temper.[5] Sampson replied conciliatingly. He reminded Shafter that the channel was mined; without countermining, which would consume much time, he could advance only by inviting the loss of his ships, which were irreplaceable.[6] The matter was referred to the Secretary of War. Alger, taking Shafter's part in the squabble, appealed to McKinley as commander-in-chief and submitted three

---

[1] Cf. Chadwick, Span. Am. War, vol. ii, chaps. iv. and v.

[2] Report of Sec. of War for 1898, p. 103.   [3] Ibid.

[4] Ibid., pp. 104–5.

[5] See, e.g., his despatch of July 2nd in which he said: "I am at a loss to see why the navy cannot work under a destructive fire as well as the army." Sampson was asked "to fire on everything in sight" until it was demolished.—Report of Dur. of Nav. for 1898, app., p. 504.

[6] Cf. Report of Sec. of Navy for 1898, p. 13.

plans for the President's adoption. He proposed (1) that the navy should be ordered to force an entrance to the harbor at once; (2) that the navy should give one of the smaller ships of the fleet to the army which should attempt to break its way through the mines; and (3) that the army should take one of its own transports, protect the pilot house and upper deck with bales of hay, call for volunteers from the army, who should attach an anchor to a tow line and drag the harbor for torpedoes, when, if the movement should be successful, the navy could follow.[1]

While these parleys were in progress Cervera determined to dash out of his "bottle," past the blockading fleet, and take to the high seas. He had come across the ocean hopelessly. Repeatedly he had made representations to the Ministry of Marine in Madrid bearing upon the condition of his ships. The government, he said, had learned nothing since Trafalgar.[2] His men were not paid, his vessels were half armed, requisitions for material went unanswered. Three men were drowned on one occasion, when he had ordered a salute, by the breaking of an old ridge rope for which he had asked replacement fifty days before.[3] He knew that he was going to certain destruction when he left the Cape Verde Islands. He knew now that his chances of escape, after leaving the harbor of Santiago, were of the smallest. It was a "direful enterprise." [4] But he would be caught if he remained and he had better make the trial than die ingloriously in a trap.

[1] Alger to McKinley, July 5, 1898, in McKinley Papers.
[2] Cervera's Docs., p. 36.
[3] Ibid., p. 35. Cervera's statements to his government regarding the defenceless condition of its navy in case of war with the United States were made not without reproof. After the explosion on the *Maine* he wrote to the Ministry of Marine in his own defence—"Do we not owe to our country not only our life, if necessary, but the exposition of our beliefs? I ask myself if it is right for me to keep silent and thereby make myself an accomplice in adventures which will surely cause the total ruin of Spain." He begged that his opinions should be communicated to the Queen and the whole council of ministers.—Ibid., p. 30; cf. N. Y. Nation, Dec. 1, 1898 and Jan. 5, 1899; R. A. Alger, The Span. Am. War, p. 245.
[4] Cervera's Docs. p. 51. "God had withdrawn his hand from Spain."—Concas, op. cit., p. 35; cf. Tejeiro, Battles and Capitulation of Santiago, p. 111.

Sampson had left his position in the line and, with the *New York*, had steamed up the coast—to the east—to confer with Shafter at Siboney, when, on the morning of Sunday, July 3rd, Cervera, without a coal supply, without food, indeed, for his men in his beleaguered position,[1] in response to orders from the authorities in Madrid and the peremptory command of Captain-General Blanco, set forth for, as he described it, his "horrible and useless hecatomb." [2]

The battle ship *Oregon* had, by this time, arrived from the Pacific, after her long voyage around the Horn, which the whole country followed with bated interest, and had her place in the line.[3] In Sampson's absence Commodore Schley on the *Brooklyn* seems to have directed the movements of the fleet. He was next in rank. Sampson, in taking his departure, had signalled the captains to disregard the movements of the commander-in-chief,[4] and, although they had had their orders and their action had been predetermined, in the event of Cervera's attempt to escape, it is incontrovertible in fact, in spite of denials which made their appearance in later disputation, that Schley had, or should have had, more than a captain's part in the battle, which was brief and decisive.[5] Nearly all had been done, to Sampson's great mortification, before he could return, and, when he did so, it was to trail his fleet, since Cervera had chosen to head away from him toward the west. The squadron opened fire on the unfortunates as they one after another, led

---

[1] Cf. Report of Bur. of Nav. for 1898, app., p. 563.

[2] Cervera's Docs., p. 112. The admiral had been put under the orders of the Captain-General. It was for him (Blanco) to decide, Cervera said, whether he was "to go out to suicide, dragging along" with him "those 2,000 sons of Spain."—Ibid.

[3] The Oregon left San Francisco on March 19th and arrived in Jupiter Inlet in Florida on May 24th.

[4] Chadwick, Span. Am. War, vol. ii, p. 130.

[5] It was said that he issued no orders as a commander to the fleet. But he flew a signal not seen on the other ships—"Clear for action," which Sampson's captain, Chadwick, dismisses with the observation that it was "scarcely needed," and at least one other—"Close up." (Record of Court of Inquiry, vol. ii, Signals, p. 22; Chadwick, Span.-Am. War, vol. ii, pp. 132, 134; cf. G. E. Graham, Schley and Santiago). In a like case, before Havana, Sampson having gone away, "Fighting Bob" Evans says that, as senior officer present, he was in command of the fleet.—A Sailor's Log, p. 412.

by the *Infanta*, Cervera's flag ship, came down the bay. They were riddled with shot, their magazines exploded, they were sunk or beached. Only the *Vizcaya* and the *Colon* led our navy a chase. The *Colon* ran 50 miles before she was overtaken. Approximately 300 of the men and officers on the Spanish ships were killed or drowned—the remainder, numbering about 1800, were made prisoners and were carried as such to the United States.[1] One American, on the *Brooklyn*, was killed; three men were wounded. The vessels, except the *Brooklyn*, Schley's flag ship, upon which the Spanish fire for a time was concentrated, being, as Admiral Cervera said in his official report, "the vessel most dreaded on account of her speed,"[2] and the *Iowa*, commanded by "Fighting Bob" Evans, escaped with few marks of combat.[3] Schley not unnaturally expected recognition. His signals to the admiral reporting a victory were ignored, or coolly replied to. The seeds of a great bitterness were being sown. "The fleet under my command," Sampson telegraphed the Secretary of the Navy, "offers the nation as a 4th of July present the whole of Cervera's fleet."[4]

The 4th of July in the United States was, in truth, a day of celebration. The President telegraphed Admiral Sampson "the gratitude and congratulations of the whole American people."[5] And he, on July 6th, asked the nation on the following Sunday to "reverently bow before the throne of Divine grace and give devout praise to God, who holdest the nations in the hollow of His hands and workest upon them the marvels of His high will" for leading "our brave soldiers and seamen to victory." Almighty God "in his inscrutable ways" had brought us our "unscathed triumph," and He still was guiding our "gallant sons" in a "strange land through the dread shadows of death."[6] The victory the President described on another occasion as "astounding"; he thought that "neither ancient nor modern

---

[1] Chadwick, The Span. Am. War, vol. ii., pp. 176–7.
[2] Report of Bur. of Nav. for 1898, app., p. 558.
[3] The Brooklyn, Commodore Schley said, bore 41 scars as a result of her participation in the battle.—Ibid., p. 519.
[4] Ibid., p. 505. His fuller report is in ibid., pp. 506–11.
[5] Richardson, vol. x, p. 213.   [6] Ibid., p. 213.

history" had afforded a parallel "in the completeness of the event and the marvelous disproportion of casualties." [1]

Santiago was now at Shafter's mercy. He had been ill from mental strain and the gout and had not taken food for four days—on which account the Secretary of War bade him be "very careful" of himself—but, as the band played "The Star Spangled Banner" and "There'll be a Hot Time in the Old Town Tonight," and, amid the cheering of the troops, who for five days had been without shelter tents in the soaking tropical rains, he was "inspired" and repeated his demand for the surrender of the city. He again spoke of shell fire and again rather uncivilly importuned the navy for cooperation which, when it was given him, Admiral Sampson observed, was not returned. [2] The requests for bombardment were made and withdrawn, made again and again withdrawn, while Shafter negotiated with the enemy. His conduct was difficult to understand. He seemed to be fighting the war, Sampson said, through the newspapers. [3]

General Miles was still in Washington, but he came, on board the *Yale*, from Charleston with reinforcements, arriving on the 11th. Shafter had been assured by Alger that he would not be superseded in command and he now so told Miles who, as general of the entire army of the United States, was able to defend his appearance on the scene. [4] Miles participated in the negotiations concerning capitulation, though he soon left the field to Shafter and gave his care to the direction of the arrangements for the departure of a body of troops for Porto Rico. Sampson asked that he should be present at the surrender or that, in any case, he should have a representative on the ground in token of the navy's part in the taking of the city, to find his

[1] Richardson, vol. x, p. 170.

[2] Report of Bur. of Nav. for 1898, app., pp. 607–8, 609; Rep. of Sec. of War for 1898, p. 110.

[3] Sampson on July 15, 1898, reported to Secretary of the Navy Long "the apparently extraordinary openness with which every detail of hope, effort or suggestion on the part of the army" was published. "The unwisdom of such procedure," he added, "is too manifest for discussion."—Rep. of Bur. of Nav. for 1898, p. 611.

[4] Report of Major Gen. Commanding for 1898, p. 26; Report of Sec. of War for 1898, p. 111; cf. Report of Comm. to Invest. the War, vol. ii, pp. 1085–6.

requests inhospitably received. No attention had been shown the army in the admiral's report of the destruction of the Spanish fleet on July 3rd, it was complained—no honors, Shafter said, need now be shared with the navy.[1]

On the 17th our forces entered the city. General Toral, under stern duress, had agreed to yield the province of Santiago and the troops within its boundaries. All, except such volunteers as might desire to remain in the islands, would be transported by the government of the United States back to Spain. The Spaniards should locate and assist in removing mines in the harbor.[2] Our losses during the army's operation of investing and capturing the city were 260 killed and 1431 wounded.[3]

It was now Shafter's turn to receive the meed of praise which he so eagerly coveted, and which he would enjoy for so brief a time. He and his soldiers had triumphed over all obstacles; the President sent "the profound thanks of the American people" to them for their "most conspicuous gallantry" and their "brilliant achievements." [4]

Interest was now transferred to Porto Rico. Cuba would be allowed to rest except for a few minor adventures by the navy, which bombarded divers forts and destroyed ships in harbors, until Spain should be assailed in another quarter. It was deemed inadvisable to take to Porto Rico the troops who had been engaged in and around Santiago, on account of the fever with which so many of them were infected, and General Miles, as a nucleus for his expedition, used about 3,000 men at Guantanamo Bay, who had not yet been disembarked. They were turned toward the neighboring island which, at the earliest feasible day, was to be invaded and occupied.[5] The troops were put ashore at or near Ponce on the side of the island opposite San Juan, the principal seat of Spanish power. Other units, mostly volunteers who had served as militiamen in their respective states, arrived under General James H. Wilson,

---

[1] Report of Sec. of Navy for 1898, p. 15; Report of Bur. of Nav. for 1898, app., pp. 628, 630; F. E. Chadwick, Span. Am. War, vol. ii, pp. 247–8.
[2] Report of Sec. of War for 1898, pp. 122–3. [3] Ibid., p. 5.
[4] Richardson, vol. x, p. 216.
[5] Report of Comm. to Investigate the War, vol. vii, p. 3249.

General John R. Brooke, General Theodore Schwan and General Henry. There was little resistance. The people came out to hail the invaders as deliverers, women gave them nosegays, men cried "Down with Spain." [1] The expedition by accretions came to number about 17,000 men.

One hundred American flags were sent to Miles to be unfurled in the towns as the army occupied them and proceeded on its triumphant way.[2] The plan of campaign called for pressure from the interior upon San Juan which was blockaded by the fleet. There could be no escape for the enemy had it planned any, though our army was hampered by obsolete equipment and the omissions and neglects of the controlling authorities at Washington,[3] who were now receiving from politicians in the states the most importunate demands that regiments from those states be sent to the front. The sons of Indiana, Texas, Minnesota and so on must be given a sea voyage and have an opportunity to display their prowess before the war should be done.[4] The groups which it had been determined to favor were being assembled for "Wade's picnic," as it was called, since the division was to be commanded by General Wade, son of Ben Wade, the old Radical of Ohio.[5] The armistice interrupted this enterprise, as well as Miles's campaign, before it was completed. The operation, up to the time when it ceased, resulted in the loss of only 3 killed and 40 wounded.

Meantime, in Asia, Dewey stood in the harbor of Manila. Aguinaldo, who had been set ashore from an American war ship,[6] was pressing the Spaniards from the rear with the support of our militant consul who was performing his duties on board

[1] N. Y. Times, Aug. 17, 1898.

[2] Report of Sec. of War for 1898, pp. 134–5.

[3] General Miles in Report of Major-General Commanding, pp. 29–3; General Brooke in ibid., p. 139; Report of Sec. of War for 1898, p. 135.

[4] For these telegrams from senators and representatives in Congress, governors, etc. see Report of Comm. to Investigate the War, vol. ii, pp. 1126 et seq. and 1395 et seq.

[5] Such a "politicans' expedition" was denounced by the New York Times as "a scandal and an outrage."—Issue of Aug. 3, 1898; cf. ibid., Aug. 5, 1898.

[6] Report of Bur. of Nav. for 1898, app., p. 100; Autobiog. of Dewey, p. 246.

the *Baltimore*, and whose hope it was to make "this magnificent insular empire part and parcel of the United States of America" before the coming 4th of July.[1] Aguinaldo boarded the *Olympia* from time to time to confer with Dewey, and organized his army under the protection of our guns.[2]

It had been determined in Washington, supported by Dewey's advice,[3] to send out an expeditionary force for land operations under General Wesley Merritt, who was at Governor's Island in New York harbor in command of the Department of the East. He was ordered to San Francisco, and there to assemble two or three divisions, for the most part men from the Pacific and Rocky Mountain states, to be called the Eighth Army Corps. In adopting the policy, which was later to become the subject of so much discussion, President McKinley said that he had two purposes in view—"the reduction of Spanish power in that quarter" and the giving of "order and security to the islands," while they should be in possession of the United States, which as yet, however, they were not. We held only the bay of Manila and what lay ashore covered by the range of our guns—in a territory of greater area than New England, New York and Pennsylvania we had a foothold not so large or so populous as Staten Island.[4] The "commander-in-chief" of the new "Department of the Pacific" upon his arrival on the ground would announce that we came "not to make war upon the people of the Philippines, nor upon any party or faction among them, but to protect them in their homes, in their employments and in their personal and religious rights." But, in the event of resistance, General Merritt was empowered "to adopt measures of a different kind," under the guidance of "his judgment and his experience and a high sense of justice." While the President described our activity as that of a "military occupant" he also spoke of conquest. The assurances given to Cuba of our retirement, after the completion of our task, as it was stated in the so called "Teller amendment," was omitted,

---

[1] Senate Doc., 56th Cong. 3rd sess., no. 62, pt. 1, p. 329.
[2] Report of Bur. of Nav. for 1898, app., p. 103.
[3] Ibid., pp. 97–8.   [4] N. Y. Nation, Aug. 4, 1898.

in the case of the Philippines. No intimation of our withdrawal escaped the President.[1]

Now again here, as in reference to Porto Rico, United States senators, governors, mayors, newspaper editors and politicians generally were importuned by commands that were eager to join the expedition and they, in turn, pressed the War Department to favor this or that body of recruits who wanted the adventure attendant upon a trip to Asia.[2] Brigadier-General Thomas M. Anderson who commanded the first contingent to go out arrived in Manila Bay on the last day of June with 2500 men. He was followed by a second expedition under Brigadier-General F. V. Greene with 3500 and a third in charge of Brigadier-General Arthur MacArthur with some 4800 men, so that the force in this far away place comprised about 10,000 men, a number soon increased to 15,000, of whom 2000 were regulars.[3]

Aguinaldo had been cooperating, in a measure, with us and had succeeded in deceiving Dewey as to his purposes. In some statements by General Anderson and General Merritt, after the commander-in-chief came on July 25th, there was no recognition of the native chieftain as an ally, whereupon he became "aggressive and even threatening."[4] He addressed President McKinley; he sought the sympathy of a people who had won their own independence by revolution.[5] He was dignified by no official attention and was made to understand that our activities were not in the interest of his "republic." He was not wanted as an ally by our army except as he might serve his temporary use in the overthrow of Spanish power. He and the forces which he had assembled stood in positions overlooking Manila, interfering with our operations, and, as he offered us no assistance, our commanders must pass around him and move forward on independent lines. On August 7th Dewey and

---

[1] Richardson, vol. x, pp. 208–12.
[2] Report of Comm. to Investigate the War, vol. ii, pp. 1284 et seq.
[3] Ibid., vol. vii, p. 3265.
[4] Under date of July 30, 1898, Dewey to Long, R. A. Alger, The Span. Am. War, pp. 350–1; Report of Bur. of Nav. for 1898, app., p. 118.
[5] Senate Doc., 55th Cong. 3rd sess., no. 62, pt. 1, pp. 360–1.

Merritt demanded the surrender of the city. The Captain-General refused and preparations for combined movements by the army and navy commenced. Joint attack on the 13th was answered by a white flag on the fortifications of the walled town. Our troops marched into Manila at once,[1] and the formal capitulation which brought us 13,000 prisoners and much war material followed the next day, the 14th. It was seen that the insurgents, with their love of rapine and pillage, could not be allowed to enter the city and, by order of President McKinley, to whom the question was referred, they were informed that they must recognize the military occupation and authority of the United States.[2] The Spaniards put themselves under the protection of our troops.[3] General Merritt, as military governor, appointed General MacArthur to be military commandant and provost-marshal-general of Manila. General F. V. Greene was given control of fiscal affairs. A beginning was made in the work of establishing order in the city and the adjacent territory.

Spain had done, and could do, nothing to sustain her military and administrative forces in the islands. She had held in reserve a small fleet under Admiral Camara. The descent upon our coasts of this more or less mythical squadron was talked of after Cervera's ships had been destroyed. As a matter of fact it had been directed toward the Philippines. But when it reached the Suez Canal the units were in such a condition that further progress was plainly futile. They were refused coal in Egypt because of the obviously hostile purpose of their voyage and they hobbled home, their return movement being hastened by a threat on our side of the despatch of an "Eastern Squadron" under Commodore J. C. Watson which, on the way to join Dewey, it was said in the newspapers, might harass the coast of Spain.

The *Charleston*, bound for Manila with troop ships in convoy, had halted at Guam in the Ladrones long enough to fire at two abandoned forts, an attention which the Spaniards mistook for a

---

[1] Report of Bur. of Nav. for 1898, app., pp. 119–21.
[2] Report of Comm. to Investigate the War, vol. ii, p. 1310; cf. R. A. Alger, The Span. Am. War, pp. 338–9.
[3] Report of Maj. Gen. Commanding for 1898, pp. 39–46.

salute, since they had not heard of the outbreak of the war. The governor was told to surrender himself and his islands, which he did. The garrison of 60 men were disarmed and taken on to the Philippines as prisoners of war and, as a token of conquest, our flag was hoisted to fly where Spain's had been in this lone and distant spot.[1]

Some months since the scheme to annex Hawaii had been declared to be dead beyond hope of resurrection.[2] Quietly and certainly the promoters of the project, who had never left the ante-rooms of the State Department, were going forward with it to the end which they had in view. The friends of the treaty could not secure a two-thirds vote in the Senate—annexation could not be effected by that course. Long ago Morgan, the boisterous jingo from Alabama, had foreseen the possibilities of annexation by joint resolution.[3] A mere majority vote in each house would, in an instant, add the Sandwich Islands to the United States. With eyes set on the Philippines thousands of miles farther away Honolulu was, by comparison, at our very door. The needs of the navy, day by day, now that our troops were being shipped over the bosom of the Pacific, and national security, if we were to hold our ground in the East, made the taking of Hawaii imperative,[4] wherefore, on June 15th, the House, by a vote of 209 to 91,[5] though Speaker Reed said that, after the destruction of the fleet at Manila, it was not more necessary to annex Hawaii in order to conquer Spain than to annex the moon,[6] and the Senate, on July 6th, by a vote of 42 to 21, passed the resolution.[7] The President approved it the next day, July 7th, and, on August 12th, Rear Admiral Miller on the *Philadelphia*, who had been despatched to Honolulu for the

---

[1] Report of Bur. of Nav. for 1898, app., pp. 151–7.
[2] N. Y. Nation, July 14, 1896.　　[3] N. Y. Times, July 1, 1897.
[4] J. W. Foster, Diplomatic Memoirs, vol. ii, p. 174.
[5] Cong. Record, 55th Cong. 2nd sess., p. 6019.
[6] S. W. McCall, T. B. Reed, pp. 234–6; cf. Corr. of Roosevelt and Lodge, vol. i, p. 302. Cleveland told the Associated Press that it was "a perversion of our national mission"—the mission of the nation was "to build up and make a greater country out of what we have instead of annexing islands."—A. Nevins, Letters of Grover Cleveland, p. 492.
[7] Cong. Record, 55th Cong. 2nd sess., p. 6712.

purpose, officially received the islands in a ceremonial transfer, the stars and stripes were raised on the public buildings and flung out in the streets, and the administrative officers affirmed their allegiance to the Constitution of the United States.[1]

The war with Spain had run its course. A minister of the government in Madrid, in defending himself from the charges of unreadiness, expressed a truth with some of the grace of his people. No amount of foresight, said he, could alter the fact that the Americans outnumbered the population of Spain in the ratio of four to one, and that they were fighting near their base of supplies. The Spaniards were a fatigued race who had once marched over the world as conquerors, but now exhibited their glorious cloak full of rents.[2]

On July 26th, three brief months after the declaration of war, Jules Cambon, the French Ambassador to the United States to whom the interests of Spain, upon the rupture of diplomatic relations with us, had been committed, sought a meeting with the President. It was held in the library of the White House. The President was accompanied by Secretary of State Day, the Ambassador, by his secretary. The Ambassador read a message from the Minister of State at Madrid who, in the name of the Queen Regent, asked for the terms of peace. The President was ready with his reply. He said that Spain must relinquish all claims to sovereignty in Cuba and should withdraw from the island at once. Porto Rico should be ceded to the United States, together with such adjacent islets as Spain held in the West Indies. These requirements would admit of "no negotiation." She should yield to us an island in the Ladrones. The United States would hold the city, harbor and bay of Manila pending the conclusion of a treaty of peace and the determination in that treaty of the "control, disposition and government" of the Philippines.[3] If these conditions, as the President stated them, should be accepted the United States would appoint commissioners to meet commissioners

[1] Report of Bur. of Nav. for 1898, app., pp. 145-7; App. Ann. Cyclop for 1898, pp. 189-94.
[2] App. Ann. Cyclop. for 1898, p. 706.
[3] Foreign Relations for 1898, pp. 819-21; McKinley Papers.

representing Spain. There were allusions, in return, to the demand for the relinquishment of Porto Rico, which "strips us," said the minister of state, "of the last memory of a glorious past and expels us at once from the Western hemisphere, which became peopled and civilized through the proud deeds of our ancestors." [1] But a protocol was signed on the basis of our demands by Secretary of State Day and Ambassador Cambon on August 12th, and naval and military commanders were ordered to cease hostilities.[2] The blockade of Cuba was raised. Upon leaving Santiago, on August 24th, Shafter transferred the command to General Lawton, General Wood having earlier been put in charge of the city. Upon Lawton's retirement all passed to Wood who was to perform notable service in cleaning the region of filth and reducing the prevalence and fatality of disease, a subject which, as a doctor, he understood.[3]

Commissioners were named on each side to proceed to Havana and San Juan to arrange for the Spanish evacuation.[4] Steamships to carry away the 130,000 men in the Spanish army and some 15,000 other persons, for the most part Spanish civil servants with their families, were not immediately at hand and the work was delayed. On October 18th the last man had left Porto Rico. At noon of that day the flag of the United States was raised over the island. But it was the 1st of January, 1899, before Havana was surrendered by the Captain-General to Major-General Brooke who had been appointed military governor of Cuba,[5] an office which he held for a year, when he was succeeded by General Wood. Fitzhugh Lee, who had been chafing under inaction at Jacksonville, was ordered to Cuba in November; he would be governor of the provinces of Havana and Pinar del Rio, a sweet *solatium* for one who, as consul-general there, had been under so much criticism, not

[1] Foreign Relations for 1898, pp. 821–3; McKinley Papers.
[2] Foreign Relations for 1898, pp. 823–30.
[3] Cf. his report to Alger in N. Y. Times, Oct. 1, 1898.
[4] Richardson, vol. x, pp. 174–5; Foreign Relations for 1898, pp. 801, 806.
[5] N. Y. Times, Jan. 2, 1899.

at all unearned, for his froward conduct prior to the outbreak of the war.

The negotiation of the treaty of peace on our side required the services of William R. Day, who resigned his place as Secretary of State, to be succeeded by John Hay, brought home in ill health, and very reluctantly, from the embassy in London.[1] Who now would be sent to England? Platt would be heard from again. He visited President McKinley and then wrote to enforce his objections to Whitelaw Reid, whose eyes were constantly set on the post. Platt cited "understandings ignored and agreements violated." Reid was "both selfish and unscrupulous." He had "a uniform record of broken promises, promises only half performed, promises kept only while the present favor lasted." He was a friend "just so long as his friendship was paid for." The Tribune's "diabolical blackguardism of the organization as an organization," Platt averred, "had rendered the name of Whitelaw Reid so odious to Republicans generally that his advancement now would be regarded as a personal insult to every loyal member of the party." Platt had never thought that McKinley would contemplate "this particular and extreme injury."[2]

Reid would again be quieted for a time by an appointment as a member of the Peace Commission. Mr. Day would be its chairman. Their associates would be Senator Cushman K. Davis of Minnesota, Senator William P. Frye of Maine and Senator George Gray of Delaware, Gray being named as a Democrat after Chief Justice Fuller and Justice Edward D. White had declined to serve. The English mission was offered to Senator George F. Hoar of Massachusetts who declined it.[3]

[1] Hay to McKinley, Aug. 15, 1898, in McKinley Papers; A. Nevins, Henry White, pp. 138–9; W. R. Thayer, Life of Hay, vol. ii, pp. 173–5; Tyler Dennett, John Hay, pp. 195–6.

[2] Platt to McKinley, Aug. 14, 1898, in McKinley Papers; cf. Platt to McKinley, Aug. 23, 1898, in ibid.

[3] Who was opposing the President's expansionist policies in the Senate (with reference to the Philippines, though he had brought himself by some mental process to approve of the annexation of Hawaii) and who might, in this way, be removed from the scene.—G. F. Hoar, Autobiog. of 70 Years, vol. ii, pp. 295, 307; W. B. Parker, Justin S. Morrill, p. 347; Hoar to McKinley, Sep. 14, 1898, in McKinley Papers.

Platt suggested Elihu Root,[1] but would accept Joseph H. Choate [2] who received the appointment,[3] though Reid was not to be long out of the President's mind. The consul-general in London said that the ambassador there should be able to spend from $30,000 to $50,000 a year out of his own income, a condition which seemed to point in one direction,[4] and the peace commissioners were not done with their voyage to France, before Mrs. Day and George Gray were quite captivated by the editor of the Tribune and his wife, and wrote to the President to speak of the remarkable fitness of their travelling companions to represent the country at the court of St. James.[5]

The signing of the protocol, when it was announced in August, was the signal in the United States for a celebration of the victory. Cities appropriated money for the erection of dazzling white triumphal arches. Electric lamps blazed in "courts of honor." Soldiers marched, bands played, flags decked public and private buildings, the glory of our successful arms thrilled the popular heart. The dull and respectable life which the nation had been leading in the last two decades of the century, disturbed by no more beating of drums than could be introduced into recurring tariff campaigns and the torchlight processions, which were formed to advance the fortunes of Presidential candidates, had now been broken by the pomp of war. Hannibal, Caesar and Napoleon had had their battles—they had brought home the tokens of their conquests. This was our day for the tumult and the shouting, and in New York, Philadelphia, Chicago, Omaha, Atlanta and in other cities, North and South and West, it was enjoyed in overflowing measure, the celebration reaching its climax in New York on August 20th, when Sampson came home with his fleet and paraded it up the Hudson River.[6]

[1] Bliss to McKinley, Sep. 30, 1898, in McKinley Papers.
[2] Morton to McKinley in ibid.
[3] Choate to McKinley, Jan. 24, 1899, in ibid.; E. S. Martin, Life of Choate, vol. ii, pp. 74–8.
[4] Osborne to McKinley, Sep. 6, 1898, in McKinley Papers.
[5] McKinley Papers; cf. W. R. Thayer, Life of Hay, vol. ii, pp. 193–7 Autobiog. of Platt, pp. 258–64; A. Nevins, Henry White, p. 141; Tyler Dennett, John Hay, p. 209. [6] App. Ann. Cyclop. for 1898, p. 505.

How small a military performance the war had been was
plain when on fronts in Asia, as well as in this hemisphere,
it appeared that in the navy only 18 had been killed in battle.
The army had lost 290 in killed and 65 had died of their wounds,
though there were no less than 274,717 enlisted men, 50,000
of whom had been transported out of the country for active
service. But there had been death from disease; 2910 soldiers
fell a prey to fevers. There must be a reckoning; blame must be
placed where it belonged.

The newspapers found in the management of the war scandals
which they proclaimed in lurid terms. Theodore Roosevelt,
who had been a free critic of our naval policies, and had been
put by the correspondents in the centre of the fray in Cuba,
now turned his attention to the War Department. He had
been eager to go with his men to Porto Rico for new adventure,
and wrote to Secretary Alger to say that they were "as good as
any regulars and three times as good as any state troops,"
who, he added, undiplomatically enough, were armed with
"archaic weapons." The Secretary of War replied that the
Rough Riders were "no better than other volunteers," they
should be thankful for their modern arms, and denied the request,[1] whereupon Roosevelt turned his attention at once to
conditions around him at Santiago. His prestige as a late
Assistant Secretary of the Navy, and for other reasons, made
his voice one that would be heard. His concern now was for
the health of the troops. The volunteers, because of their
want of training for the exposures and privations of military
life, were particularly open to the attacks of disease. Neither
regulars nor volunteers were inured to a tropical climate in
summer with its "blistering heat," its "drenching rains," and
the night dews which were as wetting as the floods from the
sky.[2] They were, however, beyond the possibility of denial,
subjected by the Department at Washington to neglect and
hardship from which an expeditionary force should have been

[1] N. Y. Times, Aug. 5, 1898; Corr. of Roosevelt and Lodge, vol. i, pp.
330, 331–2.
[2] Chief Surgeon of the Fifth Corps in Report of Sec. of War for 1898,
p. 788.

secure; and suffering imposed upon the men awaiting call at the camps in the states reflected still more painfully on the system under which the army was operating. Camp Alger, as it was called, in Virginia, within a few miles of Washington was described as a "pest hole." Because of the water supply a defective sewerage system, and the crowding of the tents it became a "nursery of typhoid." [1]

The army was set in an antiquated frame, its organization and control were bound by routine and corrupted by the expediencies of "politics." Proper and wholesome food, tentage, preventive medicines would have obviated much sickness and many deaths.[2] The refugees who came out of Santiago for protection during the investment of the place had brought yellow fever and other fevers with them. The men, without other covering, sought shelter from the rains in infected buildings and palmetto huts. Miasma was exhaled from the soil as they dug defensive trenches in the hot and soggy earth.[3] The sick were put with the wounded in the hospitals. Shafter, on July 27th, reported 3770 sick men in his command; the next day the number was 4,122, and the medical stores, always inadequate, were practically exhausted.[4]

The men were being invalided home as rapidly as possible, though not without complaint as to the treatment they received in transit. Conditions gave no sign of mending. General Miles said, as early as on July 21st, that there was not a single regiment of regulars or volunteers in the command that was not infected—from one man in an Ohio regiment to 36 in a Michigan regiment.[5] Shafter would take them into the mountains but he was told that it was as insanitary on higher ground as in the camps near the coast.[6] Roosevelt, who found that

---

[1] N. Y. Times, Aug. 6, 1898.

[2] These statements are abundantly confirmed in the Report of the Comm. to Investigate the War; also in R. A. Alger, The Span. Am. War; cf. Roosevelt's letters to Lodge in Corr. of Roosevelt and Lodge, vol. i.

[3] Report of Sec. of War for 1898, p. 784.

[4] Report of Chief Surgeon in Rep. of Sec. of War for 1898, p. 781; Report of Comm. to Investigate the War, vol. ii, p. 1062.

[5] Report of Maj. Gen. Commanding for 1898, p. 27.

[6] R. A. Alger, The Span. Am. War, pp. 262-4.

nothing had been done as it should have been, barring his own part in the war, of which his boasts were free,[1] addressed General Wheeler, his brigade commander.[2] He also wrote to General Shafter. The whole army, he said, was in so weakened a condition "as to be ripe for dying like rotten sheep." Not 10 per cent. were fit for active duty. One half of the men, if they were kept in Cuba during the sickly season, would die. "To avert a doom so fearful" they should be taken to the coast of Maine or to some other place in the north,[3] a statement made only ten days after he had written to Alger seeking permission to transport his particularly brave and, presumably, fit command to Porto Rico.[4] The general and medical officers held a "town meeting," as Secretary Long called it, to discuss the grave state of affairs.[5] The division and brigade commanders, including Wheeler, Sumner, William Ludlow, Adelbert Ames, Chaffee, Leonard Wood, Kent and Lawton (the latter with important reservations) signed a "round robin," and addressed it to Shafter, who, in turn, sent it on to Washington with his own recommendations, which coincided with those of his officers and which were peremptory. The paper, through Roosevelt's activities—indeed his hand was seen in the whole rising—was given to the press before it reached the War Department, Shafter said even before it came to him.[6] Roosevelt's excited letter to Shafter and a statement by General Ames were also given to the newspaper correspondents, all to be published throughout the United States by the Associated Press on August 5th.[7] The authors of the "round robin" spoke as Roosevelt had spoken—they declared that malarial fever which now raged was certain to be followed by yellow fever. "This army," they said, "must be moved at once or

---

[1] See his letters to Lodge in Corr. of Roosevelt and Lodge, vol. i.
[2] Ibid., vol. i, pp. 335–7.   [3] N. Y. Times, Aug. 5, 1898.
[4] Ibid.   [5] J. D. Long, America of Yesterday, p. 212.
[6] Roosevelt's version is different. See his Autobiog., pp. 267–8. According to his account he was the good boy who was put forward by the bad men to do what they were afraid to do.—Cf. Hagedorn, Leonard Wood, p. 201.
[7] Cf. N. Y. Times, Aug. 5, 1898; Walter Millis, The Martial Spirit, pp. 352–3; H. F. Pringle, Theodore Roosevelt, p. 197.

it will perish." Those who should try to prevent such a movement back to the northern part of the United States would be making themselves "responsible for the unnecessary loss of many thousands of lives." Five army surgeons added their testimony—action should be immediate.[1] Alger, highly incensed, said that he had done what he was now so uncivilly asked to do before the remarkable paper reached him. He had telegraphed Shafter the previous day, August 2nd, that it was "going to be a long job at best to get so many troops away."[2] But he had an awakening now.[3] A little prior to the receipt of the "round robin," as he declared, or simultaneously, or immediately after it came to him, he understood the need of action and he ordered the troops to Montauk Point, 116 miles from New York City. No community wished to have so many fever patients thrown into its midst—there was worse panic than when the people saw visions of Cervera's advancing fleet. But all would be well in this remote northern end of Long Island where the returning troops, by direction of the President, were to be cared for, without regard to expense.[4] At the same time Alger reproved Shafter, in the name of the President, who was astounded at such a breach of military discipline.[5] On no account should communications be given to the newspapers without the authorization of the War Department.[6]

The censure was deserved. The language of the letter was intemperate. The announcement of such a state of affairs was astounding in its suddenness. How could it be that in less than three weeks after the surrender an army, in hourly telegraphic communication with Washington, accompanied by watchful newspaper correspondents, should have come to the

[1] Report of Comm. to Investigate the War, vol. i, pp. 216–7 and vol. ii, pp. 1068–70; R. A. Alger, The Span. Am. War, chap. xvi; W. H. Carter, Life of General Chaffee, pp. 151–3.
[2] Report of Comm. to Investigate the War, vol. ii, p. 1063.
[3] N. Y. Times, Aug. 6, 1898.
[4] Report of Comm. to Investigate the War, vol. i, p. 218 and vol. ii, pp. 18, 49.
[5] Olcott, Life of McKinley, vol. ii, pp. 81–2.
[6] Report of Comm. to Investigate the War, vol. ii, p. 1070.

verge of complete annihilation by disease without public knowledge of its plight?[1] The families and friends of the soldiers in Cuba were alarmed and subjected to needless distress by such extravagance of statement. The Department was embarrassed and discredited beyond its deserts. An enemy with spirit and power greater than Spain's, by such a declaration of weakness, would have been given courage to refuse a peace. We were exhibited in a strangely unfavorable light in the sight of the world.[2] Roosevelt deserved to be court-martialled for insubordination, though no one believed that he would suffer greatly for what he had done.[3]

The order from Washington for departure, when it reached Cuba, was instantly obeyed. A few regiments of what were called immunes would remain on the ground, while the rest, as rapidly as possible, were piled into transports which, it was said with too much truth, were inadequately supplied with provisions and medicines.[4] About 23,000 men were taken to Montauk Point from Santiago, half of whom upon their arrival were so ill as to be scarcely able to walk—10,000 required treatment in the hospitals.[5] Eighty-seven men died on the way from Cuba and about 200 more after coming north.

It was nearly as bad elsewhere. At Chickamauga Park, where so many of the soldiers who were received for the war were being drilled and made ready for service, 425 died of typhoid fever. Other camps, as at Tampa, from which place 7,000 or 8,000 were taken to Montauk Point to join the invalids from Cuba, Jacksonville, Falls Church, Va., and Middletown, Pa., added their toll and, to check the dangers of contagion, the policy of large camps (there were at one time

---

[1] Cf. N. Y. Times, Aug. 5, 1898.

[2] Captain Chadwick describes it as "a most inconsiderate and unwarrantable breach of discipline and good sense."—F. E. Chadwick, Span. Am. War, vol. ii, p. 258; cf. Alger, Span. Am. War, pp. 269–70; J. D. Long, America of Yesterday, p. 212.

[3] Possibly because Alger was so "fond" of him.—Autobiog. of Roosevelt, p. 238; cf. N. Y. Tribune, Aug. 5, 1898; N. Y. Times, Aug. 6, 1898.

[4] Cf. Corr. of Roosevelt and Lodge, vol. i, p. 341; Rep. of Sec. of War for 1898, p. 785.

[5] Report of Comm. to Investigate the War, vol. ii, pp. 19, 22–3, 29, 52.

at Chickamauga Park 56,000 men) was abandoned and the
recruits were assembled in a greater number of centres with
fewer men at each. Under criticism, and with somewhat
improved administration, as a result of experience, the death
rate diminished, even before the cooler weather of autumn
came to interpose its more salubrious influences.

In front of Santiago the infantry had not had suitable
artillery support. The black powder which was in use revealed
their precise location—after discharge the men who had fired
were targets for an enemy which was supplied with smokeless
powder.[1] Many of the soldiers were armed with old Springfield rifles instead of magazine guns. General Shafter had
left ambulances behind when he had embarked; only three
were carried on the transports.[2] The wounded must be put in
rough wagons and carts bedded with hay. There were few
litters. The chief surgeon said that there should have been
ten for each regiment—there were often but two and sometimes none at all.[3] There were not enough surgeons and nurses.[4]
Medical supplies which should have been with the army were
not taken from the ships or had not been furnished by the
Department at Washington.[5] Transport on land had not been
provided and material could not be brought to the front as the
troops advanced.[6] When there were vehicles there were no
roads. The wagons after the rains began to fall were mired;
horses and mules as well as teamsters took sick and died.[7]
Neither enough nor the right kind of food, because of defective

[1] Cf. Autobiog. of Roosevelt, p. 247.

[2] Cf. R. A. Alger, The Span. Am. War, pp. 290-1; Chadwick, Span.
Am. War, vol. ii, pp. 103-4; Report of Sec. of War for 1898, p. 783.

[3] Report of Sec. of War for 1898, p. 780.

[4] Ibid., p. 788; cf. testimony of wounded men, as J. Bigelow, Jr.,
Reminiscences of Santiago Campaign, and Stephen Bonsal, The Golden
Horshoe.

[5] R. A. Alger, The Span. Am. War, p. 291; Report of Sec. of War for
1898, pp. 780-1.

[6] It was not until the last week in July and the first weeks in August,
when the war was done, that tents and other equipment began to be unloaded from the ships and carried to the camps.—Chief Surgeon Pope in
Report of Sec. of War for 1898, vol. i, p. 785.

[7] Miley, In Cuba with Shafter, pp. 84-9; Report of Sec. of War for
1898, p. 783.

commissary arrangements and the improper management of the transport service, was ever at hand. At one time Roosevelt said that the Rough Riders were eating the meat of horses and mules. When their shoes wore out they could not get new ones.[1] He himself had, he said, "neither blanket nor coat," [2] though, "being as strong as a bull moose," he cared "nothing for that" so long as he "got into a fight." [3] The men were clad, he observed, as if the campaign were to be carried on in Montana in the fall rather than in the tropics in July. They were sent to Cuba with flannel shirts and winter underwear.[4] Staff officers drawn from civil life were wholly incompetent for their tasks.

A notorious scandal developed on the subject of beef. In the contracts it was stated that it must be so refrigerated as to be fit for use 72 hours after delivery. Much of it, so it was said, was spoiled before it reached the camps—it was "embalmed," it smelled and looked, too, as if it had been treated with some preservative fluid.[5] The canned meat was of such a quality that the soldiers were nauseated by it. Some of it, upon coming to Cuba, was in a putrid state; if it were unloaded at all it was, because of its stench, buried in the earth.[6] Miles rejected 300,000 pounds which arrived at Ponce the day the protocol was signed and it was thrown overboard.[7] Not a quarter, not a tenth part of what was provided, Roosevelt averred, was or could be eaten.[8] An army in the tropics, General Miles said, should have received its supply of beef on the hoof.[9]

The demands for Alger's resignation, which had been heard

[1] N. Y. Times, Dec. 23, 1898.

[2] Corr. of Roosevelt and Lodge, vol. i, p. 317.   [3] Ibid., pp. 315, 322.

[4] Report of Comm. to Investigate the War, vol. v, p. 2263; cf. J. C. Hemment, Cannon and Camera, p. 175.

[5] See testimony of General Miles in Report of Comm. to Investigate the War, vol. i, pp. 155–6 and vol. vii, pp. 3256 et seq.; N. Y. Times, Feb. 1, 1899.

[6] Cf. N. Y. Times, Jan. 24, 1899.

[7] Ibid., Jan. 4, 1899.

[8] Report of Comm. to Investigate the War, vol. v, pp. 2258–9; cf. N. Y. Times, Jan. 14, 1899.

[9] Report of Comm. to Investigate the War, vol. vii, p. 3256.

for many weeks, increased.[1] He had been the cause of all the lazy blundering. His appointment in the first place had been entirely ill advised. His private wealth, his political ambitions which had been so unquiet, his low standards for the public service were recalled.[2] The most eager of all the members of the cabinet for war he and his Department, upon which most of its burdens would fall, were the least prepared for it.[3] Even criminal neglect was indicated. Alger resented such imputations. Investigation was demanded. There would be none, he said, because there was nothing to investigate,[4] though it was plain enough that the Secretary of War, like the army itself had been the victim of a stupid system, whatever his own culpability or that of the men who surrounded him.[5] The President, bending under the storm of popular indignation, appointed a commission of which General Grenville M. Dodge was the president, to examine into the conduct of the War Department in all its branches.[6] The members, nine in number, when they were found—for it was not easy to bestow the honor of such an appointment upon any candid and useful man—met first in Washington, then in New York and Chicago, supplementing the hearing of witnesses with personal visits to various soldiers' camps. While the report dealt gently with Alger and his Department, since "Algerism" as it was called, was to be "whitewashed," [7] and entirely exonerated

[1] Cf. N. Y. Times, which on May 21, 1898, called his continuance in office "a national disgrace." His remaining in the War Department cost the country "$100,000 a day in general inefficiency." "War—under Alger—is Hell," the Times said again.—Issue of Aug. 31, 1898.

[2] Cf. N. Y. Nation, Sep. 15, 1898, for Alger's appointment to the cabinet, where a theory which connects him with Ohio politics is advanced. He had played his part in perfecting the bargain by which Hanna was enabled to take Sherman's place in the Senate.—Alger to McKinley, Jan. 11, 1897, in McKinley Papers.

[3] John D. Long, America of Yesterday, p. 188; Miles, Serving the Republic, p. 269.

[4] N. Y. Nation, Sep. 1, 1898.

[5] For a defence of Alger see General Boynton in N. Y. Times, March 7, 1899, and Alger, The Span. Am. War.

[6] Report of Comm. to Investigate the War, vol. i, p. 237.

[7] The report was, as it was intended to be, said the N. Y. Nation, "nine-tenths whitewash and one-tenth apology." —Issue of Feb. 16, 1899; cf. N. Y. Times, Feb. 10 and 14, 1899.

him and his agents of corrupt action,[1] many facts that were
discreditable to the service were disclosed. The effort to rule
out the damaging testimony of Miles because he had refused
to take the oath prescribed by the board gave its findings an
entirely unjudicial and partisan turn. One man was cornered
and disgraced, General Charles P. Eagan, Commissary General
of Subsistence. On the stand, as a witness, he accused General
Miles of lying and generally covered the commander-in-chief
with abuse. His attack upon his superior officer was so coarse
and violent that the commission ordered him to amend it and
it underwent expurgation before being "accepted" and printed.[2]
Eagan was court-martialled and condemned to be dismissed
from the army, a sentence which President McKinley com-
muted to a suspension from duty for six years.[3]

The disgrace of Eagan was quickly followed by the appointment of a court of inquiry to give further attention to the
charges of mismanagement, especially with a view to discrediting Miles for whom Alger had by this time come to feel
an intense dislike. The commission's report had not satisfied
public opinion and Alger, as well as the President himself,
who was unwilling to send away his Secretary of War, at
any rate under the fire of angry criticism, would have vindication, if it were procurable. Three army officers, General
Wade, General George W. Davis, and Colonel George L.
Gillespie, would establish the facts.[4] These men heard the
witnesses again, visited the packing houses and employed
chemists to examine the beef. In May, 1899, they made their
report to the President, denying that the fresh beef furnished
the government was "embalmed," but declaring the canned
beef to have been unfit for the use of the army in the tropics,
though of the same quality as that which was distributed to

[1] Report of Comm. to Investigate the War, vol. i, pp. 110–1.

[2] Ibid., vol. vii, pp. 3564–81; N. Y. Times, Jan. 13, 14, 17 and 18, 1899;
N. Y. Nation, Jan. 19, 1899.

[3] Cf. N. Y. Nation, Feb. 16, 1899; N. Y. Times, Jan. 19 and following
issues. Eagan is defended by Alger in his book, The Span. Am. War,
chap. xxii.

[4] N. Y. Times, Feb. 10, 1899.

the trade generally. Miles was censured for not promptly notifying the Department of the character of the rations furnished the troops.[1] The conclusions still failed to convince the public that the truth was not being suppressed. The primary duty of the court, the New York Times said, was to shield Alger. It was "a very shameful report, an indecent and disgraceful report," that newspaper continued.[2] Others expressed a like opinion and demands that the Secretary of War should resign were renewed.

The whole war had been but a not too well organized spectacle in the hands of an amateur army and navy. No plan of campaign had been devised beforehand and none was followed.[3] Our democracy has been seen in lights which suggest burlesque rather than sober history. It was so now. The sight of the navy scouring the seas for weeks for a few disabled ships from Spain, and not finding them before they had come to anchor in a protected harbor, and its subsequent efforts to discover whether all or only a part of them were in that harbor, which were futile,[4] until after a youth had dramatically made a tour overland on a mule to peep at them through a field glass; the sight, too, of another young naval officer sinking a weighted collier in a channel to "bottle up" the fleet, and of a nation acclaiming him as its first citizen,[5] though he had failed to execute his purpose,[6] furnish the elements of farce. The coming out of the ships at length, not to battle but to certain destruction, and a long and angry dispute of commanders as to which should have the glory attached to the shooting down of the

---

[1] He had not done so, it was suggested, because of knowledge that protest would be without avail.—J. Bigelow, Jr., Reminiscences of the Santiago Campaign, pp. 100–1.

[2] N. Y. Times, May 8, 1899; Report in Senate Doc., 56th Cong., 1st sess., no. 270, 3 vols. of about 3000 pp.

[3] Cf. F. E. Chadwick, Span. Am. War, vol. ii, p. 4.

[4] Cf. R. A. Alger, The Span. Am. War, pp. 224–6.

[5] Cf. description of a reception tendered him at the Metropolitan Opera House in New York.—N. Y. Times, Aug. 5, 1898.

[6] Described by the Secretary of the Navy, nevertheless, as "one of the well known historical marvels of naval adventure and enterprise," entitling its leader to "undying fame."—Report of Sec. of Navy for 1898, p. 11.

helpless victims, form a chapter adding but little lustre to the
national name.

The controversy between Sampson and Schley raged with
intensity for many years. That Sampson had gone up the
coast for a conference with Shafter, and that before he could
turn his ship about and could catch up with the rest of the
fleet the battle was done was true. He on the *New York* was
not at any time, as he said himself, "within range of the heavy
Spanish ships." [1] He was commander-in-chief of the squadron.
But he had gone away. Schley, the second in rank, was in the
thick of battle. But of him Sampson, in telegraphing the
report of the day's events to the Navy Department, made
no mention. In his later official report there was but casual
and, as it seemed, grudging reference without praise.[2] Schley's
report to Sampson was restrained in its tone. He had "never
in his life served with a braver, better or worthier crew than
that of the *Brooklyn*," working though they did under "a storm
of projectiles passing ahead, astern and over the ship." He
congratulated his chief and spoke of his satisfaction in having
had "the opportunity to contribute in the least to a victory"
which, he continued, "seems big enough for us all." [3]

The partisans of Schley, in newspaper, magazine and book,
as well as in Congress,[4] instantly took up his cause. He was
a man who seemed to have legions of friends. He had out-
ranked Sampson in point of service and that he had not been
preferred for appointment to the highest command at the outbreak of the war was, in the sight of many, due to the maneuvers
of enemies in the Department at Washington, particularly
Admiral Crowninshield whose removal was demanded. Schley
was being "persecuted." Thousands of men and women wrote
to him, sent him laudatory poems, asked for his autograph

---

[1] Report of Bur. of Nav. for 1898, app., p. 507.
[2] Ibid., pp. 505–11. That Schley felt it to be so is attested in his letter
to James Parker in Parker's book, Schley, Sampson and Cervera, p. 332,
and elsewhere.
[3] Report of Bur. of Nav. for 1898, app., pp. 517–20.
[4] As soon as that body got hold of the subject as a result of President
McKinley's recommendation that both men be appointed permanent rear
admirals, Sampson to be advanced by 8 numbers and Schley by 6.

and for buttons from his coat.[1] He was offered and accepted receptions, dinners, medals and jewelled swords from his admirers in cities and states.[2] When he appeared in public the "shouting and enthusiasm" which his figure evoked was described as "something enormous." When Sampson was also present this attention was the more marked, for Sampson in turn was ignored.[3]

Under attack Sampson and the Department retorted making charges which reflected upon the skill, even the courage, of Schley, while the fleet was muddling about in the Caribbean in quest of the ships of Spain [4]—that he had for two days left the entrance of Santiago harbor unguarded, while he went out to seek coal of which, they said, he had an abundant stock; even that he had maneuvered his flag ship in an unprofessional, if not cowardly, way in the battle. Sampson called Schley's conduct "reprehensible." He unquestionably displayed an infirmity of purpose, if not a want of bravery, little to his credit in the sight of the Navy Department and many, perhaps most, of his associates in the service. If the facts had been fully known at the time Secretary Long said that they would "undoubtedly have been regarded as cause for relieving him from command, if not for further disciplinary proceedings." [5]

[1] N. Y. Times, Aug. 2, 1898. An example of the poetry which the event inspired may be found in the following from Ohio—

> "Hurray for Schley,
> He chased 'em,
> And placed 'em,
> And waited round to
> Baste 'em,
> And shot 'em,
> And got 'em,
> And sent 'em to the
> Bottom."—Ibid., Aug. 4, 1898.

[2] With sufficient modesty, as when he said, after a dinner in his honour in Brooklyn—"If I were entitled to one-millionth part of the acclaim which has come to me I feel that I could share that fraction with all my comrades, and have enough left for a life time of satisfaction."—Ibid., Dec. 7, 1898.

[3] Halstead to McKinley, Oct. 1, 1899, in McKinley Papers.

[4] Cf. N. Y. Times, Nov. 28 and Dec. 20, 1898, and Feb. 21 and 24, and March 7 and 8, 1899; J. B. Foraker, op. cit., vol. ii, pp. 33–7.

[5] Long to McKinley, July 3, 1899, in McKinley Papers. Cf. F. E. Chadwick, Span. Am. War, vol. i, pp. 306–7, 316–7; R. D. Evans, An

The two men and their partisans made their relations into a public quarrel which they themselves, trained to the service, lived to deplore, especially when, three years after the event, it led to the appointment of a court of inquiry. This court, to which the case was referred, was composed of Admiral Dewey, chairman, and Admirals Benham and Ramsay. Again charges of persecution were made in the newspapers. Schley was the victim of a "conspiracy." Alexander K. McClure of the Philadelphia Times, Felix Agnus of the Baltimore American, Murat Halstead of the Cincinnati Commercial Gazette, who said that Sampson had "as much to do with the battle of Santiago as the King of England had with the battle of Waterloo, and no more,"[1] and other newspaper editors could not be silenced. The charges, Secretary Long repeated, were "gratuitous and unjust." Crowninshield's detachment from the service in answer to such "shrieking" would be "simply monstrous." Schley himself made no complaint of his treatment by the Department.[2] The renewal of the great dispute was due to the publications of a naval historian, Edgar S. Maclay. His statements Schley's friends declared to be defamatory, and, as they were said to have the favor of high officials of the Navy,[3] Schley reluctantly, and under what seemed to be compulsion, on July 22, 1901, asked for an investigation of his conduct. The whole subject was reviewed for weeks in September, October and November of that year in one of the buildings at the Navy Yard in Washington before a crowd of curious spectators. At the end the court quite liberally condemned Schley, though Dewey dissented on a number of points. Dewey further found that Schley had been in command at Santiago when the Spanish fleet was destroyed, although this question was not involved in the investigation. Still

---

Admiral's Log, chap. i; John D. Long, The New Am. Navy, vol. i, pp. 275–82; Nauticus, The Truth about the Schley Case; W. A. M. Goode, With Sampson through the War, chaps. v and vii; H. C. Lodge, The War with Spain, chap. v; N. Y. Nation, Feb. 16, 1899.

[1] Halstead to McKinley, Nov. 26, 1899, in McKinley Papers. The letters of McClure and Agnus are in ibid. under dates in August, 1901.

[2] Long to Cortelyou, Aug. 26, 1901, in ibid.

[3] E. S. Maclay, The Hist. of the Navy, vol. iii.

nothing was gained, for Schley's friends continued to assert that he had done no wrong before July 3rd and that on that eventful day he had been the commander of the fleet. The court had been under the influence of the same hostile clique in the service which had denied him justice in the first instance.[1]

The army and navy throughout the war were acting at cross purposes. Neither had a staff system. There was no common plan of action.[2] The disagreement of view regarding transport, the convoy of troop ships, which added to the confusion and delay at ports of embarkation, especially at Tampa,[3] the want of lighters and other small boats to take off the men and the equipment upon their arrival in Cuba and Porto Rico indicated incompetency of method as well as of personnel difficult to comprehend. Shafter did affront to the newspaper men who wished the war to be fought for their convenience. When they were not indulged they painted him black. Much of the time, they said, he lay in a hammock with attendants at his side to fan him and to scratch his head for a scalp disease. He was ridiculed beyond his due, though he was, without question, a very dunderhead by all the rules set up for a soldier.[4] His dispute with Sampson as to the conduct of the Santiago campaign, with innuendoes bearing upon the relative efficiency of the two arms of the service at the taking of that city, did but little honor to the nation and those who are appointed to fight its wars.[5] Shafter's charge amounting

[1] Cf. James Parker, Schley, Sampson and Cervera, pp. 317 et seq; Record of Proceedings of the Court in two great volumes; J. D. Long, The New Am. Navy, vol. i, pp. 258 et seq; R. D. Evans, An Admiral's Log, chap. i.

[2] Chadwick, Span. Am. War, vol. ii, p. 58.

[3] Report of Comm. to Investigate the War, vol. v, p. 2258; cf. Corr. of Roosevelt and Lodge, vol. i, pp. 3119–20.

[4] Roosevelt said that he was "too unwieldy to get to the front." (Corr. of Roosevelt and Lodge, vol. i, p. 317.) Again that Shafter had never come within three miles of the line—"not since the campaign of Crassus against the Parthians" had there been "so criminally incompetent a general." (Ibid., p. 318). He was "utterly inefficient."—Ibid., p. 321.

[5] Report of Sec. of Navy for 1898, p. 15; R. A. Alger, The Span. Am. War, who, of course, defends Shafter, chap. xv; cf. Stephen Bonsal, The Golden Horseshoe, p. 2; N. Y. Nation, Dec. 8, 1898; J. D. Long, America of Yesterday, pp. 203–4.

to cowardice, which he made to the War Department and to the newspapers, regarding Sampson's failure to cooperate with the army earned him official reproof which he did not receive.[1]

On the other hand it was true that Sampson had asked for only 10,000 troops at Santiago, saying on June 7th, too hopefully it would seem, that if such a force were on the ground the city and the Spanish fleet "would be ours within 48 hours";[2] and it was the navy which, when the transports were ready to sail, kept the men in their hot and cramped quarters on the ships in Tampa Bay in fear of a "phantom" squadron which officers of that navy declared that they had seen in Nicholas Channel.[3]

Alger's vindictive treatment of Miles who had dared to speak plainly of the frightful conditions imposed upon the army at Tampa and elsewhere,[4] and Shafter's petty jealousy of Miles, his commanding officer, and his determination, with the support of his friend, the Secretary of War, to direct the Santiago campaign for his own glory remain blemishes upon the service. Indeed every one who chose to enter the lists was attacking every one else who lay in his way, with the aid of an irresponsible press, and the country and the world were treated to an unbelievably strange story. Fires were fanned by the political ambitions of the authors of so much detraction and malignity. Alger, Miles, Roosevelt, and it is not clear how many more, would use the war, if possible, for their advertisement as candidates for high office. We had "remembered the Maine," but this memory had been obliterated by the factionists, each of whom was engaged in trying to discredit the other that he himself might have the greater share of popular fame.

Sons and favorites of politicians pressed the War Department for captaincies, majorities and colonelcies, and had

[1] Report of Bur. of Nav. for 1898, app., pp. 608–14.
[2] R. A. Alger, The Span. Am. War, p. 71.
[3] Ibid., p. 72.
[4] They were "always at swords' points."—J. D. Long, Am. of Yesterday, p. 194.

received them.[1] Many of the volunteer officers belonged in
opera bouffe rather than on the battle field. All was done under
the eyes of newspaper reporters who were entirely without
experience in observing and reporting the movements of an
army and whose writings were grotesque. The yellow journals
had brought on hostilities for the excitement of the masses
whose patronage they required if they were to attain their
ambition for an ever-widening sale of their papers; they now
felt it incumbent upon them to prosecute the war. The correspondents and "artists" hung upon the heels of the civilian
officers whose manners tended to corrupt the gravity of men
trained to arms.[2] The smallest feats of amateurs were magnified into heroic actions. Vivid and sensational descriptions,
pictures, belching headlines in New York proclaimed the
progress of the war which would not, under any pressure,
assume important proportions, or give promise of lasting even
through one summer.

Nothing was quite so picturesque as the figure of Theodore
Roosevelt at the head of the "Rough Riders." He made
certain, with the assistance of his friend Lodge, that he and
his command should be included in the first contingents sent
to Cuba.[3] His ready pronouncements and his attitudinizing,
as if he were in front of a camera for a picture, provided material
for the journalists day by day to their profit and his delight.
It was reported on June 25th by Leonard Wood to his superior
officer, General Young, commanding the Second Brigade, that
Richard Harding Davis, who was not in the service, had been
"with Colonel Roosevelt during almost the entire action" at
Las Guanimas.[4] Representations of him in a sombrero and
"chaps," riding a broncho up San Juan hill, waving a sabre
like a Berserker, in eye glasses, without which he could not

[1] The New York Times spoke of the appointment of John Jacob Astor
to be a lieutenant-colonel, of a grandson of Ulysses S. Grant, a son of
James G. Blaine, a son of John A. Logan, two sons of Calvin Brice, "the
son of that senator and that representative" in Congress without "relevancy
to the good of the service."—Issue of May 21, 1898.
[2] Cf. R. A. Alger, The Span. Am. War, p. 295.
[3] Corr. of Roosevelt and Lodge, vol. i, pp. 301, 302.
[4] Report of Maj. Gen. Commanding for 1898, p. 345.

have distinguished a Spaniard from the bole of a banana tree,[1] shouting and showing his teeth as if he would eat the enemy raw, amused all beholders. He never gave his orders in a military way but addressed his command as "boys."[2] "Teddy's Terrors" were on every tongue. This young man was at last in one of the wars which he had been recommending to the nation for the development of its finer traits.[3]

The race of the *Oregon* out of the Pacific and around the Horn, as if the fate of the war depended upon her presence in the Caribbean Sea, with many predictions in the newspapers that she would be caught and sunk by the dreaded Cervera, had the thrill of sport.[4] Of the Philippines it has been said that the American people generally, at the time, did not know whether they were islands or canned goods.[5] President McKinley himself confessed that, when he received the news of Dewey's feat, he had had to seek their location on a revolving tin geographical globe—if he had been asked he could not have "told where those darned islands were within 2,000 miles."[6] Guam, an amusing syllable which the people now saw in the newspapers, was still more mystifying—it was known only to the cartographers. The picking up, quite casually, of this dot in the sea as a ship passed by on the way to Manila and the capture of a garrison which had not yet learned that their government was at war was another piece of stage play. A few of our consular officers had taken it upon themselves to confer with a native insurgent chief in exile with a view to carrying him back to the Philippines. He was returned to the scene of his rebellion in an American war ship soon to become

[1] He had a dozen pairs in reserve in his trousers and his hat, in case those he was wearing should fall off or be shot away.

[2] N. Y. Times, Aug. 25, 1898.

[3] Upon his return from Cuba he said, "We had a bully fight. This is a fine regiment and all a lot of crack-a-jacks."—N. Y. Times, Aug. 16, 1898.

[4] Captain Concas, Cervera's chief of staff, has said that the whole American force in Cuban waters before the arrival of the Oregon might have been divided into four squadrons "each overwhelmingly stronger than ours."—Concas, The Squadron of Admiral Cervera, p. 26.

[5] Cf. A. C. Coolidge, U. S. as a World Power, p. 149.

[6] H. H. Kohlsaat, From McKinley to Harding, p. 68.

the leader of a protracted and savage war upon the army of the United States. The American consul at Manila, who had but lately arrived at his post, stood at Dewey's side on the bridge of the flag ship of our fleet during the engagement to sing that hero's Odyssey. There was "no couplet to form a comparison" with such a naval action, said the enthusiastic consul. The crews were "all hoarse from cheering" when the firing ceased, suffering, he said, for cough drops instead of liniments and the services of surgeons.[1] Even this event would be seen at length in less rosy lights.

The 400 killed on land and sea in the war were only a few more than had gone down in the *Maine*. Even adding those who had succumbed to disease at the camps in the United States, as well as in the tropics, which raised the number to just above 3,000, the entire loss was less than the total number of deaths in the Johnstown flood. All told it was equal to only a morning's slaughter in one of the several great engagements in the Civil War. For at Antietam on both sides 23,000 were killed and wounded, at Chancellorsville 30,000, at Gettysburg 33,000 (nearly 6,000 were killed), in the Wilderness probably 40,000, with 18,000 more a few days later at Spottsylvania, on the Union side alone, and 12,000 more, again without taking note of the Confederate losses, at Cold Harbor. In the war with Spain we did not lose a gun, a flag, or a ship, and, with the exception of Hobson and his little crew, not a soldier or sailor was taken prisoner.[2] The perils that lay in the war area in the sickly season had been understood—they were repeatedly alluded to in the diplomatic and military correspondence before and during the first weeks of the war. Spain had lost 75,000 from disease in the three years during which she had been engaged in trying to suppress the rebellion in Cuba; that we should escape a like experience no rational person had the right to believe—deaths from this cause were certain, when, contrary to sound advice, we persisted in taking our

[1] Senate Doc., 55th Cong 3rd sess., no. 62, pt. 1, p. 326.
[2] Richardson, vol. x, p. 172; Report of Maj. Gen. Commanding for 1898, p. 37.

troops into the tropics in the heat and fetid moisture of mid-summer.[1]

The condemnation of Alger and his whole Department ran beyond bounds. Men wrote to the President to say that their sons had left "good homes"—they should not be treated like pigs.[2] The truth is that war had lost its glamour. Its poetry, as General Corbin observed, had dazzled the young; they had now encountered "solid facts" and were repelled by some of its realities.[3]

On August 7th, 46 days after the date of the landing of General Shafter's army in Cuba and 21 days after the surrender, the troops began to embark for home and, on August 24th, practically the entire force was again on our soil, having been absent from the country for only two months.[4] The volunteers, as soon thereafter as possible, were mustered out and discharged from service.

The peace commissioners met in Paris on October 1st. The Spanish representatives demanded the withdrawal of the American forces from Manila, which had been captured, as they declared truly enough, after the signing of the protocol. This point, however, had been disposed of by the President. The city, he had said in his instructions to the commissioners, had fallen to our arms before the commanders of our forces in the Philippines could be apprised of the peace; the islands were ours, therefore, by conquest as well as by virtue of the protocol.[5] The discussions passed to Cuba. Spain having agreed to relinquish her sovereignty intimated that the island might be annexed to the United States, a wish which many Americans also expressed, though it had been declared in the

---

[1] N. Y. Nation, Aug. 25, 1898.

[2] Cf. Report of Comm. to Investigate the War, vol. viii, pp. 3, 68.

[3] Ibid., vol. vii, p. 3299. "The frantic efforts for places on the transports [at Tampa] were only equalled by similar efforts to get back to the United States after the expedition had been in Cuba a short time."—J. D. Miley, In Cuba with Shafter, pp. 27–8.

[4] Richardson, vol. x, pp. 172–3.

[5] Foreign Relations for 1898, p. 906. The city fell on August 13th. General Merritt received notice of the cessation of hostilities on the 16th.—Report of Major General Commanding for 1898, p. 44; Chadwick, The Span. Am. War, vol. ii, p. 425.

Teller amendment, and other assurances had been more or less officially and publicly given, that it was our intention to withdraw when our mission had been performed. The Spaniards, it plainly appeared, were not single hearted. Their bitterness against the rebels prevented them from desiring gain to come to the body of men who had cost the government at Madrid so dear, and whose activities had brought on intervention by the United States. Spain had said that there was no Cuban "republic." [1] Moreover she had debts which might be repaid her if we should take over the island.[2] There were many holders of Spanish and Cuban bonds in France, as well as in Spain, and much was made of this subject in the Paris newspapers.[3] The American delegation firmly repelled the suggestion of any assumption of jurisdiction in Cuba. The treaty should confine itself to the issue made in the protocol, namely, Spain's relinquishment of title to, and sovereignty in, the island. Porto Rico would be taken and added to the national domain, but Cuba we were occupying with a temporary purpose. Guam would be held as a naval station.

The principal difficulties in the way of agreement arose on a return to the question of the Philippines, concerning the possession of which a considerable amount of official as well as popular opinion was being expressed. Indeed it had been for weeks, and it remained, one of the principal topics of discussion among politicians and in the press. Young nationalists, like Lodge [4] and Roosevelt, were actively opposed to retirement from the islands. Germany, Japan or some other power would occupy them at once should we withdraw.[5] As for the masses of the people, they cared little or nothing about the subject, and for support from this quarter politicians had but to make allusion to the possibility of "hauling down the flag." [6]

[1] Cf. Foreign Relations for 1898, p. 588.
[2] Ibid., pp. 924, 927, 930, 931; N. Y. Nation, Oct. 20, 1898; Cortissoz, Life of Whitelaw Reid, vol. ii, pp. 232–43.
[3] McKinley Papers, especially Day to McKinley, Oct. 23, 1898.
[4] A. Nevins, Henry White, pp. 136–7.
[5] This view was instilled into the President's mind.—G. F. Hoar, Autobiog. of 70 Years, vol. ii, pp. 307–8.
[6] Cf. N. Y. Nation, Aug. 18, 1898.

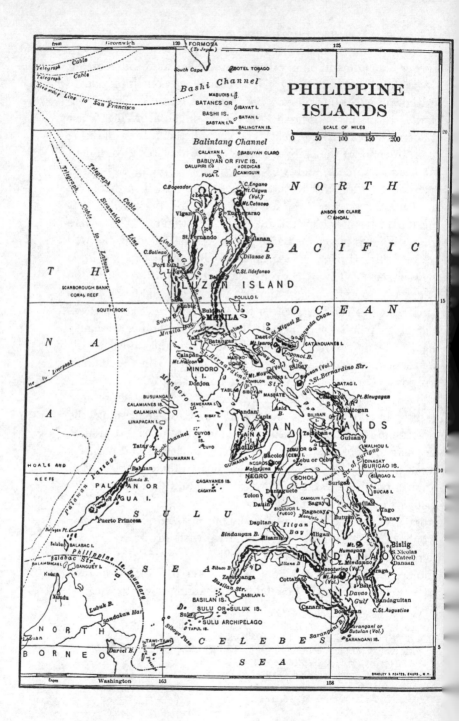

Manufacturers and business men, who were in more intimate relationship with McKinley, perhaps, than with any President whom we have ever had, were, in many instances, favorable to our holding the islands; they were nearly unanimous in believing that this policy would increase shipping, develop commerce and raise the nation to a higher place in world trade.

The commission in Paris drew to it advisers who gave it information in regard to the ethnic character of the tribes inhabiting the islands, their relations one to another, their religious and social customs, their disposition toward the United States, the resources of the country and its probable fate if our military and naval forces were withdrawn. The military governor, General Merritt, had been ordered, at the end of August, to leave his command, which he turned over to General Elwell S. Otis, who had arrived after the fall of Manila, and to proceed to Paris.[1] He was questioned and gave his testimony to the commissioners.[2] Statements from Admiral Dewey whose prestige was immense were taken to be favorable to our retention of the islands. Rumor and opinion were mixed with fact. What came to hand in Paris was reported to Washington, what came to the President and the State Department was forwarded to Paris.

Whitelaw Reid would have us regard him as the annexationist of the commission.[3] Others spoke of holding some of the islands—he would keep them all. Others had reservations— he would yield nothing to Spain and nothing to the sentiment in the United States which was averse to our involving ourselves in the work, first of pacifying a disturbed distant area and then of permanently administering its affairs. Davis and Frye were easily brought to Reid's side, he said, though their zeal, since they were famous jingoes, was probably as great as Reid's, and these three men, a majority, signed a state-

[1] Report of Maj. Gen. Commanding for 1898, p. 45.
[2] Senate Doc. 55th Cong. 3rd sess., no. 62, pt. 1, pp. 362 et seq.
[3] Reid was an expansionist. "Some day we will have Cuba as well as the Sandwich Islands," he wrote to McKinley on December 5, 1896. "To get both in your administration would put it beside Jefferson's in the popular mind and ahead in history."—McKinley Papers.

ment and forwarded it to the President.[1] Mr. Day, in dissenting, said that our experiments in colonial expansion should be
"kept within bounds." [2]   He would take only Luzon and,
perhaps, some adjacent parts of the group, while George
Gray was opposed to our retaining the islands, either in whole
or in part, as a reversal of American policy and a "shameful
stepping down from the high moral position" which we had
occupied upon entering the war.[3]

Reid's influence with McKinley may have been strengthened
now that John Hay had become Secretary of State,[4] though
Hay's enthusiasm for annexation was not great.[5] The President,
in his instructions to the commissioners, when they departed
for Paris in September, seems to have taken it for granted
that we would hold Manila and at least a portion of the archipelago. The war, he said, had brought us "new duties and
responsibilities"—they must be met and discharged in a manner
becoming "a great nation on whose growth and career, from
the beginning, the Ruler of Nations" had "plainly written the
high command and pledge of civilization." It was noted that
there were commercial opportunities in that quarter—to these
considerations "American statesmanship" could not be "in-

[1] Foreign Relations for 1898, pp. 932–3; Cortissoz, Life of Reid, vol.
ii, chap. xiii.

[2] He wrote privately to McKinley—"As I have always said to you the
acquisition of this great archipelago with 8 or 9 millions of absolutely
ignorant and many degraded people with a capacity of supporting a population of 50 millions seems like a great undertaking for a country whose
pride it is to rest its government on the consent of the governed."—Oct.
28, 1898, in McKinley Papers.

[3] Foreign Relations for 1898, pp. 934–5. Regarding Gray's character
and his later surrender see Cleveland to Olney, A. Nevins, Letters of
Cleveland, p. 495.

[4] Hay's friendship for Reid was not idolatry. He described Reid's
hunger for office as "insane."—Tyler Dennett, John Hay, pp. 193–4, 197.
Cf. Reid's letters to McKinley in C. S. Olcott, Life of McKinley, vol. ii,
pp. 123–8; W. R. Thayer, Life of Hay, vol. ii, pp. 197–200; Cortissoz,
Life of Reid, vol. ii, p. 256.

[5] He wrote to John Bigelow, Sep. 5, 1898, in answer to a letter of protest—"I fear you are right about the Philippines and I hope the Lord
will be good to us poor devils who have to take care of them." (Letters
and Diary of Hay, vol. iii, p. 134.) His views, however, were undergoing
change upon learning from Lord Salisbury that England favored our retention of the islands. (Tyler Dennett, John Hay, p. 191.) He cabled
this information from London to Secretary Day.—McKinley Papers.

different." [1] Most of the members of the cabinet advocated the retention of the entire Philippine group.[2] Lodge was working upon McKinley to rid him of his timidity.[3] There is an explanation of the President's development as an expansionist founded on revelation. One evening, when he was pondering the problem, after prayer to Almighty God, he was made to see it in its true light—"There is nothing left for us to do," he said to himself while under the spell of this exaltation, "but to take all the islands and to educate the Filipinos, and uplift, civilize and Christianize them and, by God's grace, do the very best we can for them as our fellow men, for whom Christ also died." Then he went to bed, fell asleep and slept soundly.[4]

So much naïveté or cant, however it may be regarded, but ill concealed the fact that the President had been brought under the influence of Reid, Lodge, Roosevelt and the expansionists who were taking control of the Republican party. Germany, Russia and Great Britain had seized footholds on the Chinese coast. We must be on guard nearby.[5] Germany's attitude was particularly disquieting and a movement made by an admiral of a visiting German squadron, while Dewey stood at Manila, was viewed with great alarm.[6] Newspapers, party conventions in the states, politicians who would be elected to Congress in the autumn of 1898 fanned the fires of expansion.[7] President McKinley made a pre-election tour in the West, ostensibly to attend a series of "Peace Jubilees," sounding during his journey as well as guiding public sentiment. Upon

[1] Foreign Relations for 1898, pp. 907-8.
[2] C. S. Olcott, Life of McKinley, vol. ii, pp. 61-3.
[3] Corr. of Roosevelt and Lodge, vol. i, pp. 323-4. "If old Dewey had just sailed away when he smashed that Spanish fleet," McKinley said to friends on one occasion, "what a lot of trouble he would have saved us."—H. H. Kohlsaat, From McKinley to Harding, p. 68.
[4] Olcott, Life of McKinley, vol. ii, pp. 110-1, on authority of a conversation of the President with a group of Methodist preachers who visited him, reported in the Christian Advocate, Jan. 22, 1903.
[5] Walter Millis, The Martial Spirit, pp. 123, 221, 251; Autobiog. of Dewey, p. 181.
[6] Autobiog. of Dewey, chap. xvii; Millis, The Martial Spirit, pp. 331-3.
[7] N. Y. Nation, Sep. 1, 1898; Corr. of Roosevelt and Lodge, vol. i, p. 313; J. D. Long, America of Yesterday, p. 215.

his return he announced that the people were in favor of holding the islands.[1]   He wrote to Mr. Day who was so reluctantly cooperating with the annexationists in Paris, on October 25th, that the question was receiving the "thoughtful consideration" of the nation and that it was the "well considered opinion" of a majority that duty required us to "take the archipelago." [2] The next day he officially instructed the commission, with the approval of the entire cabinet, to make this demand,[3] which it was clear enough, after the pollings in November,[4] that Spain could not resist.

As a *douceur* $20,000,000 would be paid her to reimburse her for expenditures in the Philippines and her ships and merchandise, entering Manila and other ports, would enjoy equality of treatment with ships and merchandise of the United States.[5]   Our representatives held their ground firmly. The victors' terms were declared to be hard, but, the impossibility of gaining further concessions by argument [6] being understood, the treaty was signed on December 10, 1898.[7] We had taken every other outlying possession of Spain—how had it been, Commissioner Frye in Paris asked, that we had overlooked the Carolines? [8]   Reid also regretfully noted the omission with reference to that insular group,[9] though they seem to have been eliminated because of German claims, and because Spain, it was believed, would not be able to hold them for long in any case.[10]   The ratifications were to be exchanged

---

[1] N. Y. Times, Dec. 1, 1898; Hoar, Autobiog. of 70 Years, vol. ii, pp. 311–2.

[2] McKinley Papers.   [3] Foreign Relations for 1898, pp. 935, 937–8.

[4] "A splendid victory for an off year and a splendid tribute to your administration."—Hanna to McKinley, Nov. 10, 1898, in McKinley Papers.

[5] The President's "great concern," Secretary Hay telegraphed Mr. Day, was that the treaty should be in terms "which will not only satisfy the present generation but, what is more important, be justified in the judgment of posterity."—Foreign Relations for 1898, p. 941.

[6] A wag in a Spanish newspaper seeing the humor of the scene said that in leaving the Foreign Office the Spanish commissioners were "stuffed with arguments," while the Americans were "stuffed with archipelagoes." —McKinley Papers.

[7] Foreign Relations for 1898, pp. 831–40.

[8] Chadwick, The Spanish Am. War, vol. ii, p. 464.   [9] Ibid., p. 466.

[10] Day to McKinley, Dec. 12, 1898, in McKinley Papers.

in Washington within six months. "What a mighty empire has thus crumbled and fallen!" wrote Secretary Day to President McKinley, not without pity for the foe from whom so much had been exacted by the commission,—"Once the mistress of the world—now a broken, defeated and bankrupt people, with the dynasty itself in doubt." [1]

It was said by Mr. Cannon at the end of the second session of the 55th Congress that a total of $361,788,095 had been appropriated to meet the costs of the war,[2] an estimate which he, a few months later, increased to $482,562,083.[3] But such a statement of our outlays for the liberation of Cuba, the purpose with which we had set out, is incomplete. Many other charges were incurred which have been continuing to this day.

The establishment of a government suited to the native population of Porto Rico might be no insuperable task even for a civil service like our own, which was in no way prepared for colonial administration. But the assumption of such responsibilities was a distinct departure for a republic which had been founded in the tradition that it should avoid entangling foreign connections and remain at home for the development of its own ample territories. Our interests, our experiences, our racial stock belonged in the temperate zone. We had neither liking for life, nor genius for problems of government, in lands under the Equator. Our success in the management of our affairs in a contiguous continental area in North America was incomplete, as all men could see. This and more was said concerning Porto Rico, and it applied as forcefully to the Sandwich Islands which at the same time were falling under our control.

The resolution to quit Cuba met with the approval of most enlightened men. The eyes even of the jingoes were opened to the perplexities which the government of such a congeries of negroids, mestizos and other people of mixed and alien races would certainly entail. But the pledge to leave the island it was

[1] Day to McKinley, Dec. 2, 1898, in McKinley Papers.
[2] App. Ann. Cyclop. for 1898, p. 210.   [3] Ibid. for 1899, p. 229.

feared in some quarters in this country, as well as in Cuba, might not be kept. Discussion raged over the possibility that our politicians would find an excuse in the existing state of affairs to remain for an indefinite period, thus involving us for long in military and naval liabilities, and in unending expense. The behavior of the Cuban "patriots," after we had entered upon the war for their liberation, was so astoundingly unlike what the "Cuba Libre" junta and the yellow journalists had led us to suppose their conduct might be that even their advocates were disillusioned. As allies in a war commenced for their benefit they won no respect. Treasons and stratagems were their idea of statecraft. One group elected a president; another group elected a president; each asserted its claim to autonomy and would have us regard it as the "republic" which, prior to our declaration of war upon Spain, we were to recognize with a grant of "belligerent rights" or of "independence." Bushwhacking and banditry, assassination and massacre the Cubans called war. Their predaceous spirit, their cruelly vindictive measures were a disgrace to the profession of arms. An enlisted man in the Spanish army, after the surrender at Santiago, wrote a letter, in behalf of himself and 11,000 Spanish soldiers, which he addressed to the "Soldiers of the American Army," contrasting our method of fighting face to face with that of the Cubans, "a people without religion, without morals, without conscience and of doubtful origin—the descendants of Congos and Guineas, mingled with the blood of unscrupulous Spaniards and of traitors and adventurers," who, instead of confronting the enemy, shot their victims "from ambush and then immediately fled." [1]

The Cuban army was, it was said, not one-fifth as large as it had been reputed to be. It was made up of laborers—negroes and poor whites—over 90 per cent. of them being illiterates. In their "great battles" which had lasted all day only one or, possibly, two men had been killed.[2] They plun-

[1] Chadwick, Span. Am. War, vol. ii, p. 263.
[2] C. F. Allison of U. S. Commission in Havana to McKinley, Nov. 30, 1898, in McKinley Papers.

dered the camps of the American troops who had come to befriend them.[1] Their commanders, in general, were self seeking men who would not keep pledges or agreements. They could not be made to work on entrenchments or in the transport service.[2] They, or native renegades indistinguishable from them, killed the wounded and mutilated and robbed the dead. They shot at Cervera's sailors clinging to the Spanish wrecks at Santiago while the Americans were endeavoring to save the poor fellows, and they desisted only when our naval commanders threatened to shell them in the retreats in which they were loading their guns.[3] Garcia, who had at hand only a few ill clothed, meagerly accoutered, undisciplined men during the siege of Santiago disregarded Shafter's request and failed to meet or to check the advance of Spanish reinforcements from the north.[4] When the Spaniards surrendered, he was not allowed to enter lest the imps in his train should sack the city. In injured pride he withdrew and returned to the hills. Such was the picture generally given of the Cubans after our troops and our newspaper correspondents had met them on their own ground. Undoubtedly there were among that portion of the population which had been prolonging the rebellion against Spain some men of patriotic views and pure purposes. They had believed that we would give them a greater part in the victory over their old enemy and, as the war was begun to make them free, when this end had been gained, that the island would be surrendered to them at once.

Meantime the poor non-combatant inhabitants were still

[1] Cf. J. Bigelow, Jr., Reminiscences of the Santiago Campaign, p. 108.
[2] N. Y. Times, July 23 and 29, 1898; N. Y. Sun, July 23, 1898; H. H. Sargent, The Campaign of Santiago, vol. ii, pp. 165–6.
[3] N. Y. Nation, July 7, 1898; Nat. Cyclop. of Am. Biog., vol. ix, p. 15; The Span. Am. War by Eye Witnesses, p. 172.
[4] Report of Bur. of Nav. for 1898, app., p. 609; R. A. Alger, The Span. Am. War, pp. 186–7; Miles, Serving the Republic, p. 28. It is but fair to say that Miles and Sampson had a better opinion of the Cubans, though their opportunities for contact with them were fewer, and both were not averse to throwing discredit upon Shafter and his management of the situation at Santiago.—Report of Bur. of Nav. for 1898, app., pp. 449–50; Stephen Bonsal, The Fight for Santiago, pp. 441–5; Report of Comm. to Investigate the War, vol. ii, p. 1052.

suffering for lack of the common necessaries of life. During the blockade it is very likely that they were speaking the whole truth when they said that there were more pinching want, more distress, starvation and death among them than there had been under Weyler when he kept the country people in concentration camps. The Cuban army, after the armistice, generally refrained from further attacks upon the Spaniards who, at our demand, had retired to the garrison towns. The Cubans were told in definite terms from Washington, through our commanders in the island, that the war was over.[1] But, released from control, they, like the civil population, without food to eat, resorted to lawless pillage. In November two million rations were issued by the government of the United States to relieve the starving and Calixto Garcia and Maximo Gomez, after nursing their pique for a time, recommended their troops, as well as the people, to accept the promises of the United States with reference to eventual independence. The "army" elected an Assembly which, at Santa Cruz, on November 7, 1898, chose Domingo Mendez Capote president, who, with a vice-president and secretaries, should exercise administrative authority when the Assembly should not be in session.

The Cubans gave themselves up to jealousies and quarrels. Factions distrusted one another. Garcia headed a commission which visited Washington where he died, his remains, in the interest of improved relationships, being returned to Cuba by the United States government in a man-of-war.[2] The insurgent "army" could not be disbanded until the men had been paid. They asked the United States for $60,000,000 and, no other resource being at hand, finally, in the interest of the law and order which we had set forth to restore, $3,000,000 were advanced for this use, on the condition that the Cuban "soldiers" would lay down their arms, go home and give their minds to peaceful pursuits. Though the Assembly voted to impeach Gomez, the general-in-chief, for acceding to the pro-

[1] N. Y. Nation, Aug. 25, 1898.
[2] N. Y. Times, Nov. 22 and Dec. 12, 1898, and Feb. 10, 1899.

posal and dismissed him from his command, the negotiations continued and the desired result was gained.

It was a comedy indeed. We had won a great military and naval victory over another power—we so described it. We carried the prisoners which we had taken in the war, troops which had been used against us, back to their homes. We fed the population of Cuba. We paid off the Cuban "army." And then we agreed to give Spain $20,000,000 to recoup her in some degree for the trouble of waging the war upon us, an example in openhandedness which is not to be compared with anything in the military history of the world.[1]

[1] Cf. N. Y. Times, Aug. 10, 1898.

CHAPTER XXXIX

THE political campaigns of 1898 involved the election of members of the House of Representatives, some governors of states and some state legislatures which would choose United States senators. The war with Spain had been productive of issues which would be taken to the people by the two parties. Its conduct, especially with reference to the management of the army and the expansion of national interests to cover insular possessions, some a few miles, others thousands of miles from the continental area, to which the American idea of government had hitherto been confined, were questions in all men's minds. The war had been won with brilliancy, skill and despatch and the people were in a martial furore increased by "jubilees," in which the ships that had participated in successful engagements, generals and admirals who had seen bloodshed, soldiers in uniform, flying flags and beating drums were paraded for all to see. The avidity for military glory had not been sated and, while Alger and the War Department were subjected to the most scathing condemnation, new and more wars were in the national heart. The Republican party was to be purged of Alger and Algerism. All the blunders were laid at the door of this man—he was to be cast out—the party could then take the credit and enjoy the prestige of the greatest of victories. The lesson, aside from his incompetency and implied corruptions, was the instant need of a policy which was described as "preparedness." There should be a larger standing army, a reorganized departmental system, a greater navy, coast defences, a canal at the Isthmus which would permit of the faster movement of vessels from the Pacific coast to protect our Atlantic seaboard from the European powers, the faster movement of vessels from the Atlantic coast to keep our Pacific shore line safe from the hostile assaults of Japan. The memorable voyage of the *Oregon* put before the eyes of the dullest the dangers besetting the country, especially now since we had flung out our flag in Hawaii and at Guam, and were on the point, as was plain, of remaining in the Philippines. No more would the republic be what it had been, the home of a quiet domestic people, averse to the "entangling alliances" of which so much had been heard, wrapping itself in its Monroe Doctrine—it had gone out on a new way, its eyes set on foreign colonies and a place among the empires on whose lands, as was proudly said of England, the sun never set.

There was a moral issue involved. We had commenced the war to free Cuba. We had prosecuted the war and brought it to an end without taking too much account of the inhabitants. We had seized Porto Rico. We had seized an island in the Ladrones. The taking of the Philippines would be by conquest not only of Spain, which long had held them, but also of the native tribes which were intent upon self government. Only the white people settled in the Sandwich Islands welcomed annexation to the United States and plots and risings might face us, if not at once, in a future time in that quarter. The treaty of peace was being concluded by the commissioners in Paris. All was unsettlement as the political campaign of 1898 drew nigh. The President, as has been related, visited many parts of the country to attend "Peace Jubilees" and deepen the popular sense of a great victory over a foreign foe. But the criticism of the management of the War Department which found vent upon the head of Mr. Alger, the call for reforms in our administrative system which would better prepare us for martial contest, when we should again essay it, and the attack upon the whole scheme of holding and governing distant insular possessions, especially when our assumption of sovereignty was resented by the inhabitants, created enough division of sentiment to insure a lively struggle at the pollings of November.

The Democrats generally, it was believed, would array themselves in opposition to the policy of annexing foreign territory, and especially the governing of native peoples against their will. They also found fault with the conduct of the war, though this advantage was stolen from them by Theodore Roosevelt, who had no sooner landed at Montauk Point, with his sabre at his side, than he was taken to be the leader of that party within the Republican party which would purge it of the rascals and incompetents who had done everything wrong in Cuba. He was an expansionist. He voiced popular sentiment as it was generally expressed in regard to the Philippines. But he spoke softly of Alger of whom he would make later, as he had made earlier, use, in spite of the fact that to most other men the Secretary of War was the symbol of all evil. Roosevelt's denunciations were expended upon the system.[1] He unfurled the banner of "preparedness"—we should not again fight a war without cleaning the national house and establishing ourselves on a footing which would make us a military power to be respected and feared by the nations of the world. He had begun in Cuba his campaign for some elective office and he was invited at once, upon his return, to be the Republican candidate for governor of New York.[2]

The advantage which had been gained in New York City by the reform movement of 1894 and the election of William L. Strong over Croker's candidate for mayor had been undone in 1897. The respectable civic forces, in the usual way, disintegrated in the face of the superior organization of an entrenched machine. They divided their strength. Some voted for ex-Secretary of the Navy Tracy, the Republican; others, a greater number, for Seth Low, a "Citizens' Union" candidate, but Robert A. Van Wyck, the Tammany candidate, was

[1] Alger's shortcomings he, in some degree, excused—they were "congenital." (Corr. of Roosevelt and Lodge, vol. i, p. 340). The response of the War Department—a not unnatural one—was a denial to Roosevelt of the medal of honor, which he dearly coveted. That he could not get it excited his ire—he had earned it, he had killed a Spaniard with his own hand, he told his friend Lodge, a feat, but not a large harvest for so much bellicosity.—Ibid., p. 366; H. F. Pringle, Theodore Roosevelt, p. 207; N. Y. Times, Jan. 7, 1899.
[2] Cf. Autobiog. of T. C. Platt, pp. 368–9.

elected by a substantial plurality. By this time New York had become a "Greater New York"—the city had come to include Brooklyn, as well as outlying urban communities, which were consolidated into "Boroughs" called Queens, Richmond and the Bronx. The prize, therefore, was the more worthy of Tammany's skilful efforts to capture it.

Richard Croker in 1898, being again in complete control of the city, now a greater city, and more powerful than ever before, would, if he could, control the state. Tammany would nominate another Van Wyck, a justice of the supreme court of New York, the mayor's brother, for governor. The Republicans, under Platt's influence, had made Black governor in 1896. But public feeling was disturbed. Could Platt name a governor again amid the resentments which the war had awakened? Rather than forfeit control to the Democrats it were better to put at the head of the ticket a "war hero," a refractory person and an unwelcome choice, but one who, in the present state of the popular temper, might catch the votes of enough excited men to bring victory to the party. Roosevelt was eager to secure the nomination and he again put away his pride, truckled to Platt,[1] who at the time was involved in unsavory scandals in connection with the management of the state canals, and gained the favor of that potential personage. By the convention at Saratoga Springs, at the end of September, he was made the Republican candidate for the governorship and, throughout October, stumped the state with his peculiar impetuosity. He had taken the nomination from a man of whom he had frequently expressed his distrust, and found on the ticket with him those who were not in good repute among the friends of good government. These facts called forth unpleasant comment.[2] It was said, too, that he drew too much upon his fame as a warrior in Cuba.[3] On the platform with him when he spoke were Rough Riders and other

[1] Cf. N. Y. Nation, Sep. 22, 1898. [2] Cf. ibid., Oct. 27, 1898.
[3] "He talked and he talked and he talked,
  He talked in the wind and the rain,
  And the burden of all he could say was
  That I, Teddy Roosevelt, licked Spain."

returned soldiers in uniform. He neglected state issues and prated about preparedness and expansion, about new foreign foes and new wars,[1] though, as the campaign progressed, he gave more attention to the question of good government in New York state, and made friends of some who had looked upon him on Platt's ticket as no better than the Democrat, who was Croker's man. Roosevelt was elected, but there was little to spare. His plurality was less than 18,000 and he carried his associates on the Republican ticket to victory, though by smaller margins of safety. Black in 1896 had had a plurality of more than 200,000. The consideration of these facts was not designed to increase the successful candidate's assurance of the esteem in which he might be held, but it placed him in a position of great political influence which could be used, as it proved, for advancement into a still larger field.

In Pennsylvania a stubborn contest had been waged within the Republican party against Quay. He was its unquestioned "Boss," and had ruled it arbitrarily since the withdrawal of Cameron's hand. Men had risen in his path but none made such unyielding war upon his leadership as John Wanamaker, the Philadelphia merchant, who had been in Harrison's cabinet where, as Postmaster General, he had greatly improved the postal service. It was said that Wanamaker had asked for a favor which was denied him and that his course now was ascribable to this fact.[2] At any rate he had become Quay's active enemy and rose to unexpected rank as a speaker and campaign manager in the organization of independently minded voters in Pennsylvania. In 1898, while Quay's nominee for governor was elected, he himself was retired from the United States Senate, being at the same time faced with criminal proceedings affecting the use of public funds. A deadlock in the legislature had prevented his election and, when he was reappointed by his friend, the governor, he was not received in the chamber in which he had held a seat for so many years.[3]

[1] Writings of Carl Schurz, vol. v, pp. 520, 523–4; Autobiog. of Platt, p. 373; H. F. Pringle, Theodore Roosevelt, pp. 205–6.

[2] A. K. McClure, Old Time Notes of Pa., vol. ii, pp. 596–8.

[3] Cf. ibid., chaps. civ and cv.

The new Congress as a result of the elections of 1898 would remain Republican in both branches, by a reduced majority in the House of Representatives, but with an increase of strength in the Senate.[1] Speaker Reed who had resigned as a member of the House of Representatives, because of his dissent from the policy of the administration in the making of a war of conquest and the annexation of foreign territory, was succeeded in an office which he had made so powerful by David B. Henderson of Iowa. President McKinley's message, as he welcomed the Congress at its short session in December, 1898, after the elections, reviewed the successes of his administration in the period of nearly two years which had elapsed since he had come to his office—the tariff law, the resultant prosperity of the people, the improvement of the national credit because of public confidence in the government's intent to give the country a sound currency. The causes of the war were re-stated, the history of its events recounted and the progress of the negotiation at Paris of a treaty of peace referred to with the expression of a confident hope of definitive results at an early day. Cuba was to be guided toward self government. The discussion of future policies in reference to "new possessions" would await the ratification of the treaty with Spain. The Nicaragua Canal Commission, under the chairmanship of Admiral John G. Walker [2] which had been appointed on July 24, 1897, to make observations supplementing the work of the board appointed by President Cleveland on April 25, 1895, headed by Colonel William Ludlow [3] had, it was said, nearly completed its labors. The construction of such a maritime highway, in view of "the prospective expansion of our influence and commerce in the Pacific," President McKinley declared, was now more than ever "indispensable." The doctrine that steamship lines should be subsidized from the Treasury was again expounded. The regular army should be held at not less than 100,000 men. The navy was to be strengthened by the con-

---

[1] Cf. Croly, M. A. Hanna, pp. 292–4.
[2] His associates were Colonel Peter C. Hains and Lewis M. Haupt.
[3] Report in House Doc., 54th Cong. 1st sess., no. 279.

struction of three new battle ships and twelve new cruisers.

The treaty of peace soon came to the Senate to meet with a vehement calling of the administration to account for its apparent readiness to surrender our traditions as it went into the seven seas for new territory, and took over the business of forcibly governing foreign races. None surpassed Mr. Hoar in his exposition of American principles and his pleas that they be not departed from. But there were others, both in and out of Congress—ex-President Cleveland,[1] ex-President Harrison, ex-Senator Edmunds of Vermont, ex-Speaker Reed, John Sherman,[2] Carl Schurz, Mr. Godkin whose health now was tottering under the strain of long service, and the New York Evening Post and the New York Nation; ex-Secretary of the Treasury George S. Boutwell, President Eliot of Harvard, Theodore Woolsey and William G. Sumner of Yale; Andrew Carnegie the iron master;[3] Edward Atkinson, Moorfield Storey, Charles Eliot Norton,[4] Charles Francis Adams, William James and James Schouler of Boston; David Starr Jordan, president of the new Stanford University in California; John G. Carlisle, ex-Postmaster General William L. Wilson, ex-Senator John B. Henderson, Bishop Henry C. Potter and Henry van Dyke.

These and other men of high discrimination profoundly regretted the step which had been taken. They cordially disliked the outlook which embarkation upon a colonial policy afforded. They especially deplored the prospect of the slaughter of native races as a preliminary to the establishment of colonial government. They believed and said, with Carl Schurz, that the American democracy was losing its honor, that "ruthless violence" was being done to "the spirit of the Constitution."[5] They took counsel together. An Anti-Imperialist League was

[1] Who spoke of it as "this fatal imperialistic folly."—A. Nevins, Letters of Cleveland, p. 506.

[2] Who said that we should recognize the independence of the Philippines and withdraw the troops.—Sherman to McKinley, Feb. 16, 1899, in McKinley Papers.

[3] Cf. W. R. Thayer, Life and Letters of John Hay, vol. ii, p. 199.

[4] Cf. Letters of Norton, vol. ii, p. 290.

[5] Writings of Schurz, vol. v, pp. 77–9.

formed which held conferences and adopted resolutions.[1] Dewey, after destroying the Spanish ships at Manila, might better have sailed away—the troops might better now be withdrawn and the people be left to their own dispositions.[2]

There were in the Philippine group as many as 1650 islands bearing names and 1500 more so small as to seem not to merit such dignity.[3] They, all together, had a land surface of approximately 120,000 square miles. Probably 7,000,000 people dwelt upon them, one half of whom found their livelihood in Luzon, as large as the state of Ohio, upon which Manila, the principal city, with a quarter of a million people, was situated. The cost of our resolution to take this tropical archipelago and to be responsible for its government and for its defense against other powers which might, in the future, have designs upon it would be dear. The sending out of one transport laden with troops called for more ships, more men, more munitions, more fighting, more casualty lists, more death from disease. Over 7,000 miles from San Francisco, in the heat of the Equator, amid strange little brown people, our flag took its way and there, unless opposition should become more eloquent at once, it would remain.

Argument and protest might not avail. The masses in a democracy are whipped into hysteria by wars, economic panics and other great national disturbances under leaders who are ready to play upon ignorance and prejudice. Three senators had joined in the preparation of the treaty—one, Mr. Gray, reluctantly, though he now appeared as its advocate [4] and they led the battle for its ratification. Always there were calls to "duty" and appeals to "destiny." We were on the ground—it was ours—we were to pay $20,000,000 for the Philippines—the trade of the East invited us—if the islands were left to themselves the natives would fall to butchering one

[1] Writings of Schurz, vol. vi, pp. 77–9.
[2] Cf. N. Y. Nation, May 19 and 26 and Aug. 4, 1898; S. W. McCall, Life of T. B. Reed, pp. 237–8.
[3] The number is variously given. Cf. J. H. Blount, Am. Occupation of the Philippines, p. 227.
[4] Cf. N. Y. Times, Jan. 17, 1899.

another—some other power would enter and seize and hold what it was proposed that we should now cravenly reject. If we were to leave the Philippines to their fate we could better ratify the treaty and retire at our leisure at some later time.[1]

The Filipinos in this emergency exerted themselves to the utmost. They had juntas in London, Paris, Madrid and Hong Kong. Attempts were made to organize the sentiment of the world in behalf of the cause of their independence. It was reported repeatedly that Germany would aid Aguinaldo. He announced a cabinet, the "republic" was provided with a new Minister of Foreign Affairs, new Ministers of the Interior, Finance, War and Public Works. They were clever men— lawyers, engineers and soldiers. At least one of the number had been educated in England. Intelligent envoys appeared in this country. They spoke to groups of citizens; they were interviewed by the newspapers, visited the State Department to deliver notes of protest which were not answered, met and talked to senators who were to vote for or against the treaty and sought an audience with McKinley which was declined.[2] Aguinaldo made a formal plea to the United States for the recognition of his government.[3] The presence and activity of his emissaries in this country gave support to the anti-expansionists. Proof was at hand that a people intent upon the enjoyment of freedom dwelt in the territory, which we proposed to annex; proof was at hand, also, if it were required, that they would resist our efforts to occupy their islands and control their affairs.

Instead of softening his tones the President issued an order to the Secretary of War which was cabled to General Otis who was to bring it to the notice of the Filipinos. Our policy was re-stated. There would be no turning back. The army would aim "to win the confidence, respect and affection of the inhabitants," who should be assured of a "full measure of individual rights and liberties which are the heritage of

[1] Cf. N. Y. Times, Jan. 4, 1899.

[2] Ibid., Jan. 24, 25, 28 and 31, 1899.

[3] Ibid., Jan. 18, 1899; cf. Report of Maj. Gen. Commanding, pt. 2 pp. 76–8.

ll free peoples." The "high mission" of the United States
vas to be "one of benevolent assimilation, substituting the
mild sway of justice and right for arbitrary rule," and so on.[1]

Bryan who had come home unscathed from a few weeks in
a camp with a squad of would-be soldiers from Nebraska
vas again in civilian habiliments, and he was quick to see in
'Imperialism," as it was coming to be called, a new issue for
he party which he still led.

The issues of the war, since he had enlisted in it, had changed,
e told McKinley, whom he visited at the White House. The
roops had "volunteered to break the yoke of Spain in Cuba
nd for nothing else. They did not volunteer to attempt the
ubjugation of other peoples."[2] Overwhelmingly defeated as
ts Presidential candidate in 1896 Bryan would now put another
vord upon his banner and go with it to the people in 1900.
Ie would be more Jeffersonian than he had thought himself
n 1896; for he would now deny the right of the opposing party
o convert the republic into a despotism which would govern
vithout the consent of the governed. Plainly the Filipinos
id not want us in their islands; they could be made amenable
nd would submit to our rule only under military compulsion.
Vas this Jeffersonism or Americanism? We could not afford
o erase from the constitutions, state and national, the bill
f rights. The impassioned appeal—"Give me liberty or give
e death" still echoed around the world.[3]

If Bryan could induce his party to take the position which
e had taken, men in other parties might be attracted to it
nd might vote for its candidates. But first, as it appeared, the
reaty must be ratified, else there would be no opportunity
o wage so propitious a battle in the newspapers and on the
ustings in the following year. Bryan, therefore, visited Wash-
gton. He denounced conquest and most of the representatives

[1] N. Y. Times, Jan. 6, 1899; Report of Maj. Gen. Commanding for 1899
. 2, pp. 68–9; J. H. Blount, Am. Occupation of the Philippines, chap,
ii.

[2] L. J. Gage, memo. of conversation in White House, Sep. 24, 1898,
McKinley Papers.

[3] Cf. Bryan's Jackson Day speech in Cincinnati on Jan. 6, in N. Y.
mes, Jan. 7, 1899; also his speech in Denver in ibid., Jan. 18, 1899.

of the party in the Senate who now looked to him as their guide
and mentor were induced to subscribe to this principle, though
they had been foremost in fomenting the turmoil which had
brought on the war. The fate of the treaty hung in the balance.[1]
The Anti-Imperialists were roundly scored. They were "sleeping life away and opposing progress." Excited patriots called
them "traitors." G. A. R. "Encampments" passed resolutions,
branding them as "unworthy of the name of American citizens." [2]

They were undeterred. Andrew Carnegie, in the course
of his opposition, in his effort to give McKinley the "real truth'
about "the pains and penalties arising from distant possessions,'
quoted letters from Sir Henry Campbell Bannerman, leader
of the Liberal party in England, who would, if he could, protect
the President from friends who were tempting him "to plunge
the country into the vortex of the Far East." Campbell Bannerman wrote to Carnegie—"Now that your great republic
has gone in for a big army and powerful navy, numerous colonies
and all the other appurtenances of empire you will encounter
some of the difficulties for which our cast iron system has been
created. We all wish you luck in your new career, but, if you
had our experiences, there would be more support given to
yourself and those who are with you in trying to preserve
your happy immunity." [3]

Carnegie used all his influences to prevent the ratification of
the treaty, and there was no certainty of the result until the
end. One word from Bryan, Carnegie said, and the treaty
would be beaten.[4] If it could not be defeated it must be modified—there must be a pledge, Bryan was told, that the Filipinos
should be given their independence. On the other side Lodge
and Aldrich labored with might and main for ratification

---

[1] Lodge to Roosevelt in Corr. of Roosevelt and Lodge, vol. i, p. 368.
[2] McKinley Papers.
[3] Carnegie to McKinley, Feb. 21, 1899. Campbell Bannerman's letter
is dated Jan. 20, 1899, in McKinley Papers.
[4] Bryan Papers, cited in W. S. Holt, Treaties Defeated by the Senate,
pp. 165, 167; Autobiography of Carnegie, p. 364.
[5] Corr. of Roosevelt and Lodge, vol. i, pp. 391–2.

Offices were bartered for votes.[1] But it is correctly held to have been Bryan who saved the day for the annexationists. He determined the course of a sufficient number of his pliant friends to make up the necessary two-thirds.[2] On February 6th when 84 senators voted on the subject there were 57 yeas, one more than the Constitution required. Thirty-nine Republicans, 10 Democrats and 8 Populists and Silver Independents were numbered with the ratificationists; 22 Democrats, 2 Republicans[3] and 3 Populists voted against the treaty.[4] Once it was approved and the Philippines were annexed Bryan could go forward with his program.

An opportunity to discuss the provisions of the treaty was afforded the members of the House when that body was called upon to join the Senate in appropriating the $20,000,000 to be paid to Spain as a salve for her wounded dignity. But when the vote was taken it was a feeble protest; only 33 men stood their ground and opposed the carrying out of the bargain.[5] A spur to action in the Senate had been provided in Manila. Aguinaldo and his forces had faced the American army on the outskirts of the city while the treaty pended, and neither side could be restrained much longer. When the news was cabled to the United States that, on February 4th, four Filipinos had approached an American outpost and, refusing to heed a command to halt, had been fired upon,[6] sentiment among the masses, if not among our intellectuals, underwent a change. The New York Times, by some process of reasoning, reached the conclusion that the outbreak was a demonstration of the

[1] Holt, op. cit., pp. 171–3; Pettigrew, Imperial Washington, p. 206.
[2] Cong. Record, 56th Cong. 1st sess., p. 1940; Hoar, Autobiog. of 70 ars, vol. ii, pp. 322–3; Hoar in N. A. Review, Oct., 1900; W. S. Holt, Treaties Defeated by the Senate, pp. 174–7; Pettigrew, Imperial Washton, pp. 270–1.
[3] Hoar of Massachusetts and Hale of Maine.
[4] Cf. Holt, op. cit., p. 169; C. S. Olcott, Life of McKinley, vol. ii, pp. 40.
[5] Cong. Record, 56th Cong. 1st sess., p. 1941.
[6] Report of Maj. Gen. Commanding for 1899, pt. 2, pp. 92, 96–103; C. Coolidge, The U. S. as a World Power, p. 155; C. B. Elliott, The Philippines to the End of the Military Regime, p. 452. Conditions preceding the outbreak are fully described in J. A. LeRoy, The Americans the Philippines, vol. ii, pp. 1–9.

Filipino's "incapacity for self government." [1] In any event it was an "attack upon the flag" which, at no time, is to be viewed with tolerance. Agoncillo, the Filipino envoy in Washington whose cable messages were immediately put under strict censorship, moved his headquarters to Montreal,[2] and the junta soon took flight also.[3] New commissioners who were on their way to Washington to labor for independence, hearing upon landing at the pier in San Francisco of the commencement of hostilities, also headed toward Canada.[4]

Spain had called it a rebellion, we had fallen heir to it. It was now our rebellion. The insurgents were driven from their trenches around Manila with heavy losses and were pursued into the hills. In two months, in February and March, 1899, 184 American officers and men were killed and 976 wounded. These numbers were increased at the end of seven months, in August, 1899, to 361 killed and 1412 wounded. Several hundreds more had succumbed to disease. General Otis's army had come by this time to be a body of 31,000 men.[5]

The short and closing session of the 55th Congress, barring the ratification of the treaty of peace, was productive of little action. The Senate by a vote of 26 to 22, as many as 42 members not voting, passed a meaningless resolution stating that it was not our purpose to "permanently annex" the Philippines "as an integral part of the territory of the United States." Measures looking to a reorganization of the army and the navy which were far from what they should have been, had Congress really taken to heart the lessons of the war, were adopted in the final days of the session and were approved by the President.

A commission, that resource of public ministers when they are about to adopt a course which may bring them unpopularity and again, when caught in an eddy of public opinion, they are debating retreat from a position which they may have occupied

[1] Issue of Feb. 7, 1899.
[2] N. Y. Times, Feb. 7, 1899. For facts regarding Agoncillo see F. Greene to Hay, Feb. 2, 1900, in McKinley Papers.
[3] N. Y. Times, Feb. 8, 1899. [4] Ibid., Feb. 11, 1899.
[5] Report of Maj. Gen. Commanding for 1899, pt. 2, pp. 142–3.
[6] Cong. Record, 55th Cong. 3rd sess., pp. 1846–8.

was appointed by the President to visit the Philippines. President J. G. Schurman of Cornell University, Charles Denby, for many years minister to China, and Professor Dean C. Worcester of the University of Michigan, who had written authoritatively of the people, the climate and the productions of the islands, were asked, in conjunction with Admiral Dewey and General Otis, to study the problem and make a report.[1]

These gentlemen, upon their arrival in Manila on March 4, 1899, met with little more sympathy when they proclaimed our philanthropic purposes than had our military commanders, though there were elements in the population which were appreciative of the prospect of our friendly protection. The interest in us expressed by these classes, however, was largely selfish, based upon a feeling that their lives and property would be safer under the honest and equitable government which it was believed that we would establish.[2] The ports were declared open to commerce on December 11, 1899. Our severe Chinese exclusion laws were, by military decree, extended to the territory to keep that people out of it.[3] It was said that Aguinaldo had at his call 70,000 men, many of whom had served in the Spanish army where they had gained experience in trench digging and the use of arms. But his troops were not well supplied with rifles—a third of his men, at least, were provided only with the native weapon, the bolo, a long, sharp knife, ground to a point, a nasty implement at close range and in the hands of an agile antagonist.

In their retreats in Luzon to which we had driven them they were pursued persistently, but were not subdued. Expeditions were sent to the smaller islands to deal with risings and unfurl the flag of the United States where it had not been seen before. Garrisons were left to do police duty while the body of our troops moved on with a view to putting the entire archipelago under military control. In this process many of our soldiers were

Report of Comm. in Senate Doc., 56th Cong. 1st sess., no. 138; cf. Report of Maj. Gen. Commanding for 1899, pt. 2, p. 149.
Cf. C. B. Elliott, The Philippines to the End of the Military Regime, 158; J. G. Schurman, Philippine Affairs, p. 6.
Foreign Relations for 1901, p. 93.

captured and carried off. Spanish prisoners had not been
returned to Spain. Our intervention in behalf of the unfortunate
men, who had been taken before our occupation, and were
still in captivity under conditions which were exasperating,
was sought. Aguinaldo demanded of Spain a large ransom
for her nationals, a proposal which was looked askance at
in Madrid and was entirely inadmissible from our standpoint,
since the sum so paid him would certainly be used to prolong
the war.[1] About 5,000 Spaniards who had been released from
time to time as our army advanced asked for transportation
back to their homes. Although their return was not required
of us we again displayed a handsome magnanimity—they
were landed at Barcelona at the expense of the government o
the United States.[2]

Throughout the rainy season in 1899 the campaign wa
prosecuted as energetically as the conditions unfamiliar to ou
troops would allow. Their trials on expeditions into unknow.
country, the sniping at them by the enemy, his treachery i
shamming death and then shooting them from the rear, c
knifing them, incensed them to such a degree that it was impo:
sible to conduct the contest in entire accordance with the prin
ciples of civilized combat. It is not surprising that the soldie
resorted to tactics which had been adopted in dealing with th
Indians on our Western plains, and the idea in mind, as th
evidence of the feints and deceits of the Filipinos increase
was extermination. Stories about the cruelty of our troop
appeared in the American newspapers.[3] The humanely minde
with whom all men are brothers and for whom Aguinaldo w:
a kind of liberator struggling against fearful odds to gain freedo
for his people, made grave charges against the army and i

---

[1] Foreign Relations for 1899, pp. 682–93.
[2] Report of Lieut. Gen. Commanding for 1900, pt. 2, p. 474; cf. ibi
pt. 4, p. 286.
[3] J: L. Laughlin, Patriotism and Imperialism, Liberty Tracts, no.
Sec. Root's Record, Marked Severities in Philippine Warfare, a pamphl
Boston, 1902; J. F. Rhodes, McKinley and Roosevelt Administratio
pp. 204–5; J. H. Latané, America as a World Power, p. 96; J. H. Blou
American Occupation of the Philippines, pp. 203–4; A. C. Coolidge, T
U. S. as a World Power, p. 157.

commanders. We were, it was said, prosecuting a ruthless war in a savage manner on a helpless race.[1] But war it was, and it went on. General MacArthur, General Lawton, General Wheaton pressed the Filipinos, large numbers of whom were killed and captured. Their stores were taken and destroyed, but always Aguinaldo himself eluded us and retired to new fastnesses. To suggestions of a truce, demands that he surrender, proffers of a form of government with mixed native and American tribunals he remained obdurate. General Lawton whose vigorous blows had made much impress upon the natives was, at the end of the year 1899, slain by a sharpshooter,[2] a sacrifice which intensified the determination to pursue the contest relentlessly.[3] The American army, by this time, had been increased to 65,000 men.[4] A member of General Otis's staff, upon his return home, said that to subjugate the Philippines and hold them would require a body of 100,000 or 150,000 soldiers.[5] Commissioner Schurman held similar views. But, he said, the President should be given all the men and all the money that, "in any contingency," could be needed to suppress the insurrection.[6] Mr. Schurman had been at the moment of his appointment opposed to the Philippine policy of the administration.[7] He was now an advocate of staying in the islands to the bitter end.

The commissioners made a preliminary report in November, 1899. They described the population. There were many tribes, speaking many languages. Only one, the Tagals or Tagalogs, were under arms. The commission, indeed, called it the "Tagalog rebellion." [8] The people, when pacified, might, with our guidance, cooperate with us in the administration of local affairs, from Manila as a centre. As they came under

[1] Cf. Writings of Schurz, vol. vi, p. 98.
[2] J. A. LeRoy, The Americans in the Philippines, vol. ii, pp. 158–9; N. Y. Times, Dec. 20, 1899.
[3] Cf. N. Y. Nation, Dec. 28, 1899.
[4] Report of Sec. of War for 1899, p. 8.   [5] N. Y. Nation, July 8, 1899.
[6] N. Y. Times, Oct. 20, 1899.
[7] J. G. Schurman, Philippine Affairs, p. 2.
[8] Cf. Schurman in N. Y. Times, Oct. 20, 1899; ibid., Philippine Affairs, p. 7; N. Y. Nation, Oct. 25, 1900.

the influence of our educational system they could be given larger powers and be put on the way toward the independence which Aguinaldo and others in his following coveted. The answer of the commission to those who advocated a withdrawal of the United States was that such a movement would lead to anarchy which would excuse, if it should not necessitate, the intervention of other powers, and eventually to the division of the islands among these powers. Only through continued American occupation was the idea of a free, united and self-governing commonwealth conceivable.[1]

A reception for the greatest conqueror in the world's history awaited Dewey when he should come home. Already in May, 1899, New York City was preparing for it. Hundreds of thousands of dollars were appropriated from public funds and collected from the people for expenditure on the celebration. The admiral on the *Olympia* was returning by way of the Suez Canal, taking his honors at ports of call as he advanced. Sampson and the North Atlantic squadron were at hand in New York to meet him. Some thought that the President should leave Washington to welcome the hero, but better advice prevailed. McKinley being commander-in-chief of the army and navy it was determined that Dewey should come to him.[2] A naval parade up the Hudson River on the 29th of September and a procession down Fifth Avenue in which 30,000 marines, regulars and state militiamen participated followed on the 30th. "Welcome Dewey" in "letters of light," 50 feet high, on the Brooklyn Bridge; a great arch in Fifth Avenue, at 24th street, with colonnades designed by leading American sculptors, a copy of the arch of Titus and Vespasian in the Forum at Rome which, it was recalled, had been erected by Domitian in commemoration of the taking of Jerusalem by Titus; a gold loving cup in Roman form with a capacity of 4½ quarts, presented to the guest; ceremonial dinners; pyrotechnical displays and other festal elegancies illustrated the

[1] Report of Commission, Senate Doc., 56th Cong. 1st sess., no. 138; cf. N. Y. Nation, Nov. 9, 1899. A final report in 1900–01 is in four volumes.

[2] Hay to McKinley, Aug. 28, 1899, and Long to Cortelyou, Aug. 29, 1899, in McKinley Papers.

national opulence as well as the popular emotion. The celebration was continued in Washington where the admiral received at the hands of the President the jeweled sword voted him by Congress, attended dinners and balls, reviewed parades and enjoyed other honors as the "nation's guest."

A subscription was opened by a newspaper; the great man was presented by the "American people" with a handsome home in Washington,[1] which encouraged him, a widower, to marry a widow. He was in the United States not six weeks before this project was consummated.[2] Tradesmen added their contributions for the advertisement of their wares and furnished the mansion. When soon he transferred the house and its contents to the lady, whose personal fortune was so large as to require no such accretion,[3] the national countenance fell, and that his feet were of clay was made still more plain to the huzzaing crowds when it was seen shortly that he was a candidate for the Presidency of the United States.

While the militaristic sentiments of the people were being so carelessly indulged there were reminders of a deep love of peace in the hearts of many men. During the summer of 1899 the nations, at the invitation of the Czar of Russia, had appointed delegates to a conference. It met in the "House of the Wood," an old palace in the capital of Holland. Twenty-six governments were represented. Eminent statesmen were in the company—de Staal, the Russian Ambassador in London, who presided; de Martens, also a Russian; Count Munster from Germany; Leon Bourgeois from France; Sir Julian Pauncefote in the English delegation; Andrew D. White, Seth Low and Captain A. T. Mahan from the United States. The object was a revision, in the interest of humanity, of the laws of war, and especially the development of a system by which international disputes might be referred to arbitration. The negotiations and debates were tedious—general apathy on the subject and the hopelessness of endeavoring to accomplish so much

---

[1] N. Y. Times, Oct. 7, 12 and 27, 1899. McKinley subscribed $100.—May 26, 1899, in McKinley Papers.

[2] N. Y. Times, Oct. 31 and Nov. 10, 1899.   [3] Ibid., Nov. 21, 1899.

by the consultative process, as well as the jealous opposition of the German Emperor to the aims of the meeting, were to be overcome,[1] a result at length achieved. The United States became a party to the convention upon its ratification by the Senate in February, 1900.[2] A permanent court, usually known as the Hague Tribunal, was established—a body to which difficulties could be referred voluntarily (obligation was not in mind) for quiet adjustment in the interest of a civilization which should know war no more. The American delegates received a whelming mass of evidence from the United States that many of its people were peace loving, and that there was a determination among those who, if they were quite clearly, in many cases, goodly idealists rather than practical men, sought to secure greater guarantees of usefulness from the meeting than could possibly flow from its agreements.[3]

The course of affairs in the Philippines, no less than in the United States, was influenced by the early prospect of further expressions of popular sentiment at the polls in November, 1899, and in the general Presidential election of 1900. Aguinaldo and his friends, though much that was disparaging was said of them as the war proceeded, and as the attempt to put them down enraged our soldiers who were detained unwillingly in a strange tropical land in the China Sea, were not without a shrewd intelligence, which had been proven in the campaign of their envoys in this country to defeat the ratification of the treaty. They quite well knew that feeling in the United States regarding the war was not unanimous and, as Bryan and the Democratic

[1] Cf. R. B. Mowat, Life of Lord Pauncefote, pp. 234–5. Pauncefote's services in the cause were of the first importance.

[2] N. Y. Tribune, Feb. 10, 1900; N. Y. Nation, Feb. 15, 1900; Senate Ex. Journal, vol. xxxii, p. 375.

[3] Cf. Autobiog. of A. D. White, vol. ii, chaps. xlv–1; J. W. Foster, Arbitration and the Hague Court; F. W. Holls, The Peace Conference at the Hague. Cleveland declined President McKinley's appointment to be an arbitrator under the terms of the convention on the ground of disinclination "to interrupt the comfort of absolute freedom from public duty." (Cleveland to McKinley, Aug. 29, 1900, in McKinley Papers.) He thought that the conclusions arrived at by the conference were "lame and disappointing." (Nevins, Letters of Cleveland, pp. 536–7.) Ex-President Harrison accepted the tender of an appointment to the court.

party espoused their cause, and would take to the people
the question of the withdrawal of our military forces, they continued to fight.

Still complaint was heard that it was not civilized warfare.
The impossibility of the insurgents meeting a well equipped
body of American troops was plain. Their losses in such encounters had borne tribute repeatedly to the overpowering
weight of our advantage. They, therefore, resolved, at the
end of 1899, to disband their field armies and carry on their war
as guerrillas. The enemy now was not in uniform—he was
indistinguishable and was met with at every hand. Treachery
in each community was commended by that community.
The natives applauded one of their number who would, by
whatever means, kill an American and they would block
the efforts of our commanders to extend our military power
and bring the country under our control. No soldier knew when
or by whom he would be shot or run through by a knife.[1]
It is certain that no service with which our army, or, perhaps,
any army in the world, was ever charged in modern times was
so arduous, exasperating and revolting as the service, nearly
interminable as it promised to be, in pacifying such a foe. More
suffering and peril faced the troops sent to the Philippines
than had ever excited the pity and resentment of the country
during the few weeks in Cuba. But they, month by month,
and year after year, performed their dangerous and disagreeable
duties, in compliance with orders, without publishing their
cause or demanding popular sympathy. Rains, great heat,
fevers marked the months of summer. The food provided for
their use, especially the meat, was as unpalatable as that at
Santiago which had stirred Miles and Roosevelt to violent
statement.[2] The beef, when it reached the camps, many of
them among the distant hills of Luzon or on the smaller islands,
was at times utterly unfit for use. The men were 6000 or 8000
miles from their homes, with which they could communicate
only slowly and under great difficulty. They could have no

[1] Cf. Report of Lieut. Gen. Commanding for 1901, pt. 2, p. 89.
[2] Cf. R. A. Alger, Span. Am. War, p. 341.

interest in the result of such a war. It was an unjust, unholy application of a conqueror's force upon a weak race which was doing no more than any people would do were its land invaded by foreign troops. It was a soldier's task but the most unwelcome that could be given to an American, with his country's ideals before him, especially if he be a volunteer, without that training to unquestioning obedience which is associated with the profession of arms. News about the war was subjected to strict military censorship, but the men in each regiment as they returned home brought dismal tales concerning their service, the magnitude of the task and the protracted period which would be required for its performance.[1]

By this time Alger had been relieved from duty as Secretary of War. He had been treated indulgently by the President in the view of practically the entire country.[2] He should not have been appointed to his post; he should have been removed from it immediately after the war, said the New York Nation, "for demonstrated incompetence and for being the best hated public man" in the United States. His time finally came in July, 1899, when it was announced that he was a candidate in Michigan for election to the United States Senate. Mr. McKinley, eager to be rid of so great an encumbrance as Alger was held to be by the President himself and the leaders of the Republican party whose eyes were set on the elections of the autumn, which would fix the pace for the voting in 1900, found in the Secretary's activity in the politics of his state an excuse for a request for a resignation, which, with some politeness, insincere on both sides, was given and accepted, whereupon Elihu Root of New York who stood high in public favor was put in the place.[3] It was predicted that

[1] Cf. N. Y. Nation, Aug. 3 and 24, and Sep. 7, 1899. For the "horrors" of the war see D. S. Jordan's article written for N. Y. Outlook but not published, April 27, 1899, in McKinley Papers.

[2] Cf. Corr. of Roosevelt and Lodge, vol. i, p. 412.

[3] To the great displeasure of Whitelaw Reid who was "simply frantic," (John Hay to McKinley, Aug. 4, 1899.) and began to attack the administration in the New York Tribune. (J. W. Griggs to McKinley, Sep. 27, 1899, in ibid.) Platt eagerly took the credit for the appointment.—Platt to McKinley, March 7, 1901.

there would be no scandals while he should be at the head of the Department.[1]

Root was needed to strengthen the President's position before the country and he and all the members of the Cabinet, together with Roosevelt and others whose voices the populace was eager to hear, were put upon the stump in September and October, 1899, in defence of expansion and the war in the Philippines. The President attached a number of them to his retinue as he went forth on a vote-begging expedition in a railway train in the West.[2] Plainly the McKinley administration with its "Imperial" program stood well with the people. Crowds acclaimed him at every little town as he entered it and the elections in November signalized the power which the taking of foreign territory exerted upon the imagination of the masses. Flag 'waving, missionary work in distant parts of the world to "uplift" savage tribes, the enlargement of opportunities for trade, and the prospect of making a prosperity, already marked, a further agency to enrich the country and all its inhabitants, brought voters to the polls and created majorities. In Ohio, the President's own state, where opposition to him and Hanna was active and factions were angrily contending for the offices, his policies received satisfactory endorsement. The plurality of the Republican candidate for governor was nearly 50,000. The Republican running for governor in Iowa on a platform calling for the prosecution of the war in the Philippines against a Democrat, who denounced the President's course as militarist and Imperialist, won by a plurality of nearly 60,000. In other states the trend was in the same direction. The Democracy in its demoralized condition offered no resistance to the Republican sweep. Bryan was still its prophet. No one appeared to contest his control. Men of ability and character in the party who had stood at Cleveland's side foresaw that it would again suffer the wreck which it had faced in 1896.[3] The candidacies for 1900 were

---

[1] N. Y. Nation, July 27, 1899; J. F. Rhodes, The McKinley and Roosevelt Administrations, p. 195.

[2] Cf. N. Y. Nation, Oct. 12 and 19, 1899. [3] Ibid., July 27, 1899.

definitely indicated. It would be McKinley on the one side and Bryan on the other.[1]

The President's references to the war in his message to Congress in December, 1899, would have been regarded as cant had it not been rather plain that he was expressing what, in his simplicity, he had somehow come to believe and what the prevailing sentiment of the country required of one in his position were he to continue to think of himself as a "great heart, beating rhythmically with the pulses of the commonalty."[2] Roosevelt who was still babbling about the invigorating value of war,[3] Lodge, Admiral Dewey and others—these were prominent types—were stirring the military spirit of the country. The people had new interests, new aims, new purposes. Mr. McKinley—now the swashbuckler, now the Christian missionary, now on the war path, now the minister of sweetness and light, and again the commercial salesman, advertising our products to the world[4]—in his Protean role, merely recorded the flow of popular thought. He retold the story. He had instructed General Wesley Merritt to say, when the first expedition set foot on the Philippine Islands, that we had come "to protect" the people "in their homes, in their employments and in their personal and religious rights." Notwithstanding this and later utterances in the same sense the "sinister ambition of a few leaders" had induced an attack upon our troops which had resulted in "a terribly destructive and sanguinary repulse of the insurgents." It was a "rebellion," Mr. McKinley said, and it "must be put down." The barbarities of the enemy were emphasized for the justification of our course. It was an "unwelcome but most righteous campaign." The "noble self sacrifice" of our army formed "one of the brightest pages in our annals." "Under the protection of our sovereignty" the people would "enjoy a prosperity and a freedom which they have never before known." The "beneficent intentions" of this government would soon be understood.

[1] N. Y. Nation, Nov. 16, 1899.
[2] Ibid., Oct. 12, 1899; cf. ibid., July 13, 1899; Writings of Schurz, vol. vi, pp. 273–5.
[3] N. Y. Nation, July 6, 1899. [4] Cf. ibid., Aug. 24, 1899.

The islands had become "ours by every title of law and equity." Should we desert them they would be left at once "to anarchy and, finally, to barbarism." We should be flinging them, "a golden apple of discord, among the rival powers no one of which could permit another to seize them unquestioned. Their rich plains and valleys would be the scene of endless strife and bloodshed." Dewey's coming to Manila Bay, instead of being "the dawn of a new day of freedom and progress," would be but "the beginning of an era of misery and violence," worse than any seen before. "Our flag," the President said finally, "has never waved over any community but in blessing. I believe the Filipinos will soon recognize the fact that it has not lost its gift of benediction in its world-wide journey to their shores."

The intention to withdraw from Cuba, the President avowed, was a pledge, and it should be "sacredly kept." We held the island "in trust for the inhabitants" and the acceptance of the trust called for "the sternest integrity of purpose and the exercise of the highest wisdom." But the Cubans were not to come into their own at once. Before the people should be cast adrift we would "see to it that free Cuba be a reality not a name, a perfect entity not a hasty experience, bearing within itself the elements of failure." The people should first "attain to that plane of self-conscious respect and self-reliant unity" fitting "an enlightened community for self government" before we should release our hand. When that day should arrive would be determined "in the ripeness of events."

Porto Rico remained under provisional military control. Congress should devise for the island a system of civil government. Before recovering from the ravages of the war it was swept in August, 1899, by a hurricane which killed 2,000 of its inhabitants and injured 3,000 more, destroying at the same time many millions of dollars' worth of property. The people must be fed by the army of occupation. Private charity supplemented the relief afforded through the War Department. Here, as in the Philippines and Cuba, the President made much of the Americanizing influences of education, were the people subjected to it. "The free school house," said he, "is the best preceptor for citizenship." By this means would the Porto Ricans come to know "the blessings of free government."

Hawaii, too, made demands upon the President's attention. He had appointed a commission of five members, headed by Senator Cullom of Illinois, to visit the islands and consider their needs. The result of the commission's observations during the summer of 1898 had been transmitted to Congress in December of that year. They recommended that Hawaii be given a "territorial government." The President endorsed their views, alluded to the conditions which prevailed, pending legislation, and asked for action at once.

How far interest in the new colonial questions had supplanted the public concern for purely domestic matters, such as the tariff and the currency, was illustrated by the relatively subordinate place now accorded to these topics in the message. The President observed that the revenues of the government were increased in so marked a degree—he would have it inferred that such prosperity was due to the policies of the Republican party—that the troubles incident to the greenbacks, of which so much had been heard during the Cleveland administration, had not recurred. Nevertheless he urgently commended to Congress such legislation as would put the notes out of the way permanently, and place the country firmly on a gold basis.

Finally, after more than three decades of contention with the Greenbackers, the silver men and other advocates of cheap money, in the whirl of national exaltation which ensued upon the war and in the midst of industrial prosperity seldom seen—of which more is to be said—a financial measure, such as had so long been sought, was passed by Congress, receiving the President's approval on March 14, 1900. At last the country was safely and soundly on a gold money standard. A definite amount of gold in a dollar became specifically, by statute, the unit of value and it was declared to be the duty of the Secretary of the Treasury to maintain all other forms of money at a parity with this dollar. Adequate provision was made for the retirement of the greenbacks. The Bryanites in the House, and Teller, Jones and the silverites in the Senate yielded their ground only under protest, but opposition was listless. Their day had come. They were overborne by a vote of 190 to 150 in the House and 46 to 29 in the Senate.[1]

If this were one of the triumphs of history, ending an era in which the poor man, who believed that more money and cheaper money would remove the burdens from his back, and the miners of the Western mountains intent upon getting from the government a subsidy for their product, acting together, had threatened the foundations of democracy, the passage of the bill at the time seemed to be merely an incident in a greater play. The long war with the rabble had been won in 1896 and Congress was now merely affirming the decision and putting the subject securely out of the range of daily strife.[2]

The eyes of the country were fixed on colonial problems. The Philippines and Cuba did not press for attention; they remained under military control. Porto Rico, on the other hand, made demands upon the wisdom of Congress. The hurricane, tariff arrangements to afford the island outlets for its coffee, sugar and tobacco, as well as other considerations, combined to render immediate action imperative. The President in his message had said that it was "our plain duty to abolish all customs tariffs between the United States and Porto Rico and give her products free access to our markets." The Secretary of War in his annual report declared that "justice and good faith" demanded the removal of such provisions of law as were in restraint of trade.[3] The people were in distress. Their coffee bushes, the principal source of their exportable wealth, had been destroyed by the great storm.[4] They were holding mass meetings and petitioning Congress for relief.[5]

[1] Cong. Record, 56th Cong. 1st sess., pp. 572, 1835.
[2] Cf. N. Y. Nation, Dec. 21, 1899, and Feb. 22 and March 15, 1900; N. W. Stephenson, N. A. Aldrich, p. 162.
[3] Cf. Cong. Record, 56th Cong. 1st sess., pp. 1051, 2168, 3506.
[4] Cf. A. C. Coolidge, The U. S. as a World Power, p. 145.
[5] N. Y. Nation, March 29, 1900.

At first there seemed to be general agreement with the President. But, in the development of a liberal policy, he was confronted by the old-fashioned protectionists who abounded in the Republican party and had hitherto had a firm hold upon him. Many pretended to fear free sugar and free coffee from Porto Rico; if these things came in without duty might there not, in no long time, be free trade with the Philippines and Cuba? It was our duty, said Representative Payne of New York, chairman of the Committee on Ways and Means, which had abandoned the new McKinley view of the subject under protectionist attack,[1] with some of the President's own unction, "to take these poor people and educate them, and lift them up, and give them the privileges of the Constitution." They should be elevated to "the full level and stature of American manhood."[2] Therefore, we would extend the provisions of the Dingley law to imports from other countries into Porto Rico, while taking its market, whatever it might be worth, for ourselves, asserting our right at the same time to tax colonial commerce. We would collect duties equal to 25 per cent. of the Dingley law rates on Porto Rican goods coming to our continental ports, while they should levy a similar tariff on American goods entering their island. On some articles, indeed, the duties would be in excess of 25 per cent. to countervail internal revenue taxes laid on such articles in the United States and in Porto Rico respectively.[3]

The Democrats said that "unequal taxation" of this kind for the people residing in a territory, which, by this act, was accepted and acknowledged to be a part of the United States, was "the baldest form of Imperialism."[4] The Constitution should follow the flag. The Porto Ricans had come under our sovereignty with confidence in our sense of justice. Equality was equity and the soul of liberty. We were breaking faith. The bill provided for taxation without representation

---

[1] N. Y. Nation, March 1, 1900; Cong. Record, 56th Cong. 1st sess., p 2331; N. Y. Tribune, Feb. 1, 1900.
[2] Cong. Record, 56th Cong. 1st sess., pp. 1946-7.
[3] Ibid., p. 1940.   [4] Ibid., p. 1947.

The people of the island were to have no voice in determining the method of taking money from them or the use that would be made of it. The advocates of such a measure had the political morals of George III. Our policy was a "robber policy." The Republican party had brought on the Civil War to free the negroes; the same party now ignored the Constitution, the Bill of Rights, even the Ten Commandments, in order to enslave yellow, brown and black men in the islands of the seas.[1]

Some Republicans spoke in the same strain. Representative McCall of Massachusetts was heard. Either Porto Rico was a part of the United States or it was not. We were degrading the idea of constitutional liberty. He denounced with all his energy the "hateful notion" of honor and right at home and tyranny toward a poor people who had been brought under our care abroad.[2] Littlefield of Maine also protested. The scheme, he said, was "un-Republican, un-American, unwarranted, unprecedented and unconstitutional."[3]

Under so much criticism the tax at length was reduced to 15 per cent. of the Dingley rates and the bill was passed on February 28, 1900, by a vote of 172 to 160.[4] The Senate had a bill of its own, prescribing a form of civil government for the island, which had come to bear the name of Mr. Foraker, chairman of the Committee on Pacific Islands and Porto Rico. It, like the Payne bill in the House, had at first provided for free trade. But all now was changed. The Senate would accept the rates of duty on imports which had been named by the House amid further protest. "The good faith of the American people," Senator Proctor of Vermont said, "should stand unquestioned wherever the stars and stripes are seen." We must deal with these questions "in the spirit of American institutions and American civilization."[5] Senator Wellington of Maryland denounced the bill as transgressing "every principle of national honor, of patriotism, good faith and benevo-

[1] Cong. Record, 56th Cong. 1st sess., p. 2365. [2] Ibid., pp. 2091-2.
[3] Ibid., app., p. 57; N. Y. Nation, March 1, 1900.
[4] Cong. Record, 56th Cong. 1st sess., p. 2429 [5] Ibid., pp. 3507-9.

lence." [1] Outside of Congress ex-President Harrison declared that the taxing of Porto Rican products coming to the United States was "a very grave departure from right principles," [2] while ex-Senator Edmunds of Vermont said that in the passage of such a measure we were imitating and paralleling the acts of the British Parliament which had resulted in the Revolutionary war, the creation of a government founded on the "principles of liberty, justice and equality of rights," and the establishment of a Constitution which explicitly forbade such discriminations. [3]

The bill was passed by the Senate on April 3, 1900, by a vote of 40 to 31 and, after conference, reached the President who, though he had distinctly spoken for free trade, drifted with the strong protectionist wing of his party. [4] Indeed he had urged Congressmen to vote for the bill. [5] He signed it on April 12, 1900. When the duties were collected the protectionists were willing that the money should be paid back to Porto Rico to educate the people and construct public works, [6] but they would yield nothing on the subject of the protective principle in dealing with colonies. [7]

The system of civil government in the melded House and Senate bills, still called the Foraker act, [8] provided for a governor to be appointed by the President, established an executive council of eleven members to be named by the President, at

[1] Cong. Record, 56th Cong. 1st sess., p. 3687.   [2] Ibid., pp. 3507–9.
[3] Ibid., p. 3507.   [4] N. Y. Nation, Feb. 1, 8, 15, 22 and March 8, 1900.
[5] Ibid., March 15, 1900; Cong. Record, 56th Cong. 1st sess., pp. 3687, 3748. His backbone was cartilage, said the New York Nation. (Issues of March 15, 1900, cf. ibid., Jan. 25, Feb. 1, 8, 15 and 22 and March 1, 1900.) McKinley changed his policy, his biographer says, in the interest of "party harmony." (C. S. Olcott, Life of McKinley, vol. ii, pp. 216–8.) "I'll tell you exactly how it was done," Hanna said to H. H. Kohlsaat. "We received notice from 250,000 Union cigar rollers that if we admitted Porto Rico cigars free of duty each of the 250,000 would get three other Union men to vote against the Republican party in November, 1900, making 1,000,000 votes against McKinley."—H. H. Kohlsaat, From McKinley to Harding, p. 71.
[6] This was "charity," not justice, said Senator Proctor.—Cong. Record, 56th Cong. 1st sess., p. 3509.
[7] N. Y. Nation, March 29, 1900.
[8] U. S. Stat. at Large, vol. xxxi, pp. 77 et seq.

least five of whom should be natives, and laid down rules for the election of a house of delegates to be chosen by the people which would constitute, with the council, a local legislature. It was further specified that any bill, though it should pass the house of delegates and the council and be approved by the governor, might be annulled by Congress, thus quite denying the people anything like self government. They were no longer citizens of Spain—they were not now citizens of the United States.[1] Charles H. Allen was named by McKinley to be the first governor and various authorities upon education and other subjects were sent out to develop agencies for the social regeneration of the people and to justify the promise which we had made to improve their condition.

In an act to provide a government for Hawaii the protectionists were not able to make the arrangements which were devised for Porto Rico. Trade would be free.[2] Very clever white men had been in control of the republic which had been established after the Queen had been deposed. They had proven their skill in politics as well as their tenacity of character in the pursuit of their design to secure annexation to the United States. They would receive consideration again. The report of the Cullom commission had been transmitted to Congress in December, 1898. It found and declared that the inhabitants of the islands were "capable of self government," going far out of its way to say, at the same time, that the Porto Ricans and the Filipinos were not possessed of such fitness—a subject which it was not invited to examine, though, in its opinion, the interests of the administration might be forwarded if it should particularly state that its recommendations as to this one insular people should not be regarded as the laying down of a rule for dealing with other annexed populations.[3]

[1] Cf. J. B. Foraker, Notes of a Busy Life, vol. ii, p. 84; L. A. Coolidge, O. H. Platt, chap. xxvii.

[2] Cong. Record, 56th Cong. 1st sess., pp. 3425, 3748; Phila. North American, March 9, 1900.

[3] Senate Doc., 55th Cong. 3rd sess., no. 16; N. Y. Nation, Feb. 22 and March 8, 1900.

The suggestions of the commission which had been neglected for a year were now given serious attention and separate bills bearing on the subject were passed by the Senate and the House, to be joined in April, 1900, in a plan which was sent to the President.[1] Congress gave the islands "territorial government," a form of government such as Arizona and New Mexico still enjoyed, that government provided for the Western territories before their admission into the Union as states. They would have their own elective legislature with the privilege of sending a delegate to Congress. The tariff and navigation laws were extended to the archipelago and the trade between its ports and the ports of the United States became coastwise in character. Duties after June 15, 1900, would no longer be paid on Hawaiian products brought to San Francisco and other ports, or on American products entering the Sandwich Islands. President McKinley appointed the president of the late Hawaiian republic, Sanford B. Dole, to be the first American governor of the islands.[2]

Nor was Alaska forgotten—that expansive empire in the northwest for which practically no provisions for civil government existed except such as were found in the act of May 17, 1884. The discovery of gold had sent a multitude of men into the north. The development of other industries had increased the requirements of the people. Yet it formed but one judicial district. It had but one judge, one marshal and one district attorney. Municipal organization had not been, nor could it be, effected under authority of law. Local police control was wanting and peace and order could be maintained only by irregular and voluntary action by the people. Congress now enacted an elaborate code for the administration of affairs in this vast territory, so long neglected.[3]

The Nicaragua Canal, never out of mind, was again under discussion. The commission, headed by Admiral Walker, which had been appointed in 1897 to continue the surveys begun by

[1] Cong. Record, 56th Cong. 1st sess., pp. 4648–51, 4766, 4892.
[2] U. S. Stat. at Large, vol. xxxi, pp. 141, et seq.
[3] Cong. Record, 56th Cong. 1st sess., pp. 6637, 6710, 6867.

the Ludlow board of 1895 made its report on May 9, 1899, confirming earlier statements as to the practicability of the route. The cost was now estimated at about $118,000,000, though one of the members, Colonel Hains, thought that it might reach $135,000,000.[1]

It was certain that, ere long, action would be demanded. The people, since the war, were burgeoning with commercial energy and national pride, which nearly reached arrogance. The Senate, on January 21, 1899, at first without a roll call, and, upon reconsideration, on the ground that such action was "unprecedented," by a vote of 48 to 6, passed a bill authorizing the issuance of Treasury warrants to purchase the rights of the company, which had been engaged since 1899 in trying, with private capital, to build the canal through Nicaragua, and to proceed with the work at a cost of $115,000,000.[2] Foreseeing failure to secure the concurrence of the House Morgan, who so long had pursued the subject with almost fanatical pertinacity, inserted an amendment in the River and Harbor bill and, by a vote of 50 to 3, the Senate would give $10,000,000 for making a commencement on the work so near to his heart. This scheme also failed to receive the endorsement of the other branch of Congress.[3]

As the conviction that a canal must and soon would be built deepened, opinion called for more intelligent consideration of the subject than it had yet received. President McKinley and Senator Hanna, as well as many other men, had come to feel a doubt as to the wisdom of taking too much for granted.[4] Might it not be, after all, that the Panama route were the better one? This idea was fostered and advanced by a lobby which the new Panama Canal company had set up in Washington and, instead of Morgan's amendment in the River and

---

[1] Report of Nic. Canal Comm., 1897-9; cf. Report of Isthmian Canal Comm. of 1899, Senate Doc., 57th Cong. 1st sess., no. 54, p. 59.

[2] Cong. Record, 55th Cong. 3rd sess., p. 911. The various bills in Congress favoring the canal, from 1891 to date, were brought together in ibid., pp. 895-910.

[3] Cf. Tyler Dennett, John Hay, p. 227.

[4] Croly, M. A. Hanna, p. 378.

Harbor act, appropriating money to proceed with the work on the Nicaragua route, another was adopted authorizing the President to appoint a new commission, usually called the Isthmian Canal Commission, in recognition of a larger scope of purpose, to consider and give advice as to the relative feasibility of the two lines by which ships might pass from sea to sea. Admiral Walker, who would again be the chairman, and his two associates on the old commission, were reappointed. Six others were added to make it a board of nine men. They organized for work on June 15, 1899.

Meantime John Hay, Secretary of State, after the way had been prepared in England by Henry White, whom he had left in London as secretary of the embassy, and Sir Julian Pauncefote,[1] the British Ambassador to the United States, were preparing a treaty which would modify the terms of the old Clayton-Bulwer treaty of 1850. This convention had been a bugaboo in all discussions of the question of an isthmian canal. Whether it would or would not prevent our constructing this waterway, whether, when built, it would interfere with our untrammeled use of the work, or whether, indeed, it still remained in force and was operative as between Great Britain and the United States, an untenable contention,[2] were subjects of argument in and out of Congress. It was clear that men who knew, and cared, nothing about the law of nations would in no long time, if diplomacy were not invoked to clear the way, take command of the situation and precipitate unpleasant complications. The discussion and passage of bills authorizing the construction of the work were proof that zealots in Congress were without respect for international obligations. The Clayton-Bulwer treaty, if possible, must be amended. It would now be stated specifically in a new treaty which was signed on February 5, 1900, that, if the government of the United States should build such a canal, we should have the "exclusive right" of regulating and managing it after comple-

---

[1] After August 18, 1899, Lord Pauncefote.
[2] See Senate Doc., 56th Cong. 1st sess., no. 268; N. Y. Nation, July 6, 1899 and Feb. 22, 1900; Tyler Dennett, John Hay, p. 248.

tion. "Neutralization" should be effected on the terms secured
in the case of the Suez Canal. All nations, without discrimination, in war as in peace, should find the American interoceanic
waterway as free and open for their navies as for their merchant
ships. After the convention should be ratified by the United
States and Great Britain other powers would be invited to
adhere to its provisions.[1]

Success in bringing England to the point of making so liberal
an arrangement was due to Hay's pleasant acquaintance with
Lord Salisbury and other British statesmen, some of whom
had wished to join the canal negotiation with the Alaskan
boundary question, which had been referred in 1898 to a
Joint High Commission. This commission was appointed and
convened to consider the location of the international line,
the protection of the seal herds (a matter still not at rest)
and other questions—in all twelve issues affecting the relations
of Canada and the United States.[2] It held sessions in Quebec
and Washington and adjourned, without having gained any of
its ends, in 1899. But Hay now, by happy address, after a
modus vivendi as to Canada had been effected,[3] won the point
with reference to the Clayton-Bulwer treaty without confusing
subjects, and he, as well as his friends, felt that he had achieved
a triumph. More, reasonably, could not have been asked of
England which had made the most important concessions.[4]
If we should be able to get the needed rights for the construction
of the interoceanic highway from the governments of Costa
Rica and Nicaragua through which states it would pass, such

[1] Foreign Relations for 1901, pp. 237–43; Senate Doc., 57th Cong. 1st
sess., no. 85.
[2] R. B. Mowat, Diplomatic Relations of Great Britain and the U. S.,
pp. 278–9; W. R. Thayer, Life of Hay, vol. ii, pp. 203–7; Tyler Dennett,
John Hay, pp. 217, 224–39; J. W. Foster, Diplomatic Memoirs, vol. ii,
pp. 186–9, 191–3; A. Nevins, Henry White, pp. 145–6; Letters and Diary
of Hay, vol. iii, p. 142; A. L. P. Dennis, John Hay, in Am. Secs. of State,
vol. ix, p. 128; R. B. Mowat, Life of Pauncefote, pp. 274, 278–9.
[3] Tyler Dennett, John Hay, pp. 230–9.
[4] "All that I have ever done with England," Hay wrote to J. W. Foster
on June 23, 1900, "is to have wrung great concessions out of her with no
compensation." This was one of her "great concessions"—W, R. Thayer,
Life of Hay, vol. ii, p. 234. Cf. Mowat, Life of Pauncefote, pp. 277–9.

guarantees from Great Britain should have been sufficient for all but nationalists of the most unyielding kind.[1]

But it was seen that to secure immediate action in the Senate would not be easy, if it should, indeed, be possible at all. McKinley viewed the subject with amiable idleness and left all to his Secretary of State. Hay had assurances of support from a number of senators. Since the war, as has been indicated, the popular attitude toward England in the Republican party had undergone material change.[2] Whitelaw Reid and the New York Tribune endorsed the treaty as a happy ending of "an ancient and sometimes vexatious controversy." The "vast majority of the people of the United States" would, the Tribune said, hail its signing and ratification "with joy."[3] It seemed to have the favor of a weighty portion of the press in all parts of the country.[4] The Committee on Foreign Relations to which it was referred in the Senate reported in its favor.[5] Lodge[6] had expressed his approval of the convention, and it is possible that but for his turning upon it, with his friend Roosevelt's active cooperation,[7] it would have received the necessary number of votes in the Senate with comparatively little discussion.

It was a "Presidential year" and the prospect of gain from nursing old grievances and opening old sores was bright. The American public generally overlooked the fact that progress could not be made at London with pending questions in relation to Canada without tedious negotiation with, and the assent of, the Dominion politicians, but these old questions were in mind. Two arbiters to which the subject of damages

[1] Cf. N. Y. Nation, Feb. 15, 1900.

[2] Writings of Carl Schurz, vol. v, p. 465; B. A. Reuter, Anglo-Am. Relations during the Span. Am. War, chap. vii.

[3] N. Y. Tribune, Feb. 6, 1900; cf. ibid., Feb. 7, 1900, and subsequently.

[4] W. S. Holt, Treaties Defeated by the Senate, pp. 187–92; R. B. Mowat, Life of Paurcefote, p. 283.

[5] Senate Doc., 56th Cong. 1st sess., no. 268.

[6] "The delectable Lodge," Cleveland called him; "Massachusetts' sweet scented scholar in politics."—A. Nevins, Letters of Cleveland, pp. 495, 532.

[7] Cf. N. Y. Sun, Feb. 8, 1900; A. L. P. Dennis, John Hay, in Am. Secs. of States, vol. ix, pp. 154–6, 159.

for the seizure of Canadian sealing vessels had been referred
had awarded $425,000 to British claimants. This sum which
was held to be exorbitant before, when settlement on this basis
was proposed, must now be paid, and that episode awakened
unpleasant popular reactions.[1]

The Germans were madly anti-English because of racial
sympathies for the Boers in the war raging in South Africa;
the Irish held to their well known spites.[2] The Democrats in
their convention in Ohio in 1899 charged Hay with having
entered into a secret alliance with Great Britain. The Bryanites in many states were putting anti-English planks—no new
shibboleths for them—into their party platforms.[3] They must
not have the undisputed advantage of such support. The
Republicans must enter the field. It was easy to make men
whose seats in the Senate might be taken away from them, if
they did not carry themselves well in the campaign, timid and
fearful and, when they were told that to accept a treaty giving
the country anything less than a fortified and exclusively
American canal was "political suicide," they abandoned a
cause which just a little while since they had promised to
espouse.[4]

Lodge, Roosevelt and the jingoes intimated, and plainly
said, that Hay had been tricked—he was surrendering American
liberties. On March 13, 1900, "in profound disgust" at the
"howling fools" in the Senate, as the Secretary of State wrote
his friend Henry White,[5] he forwarded his resignation to
President McKinley, who promptly declined to receive it.[6]
Now the House, Speaker Reed's hand having been with-

---

[1] W. R. Thayer, Life of Hay, vol. ii, p. 166; Mowat, Life of Pauncefote,
p. 208; N. Y. Nation, Dec. 30, 1897.

[2] Thayer, Life of Hay, vol. ii, pp. 219, 220, 221, 234-5, 253; Mowat,
Diplomatic Relations of Great Britain and the U. S., pp. 284-5.

[3] Thayer, Life of Hay, pp. 220-1; Tyler Dennett, John Hay, p. 233.

[4] N. Y. Nation, Feb. 15, 1900; N. Y. Tribune, Feb. 13 and 27, 1900;
Thayer, Life of Hay, vol. ii, pp. 229-30; A. Nevins, Henry White, pp.
150 et seq.; N. W. Stephenson, Nelson W. Aldrich, pp. 167, 449; Letters
and Diary of John Hay, vol. iii, pp. 156-7; 159-60; Corr. of Roosevelt
and Lodge, vol. i, p. 453; A. L. P. Dennis, Adventures in Am. Diplomacy.

[5] Nevins, Henry White, p. 152.

[6] Thayer, Life of Hay, vol. ii, pp. 226-8.

drawn, was out of control. The representatives, not to be behind the senators in popular favor, while the excitement was at its height, on May 2, 1900, with practical unanimity (224 yeas to 36 nays) passed a bill authorizing the Secretary of War, treaty or no treaty, to put the Nicaragua canal under contract at an expenditure of $140,000,000.[1] Nothing came of this outburst. It was for "campaign purposes only."[2] It was plain that the question in all its aspects must await the outcome of the election of 1900.[3]

At the same time our interest was, perforce, extended to Samoa where, by a tripartite agreement, we were exercising, with Great Britain and Germany, a kind of suzerainty. A revolution had broken out at the death of the king. One chief and his adherents had fallen upon another and his following. A commission was appointed to visit the islands in the interest of order, our representative being Bartlett Tripp, who, in spite of his self vaunting reports to Mr. Hay, probably rendered a service in that quarter. Peace was restored and, it being plain that jurisdiction should not be divided,[4] a convention was drawn up and ratified in February, 1900, bringing the tridominium to an end. By the new arrangement Great Britain and Germany renounced all their rights and claims with respect to the islands east of longitude 171 degrees west of Greenwich, and henceforward we should have sole responsibility in the major part of the area in which the three powers had functioned with too little success side by side. We thereby gained Tutuila and its adjacent islets, including the fine harbor of Pago Pago.[5]

---

[1] Cong. Record, 56th Cong. 1st sess., pp. 5014–5.

[2] N. Y. Nation, May 10, 1900.

[3] Nevins, Henry White, p. 153; cf. Letters and Diary of Hay, vol. iii, p. 166. Lord Pauncefote wrote to Lansdowne, Secretary of State for Foreign Affairs—"The language held by certain senators reveals, I regret to say, a complete disregard of the obligatory force of treaties."—Quoted in R. B. Mowat, Life of Pauncefote, p. 283.

[4] Cf. R. B. Mowat, Life of Pauncefote, p. 223.

[5] Foreign Relations for 1899, pp. 604, 73; McElroy, Grover Cleveland, vol. i, p. 262; A. L. P. Dennis, John Hay in Am. Secs. of State, vol. ix, pp. 132–3; R. B. Mowat, Life of Pauncefote, pp. 222–5; ibid., Dip. Relations of Great Britain and the U. S., pp. 234–9.

While the Secretary of State was engaged upon his enlightened negotiations with Great Britain in the interest of a neutral canal across the isthmus he interested himself also in American rights in China. The recent advances of the European powers in "slicing China alive"—as the shrewd Chinese statesman, Li Hung Chang, denominated the process of seizing her territory through innumerable mining, railway and commercial concessions and the establishment of "spheres of influence"—she was powerless to resist. Russia, Germany, Great Britain, France and a neighbor, Japan, in turn, had secured their portions and our possession now of a foothold in the Philippines made a statement of their intentions and purposes extremely desirable from our point of view. What would our position be with reference to trade in this awakening continent? Mr. Hay's aim was to establish what had come to be called in England, where the subject was under discussion, the "open door." Notes were addressed to Great Britain, France, Germany, Russia, Italy and Japan and the result was a guarantee that the citizens of all should have equal consideration. Each nation having a zone of interest in China should accord to us and other nations precisely the same rights and privileges in this zone of interest. None should be subjected to exceptional tariffs, harbor dues, railway or other charges to afflict the trade and commerce of one country at the expense of another. On March 20, 1900, Mr. Hay, in a letter forwarded to American representatives abroad, announced that the powers concerned had accepted his suggestion and that their consent was to be regarded as "final and definitive." [1] It was, said the New York Nation, "a splendid instance of American sagacity winning a peaceful victory." [2] It was "a fine triumph of American diplomacy," said the New York Tribune. Secretary Hay could be congratulated upon the result—it was an event of which the United States could "properly be proud." [3] Lord Salisbury and other English

---

[1] Foreign Relations for 1899, p. 142; Tyler Dennett, John Hay, chap. xxiv; cf. A. C. Coolidge, The U. S. as a World Power, p. 181.

[2] N. Y. Nation, April 5, 1900.

[3] N. Y. Tribune, March 29, 1900.

statesmen hailed the achievement—it was a work which would
be of great importance and utility to the world.[1]

The value of the advantages thus gained, whatever they
were and however valuable they may have been,[2] was to be
impaired at once by a general rising of the Chinese people
who looked on at the partitioning of their empire with a not
unnatural resentment, and they would make violent protest.
The masses were seething with hatred of the foreigner. The
trouble began in 1898 when the Empress Dowager, who, hitherto,
had been taking the counsel of Li Hung Chang and other
enlightened Chinamen, fell under reactionary influences.
Palace politics led to the adoption of policies which pointed
directly to what was to follow. The European powers were to
be defied and, if possible, the grants of territory and privilege
which they had gained by one means or another, because of
the inability of the government to offer any kind of effectual
resistance, would be annulled. The new government at Pekin
was distinctly anti-foreign. Modern arms had been purchased
and the outlook was threatening in the sight of missionaries
who were engaged in carrying the Christian religion to the
people, in the sight of their native converts, traders and the
consular and diplomatic officers stationed in China. Such an
attitude in government circles fanned the enthusiasm of some
old secret societies, the chief among them being the I-Ho-
Chuan, the League of United Patriots. Since Chuan may
also be translated as fists and since members of the organization
took part in athletic contests foreigners in China called the
members "Boxers." They were widely scattered, in groups,
and, when they added their fuel to the flame and carried the
idea of a demand upon the government for the expulsion of
the "foreign devils" to the ignorant and fanatical settled in
small towns and in the country, the way was prepared for the
"Boxer Rebellion." From sporadic attacks on, and massacres
of missionaries, the destruction of convents and places of
worship, the torture and murder of Christian converts, Catholic

---

[1] Nevins, Henry White, p. 167; cf. Tyler Dennett, John Hay, p. 295.
[2] Cf. A. L. P. Dennis, John Hay, in Am. Secs. of State, vol. ix, pp. 134-44.

and Protestant—the feeling against those who had deserted the faith of their fathers was intense—disorder became general. The graves of foreigners were opened and the remains of the dead scattered. It was fortunate for the legations in Pekin that guards had been brought up from war ships which had been assembling at Taku before communication should be interrupted and the diplomatic quarter should be besieged.[1]

Further protection was imperatively needed and a mixed force of British, Germans, Americans, Russians, French, Italians and Austrians was put in motion in June in answer to the call for help. The troops, including marines and seamen, all together, numbered less than 2,000 men, and they set forth for Tientsin. They were obstructed at every point by incensed mobs armed with bludgeons, pitchforks, pikes, swords, and some trained soldiery with guns—all intent upon driving the dogs of foreigners into the sea. Hundreds of Chinamen were slain, but the rising had assumed such a dangerous form that, after the little allied army had fought its way to Tientsin, where the foreign colony was valiantly defending itself from the crazed people, their further progress was checked. At this juncture the European powers resolved upon the immediate reduction of the Taku forts which had been strengthened in anticipation of attack. Storming parties were landed to support the bombardment from the ships and, after a few hours' stubborn fighting, the defenses, which extended for a distance of two miles, were destroyed and the Chinese who were not killed or had not scuttled across the paddy fields were taken prisoners. The allied naval commanders issued a proclamation—the powers were not making war on China—their only object was to rescue their countrymen and to suppress a rebellion which rendered the land uninhabitable for foreigners.

The capture of the forts on the coast served but to increase the fury of the Boxers at Tientsin whose forces were augmented by regular troops. Property was destroyed, houses in the European compounds were burned and the people were put under shell fire. The progress of reinforcements was impeded,

[1] Foreign Relations for 1900, pp. 132–3.

but they came and, on July 14th, captured the city, the leader of our contingents which were acting with the British, a gallant soldier, Colonel E. H. Liscum, falling in battle. The allies lost in this engagement 800 in killed and wounded. Troops were despatched from the nearest points of supply for the advance upon Pekin which began on August 4, 1900. The combined force at this time attained a strength of about 20,000 of which the Japanese, because of their nearness to their base, provided more than a third. England had drawn some native troops from India. Our contribution to the conglomerate foreign army was a body of 2500 men, under General Chaffee, who arrived at Taku on July 28th, withdrawn for the most part from the Philippines.[1]

Action with reference to Pekin was required at once. No less than 80,000 men were needed, of whom it was determined, by the allied commanding officers on the ground, that we should supply 10,000, whereupon a number of regiments of infantry, cavalry and artillery were set in motion at various stations in the United States and transported to the Pacific coast for despatch to China. The President appointed W. W. Rockhill, familiar with conditions in the East, a special envoy. He proceeded to the scene as an agent of the State Department. News from the legations at Pekin, when at irregular intervals it was received, was of the most disquieting character. Now and again the newspapers announced that all the inmates had been slain.[2] The guards which were got through for their defence numbered only 350. The imprisoned people were without food, they were under repeated attack. The Austrian legation was burned, the German minister, Baron von Ketteler, was murdered by soldiers of the regular Chinese army, a Japanese attaché was killed. Finally the entire diplomatic corps with their wives and children and retinues retired to the British legation and some adjoining buildings where, for eight or nine weeks, behind improvised barricades, in fear of their lives from fire and bombardment, or of capture and

[1] Report of Sec. of War for 1900, p. 63.
[2] Cf. N. Y. Tribune, July 16 and 20, 1900.

cruel slaughter by the inflamed population, they awaited relief. It was on August 14th that the allied troops made their entry into Pekin and Li Hung Chang, being recalled, was empowered to conclude peace.[1]

"It was an unique situation for the foreign representatives to be bitterly attacked and persistently besieged by the government to which, in the most friendly way, they were duly accredited," said our minister, E. H. Conger, in a letter to President McKinley, thanking him and "the brave army under General Chaffee" for the rescue of the party. "The strain upon all has been great, but we never for a moment lost faith in timely Providential deliverance." [2] The letter was soon followed by a shipment by Mr. Conger through the State Department of a lot of Siberian sable furs from which coats could be made for the President and Mrs. McKinley.[3]

The new looking abroad, so absorbingly reflected in our statesmanship, which was communicated to the people by our politicians and by the press, could not quite obliterate interest in domestic subjects. Some matters at home were still in mind. The currency question might be put away, as it seemed to have been. It might not be profitable for politicians any longer to say that the people were being robbed by the "gold bugs"; there were signs that the next "black beast" would be the "trusts." Here was an old theme, but many thought that it had potentialities which had not yet been fully exploited. For twenty years it had been said by the free traders that protection was the promoter of monopoly which destroyed competition and raised prices. The tariff had been dubbed the "mother of trusts"—this it still was. Manufacturers procured high duties from a favoring Congress and in the shelter of such a barrier, safe from foreign competitors, they built up inordinately profitable businesses. They preyed upon

[1] The diplomatic movements in connection with the Boxer rebellion, in so far as we participated in them, are presented in Tyler Dennett, John Hay, chap. xxv. See also W. R. Thayer, Life of Hay, vol. ii, pp. 231–49.

[2] Conger to McKinley from Pekin, July 7, 1900, in McKinley Papers.

[3] Conger to McKinley, Oct. 1, 1900, in ibid.

the poor man. Though their methods might be obsolete and their goods of inferior make they were secure. The so-called Sherman Anti-Trust law of 1890 had been passed by a Republican Congress as an answer to criticism directed at the party on this point.[1]

Republicans were friends of the tariff but they were not to be caught defending the evils and abuses, which might or might not be the outgrowth of the economic policy they had advocated during their twelve year war upon Cleveland, who had led the cause of those who would reduce customs duties in the interest of lower prices and a larger welfare. Some business combinations were treated as trusts, coming within the purview of the Sherman law. A few definitions were extracted from the higher courts.[2] But the restraint put upon these agencies of evil, as they were said to be, was not great and they were thriving on every side. The "sugar trust" was in every one's mind. It was regarded as a most opprobrious monopoly. It visited its will upon Congress, made its own rates in tariff laws and defied public opinion. Though the answer was that sugar never was better and cheaper, that the trust, by economies in production and general efficiency of management, had brought it to the coffee cup of the poorest man, the circulation of charges that it was a nefarious business organization never ceased. The Standard Oil Company, which had crushed its way to power over the ruins of small competitors, was another name which all men knew and execrated, especially after its methods became the subject of an extended review in a popular magazine.[3] The men at its head, beyond the possibility of denial, had left wreckage in their path. They dominated railroads, legislative bodies and courts of law, yet the answer again was that they had refined oil in such a way that kerosene would no longer explode in a lamp and set fire to houses and towns, that it was so cheap that it was within the

---

[1] John Sherman's Recollections, vol. ii, pp. 1071–5; T. E. Burton, John Sherman, pp. 353–65.

[2] Cf. D. R. Dewey, National Problems, pp. 201–2.

[3] Cf. J. F. Rhodes, The McKinley and Roosevelt Administrations, pp. 157 et seq.; Ida M. Tarbell, Hist. of the Standard Oil Co.

reach of every one. It had supplanted whale oil and the
candle and, though gas had appeared as an illuminant, the
steady glow from refined petroleum caused men to prefer
it in lamps by which at night they read newspapers and books.[1]

Impetus was given to the movement against trusts by the
mergers and consolidations of companies which set in after the
Spanish American War. We were in a new and marvelous
era of prosperity. The assurance which men of initiative and
enterprise gained by the election of McKinley over Bryan,
whose pretensions had so thoroughly alarmed and so deeply
disturbed them, was immediately communicated to trade. The
war, which soon followed, had invigorated a number of industries in receipt of government contracts. The prospect of
colonial possessions, the visions of a market in China and of
other foreign outlets for our products stirred the imagination
profoundly.[2] Indeed, at the moment, the possibilities seemed
to be illimitable. If we should not supersede England in world
trade we should contest the field with her and take our place
beside her in shipping and exportation. From a sense of
inferiority which our entire attitude toward the outer world
had reflected, often in the most ludicrous ways, we had come
to feel that the nation was really a peer of the first powers of
Europe. Money was abundant and it was lent to business
men confidently. Credit was extended. A rising stock market
brought investors and speculators into Wall Street. The
avidity for shares suggested the sale of the securities of new
companies which multiplied at a rapid pace. Promoters
appeared, bankers cooperated in the work of combining and
enlarging corporations. The owners of mines and manufactories, of banks, railroads and steamship lines were approached
by unctuous gentlemen who laid before them plans for the
recapitalization of their businesses. These were enticing,
providing, in many cases, cash, bonds and stocks in such
generous amounts as to promise ease, with riches, to men who

[1] For a defence of trusts see C. R. Flint and others, The Trust: its
Book; C. R. Flint, Memories of an Active Life, chaps. xx and xxi; cf.
G. H. Montague, Trusts of To-day.
[2] Cf. N. Y. Nation, Oct. 19, Nov. 2 and Dec. 14, 1899.

had long been plagued with difficulties, and who sought comfortable retirement. Groups of works were combined to form an Amalgamated Company. These were confederated in a few months with other companies to form a larger new company, the United This or That, to be joined again in a short time with other industrial properties under a still more impressive name. The combinations were "trusts," said those who were looking for issues in the campaign of 1900. Actually they were created to yield commissions and stock bonuses to brokers, bankers and other promoters, yet their power for evil in narrowing markets for buyers and increasing prices might be monstrous.[1]

The malevolent influence of great combinations already in existence was exposed by such newspapers as the New York World and by a number of magazines which gained a reputation for similar investigation and disclosure, activity which was generally referred to as "muck raking." Neither political party was to be caught sleeping in the face of such a stirring of the prejudices of the voting population by this rapidly increasing distrust of large corporations. The Democrats would denounce aggregations of capital which were held to promote monopoly and to increase the cost of living. Their course was foreseen, their denunciations would have a familiar sound. It remained for the Republicans to assert and prove that they were, in equal measure, opposed to the "trust" and all that the name implied. Large companies which sought to control production, fix prices and mulct the consumer must be condemned and dealt with restrictively by law. The platforms of the party in the state campaigns in 1899 were clear on this point. In Ohio such combinations, "inimical," as they were, "to the interests of the people," were denounced. In Iowa, Massachusetts, and wherever opportunity offered, conventions adopted resolutions, party speakers in these conventions and on the stump rose to heights of eloquence and Republican newspapers were filled with trenchant writing abusive of monopoly in industry, with, now and again, ad-

[1] Cf. N. Y. Nation, Oct. 26, 1899.

monitory references to the fictitious capitalization of corporations. No one—not even Bryan—would make such impetuous assault in such excess of statement upon the "trust" as Theodore Roosevelt. ·Already as governor of New York his speech betokened his entry into this field. State legislatures passed new laws, or strengthened old ones, restricting company management.

An Industrial Commission had been created by an act of Congress of June, 1898. It had been calling witnesses and publicly cross-examining them preparatory to the presentation of a report. President McKinley in his message in December, 1899, dealt extensively with the subject and said that it should "early claim the attention of Congress." This body occupied itself with a variety of measures which were meant to impress the people in the impending Presidential campaign with the idea that the Republicans were quite as hostile to "trusts" as the Democrats. Bills were introduced proposing drastic regulation of business. One was designed to prohibit corporations from making profits in excess of four per cent.; the use of the post would be denied to violators of the law. They would be fined, their goods would be confiscated, if they should engage in interstate commerce. As if statute were not enough constitutional amendments were proposed to put the matter away from Congress and make the "trust" unlawful for all time to come.[1] Speech was loud and angry—all without result; it was intimated that none was intended except to plant the fact in the popular mind, if possible, that the Democrats had no patent right to this particular kind of vote-getting propaganda.

The arrangements which the two parties seemed to be on the point of making with reference to nominations were disturbed by a suggestion that Dewey should enter the field as a Presidential candidate. His self esteem had been so much increased by the extraordinary attention which was shown him upon his recent return to this country that it affected his quite restricted understanding. Indeed the idea found lodg-

[1] Cf. N. Y. Nation, March 29, May 24 and June 7, 1900.

ment in his mind before he had left the Philippines.[1] A few flatterers had made him think that the nation, having showered him with honors, would bestow upon him this other one, and place him and his new wife in the White House. His principles were hazy. He did not know whether he was a Republican or a Democrat,. whether he could better seek the nomination of one party or the other, a difficulty which at one time had beset General Grant. He was unable to see that the way was definitely prepared for McKinley's renomination—by nothing, in the range of human probability, could the plans which the President's powerful friends had made be overset. Nor would it be practicable, so far as even the simplest mind could judge, for the leaders of the Democratic party to turn to Dewey, or Schley, or Wheeler, or Fitzhugh Lee, or any other "war hero"; [2] they were attached under an almost hypnotic influence to Bryan and would make their campaign principally on the subject of Imperialism.

The issue had been brought into our politics by the well known activities of Dewey himself at Manila. But even his views on this subject were in doubt. He had spoken in a sense indicating his opinion that we had better withdraw from the Philippines and permit the people to govern themselves. But later he had signed the report of the Schurman commission recommending another policy.[3] The Anti-Imperialists who had been somewhat interested in his views now definitely cast him off. He, moreover, treated the office quite casually and, in order to bring himself within the range of a candidacy, uttered the opinion that it was "easy enough to be President." The occupant of the office merely took orders from Congress, and he had been obeying orders all his life. Men now laughed at him whom they had lately held to be one of the first heroes of all time. Neither McKinley nor Bryan thought that any-body was fit to be President, nor did their respective admirers and friends. The historian and philosopher might study the

[1] Rounseville Wildman to J. A. Porter, June 10, 1899, in McKinley Papers.
[2] Halstead to McKinley, Nov. 26, 1899, in McKinley Papers.
[3] N. Y. Nation, April 12, 1900.

records of the United States and he would conclude, after pondering the lives of a number of the Presidents, that Dewey's estimate of the character needed for a chief magistrate was not far amiss. But the people, under challenge, were not willing to admit that their choice of the head of their republic was made haphazard from the ranks of average citizens, and before the conventions met, having said that he would serve his countrymen, if they wanted to have him do so, he thanked God that this sacrifice of his ease and comfort would not be required.[1]

Nothing remained before the Republican national nominating convention, which would meet in Philadelphia on June 19th, but the selection of a candidate for Vice President. Hobart had died—if he had lived a belief was expressed that he would have been renominated, though nothing can be definitely vouchsafed on this point. The situation was canvassed attentively by Hanna and the leaders of the party. The purpose of a Vice President in the sight of those who name him for the post, is not, principally, to preside over the United States Senate, nor yet to succeed the President in case of that officer's disability or death. He is to add strength to the ticket, conciliate disappointed factions, represent, perhaps, phases of opinion which are not the President's and draw to the party support which the President alone might not command.

There was some reason to suppose that Secretary of the Navy Long might be the nominee.[2] The subject had been canvassed by the leaders of the party; it had been discussed with McKinley.[3] Now and again Roosevelt's name had been mentioned without receiving the President's favor. It was plain that he had friends in the West.[4] His impetuosity was taken to be in some ways an expression of the feeling of that part of the Union with which he had identified himself by his life

[1] Cf. Corr. of Roosevelt and Lodge, vol. i, p. 455; N. Y. Nation, June 21, 1900.
[2] N. Y. Nation, May 31, 1900.
[3] Quay to McKinley, May 21, 1900, in McKinley Papers.
[4] N. Y. Nation, May 31, 1900.

on the plains, by his attachment to his Rough Riders and his writing and speech. He was the ranchman, the cow boy, wild America incarnate, and a considerable amount of sentiment favorable to his nomination was evident in the state conventions and in the press. But he was governor of New York and he was in the midst of an administration which now was boldly enough for the public good, though again wilful and apparently in the interest of self advancement. He combated Platt, but at the same time consorted with the Republican "Boss" with a view to gaining his personal ends.[1] Platt, never deceived by the young man's tactics, took what he could salvage from the wreck of his hopes which Roosevelt, had his sincerity befitted his professions, might have made complete. The governor of New York said, on February 12th, that he would, "under no circumstances," accept the nomination for Vice President. His "duty" was at Albany where he had commenced a great work—he would carry it to a "successful conclusion." This statement was made for public use, for he and Lodge had been dallying with the idea of the Vice Presidency for months, sometimes favoring one side and sometimes the other, in their attempt to reap the greatest advantage from their partnership in public life.[2]

As the time for the convention to meet approached Roosevelt reiterated his declaration that he was not a candidate, though all the while his points seem to have been extended in the hope that the lightning might strike them. His decision was "irrevocable"—he would refuse to accept, though the convention

[1] N. Y. Nation, May 10, 1900; Corr. of Roosevelt and Lodge, vol. i, p. 444; Autobiog. of Platt, pp. 374–5; H. F. Pringle, Theodore Roosevelt, pp. 210–2, 214–5.

[2] Roosevelt wrote Lodge in July, 1899, that he would welcome the nomination. (Corr. of Roosevelt and Lodge, vol. i, p. 404.) Lodge in the exchange of opinion usually quite warmly advocated advancement by this route. (Cf. ibid., p. 450.) Roosevelt was also ready to leave the governorship of New York to become Secretary of War and was frankly disappointed when, after Alger's dismissal, Elihu Root was preferred over him for the post. (Ibid., pp. 414–5). He was again a candidate for the Secretaryship when it was suspected that Root might be nominated for Vice President, (Ibid., pp. 428, 430.) and was, all the while, hoping that he might be chosen to be the first civil governor of the Philippines.—Ibid., pp. 437, 439.

should nominate him for the office.[1] His reputation as a resolute
man deceived many who gave his pretensions no further
thought and proceeded with their plans to make the ticket
McKinley and Long, or, possibly, to give the nomination
to Cornelius N. Bliss, or Senator Allison, or Senator Fairbanks.[2]

But there was activity in other quarters. Platt looked upon
the mention of Roosevelt's name with sly delight. He would,
if possible, put another term as governor of New York out of
the young man's reach.[3] The prospect was pleasing—therefore
those cajoleries which earlier had been practised upon Roosevelt
by the old fox of Republican politics were resumed and the
way was prepared for the unsettlement of arrangements.
He found a congener in Quay who had been waging a losing
battle for his seat in the Senate and who now, with a delegation
of admirers around him in the convention and a claque in the
gallery, easily assembled in the principal city of his own state,
where his friends abounded, would defy his enemies and assert
his power. When he had been defeated in the legislature for
reelection, as has been related, he had been appointed by a
servile governor to fill the vacancy which its failure to make
a choice had created. When he had presented such credentials
in the Senate, where he had sat for years, that body refused
to receive him. Mark Hanna's support had been anticipated—
indeed Quay said that it had been promised him.[4] But that potential personage's influence was used against the claimant
with the result that Quay was compelled to return home as
a private citizen. It was known that Hanna cordially disliked
the idea of the nomination of Roosevelt whose fulminations
were so disquieting to business men. He consulted McKinley.
"You know," Hanna said on one occasion, "a President sometimes dies and where would we be if Roosevelt should come

---

[1] N. Y. Nation, June 28, 1900.
[2] Cf. Croly, M. A. Hanna, pp. 308–9. Hay and Root were also in mind.
—Letters and Diary of Hay, vol. iii, pp. 163, 179.
[3] Cf. Corr. of Roosevelt and Long, vol. i, pp. 449, 456.
[4] Cf. N. Y. Nation, May 3, 1900; Croly, M. A. Hanna, pp. 283–4.

to the White House?" But, after McKinley had used all
the influences which he could quietly exert to avert the result,[1]
he sagely avoided involving himself in the business of choosing
a candidate for the office. The convention, he said, must
make the nomination, not the President.[2]

The way was open. Quay, for his own reasons, instantly
took his place at Platt's side. Both these eminent practitioners
in the art of politics, one not less than the other, were opposed
now, as in the past, in sympathy and action, to the principles
which Roosevelt defended as a "reformer," but for the moment
they had other ends in view and would, if possible, see that
the nomination should come to him in so flattering a guise
that he could not refuse it.[3] If he had not wanted the nomination and had been intent upon the performance of his duties
at Albany he would not have attended the convention in Philadelphia. His friend Lodge, foreseeing the result, urged him
to come, and he could not put away the impulse to be present
and to hear the shouting which the mention of his name might
evoke.[4] That no one could mistake his figure as he walked
the aisles of the hall he wore his cow boy sombrero.[5] The
stage was set and the play went on. Platt's New York delegation and Quay's Pennsylvania delegation made it clear to the
young man that he must, as the New York Tribune said,
"eat the professions of repugnance toward service in the Vice
Presidential chair in which his utterance had abounded for
several months past." [6] California and other states forwarded
Platt's cunning scheme and the result was practically assured
before the convention was organized. At the last moment

---

[1] Cf. J. B. Foraker, Notes of a Busy Life, vol. ii, pp. 90, 93; Thayer,
Life and Letters of Hay, vol. ii, p. 342.

[2] C. S. Olcott, Life of McKinley, vol. ii, pp. 271–2, 279, 283. The
nomination was "anybody's persimmon," Hay said on June 15, 1900.
"The utmost artesian boring" had not "availed to elicit from the President
his choice."—Letters and Diary of Hay, vol. iii, p. 179.

[3] A. K. McClure, Old Time Notes of Pa., vol. ii, pp. 611–2; Croly, M. A.
Hanna, pp. 309–17; J. F. Rhodes, McKinley and Roosevelt Administrations, pp. 133–5; H. F. Pringle, Theodore Roosevelt, p. 223.

[4] Corr. of Roosevelt and Lodge, vol. i, pp. 459, 460, 462.

[5] H. F. Pringle, Theodore Roosevelt, p. 220.

[6] N. Y. Tribune, June 19, 1900.

Roosevelt made another statement deprecating the action of his friends, while Hanna, whom Roosevelt had told that, if he were nominated, he would rise in his seat and positively decline the honor,[1] deplored the selection of a man who was indisposed to run. But nothing could stop the movement which, at the end, took the form of a stampede.[2]

Wolcott of Colorado, after Hanna had called the meeting to order, was appointed temporary chairman with the task of making an opening speech laudatory of the party, with particular reference to its feats during the McKinley administration. He was chosen because of the facility of his tongue and also because he had been an outspoken silver man. The prominence given him now would signalize the healing of the breach which had been created by differences in the party over the currency question. Lodge was made permanent chairman and from him came another political oration.

On the morning of the third day, after a prayer by a Catholic archbishop, after Foraker and others had presented McKinley's name, the President, in accordance with every plan, was nominated as his party's candidate for a second term by a unanimous vote of the delegates amid the horse play which has always characterized such bodies of men. The seconding speeches had brought Roosevelt to the platform. "He faced the multitude," a writer in the New York Tribune said, "with the same determined look and with jaw as firmly set as if a howling mob were at his heels and wished to rend him," though the occasion may not have seemed to demand such a defiant attitude. At any rate he was seen as "the real hero of the convention." He "stood flushed and almost dazed by the tremendous character of his greeting." His speech, when he began it, was "sharp, intense and at times hissing with the steam of over pressure." [3] In a short while when it was time to nominate

[1] C. S. Olcott, Life of McKinley, pp. 275–6; cf. J. B. Foraker, Notes of a Busy Life, vol. ii, p. 92.

[2] N. Y. Tribune, June 19, 1900; N. Y. Nation, June 28, 1900; cf. Autobiog. of Platt, pp. 383–97; H. H. Kohlsaat, From McKinley to Harding, p. 88.

[3] N. Y. Tribune, June 22, 1900.

candidates for the Vice Presidency he was the convention's unanimous choice for the office except for his own vote, and the ticket was McKinley and Roosevelt. Platt's happiness was complete—Roosevelt would leave the waters which his personality had ruffled in New York state. Hanna made graceful acquiescence. "We have done the best we could," he told his friend McKinley. "Now it is up to you to live." [1]

The platform which had been adopted on the second day of the convention rang with familiar phrases. The achievements of the party, particularly the enactment of a protective tariff and the law making gold the standard of value, were vaunted; the delinquencies of the Democrats were held up to view. McKinley, "walking untried paths and facing unforeseen responsibilities," had proven himself "in every situation the true American patriot and the upright statesman, clear in vision, strong in judgment, firm in action, always inspiring and deserving the confidence of his countrymen." Trusts must be restrained and foreign markets must be opened to American products by "the policy of reciprocity." The need of legislation to encourage American shipping was not mentioned, as it had been in 1896 and in earlier national platforms. Reference to the Nicaragua Canal was also omitted and the recommendations on this point were made to apply to an "isthmian canal." [2]

The platform was scanned by the Anti-Imperialists for statements concerning insular annexations. The acquisition of Hawaii was, in a few words, "approved." To Cuba "independent and self government" had been assured; "to the letter this pledge will be performed." Nothing was said about Porto Rico or the Philippines except to indicate that they had inevitably come to us as a result of the destruction of Spanish sovereignty. Thereby was "our responsibility before the world"

[1] A. K. McClure, Old Time Notes of Pa., vol. ii, p. 612; H. H. Kohlsaat, From McKinley to Harding, pp. 101–2; Hanna to McKinley, June 25, 1900, in McKinley Papers. Roosevelt wrote to Bellamy Storer on July 27, 1900: "The demand for me, especially in the farther west, was so strong that to refuse would have been to give a black eye to the ticket."—M. L. Storer, In Memoriam, p. 36.

[2] Cf. Croly, M. A. Hanna, p. 378.

for the "maintenance of law and order" created. "Whenever sovereign rights were extended it became the high duty of the government to maintain its authority, to put down armed intervention and to confer the blessings of liberty and civilization upon all the rescued peoples." [1]

Thus was the way prepared for the Democratic convention which would re-nominate Bryan. That meeting would be held in Kansas City on July 4th. The "Great Commoner" and his isms had so indoctrinated the party that Mr. Cleveland and his admirable friends who had been set aside in 1896 were, it was plain, still unwanted in the councils of an organization, whose purposes and aims they had done so much to elevate and make honorable in the sight of the world. The officers of the old Farmers' Alliance had met in Washington in February and pledged Bryan their support on a platform calling for silver currency at the ratio of 16 to 1. The People's party in May, at Sioux Falls in South Dakota, had formally nominated Bryan; he was made their candidate by acclamation on a radical platform condemning the "gigantic money trust" which was pressing blood out of the poor, and demanding "the free and unlimited" coinage of silver and great issues of rag money. They would abolish the representative system and put the agencies of government in direct control of the people. It was remarked that nothing remained for the Democratic party but to hold a ratification meeting. The Populists who had controlled it in 1896 and who were undoubtedly still in command had but to ratify in Kansas City what had been done at Sioux Falls.[2]

When the Democratic convention met Bryan was to have been named at once on the 4th of July, with allusions to the day and its significance in American history, but the plan miscarried and the result was not attained until the 5th. Then the inevitable came to pass. The "peerless leader" was nominated by acclamation. Opposition to Bryan was existent in some states but it could not be made effective against the

---

[1] For comment cf. N. Y. Nation, June 28, 1900.
[2] N. Y. Nation, May 17, 1900.

fanatical force of the Socialistic and Populistic elements which
had gained control of the organization in the West and South.
States like New York, New Jersey and Pennsylvania deprecated
such radicalism, they knew that "free silver" had led to defeat
in 1896 and would lead to the same result in 1900, but the delegates were men of so little principle and resolution that they
easily fell a prey to the intolerant proscription which was
applied to every independent mind. Hill made his reappear-
ance. He sat with Murphy and Croker in the New York
delegation which, however, showed him few honors. Croker
controlled the delegation.[1] There had been a time when he
was viewed as a state and national leader and his name and
figure still evoked demonstrations of approval. There were
moments, if he had been a man of personality and oratorical
power, when the convention might have turned to him, and
rebellion against Bryan's dictatorship would have made the
fettered delegates free agents in the naming of a candidate.[2]
But he had never been and was not now a magnetic character.
A really earnest effort was put forth by at least a part of the
delegates to nominate him for the Vice Presidency, after he
had made the most abject surrender to Bryan in a speech
"seconding" that champion of the liberties of the people, but
it failed, partly because of his objections and protests and partly
because of the indisposition of the convention to have aught
to do with New York and the East. Enthusiasm was reserved
for Adlai E. Stevenson, the man who had been the associate
of Mr. Cleveland on the ticket in 1892, who had served for
four years as Vice President, but who in 1896 had renounced
the Cleveland leadership of the party on the silver issue. When
the ballot was taken there were 559 votes for Stevenson, 200
for Hill and 89 for Towne, one of the "martyrs" who had
walked out of the Republican convention with Teller in 1896,
and who in May had been named at Sioux Falls by the People's
party as Bryan's "running mate."

The platform was a saner expression of sentiment than
Bryan's personality or the Populist party, of which he was the

[1] Cf. N. Y. Nation, July 12, 1900.   [2] N. Y. Times, July 5, 1900.

symbol, gave right to expect. As a matter of fact controversy
in the Committee on Resolutions had raged furiously and expediency eliminated much material which otherwise would
have found its way into it. It was stated and argued that free
silver should be omitted from the platform. That issue had
been forced in 1896; it had brought disaster; it should be cast
away in the interest of success, if on no other account. But
Bryan had said so much about the ruin which had been visited
upon the country by gold, and his following was still so maliciously bent upon mulcting the creditor for the advantage
of what was called the "debtor class" that he would hear of
no compromise on this point.[1] Nevertheless there was but
one vote to spare in the committee—26 favored the old 16 to 1
plank, while 24 would have dropped it.[2] He had barely saved
his face. The party would again confront the country as an
advocate of "free silver."

"Imperialism" would be condemned. The resolutions purported to plant the party on the Declaration of Independence.
The Constitution must follow the flag. The consent of the
governed was a fundamental principle of a republic, without
this it became a tyranny. A colonial policy had been adopted
inconsistent with free institutions. The "greedy commercial-
ism" which had dictated our course in the Philippines, "the
war of criminal aggression against the Filipinos," and the rest
of it, were roundly denounced. This question was declared
to be "the paramount issue of the campaign." "Militarism"
was brought to account—it was denounced as "un-American,
undemocratic and unrepublican" and "a subversion of the
ancient and fixed principles of a free people." Ringing sentences were aimed at trusts and private monopolies which
had been fostered and were protected by the Republican party.
England was assailed in the old way, not only for her money
system, an echo of the campaign of four years ago, but for her
effort to take advantage of us in the pending Hay-Pauncefote
treaty and for her conduct of the South African war. The men
who made the Democratic platform, speaking "for the entire

[1] N. Y. Nation, July 12, 1900.   [2] N. Y. Times, July 6, 1900.

American nation, except its Republican officeholders, and for all free men everywhere," extended their "sympathy to the heroic burghers in their unequal struggle to maintain their liberty and independence." The party denounced the extravagance of recent Congresses, the squandering of money on "barefaced frauds upon the taxpayers" and asked for the reduction and repeal of "war taxes" and a return to "the time-honored Democratic policy of strict economy in government expenditures."

A small body of "Silver Republicans" met in Kansas City in the days following the adjournment of the Democratic convention to endorse Bryan and Stevenson. Some members of the Anti-Imperialist League which had been formed to combat McKinley's policy in the Philippines also called for Bryan's election over McKinley, who, "whether in weakness or of wicked purpose," had used his authority to subvert the character of the government and to destroy national ideals. Other Anti-Imperialists who could not endorse Bryan's views on the money question nominated other candidates who, however, shortly withdrew from the contest. The Populists who called themselves "Middle of the Road" men and would not accept the idea of fusion with the Democrats met in Cincinnati and, after adopting a strange platform, nominated for President Wharton Barker, a broken banker of Philadelphia of erratic views, who had earlier been an uncompromising high tariff Republican, and for Vice President the picturesque Ignatius Donnelly of Minnesota. One group of Socialists offered as its Presidential candidate Debs, the Laborite, who had led the rioters in the Pullman strike; another group found a candidate in Massachusetts named Malloney. Two Prohibition parties and a party which would do away with representative government and give all power into the hands of the people to be exercised directly also put candidates in the field. After surveying the scene the Independent Gold Democrats who had nominated Senator Palmer in 1896 resolved not to make separate nominations in 1900.

Indeed, from the hour of his nomination, Bryan's defeat

was as certain as any prophecy that may be applied to human events. There was "full confidence," said the New York Times, that the American people would decide the question as they had decided it four years ago. It was an issue "between national honor and dishonor, between ruin and safety." There was but one issue and it was "sharp and clear." [1] Bryan was the Democratic party's "old man of the sea," said the Richmond Times. The test of Democracy was no longer faith in principle but obedience to "a fanatical rhetorician." "The boy orator of the Platte" was "gripping his knees around the Democratic neck;" it would be a glorious day for the party when it should be "thoroughly rid" of him. [2]

Be as confident as they might the Republicans were on their guard. "Nobody knows," said John Hay, "what Jack Cade may do." [3] Apathy was complained of. [4] Hanna who was directing the campaign would relax no effort. But he was not sufficiently frightened to entertain a suggestion of Wharton Barker who made as singular a proposal to McKinley as ever was made by one candidate for the Presidency to another. Barker would carry Georgia and, probably, Texas and Alabama, he said. All the votes which should come to him would be taken away from Bryan. In a "strictly private and confidential" letter to McKinley he asked for money that he might prosecute a more aggressive campaign. [5] Platt who was to be freed from the troubles which Roosevelt had brought upon him, presented Benjamin B. Odell, Jr., as the Republican candidate for governor of New York, a name which met with favor. The outlook on every hand was encouraging to the managers of the party. On July 12th McKinley was notified of his nomination at his home in Canton, whither he had gone for the ceremony, by a committee of which Senator Lodge was the spokesman. On the same day Roosevelt at Oyster Bay received a delegation bent on informing him of his selection as a candidate for the Vice Presidency. The speech was made by Senator Wolcott

[1] Issue of July 6, 1900. [2] Quoted in N. Y. Times, July 9, 1900.
[3] Letters and Diary of Hay, vol. iii, p. 202.
[4] Hay to McKinley, Sep. 3, 1900, in McKinley Papers.
[5] Barker to McKinley, Aug. 11, 1900, in ibid.

of Colorado. Both McKinley and Roosevelt responded expounding the issues of the campaign—McKinley inventing
a phrase with reference to the opponents of his course in the
Philippines. "There must be," he said, "no scuttle policy." [1]

The stump speakers travelled far and talked eloquently,
though McKinley himself took but a small part in the campaign
beyond his letter, in August, accepting the nomination which
was given wide publicity. He now and again visited Canton
to reattach himself to the voters of Ohio, though he forewent the
exacting exercise of receiving and addressing visiting delegations,
the course which had been followed in 1896. His managers
now advised attention to public duty. Roosevelt who seemed
to captivate the public fancy, and who was overflowing with
energy for the task, would take from the President the burden of
travel and speech making.

Already in July Roosevelt found occasion to visit the West
to attend a reunion of his Rough Riders in Oklahoma City.
Going to it and returning from it his railway train was that
of a travelling showman. Crowds came to see him and hear
him from the rear platform. He waved his wide brimmed
sombrero at his admirers as they shouted their approval.
He had been "Teddy" before, but this name was now fastened
upon him by a seal from which he could never escape.[2] It was
a new sight. A man who, in his whole life, had never put a hand
to manual labor, whose bubbling activities found vent in useless
sport, born to luxury and wealth, moved over the surfaces of
the republic as the people's friend. He gained their ear and
won their trust. It was a play that he enjoyed as well as they,
and it was to hold the stage for many years.

A fortnight later Roosevelt was again in the West addressing
the National League of Republican Clubs in St. Paul.[3] It was
said that he would postpone further campaigning until September, but in a few days he was in Atlantic City talking to
a Jewish Chautauqua society.

[1] N. Y. Tribune, July 13, 1900.
[2] Cf. N. Y. Times, July 4 and 6, 1900; H. H. Kohlsaat, from McKinley
to Harding, p. 77.
[3] N. Y. Times, July 18, 1900.

Bryan had been pouring out his oratory at his home in Lincoln, Nebraska, whenever opportunity was at hand. He and Stevenson were to be notified of their nominations in Indianapolis on August 8th. Large numbers of prominent adherents came to that city by the railway trains to attend. In their speeches neither candidate said one word about silver which was a confirmation of the statement of the convention that Imperialism was the "paramount issue." The country had been heard from. The disfavor with which Bryan's insistence that the old 16 to 1 plank should be inserted in the platform was regarded by the party leaders and the party press in the East had come to plain expression. Bryan was attacked by the Republicans because he was Bryan; the Democratic party was assailed because it had been and remained, by the official statement of its principles, unsound on the money question. The campaign was to be prosecuted by the Democrats in the East and the Middle West on the colonial issue, with particular reference to the Philippines and the war for the subjugation of a native race. There were Cleveland Democrats, Mugwumps and some Republicans who had refused to support Bryan in 1896, who now said that they would do so. The wrong of using the army of the United States to conquer a people on islands off the coast of Asia who were intent upon the enjoyment of political independence was so monstrous in their sight that even the ruin of the currency seemed a minor thing. They observed for their own consolation that gold was now the money standard by definite statement of law. Bryan, if he were elected, could not change it.[1] The issues were militarism and Imperialism—the republic was in danger, its meaning was being lost and its form was on the point of being destroyed. On the other hand most of the Democrats who had voted for McKinley or Palmer, in 1896, still withheld their favor from Bryan. Don Dickinson, John G. Carlisle, George Hoadly, Charles S. Fairchild, J. Sterling Morton and other members of the Cleveland cabinets again made it clear that the Democratic party was not this, but a new Populist party. Until it should be freed of Bryan

[1] Cf. Writings of Schurz, vol. vi, pp. 204 et seq.

and his like they would have none of it.[1] Efforts to involve
Cleveland himself in the campaign utterly failed. His friends
knew that while he remained there would be at least one stout
enemy of the socialistic schemes which Bryan was parading
under the party name. He wrote a friend that he was "by
no means free from the perplexity which now afflicts thousands
of those who love the principles of true Democracy." And
he thought, therefore, that he should be permitted in his retirement "to avoid the irritation and abuse" which his "interference at this time would inevitably invite."[2] "Bedlam was
at its height"—he would keep silent.[3] With the arrival of
every mail he cursed "the animals who had burglarized and
befouled the Democratic home," but he did this under his
breath, remaining "only an intensely anxious looker-on."[4]

In September the Anti-Imperialists made a final effort to
capture McKinley. They had a hope that he could be induced
to include a statement in favor of Philippine independence in
his letter of acceptance.[5] It was a vain hope. Nothing of this
kind, when the paper appeared, was to be found in it. Courtiers
gave it praise, Hay saying that it was "the greatest document of
the sort in our history."[6] Lodge read it with "profoundest
satisfaction and with great admiration,"[7] while Long declared
it to be "a whole campaign in itself."[8] The men who wished
the republic to be an "empire" were in firm control of the President. Roosevelt had been exchanged for leaders like Benjamin
Harrison who, while he must prefer McKinley to Bryan,
was so much out of sympathy with the policies adopted
with reference to the Philippines and Porto Rico that he
would not speak for the ticket.[9]

Bryan's stumping tours brought him to New York City on

[1] Cf. N. Y. Nation, Aug. 23 and Oct. 11, 1900.
[2] N. Y. Times, Aug. 31, 1900.
[3] A. Nevins, Letters of Cleveland, p. 535.
[4] Ibid., p. 532; cf. ibid., pp. 534, 536–41.
[5] Hoar to Hanna, Sep. 3, 1900, in McKinley Papers.
[6] Hay to McKinley, Sep. 11, 1900, in ibid.
[7] Lodge to McKinley, Sep. 10, 1900, in ibid.
[8] Long to McKinley, Sep. 10, 1900, in ibid.
[9] Manley to Cortelyou, Oct. 3, 1900, in ibid.

October 16th. His patron was Richard Croker, the chieftain of Tammany Hall, a most inappropriate ally for one who professed to be a social reformer. He was received and commended to the voters by one of the most corrupt and otherwise opprobrious "bosses" which our politics has ever produced.[1] He was, nevertheless, welcomed and pursued by crowds. He made a number of speeches, one in Madison Square Garden, the great auditorium in which he had been heard with curiosity in the campaign of 1896. He was still a harlequin whom every newspaper advertised. No one expected as the phrases flowed from his mouth to be instructed; men would not vote for him because of proper reasons which he should give them for doing so. Republicans said that he was "his own best opponent." Whenever he took to the "hippodrome" his "slack jaw" sent him farther and farther down the road to defeat.[2]

Against such a campaigner it was natural that Hanna and the Republican managers should pit Roosevelt. He had a similar talent for rough and tumble campaigning. The crowd ran agape after them both. They stood side by side in Chicago on Labor Day to watch a great trades union parade, and spoke to the assembled workingmen. Roosevelt went home to address the Republican state convention at Saratoga which nominated Odell for Governor, but soon he set forth on a tour which, beginning in Michigan, carried him through the Northwest, the Rocky mountain states as far away as Utah, and east again through Kansas, Nebraska, Iowa, Missouri, Indiana, Kentucky, West Virginia and Ohio. Rough Riders and other soldiers of the Spanish war came to greet him wherever he went. Cow punchers, yelling and shooting into the air, galloped in his train as he bestrode a horse among them. Indians in native dress, Indian bands of music, Indian maidens riding in wagons, white girls in "Roosevelt hats" came out in the Dakotas and Montana to hurrah for "Teddy." In Nebraska, in Bryan's own state, Roosevelt was making 13 speeches a

---

[1] Cf. J. F. Rhodes, The McKinley and Roosevelt Administrations, p. 142.
[2] Hay to McKinley, Sep. 3, 1900, in McKinley Papers.

day. Buffalo Bill who met him in Kansas said that he was the "American cyclone"—the Democrats were taking to their cellars wherever he appeared. He was the embodiment of a flaming nationalism—he defended armies and colonies, extolled national duty and world power, ridiculed the anti-Imperialists. "We are a nation of men not a nation of weaklings," he would shout. We as little feared "to face our duty in the far islands of the Eastern seas as to face our duties at home." [1] States which had given Bryan majorities in 1896 would not do so in 1900. The jingo was called forth in the silver man and he was a Republican again. After an absence of 46 days from New York Roosevelt returned for a great mass meeting at Madison Square Garden, which was organized to welcome him home and for a tour of New York state in the interest of the election of Odell as governor, and the Platt ticket.

A statement by one of the major political parties of the United States that the retention of the Philippine Islands was the "paramount issue" of the Presidential campaign gave encouragement to Aguinaldo. He gained recruits. Resistance increased and our army must be reinforced. Disproof of General Otis's prediction that the "rebellion" was "over" came by every cablegram from Manila.[2] The native leaders were so far heartened that they renewed their appeals to the American people for sympathy. They addressed the European powers and reorganized their juntas for the dissemination of propaganda in the interest of their cause.

In southern Luzon and the Visayas, lying south of Luzon, hostilities taxed the ingenuity of our commanders. Although 65,000 men were in the service in various parts of the archipelago conditions were again highly disturbed. Terrorism reigned. Even in Manila Americans and American sympathizers felt that they were unsafe and they took ship for Hong Kong. General MacArthur must have more soldiers else he could not escort his wagon trains engaged in carrying supplies

[1] N. Y. Times, Sep. 6, 1900.
[2] N. Y. Nation, June 14, 1900; J. H. Blount, Am. Occupation of the Philippines, pp. 39–40.

to distant garrisons, protect government property and guard peaceful natives from guerrillas and ladrones.

It was believed that, up to this time, in the course of the war, we had killed 30,000 Filipinos.[1] John Foreman, a foremost authority on the Philippines, where he had resided for many years, said that we occupied barely one-five hundredth part of the total area of the archipelago in places inaccessible by water. In other words we held only so much as we could defend by force of arms. He thought and said in the midst of the campaign that without a great permanent army to occupy the country we could do nothing in the interior, and we ought to extricate ourselves from such a situation in whatever way we could at the first good day.[2] The army, after new contingents arrived, attained a strength of 75,000 men.[3]

An unofficial adviser appeared in the person of "Fighting Joe" Wheeler. It seemed to be not in the heart of McKinley to refuse anything to so redoubtable a "rebel," who was so intent upon signalizing his attachment to the reunited country, and, after coming home from Cuba, he was sent to the Philippines. He was serving there under General Otis, but he made frequent reports directly to the commander-in-chief in the White House, a relationship which must have been invited by the President. At any rate the tender of so much letter writing was not repelled. Little that was being done in the Philippines commended itself to Wheeler's judgment. He could not run into the jungle on his own account, as he had done in Cuba under Shafter. He was ignored by Otis and MacArthur which did him deep affront. They did not draw him into council. They needed cavalry, he said. The troops were inactive. The war was costing the government two millions a week. The President was urged to cable Otis to pursue the Filipinos and capture them at once; nothing would do so much to "energize" the army. If Wheeler were not allowed to fight he wished to come home and take his seat in Congress where he

---

[1] N. Y. Nation, Aug. 16, 1900.
[2] National Review for Sep., 1900; N. Y. Nation, Sep. 20, 1900. But see J. A. LeRoy, The Americans in the Philippines, vol. ii, p. 62.
[3] Report of Sec. of War, for 1900, p. 4.

could defend the McKinley policy of annexation. He was more than a military genius—he deemed himself an ambassador to increase national trade and commerce. He had the vision of Colonel Mulberry Sellers. Civilization was turning toward the setting sun. The United States was on the verge of a splendid new prosperity. We had been brought within reach of 500 millions of people on the eastern shores of the Pacific Ocean. Each one needed four suits of clothes a year, i.e. 36 yards of cloth. These suits, being of a white stuff, must be washed often, consequently they would wear out rapidly. The average price of such a fabric per yard was 30 cents Mexican or 15 cents gold,—for 500 millions of people a gross sum of 2 billion 700 million dollars. Then this multitude must have shoes, stockings and undershirts which would mean to us 2 billion 700 million dollars more.[1] Otis bore with so insubordinate an officer, merely saying that Wheeler seemed to be in a "highly excited mental condition," [2] and, that he might not further trouble the administration, military and civil, he was in a short time made a brigadier-general in the regular army and retired from the service.[3]

Meanwhile a new Philippine commission appeared upon the scene. President Schurman of Cornell University and his associates on the first commission had furnished McKinley with the defence which he needed for taking and holding the islands. They had made a number of proposals in regard to provincial governors and municipal administration, and had cooperated with the military authorities in organizing justice courts and other agencies promising civil order.[4] Congress still failed to act and the subject remained in the hands of President McKinley whose authority was found in his war powers. The new commission reached Manila on June 3, 1900. It was headed by William H. Taft, who, at the President's particular request, following a recommendation of

[1] Wheeler to McKinley, Jan. 14, 1900, in McKinley Papers.
[2] Otis to Adjutant General, Jan. 10, 1900, in ibid.
[3] Wheeler's many letters are in the McKinley Papers under dates in 1899 and 1900.
[4] Cf. Report of Comm., Senate Doc., 56th Cong. 1st sess., no. 138.

ex-Secretary of State Day, laid down a Federal judgeship in
Ohio and accepted the post.[1] With this young man—he was
still but 42 years of age—were Dean C. Worcester, the authority
regarding the people and the islands who had been on the
Schurman commission; Luke I. Wright of Tennessee; Henry
C. Ide of Vermont, and Bernard Moses, a professor in the
University of California, who had earned respect in the fields
of history and political science. The labors of these men were
vain until order could be restored by the troops, though they
continued the development of plans for the establishment of
civil administration which had been proposed and discussed by
the preceding commission and were being put into execution
with indifferent success by officers of the army. This commission would take over the tasks of government from the military
authorities and represent the President.[2]

It was a colossal work to formulate agencies for the government of the people which would be feasible. Their customs,
traditions, as well as their actual needs, must be considered.
Justice must be administered with an even hand. Public
franchises, mining and timber claims, transfers of land, the
construction of roads and bridges, internal improvements had
awaited the pacification of the country by the troops. The
solution of these problems, in turn and at length, would be
factors in effecting and maintaining peace and good order.
There were, too, difficulties with the Catholic Church in which
the natives were involved. Never before were such tasks
faced by men having to do with government in this country.
We had no body of civil servants familiar with colonial administration. But Judge Taft and his associates had one
advantage in that they were working in a field far away from
the disturbances of American politics. Once it should be
determined at the polls in November, if it should be determined,

---

[1] C. S. Olcott, Life of McKinley, vol. ii, pp. 174–7; Woodard to McKinley, March 25, 1900, in McKinley Papers; N. Y. Tribune, Feb. 7, 1900;
speech of Taft in N. Y., Dec. 13, 1908, cited by J. F. Rhodes, McKinley
and Roosevelt Administrations, pp. 196–7.

[2] See instructions of President of April 7, 1900, in Report of Sec. of
War for 1900, pp. 72–6; C. B. Elliott, The Philippines to the End of the
Military Regime, pp. 496 et seq.; N. Y. Nation, Feb. 15, 1900.

that the Philippines were to be held by the United States, that it was our purpose and right in the sight of a majority of our citizens to take an alien people under our care and to govern them without their consent, the public interest in the subject would, it was believed, abate and the commission could quietly unfold its plans and proceed with the performance of its important duties.[1]

McKinley received nearly a million more votes than Bryan. He carried all the so-called doubtful states—New York, Indiana, New Jersey, Connecticut and West Virginia. Outside of the Solid South he picked up, on the silver issue, the electoral votes of only Colorado, Idaho, Montana and Nevada, a pitiful company in their contribution to his total. There were 292 votes for McKinley and 155 for Bryan, 21 votes less than he had received in 1896. He lost his own state of Nebraska. New York gave McKinley a plurality of 143,000, Pennsylvania 288,000, Michigan 104,000, Wisconsin 100,000, Iowa 98,000. The Prohibitionists, Socialists and other minor parties altogether polled less than 400,000 votes.[2]

The overwhelming defeat of Bryan in his second appeal to the people brought with it increased Republican majorities in both branches of the next Congress. In Pennsylvania Quay was assured of reelection by the legislature to his old seat in the Senate. Alger in a short time would be a senator from Michigan. Platt had gained his ends in New York. Such sweeping party victories meant success for those whom the public service could very well spare. Hanna's influence in Ohio and in the country generally was enlarged. During the campaign he had appeared in defence of the McKinley administration and had proven himself an acceptable and effective speaker.[3] The development of policies which would give opportunities to business enterprise and increase the prosperity

---

[1] First report of Taft Comm. in Senate Doc., 56th Cong. 2nd sess., no. 112.

[2] Barker had predicted that he would receive 1,000,000 votes; he got 50,000.—N. Y. Times, Oct. 8, 1900.

[3] Croly, M. A. Hanna, pp. 331–40; J. F. Rhodes, The McKinley and Roosevelt Administrations, pp. 140–1.

of the people was assured. The general feeling of confidence was reflected in the stock markets. Capital was abundant, owners lent it hopefully. New issues of securities, further and larger mergers of companies on the strength of profitable markets for the products of industry were under discussion and would be not long delayed.[1]

As on election day in 1896 the offices of stock-brokers were kept open all night that they might take orders for purchases or sales at the opening of the London market at 4 A. M. Chicago time and 5 A. M. New York time, five hours before business could be transacted in American exchanges. The rise in the value of securities between November 2nd, the day before the Bryan fright had ended in 1896, and November 5, 1900, the day preceding the turning back of his second assault upon order and security, was impressive. American Cotton Oil stock which had been quoted in 1896 at 14⅛ sold four years later at 36. Other advances were—for American Tobacco, from 78¾ to 98, Brooklyn Rapid Transit from 22 to 62, Chesapeake and Ohio from 17 to 31, Chicago, Burlington and Quincy from 77⅞ to 129⅞, Chicago, Milwaukee and St. Paul from 76 to 117¾, Rock Island from 67¾ to 110⅛, Colorado Fuel and Iron from 20 to 40⅛, Missouri Pacific from 23¼ to 57, New York Central from 95¼ to 133, New Jersey Central from 105 to 136, Tennessee Coal and Iron from 27⅛ to 57¼ and so on.[2]

The stampede to buy stocks began as soon as the news of McKinley's election was known—first, as was expected, in London. A greater number of excited brokers than had ever before occupied the floor of the exchange in New York awaited the fall of the gavel which signalized the opening of business in that city. The galleries were crowded. Wall Street was filled with men and women eager to place their orders to buy. Gains of $3, $4 and $6 a share were recorded before the day was done. Standard Oil was sold at $650, an advance of $25. Two million shares were traded in on the day following the election, more than on any day in the history of the Exchange.

[1] Cf. N. Y. Nation, Nov. 15, 1900. [2] Cf. N. Y. Times, Nov. 7, 1900.

Bankers and brokers radiated hope and good cheer. Providence was smiling on the United States. The country, rid of Bryanism, Populism and the other "crazy vaporings of reckless agitators," would have four years of "the greatest prosperity in the history of the world."[1] Satisfaction because of the result was general in England. That Bryan had been defeated and again put aside, that the people had refused to strike the Stars and Stripes in the Pacific, were subjects of congratulation in the London press. The Times complimented us upon the "splendid pronouncement made on behalf of the principles which lie at the base of all human society."[2] The result, Ambassador Choate said, gave the English people as much pleasure as was felt in the United States.[3]

Nor did the excitement in the stock market subside. One two-million share day followed another with paralysis of the machinery for registering transactions, and with sensational advances in price. Foreign trade was increasing. Manufacturers who had been concerned principally with the domestic market now saw opportunities in all parts of the world for the consumption of the products of their mines, furnaces and mills. In the fiscal year ending June 30, 1900, the value of exported and imported goods reached a total of $2,200,000,000, the greatest amount ever recorded in our history—it had been approximately $1,900,000,000 in 1899. And there was a favorable balance of trade—exports exceeded imports by from $500,000,000 to $600,000,000 annually. The mounting quantities of machinery and other manufactures of iron and steel, a total of itself in excess of $230,000,000, of leather, of cotton goods awakened the enthusiasm of those who spoke and wrote about the future of the United States. It was computed and stated, notwithstanding the Spanish war and its resultant costs, that the government had an excess of income over and above its expenditures for the fiscal year ending June 30, 1900, of about $80,000,000.

The general spirit of optimism pervaded the message which

[1] N. Y. Times, Nov. 8, 1900. [2] Quoted in ibid.
[3] E. S. Martin, Life of Choate, vol. ii, p. 174.

President McKinley addressed to the 56th Congress when it assembled in December, 1900, for its concluding short session. There were "evidences on every hand," he said, "of individual and national prosperity" and "proof of the growing strength and increasing power for good of republican institutions." Popular government had demonstrated in its 124 years of trial on this continent "its stability and security, and its efficiency, as the best instrument of national development and the best safeguard to human rights." Very little contained in the message spoke of departures in policy or stirred public comment. It was a review of what had been done and a confirmation of the public estimate which had been formed of McKinley's character. He breasted no popular current but went with it as gracefully and unresistingly as any one who ever held the Presidential office in the United States. Some passages in regard to reciprocity were taken to be indicative of an enlargement of the President's view. It was in reality an evidence of the awakening of ambition in the minds of our larger manufacturers whose eyes were not set so fully as formerly upon the "home market," and who saw abroad an outlet for their industrial enterprise and skill. His references to China were a mere review of what had been done to rescue the legations and for the protection of treaty rights. What he should say about the late Spanish insular possessions, especially the Philippines, which had been bandied about in the earnest discussions connected with the campaign, was naturally awaited with interest. It appeared, in the first place, that the gentlemen at Paris who had arranged the treaty of peace with Spain had been but badly coached in their geography. They had carelessly omitted some of the many islands in the archipelago which they had intended to take and $100,000 must be added to the $20,000,000 set aside as *solatium* and purchase money so that our sovereignty should be complete.[1] Congress had already provided a civil government for Porto Rico—it was, the President said, in "successful operation." Courts had been established. The garrisons had

[1] Cf. N. Y. Nation, Jan. 10, 1901.

been reduced to 1636 men, of whom one-half were natives enlisted for the service.

General Wood as governor of Cuba had reported a state of affairs in that island so favorable to peace and order that Mr. McKinley on July 25, 1900, in the midst of the Presidential campaign, not without the wish to disarm, in some degree, his critics, who freely predicted that Cuba, as well as Porto Rico and the Philippines, were destined to become a part of the American "empire," directed the issuance of a call for the election of members of a convention to frame a constitution for a free and independent government of the island. General Wood acted at once. The election would be held on September 15th, and the committee would meet in Havana on November 5th. Wood, representing the President of the United States, called the assembly to order and made some statements, as he was authorized to do, defining the duties of the delegates. The constitution must be "adequate to secure a stable, orderly and free government." A dictatorship, characteristic of the Latin Americans, when the people should be left to themselves for the development of a democratic system, was feared. The convention was warned—the distinction between "true representative government and dictatorship," Wood said, as he stood before the delegates, is that, under a representative government, "every representative of the people, in whatever office, confines himself strictly within the limits of his defined powers." Nearly 6,000 troops remained in Cuba. For the present, Mr. McKinley said, the force could not be withdrawn or materially reduced.

The portions of the message relating to the Philippines were read with the most eagerness, especially as the policy to be pursued there had been veiled in a good deal of mystery during the campaign. That the islands were being held, that the Taft commission was on the ground trying to evolve a system of administration, that all was under the control of the President, lacking action by Congress, were known and accepted facts. In the election the people had endorsed the administration and put further trust in the President. His statement now was a publication of his instructions to Taft and the other members of the commission which had been issued in April, promise to lay before Congress the reports of the body and some hopeful and pleasing predictions, resting again on high ground, with reference to the future of the islands which were to stand under "our fostering care." "The fortune of war," he said, had "thrown upon this nation an unsought trust which should be unselfishly discharged," and had brought the government "a moral as well as material responsibility toward these millions" whom we had "freed from an oppressive yoke." The Filipinos were "the wards of the nation." Duty bade us "treat them that our flag may be no less beloved in the mountains of Luzon and the fertile zones of Mindanao and Negros than it is at home—that there, as here, it shall be the revered symbol of liberty, enlightenment and progress in every avenue of development." No limit could be fixed "to the degree of culture and advancement yet within the reach of these people, if our duty toward them be faithfully performed."

Such rhetoric was McKinley-esque. To the Anti-Imperialists it was sheer nonsense and hypocrisy. It answered no objection which had been made to the war upon the natives and the assumption of power over them "without their consent." It contained no assurance of an intelligent will, much less the skill and ability, to contribute to the culture and advancement of a strange and unstudied race, even when it should be subjugated by force of arms. The President said that he would need from 45,000 to 60,000 troops in the Philippines "for some time to come." He recognized that "the grave responsibility" for the future government of the islands rested with members of Congress, who should read the reports of the Taft commission—whatever legislation should be passed should be along the "generous lines" suggested by that body.

The present strength of the American army was 100,000 men—without new legislation there would be, on June 30, 1901, a reduction to about 30,000. The President recommended a permanent regular army of 100,000. The navy was not large enough. New vessels were in course of construction—more should be built.

Congress having its ways well oiled by its existing majorities, with the promise of larger ones in the following years as a result of the Republican triumph over the unsoundly led and disorganized opposition, faced its tasks at once. It would brook no delays and, lest objection be interposed, the Cuban and Philippine subjects would be dealt with in an underhanded way. Amendments were tacked to the army appropriation bill and those who should be minded to vote against what was proposed were to be put in the false position of withholding money for the national defense. The scheme in both cases originated in the Senate. The amendment relating to Cuba bore the name of Mr. Platt of Connecticut, who reported it from the Committee on Relations with Cuba on February 25, 1901, shortly before the day set for adjournment.[1] The convention at Havana had adopted a constitution for the people of the island on February 11th,—the delegates signed it on February 21st. It was based upon and followed the pattern of the Constitution of the United States. The division of powers, the checks and balances of our system would, it was felt, insure the government our favor. Indeed no other model for a republic readily suggested itself in view of our growth to power and prosperity under institutional forms which were generally held to be beneficent. But more had been asked of the convention—it should make a statement, General Wood said when he addressed it on the opening day, concerning the relations which in future, after the establishment of self-government, should exist between Cuba and the United States. On this point it had been proposed that we should stand on the same ground as other powers. But a body of opinion in this country was quickly formed expressive of a complete disapproval of such a divorce of interest in, and concern for the welfare of, a people whom we had quixotically delivered from the oppressions of Spain. It was powerful and Platt came forward to give it force in Congress.

[1] Cong. Record, 56th Cong. 2nd sess., p. 2954.

Our relations with the Cubans hereafter, upon the establishment of their government under a constitution, should be based on several principles, the most important of which was a recognition of our right "to intervene for the preservation of Cuban independence, the maintenance of a government adequate for the protection of life, property and individual liberty, and for discharging the obligations with respect to Cuba imposed by the treaty of Paris on the United States." The Isle of Pines should not be included within the boundaries of the new Cuban republic, title to it being left to future adjustment by treaty; and the United States, in order that it might "maintain the independence of Cuba and protect the people thereof, as well as for its own defence," should have the right to buy and lease lands for coaling and naval stations at points to be selected by the President of the United States.[1]

The Cuban amendment was before the Senate and the members could take it or leave it, with knowledge that, if the army were not paid, they would be called together in extra session running through a hot Washington summer. The conditions, in effect, would impose upon the Cuban convention an acknowledgment of American suzerainty. The Senate's approval of the amendment was by a vote of 43 to 20.[2]

Another amendment to the army bill—this one bearing the name of Senator Spooner, since he had brought its provisions before the Congress at its last session in another form,[3] vested "all military, civil and judicial powers necessary to govern" the Philippines in "such person and persons" as the President might appoint, to be exercised in such manner as he should direct, to the end that the inhabitants should be protected in "the full enjoyment of their liberty, property and religion." The establishment of a "permanent civil government" was postponed—all would be subject to such arrangements and dispositions as the President might devise and sanction. This amendment was adopted by the Senate by a vote of 45 to 27.[4]

[1] Report of Sec. of War for 1901, p. 48; C. S. Olcott, Life of McKinley, vol. ii, pp. 209–14; L. A. Coolidge, O. H. Platt, chap. xxvi.
[2] Cong. Record, 56th Cong. 2nd sess., pp. 3151–2.   [3] Ibid., pp. 2957–8.
[4] Ibid., p. 3145; Report of Sec. of War for 1901, pp. 57–8.

Here was more arbitrary action precipitated upon the country, the Anti-Imperialists said, not only without the consideration which such subjects demanded but also without regard for the rights of the minority party.[1] The speed with which these important policies were presented and were approved by the Senate met with protest, but their progress in the other chamber was still more rapid. Both amendments were in the appropriation bill when it appeared on March 1st for passage by the House. There was a motion for concurrence—two hours would be allowed for debate. Nothing could be done. The House had been called a "bear garden" but its rules now, for several years, gave the majority such despotic power that peace was enforced upon the wildest spirits. A few words were said, which the speakers were allowed to expand for publication in the Record, about the "offensive, obnoxious and unconstitutional provisions" which had been engrafted on the bill, about the policy of "greedy and damnable conquest," about the "tyranny" of the majority, about the "gradual dry rot" which was "taking place in the American conscience," about the "breaking of faith" with the Cubans—"to lie or not to lie," one member said during the debate, was "the question before the American people" [2]—about the violation of "practically all the ten commandments" in carrying on a war of "slaughter and extermination" in the Philippines. The amendments were concurred in by a vote of 161 yeas to 137 nays,[3] and the bill was signed by the President on March 2, 1901.

At the same session Congress relieved the country of some of the war taxes and reorganized and increased the size of the army. The President had asked for authority to enlist loyal Filipinos to help in the work of pacifying the islands, and it was granted to him. The Secretary of the Navy was directed to prepare plans for the construction of two new battle ships and two armed cruisers. The 56th Congress had appropriated for two years $1,444,062,545, about $128,000,000 less than the preceding Congress which had financed the war. However, as

[1] Cf. Cong. Record, 56th Cong. 2nd sess., pp. 2957 et seq.
[2] Ibid., p. 3360. [3] Ibid., p. 3384.

the Democrats observed, this was nearly $400,000,000 more than the appropriations to defray the costs of government by the 54th Congress, that one preceding the war. Then in two years but $46,000,000 had been voted to the army, now for two years the total was $230,000,000. The naval appropriations in the same time had risen from $63,000,000 to $144,-000,000.

The Senate found itself face to face, as in the last session, with the Hay-Pauncefote treaty which would prepare the way for the construction of an isthmian canal. Admiral Walker's enlarged commission, appointed in 1899, did not make a report until November, 1901,[1] but a preliminary statement of its conclusions was ready when Congress met in December, 1900. It expressed its favor for the Nicaragua route and declared that the cost would be $200,000,000, very much more than any earlier estimate, because of the greater dimensions of the cut, which, it was said now, must accommodate the largest modern ships. The isthmus at Panama offered the most satisfactory engineering prospects. The estimated cost of completing the canal here, at its narrowest width, where work had been resumed by the French, would be about $142,-000,000, therefore $58,000,000 less than must be expended on the Nicaragua route. But the new Panama company was indisposed to sell its property, and, since it held an exclusive concession from the government of Colombia, independent activity on our side at that place was barred. Nicaragua and Costa Rica, on the other hand, were "untrammelled by concessions," and, if they were prepared and willing to grant us the necessary rights, this, in view of all the facts and circumstances, must be held to be "the most practicable and feasible route." [2]

The Clayton-Bulwer treaty with England still stood athwart the way and the pending proposals for its modification called for the action of the Senate. Lodge and Roosevelt, playing

[1] Senate Doc., 57th Cong. 1st sess., no. 54. The final report was not received until January, 1902.
[2] Cf. N. Y. Times, Dec. 5 and 6, 1900; N. Y. Nation, Dec. 13, 1900; J. W. G. Walker, Ocean to Ocean.

their familiar parts, which gave them places as our most redoubtable nationalists, had reawakened jingo sentiment on the subject of England. They continued their popular agitation. They thus met and affronted Secretary of State Hay who belonged to their social and intellectual caste, and who was at least equal to them in the esteem with which he was regarded in the literate world. He had labored diligently and patriotically to negotiate the treaty. It was an enlightened measure in the interest of international harmony and peace. Yet two men who had suddenly come to influence in the Republican party, of better knowledge than was possessed by those whom they would sway, seeing an opportunity to improve their position, led a hue and cry against the treaty.[1] The New York Sun, always jingoist and the New York Journal, speaking to its ignorant foreign audience, broke out in fury and inflamed other sections of the press.[2] The campaign had been launched before, and had been continued throughout, the Presidential canvass.[3] It had gone far. The steps taken could not be retraced. More men who had been in favor of the treaty when it first appeared slunk away from it, or actively opposed it. In his message to Congress in December, President McKinley only casually commended "the convention with Great Britain" to the "early attention of the Senate." He had been bent by the winds and left the contest to Hay, who suffered alone in the storm of cowardly unreason, while the crowd, as he complained, "blathered away at England."[4] Senators asked for consulships. They would sell their votes for offices.[5] Hay again tried to resign.[6] The course of a few politicians, pursued

[1] Cf. Tyler Dennett, John Hay, p. 257.

[2] Nevins, Henry White, pp. 151-2; Tyler Dennett, John Hay, pp. 233, 254-5.

[3] Tyler Dennett, John Hay, pp. 233-4.

[4] Nevins, Henry White, pp. 151-2; Holt, op. cit., pp. 184 et seq.; N. Y. Nation, Dec. 20, 1900. The public mind at the moment, Secretary Hay said, was "morbid" on the subject of England. (C. S. Olcott, Life of McKinley, vol. ii, p. 259.) He wrote J. W. Foster of "the mad dog hatred of England."—Thayer, Life of Hay, vol. ii, pp. 234-5.

[5] Cf. Letters and Diary of Hay, vol. iii, pp. 176-8; Holt, op. cit., p. 193; Education of Henry Adams, pp. 375, 394.

[6] Nevins, Henry White, p. 154.

merely for the acclamation of the cheap and uninstructed—international complications, even war, were not absent from the calculations of Lodge and Roosevelt, who would have abrogated the Clayton-Bulwer treaty no matter what the consequences [1]—was soon confused with public sentiment. The American people, Lodge said, would never give their assent to the building, at their own expense, of a canal which they must guard for the benefit of the world's commerce unless they could have "virtually complete control of it." [2] Therefore, in December, 1900, upon the convening of Congress, the paper which Hay and Pauncefote had prepared was re-written in the Senate under Lodge's leadership. [3] Amendments were suggested and adopted. In the first place, it must be clearly stated that the old Clayton-Bulwer treaty was being superseded by the new treaty; secondly, that rules made for the use of the canal should take into account the exceptional measures which the United States might adopt for its own defense, or for the maintenance of public order; and, finally, that there should be no requirement for the adherence of other powers—they were without rights in the case. The first and third amendments were approved by unanimous votes and the second by a majority of 65 to 17. The Democrats who strove to gain more political advantage for themselves than could accrue to the Republicans proposed other amendments still more anti-English in tone, but failed to achieve their ends. The treaty, after having been revised in this material way, received "the advice and consent" of the Senate by a vote of 55 to 18. [4]

The British government refused to accept it in its new form—the Senate had removed the idea of neutrality—they would prefer to continue to abide by the provisions of the Clayton-Bulwer treaty, which was "an international compact of unquestionable validity," and which "ought not to be abrogated

---

[1] Corr. of Roosevelt and Lodge, vol. i, pp. 484–8, 494; Nevins, Henry White, pp. 155–8.

[2] Nevins, Henry White, pp. 154–5.   [3] N. Y. Nation, March 14, 1901.

[4] Senate Doc., 57th Cong. 1st sess., no. 85; cf. ibid., 63rd Cong. 2nd sess., no. 474.

or modified, save with the consent of both the parties to the contract." [1]

The ceremonies attendant upon the beginning of McKinley's second term on March 4, 1901, followed the accustomed forms with parades in the streets of Washington and an inaugural ball. The members of the cabinet, one and all, resigned to be reappointed, Hay to the State Department, Gage to the Treasury, Root to the War Department, Long to the Navy Department, Emory Smith to the Post Office, E. A. Hitchcock of Missouri, who in 1898 had succeeded Cornelius N. Bliss, to the Interior Department, James Wilson to the Department of Agriculture and Griggs as Attorney General whose place was very shortly taken by Philander C. Knox, after an effort had been made to secure Mr. Choate, who preferred to remain in London.[2] The government would proceed in the course it had taken in the four years completed and past.

In the spring and summer of 1901, after Congress had adjourned, the popular mind was concerned with the developing prosperity of the country. The impetus given to business by the election did not abate. Though there were increased expenditures by the government, the revenues were ample for every need. The deposits in banks, their loans of money to the people, transportation by land and sea, prices of agricultural crops, employment for wages evidenced a confident feeling which continued to be reflected in the stock markets. The prospect of recapitalizing companies and of forming new corporations of hitherto unheard of magnitude invited promoters and bankers, and this movement which had been in progress for two or three years was soon at full tide. The expansive minds of the promoters of the combinations was understood when, upon scanning the list of shares dealt in on the New York Stock exchange, it was seen that 27 bore the name American, many more National and International, North American, United States, Federal, General, Union and Republic. The

---

[1] Lord Lansdowne to Lord Pauncefote in the American newspapers of March 26, 1901; Senate Doc., 61st Cong., 3rd sess., no. 746; N. Y. Nation, March 28, 1901; R. B. Mowat, Life of Pauncefote, p. 283.

[2] Choate to McKinley, Feb. 9, 1901, in McKinley Papers.

high point was reached in the formation of the United States Steel Corporation with an authorized capitalization of $1,-100,000,000 in stock and $304,000,000 in bonds, a total of nearly one and a half billions, a staggering sum reckoned by all previous standards. Three men, principally, were involved in this operation—Elbert H. Gary, a Western farm boy, who had studied law and had made himself the head of the Federal Steel Company which had been chartered in 1898 and was a combination of the Illinois Steel Company and other companies, with works situated, for the most part, at or near Chicago; Andrew Carnegie, a Scotsman, who had come to America as a lad and who, by extraordinary acumen, had built up a great steel business at Pittsburgh, and J. Pierpont Morgan, the head of the banking house bearing his name in New York.

The manufacture of steel in this country had, in a few years, undergone an amazing development. The great supplies of coal and iron, the intelligence and skill of our iron masters, the efficiency of our processes, especially that one which replaced the Bessemer converter with the open hearth method, the cheapness of the product, the wide variety of new uses to which it was put were adding stirring pages to the industrial history of America. Fortunes had been made in iron—greater ones in steel. But it was an adage that the business was "prince or pauper"—it was, Carnegie had once said, "a ticklish witch." [1] For a time it would be highly prosperous—suddenly, with a fall in the demand, employees must be discharged and the works closed. Mr. Gary had visions of a foreign trade which our facilities for cheap manufacture would enable us to supply. More economies by mergers of plants remained to be effected. Gary's furnaces and mills were situated at too great a distance from the seaboard for the export trade. While his own company was large Carnegie's at Pittsburgh had a yet greater output. Its supplies of ore in the newly discovered ranges in Minnesota on the shores of Lake Superior, and coke, since it had effected alliances with Henry C. Frick, gave it advantages which embarrassed its competitors. Efficient

[1] B. J. Hendrick, Life of Carnegie, vol. ii, p. 18.

administration by a group of capable young men, under the bold and implacable direction of Carnegie, who stood at their head, made it impregnable on the subject of production costs and quality of output. From $160 a ton for steel rails in 1875 the price in 1898 had fallen to $17, and Carnegie spoke of making three pounds of steel for two cents. The profits of his company were $21,000,000 in 1899 and $40,000,000 in 1900 of which he himself received $25,000,000.[1] But he was eager to devote his remaining years to philanthropy, an ideal which he had formed as a young man. There were clashing interests in the industry and indeed among his own partners.[2] To meet threats of a really dangerous competition was a disturbing prospect to a man of his age as determinedly and defiantly as he was wont to treat those who opposed his will. He, therefore, seemed ready, though he acceded reluctantly, to consider suggestions for the sale of his great properties. No plan met his favor until the offer came through Mr. Morgan. The proposal which was accepted called for a price of $400,-000,000, increased in the course of the negotiation by a further payment of $90,000,000 in common stock of the new corporation. Carnegie himself received about $225,000,000 in five per cent. gold bonds. His partners contented themselves with preferred and common stock. Upon the completion of the arrangements Morgan, in taking Carnegie's hand, congratulated him on having become "the richest man in the world." His methods in business had made him but few friends—he could now bring bays to his brow by generous giving.[3]

With the Carnegie and Federal companies Mr. Morgan joined five other companies bearing the name "American" and two bearing the name "National," all themselves mergers of smaller companies effected in 1898, 1899 and 1900, together with a Lake Superior ore company, to form the new "Steel Trust." The principals in the coalition were brought into relationship for a discussion of the scheme in December, 1900,

[1] B. J. Hendrick, Life of Carnegie, vol. ii, p. 53.
[2] Ibid., pp. 114–7.
[3] Cf. J. F. Rhodes, McKinley and Roosevelt Administrations, pp. 145, 147.

the new corporation was chartered on February 25, 1901, and
the great billion dollar business was organized and put into
operation on April 1st following, amid many statements that
it had been overcapitalized and prophecies that it would fall
of its own weight. The corporation had producing equipment
in 149 steel works of 9,400,000 tons of finished steel annually.
It had 78 blast furnaces capable of making 7,400,000 tons of
pig iron in a year, 50,000 acres of coke land, untold supplies of
ore, 1,000 miles of railroad and a fleet of 112 ships on the
Great Lakes, docks and other properties. Though, by economies of operation immediately introduced by the management
and by an unabated demand for its products, the company
paid seven per cent. on its preferred stock and four per cent.
on its common stock from its earnings for the first year or
two, it soon met with reverses in trade comprehending the
country, which proved to be temporary, but which seemed,
for a time, to be confirmatory of popular fears.[1]

Other mergers of mergers, consolidations of companies which
had themselves but lately been consolidated, occupied the
attention of bankers and brokers as their stocks and bonds
came upon the market for distribution to a public eager to
participate in fortune making, founded upon a confidence in
the wealth and grandeur of the United States.[2] At the end of
April and in the first days of May, 1901, speculation in New
York City reached proportions never attained before. On the
last day of April over 3,000,000 shares were traded in by
brokers. In the month of April the transactions totalled
nearly 42,000,000 shares, three times as many as in the same
month in 1900, seven times as many as had been customarily
dealt in in a month prior to 1898.[3] The avidity of those in
whom the gambling spirit dwelt, and by whom it was freely
indulged, attracted widespread attention, and, at the same

---

[1] See J. H. Bridge, Inside Hist. of the U. S. Steel Corp.; B. J. Hendrick,
Life of Carnegie; George Harvey, Henry C. Frick; Ida Tarbell, E. H.
Gary, chap. v; A. Cotter, Hist. of the U. S. Steel Corp., chaps. i–iii.

[2] A. C. Coolidge, The U. S. as a World Power, pp. 175–6.

[3] Cf. N. Y. Times, May, 1, 1900; cf. A. D. Noyes, Forty Years of Am.
Finance, p. 301.

time, induced much homily. But enormous stock issues would be distributed so long as it should be profitable for those engaged in the pursuit. The bubble burst and panic ensued as a result of a "corner" in the shares of the Northern Pacific Railroad in May.[1] It was not the end but reaction was at hand, and a number of great companies, launched too late, fell before their organization could be completed.[2]

More was to be said about trusts, their monopolistic nature, and the increase of profits reaped behind tariff walls reared by Republican Congresses in league with manufacturers. - It had been stated in the campaign by both parties that great aggregations of capital for the control of industry should be put under restraint. The trusts were growing more menacing—they were embracing a greater number of industries. Their output needed larger markets.[3] More and more were manufacturers turning their minds to foreign countries. It was increasingly plain to men of vision that trade, if they would expand it, lay in other fields. As England had grown rich from her export business so would America profit if she should study the needs of other peoples, improve shipping and banking facilities, obtain tariff concessions and open foreign trade routes. Manufacturers of steel, locomotive engines, agricultural and other machinery, cotton goods, hats, shoes and many other articles had a new outlook. Instead of pleading weakness and inferiority which had been at the bottom of the protective tariff campaigns our industrialists were ready to boast that they were leading the world. Many of them had come to care less and less about the "wall," though they were the same men who a while ago had said that they would be prostrated by free trade. Their way out was by reciprocity, a bargaining for lower tariffs on goods exported to selected countries in return for remission of charges on the products of these countries coming to the United States. There had been

---

[1] Cf. J. G. Pyle, Life of J. J. Hill, vol. ii, pp. 150-1; Noyes, loc. cit., pp. 305-6.

[2] Cf. J. F. Rhodes, McKinley and Roosevelt Administrations, pp. 155-6; A. D. Noyes, loc. cit., pp. 308-10.

[3] Cf. G. H. Montague, Trusts of To-day.

such giving and taking in the Harrison administration at the direction of Blaine under provisions of the McKinley law. Negotiations were renewed under the Dingley law and it was a subject which had been entrusted to John A. Kasson, a special agent of the Department of State. No less than 11 such arrangements in treaty form were made ready in 1899 and 1900 and sent to the Senate for ratification, relating for the most part to Bermuda, Jamaica and British possessions in the American hemisphere, to countries in the "Pan America" which Blaine had introduced to the national consciousness, and to France.[1] They were but small loopholes in the barrier, but the men who were opening their minds to the world had brought McKinley into sympathy with their larger aims and he, while many of the old high tariff advocates were amazed at the signs of what they considered to be a kind of treason, boldly for him, took his stand beside the more intelligent "captains of industry" in the Republican party.[2]

As the Senate had balked at the Hay-Pauncefote treaty so did it refuse to ratify the Kasson trade treaties. The President urged action. He sincerely sought it. When the period named in the treaties, two years, had expired without ratification extensions were secured from the parties to them. The policy of reciprocity, McKinley said, rested "so manifestly" upon "the principles of international equity," it had been "so repeatedly approved by the people of the United States" that he could not understand how the Senate could fail to give it "full effect." [3]

---

[1] Treaties in Senate Doc., 56th Cong. 1st sess., nos. 20, 21, 22 and 225; J. A. Kasson, Address on Reciprocity before Illinois Manufacturers' Association, Oct. 24, 1901; cf. N. Y. Nation, Jan. 17, 1901.

[2] This group was vigorously represented by Theodore C. Search of Philadelphia, president of the National Association of Manufacturers. The author of this work was in his confidence as the editor of "The Manufacturer." For this subject in this period see the files of that paper in the Library of the Historical Society of Pennsylvania and the proceedings of the annual conventions of the National Association of Manufacturers in Philadelphia, Cincinnati, New York, Boston and Detroit. Cf. testimony of T. C. Search before Industrial Commission, House Ex. Doc., 56th Cong. 2nd sess., no. 495, pp. 125–38; N. Y. Nation, June 13, 1901.

[3] Cf. W. S. Holt, Treaties Defeated by the Senate, pp. 195–7.

The Platt amendment which formulated the American demands upon the constitutional convention at Havana, if the island were to be rid of the American army, met with objection from the Cubans. It could not be supposed that such delimited independence would receive favor, though it was a matter of no great importance to us whether it should be so or not. We had fought and won the war and we had imposed our own terms upon Spain—we should do a like thing with the Cubans.[1] They despatched delegates to Washington to discuss the subject. These emissaries were informed emphatically that the Platt amendment was an expression of national sentiment. Nothing less would be accepted, nothing more would be granted. From the President, from Secretary of War Root and from others the Cubans received explanations and interpretations, but no concessions. They were told where the coaling stations would be established. We should decide later what should be done with the Isle of Pines. Nothing remained to the convention, upon the return of its commissioners, but the adoption of the principles embodied in the Platt amendment, an object which was attained in June, after three months' debate, by a majority of five votes.[2] Political parties in Cuba divided on the issue of the relations of the republic with the United States and preparations were made for the election of a president and other officers, so that, at as early a day as possible, there should be a transfer of sovereignty and the American army would embark and sail away.

That the Philippine insurrection was at an end had been stated officially and unofficially many times.[3] It was said frequently in the campaign that McKinley's reelection would terminate the war.[4] Roosevelt on the stump asserted repeatedly that Bryan and the Democratic party were alone responsible for its continuance.[5] It is true that hope had given way to

[1] Cf. N. Y. Nation, Oct. 25, 1900, and Feb. 28, 1901.

[2] Report of Sec. of War for 1901, pp. 107-27.

[3] N. Y. Nation, Dec. 20 and 27, 1900; J. H. Blount, Am. Occupation of the Philippines, p. 306.

[4] Cf. statement of Taft's Philippine Commission in Report of Sec. of War for 1900, p. 81.

[5] N. Y. Nation, Nov. 1, 8 and 15, 1900.

discouragement in the minds of the natives upon their receipt of the news of McKinley's victory and the signs which they saw around them of our intention to prosecute the work of their subjugation vigorously. Prominent insurgent leaders who were captured were deported to Guam.[1] But the will of the people was not yet broken. Petitions from leading Filipinos still reached Congress.[2] Though the expression of popular feeling in the election of 1900 was clear it could be said that the issue had not been fairly drawn in that there were many Anti-Imperialists who had voted for McKinley.[3] Early in 1901 the "guerrillas" employed an army of 60,000 American troops distributed at more than 500 stations. Upon the return of 30,000 volunteers to San Francisco, where they were mustered out of service, the number of regulars remaining in the islands was stated to be about 45,000.[4] There had been from May 5, 1900, to June 30, 1901, General MacArthur said, 1026 "contacts" with the insurgents in which 3854 had been killed and 1200 wounded, while the captured and those who voluntarily surrendered numbered 30,000. In imposing this punishment upon the enemy 245 Americans had been killed and 490 wounded.[5]

When order was restored in one island trouble commenced in others. The "rebels" moved from place to place in native boats. Thousands of men, pretending, perhaps, to friendship for the United States which they renounced as soon as the soldiers passed on to another centre of disturbance, were enlisted in the movement to hamper the establishment of American sovereignty. The Spanish government and the church had long exploited the country. Spain had gone—the Filipinos demanded the expulsion of the friars. The people had no assurance that the United States would solve this question which was given as one of the principal grounds for

---

[1] Report of Sec. of War for 1901, p. 31; Report of Lieut. Gen. Commanding for 1901, pt. 4, pp. 422–32; ibid., pt. 2, pp. 94–6.
[2] N. Y. Nation, Jan. 17 and 24, 1901.
[3] Writings of Schurz, vol. vi, pp. 257 et seq.
[4] Report of Sec. of War for 1901, pp. 32–3.
[5] Report of Lieut. Gen. Commanding for 1901, pt. 2, p. 98.

continuing resistance to our arms. The enlistment of native troops in aid of the American cause was, perhaps, the most influential factor finally in the restoration of peace. They assisted in the capture of Aguinaldo who was still at large. He may have been, to many of the insurgents, a mere legend. But he must be captured, if it were only to convince the people that their leader was no longer in the field. If he were taken they could well surrender and return to peaceful pursuits. General Frederick Funston who had had experience in bushwhacking with the Cuban insurgents against Spain before we had entered the war, and then had served in our volunteer army, now, for some time, had been a figure in exploits in the Philippines which were frequently described in the newspapers. He devised a plan, with the assistance of trusted natives, to capture the wily chieftain who was in a camp at Palanan in the province of Isabela in northern Luzon. By decoys, the forging of letters and other ruses, fit for kidnappers and bank crooks, rather than soldiers of the United States,[1] Aguinaldo was trapped in March, 1901, and carried back to Manila.[2] A manifesto was exacted of him declaring his allegiance to the United States and, upon its publication, other leaders, with their followings, yielded. This was described by the Philippine Commission, on October 1, 1901, as the "collapse of the insurrection." [3]

The civil government under the Taft commission was so far organized that on July 21, 1901, President McKinley appointed Judge Taft to be civil governor of the islands and he was installed at Manila, under this order, on the 4th of July following. The event was converted, in so far as it could be, into a patriotic occasion befitting the anniversary day of American independence. Taft addressed the company of Malays assembled before him as "My Fellow Countrymen." At the same time General MacArthur relinquished his command as

[1] Cf. N. Y. Nation, April 4, 1901.
[2] Report of Lieut. Gen. Commanding for 1901, pt. 2, pp. 99–100; Funston's report in ibid., pt. 3, pp. 122–30; Funston, Memories of Two Wars, chap. vii.
[3] Report of Commission, pt. 1, p. 7, in Report of War Dept. for 1901.

military governor to General Chaffee who had just completed his service in China.[1]

A new tariff law went into effect in November, 1901. It would reduce the cost of living. American products heretofore excluded could now enter the islands. But on the point of the admission of Philippine products coming to the United States the commission asked for greater "generosity" on the part of Congress in duties on tobacco, hemp and sugar—then trade would "increase by leaps and bounds." [2]

Though there had been hope that Aguinaldo's capture and the subsequent surrender of various bands of insurgents would end the war it was not so. There were still four or five important provinces in which disturbance continued.[3] General Chaffee warned his soldiers against "overconfidence in assumed pacified conditions." He believed that President McKinley had been misled. In no province, he said, had there been complete civil control in the past, and he doubted whether now the troops could be withdrawn anywhere with safety.[4] Truces were followed by ambushes and massacres. Peaceful industry was obstructed. From the smaller islands to which the insurgents in Luzon had fled came stories of murder and robbery. As many as three officers and 40 or 50 men in garrison in Samar in September, 1901, were killed by natives who, lately masquerading as friends, fell upon them with bolos and then mutilated and burned their bodies.[5] So the war proceeded in desultory fashion fit in manner for place in the annals of our campaigns against the Indians with cumulative gains indeed, promising complete success at length, while the commission at Manila strove to establish a system of civil government in which gradually, in the fullness of time, it made commendable progress.

[1] Report of Sec. of War for 1901, pp. 12–3; Report of Philippine Comm., pt. 1, p. 16 and app. D in pt. 2 in Report of War Dept. for 1901.

[2] Report of Comm. for 1901, pt. 1, pp. 28, 121-2, 149; cf. ibid. for 1902, pp. 6–7; J. G. Schurman, Philippine Affairs, pp. 72–6.

[3] Report of Commission for 1901, pt. 1, pp. 7–8.

[4] Report of Lieut. Gen. Commanding for 1901, pt. 5, p. 12.

[5] Report of Lieut. Gen. Commanding for 1902, pp. 625–34; W. H. Carter, Life of Chaffee, pp. 245–6.

The Supreme Court, many of the Anti-Imperialists said, would support their declarations that the government proposed for the islands gained in the war with Spain was not only un-American in theory but unconstitutional in fact.[1] Cases came to the tribunal arising from the collection of customs duties on tobacco, sugar, oranges, whiskey, brandy, diamond rings and jam which importers, when demands were made upon them, paid under protest with promise of legal contest. These were grouped in the public mind and reached the court as the "Insular Cases." The most accomplished lawyers in the land were engaged to represent the appellants. The Constitution, the debates in the convention which framed it, the proceedings of Congress, the whole record of judicial decisions, legal lore generally, as it had been brought into books by its exponents throughout the world, were explored for supporting judgment and precedent. Argument and citation filling more than 1,000 pages were assembled and put into print pursuant to concurrent resolution of Congress.[2]

Had Porto Rico and the Philippines become parts of the United States, or were they "foreign countries"? From a consideration of this question came opinions as to the right to annex distant possessions and to incorporate them, in one mode or another, in the republic and to govern their populations under systems not applied to the American people. There was division in the highest court. On the general point as to whether it was foreign or domestic territory, and whether duties were collectible at our ports upon merchandise and wares imported from Porto Rico and the other islands Justice Henry Billings Brown [3] delivered the opinion for himself and four of his associates, on cases arising from the payment of duties on articles from Porto Rico in the period following the ratification of the treaty of Paris and prior to the passage of the Foraker act, found for the complainants, and said that the money collected by the customs officers had been illegally taken from

[1] Cf. N. Y. Nation, Oct. 18 and Dec. 27, 1900.
[2] House Doc., 56th Cong. 2nd sess., no. 509; cf. Senate Doc., 56th Cong. 1st sess., no. 234.
[3] Appointed by President Harrison in 1890 from Michigan.

the importers and that these importers should be reimbursed. The strict constructionists seemed to have won a victory over McKenna, Shiras, Edward Douglass White and Horace Gray, though there were opinions and concurring opinions and opinions and dissenting opinions, and no two justices seemed to be of one mind.[1]

At this point Brown changed his ground. He took one position with reference to events in the transitional phase of our insular relations, but on the question of the Foraker act allied himself with the Imperialists.[2] In the latter case he declared that conditions might arise, and presumably had arisen, to render "the annexation of distant possessions desirable." They might be inhabited by "alien races, differing from us in religion, customs, laws, methods of taxation and modes of thought," on which account "the administration of government and justice, according to Anglo-Saxon principles" might, "for a time, be impossible," when the question must arise as to whether "large concessions ought not to be made for a time," so that, "ultimately, our own theories may be carried out and the blessings of a free government under the Constitution extended to them." The idea that all the inhabitants of annexed territory were made citizens *ipso facto*, by the act of annexation, could not be defended. "A false step" at this time might be "fatal to the development of what Chief Justice Marshall called the American Empire." Porto Rico, Justice Brown said, was "a territory appurtenant and belonging to the United States, but not a part of the United States within the revenue clauses of the Constitution."

The minority, the Chief Justice and Justices Harlan, Brewer and Peckham, said that, under the Constitution there could not be one rule of taxation in one territory and a different rule in another. There could not be, anywhere in the United States, a departure from the established system of representative government in favor of a "system of domination over distant

---

[1] De Lima v. Bidwell, Goetz v. U. S., Crossman v. U. S., Dooley v. U. S., Armstrong v. U. S.—all in 182 U. S., October term, 1900.
[2] Cf. N. Y. Nation, June 6, 1901; N. Y. Times, May 29, 1901.

provinces," wherein Congress should exercise "unrestricted power." [1]

In the confusion of mind and contradiction of statement in which the justices had involved the subject the country was left in a haze as to what they meant, though it seemed to be clear that McKinley and the administration had found a justification, if a limping one, for their courses of the past three years. The Imperialists were outspoken in expressing their satisfaction and in congratulating themselves upon the happy result.[2] The court, as it was wont to do in a time when great forces are at work, and the government is manifestly undergoing fundamental transformations of character, had yielded and followed the course of events. If the sages, in their hearts, had wished to defend the teachings and principles familiar to them, they were not brave enough to face the consequences of their honesty.[3]

The Anti-Imperialists, on their side, viewed the result without great surprise. The division of opinion in the court was consolatory. They would still protest against "the policy of conquest." [4] But there was little reason, in the judgment of those who did not delude themselves, to suppose that any step backward was now to be taken when we had gone so far down a new road. If this were the "American Empire" which Chief Justice Marshall had foreseen it was at hand.

Mr. McKinley at once, upon assuming the Presidency, had gained a reputation for accessibility. He found opportunities to meet the people. He responded freely to calls upon him for speeches and appeared before audiences in many parts of the country at which he expounded public questions in pleasant phrases, often in language which was not his own, but which

[1] Downes v. Bidwell in 182 U. S.

[2] Cf. N. Y. Times, May 28, 1901.

[3] Cf. ibid., May 30, 1901. This truth was expressed by a humorist of the time writing as Mr. Dooley—"No matter whether the Constitution follows the flag or not the Supreme Court follows the illiction returns."— Cited in C. W. Elliott, The Philippines to the End of the Military Regime p. 496; cf. Latané, America as a World Power, chap. viii; A. C. Coolidge The U. S. as a World Power, p. 141.

[4] N. Y. Nation, Jan. 17 and May 30, 1901; Writings of Schurz, vol vi, p. 275.

his facility as an orator enabled him to assimilate and utter with great effect. When he was pressed with invitations to come here and go there he would say that he would speak if the address should be prepared for him. When it was put in his hands he delivered it with a zest which made it his own.[1] He was fond of rounded periods and happy sentiment. Men like Griggs and Charles Emory Smith were drawn into his official family largely because of their rhetorical gifts.

On April 29, 1901, the President set out for the Pacific coast by way of New Orleans accompanied by members of the cabinet,[2] who held their meetings on the train as they passed along, Senator Hanna and a number of other friends. He was off on a 10,000 mile trip to inform himself of the "needs, desires and aspirations" of the nation of which he was the official head. It was a journey, said the New York Times, with no precedent in the history of the American Presidency.[3] He spoke frequently on his way, though the program must be curtailed because of the dangerous illness which overtook Mrs. McKinley in California.[4] If he dealt in his familiar platitudes, he delighted the crowds who came to greet him and listen to his hope-giving words about duty, obligation, purpose, policies of right and justice and the glories of the future in America under God.

But he also had practical suggestions which arrested attention. He spoke of larger markets for a greater United States, a matter to which he had referred in the address on the occasion of his inauguration as President for a second term on March 4th last. He had then pleaded for "broader commercial relations" and now he would present his program to the people of the South and West. In Roanoke he alluded to our "expanding markets" and the need of foreign outlets for our "surplus";[5] at Corinth, Miss., to an industrial policy that would "open up the widest markets in every part of the world for the products

[1] E. P. Oberholtzer, Memoir of J. B. McMaster in Pa. Mag. of History, Jan., 1933, p. 20.
[2] John Hay among them.—Letters of Hay, vol. iii., pp. 206–8.
[3] N. Y. Times, April 30, 1901.   [4] Letters of Hay, vol. iii., p. 209.
[5] N. Y. Times, April 30, 1901.

of American soil and American manufacture." [1] Not maxims but markets, he said at Memphis, were the need of the United States, and measures to be taken to secure them were problems to be solved "untrammelled by the past." The "open door" in China, reciprocity with South America now commanded his sincere interest, though he had been the chief of the "home market" men. [2]

A Pan-American Exposition had been projected in Buffalo in 1901. As its name indicated it was a link in the old scheme to improve feeling between the people of the Western continent, especially with a view to the betterment of their commercial relations. The proximity of Buffalo to Niagara Falls would, it was believed, draw crowds. Sums of money were appropriated by the Federal and state governments. Latin American states avowed a willingness to forward displays of their natural resources and of their arts and crafts, and the exposition was visited at the end of the summer by President McKinley, who was again accompanied by several members of his cabinet. He would deliver an address on Thursday, September 5th, "President's Day." This speech breathed the spirit of international good fellowship. Reciprocity, that trade might be extended, was one of its messages. "No narrow, sordid policy" would serve the uses of the country. A system providing for "a mutual exchange of commodities" was essential to our continued growth. "The period of exclusiveness," he said, was past— retaliation, commercial wars were unprofitable. The country could not repose in a "fancied security" that it could "forever sell everything and buy little or nothing." If tariffs were no longer needed for revenue or for protection why should they not be employed to extend and promote our markets abroad

Coming from a Republican leader who had been identified so prominently with the idea of high protection McKinley' advocacy of lower tariffs seemed to many men highly significant The press at home and abroad was commenting upon the enlargement of his views [3] when, on the afternoon of the following

---

[1] N. Y. Times, May 1, 1901. [2] Cf. N. Y. Nation, May 9, 1901.
[3] Cf. N. Y. Times, Sep. 6, 1901.

day, September 6th, in a hall on the exposition grounds where he was bowing to, and shaking hands with, the people who passed before him, he was shot by an anarchist and dangerously wounded. The man had concealed a pistol in a bandage which he had wrapped around his hand. One ball glanced from the President's breast bone, another lodged in his abdomen. Hope for his recovery was expressed, but the best medical skill could not arrest gangrene poisoning which resulted from the wound in the abdomen. He died eight days later, whereupon [1] Theodore Roosevelt, the Vice President, immediately took the oath of office and became President. Mr. McKinley's funeral services in Washington were attended with honors befitting the head of the republic. In England and throughout the world the day was marked by eulogies of his character and the saying of prayers. The hideousness of the crime, the sudden sacrifice of the life of an innocent man, kindly, sympathetic, democratic, sincere, well meaning, if he were not to be reckoned among the forceful or the great, stirred the emotions of all classes of the people. Though he opposed others they were not his enemies. His conciliatory attitude, of which so much was said in criticism of him as. a public man, saved him from the enmities which definite convictions must always invite. To his party, to his friends in the party, to Americans to whom he was the embodiment of Republican principles, his loss seemed to be irretrievable, so soon as it was understood that he was gone and that Roosevelt would be President in his stead. Had not this stormy petrel of the party been taken out of the governorship of New York and nominated for Vice President that he might be reduced to some degree of order? [2] Now, barely six months

---

[1] The assassin, Czolgosz by name, was instantly seized, convicted of murder on September 26th, less than a fortnight after the President's death, and a month later expiated his crime in the electric chair at Auburn prison.

[2] Cf. N. Y. Nation, Sept. 19, 1901. Senator Platt of New York when asked if he would attend the inaugural ceremonies at Washington on March 4, 1901, said, "Yes, I am going to see Theodore Roosevelt take he veil." (H. H. Kohlsaat, From McKinley to Harding, p. 89.) "Now look," said Hanna to Kohlsaat after McKinley's death, "that damned cowboy is President of the United States.—Ibid., p. 101.

after McKinley had been inaugurated for the second term, with 3½ years of his term not yet run, this headstrong egoist was in the first office in the land. The army was still in Cuba. The bolo men of the Philippines were still ambushing our soldiers and, with or without a treaty with England, a canal was to be built across the isthmus to connect the Atlantic and Pacific Oceans. An advocate of a large army and a powerful navy, one who spoke inconsiderately of blood and wars, had come, by accident, to the head of a government which had abandoned its traditions and recast its principles and was placing itself on the world's stage beside the European powers. Those who had been McKinley's advisers would, in all probability, have but little part in the administration of his successor, if, indeed, he should be receptive to counsel. A breaking up of the cabinet must soon ensue though the new President, in a happy gesture, invited all the heads of departments to remain in their places.[1] Business paused, confidence was disturbed by the uncertainties which were attached to the exchange of a President who was amiable and tactful to a high degree for another whose brain was often in storm, and who was given, if his past courses in politics were prophetic of the future, to sudden resolves and arbitrary action. For party government would be substituted a flashing, theatrical personal government, and the nation would go down new ways.

[1] Though he seems to have contemplated the immediate removal of Hay and Gage.—H. H. Kohlsaat, op. cit., pp. 97–9; Tyler Dennett, John Hay, pp. 341–2.

CHAPTER XL

THAT another era was at hand, that, after the Spanish War the American people had passed from one phase of their life into a new world of feelings and interests as fundamentally as they had done this as a result of the Civil War was plain to be seen. The United States which had lived comfortably and prosperously within a definite continental area, apart from the ambitions and rivalries of the European powers, had put itself beside them. We now, as they, possessed distant colonies. Hereafter we should need a greater army and a greater navy, a new diplomacy, a new statesmanship. A price would be paid for grandeur. The multiplication of public offices, ever increasing taxation, a central government rising in the complexity of its powers, with encroachments upon the liberty of the citizen, were immediately in view. It was a road from the simple, pleasant freedom, which, in the 18th century, we had fought to gain, into an involved future, from which, it was clear, to instructed and candid persons, and, as the event has proven, there could be no turning back. We were at the cross ways—a few eager and adventurous young politicians brought before the eyes of the masses glories among new scenes, and thither, with bugles blowing and drums beating, we were led.

Queen Victoria died on January 22, President McKinley on September 14, 1901. It seemed, indeed, to be the end of an era, not only for the United States but for the English-speaking race. Progress and achievement in many directions had been unprecedented. The material advancement of mankind to which England and America had contributed in preeminent ways was reviewed, and our part in forwarding the civilization of the world could be regarded with honest pride. Expositions

677

in Philadelphia in 1876, in Chicago in 1893, in Buffalo in 1901, together with smaller sectional fairs and exhibitions attested to our varied and abundant resources and the inventive ingenuity of our people.

The Twelfth Census of 1900 was intelligently planned and it gave a correct and valuable view of prevailing social conditions. The population of the country had been 50,000,000 in 1880, 63,000,000 in 1890—it was over 75,000,000 in 1900, not including Alaska, the Indian Territory and Hawaii. The first five states in the number of their inhabitants were as they had been in 1890—New York with 7,268,000, Pennsylvania with 6,302,000, Illinois with 4,821,000, Ohio with 4,157,000 and Missouri with 3,106,000. Notable increases in the population of Texas and Oklahoma told of discovered opportunities in that quarter, while a loss in Nevada afforded material for homily as to the premature making of states of territories and of inviting their politicians to Washington, especially to the United States Senate, to lower the dignity of our public life.

Among the cities New York easily led; since Brooklyn and surrounding ground had been brought into the metropolitan area its population had increased to 3,437,000, nearly one-half that of the state of New York. Chicago had 1,698,000 inhabitants and Philadelphia 1,293,000. The cities next in rank were St. Louis with 575,000 and Boston with 560,000.

It was observed with disquietude by those who gave their attention to the evils of immigration that 10,000,000 persons in the country were foreign born, while 15,000,000 more came of parents of foreign birth. Here were about 25,000,000, or one-third of the population, to be weighed against 50,000,000 of older American stock.[1]

The waxing industrial and commercial potentiality of the United States in the last years of the century, embracing almost every community, induced a feeling of comfort and ease in the people. A spirit of invincibility pervaded the nation. A tariff law of the kind which a large body of the people unquestionably believed was associated with their welfare, a stable cur-

[1] Abstract of Census of 1900.

rency of which there was assurance for a long time to come,
bumper crops of the cereals, cotton, wool, tobacco and food
animals, new discoveries of mineral deposits—gold in Alaska,
iron ore on the shores of Lake Superior, petroleum in Texas
and California—developing manufactures, large consumptive
capacity at home among a people who were raising their standards of life, and foreign outlets in a world which was enjoying
an ordered peace—all spoke of "good times" which were at
hand and seemed to be predictable indefinitely in the future.
Never in history, it has been said, had such a spectacle been
witnessed on so tremendous a scale.[1] American exports underwent great increase—they nearly doubled in value between
1896 and 1906, and in 1901 passed those of England so long
preeminent in the field of foreign trade. Immigrants poured into
our Atlantic ports to meet the demand for labor. Capital was
accumulated and sought investment abroad. London had been
the centre for international banking. English money was lent
to foreign governments and to foster enterprise in every part
of the world. Now, too, at New York money, in its abundance,
sought remunerative outlets and our capital was flowing to
Cuba and our new dependencies, to Europe and South America.
There was, indeed, a new outlook which came with a sense
of strength, an outlook which the nation had not had before.

The railroads were pressed to transport the freights which
busy mines and factories offered them and, while the era of
their greatest development in new building had passed, since
the continent was netted with their tracks, capital was still
flowing into their stocks and bonds for extensions and improvements. The length of these roads in 1901 was 192,162 miles,
with second tracks and side lines measuring 66,000 miles more,
making in all about 258,000 miles of track of which, by this
time, all but 18,000 miles were of steel.

The total revenue from traffic was more than a billion and
a half dollars annually. We had come into a period when the
lines were being collected and co-ordinated. As in manufacturing industry separate smaller units were being assembled and

[1] A. C. Coolidge, The United States as a World Power, p. 174.

merged. The roads were being formed into groups and "systems" in the interest of efficiency of operation and more economical administration. Powerful figures had appeared in the history of railway building and management in the United States—Vanderbilt, Thomas A. Scott, Jay Cooke, Henry Villard, J. Edgar Thompson, Jay Gould, Collis P. Huntington, Leland Stanford and the Californians. At least two more names were to be added to the roll as the century came to an end— James J. Hill and Edward H. Harriman. Hill, the Colossus of the Northwest, brought his railroad, the Great Northern, on a line lying north of the Northern Pacific, to Puget Sound in January, 1893. A switchback was used to scale the crest of the Cascade Mountains. It was not until December, 1900, that the tunnel, more than two and a half miles in length, was finished and trains ran through this great excavated passage way. Mr. Hill gave the attention of a remarkably able and pertinacious individuality to the interests of his railroad and the country which it penetrated. He was, in every sense of the word, an empire builder. The welfare of his company and the well being of the Northwest, in his mind, were indissolubly linked. To provide his road with revenues the population tributary to it was rapidly increased by settlement. He sought in the Eastern states outlets for trade in the products of the country. That his cars might not be carried back empty he built steamships and developed commerce with China and Japan. Largely through his influence the exports of the customs district of Puget Sound in the decade 1893–1903 increased 540 per cent.[1] Seattle would become, Mr. Hill believed, the first seaport on the Pacific coast.

In the work of upbuilding the states through which his lines passed and of forwarding the interests of his company his eyes were set upon the older Northern Pacific Railroad, which in the panic of 1893 had again met wreck. He had built his road out of earnings. He had directed its affairs prudently. He comfortably outrode the storm and he would, if he could, gain control of the parallel road, now insolvent, and in the hands

[1] J. G. Pyle, Life of J. J. Hill, vol. ii, p. 60.

of receivers, reorganize it and manage the two properties coop-
eratively. The plans for such a junction of interests were carefully laid. The bondholders, many of whom resided in Europe,
had been so deeply troubled by their Northern Pacific investments that they were ready to sell to anyone at almost any
price and "wipe its name from the face of the earth."[1] Hill
took counsel with J. Pierpont Morgan and, as the road had "run
its length,"[2] they would try to rehabilitate it financially and
establish a "community of interest." The negotiations occupied
many months on both sides of the Atlantic and an agreement
was concluded in London by which the desired result might be
gained.[3] As soon as it was announced that the roads were to
be merged the farmers of the West, who had so long been taught
to ascribe their woes to the railroad companies, and the demagogues of the East who prated about trusts and monopolies, as
they angled for votes in the ranks of the ignorant masses,
violently attacked the scheme. Hill and Morgan were about to
fasten their hold on the entire Northwest. Competition was to
be destroyed. A Great Northern stockholder brought suit in a
Federal court to see if an anti-monopoly statute of Minnesota
was not being infringed, and, on March 30, 1896, the Supreme
Court of the United States said that the plan of reorganization
must be abandoned.[4] The same ends, therefore, must be gained
by other methods. A group of men headed by Mr. Morgan,
friendly to Hill, purchased enough stock to control the company
and their interests were put into the hands of voting trustees.
Both roads, henceforth, had the advantage of Hill's capable and
intelligent management and the results were soon seen.

In the belt across the plains and the mountains south of
Hill's broad domain a figure of another kind appeared. He was
not a borderer like Hill but a product of Wall Street. By inheritance his claims upon success were, probably, greater than
those of the Irish boy who had come into the United States from
Canada. His forebears for several generations had been settled
in this country. His father was a clergyman of the Episcopal

---

[1] Pyle, op. cit., pp. 19–20.   [2] Ibid., p. 4.
[3] Ibid., pp. 14–6.   [4] Cf. ibid., pp. 18–9.

church, one of no note in his calling though others in the family had gained position and influence. The boy at fourteen became a messenger in a broker's office in New York. He, after the Civil War, founded a Wall Street house of his own, executing purchases and sales for others, and engaging in speculation on his personal account. After an experiment with the reorganization of a railroad in northern New York state he made himself a factor, with his friend, Stuyvesant Fish, in the direction of the affairs of the Illinois Central, a property which grew prosperous with Chicago. From this came new opportunities which he embraced with singular ability. A small, rather saturnine and sufficiently cunning man, whom others of larger experience found it difficult to like, he made his way from this point to one of the first places in railway management in this country.

As the Northern Pacific had succumbed in 1893 so had 155 other railroad companies with a total capital of near two and a half billion dollars. One of these was the Union Pacific, the first Pacific railroad, which stretched its tracks, aided by government grants, across the plains from Omaha on the Missouri to Cheyenne, and over the Rocky Mountains to Ogden in Utah, where it met the Central Pacific which extended to California. With the debt it owed the United States and other burdens its position was such that reorganization seemed to be hopeless. J. Pierpont Morgan, to whom its case was referred, despaired of its future. It was carried to another banker in New York, Jacob H. Schiff of Kuhn, Loeb & Company. At length this firm brought new men into a committee which took up the work of presenting the subject to capitalists and investors. Obstruction appeared, especially in Congress, without whose cooperation little could be achieved. It was discovered that these hostile influences proceeded from "that little fellow Harriman," as Mr. Morgan, by whom he was not admired, described him.[1] When faced with the charge Harriman frankly told his inquisitors that he had the intention of reorganizing the road in accordance with plans of his own in

[1] George Kennan, E. H. Harriman, vol. i, p. 123.

connection with the Illinois Central, whereupon he was, after a time, admitted to the syndicate, with the promise of a place on the board of directors. It was November, 1897, before the property passed into the hands of Mr. Schiff and his friends for a price exceeding $81,000,000. Harriman sat on the board to which he had been reluctantly elected with but few duties. He was regarded as an upstart by most, if not all, of his associates, and his manner of projecting himself into their company caused him to be viewed with a good deal of distrust.

But it soon appeared that, if he had come into railroading from a stock broker's office, his knowledge of the business was. comprehensive and detailed. He laboriously investigated the needs of the road. He travelled over it observing its condition and talking to the company's employees. He was, by this time, a man of large means, and, all the while, he was buying its common shares, knowing that the improvements which he had in view would increase their value. In May, 1898, he was chosen by Mr. Schiff to be chairman of the executive committee and, from this time onward, Harriman was preeminently the Union Pacific and the Union Pacific was Harriman. The road was practically rebuilt at an initial cost of $25,000,000. It was supplied with new cars, locomotives and mechanical equipment. Feeding lines which had belonged to the system and had been lost to it were re-acquired, and more was soon to come. The road, if it were to be useful and profitable, must have connections to the coast; there must be like efficiency of operation on the link from Ogden to San Francisco, therefore, on the Central Pacific, which had been taken over by the Southern Pacific Company and was being run under its management. The death of Collis P. Huntington in 1900 opened the way for the acquisition of this road, but it could not be obtained except by the purchase of the entire Southern Pacific system. More than $50,000,000 must be paid to secure control, an obstacle far from insurmountable. Bonds were issued on the security of the Union Pacific properties and, with the proceeds, Kuhn, Loeb & Company soon entered the market to obtain stock, though not enough shares could be had until after a treaty had been made with the managers of the Huntington estate, a result gained in March, 1901. While the negotiations were undertaken merely with the object of obtaining an outlet to the coast Harriman now came into possession of what was regarded as the greatest transportation system in the world.[1] In addition to the Central Pacific he had a continuous main line from Portland, Oregon, to New Orleans by way of San Francisco, Los Angeles, Yuma and El Paso, with extensions into Mexico. The trackage of the system was nearly 9,000 miles and it operated two or three steamship lines to Havana and New York in the east, and to Yokohama, Shanghai and other Asiatic ports in the west. Harriman said that he had bought more than a railroad—he had bought an "empire." [2]

So much, it could be supposed, might have satisfied his ambitions but more was in his mind. He would invade the north and trench upon the ground held by Mr. Hill. In this field there would be a head-on collision. Hill was not to be dealt with in any casual way. He knew the country through which his lines ran with the unfailing instincts of one who long had dwelt in it and had watched and fostered its growth. He had the great figure of Morgan at his side. Harriman had still done nothing to instate himself in the esteem of the first of American financiers. A connection with Chicago and the Middle West and with the South that freights might be assembled for transport to Puget Sound over the Hill lines was needed and desired. Any one of three systems serving this territory might have been put to the use—the Chicago and Northwestern with 5576 miles of line, or the Chicago, Milwaukee and St. Paul with 6746 miles, or the Chicago, Burlington and Quincy, "the Burlington," with 7,911 miles. The latter, from Mr. Hill's standpoint, was the best in point of construction and management, as well as for the country which its tracks penetrated. He brought Mr. Morgan to his view. The road could be acquired; it was for sale. Harriman and his banker, Mr. Schiff, of Kuhn, Loeb & Company, had formed a pool and were buying the stock in the open market with the intention of linking it with the Union

[1] George Kennan, E. H. Harriman, vol. i, p. 240.   [2] Ibid., p. 241

Pacific system. Mr. Hill and Mr. Morgan approached the directors of the company—a price was agreed upon in March, 1901, and the purchase was made for the joint account of the Great Northern and Northern Pacific for more than $200,-000,000, control passing at once, and without contest, to Mr. Hill,[1] who was now in a comfortable position. He had again usefully served the Northwest.

The affront done Harriman by the *coup* inspired that man to prompt and savage rejoinder. He had asked Hill for an interest in the Burlington as soon as he knew that it was about to pass into the hands of the Great Northern and the Northern Pacific, and he offered to furnish a third part of the purchase money. Such a participation in the ownership was not to be thought of, and Harriman laid his plans. If he could not gain a share in the management of the Burlington by one means he might secure it by another. He would take the larger to obtain the smaller; he would buy the Northern Pacific. By a sudden and secret movement he would acquire more than half the capital stock of the company through Kuhn, Loeb & Company and affiliated brokerage houses in Wall Street. Such methods were the highwayman's. Harriman, should he succeed in accomplishing his design, would entirely break up a rival trade route, and with the Southern Pacific, the Union Pacific and the Northern Pacific would dominate the railway business in the entire continent beyond the Mississippi River. Mr. Morgan had sailed for Italy, satisfied with his successful management of the Burlington deal, and Mr. Hill was on the Pacific coast. Hill came home on a fast special train to find that Harriman and his friend Schiff were taking all the Northern Pacific stock which they could bring into their nets at constantly rising prices, including large amounts disposed of by the Morgan house and other friends of Mr. Hill, without a suspicion of the trick. Such absurdly high bids brought large blocks into the market. Morgan by cable authorized purchases which stopped Harriman's progress, though not before he had secured 370,000 shares of the common

[1] J. G. Pyle, Life of Hill, vol. ii, chaps. xxvi and xxvii; George Kennan, E. H. Harriman, vol. i, chap. xi.

and a majority of the preferred stock of the company. The contest attracted speculators, and their urgent needs for stock for delivery to cover their "short" sales led to a "corner" on May 9, 1901, and a disastrous crash in Wall Street. Each side believed that its position was secure, though Harriman was not too certain of his victory, and blamed his bankers for not purchasing more common stock which, he said, he had authorized them to do, while Mr. Hill and the Morgan interests on their side must have recourse, as they knew, to a right which the Northern Pacific Company had reserved to retire its preferred stock in order to prevent the enemy from voting it. Of this right Mr. Hill and Mr. Morgan were disposed to avail themselves at once and Harriman would be defeated in his object. His discomfiture was manifest. He was left with an insufficient amount of common stock to elect a friendly board, though, to avoid litigation which seemed to impend, he was given a place upon it by Mr. Hill and Mr. Morgan in consideration of the large financial interest in the property which he had so dramatically acquired.[1]

More was to follow at once. Hill, looking to the future of his two northern trunk railroads and the Burlington system after his death, and in the interest of a lasting peace among outstanding forces, in November, 1901, formed a holding company, the Northern Securities Company, with a capital of $400,000,000, which was said by the Supreme Court of the United States in 1904, though by the narrow majority of five to four justices, to be a combination in restraint of trade and, therefore, violative of the Sherman Anti-Trust law. It must be dissolved. Mr. Harriman had joined in the organization of the new company, since it offered him advantages, and all who surrendered their shares as a result of the judgment of the court received back what they had put into it, though not until Harriman had again raised obstructions in the renewed, though vain, hope of eliminating Mr. Hill.[2]

[1] Kennan, op. cit., vol. i, chap. xii; Carl Hovey, J. Pierpont Morgan, pp. 246–50; A. D. Noyes, Forty Years of American Finance, pp. 304–7.
[2] Kennan, op. cit., vol. i, chap. xii; Pyle, op. cit., vol. i, chap. xxix. The Northern Securities case lies outside the scope of this work.

While the steam roads were sharing in the unprecedented prosperity of the age and were reaping large profits the shadow of a competition which might assume ominous proportions was seen. The progress which was being recorded year by year in the domain of electricity was truly astounding—in lighting, in the communication of intelligence, in the propulsion of machinery and in the transportation of persons and freights. The need of better methods of moving from place to place was keenly felt, especially in urban areas. Vehicles drawn by animals were crude devices and ill adapted to the quickened pace of human life. The omnibuses in towns, with their creaking wheels, their haggard horses, their untrustworthy drivers, had been followed by street cars propelled by horses or mules on iron tracks. Though the rails on which the cars ran encumbered the streets, the rapidity and convenience of the service and the profits accruing to the stockholders of the lines quieted criticism, and these horse roads, for a time, satisfied public wants. In New York the private rights of dwellers in cities were invaded in, it would have seemed, an intolerable manner. Hideous scaffolding was built in the streets and tracks were laid on it. Small locomotives belching out smoke and soot whirled rumbling trains of cars from station to station in front of the bed room windows of the inhabitants of abutting dwelling houses. Passengers mounted stairways to the elevated roads and descended stairs again when they reached their destination. Such devices were defensible only because of the necessity of taking large numbers of persons from place to place with celerity and of relieving congestion in the surface areas below.

Invention went farther and, after the horse railroads were combined by financiers, and capital was at hand for adventure, cables were installed in tubes under the tracks. These ran endlessly by power developed at central stations, and the cars were propelled by a clutch which awkwardly reached down through a slot to take hold of the moving steel rope. Cable car lines were in operation in, or soon after, 1890 in San Francisco, New York, Philadelphia, St. Louis, Washington and other cities. Though such a metropolitan transportation system quickened communication, when it was in good repair, and released horses from a service which, while they continued in it, was viewed pityingly by the humane, it was not long before the cable car was a memory and men marvelled that they should have had aught to do with such a mechanical scheme in their search for swifter and better methods of city transit. For a long time inventive electrical engineers had been trying to solve the problem. They had labored with a car which would carry its current with it in storage. But the battery was heavy, it must be recharged frequently and, while some vehicles were equipped in this way and were more or less satisfactorily operated, both on tracks and without them, success lay in another direction. The power must be in a wire strung within reach of an arm with which the car to be moved would establish contact. It would receive the current for its motor by means of a little gadget called a trolley fixed at the end of the extending arm. Millions and hundreds of millions of dollars were invested at once in trolley roads. The wire was usually overhead—when the managers of the roads were compelled to put it in a conduit under the street they would do so. But the joy which was felt by the people in thus being given wings to carry them from place to place caused them to look with indulgence upon the ugly exposed wire and the poles erected to support it.

At a meeting of the American Street Railway Association in November, 1891, the president said that three years before, in 1888, there had been only 13 electrical roads in the United States. The number in this brief period had increased to 400, representing an investment of $75,000,000. Stables were being converted into power houses, the electrician was taking the place of the farrier and the veterinary surgeon and the drivers were being trained as motormen. The companies were selling their horse cars and purchasing "trolley cars," the manufacture of which had suddenly become a great industry. It was computed that there were no less than 13,765 miles of electric railway in the United States in 1897 and nearly 22,000 in 1902; on only 947 miles of road were horse cars used in 1897, a total reduced to 259 in 1902. There were roads operating cars by electricity in every state and territory. The capital of the various companies in 1902 amounted to nearly one and a half billion dollars.

The steam railroads which were engaged in suburban passenger traffic found that their revenues were declining. There was much complaint from this side. Without cost for terminal or local stations, or for comfortable equipment, since passengers were crowded into the "trolley cars," the effort to serve suburban travellers any longer, steam railway men said, might as well be abandoned. It was not worth while for the steam road to reduce its fares and attempt to occupy the field which had been seized by its new competitor. Cheap transit by this method carried the inhabitants of cities into the country where they found more comfortable residence. It was possible for business men, as well as mechanics and factory hands, to live farther from their places of employment. To increase their revenues the companies put upon their lines airy, open cars for use in summer and encouraged the people to ride hither and yon for recreation. That this traffic might assume even greater proportions the managers established parks in the vicinity of large centres of population where they provided bands of music and other entertainment. To these resorts, often located 10 or 15 miles away, crowds of persons were drawn for afternoon and evening concerts. "Trolley trips" were arranged. Three young women in New York set forth for Boston in 1900. For only 40 miles of the way was it necessary to use the steam railroads.[1] In some neighborhoods the electric trams were carrying the mails, parcels and light freights. Everywhere horses were frightened as the new cars sped along the roads; accidents inspired the pens of writers to the newspapers. But the "trolley" lines served a new use over short distances and ominously pointed the way to a competition which would seriously trench upon the field of steam railways.[2]

[1] N. Y. Tribune, Aug. 20, 1900.
[2] The facts in regard to street railways are largely drawn from an article by Thomas Campbell-Copeland in App. Ann. Cyclop. for 1897, pp. 739–50. See also Scribner's Magazine for April, 1890; N. Y. Times, March 31, 1890.

With the application of electricity to traction a new day dawned for the elevated railroad in New York and other cities, and for those who lived beside their dirt and din and moved beneath them in danger from chunks of coal, bolts of iron, fire, lubricating oil, hot and cold water which, as the Scientific American said, were "only a part of the droppings that fell from the rattling trains." [1] The cars running on their stilt roads could now, and would soon, be propelled by electricity. Still more important with reference to the future was the feasibility of turning city passenger traffic into subways and tunnels underground. Impracticable so long as coal burning locomotives must be used, with electricity, which gave off no smoke or soot, trains could be run in cleanliness, comfort and safety in tubes under rivers and beneath city streets. Transit problems in populous centres could be solved in a new way with hope of much happier results. A Rapid Transit Commission had been giving consideration to an underground road in New York. They selected routes and in 1897 had overcome most of the legal obstacles raised against the execution of the work. Finally, on March 24, 1900, the contracts having been let, ground was formally broken in City Hall Park for a rapid transit tunnel which was to extend as far north as 182nd street, a distance of 13 miles. A second bridge over the East River to Long Island was begun, and corporate shares were being issued in 1900 for a third bridge between New York and Brooklyn. Electricity was giving encouragement to a plan to place a tube under the Hudson River to connect New York City with New Jersey.

The telegraph had linked communities, quickened trade and commerce and made over newspapers. By cables laid under the sea distance had been annihilated, so that every part of the world, except regions which still were wilderness, was within reach of every other part. More marvelous was the invention of the telephone. The telegraph conveyed electric signals, the telephone carried the voice itself. Its beginnings were small. A young Scotsman, Alexander Graham Bell, who had been giving lessons in elocution in and around Boston, especially with a

[1] Scientific American, March 25, 1893.

view to helping deaf mutes, was experimenting diligently with
the mechanics of audition and he had so far progressed with a
momentous idea that he exhibited his apparatus for carrying
sound in waves along a wire by the use of a magnet, and changing these waves back to sound at the other end, at the Centennial Exposition in Philadelphia in 1876. It attracted curious
attention. Amateur telephonists appeared everywhere. Boys
had fitted up appliances and talked for short distances over
cords into tin cans across the mouth of which membranes were
stretched. They were taught now how to use a magnet set
behind a diaphragm to create an electric circuit. Directions for
the construction of the telephone were printed in the newspapers,[1] and it was, for a time, one of the most popular of toys.
In 1877, while Bell was lecturing at Salem, he caused messages
to be transmitted to and from Boston 20 miles away. Words
spoken in Boston were distinctly heard in his lecture room and
the applause that greeted them was audible to listeners in
Boston. At Chicago in the same year Elisha Gray, who even
earlier than Bell had been experimenting in this field, gave a
demonstration and transmitted musical sounds to Milwaukee,
85 miles distant.[2] Thomas A. Edison,[3] Amos E. Dolbear and
others gave their attention to the subject and, under so many
hands, progress was rapid. In 1878 it was said that a conversation had been carried on by telephone over a distance of 250
miles. It was predicted that the contrivance would take its
place ere long among the necessities of daily life. At first the
"subscriber" simply hired two instruments and connected them
with a wire wherever he pleased, but soon the company established the line; he was given the use of the wire as well as the
instruments, and the "subscribers" were hooked together at
central exchanges.

The wires were "noisy"; the voice was indistinct; the charges
for the service were high so that only the rich could enjoy the use

---

[1] Cf. App. Ann. Cyclop. for 1877, pp. 706–8.
[2] Cf. ibid. for 1876, p. 740.
[3] George S. Bryan, Edison, the Man and his Work, chap. viii; Ellison
Hawks, Book of Electrical Wonders, pp. 132 et seq.; F. A. Jones, Life
Story of T. A. Edison, pp. 85–7

of the new device. But when the census was taken in 1880 there were 148 companies employing 3,338 persons with 34,305 miles of wire and 54,319 receiving sets.[1] One of these—that bearing the name of Bell—gained a practical monopoly of the business. Though the inventor himself was entirely wanting in practical sense some men who had come to his side lent the business able direction, beat off rival claimants to patent rights and gave it a preeminent position. The "independent" companies which were formed fell by the way; it was manifest that such a service was for the organization which had a preponderant number of stations. In placing a telephone in his house or office the subscriber wished to have the assurance of reaching the greatest possible number of persons with whom he might desire to speak.[2] The Bell Company in 1901 had 1,354,000 miles of wire. The number of instruments in the hands of licensees was nearly two million and the number of exchange connections, or calls, daily was between five and six millions. In cities there were, in large mercantile houses, "private branch exchanges," or "switchboards," doing as much business as the telephone company's exchanges in many a small town.

The distance over which the voice could be successfully transmitted was constantly increased. New York could speak to Boston in 1884, to Washington in 1889, to Buffalo in 1888.[3] A line connecting New York and Chicago was opened in 1892. In 1896 Major McKinley in his home in Canton, Ohio, plainly heard the cheering of his name over a private wire entering his house and connected with the convention hall in St. Louis, where he was being nominated for the Presidency.[4] Many of the wires were being enclosed in conduits underground, thus ridding cities of the unsightly and dangerous network of cables suspended in the air, and insuring uninterrupted service when snow fell, ice formed on the wires to bear them to the ground, and winds blew to overset the poles. The advances in ef-

[1] App. Ann. Cyclop. for 1882, p. 785.
[2] Cf. H. N. Casson, The Hist. of the Telephone.
[3] W. C. Langdon, The Beginnings of Long Distance in Bell Telephone Quarterly, Oct., 1931, and other information from Mr. Langdon.
[4] Supra, p. 390.

ficiency which were made by the company commanded general admiration. The low price to subscribers rapidly increased the use of the telephone. It was installed in remote farm houses and many of the hardships of country life were ameliorated by its agency. The telegraph held its place in long distance communication because of a cheaper rate for messages over its wires, but the telephone company perfected its system to such a degree that in and near cities it was nearly supreme. Men bought and sold stocks, houses and lands, and every sort of merchandise by telephone. The amenities of life, as well as business of all kinds, occupied the wires as girls in the exchanges connected speaking voices with listening ears and disconnected them again endlessly, at all hours of the day and night. The telephone altered the face of living and it became an indispensable factor in all human relationships.

The discovery that messages could be transmitted by telegraph through the ether without wires was the crowning triumph in the electrical field. Marconi, an Italian, developed apparatus which arrested world-wide interest. He came to New York in September, 1899, to report the international yacht races. Bulletins telling of the progress of the boats were successfully transmitted to a receiving station on shore. The army and navy were asked to adopt a system which, if yet in its early stages of development, was plainly opening another amazing new vista to man. Wireless apparatus was installed on the large transatlantic ships and a daily newspaper in New York established a station at the Nantucket light ship to gather news of incoming vessels while they were still 200 miles from Sandy Hook.[1]

At the sight of a light shining under water at the Centennial Exposition in Philadelphia in 1876 visitors to that panorama of national progress marvelled. Feeble candles of tallow or wax, lamps which burned the fat of the pig or the whale, gas made from coal, kerosene, after petroleum was found and its uses were made known to the world, had illuminated man's ways at night, but always dimly. Electricity promised to turn darkness into

[1] Cf. D. Mazzotto, Wireless Telegraphy and Telephony.

day. Streets and buildings would hereafter be flooded with a brilliant new light which physicists and engineers, aided by capital which was at hand for this use, would put at the disposal of the people, who, in a little while, would account the service indispensable. Mines could be lighted, working hours could be lengthened in offices and factories, dark and hitherto useless portions of buildings could be illuminated, the productive capacity of man would be increased and his comforts and pleasures multiplied by the extension of his power to see. The arc lamp, creating light by the current passing between two pointed pieces of carbon, sputtered in the streets, but it was a promise of better things. As it was, with occasional lapses, it distanced gas and made travel at night on the pavements of cities safer and pleasanter than ever before. The electricians of all countries employed their wits trying to devise a cheap and commercially practicable light proceeding from incandescence.

When it was announced that Edison was turning his attention to this subject, after he had done much to improve the application of electricity to telegraphy and telephony and in other fields, it was believed that the solution of the problem was near. The result of investigations in his laboratory were made public at the end of 1879. His researches led him to platinum and similar metals fusible only at high temperatures, and his perfected lamp was a coil of wire fixed in a glass vacuum tube. From this lamp he passed to one using a carbon filament, which was at first of paper and then of bamboo, and which had advantages over wire.[1] Having devised methods of turning the light off and on, of generating the current at a central station and of conveying it into homes, office buildings and business houses the stage was set for the commercial development of electricity in illumination. Edison opened his first station for the sale of current for house lighting in New York in 1882. While the arc light, which was constantly being improved, was displacing gas in the streets and in theatres, hotels, railway stations, factories and large interior spaces the incandescent

[1] Cf. F. A. Jones, Life Story of Edison, pp. 140–61; Dyer and Martin, Edison, His Life and Inventions, vol. i, chaps. xi and xiii.

light stood at the threshold of its amazing development.

The Edison and other exhibits at an electrical exhibition in Paris in 1881, and at another in Philadelphia in 1884 dazzled the eyes of all beholders. The grounds and buildings of the exposition in Philadelphia were illuminated by lights equal, it was said, to 1,500,000 candle power. Arc lamps of many inventors and manufacturers were seen, but the Brush Company which had done much to advance this kind of lighting led all others in the size of its exhibit. In the tower it had placed a lamp of 100,000 candle power. Inside the building no less than 5,600 small incandescent lamps of Edison and other experimenters in this field, not only of the United States but of foreign countries, many in colored bulbs, were set up and strung about making it a veritable fairyland. The exposition in Chicago in 1893 and the Pan-American exposition in Buffalo in 1901 were given by electricity a brilliance new to great "Fairs." The civic jubilees attending the end of the war with Spain celebrated the triumph of the electricians as much as the nation's success at arms. It was believed, in 1899, so rapid was the growth of electric lighting as an industry, that one billion dollars were invested in it. At that time, by reliable estimates, there were 500,000 arc and over 20,000,000 incandescent lamps in service in the United States. Men flashed the names and merits of their wares into the eyes of passers by. Cities soon were literally aflame at night.

For some time machine tools had been operated electrically. Belting was done away with in factories. Power came from motors instead of from steam produced by coal. Elevators moved up and down in buildings by electric power. Electric fans were installed in offices and homes to reduce the discomforts of summer. Cataracts and rapid rivers were "harnessed." The energy represented by the fall of water could be translated into electricity and, by the perfection of processes for conveying it over wires to places in need of it for industrial uses, new possibilities were at hand. Two power companies drew upon Niagara and there was much wagging of heads as commerce touched this natural wonder. Fear was spread that the beauty of the great waterfall would be impaired. Customers for the current were found in Buffalo. It was victoriously announced in 1899 that enterprising men in California were transmitting electricity derived from a cataract to users who were located 83 miles away from the generating plant.[1] The future of this marvelous and still but imperfectly understood force seemed to be limitless and the efficiencies and economies pledged to industry by electricity were a large factor in putting into the people of the United States that unconquerable spirit with which they entered the new century.

The steam railway had met a lusty competitor in the electric road. Both were in the shadow of another revolution in the business of carrying men and their goods from place to place. Trackless transportation not only in city streets but across continents was now more than a vision—it was near at hand in practical guise. For a century or more ingenious mechanics had been trying to develop a steam carriage. This device was operated with some degree of success. There were steam vans, omnibuses and tractors which trundled over the roads in various parts of the world. Finally a Frenchman devised a peculiar water tube boiler, light in weight, which generated steam instantaneously. From this time onward small passenger carriages in a practical form were made, and there were many to believe that steam would be the motive power of a vehicle which would come into general use. Others looked hopefully to electricity and predicted the perfection of a carriage using this force upon which inventors were making so many new draughts. An electromobile was successfully built and it was manufactured in large numbers. But, when all was done that could be done, the storage battery which it must carry was too heavy and the energy in the accumulator would not propel the vehicle for more than 30 miles without re-charge, though some manufacturers laid claim to a much greater range,[2] so that the use of the vehicle was practically confined to towns and cities. Easy to control, clean, noiseless, economical of operation within its

[1] Cf. N. Y. World Almanac for 1900, p. 231.
[2] Cf. N. Y. Times, Oct. 12, 1900.

limits (the cost of running a carriage for two passengers was usually not above a cent a mile) it gained a sudden and large popularity. Women could drive it confidently and safely. For pleasure riding in parks, for shopping, for social visits the electromobile was taken out to weave its way among the horse-drawn vehicles which filled the streets at a speed not greater than theirs. Buses or stages carrying storage batteries appeared in New York and other cities.[1]

Another and, as it proved, a stronger contender for the final honors in automotive engineering appeared after an engine which would utilize gasoline was devised. Many inventors in Germany, France, England and the United States were giving their attention to this problem. But the principle of vaporizing gasoline made from petroleum, mingling it with air, igniting the mixture and exploding it to develop power to drive the vehicle was complex. So much machinery was involved in the process, indeed, that many doubted the practicability of making gasoline carriages which would be commercially useful. If they were built only expert mechanics, it was said, would be able to drive them. It was granted that a vehicle propelled by such an engine would travel long distances at high speed. The cost of operation would be low especially in a country like the United States which was discovering and opening new petroleum fields. The prospect invited industrious research and the rivalries of the three kinds of automobiles, the steam, the electric and the gasoline, were watched with keen and world wide attention.[2]

One of the obstacles to advancement in the use of the automobile was the state of the American roads. Their condition was hideous as all travellers behind horses well knew. Even the street surfaces in cities were entirely unworthy of civilized life.

[1] N. Y. Tribune, Aug. 2, 1900.

[2] A writer in reviewing electrical progress in 1899 said: "It has been pretty thoroughly demonstrated that the electromobile is the most economical and available type of horseless vehicle for use on city streets, but at the present time, when it is difficult to have the requisite storage batteries recharged outside of cities and towns, the steam propelled vehicle seems to be the best adapted for interurban or touring use."— N. Y. World Almanac for 1900, pp. 230–31.

Democracy, as we had developed it in America, had failed to give us well constructed highways. The national government had built one road into the West. The states chartered turnpike companies which, after laying stones for the wagon track, might exact toll of travellers for upkeep and for the payment of interest upon the money advanced by stockholders. Other roads were built by the local governments. But the farmers who were to bear the cost of the construction of highways over which they must carry their produce to market would not vote to tax themselves in their townships and counties at a high enough rate to give their roads more than the crudest form. The result was that their animals laboriously drew their wains through the mire in wet weather, through deep dust and sand in dry weather, up hill and down dale, while in their pleasure carriages they labored rather contentedly under the same disadvantages as they proceeded to store and church and to county town.

The sudden development of interest in the bicycle fixed the people's eyes in a new way upon the roads, especially in the vicinity of large cities. The going about on two wheels by man, woman and child as a recreation and a sport reached in the 1890's the proportions of a craze. Many factories worked day and night producing bicycles for the avid riders. Each town and city had its clubs. "Runs" and "meets" were arranged. Of a Sunday morning in fair weather cycles in endless procession filled the streets bound for country or seashore. Inns and road houses had new visitors. Those who could travel 100 miles without exhaustion formed "Century Clubs." "Century runs" were announced and were participated in by hundreds of persons. Records were made and broken, prizes were awarded. Professional riders raced on their machines, international meets drew crowds of spectators as the hardy contestants in endurance tests flew over the tracks which were prepared for their competitions. A young woman who had pedalled a cycle for 700 miles in less than 80 hours set out in August, 1900, from New York to Chicago, expecting to reach that city in nine days.[1] The record

[1] N. Y. Tribune, Aug. 21, 1900.

was 39 "centuries" in 30 days—a man had established it in Philadelphia. A woman weighing less than a hundred pounds was trying on the roads of Long Island to complete 45 "centuries" in a month.[1]

Riders who fell upon their heads berated the roads over which they bumped their ways. Suddenly the people became "road conscious." Reports concerning the state of the highways were published in the newspapers for the guidance of those who would make Sunday tours. Columns on the sporting pages devoted to cycling were filled with information about the roads and the need of paving and improving them. "Cycle paths" were built between objective points. The League of American Wheelmen, the "L.A.W.," which had 25,000 members in 1892 [2] led the campaign for "good roads." The drivers of electromobiles in 1899 formed an association, the Automobile Club of America. It joined in the crusade.[3] The farmer did not understand his own business. He, more than any one else, needed properly constructed highways, if he but knew how essential they were to his comfort and prosperity.[4] He might have his letters and newspapers delivered at his door if he would make the roads fit for travel by the mail carriers. Postmaster-General Wanamaker advanced this project and held before the country a new form of public service which was begun, experimentally, in 1891 and would be extended when the people should evidence a wish to cooperate in the work of improving communications.[5]

Meantime the automobile was being developed abroad, particularly in France, where engineers were making notable progress with the machine and where the roads were hard and smooth. A popular newspaper in Paris in 1894 projected a race, The vehicles would run from Paris to Rouen and back. One

---

[1] N. Y. Tribune, Aug. 2, 1900.
[2] Letter to Wm. E. Chandler, Jan. 9, 1892, in Chandler Papers.
[3] Cf. A. A. Pope in Forum, vol. xiii, p. 115.
[4] Cf. N. Y. Tribune, Sep. 17, 1900.
[5] H. A. Gibbons, John Wanamaker, vol. i, pp. 278–82, and vol. ii, p. 91; Marshall Cushing, The Story of Our Post Office, pp. 1001, 1004–11; President McKinley's message to Congress in December, 1900; Arthur Pound, The Turning Wheel, p. 32.

hundred and two were to have taken part in the contest.
Only 15 appeared—two were "steamers," the rest were equipped
with gasoline motors. A Daimler gas carriage won, travelling
75 miles in five hours and 40 minutes. In the following year,
1895, a race from Paris to Bordeaux and back, 705 miles,
brought out 28 vehicles of which nine completed the trip.
The victor was on the road for 48 hours and 48 minutes. Later
in the same year, 1895, in November, a newspaper in Chicago
sponsored a race from that city to Milwaukee, afterward
because of the state of the roads shortened to a trip to Evanston
and return, a distance of 54 miles. Only two vehicles finished
the race, the winner having covered the course in 10 hours and
23 minutes.

From this time onward progress, if gradual, was steady and
of absorbing public interest, the advantage remaining with
France from which we borrowed the names of the various
types of motor carriage, of its parts, of the driver and of the
shed in which to run it for shelter. Its shape in the main
followed the lines of the vehicle which had been drawn by
horses and it was, in truth as in name, a "horseless carriage."
Most of the "machines" were uncovered, exposing riders to
the weather, though some, patterned after the dearborn and
the buggy, had tops with flapping curtains. The closed car,
called a limousine, was imported from Europe and was regarded as, and denominated by those to whom its appearance
was still strange, a "human show case." The important
fact was that the automobile would run, if with much and
frequent derangement of its parts, with a speed greater than
that of the horse.[1]

An autocycle, or motor cycle, was devised. The machinery
needed to propel a carriage was compressed and put under a
seat over bicycle wheels for those who wished to travel more
rapidly and with less labor than they could pedal their way
from place to place. A "bone shaker" of this type, the first
to be made in the United States, was tested on a road on Long

---

[1] Cf. C. R. Flint, Memories of an Active Life, chap. xvii; Henry Ford,
My Life and Work, pp. 28 et seq.

Island in 1900 and developed a speed of 25 miles an hour.[1]

The first automobile show of national proportions was held in Madison Square Garden in New York in November, 1900, attracting crowds of interested onlookers. Vehicles of every sort were assembled, the product of 65 different manufacturers. A track was laid in the amphitheatre upon which to demonstrate the propulsive capacity of the machines. Here omnibuses, victorias, buggies, phaetons, runabouts and carriages of all kinds, as well as motor cycles, tandems, tricycles and quadricycles were continuously spinning around at a rate of five and, in some cases, 20 miles an hour. On the roof an inclined plane was reared on scaffolding to a height of 50 feet so that the skeptical might be convinced of the hill-climbing ability of the "horseless carriage." One of the sights in the exhibition was a machine which had been driven from Cleveland, a distance of 580 miles, in 37 hours without damage except to the rims holding the rubber tires.[2]

In 1900 it was estimated that 5,000 automobiles were manufactured in the United States—the total registration in that year, beginning with four made in 1895, and including a number of imported cars, mostly from France, was 8,000.[3] Feats of daring were many. Men's names were put into the newspapers if they, in self-propelled vehicles, should run from Newport to New York, from Philadelphia to Harrisburg, from Chicago to Milwaukee. A skilful driver succeeded in going from New York to Utica—his average speed was 15 miles an hour.[4] John Brisben Walker approached the summit of Pike's Peak in his machine. He ascended by a nearly impassable road to the height of 11,000 feet and came safely down again.[5]

If rapidity of movement over a wide travelling range were required all were agreed, before 1900, that it must come from the machine driven by gasoline, and sportsmen caused vehicles to be built for them at $20,000 and other high prices in order

[1] N. Y. Tribune, Aug. 16, 1900.   [2] N. Y. Tribune, Nov. 3-10, 1900.
[3] U. S. National Automobile Chamber of Commerce, Facts and Figures.
[4] N. Y. Times, Oct. 6, 1900.   [5] Ibid., Sep. 10, 1900.

to race with other machines of mechanical efficiency. Intrepid drivers piloted them over courses at a terrific pace. An automobile was being built in Jersey City, in 1901, which would travel at a rate of 70 miles an hour.

But no such speed could be enjoyed by drivers on country roads or city streets—in the first place, because the highways were not conducive to the attainment of speed; secondly, because automotive machinery would not enable a driver to gain great velocity, and finally, because of legal inhibitions. Horses which had a traditional right to the roads were frightened as they had been by the trolley car. Their owners who were predominant in number would for some time resent the intrusion of motor cars on the highways. Pedestrians protested and emphasized the dangers to which they were subjected. "A very small percentage of the people of Massachusetts, mainly for their own amusement, are using a new machine," Moorfield Storey observed in 1903. They wished to run it at "a very high rate of speed"; he had a neighbor who did not hesitate to travel at from 30 to 35 miles an hour, and after dark. The glaring acetylene headlights would scare "any horse that lives." Mr. Storey was "entirely unwilling" himself "to ride in one of these machines" and he had "no sympathy" with those, "who for their own sport" would imperil the lives of others. [1] Steps were taken in some communities to indict the automobile as a "nuisance" and to ban it from the roads. [2]

In New York and other cities, in 1901, no automobile was permitted to travel faster than eight miles an hour. In Hempstead, Long Island, the allowable speed was increased from six to ten miles an hour upon petition of members of the Meadowbrook Hunt Club. [3] To each machine at night a lighted lantern, visible at a distance of 200 feet, must be attached and each, too,

[1] M. A. DeWolfe Howe, Moorfield Storey, p. 189.
[2] N. Y. Times, Sep. 24 and Oct. 1, 1900. Automobiles were called "devil wagons." The Boston Evening Transcript found a prophetic allusion to them in the Bible, Nahum, second chapter, fourth verse: "The chariots shall rage in the streets, they shall justle one against another in the roadways; they shall seem like torches, they shall run like the lightnings." —John Hay, Letters and Diary, vol. iii, p. 259.
[3] N. Y. Times, Sep. 8, 1900.

must be equipped with a whistle or alarm bell to be sounded on approaching, and when crossing, intersecting streets. Automobiles must draw aside and not impede firemen in the performance of their duties. No two machines should be operated abreast without permission of the chief of police. When going aboard ferry boats the gasoline must be removed from the tanks. Drivers poured it into the gutters of the streets where, they said, it was a greater menace than it could have been on the boats.[1]

If gasoline would propel pleasure carriages and riders of bicycles it was plain that it could be made to move wagons, drays and vans, and that, in a little while, the new engine would have a large part in the transportation of goods, which would leave the railways and pass over the public roads, when they should be made firm enough to bear moving machinery. Farmers could work the soil and harvest their crops with the aid of the new engine. Extensive changes in this direction were forecast.

So long as gasoline could be purchased at ten cents a gallon it was believed that a carriage with two passengers in it could be operated for less than a half cent per mile. A low price for this fuel for the engine seemed to be assured until politicians should see in it an available source of revenue and should lay taxes upon it. The Pennsylvania petroleum fields were failing but pools which seemed to be almost inexhaustible were discovered in other parts of the country. Already, in 1887, southern California's rich supply had been tapped by the drills, and was being run in pipes to the sea for shipment to the East or to foreign ports. Three millions of dollars were invested in the business in the region around Los Angeles, which had come to be a city of 70,000 inhabitants.[2] So rapid were subsequent developments there that the output of the wells in the year 1901 was 16,000,000 barrels. The abundance and cheapness of petroleum were such that it was being used as a fuel in ferry boats and steamships and in locomotives on the South-

[1] See articles on automobiles in App. Ann. Cyclop. for 1898 and 1901; N. Y. Tribune, Nov. 6, 1900.
[2] App. Ann. Cyclop. for 1887 p. 88.

ern Pacific Railroad. Manufacturers were burning oil instead of coal for the generation of steam.[1] In 1901 oil was "struck" by a drill in Corsicana in Texas and a six inch stream was thrown into the air to a height of 175 feet. This geyser was but the first of many. The excitement was intense. In a few months production in Texas was at the rate of 1,000,000 barrels a day.[2]

Where petroleum was there too, frequently, were great volumes of inflammable gas. It was found even in regions where oil was not recoverable in commercial quantities. Beginning in 1885 wells were drilled for natural gas in western Pennsylvania, Ohio, Indiana and West Virginia, and it was immediately turned into pipes to be sent to Pittsburgh and many other centres of population for use in lighting, cooking, heating and as a fuel in manufactories. It was a boon of cheapness and cleanliness to that part of the country where bituminous coal had enshrouded industrial towns and cities with a pall of smoke.[3]

The invention of the typewriter meant another change in the habits of man, releasing as it would the amanuensis who, in long hand, had laboriously copied archival and other papers, and leading to a complete revolution in the system of letter writing. Clumsy contrivances designed to do the work of the pen had been evolved by mechanics who for a long time had been active in this field. An inventor in Massachusetts was granted a United States patent for a "chirographer" in 1843, and other machines called typographers, pterotypes and by other names appeared. The essential feature of the device which was passing to a practical form was a keyboard with letters upon it with piano forte action, the depression of the key which held the wanted letter making its mark upon paper to produce words and sentences. A man named Francis, another named Hall, and another named Sholes were working on the right principle, but it was from the Sholes machine that results came. It was exhibited and made widely known at

[1] App. Ann. Cyclop. for 1901, pp. 674, 767; N. Y. Times, July 24, 1901.
[2] App. Ann. Cyclop. for 1901, p. 767.
[3] Ibid. for 1887, p. 386; ibid. for 1888, p. 680; ibid. for 1898, p. 287.

the Centennial Exposition in Philadelphia in 1876. It was manufactured and after 1880 was sold by a firm bearing the name of Remington in Ilion, N. Y.[1] From this point progress was rapid and the business spread into other countries, with rivals such as the Caligraph, the Brooks, the Yost, the Hammond, the Smith-Premier, and many others which, if having merit, bore names that could not be made so widely known.[2] "Colleges" were established to teach the facile use of the machine to young people who entered into competitive trials of speed. In a short while no business house was without the typewriter. Its uses grew. The toilsome writing of letters by pen and ink, the copying of them in letter books ended. All commercial correspondence was typewritten. A business man read a letter in more or less legible handwriting impatiently. The machine quickened, as it facilitated in other ways, business transactions. Girls who became proficient in the use of the instrument found a new employment. Thousands of them left the home to which before women had been largely confined, and, like men, went to their tasks in town each morning. In shops and warehouses, in doctors', lawyers' and brokers' offices, in banks, in public buildings they were seen playing upon the keys of letter writing machines. Ladies employed secretaries adept in the art and much social correspondence was carried on in printed characters. Soon authors must "type" their manuscript, if publishers were to read it, and printers were to be given the task of setting it up. Public archives must be typewritten. If the labor attendant upon the use of the pen, the trouble of deciphering handwriting and the misunderstandings resulting from its indistinctions were done away with, so were many of the gentilities and elegancies which men and women had earlier put into letters. Indeed there were not a few to believe that an art which had held delights was being destroyed by machinery. All correspondence was being commercialized. As it was no longer necessary to write with the pen, the ability to do so was being lost by disuse.

[1] Geo. S. Bryan, Edison, the Man and His Work, pp. 71–2.
[2] Cf. article on Typewriters in App. Ann. Cyclop. for 1890, p. 807.

The printer, as well as the writer, was to enjoy emancipation from some of his ancient servitudes. He had been picking out little metal types from a case to form words, setting them in lines in a composing stick, which were assembled for the forms to be put upon the presses for imprint on paper. Inventors, one of them named Mergenthaler, devised a machine on the principle of the typewriter. Letters, when the levers were pressed on the board, fell down and were cast in metal in lines with a rapidity which spelled the doom of the method which, since Gutenberg's time, had been followed in the printing shop. The book, the magazine and the newspaper would hereafter be set up by a mechanical process. The compositor must learn to use it or pass from the scene, just as the amanuensis was driven to instruct himself regarding the writing machine.

At least two discoveries of far reaching significance came to affect the lives of men through medicine—the X Ray and the control of yellow fever. Wilhelm Conrad Röntgen was a physicist connected with the German university at Würzburg. In December, 1895, he appeared before a physico-medical society in that place and described researches which led to his finding a new form of energy which was radiated by passing electricity through a highly exhausted discharge tube. Since he did not know the precise nature of the rays he called them X rays, though, by others, they were often called Röntgen rays. It was observed that they would penetrate bodies opaque to ordinary light. For example, when the human hand was interposed between the tube containing the rays and a sensitized photographic plate, only the lines of the skeleton of the hand were recorded upon it. The possibilities of such a discovery in relation to medicine were immediately understood. The physician and surgeon could now see through the human body. They could diagnose many forms of disease with new intelligence. The newspapers—all people, indeed, seized upon this feature of the discovery, leaving its other importances to science. Hereafter bullets and foreign objects in the human frame could be certainly located. In the case of fractured and dislocated bones the point to be addressed was made visible—

the doctor need no longer grope blindly with reference to many of the ills that they were expected to cure or alleviate. Army surgeons made use of the X ray during the Spanish-American war. Dentists were to find it of wide and useful application in the treatment of teeth.[1]

Probably the most salutary result of the war with Spain was a Yellow Fever Commission which, in 1900, visited Cuba where experiments were conducted, and which brought to its last account an epidemic disease held to be one of the principal enemies of the human family. From the earliest years in the history of our foreign commerce ships arrived at our ports in August and September with "yellow jack." Elaborate quarantine regulations were devised and enforced to protect the country from contagion. Excited men, intent upon stopping all incoming travel, guarded the approaches of some rude communities with shot guns. Protective measures of whatever kind often failed and the disease was raging ere danger was suspected. Though much was effected in the North, in our Southern states, where the climate seemed to favor the spread of fevers, and where communication with infected areas was more frequent, each summer was looked forward to with dread. In New Orleans and other ports the disease was devastating and, before its course was stayed by approaching winter, thousands of lives would be swept away. Business was interrupted. It was computed that a visitation of yellow fever cost the country $100,000,000.[2] Our interest in prevention was now very much increased—the experience of the troops ere they could be removed from Santiago and its neighborhood in the summer of 1898 drew general attention to the disease. It was making inroads upon the army in the Philippines. The French, while they were trying to dig the canal at Panama, died like flies.[3] If we were to build an isthmian canal, which was demanded in louder and louder tones, we, too, would

---

[1] App. Ann. Cyclop. for 1896, p. 690; Wm. H. Meadowcroft, The A B C of the X Rays; A. B. Chatwood, The New Photography, pt. 1.

[2] N. Y. Times, July 11, 1901.

[3] Cf. Franklin Martin, W. C. Gorgas, pp. 20–1; M. D. Gorgas and B. J. Hendrick, W. C. Gorgas, pp. 146–7.

encounter fatal fevers. The war, indeed, had been justified in the beginning, in some degree, by the wish to "clean up" Cuba, so that it should not send us its pests.

That the mosquito spread disease was not a new theory. Recently the most important discoveries had been made regarding the anophéles, a species which had been identified as a carrier of malaria. The complete life cycle of the parasite was studied. The results of the researches of others came into the hands of Dr. Patrick Manson, a Scotsman, who in 1894 announced his noteworthy conclusions. A British army officer in the medical service in India, Major Ronald Ross, tested the theory in that country where the disease raged so fatally and advanced the investigation in valuable ways. Others visited a malarial district on the Roman Campagna to breathe the night air and expose themselves in every manner to the infection. While they dwelt in a house protected from mosquitoes, they remained in perfect health, though the population around them suffered from the malady. It was clear that the way to combat malaria was to exterminate the mosquito and in America, as in other countries, attack was made upon breeding places, such as rain barrels and stagnant pools, and malarial patients were carefully guarded so that they might not be bitten by this convicted bearer of the destructive germ.[1]

From this discovery to that concerning yellow fever may not have been far, but it involved painstaking scientific investigation along similar lines. Dr. Carlos J. Finlay, a native of Cuba, the son of a Scotsman, had persistently for many years entertained and stated the theory that the mosquito was the host of the yellow fever parasite.[2] General Leonard Wood had been left in Santiago when the infected troops sailed for Montauk Point. He immediately engaged in efforts to rid the city of filth and make its air, in so far as possible, salubrious.[3]

[1] App. Ann. Cyclop. for 1901, pp. 343–8; Howard A. Kelly, Walter Reed and Yellow Fever, pp. 104–14.
[2] Cf. Report of Sec. of War for 1901, pt. 2, Report of Surgeon General, pp. 7–9–20; M. D. Gorgas and B. J. Hendrick, W. C. Gorgas, pp. 92–8; Howard A. Kelly, Walter Reed and Yellow Fever, pp. 115–21.
[3] E. F. Wood, Leonard Wood, pp. 100–7.

When he became governor of Cuba and removed to Havana his interest in public health was extended to the whole island.[1] A physician, as he had been, he brought other men in the medical service around him and a highly important work in sanitation was done. Every city had its health officer, Major William C. Gorgas being in charge of the subject in Havana. Wood and Gorgas welcomed the appointment in 1900 by Surgeon-General Miller Sternberg of the United States Army, a distinguished bacteriologist,[2] of a commission which would give particular care to the problems connected with yellow fever. Major Walter Reed headed it.[3] With the assistance of self sacrificing volunteers from the United States army tests were conducted to develop the mosquito theory. The soiled bedding and clothing used in yellow fever hospitals were tried as a means of giving the disease to the men. So was the direct injection of blood from yellow fever patients. The volunteers were confined in rooms which were not ventilated in order to dispose of the idea that fresh air would ward off the infection. Always they were protected from mosquitoes by wire screening at the doors and windows. In another building mosquitoes were introduced. They were of the species known as stegomyia fasciata. The men who were bitten developed the disease and one of them, a valued member of the commission, who had submitted himself to experimentation, died in the interest of science. The point was established that too much emphasis had been put upon disinfection and quarantine regulations, since the danger of importing infected mosquitoes in baggage and freight, because of their brief life, was slight. Instead assault should be begun upon the insect communicating the disease to the human body, as in the case of the malaria-bearing mosquito.

[1] The truly frightful conditions under which the people lived in Havana were the subject of an investigation for the government of the United States by Col. George E. Waring, Jr. who contracted disease while in the performance of his duty and died, soon after his return home, before making his report. The preliminary data for the report were brought together in an article by G. E. Hill in the Forum for January, 1899.

[2] Cf. Howard A. Kelly, Walter Reed and Yellow Fever, chap. vi; Franklin Martin, W. C. Gorgas, p. 6.

[3] Report of Sec. of War for 1900, pt. 2, p. 532.

The application of Major Reed's findings had for its result in 1901 the practical riddance of Havana of yellow fever "for the first time in more than 140 years." [1] The "inestimable value of this service to mankind, the saving of thousands of lives and the deliverance of the Atlantic seacoast from constant apprehension," demanded, said the Secretary of War, "special recognition from the government of the United States." [2] Reed had "shown how the human race might be freed from the scourge of yellow fever as Jenner showed how it might be freed from the deadly ravages of small pox." [3] At the same time the use of the new knowledge regarding malaria materially reduced the mortality from this prolific source.[4]

Foreign immigration engaged the interest of every responsible mind. The melding of different races was a task which at times seemed to be insuperable and the reception of, and the experience of living beside, incompatible branches of the same race, brought to our shores by the transatlantic steamships, furnished problems which, if we had long ignored them, were soon to assume very disagreeable guise.

In a portion of the country which was settled by hysterical and reckless men a handful of Chinese had aroused an antipathy out of all proportion to any possible harm which had come from their immigration. Objection to them was largely based on selfishness and it was loudly voiced by the organized white trades unions. Much was said by these unions of "monopoly," but they themselves were monopolists; they would establish a monopoly of labor. The competition of cheap and efficient

---

[1] Report of Sec. of War for 1901, pp. 39–40; ibid., pt. 2, report of Surgeon General, pp. 667, 683–4; 714—40; J. F. Rhodes, The McKinley and Roosevelt Administrations, p. 178; App. Ann. Cyclop. for 1901, pp. 348–50; Franklin Martin, W. C. Gorgas, pp. 8–17; Howard A. Kelly, Walter Reed and Yellow Fever, chaps. vii and viii.

[2] Report of Sec. of War for 1902, p. 10.

[3] Ibid., p. 595; Senate Doc., 59th Cong. 2nd sess., no. 10; Senate Report, 70th Cong. 2nd sess., no. 1912; Senate Doc., 61st Cong. 2nd sess., no. 520; M. D. Gorgas and B. J. Hendrick, W. C. Gorgas, pp. 129–35; E. F. Wood, Leonard Wood, chap. xi; H. Hagedorn, Leonard Wood, vol. i, p. 280; J. H. Sears, The Career of Leonard Wood, pp. 139–45.

[4] Report of Sec. of War for 1901, pt. 2, pp. 683, 706–7; Franklin Martin, W. C. Gorgas, pp. 16–7.

workingmen was not to be tolerated and, having skins of another hue and strange habits of living, prejudice was easily awakened. That the rest of the country should not become unmindful of the sentiment on the Pacific coast outrages by mobs upon the Chinese, though not so frequent as prior to the passage of the exclusion laws, were continued. Large sums of public money were expended in badgering them. Chinese quarters in cities were raided, certificates were demanded. It was broadly asserted, and the fact was substantiated by proof, that no Chinese person in the United States was safe from arrest.[1] The cost of dealing with arriving Chinese and of making them understand that they were a species of vermin was about $50 per head. The immigration service spent as much on each Chinaman as on 28 aliens of other kinds.[2] Powderly, the ex-master workman of the Knights of Labor who had been appointed Commissioner General of Immigration by McKinley, actively aided every officer under him who was engaged in irritating Chinamen coming to our ports.[3] The exclusion laws were extended to the Philippines by military order and to the Hawaiian Islands by act of Congress, not at the desire of Hawaii, but to satisfy the demands of union labor in the United States.[4]

A Chinese minister in Washington, Wu Ting Fang, who came to his post in 1897, to remain for five years, fearlessly pleaded the cause of his people. His finesse, whether in writing or speech, his devastating satire, albeit with good humor, drew public attention to the gross injustices of our Chinese policy and led to some reactions of feeling. But politics still demanded that no quarter be given lest labor rise at the polls to wreak vengeance upon the party which should soften its attitude toward this people, though some comprehension of the foolishness of the crusade had come to pervade even the Sand Lot men on the Pacific coast when they were confronted by great bodies of Italians and other white aliens, who were capable of being disliked and who were creating foreign quarters in San Francisco

[1] Cf. M. R. Coolidge, Chinese Immigration, pp. 323–4, 326–7, 331.
[2] Ibid., p. 310.   [3] Ibid., pp. 240, 328.
[4] Ibid., pp. 240–1. See discussion of the subject in Congressional Record in 1902 summarized in App. Ann. Cyclop. for 1902, pp. 185 et seq.

and other cities as filthy as Chinatown.[1] That all their theories as to the numbers of Chinese about which they had so much concern had been ridiculously overstated was seen when it was learned that there were, in 1900, according to the Census returns, only 89,863 in the entire United States.[2] There had never been more than 100,000 or 125,000.

The negro problem, on the other hand, involved our contact with nearly nine million persons. In 1900 one in nine persons in the United States, approximately, was a negro or of negro descent from ancestors brought from Africa for labor to be performed, for the most part, in slavery. Eighty nine per cent. of these negroes were living in 14 states, the old slave states, of which 11 had seceded from the Union. They were settled on the southern Atlantic seaboard and its hinterland. In two states, Mississippi and South Carolina, the colored were still more numerous than the white population. The blacks made up more than 45 per cent. of the population of Georgia, Alabama and Louisiana. The idea of deporting them to Africa or elsewhere was nourished by few persons. The return of Afro-Americans to Liberia had practically ceased. Unfavorable accounts of the country, its climate, and the little which the ignorant and lazy negroes who had been taken there by our philanthropists had achieved, properly deterred others from leaving the shores of the United States for such a land.[3] Only about 1800 persons, barring native tribesmen, lived in the "republic." And the number was not increased. A negro named Ellis, in 1894, tried to establish a colony for people of his race in Mexico. But the scheme soon failed; the emigrants who were to plant cotton said that they had been deluded by the agents who had enticed them from their homes in Georgia and Alabama and, after the most unhappy experiences, they came home.[4]

The facts were established in the minds of rational men that

[1] Cf. M. R. Coolidge, Chinese Immigration, pp. 235–6.
[2] Abstract of Census of 1900, p. 8.
[3] For an English opinion of the experiment see Henry F. Reeve, The Black Republic.
[4] App. Ann. Cyclop. for 1895, p. 489.

we had brought the negroes to this continent over a long period of years, that they and their descendants were in our midst, that their labor, if often inefficient, was valuable and in some fields indispensable. We must adjust ourselves to them, they must adjust themselves to us, a work which was progressing more successfully than many observers would have had us believe.

Nevertheless it was undeniable that they were being treated unfairly in many particulars and did not enjoy that equal protection under the laws which humanitarians and vindictive politicians, who, in the North, had become idealists for their own ends, had earlier said that the race should enjoy. The negro must "remain in his place"—in separate coaches on the railways, in separate hotels, restaurants, theatres and schools. He was to be educated, but the facilities were meagre. The sum allotted for this use in the South was not a tenth part of what was appropriated for the support of white schools.[1]

The moral character of the negroes was not high. They perpetrated many smaller and some most heinous crimes. Because of race prejudice they were often subjected to punishments not meted out to white misdemeanants for like offences. Nor was similar care used in establishing the facts. The innocent were made to suffer with the guilty and such inefficiency in the administration of criminal law was justified on the ground that the body of the race must be, in a degree, terrorized if the whites were to dwell comfortably among them. In the same way lynching was defended. The law was too slow. For efficacy punishment should be prompt. For some kinds of crime the law prescribed penalties which did not measure its gravity— they should be more drastic if society were to be protected from the dangers with which the whites were beset in the South. It was lame reasoning, though truth was concealed in it, for legal procedure was clumsy, jails were insecure and awful sinners escaped their deserts.

Some head was being made against the famous barbarity,

[1] Cf. P. Lewinson, Race, Class and Party, pp. 62–3; J. R. Commons, Races and Immigrants in America, p. 43.

though it was slow. Lynchings were catalogued by Northern newspapers at the end of each year and the results were widely published. Preachers pictured in dark colors a civilization in which such outrages could occur. Humanitarians organized public opinion,[1] and the finger of scorn was pointed at the South whenever new hangings and burnings at the stake were announced. That the Southern people of the worthy classes felt the reproach was evidenced by anti-lynching planks in political party platforms. Governors denounced such brutishness—it was a blot on the reputation of their states. Anti-lynching laws were passed by legislatures in Georgia and North Carolina in 1893, Tennessee, Kentucky and Texas in 1897. Northern states in which there were isolated lynchings took similar measures in order to end, if possible, such disorder. Ohio in 1898 and Indiana in 1899, South Carolina in 1895 and Alabama in 1901 put like provisions in their constitutions. The various schemes increased the powers and responsibilities of the sheriffs into whose custody prisoners came, and named penalties designed to prevent these officers from too easily yielding to threat; prescribed new and harder punishment for lynchers, and, in some instances, attempted to lay on the taxpayers in local districts money damages for the benefit of the victims of mobs.[2]

In few but rude communities would men speak in defence of the practice of trying, convicting and punishing criminals by mobs instead of by legal process. But there were many parts of the South in which the people, white as well as black, were not far above savagery. Horrible crimes were committed. When they could be fastened on the negroes the blood lust of white ruffians could not be controlled by such public agencies as existed for the maintenance of law and order. Negro baiting was a sport and at such times, on the theory that community action would serve as a deterrent to new crime and under the impulsion of the hard old creed of an eye for an eye and a tooth for a tooth, lynching continued.

[1] Cf. J. E. Cutler, Lynch Law, pp. 229–30.
[2] Ibid., pp. 230–46; App. Ann. Cyclop. for 1897, pp. 11 and 813; ibid. for 1898, p. 699; ibid. for 1899, p. 323; ibid. for 1901, p. 66.

In November, 1895, three negroes, two of them females, who were charged with entering a church in South Carolina and taking a Bible, were visited by a mob at midnight, stripped of their clothing and beaten by buggy traces. Two died of their injuries. One young woman survived. Several men were identified and tried. The jury, to their shame, brought in a verdict of not guilty and the authors of the frightful outrage, as was so frequently the case on such occasions, went free.[1] A man and a woman were lynched in a parish in Louisiana in January, 1896; two men were taken from a jail in February and another in March in other parts of the state to be brutally killed by mobs.[2]

In the next year three negroes who were charged with murder, though they had not been convicted of their crimes, were taken from the sheriffs in as many parts of Mississippi and hanged.[3] In Louisiana three blacks were killed by a mob on January 20 and three more on December 12, 1897.[4] One was chained and burned to death in the woods in North Carolina on Thanksgiving Day, 1897, and in the same year mobs seized and slew a number of negroes accused of divers enormities in Georgia and South Carolina.

In 1898 Mississippi and the Carolinas furnished race disorders which shocked the country. A woman and four of her children were murdered. A negro who, it was suspected, had committed the deed was taken from the deputy sheriff by a mob, though prominent citizens tried to deter them. They put a plow line around his neck, dragged him up a hill, mounted him on a horse which was driven under a tree, to a limb of which they fastened the rope, and drove the horse away, leaving him to dangle in the air. He still lived when respectable persons cut him down, but he was seized again by the mob to be hanged until he was dead.[5] It was said that in 1898 no less than 14 lynchings had occurred in South Carolina. In a place called Lake City a negro postmaster, of whose character nothing derogatory had been said, had been twice shot at by assassins. On the night of February 21st ruffians surrounded his house,

[1] App. Ann. Cyclop. for 1896, p. 704.   [2] Ibid., p. 423.
[3] Ibid. for 1897, p. 532.   [4] Ibid., p. 490.   [5] Ibid. for 1898, p. 461.

poured oil on it and set it on fire. When the family tried to escape from the flames the mob levelled shot guns at them, killed the postmaster and a child two years old and maimed his wife, his son and two daughters.

In Georgia, in 1899, negroes suspected of starting incendiary fires were held in an improvised jail. The guards were over-powered by a mob. The men were made to stand in a row. Two volleys were fired at them. Four were killed and another was mortally wounded. A negro in another part of Georgia, for a horrible murder, was chained to a tree, tortured and burned to death in the sight of a mob of 2,000 persons.[1] Similar brutalities disgraced the South in 1900, Louisiana and Mississippi surpassing their record for lawlessness at the expense of the blacks. In 1901 one negro was burned, one was shot and five were hanged in Alabama.[2] Fourteen persons in the same year were lynched in Mississippi; two were burned, two shot and ten hanged.[3] Two negroes accused of rape were burned in Texas in 1901,[4] another in 1902[5]—all under circumstances indicating among some classes of the people a turpitude at variance with the most rudimentary principles of civilization.

A study of the subject has shown that in the decade, 1890–1900, the greatest number of lynchings in a year in the United States occurred in 1892 with a total of 235, of which 156 were of negroes. There were 200—155 negroes—in 1893; 197—135 negroes—in 1894, and 165—122 negroes—in 1897. The lowest number in a year was 107 in 1899.[6] In 22 years, from 1882 to 1903 inclusive, 1985 negroes were lynched in the Southern states, Mississippi leading with 294, followed by Georgia with 241, Louisiana 232, Texas 199 and Alabama 198. [7]

Lynchings often assumed the dimensions of riots. White-caps and regulators were a menace of which the South was not yet rid. In 1898 a mob pursued a negro in Mississippi who had

---

[1] App. Ann. Cyclop. for 1899, p. 322.　[2] Ibid. for 1901, p. 666.　[3] Ibid. p. 721.
[4] Ibid. p. 769.　[5] Ibid. for 1902, p. 806.　[6] Cutler, Lynch Law, p. 161.
[7] These compilations are only approximately reliable, but they are sufficiently so for consideration.—Cutler, Lynch Law, p. 179; cf. ibid., p. 183; Wm. P. Pickett, The Negro Problem, pp. 178–203.

had an altercation with his white employer. Blacks shot at whites from the bushes and killed their leader. In revenge the next day six negroes were killed.[1] In riots lasting for days in connection with an election in South Carolina in 1898 at least a dozen negroes were slain. Five were tied to a log and shot together.[2]

North Carolina in the same year was in a condition approaching civil revolution as a result of race strife. Because of factional quarrels between the old and intelligent elements of the Democratic party, whom the newspapers were fond of calling Bourbons, and the unpropertied whites in that party who were intent on improving their lot through issues of paper and silver money and the quack remedies of the Populists, the Republicans in 1896 had elected the governor and legislature. It was a return to the conditions which had prevailed after the war. White men were brought before black magistrates. Though the negroes held at least 1,000 offices, and some counties in which they predominated were, it was said, entirely Africanized, they clamored for more. Their numerical strength—there were in the Republican party in South Carolina, they said, 120,000 negroes and but 25,000 whites—required a fairer distribution of the fruits of victory. Relations between the races were soon intolerable. Negroes shot white men, white men shot negroes. Fear of arson, assassination and riot was in every mind. Bloodhounds were released to track blacks who ran into the swamps. The "white man's party" had been divided and negro domination again hung like a dark cloud over the homes of the state. North Carolina must be "redeemed" at the election in 1898. In August of that year, in Wilmington, where conditions were desperate, a negro newspaper editor who had said that white men were careless in protecting their women in the South, thus inviting the commission of rape, and who endeavored to condone the crime which led to, or was at any rate made the excuse for, so many lynchings,[3] was attacked by a mob. He made his escape, but his printing office was burned. Twelve negroes were

---

[1] App. Ann. Cyclop. for 1898, p. 460.   [2] Ibid., p. 700.
[3] Cf. J. E. Cutler, Lynch Law, pp. 177–8.

killed. Others were escorted to the state line and told never to
return. A white carpetbagger was taken to a railway station by
a squad of militiamen, with bayonets fixed. He was nearly
lynched before the train bound north arrived. The Democrats
won the election and jubilees were held throughout the state.[1]

There were ignorant and dangerous elements in the population
of New Orleans. White laborers on the docks who screwed, or
loaded, bales of cotton into the holds of vessels, members of a
Screwmen's Union, decided in 1894 that they would no longer
work beside negroes. The blacks were driven from the levees,
wharves were burned, cotton was destroyed and, in encounters
on March 11 and 12, 1895, four were killed and eight were seriously hurt. The militia were called to the scene.

Bloody disturbances in New Orleans in the summer of 1900
followed attempts to arrest two negroes. A policeman was shot
and a mob of hoodlums assembled and roamed the streets,
killing and maiming blacks of both sexes. A colored school
house was burned. Fourteen persons were dead and many more
were seriously hurt before order was restored.[2]

Mob violence resulting from attacks of negroes on women and
girl children was particularly difficult to control. It was impossible to deny that public opinion rather generally justified
lynching under these circumstances. In many cases, in spite
of an increasing respect for orderly punitive processes, under
forms of law, sheriffs and other guards of prisoners often released negro culprits and suspects with too little resistance.
When anti-lynching laws were to be enforced witnesses would
not inform upon or identify members of mobs. White juries
would not indict or convict white men for mob murders, though
these outrages assumed the most atrocious forms,[3] and even
judges, mayors of cities and governors of states evaded their
plain duty and defended by inaction, if not by positive declaration, the taking of summary vengeance on the bodies of blacks.
The only way to stop the punishment, i.e. burning at the stake,

[1] H. L. West in Forum for January, 1899; App. Ann. Cyclop. for 1898,
p. 598.
[2] App. Ann. Cyclop. for 1900, p. 337.
[3] Ibid. for 1899, p. 800; ibid. for 1900, p. 650; ibid. for 1902, p. 779.

the governor of South Carolina said, was to stop the crime, i.e. rape.[1] When convictions were secured and leaders of mobs were sentenced to terms in prison they would be pardoned by executive decree.[2]

It was rather generally agreed that a large part of what was intolerable in the race question in the South arose from negro suffrage. Much of the irritation which had occurred during the period of Reconstruction, and since, was induced by the fact that the blacks had been given the right to vote. So long as they enjoyed this privilege, which they, as a body, were entirely unfitted to exercise intelligently, base white men would go among them exciting their animosities and hates. They would be cajoled, massed and driven to the polls in the interest of demagogues who wished to get hold of the tax and disbursing agencies of the local and state governments, seize lucrative offices and put the honest white property-holding class in a subject place. This is precisely what had been done after the war until the reorganized states, each in its own way, had thrown off the yoke and the governments were restored to the hands of the respectable and competent white parts of the population. It is what had come to pass again in North Carolina in 1896 through the falling apart of the Democratic party.

Ignorant whites, like Tillman in South Carolina, had learned the political arts. Blatherskites with the power to speak to the tenant farmers, the hill people and the new factory workers, and to weld them into a mass, were throwing the good old traditions of Southern statecraft to the four winds. Whites of this class hated capital and property—they also hated the negro who was a competing laborer. Though the Bourbons and the poor whites fell to quarreling for the control of the machinery of the Democratic party, both together were agreed that the black man must be kept away from the polls and the wisest understood that, if there were to be order and progress, such a result must be accomplished peacefully. Any kind of violence and fraud as a means of suppressing the negro vote must give way

---

[1] Cf. App. Ann. Cyclop. for 1901, p. 670.
[2] Cf. ibid. for 1902, p. 689; J. E. Cutler, Lynch Law, pp. 246–66.

to forms of law. The danger of negro ascendency must not be in mind at every recurring election. There should be lasting assurance that government in the South would be white and, little by little, the North, excepting such parts of it as were actuated by entirely partisan considerations, came to understand that it might as well give quiet assent to this principle. The old Abolitionist elements which had stood for the equality of the races, and the guarantee and defense of the negro's political rights spoke in lower tones. Northern men who had innate and hereditary enmity for the arrogant white Southron came to an appreciation of his situation and to sympathize with him. They noted the inpouring immigration from southern and eastern Europe and they had fears, well enough grounded, that, soon or late, they would be overwhelmed at the ballot box by an ignorant rabble, even as the South had been. The enlistment of men like Fitzhugh Lee, "Joe" Wheeler and other soldiers of the Confederate army, and their sons, for the war against Spain increased, after 1898, the tolerance of the North. Therefore it was that measures to restrict the franchise taken by states in which there was a large negro vote were viewed indulgently, and the process, begun in 1890 in Mississippi, gained headway with almost no protest in portions of the country which, a short while ago, would have made the air ring with cries of treason and rebellion.

Gradually, methods making it easy for whites and difficult for negroes to vote had been contrived. Reapportionment and gerrymander limited their possible influence; poll tax requirements, confusing registration schemes and complicated ballot systems practically barred large numbers from participating in elections.[1] But statutory provisions were not enough; the state constitutions must be changed and devices to insure white supremacy incorporated in the fundamental law. Mississippi and South Carolina, each of which contained more negroes than white men, had the most reason to concern themselves with the question. The Mississippi convention would meet at Jackson in August, 1890. In a body of 134 men only one was a negro and

[1] P. Lewinson, Race, Class and Party, pp. 65–7.

only two were Republicans. The way was clear for action,[1] and when, on November 1st, the constitution was adopted and was promulgated without submitting it to popular vote, which might have led to miscarriage, the object in view was attained. Petty crime, such as many of the negroes perpetrated, disqualified an applicant for registration. He must pay a poll tax of $2 which, by a vote of the boards of supervisors of the counties, might be locally increased to $3 and, upon offering to vote, he must present his receipts. But it was another provision which definitely excluded the black masses from taking part in elections in Mississippi. A clause required that every voter must be "able to read any section of the constitution of the state," or "understand" it when it should be read to him, or "give a reasonable interpretation" of it. The election managers would determine when this condition had been successfully met. The very idea of such an inquiry intimidated, as it was meant to frighten, the negroes, and kept them from the polls.

The adoption of this scheme did not escape comment, especially in the North, and there were many to say that the Supreme Court of the United States would declare it to be an abridgment of the rights which had been guaranteed the negroes by the 14th and 15th Amendments. It was complained, that administrative officers were vested with the power "to ask all sorts of vain, impertinent questions."[2] They had the arbitrary right of rejecting any applicant for registration. By earlier laws, it was said, there had been 190,000 negro and 69,000 white electors in Mississippi, though no such number ever visited the polling places. In the Presidential election of 1888, when 115,807 ballots were cast, about 30,000 negroes were "per-

---

[1] A bishop prayed for deliverance of the convention from "pride of personal opinion, from all selfish ambition and from partisan passion and prejudices," whereupon the presiding officer, upon taking the chair, stated the principal subject confronting the delegates. "The ballot system must be so arranged" as to solve a 25 year old public problem. The rule of one race had always meant "economic and moral ruin," the rule of the other "prosperity and happiness," not to one but to all races. This rule "so just and necessary" must be insured.—Journal of Proceedings of Convention, pp. 4, 10–11.

[2] 170 U. S., p. 221; cf. Lewinson, Race, Class and Party, pp. 117–8.

mitted," as the North had been wont to say, to vote. In 1892, by virtue, principally, of the "understanding" clause, only 76,742 persons, all told, were registered. While it was alleged that over 8,000 of these were colored only 1,444 votes were cast for the Republican ticket.[1] In one county, with a population, in 1900, of 8,000 whites and 11,700 negroes, there were only 25 or 30 negro votes; in another, with 8,000 whites and 12,000 negroes, only 30 negroes were qualified to go to the polls. At the election in 1906 in a Congressional district in Mississippi with 190,883 inhabitants only 2,091 votes were cast, not one of which, it is safe to say, was a negro's.[2]

Nevertheless the abridgment of the suffrage survived review in the Mississippi courts,[3] and the subject in 1897 reached the Supreme Court of the United States, which declared, Justice McKenna delivering the opinion, that these provisions in the constitution of the state did not, "on their face, discriminate between the races," and, therefore, that what had been done by the convention did not amount to a denial of the equal protection of the laws secured to all citizens by the Fourteenth Amendment. [4]

Before the Presidential election of 1896 South Carolina followed the example of Mississippi. The legislature in 1894 had passed a registration act putting a number of new obstacles in the way of the negro when he should try to vote. Its constitutionality was questioned and an order was obtained from a Republican judge in a Federal court restraining election officers from carrying out the provisions of the law. The people were aroused. A convention to frame a new constitution was called to meet in September, 1896. The governor said that the task of this body would be to guarantee to South Carolinians white supremacy forever. The "black pall of negro domination" hovered over them—intelligent white men, constitution or

---

[1] App. Ann. Cyclop. for 1892, p. 472.

[2] G. T. Stephenson, Race Distinctions in American Law, pp. 320–1; Wm. P. Pickett, The Negro Problem, pp. 266–7.

[3] 69 Miss., p. 898 and 74 Miss., p. 270.

[4] Williams v. Miss., 170 U. S., p. 213; N. Y. Nation, May 26, 1898; W. A. Dunning in Atlantic Monthly, Oct., 1901.

no constitution, law or no law, court or no court, would govern the state.[1]

In the convention of 160 delegates six were negroes. Disfranchising clauses became a part of the new constitution when it was promulgated, as in Mississippi, without its submission to a vote of the people. Applicants for registration must be able to read any section of the constitution of the state, "or understand and explain it" when it should be read to them by the election officers. Such persons as could qualify as voters were to do so before January 1, 1898. Their names would be put upon the registration lists for life without further inquiry concerning their qualifications. After that time applicants should be subject to a mere examination in reading and writing. However no one would be permitted to vote if he did not own, and had not paid taxes on, property assessed for at least $300.[2] Such provisions in South Carolina, as in Mississippi, amounted to the nearly complete disfranchisement of the negroes. With a colored population of more than 600,000 in the state less than 3,000 negroes seem to have gone to the polls in the Presidential election of 1896.[3]

In Louisiana, a state so prolific of disorders arising from race prejudice, the negroes were to be disfranchised by amendments of the constitution which were submitted to the people in the elections of 1896. But these proposals were rejected and the next step was the calling of a convention to frame an entirely new constitution. This body met and promulgated its finished work in May, 1898, without a referendum. In Louisiana, henceforward, the applicant for registration must fill out a blank form in the English language, or in his "mother tongue," in the presence of the registration officer, "without assistance or suggestion from any person, or any memorandum whatever." There were exceptions—though he should not be able to read and write, if he should own property assessed for at least $300

[1] App. Ann. Cyclop. for 1895, p. 705.
[2] Art. ii. sec. 4 of constitution of South Carolina of 1898.
[3] Cf. App. Ann. Cyclop. for 1896, p. 706. The Republican state convention in 1900 gave the number who had been disfranchised as 100,000. —Ibid. for 1900, p. 651.

and if he should have paid all taxes due upon it, he might vote. To this was added the so-called "grandfather clause." Any man who, on January 1, 1867, had been entitled to vote in Louisiana or any other state of the Union, his sons or his grandsons, 21 years of age at the date of the adoption of the constitution, would be registered without regard to educational or property qualifications. All white men, therefore, who were qualified to vote before the adoption of the 15th Amendment establishing the political rights of the negroes, and their descendants to the third generation, were enrolled in a body without question.[1] Moreover, to increase the preponderance of white voters naturalized persons—European immigrants, in so far as they might have settled in the state—were enfranchised *ipso facto* without the application of educational or property qualifications. All persons less than 60 years of age, when offering to vote, must show their receipts for poll taxes—which the negroes habitually lost—assessed at the rate of one dollar per annum for the two preceding years. Days were set apart for the secessionists and their sons and grandsons, and for white foreigners, to visit the registration offices and to enroll, thereby creating a body which would stand as a permanent barrier on election day against the blacks. [2]

In 1896 130,344 negroes were registered in Louisiana; in 26 parishes the registered blacks outnumbered the registered whites. In 1900 only 5320 negroes were qualified to visit the polls; they were in a majority in none of the parishes of the state. In four years more the number was reduced to less than 2,000. In many parishes not a single negro was registered.[3]

North Carolina accomplished the same object by a constitutional amendment which was submitted to the people and adopted by a large majority in 1900, after the state's sorry experience with a return to Republican rule. The ability to read and write, a poll tax and the "grandfather clause" were relied upon to keep the negro out of politics in the future in that state. Men who had voted prior to 1867, and all "lineal descendants"

---

[1] Cf. N. Y. Nation, May 19, 1898.   [2] Art. 197 of Con. of La. of 1898.
[3] P. Lewinson, Race, Class and Party, pp. 81, 213–4.

were freed from any need of possessing an educational qualification for registration and, once put upon the list, they should
have the franchise "forever." [1]

Alabama and Virginia in 1900, would employ similar measures
with similar ends in view. "After an experience of 30 years,"
said the Democratic party of Alabama in a platform adopted at
a state convention in March of that year, in which time "every
necessary facility to qualify the negro for the franchise" had
been afforded him, it had been "demonstrated" that, "as a
race," he was "incapable of self government and the intelligent
exercise of the power of voting." Therefore, a new constitution,
"to perpetuate the rule of the white race in Alabama," was
imperatively demanded. No white man would be disfranchised
except after his conviction of the commission of an infamous
crime.[2]

The delegates were elected and the new constitution was
framed and adopted, and, in this case, submitted to, and ratified
by the people. In it was found a wordy and involved re-statement of the devices which had been invented in Mississippi and
Louisiana. Alabama would permanently register at once, without
hindering qualification, male residents of foreign birth, soldiers
of the war of 1812, the war with Mexico, the Indian wars, the
Civil War on both sides, and the war with Spain, and the "lawful
descendants" of these, together with descendants of soldiers of
the Revolutionary War. She would also enroll "persons of good
character" and those who should "understand the duties and
obligations of citizenship under a republican form of government." This bulwark having been set up against the negro, it
was stated that all citizens applying for registration after January 1, 1903, must satisfy the registration officers of their ability
to "read and write any article of the Constitution of the United
States," and that they have been regularly engaged in some
trade or occupation "for the greater part" of the preceding
twelve months unless they should be physically unfit for labor.
A man, whether literate or not, if he owned 40 acres of land or
other property assessed for at least $300, or if his wife owned

[1] App. Ann. Cyclop. for 1900, p. 444.   [2] Ibid. for 1901, p. 667.

such property, might vote, provided the taxes on it were paid.[1]

Simultaneously a convention in Virginia was working upon the same problem and the resulting constitution was proclaimed and declared effective without a popular vote in 1902. Here, too, permanent registration for life was assured anyone who had served "in time of war" in the army or navy of the United States, or of the Confederate States, and the sons of such. Others so favored were owners of property on which tax had been paid, those who were able to read any section of the state constitution and "give a reasonable explanation" of it, or, if illiterate, to explain, in a "reasonable" fashion, the meaning of any section of the constitution read to them by the registration officers. Thus the whites, since practically all men in the South had been in the Confederate army, or were the sons of those who had seen service in this army, were enfranchised, while the property holding qualification and the "understanding" clause could be relied upon to bar all but a few of the blacks. Those who would be enrolled as voters after 1903, the expiration of the period for permanent registration, must make application for the privilege in their own handwriting, with a recital of facts regarding their birthplace, age, place of residence and occupation, and must have complied with the further qualification of having paid their poll taxes for a prior period of three years.[2]

Thus, in one way or another, the negroes as a body, with but inconsiderable exceptions, were automatically deprived of the privilege of participating in elections.[3] The confidence that was reposed in the Supreme Court had been misplaced in the case of Mississippi. Other states now had gone farther. It was predicted that the court sooner or later, when it should be brought face to face with the issue, would intervene in the black man's behalf. But in a case out of Alabama, though there were dissenting opinions, it again evaded its responsibili-

[1] Constitution of 1901, art. viii. F. G. Caffey defends these provisions in Political Science Quarterly, vol. 20, p. 53.

[2] Constitution of Va. of 1902, art. ii.

[3] Cf. George S. Merriam, The Negro and the Nation, pp. 372–4; J. R. Commons, Races and Immigrants, pp. 44, 193; A. H. Stone, The American Race Problem, pp. 354 et seq.; G. T. Stephenson, Race Distinctions in Am. Law, pp. 320–1; Wm. P. Pickett, The Negro Problem, pp. 258–84.

ties on the ground, mainly, that the wrong complained of was "political," calling for relief, if relief were required, from the "legislative and political department of the government of the United States."[1] It is true that the "grandfather clause" many years later was declared to be unconstitutional with respect to a provision in Oklahoma when, however, it was too late to affect the result in the older states.[2] Reconstruction had been "undone,"[3] but the removal of so prolific a cause of irritation improved social relations in the South and, with the North's acquiescence, allayed sectional conflict in the nation.[4]

The problems arising from the immigration of incompatible peoples of the white race also led to outbursts of public feeling. From the beginning America had invited and welcomed white colonists to its shores. Its progress rested upon the human cargoes which ships bore to our ports from Europe. All the white inhabitants of the country had come from lands across the Atlantic Ocean, or were the descendants of such. A few thousands had arrived before 1700; the number here, as a result of immigration and increase, was a few millions before 1800. America had been, and it remained, the "asylum of the oppressed," a haven for those who sought religious and political liberty. Chinamen had lately found us inhospitable and negroes, had they still been coming to us from Africa, would have been turned back. But white immigration continued to be practically unrestricted. Opposition to the competition of so many men with hands to work as crowded the steerage quarters of incoming steamships was brewing in the labor unions, notwithstanding the fact that the masses in these organizations were themselves, for the most part, only recent migrants to the United States. From their point of view there were enough workers here. If more came by immigration wages could not be

---

[1] Giles v. Harris, 189 U. S., p. 475; cf. Giles v. Teasley, 193 U. S., p. 146; J. M. Mathews, Hist. of the 15th Amendment, pp. 125–6; G. T. Stephenson, Race Distinctions in Am. Law, pp. 313–20.

[2] Guinn v. U. S., p. 347; P. Lewinson, Race, Class and Party, p. 81; Benj. Brawley, Social History of the Am. Negro, pp. 287–91.

[3] W. A. Dunning, The Undoing of Reconstruction, Atlantic Monthly, Oct., 1901.

[4] Cf. C. H. Poe in North Am. Review for Oct., 1902.

held up, shorter hours would not be obtainable from employers and the other demands of the trades unions could not be enforced. In one decade, 1881–90, under the impetus of the economic recovery which had followed the prolonged depression into which the country had been thrown by the panic of 1873, more than 5,000,000 persons transplanted themselves to the United States from Europe and Canada, twice as many as had resided in the thirteen colonies at the time of the Revolution.[1] In the prosperous years after recovery from the panic of 1893 the movement hither of foreign labor again attained notable proportions. The number of arrivals was 311,715 in the fiscal year 1899, 448,572 in 1900, 487,918 in 1901 and 648,743 in 1902. Nearly 4,000,000 came in the five years after 1900.

The character of this immigration arrested attention—it betokened no increase of social harmony and national happiness. In the decade of the Civil War 38 per cent. of our immigrants came from the British Islands—in the decade 1881–90, 27 per cent. In 1901–05 but 9 per cent. were from this source. The contribution of Germany which in the ten years after 1860 had been 35 per cent. was less than 5 per cent. at the beginning of the new 20th century. On the other hand in these 40 years the immigration from Austria-Hungary, largely Slovaks, Poles and Jews, increased from 8 to 25 per cent., from Italy from less than 1 to 25 per cent. and from Russia from a few persons in a year to 17 per cent., principally Slavized Jews. Thus 67 per cent., a preponderating proportion of the immigration, was of races pressed out of eastern and southeastern Europe.[2]

"It is a matter of public knowledge," said Secretary of the Treasury Windom in 1890, "that transportation from any part of Europe to our Atlantic ports is so cheap and easy as practically to exclude none."[3] It was stated angrily that public bodies and private charity associations in Great Britain and on

---

[1] Cf. vol. iv of this work, pp. 397–8.

[2] Coolidge, Chinese Immigration, p. 504, quoting Report of Commissioner General of Immigration for 1906; J. R. Commons, Races and Immigrants in America, pp. 70–95; E. E. Sparks, National Development, chap. ii; J. H. Latané, America as a World Power, chap. xvii; Prescott F. Hall, Immigration, chap. iii.

[3] Report of Sec. of Treas. for 1890, p. lxxv.

the Continent were counselling and assisting paupers and criminals to emigrate to the United States.[1] The spawn of their jails and poor houses was being "dumped" upon our shores. There must be guarantees affecting the character of the incoming stream. Emigrants bound for the United States must undergo inspection before they should set sail and then again when they should reach this country.[2] An immigrant arriving at a port of entry must prove his right to land before he should be allowed to do so.[3] So long ago as 1875 a law of Congress had barred prostitutes and aliens convicted of crimes—not political —whose sentences had been remitted on condition that they should leave their own country.[4] There was no assurance that it was being enforced. By an act of August 3, 1882, the supervision of immigration became, nominally at least, a Federal matter—the Secretary of the Treasury was authorized to make contracts with state commissions and local boards for the management of the work. A head tax of fifty cents, increased in 1895 to one dollar,[5] was laid on each arriving alien—if it should not be paid it should rest as a lien upon the ship bringing such persons to port. The sums so collected were to be forwarded to the United States Treasury and should constitute a fund, called the "Immigrant Fund," to be used to defray the expense of carrying the law into effect. The state and local officers, acting under Federal authorization, should bar from admission to the country "any convict, lunatic, idiot, or any person unable to take care of himself or herself without becoming a public charge" whom they found among arriving passengers not citizens of the United States. "Foreign convicts" (again excepting those guilty of political offenses) should be returned to the countries whence they came at the expense of the ship owners. [6]

[1] Report of Sec. of Treas. for 1892, p. liv.; House Reports, 51st Cong. 2nd sess., no. 3472, p. 11; ibid., 50th Cong. 2nd sess., no. 3792, p. 2; Report of Ind. Comm., House Doc., 57th Cong. 1st. sess., no. 184, p. xiv.

[2] Cf. Report of Sec. of Treas. for 1889, p. xciii; ibid. for 1890, p. lxxv; ibid. for 1891, p. lxii; N. A. Review for April, 1892, pp. 424–38.

[3] Report of Sec. of Treas. for 1892, p. lix.

[4] U. S. Stat. at Large, vol. 18, pp. 477–8.   [5] Ibid., vol. 28, p. xcii.

[6] Act of Aug. 3, 1882.—U. S. Stat. at Large, vol. 22, pp. 214–5; Report of Sec. of Treas. for 1889, p. xcii.

In 1885 the contract labor law had been passed,[1] to meet with a good deal of not undeserved ridicule, since men coming to the country who were assured of employment might properly be held to be more desirable acquisitions than those who had no ends in view.[2] The responsibilities of the inspectors were increased. They must now make particular inquiries of each alien ship passenger as to how and why he came, whether any one had furnished him with money to enable him to come, and what his objects and purposes were in crossing the sea. Such provisions of law would be difficult to enforce—indeed their strict enforcement was impossible, especially with the agencies at hand for the work.[3] Contract laborers from Europe, it was complained, continued to arrive and were breaking down American wages.[4] The Knights of Labor had lobbied the law through Congress and they were feeling their power.[5] They demanded new legislation. Always the seat of the trouble was at New York. Here were the wharves of most of the European. steamship lines. The immigrants, after the vessels were docked, were transferred to barges which were towed to Castle Garden at the lower end of Manhattan Island and, through this station, after filing past registry clerks seated at desks for examination, which was called a "perfect farce," [6] the mass, often a half a million persons in a year, was immediately poured into the city. In Congress the House of Representatives, in January, 1889, appointed a committee to inquire into the importation of contract laborers, convicts, paupers and other obnoxious persons. They declared that the law was nearly a dead letter; the work of inspection should be entrusted to the Federal government and not to the states. It was a "matter affecting the whole Union" and was "preeminently a proper subject for Federal control." [7]

To meet criticism, which was gaining force on all sides, Secre-

---

[1] U. S. Stat. at Large, vol. 23, pp. 332–3.
[2] Cf. Report of Sec. of Treas. for 1889, p. xciv; cf. vol. iv of this work, pp. 405–6.
[3] Cf. Foreign Relations for 1894, p. 368.
[4] Cf. House Reports, 51st Cong. 2nd sess., no. 3472, pp. v-vii.
[5] Ibid., pp. ii, 632.
[6] House Reports, 50th Cong. 2nd sess., no. 3792, p. 2.   [7] Ibid., p. 4.

tary of the Treasury Windom abrogated the contract with the New York state commissioners. They were told that their administration of the office was unsatisfactory and, in April, 1896, the Treasury Department, ending dual authority, assumed direct control of the station. Castle Garden was abandoned and the arriving immigrants were taken to the Barge Office which was United States property, where the new inspectors temporarily performed their duties, not without difficulty since ships were discharging steerage passengers from their holds at the rate of 2,000 a day. On one day, indeed, 9,000 were received.[1]

It was plain that such work could not be done in space even more contracted than that accorded the state commissioners at Castle Garden and an island in New York harbor was sought, so that it might not be necessary in the future to bring the immigrants into the city, thereby freeing the people from contact with such inflowing squalor, while, at the same time, protecting the poor and ignorant passengers from the harpies lying in wait to divest them of their money. Secretary Windom chose Bedloe's Island on which the French had erected the statue of Liberty. There was objection. It was said that such a suggestion was disrespectful to the donors of the monument and unworthy of the nation which had received the gift. The Secretary returned with an opinion that the immigrant depot, if it were placed on the western side of the island, would be out of sight as ships came up the bay. Others advocated Ellis Island which Mr. Windom said was too low—its level was barely above the water at high tide. The Navy had a powder magazine there. On the other hand, Congress could dispossess the Navy Department. It should do so. Powder should not be stored in such a place; it endangered Jersey City and even New York.[2] Piling and crib work would raise the surface and the friends of the site succeeded in having it selected. When

---

[1] Cf. House Reports, 51st Cong. 2nd sess., no. 3472, pp. iii, 3–4, 1054; ibid., 50th Cong. 2nd sess., no. 3792, p. 2; Report of Sec. of Treas. for 1890, p. lxxiv.

[2] Cf. House Reports, 51st Cong. 2nd sess., no. 3472, pp. 4–18; House Ex. Doc., 51st Cong. 2nd sess., no. 146.

the shores had been built up and filled the island embraced an
area of five and a half acres. The buildings erected by the
government were ready for use in 1891 and here, after that
time, the steerage passengers on arriving ships underwent
physical examination, their papers were inspected, their boxes
and bundles were fumigated and such as were not admitted
to the country were held for deportation back to their homes.[1]

Many did not leave New York, making the city a strange
meeting ground of races speaking 60 or 70 diverse tongues.
Such a commixtion of peoples had not been seen before. It
excelled Babel. The immigrants from southern Europe residing
in New York outnumbered those from northwestern Europe in
the ratio of 19 to 1.[2] It was said in 1907 that there were nearly
as many Germans in New York as in Hamburg. The city
contained twice as many Irish as lived in Dublin, two and a
half times as many Jews as were to be found in Warsaw, one
half as many Italians as dwelt in Naples.[3] Those who did not
remain in New York usually found their way to other cities
and towns except as they might be gathered up by contractors
to live temporarily in camps near mines and quarries and in
industrial settlements. They, therefore, very much complicated
the tasks of those who were wrestling with the problems of
municipal government which in America was notoriously wanting in efficiency and honor.

The white immigrants from southern and eastern Europe,
like the Chinese, dwelt in their own quarters.[4] They were
crowded together in ramshackle buildings in slums like beasts,
ate food that was nauseating to other men and had revolting
and vicious habits. Being of the lower orders of mankind
they were repellant to those who were farther advanced in the
social scale and who had higher standards of living. Reformers

[1] Report of Sec. of Treas., for 1891, pp. lxii–lxiii. For illustrations and
maps of Ellis Island see Rep. of Comm. Gen. of Immigration for 1896.
[2] Report of Industrial Comm., House Doc., 57th Cong. 1st sess., no.
184, p. x.
[3] J. R. Commons, Races and Immigrants in America, p. 165.
[4] Cf. Report of Ind. Comm., House Doc., 57th Cong. 1st sess., no. 184,
pp. x, xlii–xlviii.

were busily employed trying to "Americanize" them. To give them better homes and more breathing space, to teach them our language and acquaint them with our institutions were objects which awakened the enthusiasm and employed the services of young men and women.[1] A variety of magazine articles and many books on America as a "melting pot" appeared and, while some spoke hopefully of our absorptive powers and the quick changes that were made in men by merely breathing the atmosphere of a free land, to others— and all of them were not labor leaders—the outlook was profoundly disturbing. Political parties in many states adopted platforms demanding the effectual damming of the stream.[2] Further control was imperatively required. There must be an "investigation" by Congress and, by concurrent resolution of the two houses, on March 12, 1890, $10,000 were appropriated for the Senate Committee on Immigration and the House Committee on Immigration and Naturalization to examine into and compile a report on "the workings of the various laws of the United States and of the several states" relative to this subject.[3] The committees visited and took testimony in New York, Boston, Detroit, Cincinnati, St. Louis and Chicago. They heard officers of the Federal government, the New York state commissioners and their inspectors and clerks, labor leaders, heads of foreign groups, slum and tenement district workers, steamship agents, editors and others, and a report comprising nearly 1100 pages was issued at the expense of the government.[4]

Many plans for limiting immigration were proposed and engaged public discussion. Some would lay a high head tax on immigrants. Others would establish a literacy test. Still others would require the passenger before he should be landed to furnish proof of the ownership of a certain amount of property. Others again would fix an age limit in order to exclude

[1] Cf. Report of Ind. Comm., House Doc., 57th Cong. 1st sess., no. 183, p. lvi.; vol. iv of this work, pp. 397–8.
[2] House Reports, 51st Cong. 2nd sess., no. 3472, p. ii.
[3] Ibid., p. i; U. S. Stat. at Large, vol. 26, p. 43.
[4] House Reports, 51st Cong. 2nd sess., no. 3472.

the old who, to a certainty, would soon be disabled for work
and might then require public aid.[1]

William D. Owen of Indiana, who was chairman of the
House Committee on Immigration and had taken an active
part in the investigation, gave his name to a bill which received
the favor of Congress and which, on March 3, 1891, was approved by President Harrison. The measure was a mere
development of the law of 1882. It called for the exclusion of
idiots, insane persons, paupers or persons likely to become a
public charge, persons afflicted with loathsome and contagious
diseases and those convicted of infamous crimes—still excepting
political offenses, unless "moral turpitude" should be involved.
Upon the arrival of immigrant ships inspectors were to board
them to see if any of the passengers belonged to the classes put
under the ban. The Secretary of the Treasury was authorized
to assume direct control of the depots at other places, as at
New York. The work generally, throughout the United States,
would be supervised by an officer attached to the Treasury
Department in Washington to be called the Superintendent of
Immigration. New provisions would, it was hoped, make
more certain the deportation of obnoxious persons at the
cost of the owners of the ships bringing them in.[2] As Mr.
Owen had been retired from Congress in the elections in Indiana in 1890 President Harrison appointed him to the new
office at a salary of $4,000 a year, with three clerks.

The managers of the political parties in 1892 believed that the
time had come to refer to the subject in their national platforms. They would still hold out the olive branch to voters of
foreign birth while uttering a few phrases to entice the members
of the labor unions into their net. The Democrats declared
that they would exert themselves to prevent the country from
becoming "the dumping ground for the known criminals and
professional paupers of Europe." They denounced "any and
all attempts to restrict the immigration of the industrious and
worthy of foreign lands," but they would keep out foreign

[1] Cf. House Reports, 51st Cong. 2nd sess., no. 3472, p. 1058.
[2] Act of March 3, 1891.—U. S. Stat. at Large, vol. 26, pp. 1084–6.

workmen who were being imported under contract "to degrade American labor." The Republicans contented themselves, after some remarks about the "manifest destiny of the republic," by saying that they would favor the enactment of "more stringent laws and regulations for the restriction of criminal, pauper and contract immigration."

When the new Congress met, the House having passed to the control of the Democrats, another investigation was set on foot in answer to another concurrent resolution which was passed in February, 1892. No advantage would be allowed to accrue to the Republicans. "Hordes of vicious, depraved, criminal and pauper elements of humanity" were still invading the land.[1] Herman Stump of Maryland, who had been active in the investigation of 1890, was appointed to Owen's place as chairman of the Committee on Immigration. The hearing of testimony was resumed. The principal object of the reorganized committee was to air scandals in connection with the work done on Ellis Island and to discredit the Republicans who had let the contracts,[2] but support was gained for the Stump bill which was making its way through Congress [3] and which, on March 3, 1893, was approved by the President. It was an act "to facilitate the enforcement" of earlier laws, and it contained one principal new feature. Many times many men, during many years, had said that the proper control of imuigration was at its source, in Europe. The Stump law required a thoroughgoing examination into the physical fitness of each prospective emigrant, with the assistance of the consular officers of the United States, before he or she should leave the port of embarkation. Other information regarding the ships' passengers was to be assembled and tabulated. Lists or manifests would be prepared aboard and put into the custody of the commanders of the vessels for the guidance of the inspectors in the United States. At Ellis Island the incomers were to be subjected to further questioning and investigation. It was again made the duty of the steamship companies to return such per-

[1] Cf. House Reports, 52nd Cong. 1st sess., no. 2090, p. iv.
[2] Ibid., pp. i-xxv.   [3] House Reports, 52nd Cong. 2nd sess., no. 1573.

sons as might be brought here in violation of law.[1] Stump soon
followed Owen as Superintendent of Immigration with the
title, after 1895, of Commissioner-General, standing at the
head of a Bureau of Immigration.[2]

Inevitably such infusions into the population increased the
demands upon the generous for charity. They made claims
upon us for hospitals and schools. They called for larger
bodies of police, gave new business to the courts and filled the
jails. Paupers, insane persons and cripples, many of them
foreigners, who had come in on the ships, cost New York state
20 millions of dollars a year. Counties along our northern line,
bordering on Canada, were pressed to take care of alien de-
pendents who were landed at Quebec, and, without let or hindrance, since there were no immigrant stations on the boundary,
entered the United States.[3]

Furthermore they were potential voters, and those whose
occupation it was to herd men and drive them to the polls,
found in these ignorant people the material to forward corrupt
political schemes. The negroes might be disfranchised—it was
not so with the Slovaks, the Poles and the Italians. They had
white skins. They came to our shores, it was said on the 4th
of July and other days given to patriotic speech, as our own
ancestors had come, to better their lot amid free institutions
which they could be taught to understand and revere. The
politicians had no wish to withhold the vote from bodies of
men so numerous who might be held in blocks and put to valuable use. It was clear enough that they were to be kneaded into
the mass which had been referred to in the Constitution as
"We, the people of the United States."

The criminal propensities of many of those who arrived were
not easy to detect by any process of examination. Some of
the groups, especially the Italians, brought their feuds with
them. Their bloody fracases were now and again described in
the newspapers. Sicilian cutthroats, assassins skilful in the use

---

[1] U. S. Stat. at Large, vol. 27, pp. 567–70.   [2] Ibid., vol. 28, p. 780.
[3] House Reports, 50th Cong. 2nd sess., no. 3792, pp. 3–4; Report of
Sec. of Treas. for 1890, p. lxxv.

of the stiletto, were a new terror in America. Their crimes were not confined to their own kind—they imperilled the lives of others in the communities in which they dwelt. And the revenge taken upon them by mobs was often as summary and savage as that which had been invented for the negroes. The removal from a jail in New Orleans in 1891 of 11 men who, it was believed, had been involved in the assassination of the chief of police and the shooting of them, since the trial of the culprits had not had a result pleasing to local sentiment, had led to international complications which, for a time, wore the gravest appearance.[1] This was not all. At Walsenburg, in a coal mining district in Colorado, in March, 1895, three Italians who were suspected of killing a saloon keeper were shot by a mob. Two who escaped were found starving in the mountains with their limbs so frozen that amputation was necessary. Diplomatic negotiations, which involved inquiries addressed to the governor of the state, were prolonged. President Cleveland asked Congress to make an appropriation of money for the benefit of the victims and, more than a year later, $10,000 were voted and paid them and their heirs.[2]

This outrage had not yet been atoned for when the scene shifted back to Louisiana. A mob overcame a night watchman at a jail in Hahnville in St. Charles parish in that state in August, 1896, seized three Italians accused of murdering two respected citizens, carried them to a stable, hanged them to the rafters and riddled their bodies with shot.[3] The Italian ambassador asked for explanations of this new "deed of blood." The President in the following year, after a tedious inquiry as to their status as citizens, requested an appropriation of $6,000 from Congress to compensate the families of the dead men.[4]

Again, on July 20, 1899, five Italians were lynched in Tallulah, a village of 500 inhabitants in Madison parish in Louisiana. A physician having been annoyed by goats which had been allowed to run at large, shot one of the animals. The owner,

---

[1] Supra, pp. 151-2. [2] Foreign Relations for 1896, p. 426.
[3] N. Y. Times, Aug. 10, 1896.
[4] Foreign Relations for 1896, pp. 396-426; ibid. for 1897, pp. 353-4.

two of his brothers and some friends, in revenge, waylaid the doctor and in a mêlée killed him. Two of the Italians were arrested but on the way to jail they were taken from the sheriff and hanged on a beam in a slaughter house. Three more who had reached the prison were taken out and suspended from an oak tree in the jail yard.[1] Again the Italian government made angry representations through the State Department and a long investigation followed, touching the citizenship of the men and the facts, generally, attending the event.[2] The names of the lynchers, the Italian ambassador at Washington said, were "in the mouths of everybody," while the local and state authorities in Louisiana made no motion to apprehend, try them for their crimes and punish them. Three grand juries declared that the perpetrators of the outrage could not be identified.[3]

Two Italians were lynched and a third was wounded by an armed mob at Erwin in Washington County in Mississippi in 1901, leading to new inquiries and demands for redress,[4] with the filing of statements that in not a case in this series of lynchings had any one been arrested, tried or punished, a course "demanded by the principles of humanity and justice" in all civilized lands.[5]

If such occurrences were proof of the crudeness of our civilization in some parts of the country and the weakness of our legal systems, if, in other cases, they reflected the growing power of the labor unions which had determined that there were already enough workers in America, they also rested on general sentiment. The lynching of these white men, like the lynching of negroes and Chinamen, was an emphatic expression of the irritation which could be excited when socially antagonistic races were brought into contact with the seasoned American stock. So long as immigrants went into the great West to settle its spreading plains it was no matter.[6] They increased the

[1] N. Y. Times, July 22, 1899.
[2] Foreign Relations for 1899, pp. 440–66. [3] Ibid., for 1900, p. 721.
[4] N. Y. Times, July 18, 1901.
[5] Foreign Relations for 1901, pp. 283–99. For summary of indemnities paid see J. E. Cutler, Lynch Law, p. 259.
[6] Cf. Report of Sec. of Treas. for 1891, p. lxi; ibid., for 1892, p. lx.

population and augmented wealth; we could still repeat the
shibboleths about the land of opportunity, about this free commonwealth which, on a happy day, was created to serve as a
haven for the peoples of less fortunate parts of the world.
Thomas Carlyle had said to Ralph Waldo Emerson—"It's all
verra well now while ye have a great deal of land and verra little
people. But wait till ye ha' gotten a great deal of people and
a very little land." [1] This day was approaching. When the
immigrating throng burdened the communal facilities of towns
and cities, especially on the Atlantic seaboard, from which they
had no wish to depart, kept their own speech, read their own
newspapers and intimate daily association with them gave the
people a view of their backward social state, enforced by the
knowledge that many of them were Catholics and many of them
Jews,[2] thus awakening religious as well as racial antipathies, the
movement for the restriction of immigration gained high mo-
mentum. It was an awkward change of ground for our thought
and speech and polity. But it was plain to be seen, men said,
that our institutions were in peril. If these hordes should continue to descend upon us, all that we had gained on this continent which was valuable would be damaged, if not wholly lost.
Only uncivilized mobs would engage in lynchings, but to practically the entire body of the people in residence in the United
States, of British descent and standards of living, the lower
classes from southern and eastern Europe as they swept into
our ports, were unwelcome additions to the population. The
school might teach them our language. Much was said each
day of the alembic of public education. The naturalization
"mills" would make them into American citizens. But the
"melting pot," as it affected the hearts and minds of these new-

---

[1] A Cranstone, Jan. 18, 1892, in W. E. Chandler Papers.
[2] A defender of the Russian Jews said of them—"Unlike the Irish they
carry no foreign politics with them to the country of their adoption."
They were law abiding. There was no need to fear a Mafia among them,
as with the Italians in New Orleans. They were seldom objects of charity.
They were taken care of at need by their own kinsmen. They were not
illiterates. They read their own jargon which was printed in Hebrew
type.—L. N. Dembitz to W. E. Chandler, April 1, 1892, in Chandler
Papers.

comers, might fail us. The assimilation, of which so much was heard, could proceed only in so far as we were given assimilable material to digest.[1]

It was said, with appearance of authority, that the children, being in our hands, could be taught our ways. But the sons were a weight greater than their parents. The first generation had been under discipline at home; the second, given privileges equal to those of our oldest citizens, breaking away from restraints, were ready to enter every portal of American life. In their adventure in freedom they, in addition to smaller errancies, made shockingly large contributions to the criminal class.[2]

The checks put upon immigration by the Owen and Stump laws were of the feeblest effect. New complaints of violations and evasions, of the entrance of undesirable classes of all kinds of aliens by way of Canada and Mexico, of collusions and conspiracies touching the good faith of the steamship companies and of our immigration officers were heard. The advocates of an educational test had not yet had their day. It came in a bill passed by the House of Representatives at the first session, by the Senate at the second session, of the Fifty-fourth Congress. The arriving immigrant, if more than 16 years of age, would be required to read and write, in his own language, 20 or 25 words from the Constitution of the United States, printed on a slip and drawn from a box at the landing place. This provision would have excluded 66,000 of 263,000 persons reaching our shores from other countries in the year ending June 30, 1896.[3] Henry Cabot Lodge was a prominent advocate of the bill.[4]

[1] Cf. F. A. Walker in Forum, vol. xi, p. 634. General Walker here in 1891 stated the fear which was in him, that soon "every stagnant pool of European population, representing the utterest failures of civilization, the worst defeats in the struggle for existence, the lowest degradation of human nature," should be completely drained off into the United States. We were suffering from "an invasion in comparison with which the invasions under which Rome fell were no more than a series of excursion parties."

[2] Report of Ind. Comm., House Doc., 57th Cong. 1st sess., no. 184, p. xxii; J. R. Commons, Races and Immigrants, p. 169–71.

[3] Report of Comm. Gen. of Immigration for 1896, p. 30.

[4] Cf. A. Nevins, Letters of Cleveland, p. 495. Lodge spoke for an "Immigration Restriction League" in Boston of which John Fiske was president.

But, it was said, it was not learning which was needed in immigrants so much as honesty and good purpose. The jails were full of men who could read and write. There were many, indeed a great majority, of the members of Congress, who would not be in their places now if such a law had been in force 100 or 150 years ago. They themselves knew, and everyone knew, that their ancestors could not read and write. Moreover, and again, it was "undemocratic and anti-American." It would be humiliating to think that the United States should ever cease to be apostrophized as—

> "She, of the open soul and open door,
> With room about her hearth for all mankind." [1]

Amendments were offered, conference committees wrought with the bill, and it was finally passed, though in the Senate by the close vote of 34 to 31.[2] It was sent to the President. Many, including the Knights of Labor and similar bodies, in letters and telegrams urged him to sign it; others hastened to denounce it roundly.[3] Mr. Cleveland was not in doubt. He disposed of the bill in terse and characteristic phrases, suggested by his political philosophy, on March 2, 1897, two days before the end of his term of office. He found the proposed plan to be "a radical departure from our national policy." Provisions of the bill were "illiberal, narrow and un-American."[4] The "stupendous growth" of the country in a century attested to the success of a "generous, open-handed course" which now was to be changed. Literacy was no proper measure of capacity for development into useful citizenship. It would be "infinitely more safe" to admit 100,000 persons who could not read and write, but who were willing to work, than "one of those unruly agitators and enemies of governmental control" who, knowing their letters, delighted in inflaming the illiterate to "discontent and tumult." The provisions of the bill, the President said,

[1] Cong. Record, 54th Cong. 1st sess., p. 1932.
[2] On Feb. 17, 1897—Cong. Record, 54th Cong. 2nd sess., pp. 1937–8.
[3] Cleveland Papers.
[4] Prof. N. S. Shaler in urging the President to veto the bill called it "undemocratic, un-American, un-Christian and inhuman."—Cleveland Papers.

were "unnecessarily harsh and oppressive." Its defects, he was convinced, "after careful examination," were patent and would "cause vexation." He, therefore, returned it to Congress without his approval.[1]

The Industrial Commission which was appointed in 1898 and made its report in 1901 gave a care to the question. That the provisions of law relating to immigration, as they stood, were violated, and, due to the manner of inspection, were unenforceable was clear.[2] If the self interest which actuated the leaders of the labor unions was more likely to come to effective expression in restrictive legislation, a powerful body of opinion was forming among the people as a whole. Newspapers, magazines and political party platforms reflected it. Societies, clubs, churches fostered the idea and, as soon as employment should slacken and important parts of this army of foreigners should become a charge upon the communities in which they had settled, new force would be given to the movement to put the subject under closer control.[3]

The association of men of this or that craft or trade for their own improvement and for social pleasure had its roots in antiquity. There were carpenters' societies and unions of gilders, wood carvers, book binders, cordwainers, hatters and stone masons. The development of mechanical industry led to the formation of new groups. When there was a society of locomotive engineers there must be one for firemen—the stokers on the engines—and for railway brakemen and switchmen, for brewers and bottle blowers, for coal miners and electricians, for garment workers and table knife grinders, for cotton mule spinners and pattern makers, for musicians and telegraphers. The growth of iron manufacture had produced an active and a powerful union with its centre in Pittsburgh called the Amalgamated Association of Iron and Steel Workers. But, all together,

[1] App. Ann. Cyclop. for 1897, pp. 164–72; Richardson, Messages and Papers, vol. ix, pp. 757–61; Senate Reports, 54th Cong. 1st sess., no. 290; J. R. Commons, Races and Immigrants, p. 234.

[2] Report of Industrial Comm., House Doc., 57th Cong. 1st sess., no. 184, pp. xv–xviii, lvii–lxi.

[3] Cf. Prescott F. Hall, Immigration, chap. x.

the various trade unions in the United States in 1892 were said to have a membership of less than 700,000.[1]

The movement developed leaders who frequently were not workingmen. They had never put their hands to labor. But with a gift for public speech, which in cases gained the dignity of oratory, and executive ability, they now and again raised themselves to eminence in directing the affairs of the unions of which they became the heads, and greatly increased the influence of their organizations. They would have it appear that the interests of employers and employed were diverse, emphasized differences as they arose, made the most of injustices done factory hands and strove to put the payers and receivers of wages into classes arrayed against each other. Capital was being massed, they said, which was true—so must labor be consolidated. Mergers and combinations were putting the employer farther and farther away from the workingman. The two no longer met. One sat in a board room in New York, while the other wrought in a steel mill in Illinois or a mine in Montana. Demands were to be formulated by labor and presented to capital with organized force. The united workingmen of a trade would go not only to one employer but to all employers in the same industry and deliver their *ultimata* as to wages, hours and other conditions of labor. If their proposals were not acceded to they would drop their tools and walk out. Powderly, as we have seen, had succeeded in gathering a quarter of a million persons into a general organization of workingmen called the Knights of Labor with a view to using labor as such against capital, a movement promoted by immigration, which was constantly adding men of socialistic proclivities from the continent of Europe to the population of the United States. It was his design to bring all workingmen of whatever kind into relationship one with another for common action. His fraternity, or order, would foster and advance the idea of trades unionism and it prepared the ground naturally for sympathetic or general strikes, a purpose which, when internal dissension sapped the strength of the organization, was carried over by the American

[1] N. Y. World Almanac for 1892, p. 92.

Federation of Labor, under the direction of Samuel Gompers, born in London of Jewish parents who had migrated to England from Holland, and had come during the Civil War to the United States. The objects of these inclusive associations were not usually attained and, when such an assertion of power was attempted, it met with the condemnation of public opinion as well as the reprobation of employers. Strikes generally were looked upon as un-American and were indefensible except under unusual provocation.[1] For workingmen to threaten, and wage war upon, those who paid them for their services increased suspicion and distrust where there should have been coopera-tion. The strike took from the workingman even that which he had—daily employment with pay for the support of himself and his family, and easily led to riots, destruction of property and loss of human life.

The passage of the unions into politics was easy. Their num-ber and power were exaggerated to influence elective officers. Such groups, when skilfully led, were listened to by those who made party platforms and sat in Congress and state legislatures. The dues and contributions of the members put at the disposal of the officers, when amassed, were ample not only to yield these men large salaries but to pay the way of lobbyists and lecturers, and for the distribution of printed propaganda by post. It became clearer and clearer that such a movement could not be stopped. The more it was resisted the faster it would grow and the issues which the labor leaders created must be met as they presented themselves, sometimes in accordance with principles of right and justice and again, unfortunately, with regard to the rules of political expediency. The Republican party would compete with the Democratic party in the bid for the labor vote, each endeavoring to hold its own adherents on this issue and to attract to it those who, from time to time, were wandering away into radical third parties. The labor men were putting a distinct impress on public policy.

So early as in 1868 a law of Congress declared that eight hours should be a day's work for all "laborers, workmen and

[1] Cf. K. Coman, Industrial Hist. of the U. S., p. 366.

mechanics" employed by the United States.[1] The provision, it was said, was not being enforced. President Grant was addressed and he issued proclamations with the hope of making it effective.[2] More must be done.[3] In 1892 Congress extended the idea to include labor employed on all "public works" of the United States or the District of Columbia, and by contractors or sub-contractors engaged on such undertakings. Penalties for violations of the law were heavy.[4] This still was not enough. The labor leaders said that the law was not worded as it should have been; it was not being interpreted as they wished it to be.[5] They pressed for the passage of a bill to extend the principle to the Territories, and, yet more important, to work done not only by the United States but for the United States, as in the case of war ships and material ordered from private manufacturers, a principle stated by officers of some of the largest firms and corporations to be such an invasion of their rights that, if the bill were passed, they would not take public contracts in the future. They could and would not make a ten hour day for private, and an eight hour day for government, work. They employed thousands of men, none of whom objected to working ten hours. Anyhow they usually paid their employees by the hour or the piece. Gompers, on the other side, said that fewer hours of labor meant "more leisure, more liberty and less slavery— higher wages, better conditions, a better standard of living." His object was to bring not only government work but all the industries of the United States to the basis of an eight hour day.[6]

By incessant agitation in writing and by speech, by negotiation, by demonstrations meant to intimidate and coerce employers, by strikes and boycotts the labor leaders made progress

[1] U. S. Stat. at Large, vol. 15, p. 77.
[2] Ibid., vol. 16, p. 1127 and vol. 17, p. 55; cf. ibid., vol. 25, p. 57.
[3] House Reports, 52nd Cong. 1st. sess., no. 427.
[4] U. S. Stat. at Large, vol. 27, p. 340.
[5] J. R. Commons, Hist. of Labor in the U. S., vol. ii, pp. 124–5.
[6] Senate Doc., 55th Cong. 2nd sess., no. 318; Gompers' history of the eight hour movement is in his Seventy Years of Life and Labor, vol. i, chap. xiv.

in reference to an eight hour day as well as other objects which they had in view. In some places in some trades they established the principle of collective bargaining—their leaders met the employers and fixed the rate of wages. Workers were not any longer self determining men to be hired for service but a mass to be dealt with through designated representatives. Elsewhere, as in cigar making and in the clothing trade, in order to combat the "sweat shop," [1] the labor men demanded and gained permission to put a "union label" on goods which the members of their brotherhoods produced. The air was filled with schemes, some of which were calculated to confer benefits on the worker, while others simply magnified the unions and pointed to despotism and tyranny.

Disputes came into the courts. Common law rules were changed and extended by statute. The states passed eight hour laws, limited in some cases to men engaged on public works, in others to women and children, in still others to workers in mines and those performing severe manual labor. In 1900, 18 states in the Union had come to have laws assuring to workers, under varying conditions, an eight hour day. In New York, Pennsylvania, Ohio, Illinois, Connecticut, Missouri, Nebraska and Wisconsin it was generally and expressly declared that a man within those states should be paid for a day when he had worked for eight hours. There were exceptions, usually, for cases in which employer and employee made contracts for a greater number of hours, and usually, too, for those engaged in farm or domestic labor. Other guarantees respecting child labor, a half holiday on Saturday,[2] the ventilation and sanitation of mines and factories, safety devices, employers' liability for injuries sustained by their employees and the management of company stores [3] were secured to workers through the state legislatures.[4]

[1] Cf. Report of Ind. Comm., House Doc., 57th Cong. 1st sess., no. 184, pp. xxiv–xxxii; ibid., no. 183, p. lvviii.

[2] In New York and Pennsylvania before 1894.—N. Y. Nation, June 8, 1893.

[3] Report of Ind. Comm., House Doc., 57th Cong. 1st sess., no. 183, p. lxi, and no. 182, pp. xxvii–xxviii.

[4] Summaries made by Carroll D. Wright in N. Y. World Almanac for

Meanwhile the labor leaders were lobbying for legislation which would aid them in organizing strikes. There must be assurance that men who had stopped work with a view to forcing their employers to accede to the demands of the unions should not be blacklisted or locked out when they desired to return to their places. In 1900 18 states made blacklisting unlawful and in eight more there were statutes which could be construed to inhibit it. Eleven states had laws forbidding employers to exact agreements from employees not to join labor unions.[1]

On the other side the employer required protection from the boycott which was instituted to frighten away his customers. This sentence of excommunication pronounced by labor leaders was terrible only in reference to small businesses. A resolution of members of a union neither to work for a man, nor to have any dealings with him directly, nor with any person who should deal with him could not be so easily enforced in reference to a large industry, as it was in the case of Captain Boycott in Ireland who gave his name to this childish game. The union could set watch on the employer and beset him in small ways; it could picket his place of business, issue hand bills and otherwise annoy him and passers by until he should yield to their demands unless, in the meantime, they should contravene police regulations, which they frequently did, or could be held to answer the greater charge of conspiracy. In 1900 three states, Colorado, Illinois and Wisconsin, directly prohibited the boycott; 20 more by implication forbade it.[2]

Congress created a Bureau of Labor in the Department of the Interior in 1884,[3] which, in 1888, was made an independent department of the government, though without representation in the cabinet.[4] In 1894 the day "celebrated and known as Labor's Holiday," the first Monday of September of each

1900, pp. 134–5. A confused account of such progress up to 1887 is to be found in G. E. McNeill, The Labor Movement, especially chap. vi. A general and valuable work published in 1918 is Hist. of Labor in the U. S. by J. R. Commons and others. Also Report of Ind. Comm. of 1898, House Doc., 57th Cong. 1st sess., particularly no. 183, pp. lx et seq.

    [1] N. Y. World Almanac for 1900, pp. 134–5.
    [2] Cf. Carroll D. Wright, Industrial Evolution of the U. S., pp. 318–20.
    [3] U. S. Stat. at Large, vol. 23, pp. 60–1.   [4] Ibid., vol. 25, pp. 182–4.

year, was designated as a legal public holiday, "to all intents and purposes in the same manner as Christmas, the first day of January, the 22nd of February, the 30th day of May and the 4th day of July" were national holidays.[1]

In many states there were bureaus, in charge of secretaries and commissioners, whose duty it was to interest themselves in the workingman. The American Federation of Labor, still under the unremitting and insistent direction of Samuel Gompers, had come, in 1900, to have about 700,000 members. It employed a force of 44 "organizers" and it and its affiliates published no less than 253 weekly or monthly papers "devoted to the cause of labor."[2]

When one point was gained another was seen rising beyond. The standards of living of the American workingman were improved in part, without doubt, because of the exertions of the unions,[3] though his prosperous condition, the protectionists said, was attributable to the tariff which freed him from competition with the "pauper labor" of Europe. There were more contributing causes than casually appeared. As a matter of fact the workers in factories and mines, and on the railroads, for it was with these classes that the union leaders were concerning themselves, were favored in a sensible way by a scarcity of labor and a consequent demand for it, so that they could pick their employers and move from place to place. A mill owner, when he made large profits, shared his gains with his work people, by his own volition, more frequently than the labor leaders would admit. In free communities, where all had the suffrage and lived, in some degree, on terms of equality, not very cognizant of social caste, self interest, if no other consideration, led employers to seek the good opinion of their men. Again it was possible for artisans to abandon their trades if they thought that they could better their lot. The more ad-

---

[1] U. S. Stat. at Large, vol. 28, p. 96.

[2] N. Y. World Almanac for 1900, pp. 134-5. A list of the affiliates of the Federation in 1898 was furnished a Congressional committee by Gompers and is published in Senate Doc., 55th Cong., 2nd sess., no. 318. Another list is published in John Mitchell, Organized Labor, pp. 85-7.

[3] Cf. Carroll D. Wright, Industrial Evolution of the U. S., chap. xix and xx.

venturous and imaginative could always move out upon free
land in the West, a fact which again operated to limit the
number of available hands and to hold up wages.

The labor leaders, however, when benefits came to the
working people, boasted of their cleverness and preened themselves before their followings as they spoke of new assaults
upon the citadels of capital.[1] They visited Washington and
threatened Congressmen with the loss of their seats in coming
elections. "Walking delegates" went in and out of factories,
addressed meetings and were constantly moving about in mill
towns, inciting the working classes to new endeavors in behalf
of their social improvement. Labor saving inventions were
introduced; new processes by application of scientific discoveries
were found and adopted by the manufacturer to enable him
to overcome increased labor costs. And this turning to the
machine was often at the expense of the workingman who found
himself, in some fields, entirely eliminated. There was no more
for him to do at any price for any number of hours in a day.
Now and again, like the man in Scripture, his last state was
worse than his first. But his help, it was believed, was in
"solidarity," in organizing and in presenting, with his fellows
in a like situation, a united front against capital and the men
who controlled capital in productive and profit-yielding processes. The worker would not complacently go back to more
work, lower wages, poorer food, a worse habitation, less recreation, or surrender any of his new privileges. The employer
entered the dawning century faced by hazards and perplexities
of the labor leaders' making which would plague him wherever
he turned.

The moral and social reforms which had occupied the attention of the people prior to the Civil War rested while that
event wound its course through our history. As the negro's
situation faded from view consciences which had been disturbed
primarily with the abolition of slavery were released for other

[1] The assumptions of inhumanity and greed on the part of manufacturers
on which the labor leaders were wont to rest their activity are plainly
presented by Gompers in Senate Doc., 55th Cong. 2nd sess., no. 318,
pp. 39–60.

philanthropic activities. Groups of men and women discussed Sabbath observance. Law and order societies gave a care to the enforcement of old ordinances on this subject, so that, with the arrival of the hordes of immigrants from Europe, we should not come to have their "Continental Sunday." Studies of prostitution and the methods of controlling it claimed attention. The laws against vice were strengthened and demands were made in cities for its repression. Women conducted effective campaigns for the protection of their sex from the "social evil." Legislatures were asked to pass laws to limit and extirpate gambling, prize fighting, horse racing and lotteries and, in answer to awakened public sentiment, progress in these directions was noted.[1]

Offense was done to the moral sensibilities of the public in a particular way by the Louisiana lottery operated with the favor of the government of that state. It had not only fastened itself on Louisiana, from whose legislature it had by corrupt means [2] during the disturbed period of Reconstruction gained its charter, but it used the United States mails to sell tickets throughout the country. A few men who held the monopoly waxed rich, while the masses given to gambling, except the small number who drew prizes, lost their money. One of the wholesome fruits of Harrison's administration was a law of Congress in 1890 denying to the lottery the use of the mails.[3] The President had urged its enactment in vigorous words, alluding to the "robbery of the poor and the widespread corruption of public and private morals" which were the necessary incidents of lottery schemes.[4] Postmaster-General Wanamaker welcomed the opportunity to prosecute under the law and to enforce its provisions. The managers of the lottery appealed to the Supreme Court and, failing there,[5] sought to bring the express companies into their service, to be foiled on this side also. Meantime the charter which had been granted in 1868, to be

[1] Cf. Forum, vol. xix, p. 238.
[2] These methods are described by C. C. Buel in Century Mag., Feb., 1892.
[3] U. S. Stat. at Large, vol. 26, p. 465, Approved Sep. 19, 1890.
[4] Richardson, vol. ix, p. 81.   [5] In re Rapier, 143 U. S., p. 110.

operative from January 1, 1869, for 25 years,[1] would expire at the end of 1893, and it was to be renewed. There was little reason to doubt that but for the vigorous action of the Federal government the lottery would be given another quarter of a century of life in which to mulct and debauch the population of the United States.

For some time a man named Morris, who stood at the head of the company, and his agents, had been making their arrangements to obtain an extension of their political grant. The company paid the state $40,000 a year under the charter of 1868.[2] They now offered $1,000,000, a sum later increased to $1,250,000 a year, for the coveted privilege, the money to be used to construct levees, to impound the waters of the Mississippi and the Red Rivers in time of flood, to support schools, to pension Confederate soldiers, to drain the city of New Orleans and for specific charitable purposes. This was a monstrous bribe.[3] But the consciences of many people in Louisiana were stirred, they could not rest under the reproach of moral obliquity and the legislature, upon which a powerful lobby was operating, rather than charter the lottery, which it had fully resolved to do, chose to put the proposal into the form of a constitutional amendment and submit it to the people. The governor vetoed it. He placed "the honor of the state above money," he said. The legislature serving the lottery company, sent the amendment to the people anyhow, after a decision of the courts, and a memorable struggle ensued at the election in April, 1892. The Democratic party divided—two conventions were held. The anti-lottery faction declared that such a method of raising revenues was "at variance with the civilization of the century" and elected its candidates by a large plurality. The amendment was rejected and the lottery, outlawed on all sides, state and Federal, after vainly seeking a lodgment elsewhere in this country, removed its offices to Honduras.[4]

[1] Sess. Laws of La. for 1868, p. 24. [2] Ibid., p. 25.
[3] C. C. Buel in Century Mag., Feb., 1892; also Forum for Jan., 1892.
[4] The door to this lottery and lotteries generally, under Senator Hoar's leadership, was still more effectually closed by act of Congress of March

The movement to bring about temperate habits in the use
of intoxicating drink had passed through a number of phases
in the middle decades of the century.   Lecturers in lyceums,
writers in the press, religious bodies, temperance societies forwarded the cause of total abstinence and pointed the way to
various legal restrictions which in at least one state, Maine, and
various local communities took the form of complete prohibition.
The evils attendant upon the prosecution of the business
increased to a really alarming extent.   No one, however much
he might berate sumptuary legislation, if he were an intelligent
observer, could deny that conditions were abhorrent.   Many
drank to excess.   This tendency was ascribed to the climate and
again to the pace of American life.   Inns were meeting places
for shabby human derelicts besotted by alcohol.   Saloons were
nuisances.   No one wished to live near them.   They were
frequently combined with houses of prostitution; gambling
and other vice flourished in the shadow of the barroom.   Saloon
keepers were not men who could be respected and a public
sentiment unfavorable to the business, root and branch, was
being rapidly formed, especially in rural neighborhoods settled
by homogeneous British-American stock.   A social cleavage
was developed between drinkers and non-drinkers, between
those who apologized for the business and those who gave it
no quarter, between churches which advocated the temperance
cause and those whose pastors were silent in the face of the
demand for reform and were, for this reason, called "whiskey
churches."

Women entered the field with an earnest determination to
close the saloon.   They prayed at the doors of dram shops and
led men away from the tempter who took their wages, starved
their wives and children and embittered so many lives.   In
Ohio this movement was known as a "Crusade"—those who
directed it were "Crusaders."   Farmers suffered from drunken

2, 1895; N. Y. Times, March 5, 1895; N. Y. Nation, March 7, 1895.   Cf.
H. A. Gibbons, John Wanamaker, vol. i, pp. 313–5; App. Ann. Cyclop.
for 1890 and 1891 under Louisiana; Sess. Laws for La. for 1892, p. 35;
McPherson's Handbook for 1890, pp. 266–7; ibid. for 1892, p. 139.

laborers, mill owners from employees who came to tasks which
their condition rendered them unfit to perform. The temperance reformers and the prohibitionists were called fanatics
and cranks. They put altogether too much emphasis on the
evil side of drinking. In any case it was as much a personal
right to drink as to eat. Drinking could not be stopped by
law; prohibition, as any one knew, would not prohibit, an
announcement by those whose habits were fixed on this subject
that they would brook no interdictions. Particularly emphatic
were the Germans in opposing the temperance movement, and
when the Italians and other eastern and southern continental
European immigrants arrived, and began to make their influence
felt, they, as warmly and more violently, in keeping with their
tempers, denounced such restraints upon their accustomed
liberties.

The agitation, however irrational it might be held to be,
proceeded. The evil at which the reformers aimed was real
and great and they were not of the fibre to yield to un-American
elements which grew stronger and stronger, especially in the
cities toward which immigrants in such numbers tended.

The prohibitionists took their case into politics. They would
support the party which promised to advance their ideas;
they would oppose the candidates of that party which denounced
the control of the liquor traffic as an infringement of individual
rights. They found most sympathy in the North in the
Republican party to which they, in general, adhered, though
extremists, as has been related elsewhere, held conventions,
adopted platforms and nominated their own candidates. Their
strength was feared by the Republicans in states in which the
parties were evenly balanced and the difficulties which beset
the campaign manager were of no mean order. On the other side
stood, not only those who had habits which were not to be
attacked, but a rich and well organized industry not to be
disregarded under threat of a curtailment of its revenues.
Neal Dow of Maine, running for President in 1880, polled
10,000 votes, for St. John of Kansas in 1884 over 151,000 votes
were cast.

To check activity which might lead to the complete abolition of the business the politicians, with the reluctant compliance of the liquor interests, were hedging it about with a variety of restrictions. Sellers must have permits and licenses for carrying on their trade. Hours of sale were limited. Saloons might not be established near churches and schools; property owners, by petition, might bar saloons from certain neighborhoods. When the temperance sentiment demanded it unusual agencies, such as county judges, who should have been saved from the performance of tasks so foreign to their functions, were entrusted with the duty of determining who, among applicants for the right to sell liquor in the county, should be given such a privilege. A form of restraint which met the favor of the politicians was the requirement that the saloon keeper should pay a large sum for his permit. It would reduce the number of sales places if the price were increased. The dirty little bar and brothel would be eliminated; liquor would be dispensed only in spacious, well-appointed saloons, for no others could meet the demands of the law. Up and down the country "high license" was recommended as a cure for intemperance.

The more the prohibition bogey was paraded before the liquor men the more feasible it was for party managers in the states to lay financial burdens upon the trade. Demands were made upon it in each campaign with promises of protection. Large sums were contributed by the distillers, vintners and brewers to political "slush funds." And so now again with "high license"; it was this for the liquor men, they were told, or, very possibly, the total loss of current profits from their business and the confiscation, without compensation, of their property under the hard hand of the prohibitionist.

But those who had gone off into the new third party and many who remained in the old parties would not be satisfied with half way measures. They denounced "high license" as "partnership with sin;" the government should not tax, or profit by, a business which "laid a curse on mankind." Anyhow "high license" improved conditions in no wise. A man could get as drunk in a saloon with mirrors and silver plate behind its bar as in a hole in the wall. Increased prices for permits merely led to the opening of an infinite number of unauthorized sales places where the business, half concealed, continued to thrive. Thousands of "speak easies" appeared wherever there were "high license" laws. If efforts were made to close them they bribed, if they had not already been blackmailed by, the police and the liquor trade was the means of corrupting politics in as foul away as before.

Nothing would do, the prohibitionists said, but the outright suppression of the traffic in the state and in the nation. Another stop on the way to the goal was seen in "local option," even more distasteful to the liquor interests than "high license," though they were often compelled to take this, too, from legislatures which were hard pressed by the temperance men. Local option had been tried before the Civil War.[1] The county or town which contained a large body of people who wished to be free of the liquor nuisance could bar it from its limits if a majority of its citizens voting at an election should decide in favor of the riddance. The party group in a state legislature which authorized such referenda committed itself in no way to the "wet" or "dry" side of the argument. In passing such a law the legislature merely referred to the people of local communities a question about which they were deeply concerned. Not much could be lost. The city, where most of the liquor which was manufactured was consumed, would not, with its foreign vote, outlaw the inn and the saloon. The city members in the legislature, therefore, would not be held too strictly accountable for permitting a local option bill to pass, while the country members were pleasing many of those to whom they owed their seats. By so generous a concession the prohibitionists might be reduced to quiet.[2]

But the struggle to attain state and national prohibition did not abate. Maine had stood alone as a prohibition state for thirty years. Other states which had joined her during the popular rising in behalf of temperance before the Civil War

[1] E. P. Oberholtzer, The Referendum in America, 1900, pp. 288–9.
[2] Cf. J. R. Commons, Races and Immigrants in America, pp. 186–7.

had left her company.[1] In 1880, the question was submitted
to the people of Kansas where an amendment to the constitution
was adopted, the vote being 92,302 for and 84,304 against the
proposal. Iowa followed in 1882. In that state 155,436 votes
were cast for and 125,677 against a prohibitory amendment,
though an unfriendly court, raising a technical objection to
the manner of submission, promptly declared it invalid, whereupon the legislature, interpreting public sentiment, prohibited
the liquor traffic by statute.[2]

In Ohio an amendment was submitted to the people at the
general election of 1883. The issue was confused with the choice
of state officers, including a governor, and also with an alternate
proposition in regard to the regulation and license of the liquor
business. The canvass was active and earnest. It was conducted on non-partisan lines. Bodies of women took the field
during the campaign and stood at the polls on election day.
Prohibition received a majority of more than 80,000 votes;
323,189 were for and 240,975 against it. The constitution
required a majority, not of the votes cast for an amendment, but
of all the votes cast at the election, in this case 721,310, and
prohibition, therefore, fell short of adoption by about 40,000
votes, a bitter disappointment to the temperance leaders who
charged the liquor men with a falsification of the returns, a
statement founded, very likely, in fact.[3]

On April 7, 1886, a prohibition amendment was submitted to
the people in Rhode Island. It had passed two legislatures
and required a three-fifths vote of the citizens going to the polls.
The campaign which was brief was successful. The liquor men
in and outside the state assembled a large sum of money to
defend their trade,[4] but the feeling against them was so strong
that they were defeated on every side. Even in the city of
Providence, which contained more than half the vote of the
state, where it was expected that prohibition would find but
little favor, the temperance forces won.[5] The prohibitionists

[1] E. P. Oberholtzer, The Referendum in America, 1900, pp. 201–3.
[2] App. Ann. Cyclop. for 1883 and 1884, under Iowa.
[3] Ibid for 1883 p. 609.   [4] N. Y. Tribune, April 7, 1886.
[5] Ibid., April 10, 1886.

were jubilant; Rhode Island was the fourth state to drive from its borders the trade in intoxicating drinks.

In the Presidential election of 1884 Blaine had been defeated by pluralities in several states, as in New York, New Jersey and Connecticut, smaller than the vote which was cast for St. John. It was not certain that the defection might not increase until the Prohibitionists should break up the party, an object which they openly said was in view. Much was made of the fact that the Whig party had gone down under Abolition. The Republican party rose in its place. It had been the "Party of Moral Ideas"—it would sink and disappear, if it should not muster enough strength and enough courage to combat the "Rum Power." Attack upon it would proceed, it was said, like attack upon slavery until it, like slavery, should be abolished.

The Republican leaders were alarmed. But, after emptying the vials of their wrath and ridicule upon a body of goodly and very earnest men, the not injudicious conclusion was arrived at that, if possible, these men had better be appeased. The prohibitionists wrote and spoke and allowed no one to forget that they had a righteous cause. They may have been perfectionists. It may have been Puritanism. They had much truth on their side when they said that the physiological effects of alcoholic drink were generally ill. It provided no nutriment for the body. Its use grew upon the user and damaged many lives. The wages of the workingman were squandered in saloons. Intoxicating liquors were increasing pauperism and crime. Proof of this fact was at hand. Factory towns were not fit to live in over Saturday nights, so vile were they with drunkenness. Politics had been debauched by a trade which was battening on the poor, the more so now that it was fighting for its life. It was taking virtue out of the American people.

Respectable figures were put forward as Anti-Saloon Republicans. Meetings were held in cities and states. Since the Democratic party was "the protector of the saloon interests" the Republican party should, "as a matter of right, become the avowed champion and defender of the home against the saloon."

The "very existence of the party" was imperilled.[1] Congress, the Anti-Saloon Republicans said, should prohibit the manufacture and sale of intoxicating liquors in the District of Columbia and the Territories. Prohibitory amendments to the constitutions should be submitted to the people in the states. Until such amendments should be adopted the business could be controlled by local option in counties and towns. When and where the saloon was not closed by law it should be highly taxed to help repair the damage which it inflicted upon society. "Scientific temperance instruction," as it was called, the teaching of the evil effects of alcohol to children in the schools, was endorsed.[2] Such a program the New York Tribune said would satisfy everyone. No more could be required. The Republican party embodied "nine-tenths of whatever reformatory and progressive tendencies" were "extant." [3]

Mrs. J. Ellen Foster of Iowa, a sturdy campaigner, spoke for women in their relation to the subject, a body of whom, ably led by Miss Frances E. Willard in the Women's Christian Temperance Union,[4] had resolved to cooperate with the separate Prohibition party. Mrs. Foster remained a Republican, in which position she became conspicuous. The Republican state conventions made such declarations as seemed to fit local requirements. The Republican national convention in 1888 was between two fires. It was on the point of adjourning without a statement of policy for the campaign when, as a kind of afterthought, a resolution was approved sympathizing "with all wise and well directed efforts for the promotion of temperance and morality," an article of faith so guarded that it could be repeated with small change in 1892 and 1896.

The liquor interests were now thoroughly aroused. They had not given up hope of repealing the law in Maine. It was not being enforced, perhaps it could not be strictly enforced in the cities on the coast. But the governor said that in three-

---

[1] N. Y. Tribune, July 21, 1886.
[2] Ibid., Sep. 16 and 17, 1886; D. R. Dewey, National Problems, p. 128.
[3] N. Y. Tribune, Sep. 18, 1886.
[4] A brief history of this organization is in App. Ann. Cyclop. for 1890, pp. 857-60.

fourths or four-fifths of the towns the sale of liquor had been "practically abolished." Nowhere was it openly sold or offered for sale; prohibition, he declared, had been of "immeasurable value." It had "increased the wealth of the state by increasing the sobriety of the people and saving the fruits of industry." [1] That the law might not be within easy reach of its enemies at each recurring election it was converted, in 1884, by a vote of 70,783 to 23,811, into a constitutional amendment.

In Kansas and Iowa the most angry assaults were made upon prohibition. Governors, courts of judicature, administrative officers, the legislatures, party conventions were called upon and used, when they could be, in a concentrated effort to nullify it. Men commended or condemned the policy according to their tastes, habits and sympathies. That the restrictions implied in such measures were effective, even when they were but partially enforced, was confirmed by the mad commotion among the distillers, brewers, vintners, importers of and jobbers in liquors, the inn and saloon keepers from the highest to the lowest, the viniculturists, the maltsters, the manufacturers of barrels, kegs and bottles whenever they were faced with prohibitory legislation. That their power might be increased they formed associations, hired lobbyists and attorneys and would contest the further progress of prohibition at every point. Drinkers, too, were exasperated as they were told of this rising threat against their freedom.

The large vote for prohibition in Ohio, where the day was saved for the liquor dealers only by trickery in the choice of the manner of submitting the question to the people, and, probably, at the end, by a false count, followed by the entirely unexpected victory of the prohibitionists in Rhode Island, was a signal for resistance at whatever cost. In a score of states bodies of temperance men and women were pressing the issue. For the legislatures to pass bills subject to approval by the people was a proceeding of doubtful validity,[2] and they would touch this highly controversial subject in no other way. They,

[1] App. Ann. Cyclop. for 1886, pp. 520-1.
[2] E. P. Oberholtzer, The Referendum in America, 1900, pp. 208-17.

therefore, put the proposals with which they hoped to conciliate the prohibitionists into the form of amendments to the state constitutions. Some were passed by one house to meet obstruction in the other. Some passed one legislature to be defeated in the next one, when, as was frequently the case, the approval of two was necessary before the referendum.

Following Rhode Island in 1886 Michigan and Oregon, in 1887, held elections upon prohibitory amendments and rejected them by small majorities, the vote in Michigan being 184,281 to 171,636, in Oregon 27,958 to 19,973. In 1888 West Virginia gave a majority of 35,000 against a similar constitutional provision. In 1889 the subject was referred to the people in Pennsylvania, Massachusetts, Connecticut and New Hampshire. Pennsylvania, because of its size and importance, offered an interesting field for a test of the power of the contending forces. The Republicans in 1888 in Pennsylvania, affirming a pledge made in 1886 to submit the question to the people, said that they recognized "the evils and abuses of the sale of liquors." They were in favor of "all laws looking in this respect to the elevation of the moral condition of the people." [1] Before doing so, however, they, in 1888, passed a high license law under which, by the use of large discretionary powers by the license granting authority, the courts of common pleas, the number of sales places in Philadelphia was reduced from 5773 to 1347.[2] This restriction, which, it was said, greatly diminished the number of arrests for drunkenness and of deaths from alcoholism, soothed public feeling in some degree, and, at the election in June, 1889, specially called and arranged for, in order that the issue might not be confused with other questions, as it had been in Ohio, the prohibitionists were defeated by a vote of 484,644 to 296,617.

In Massachusetts the vote was 85,242 for and 131,062 against the amendment; in Connecticut 22,379 for and 49,974 against; in New Hampshire 25,768 for and 30,976 against. In the same year, 1889, Rhode Island, where no attempts had been made to enforce the law, rescinded, after unremitting

---

[1] App. Ann. Cyclop. for 1888, p. 678.   [2] Ibid. for 1889, p. 688.

agitation, the action taken three years before. The provision
had been put into the constitution by more than the required
three-fifths vote, 15,113 to 9,230; it was repealed by a vote of
28,315 to 9,956, and licenses were granted again in that state.
The conventions in North Dakota, South Dakota and Washington, when submitting their new constitutions to popular
vote in 1889, also referred to the people articles prohibiting
the liquor traffic. In the two Dakotas the prohibitionists were
successful. In the state of Washington, on the other hand,
the article regarding prohibition was rejected by a vote of 19,546
to 31,487. [1]

Nebraska would vote in 1890 and, as the campaign approached, a convention of delegates from that state, Kansas,
Iowa and the two Dakotas was held in Omaha, with a view
to forming a central prohibition organization to create and
to hold as a block against the liquor power the area west of
the Mississippi River represented at the meeting. But when
the question came to a vote Nebraska was lost, 82,292 persons
approving and 111,728 disapproving the proposal submitted
to them.

In the meantime the South which had gone far with local
option, as has been related elsewhere,[2] in order to make life
safe in a community so largely inhabited by negroes, had had
two state-wide elections on the subject. Texas in 1887 rejected a prohibition amendment by a vote of 220,627 to 129,270,
and Tennessee, in the same year, by a vote of 145,197 to 117,504.

In South Carolina an effort was made to solve the problem
in another way. The political order there had been overset.
The ignorant and poor white classes, led by Tillman, had seized
the government. One of their schemes was to bring the liquor
business under state control, a policy suggested by some Scandinavian experiments. Intoxicants, after July 1, 1893, would be
obtainable only at state liquor stores from "dispensers."
Violations, convictions and litigation in the state and Federal

[1] App. Ann. Cyclop. for the years and states named; E. P. Oberholtzer,
The Referendum in America, 1893, pp. 46–7; Cyclopedia for Temperance
and Prohibition.
[2] In vol. iv of this work, pp. 581–5.

courts, even rioting which necessitated the calling out of the militia, ensued.[1]

The prohibitionists had made little progress. Their hopes faded. They had lost one state which they had gained, Rhode Island, and could rejoice over only two accessions, and these unimportant in point of the population involved, North and South Dakota.

Everywhere the ground was desperately defended by the liquor interests, while the prohibitionists, to gain their ends, exhausted their efforts through the churches, non-partisan leagues and associations of women. The temperance cause had developed many powerful advocates who industriously and zealously passed from one state to another. The liquor men, on the other hand, worked quietly through the saloons, the back rooms of which, in many instances, were the polling places; through the organized machinery of both political parties with which they maintained close relations; through the newspapers which they plenteously supplied with advertisements. They held few meetings, and, in presenting their side of the case, brought to bear upon the people little public speech. On election days all their forces were in action. They used money lavishly. Others had less reason to do so. When the prohibitionists were defeated they ascribed their failures to the men who would not trouble themselves to go to the polls. The large numbers of stay-at-home voters were presumably sympathetic with the temperance element, but not to such a degree as to come forward and register their opinions. However this may have been, while public sentiment was as it seemed to be, they were unwilling to be thought active allies and partisans of the liquor men.

Everywhere the whole vote cast for the constitutional amendments was less than the vote cast for elective officers. More than 200,000 persons who had come to the polls for the Presidential election in Pennsylvania in 1888 did not do so in 1889, when the prohibition amendment was submitted to the people. In the same way in Massachusetts, in 1889, when the total

[1] Cf. App. Ann. Cyclop. for 1894, pp. 717–8.

vote for the amendment was 216,000, 128,000 persons took no part in the election, while the number who neglected their duty as citizens in Michigan was more than 100,000. Less than half the voters in Connecticut thought it worth their while to express their views on the question when it was submitted to them. In Ohio, in 1883, nearly 160,000 persons, though they were called to the polls to vote for a governor, and voted for one or another candidate for that office, were so indifferent concerning prohibition that they failed to mark their ballots either "yes" or "no." [1]

The prohibitionists, if beaten were unbowed. But they were more and more convinced that the goal which they should hold before them, and which had never been out of mind, was national prohibition, a law comprehending the entire country and in the form of an amendment to the Federal Constitution. Not a Congress convened in which numerously signed petitions in behalf of prohibition in the nation at large were not presented in both houses. Not a Congress was without members, such as Senator Blair of New Hampshire, ready to introduce proposals to submit to the states a constitutional amendment prohibiting the liquor traffic throughout the republic. The panic of 1893 turned the attention of the people in other directions. "The free and unrestricted coinage of silver," which was known as "free silver," became the hue and cry in a region in the West which had so bravely borne the banners of prohibition. The depression at an end, the war with Spain brought still other questions to the fore. Quietly, however, local option had held its ground and increased the territory in which the people lived under prohibitory laws until soon it could be said that more than one half the superficial area of the United States, not including Alaska and the Indian reservations, from which the saloon had long been barred, was closed to the liquor business. [2]

Not far away from prohibition lay another reform, woman

[1] App. Ann. Cyclop. for the years in which the elections were held under the names of the states; cf. E. P. Oberholtzer, The Referendum in America, 1893, pp. 46–7.

[2] Cf. N. Y. World Almanac for 1908, p. 392.

suffrage. It, too, had engaged the attention of the Abolitionists and had fallen by the way when the issue of that struggle came to be bound up with a civil war. "Long haired men and short haired women" had advocated it without securing for it very much more than general ridicule. The enfranchisement of all the male negro ex-slaves after the war and the excited agitation of the Radicals who were making suffrage seem to be a human right which, when it was withheld from a black man, was the highest form of injustice, put courage into those who were engaged in trying "to break down the barriers of sex." If there were to be no color line at the polls why should there be sex distinctions? The laws in other respects were unfair to women—they were not consonant with enlightened and liberal opinion. Men, it was said, were intent upon keeping women in their "sphere," as wives and mothers. Women were treated as "domestic chattels" and their position would not be changed until they could vote as men voted, and took their place beside men in political life. The advocates of "women's rights" had their clubs and societies, some of them of considerable antiquity. Women's organizations which were formed to gain other ends espoused the cause and the advancement of the idea from year to year, if slow, was certain. Leaders like Elizabeth Cady Stanton, Susan B. Anthony and Lucy Stone had weathered contumely and were unfaltering in their labors in behalf of "equal rights." But the most important allies which the cause obtained were the prohibitionists, and especially the Women's Christian Temperance Union, with a large and active membership, actuated by the conviction that the liquor business and other nuisances and evils affecting women and the family could never be banished from the country without the female vote. So large a claim was contested, but the movement was now set forward from two sides—by the woman suffragists who were concerned about their "rights" and by the temperance people.

To say to either element that its reasoning was faulty was to invite from them charges of intolerant feeling. Many women held property, many were taxpayers, many were highly intelli-

gent and had acquainted themselves with the principles underlying government. A number, indeed, were practising law and
had entered other professions in which they were respected
figures. It could be said that fewer women than men were
endowed with the political sense. But there was temerity in
such an averment in view of the mass of ignorance which had
been thrown into the electorate when the negro had been given
the suffrage, and which was still being added to it by the authorities entrusted with the work of naturalizing foreigners. The
millions of the poorest and most obnoxious classes who came
from southern and eastern Europe in the 80's and 90's, enfranchised as they were in great bodies upon declaring their intention
to become citizens of the United States, and taking out their
"first papers," which in some states might be within six months
after their arrival,[1] without knowledge of the English language
or comprehension or appreciation of the country's institutions,
served to emphasize a discrimination which men needed no
draughts upon their chivalry to admit. It was a grave condition. Could it be improved by doubling the electorate as was
proposed? It was by no means plain that it could be. To add
the negress to the negro, the women in the steerage quarters of
the crowded incoming steamships to the male offscourings of
Italy, Hungary, Poland, Bohemia, Russia and the Balkans
spoke of no progress in a proper direction.

Men said in legislatures and in Congress, when they were
importuned by the insistent advocates of woman suffrage,
that women could have the vote when they wanted it. It was
not yet certain that any considerable number of them wished
to vote, or would go to the polls, if they were granted such a
boon. To prove this point societies against the granting of
suffrage were formed and influential figures in social life in
many communities came forward to serve as examples of women
of the best types who, for themselves, would reject the voting
privilege; they deplored the demand for it as likely to diminish
the respect in which the sex must be held, bringing no corre-

[1] For summaries of the diverse state laws giving qualifications for
voting see N. Y. World Almanac for 1900, pp. 136-9.

sponding benefits to government. The suffragists were in no way deterred and pursued their object indefatigably. Meetings which often assumed the proportions of national conventions, periodical publications, tracts and books proclaimed the growth of sentiment favorable to the reform. Its dangers were minimized or wholly overlooked. That man's view of woman might be changed for the worse were she to vote; that she would, probably, neglect her home and her domestic duties when she should enter politics might be dismissed as questions too foolish for serious attention. The effect of her vote upon government, if it were predictable, was of greater note.

It was said that when women should go to the polling places these polling places would be set in clean apartments in decent neighborhoods, elections would be disentangled from saloons where ballot boxes were "stuffed," votes were stolen and the fount of democracy was corrupted. This was a gain which might be expected to ensue upon the granting of suffrage to women, if they should make use of their new opportunities. It was said, too, and it was believed by many, that they would cohere and vote, in some degree, in a block. Standing together for prohibition of the liquor trade, for anti-gambling and anti-betting legislation, for Sunday observance and peace they would be a moral power. Because of their softer and more sympathetic natures government would be mellowed and sweetened if women should be given a part in politics. How much there may have been in such speculations would be clarified by experience at a later time. It was enough to know, as the battle raged, that an increasing number of women were averring that to vote was a "right" which should no longer be withheld from them, now since negroes and ignorant aliens were crowding the polls to express their opinions in regard to public affairs, and that men, in the face of such agitation of the question, were not debating the proposal on its merits, but were telling women, when they presented numerously signed petitions, appeared before Congressional committees and argued the case on the platform that they could have the ballot as soon as it was clear that they wanted it.

There was no complete answer, short of admission of an injustice to the woman who owned and managed a shop, or a farm, or directed a large household, when she should complain that illiterate and propertyless laborers in her employ were voting, while on election day she must remain voiceless at home. First steps would be taken in giving women votes in the choice of school officers. In this field it was obvious that they had an interest which would be close, as appeared, for example, in an exciting contest over a religious question injected into the municipal elections in Massachusetts in 1888.[1] Again, in some cases, on matters having to do with taxation they might vote. In 25 states before 1900 limited privileges of one sort or another were extended to women on points having to do with school administration and local management.

The campaign continued with fanatical energy. The territory of Wyoming was formed in 1868. The first legislature in 1870 in regulating the suffrage recognized no distinctions in sex.[2] There were only a few hundred women all told in residence in this sparsely populated region and Wyoming was not an example to the country of very great eloquence. But the .principle had been established and, when the territory, in 1890, became a state women were guaranteed the franchise in the constitution. Colorado submitted the question to the people in the form of a constitutional amendment which was adopted in 1893. Utah in 1896 entered the Union with a provision in its constitution giving women the right to vote, and Idaho, by an amendment adopted in the same year, incorporated equal suffrage in its polity. Thus in four adjoining states in the Rocky Mountains before 1900 women had privileges equal to men in Congressional and Presidential elections, as well as in reference to state and local matters. Proposals to submit constitutional amendments on this subject in other states were being presented to the legislatures each year, usually to meet with defeat, before being sent to the enfranchised male voters

---

[1] App. Ann. Cyclop. for 1888, p. 520.
[2] S. B. Anthony and others, Hist. of Woman Suffrage, vol. iii, pp. 726 et seq.

for their approval or disapproval. In Kansas, in 1894, such an amendment was rejected; there were 95,302 votes for and 130,139 against it. Similar proposals in California in 1896 and in South Dakota and Washington in 1898 met the same fate.[1]

Here again social reform disappeared under the pressure of the enthusiasms which had brought on the war with Spain, and followed it. The splendors of power which had been evidenced on land and sea, a consciousness that the country stood abreast of England and the first nations of the world, with colonies, dependencies, naval stations and an imperial mission, dazzled the American mind. A change had come over the people. New interests had been awakened in them. The philanthropic impulse, which had found expression before the Civil War and was lost in that war, to rise again, was once more submerged. The American conscience was now engaged with the right and wrong of seizing islands in the seas, shooting their inhabitants and imposing unwanted forms of government upon them. Such a subversion of the principles which lay at the foundations of the republic was revolting to many men. And what that which had been, and would be, done might mean to the helpless races being brought under our domination, as well as to our own people who were to control them against their will, stirred the souls of those persons who were called reformers to almost inexpressible protest. Idealism in familiar fields was not dead but, for a time, hearing a louder call, our humanitarian energies would be spent upon moral questions raised by a military project which, though it had been begun to bring happiness to Cuba, might, many men opined and averred, be the negation of benefit to any one.

---

[1] The progress of the movement up to 1894 is summarized in App. Ann. Cyclop. for that year under the title "Woman Suffrage"; also N. Y. World Almanac for 1900, p. 138; N. Y. Nation, April 28, 1887.

INDEX